WITHDRAWN

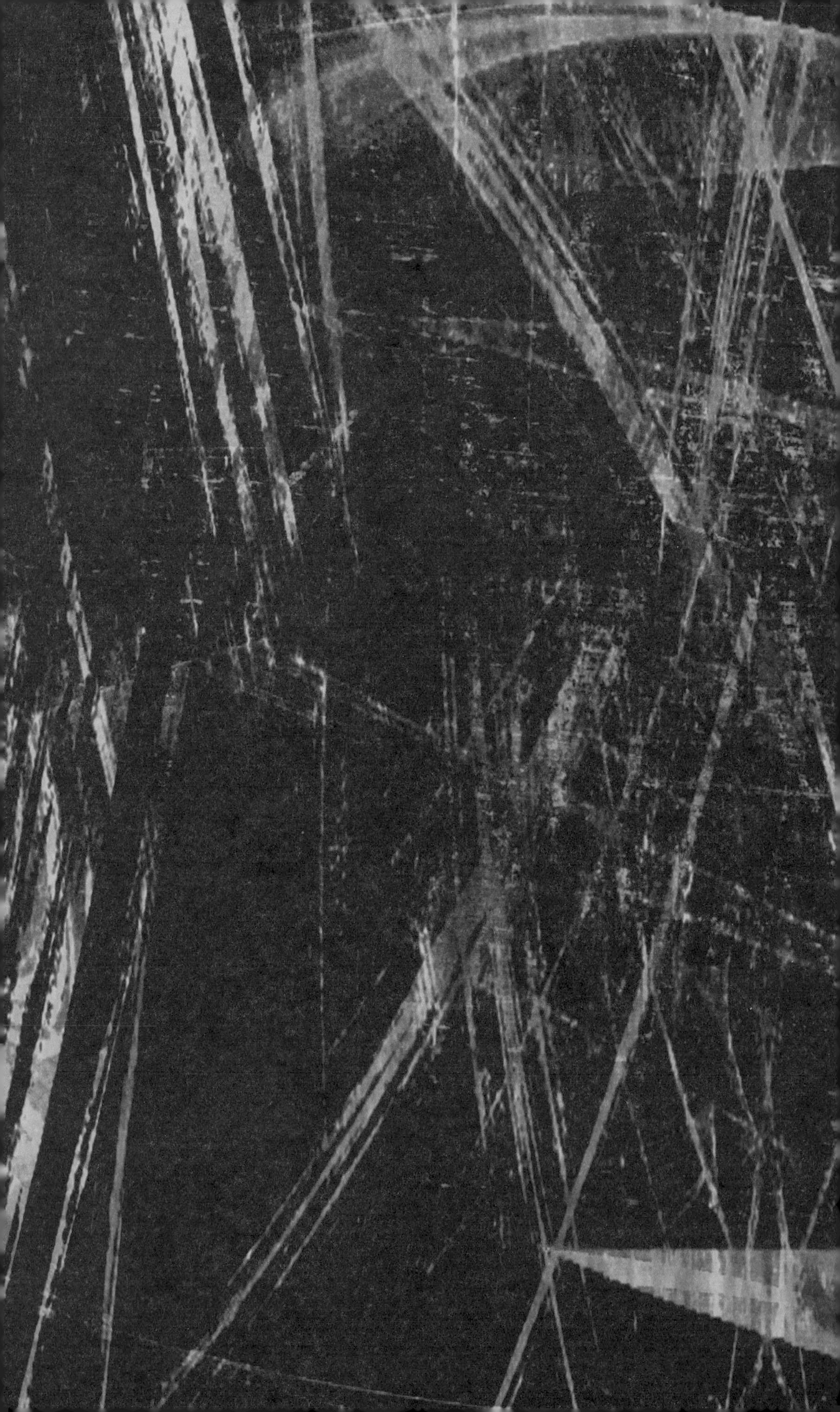

HEROES IN CRISIS

THE PRICE

AND OTHER

STORIES

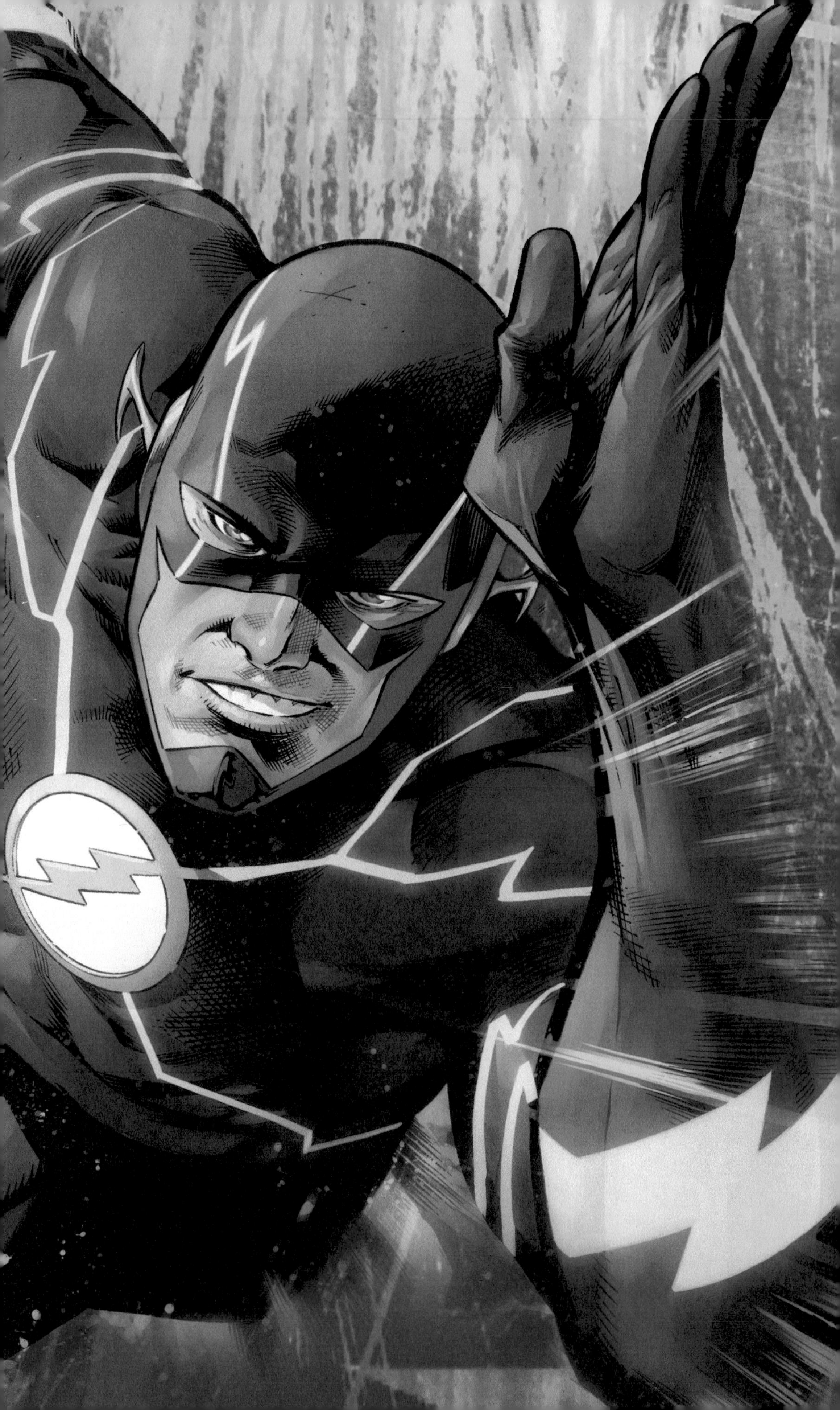

HEROES IN CRISIS THE PRICE AND OTHER STORIES

JOSHUA WILLIAMSON JULIE BENSON SHAWNA BENSON COLLIN KELLY JACKSON LANZING writers
GUILLEM MARCH RAFA SANDOVAL JORDI TARRAGONA SCOTT KOLINS JAVIER FERNANDEZ artists
TOMEU MOREY LUIS GUERRERO JOHN KALISZ colorists
STEVE WANDS WES ABBOTT ANDWORLD DESIGN letterers
GUILLEM MARCH and TOMEU MOREY collection cover artists

BATMAN created by BOB KANE with BILL FINGER
SUPERMAN created by JERRY SIEGEL and JOE SHUSTER
By special arrangement with the Jerry Siegel family

JAMIE S. RICH
PAUL KAMINSKI
KATIE KUBERT Editors – Original Series
ANDREW MARINO
BRITTANY HOLZHERR Associate Editors – Original Series
DAVE WIELGOSZ Assistant Editor – Original Series
JEB WOODARD Group Editor – Collected Editions
ROBIN WILDMAN Editor – Collected Edition
STEVE COOK Design Director – Books
LOUIS PRANDI Publication Design
CHRISTY SAWYER Publication Production

BOB HARRAS Senior VP – Editor-in-Chief, DC Comics
PAT McCALLUM Executive Editor, DC Comics

DAN DiDIO Publisher
JIM LEE Publisher & Chief Creative Officer
BOBBIE CHASE VP – New Publishing Initiatives & Talent Development
DON FALLETTI VP – Manufacturing Operations & Workflow Management
LAWRENCE GANEM VP – Talent Services
ALISON GILL Senior VP – Manufacturing & Operations
HANK KANALZ Senior VP – Publishing Strategy & Support Services
DAN MIRON VP – Publishing Operations
NICK J. NAPOLITANO VP – Manufacturing Administration & Design
NANCY SPEARS VP – Sales
MICHELE R. WELLS VP & Executive Editor, Young Reader

HEROES IN CRISIS: THE PRICE AND OTHER STORIES

DC Comics, 2900 West Alameda Ave., Burbank, CA 91505
Printed by LSC Communications, Kendallville, IN, USA. 8/23/19.
First Printing. ISBN: 978-1-4012-9964-4.

Library of Congress Cataloging-in-Publication Data is available.

PEFC Certified
This product is from sustainably managed forests and controlled sources
PEFC
PEFC/29-31-337
www.pefc.org

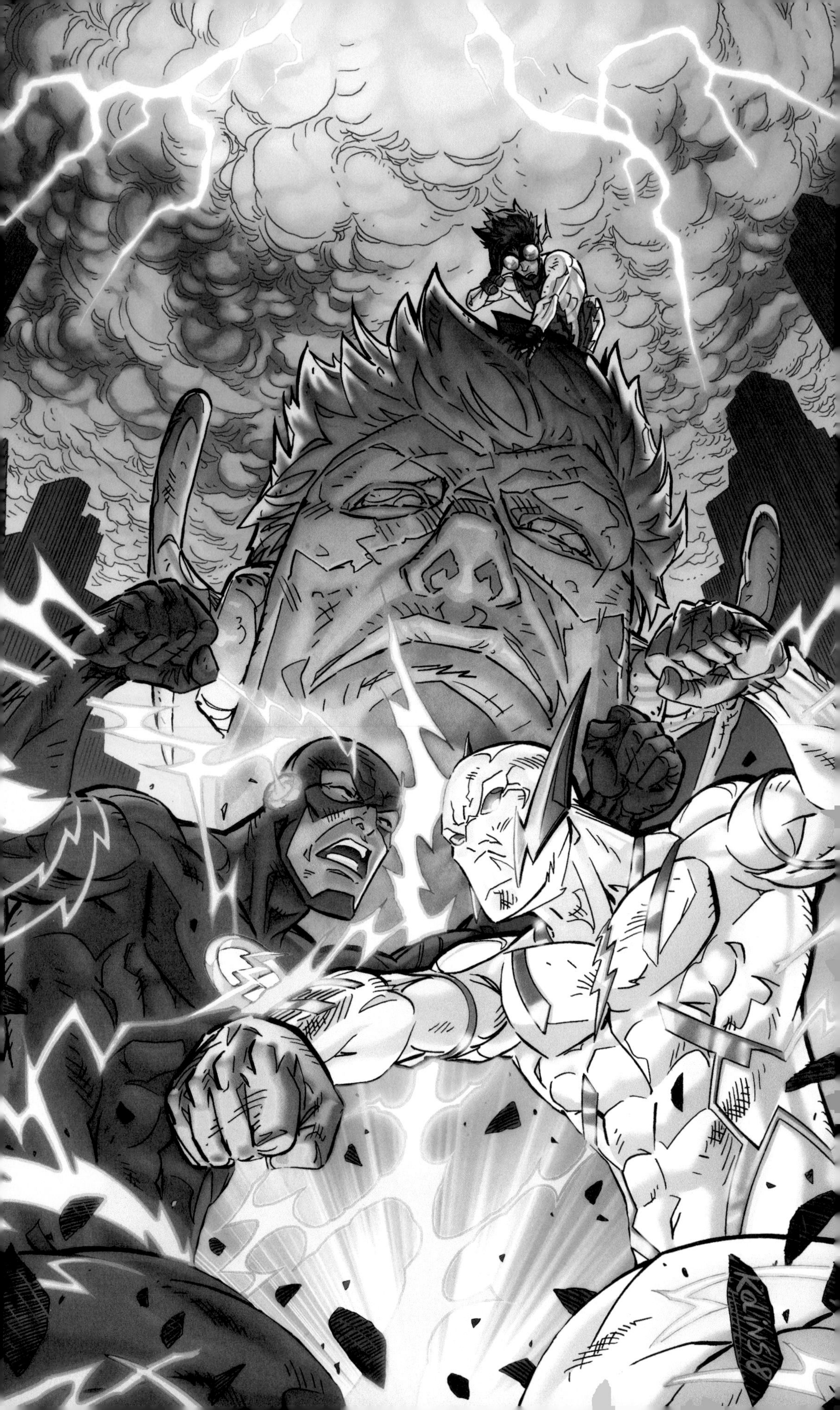

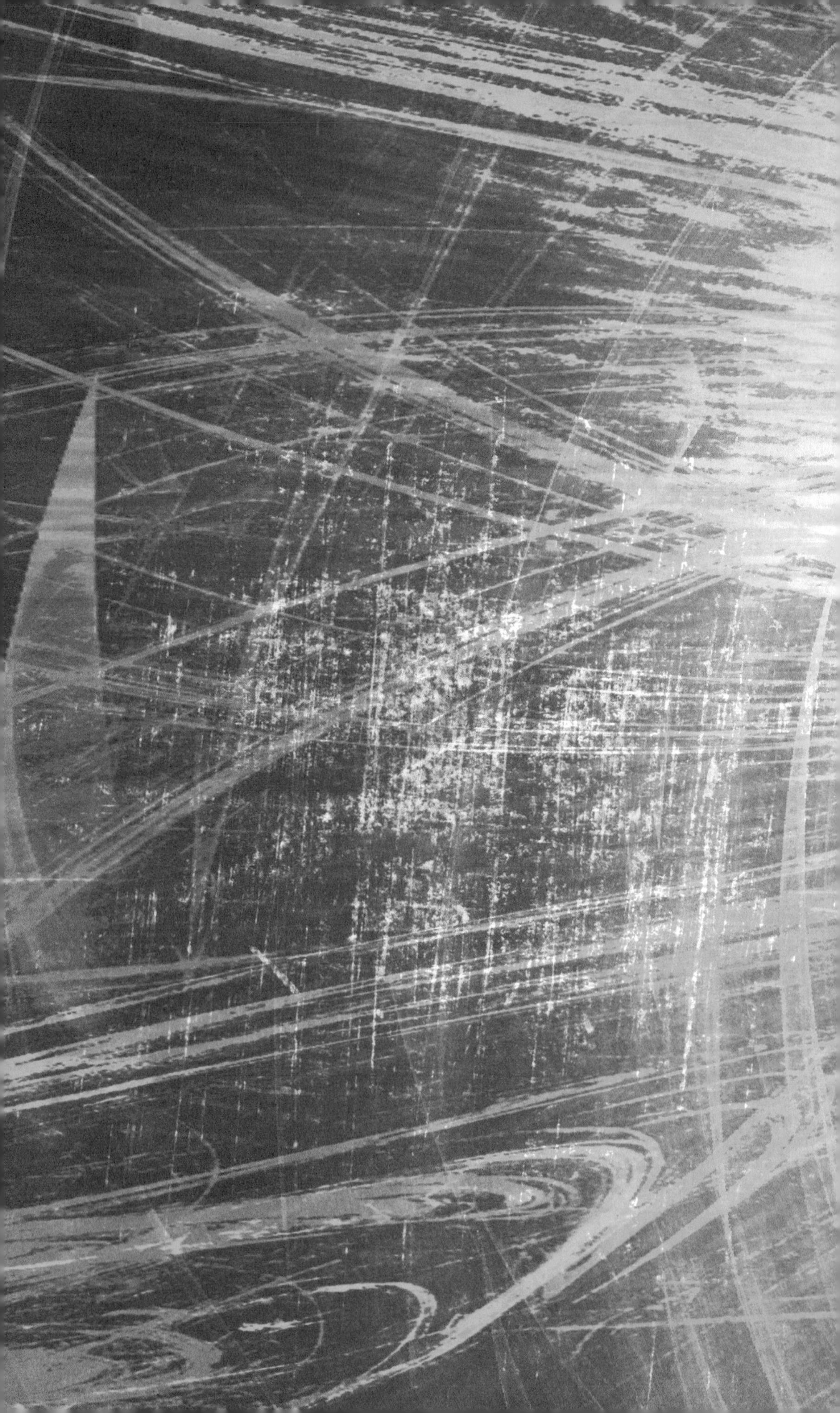

AW YEAH! CAN'T WAIT TO SEE MY FAMILY! I'VE BEEN GONE SO LONG I WONDER IF THEY'LL EVEN *RECOGNIZE* ME!

DO I OPEN WITH...IT'S ME, *BART ALLEN*, A.K.A. *IMPULSE*, A.K.A. *KID FLASH*, A.K.A. *FLASH*, FASTEST MAN ALIVE, A.K.A. *GRANDSON* OF *BARRY ALLEN*!

RAISED BY VR IN THE 30TH CENTURY BECAUSE OF MY--

NO, NO, NO, NO, MAX WOULD TELL ME I'M *OVERSHARING* AGAIN. I SHOULD JUST TRY--

YO, FAM, I'M *BACK!*

UM, *HELLO?*

HELLO?

GRANDMA?

GRANDPA?

WALLY?

WHERE *ARE* YOU?

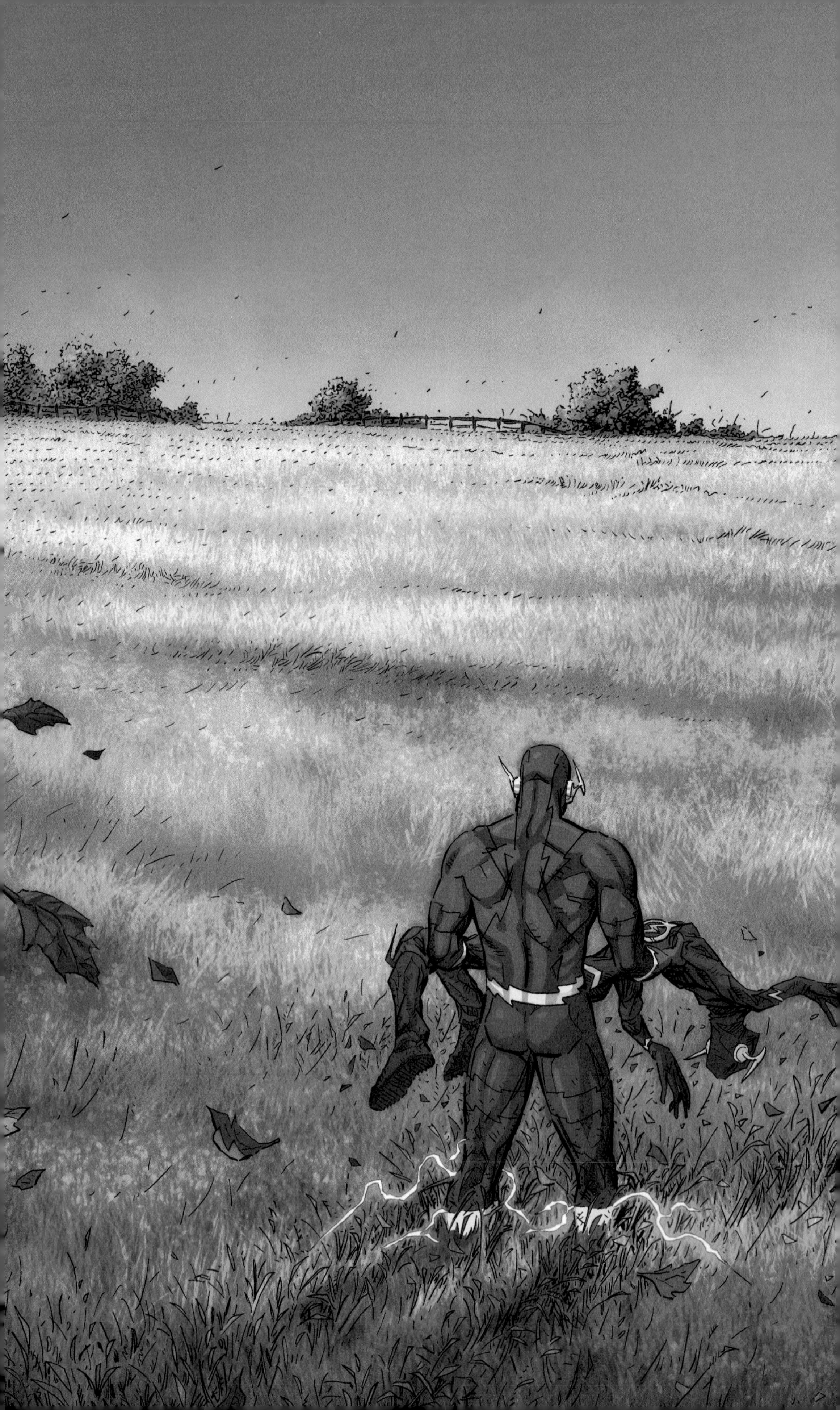

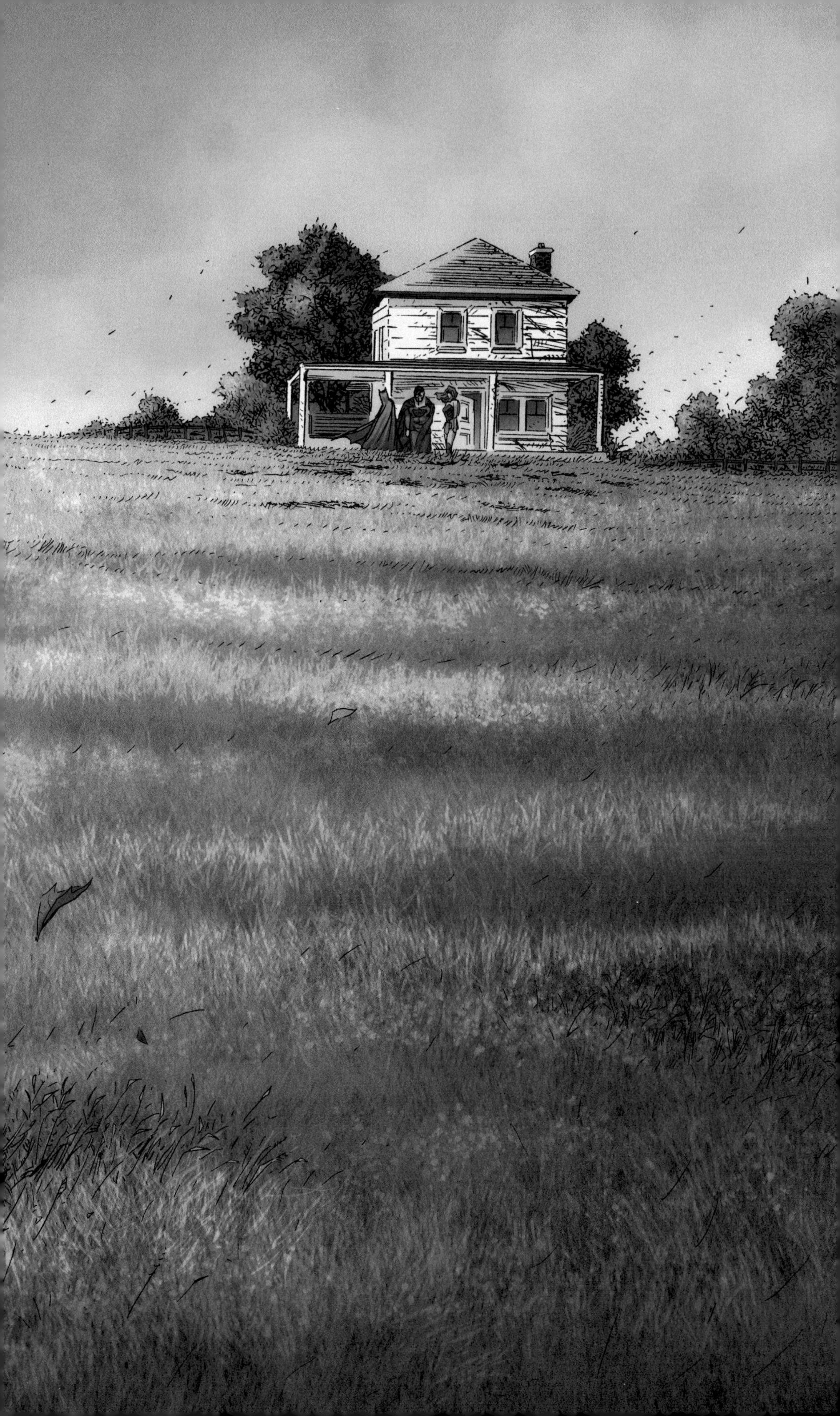

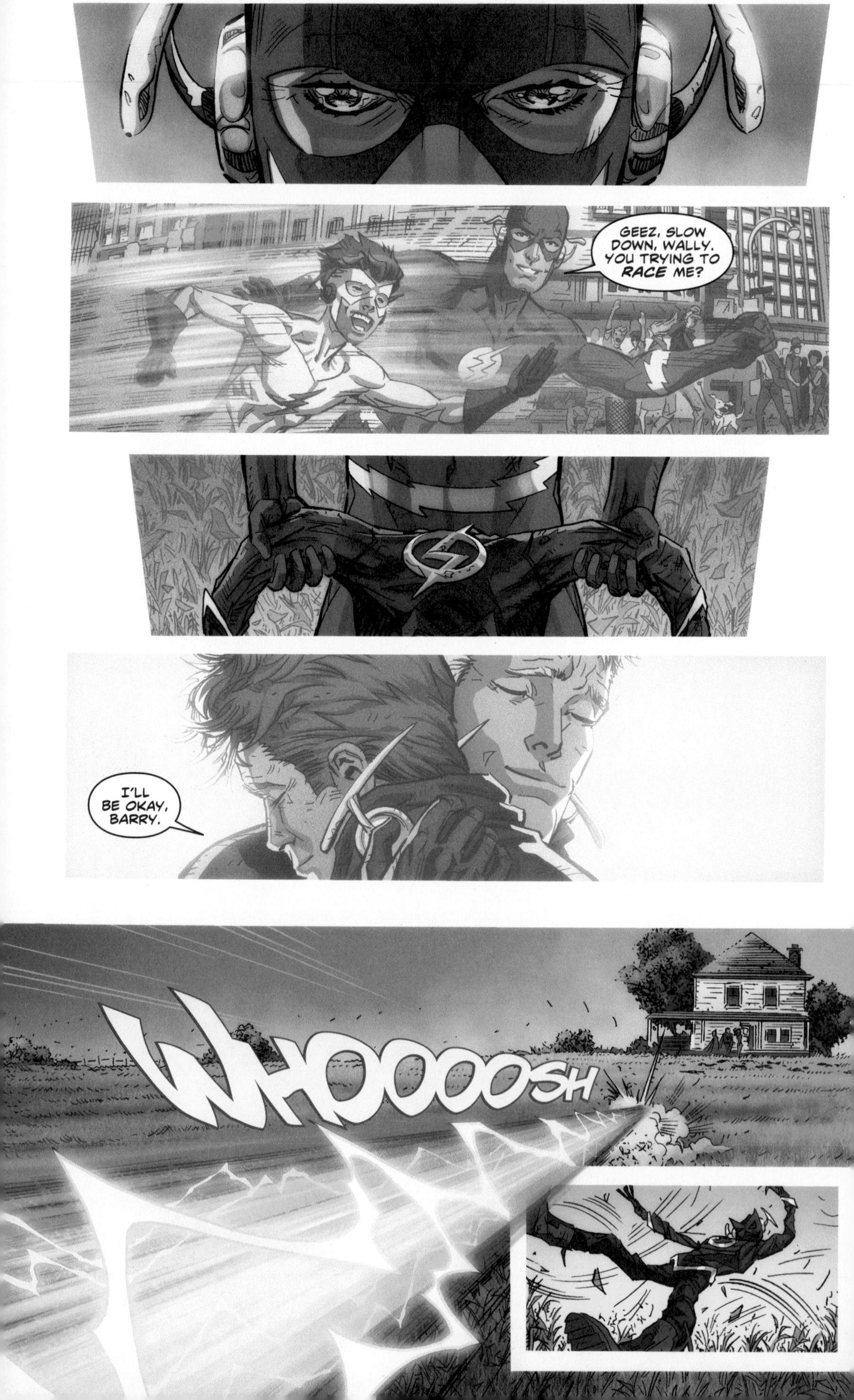
GEEZ, SLOW DOWN, WALLY. YOU TRYING TO RACE ME?
I'LL BE OKAY, BARRY.
WHOOOOSH

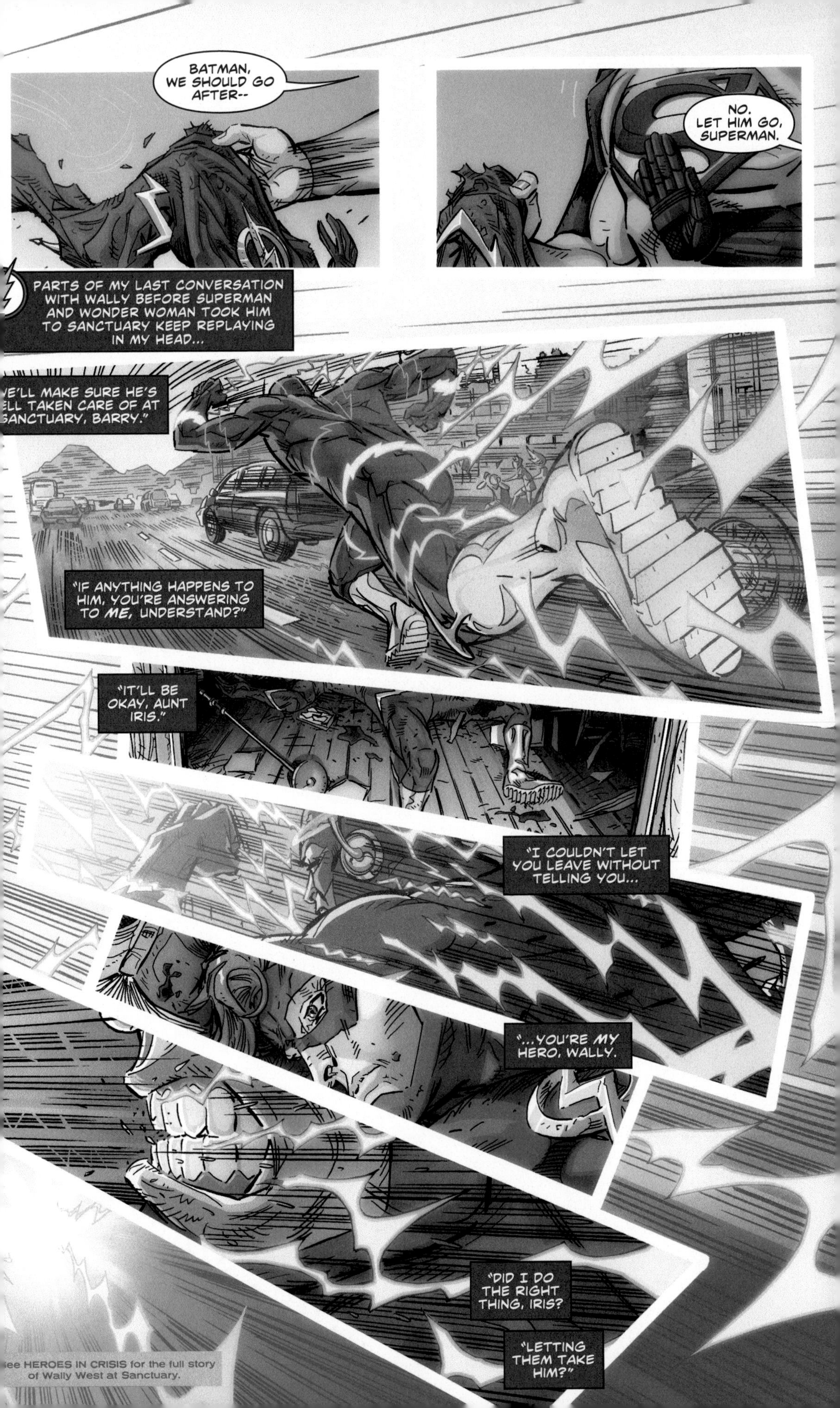

BATMAN, WE SHOULD GO AFTER--
NO. LET HIM GO, SUPERMAN.
PARTS OF MY LAST CONVERSATION WITH WALLY BEFORE SUPERMAN AND WONDER WOMAN TOOK HIM TO SANCTUARY KEEP REPLAYING IN MY HEAD...
...E'LL MAKE SURE HE'S ...ELL TAKEN CARE OF AT ...SANCTUARY, BARRY."
"IF ANYTHING HAPPENS TO HIM, YOU'RE ANSWERING TO ME, UNDERSTAND?"
"IT'LL BE OKAY, AUNT IRIS."
"I COULDN'T LET YOU LEAVE WITHOUT TELLING YOU...
"...YOU'RE MY HERO, WALLY.
"DID I DO THE RIGHT THING, IRIS?
"LETTING THEM TAKE HIM?"
...ee HEROES IN CRISIS for the full story of Wally West at Sanctuary.

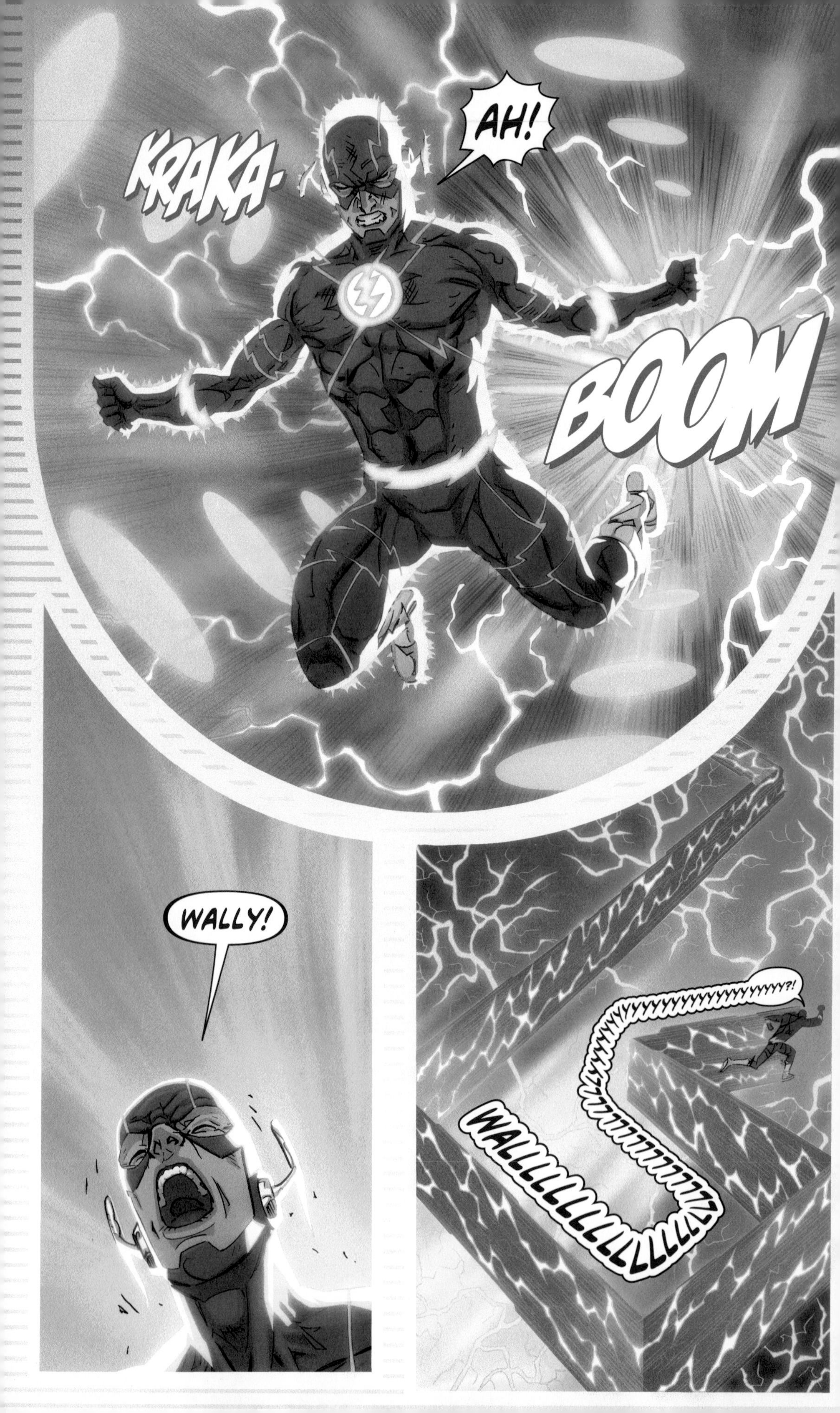
KRAKA-
AH!
BOOM
WALLY!
WALLLLLLLLLLLLLLLLLLLLLLLLLLLLLLLLYYYYYYYYYYYYYYYYYYYYYYYYYYYYYY?!

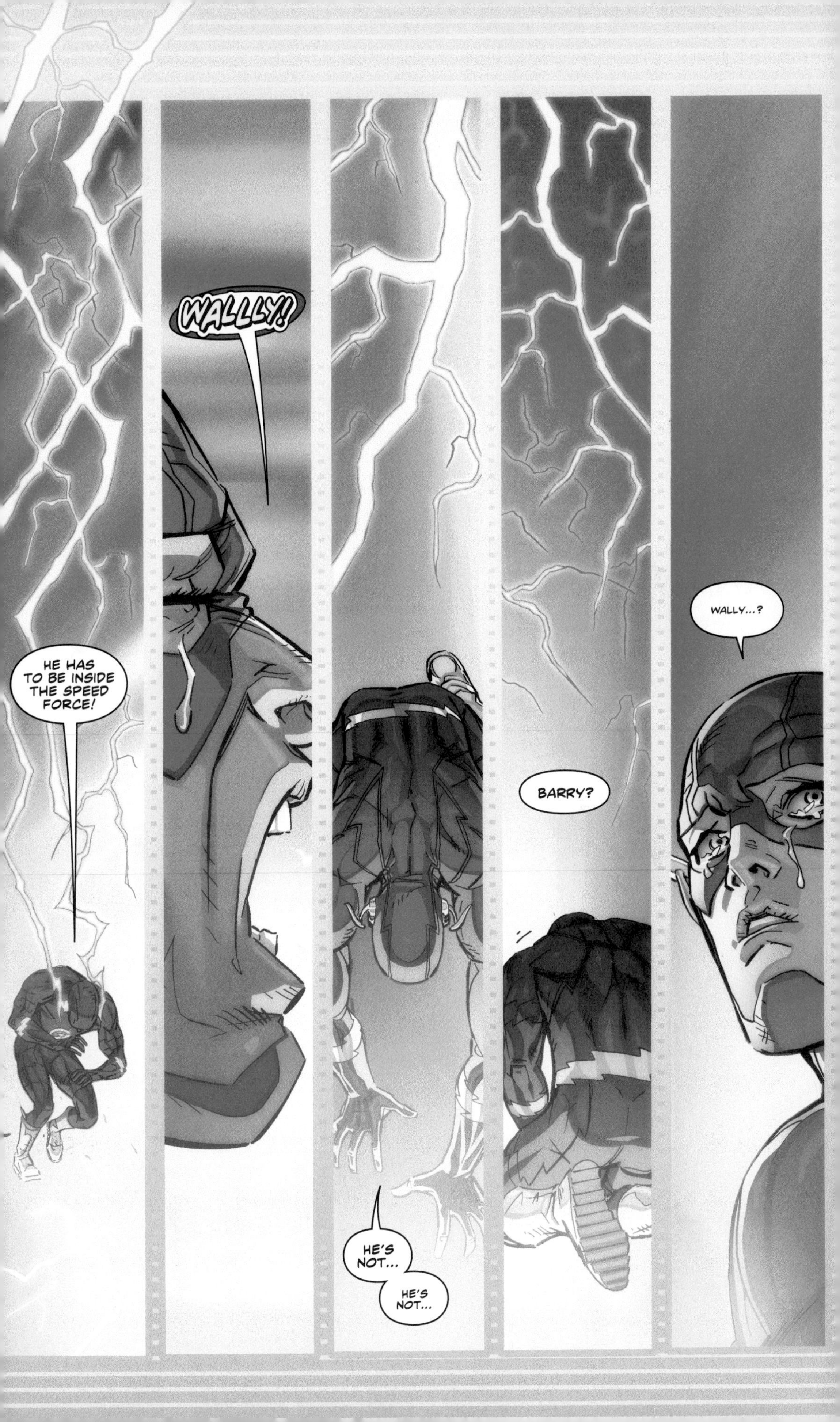
HE HAS TO BE INSIDE THE SPEED FORCE!
WALLLY!
HE'S NOT...
HE'S NOT...
BARRY?
WALLY...?

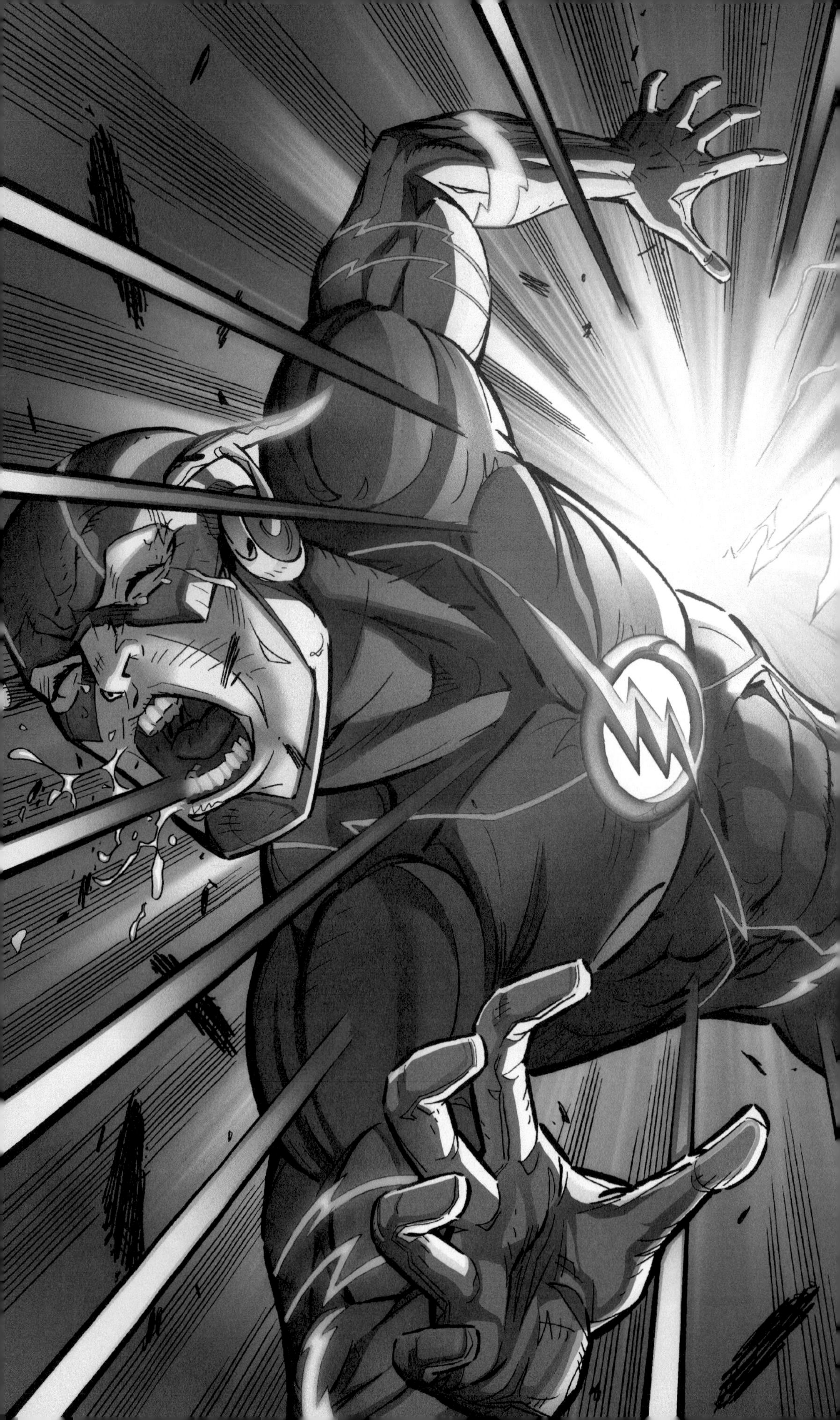

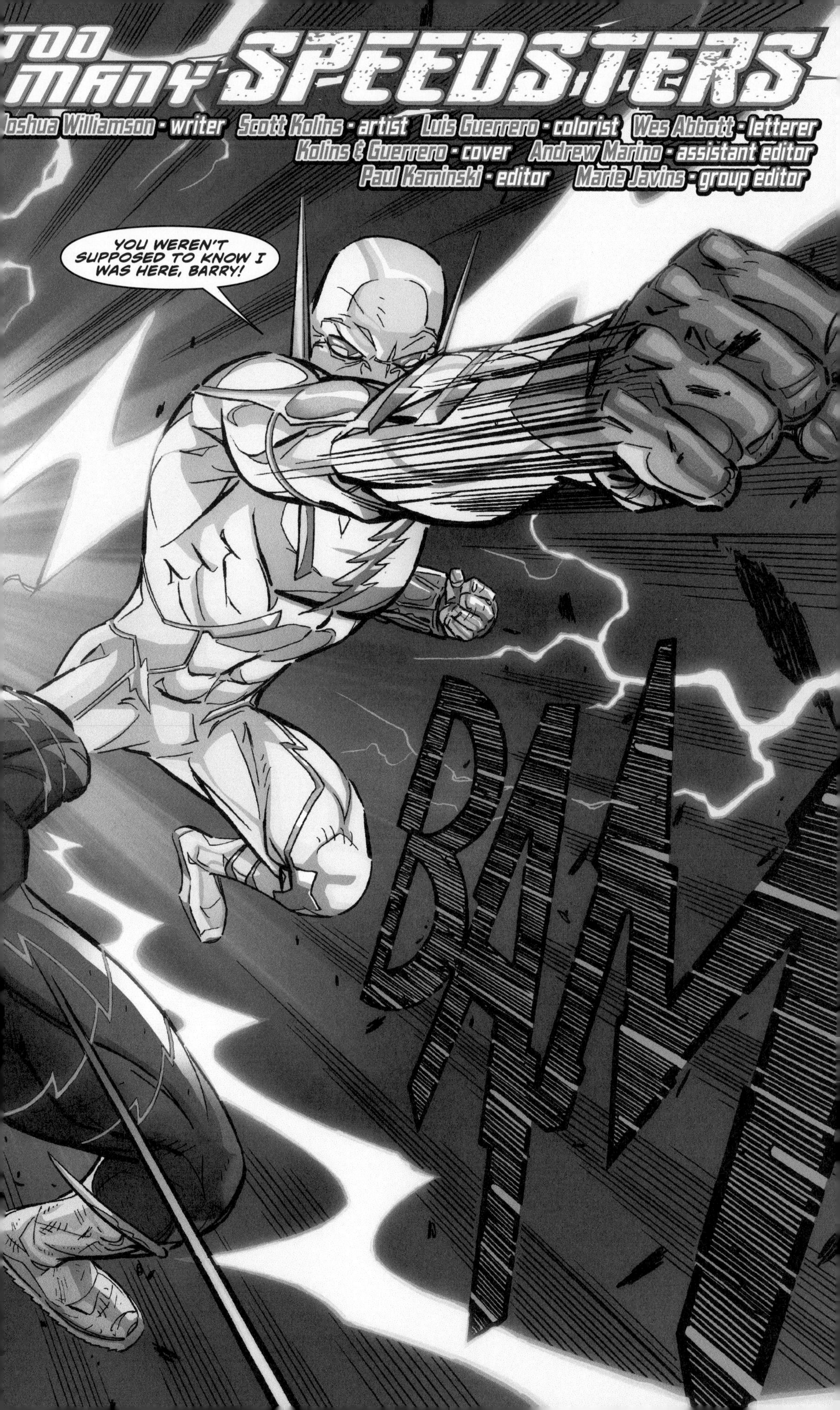
TOO MANY SPEEDSTERS
Joshua Williamson - writer Scott Kolins - artist Luis Guerrero - colorist Wes Abbott - letterer
Kolins & Guerrero - cover Andrew Marino - assistant editor
Paul Kaminski - editor Marie Javins - group editor
YOU WEREN'T SUPPOSED TO KNOW I WAS HERE, BARRY!
BAM

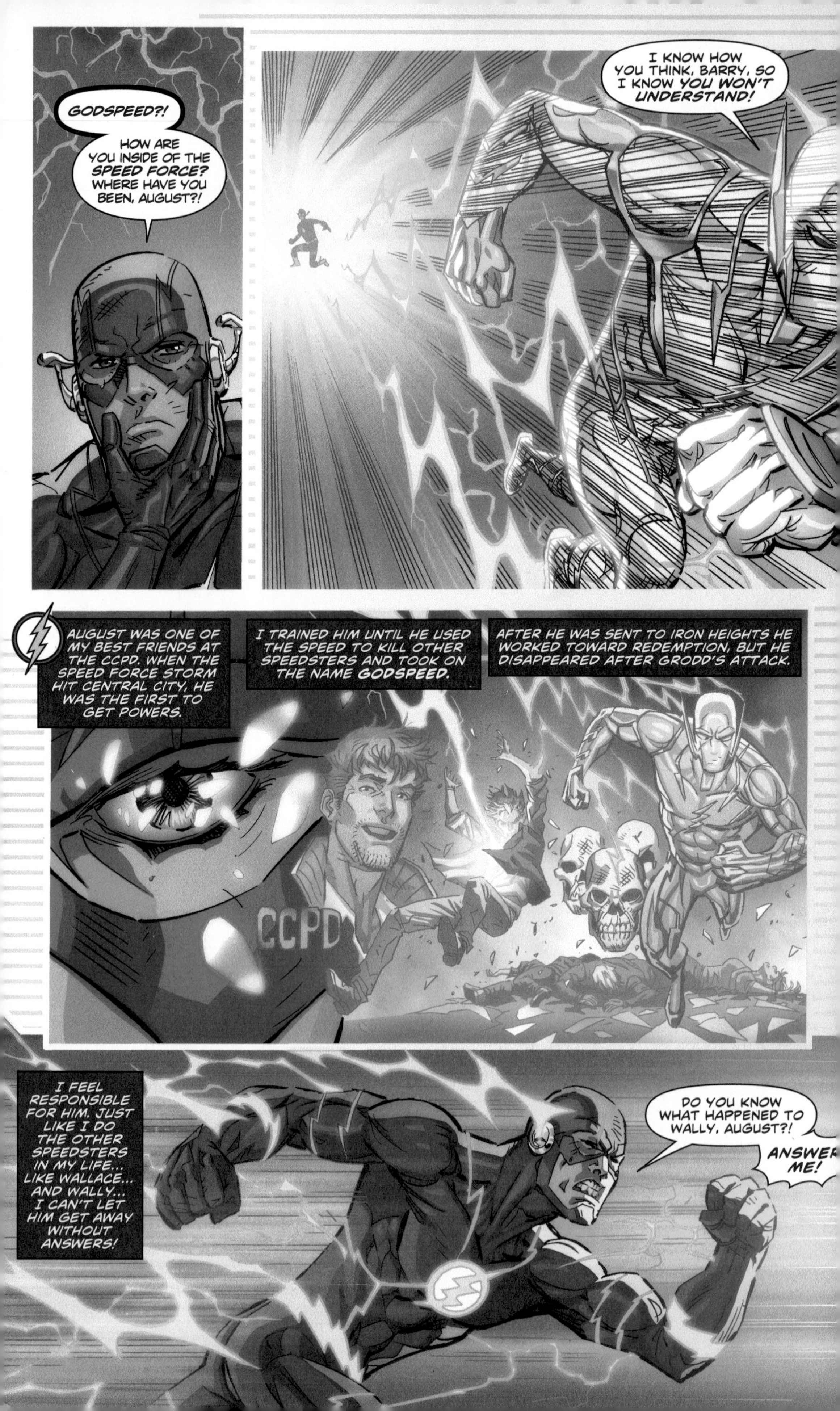
GODSPEED?!
HOW ARE YOU INSIDE OF THE SPEED FORCE? WHERE HAVE YOU BEEN, AUGUST?!
I KNOW HOW YOU THINK, BARRY, SO I KNOW YOU WON'T UNDERSTAND!
AUGUST WAS ONE OF MY BEST FRIENDS AT THE CCPD. WHEN THE SPEED FORCE STORM HIT CENTRAL CITY, HE WAS THE FIRST TO GET POWERS.
I TRAINED HIM UNTIL HE USED THE SPEED TO KILL OTHER SPEEDSTERS AND TOOK ON THE NAME GODSPEED.
AFTER HE WAS SENT TO IRON HEIGHTS HE WORKED TOWARD REDEMPTION, BUT HE DISAPPEARED AFTER GRODD'S ATTACK.
CCPD
I FEEL RESPONSIBLE FOR HIM. JUST LIKE I DO THE OTHER SPEEDSTERS IN MY LIFE... LIKE WALLACE... AND WALLY... I CAN'T LET HIM GET AWAY WITHOUT ANSWERS!
DO YOU KNOW WHAT HAPPENED TO WALLY, AUGUST?!
ANSWER ME!

YOU KNOW YOU CAN'T OUTRUN ME!

THAT A FACT?

WHAT IF I WANTED YOU TO BELIEVE THAT, SLOWPOKE?!

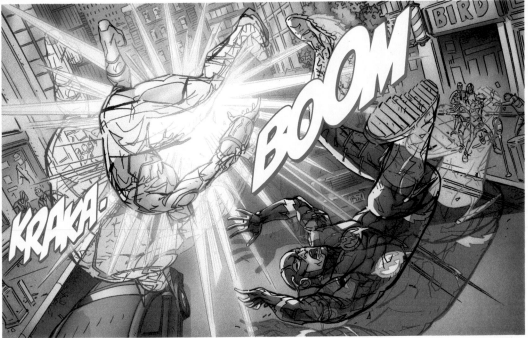

KRAKA-

BOOM

I THOUGHT YOU WANTED REDEMPTION?

THAT TAKES ACTIONS, NOT WORDS, OL' BUDDY.

HAVEN'T YOU LEARNED THAT YET? YOU CAN'T JUST SAY YOU WANT TO BE REDEEMED.

THAT'S WHY I'VE MADE IT MY LIFE'S MISSION TO HELP CLEAN UP YOUR MESS.

WHAT MESS?!

SORRY, BARRY. THE FUTURE NEEDS SAVING.

I'VE NEVER HEARD AUGUST SOUND SO...

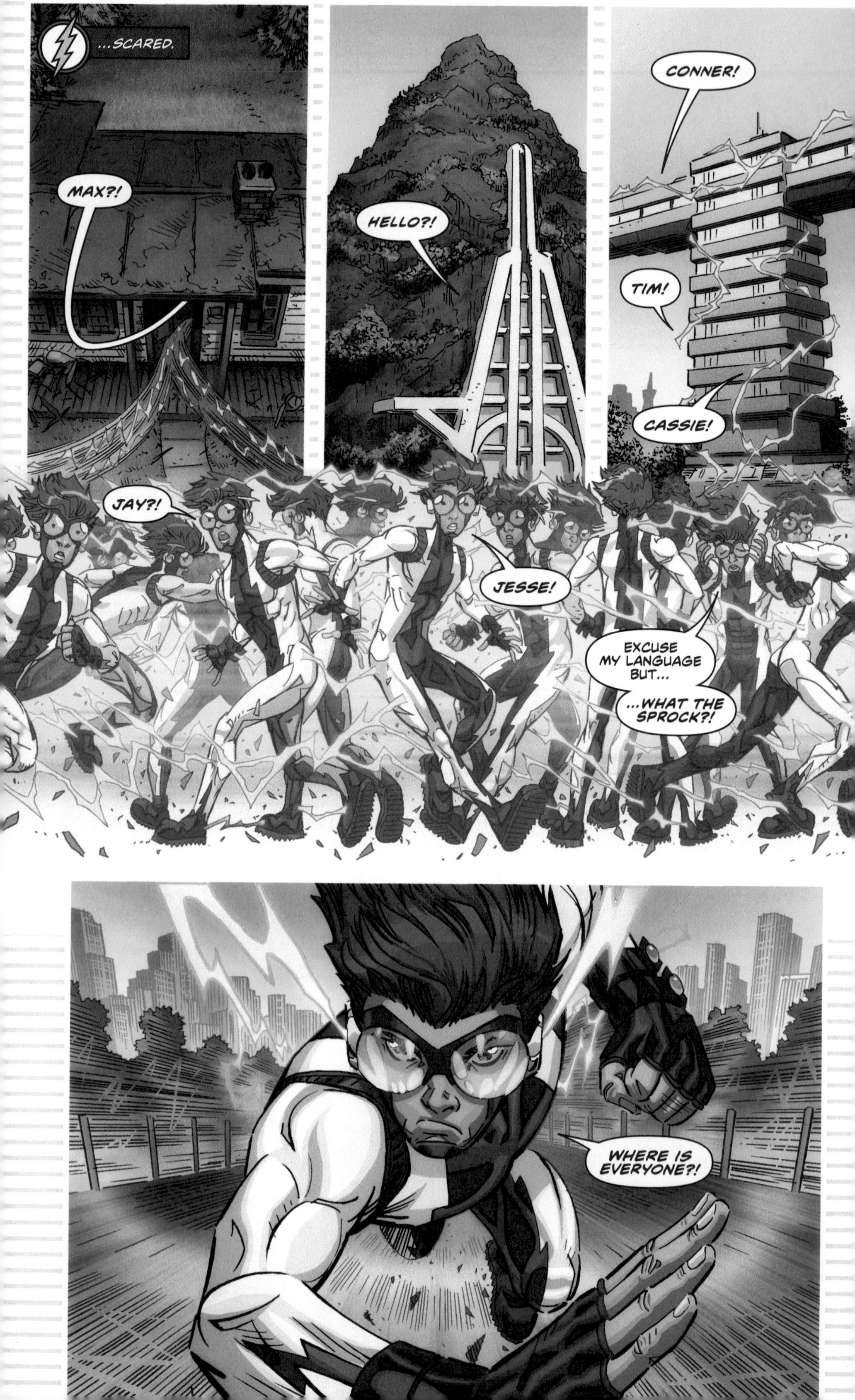
...SCARED.
MAX?!
HELLO?!
CONNER!
TIM!
CASSIE!
JAY?!
JESSE!
EXCUSE MY LANGUAGE BUT...
...WHAT THE SPROCK?!
WHERE IS EVERYONE?!

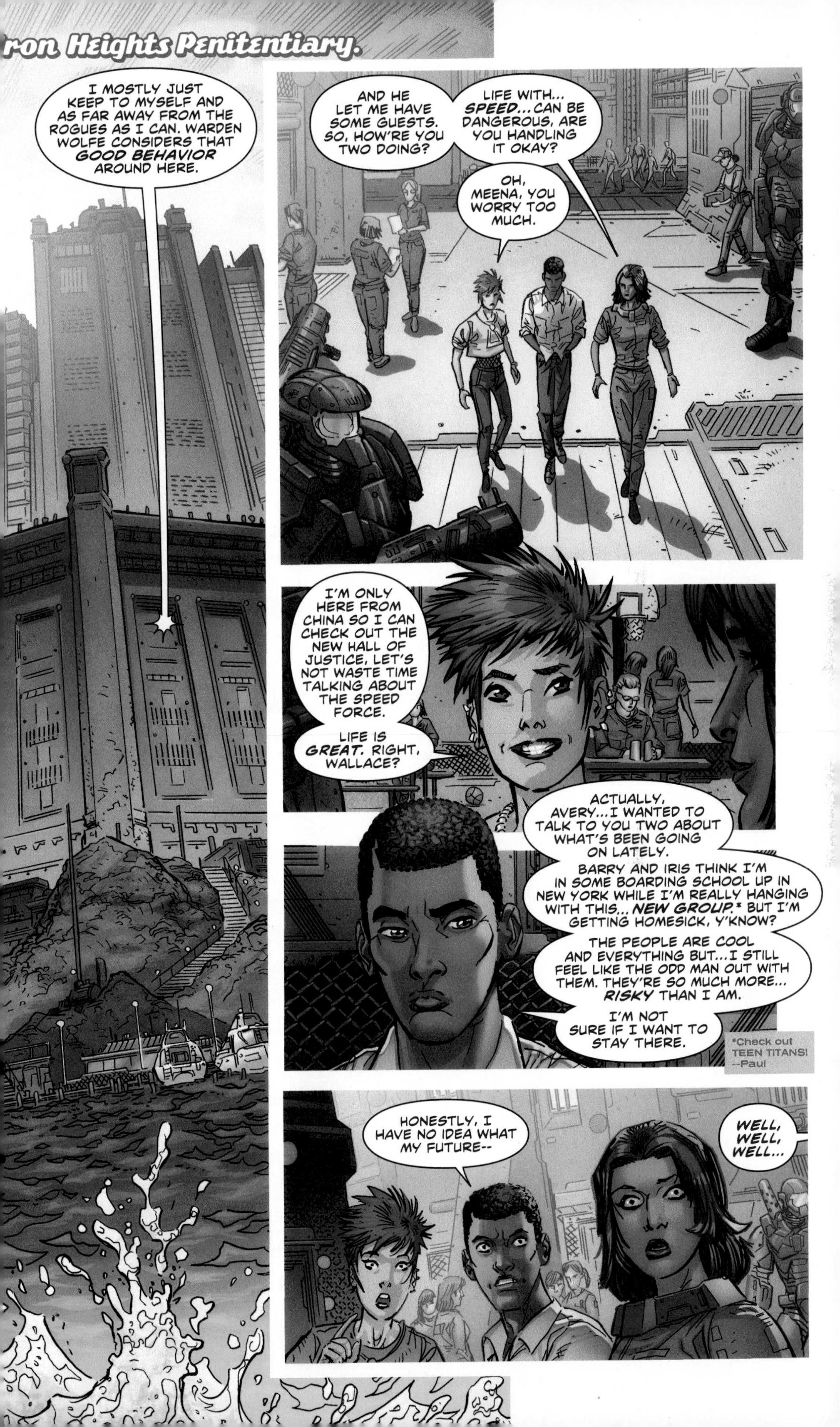
ron Heights Penitentiary.
I MOSTLY JUST KEEP TO MYSELF AND AS FAR AWAY FROM THE ROGUES AS I CAN. WARDEN WOLFE CONSIDERS THAT GOOD BEHAVIOR AROUND HERE.
AND HE LET ME HAVE SOME GUESTS. SO, HOW'RE YOU TWO DOING?
LIFE WITH... SPEED...CAN BE DANGEROUS, ARE YOU HANDLING IT OKAY?
OH, MEENA, YOU WORRY TOO MUCH.
I'M ONLY HERE FROM CHINA SO I CAN CHECK OUT THE NEW HALL OF JUSTICE, LET'S NOT WASTE TIME TALKING ABOUT THE SPEED FORCE.
LIFE IS GREAT. RIGHT, WALLACE?
ACTUALLY, AVERY...I WANTED TO TALK TO YOU TWO ABOUT WHAT'S BEEN GOING ON LATELY.
BARRY AND IRIS THINK I'M IN SOME BOARDING SCHOOL UP IN NEW YORK WHILE I'M REALLY HANGING WITH THIS... NEW GROUP.* BUT I'M GETTING HOMESICK, Y'KNOW?
THE PEOPLE ARE COOL AND EVERYTHING BUT...I STILL FEEL LIKE THE ODD MAN OUT WITH THEM. THEY'RE SO MUCH MORE... RISKY THAN I AM.
I'M NOT SURE IF I WANT TO STAY THERE.
*Check out TEEN TITANS! --Paul
HONESTLY, I HAVE NO IDEA WHAT MY FUTURE--
WELL, WELL, WELL...

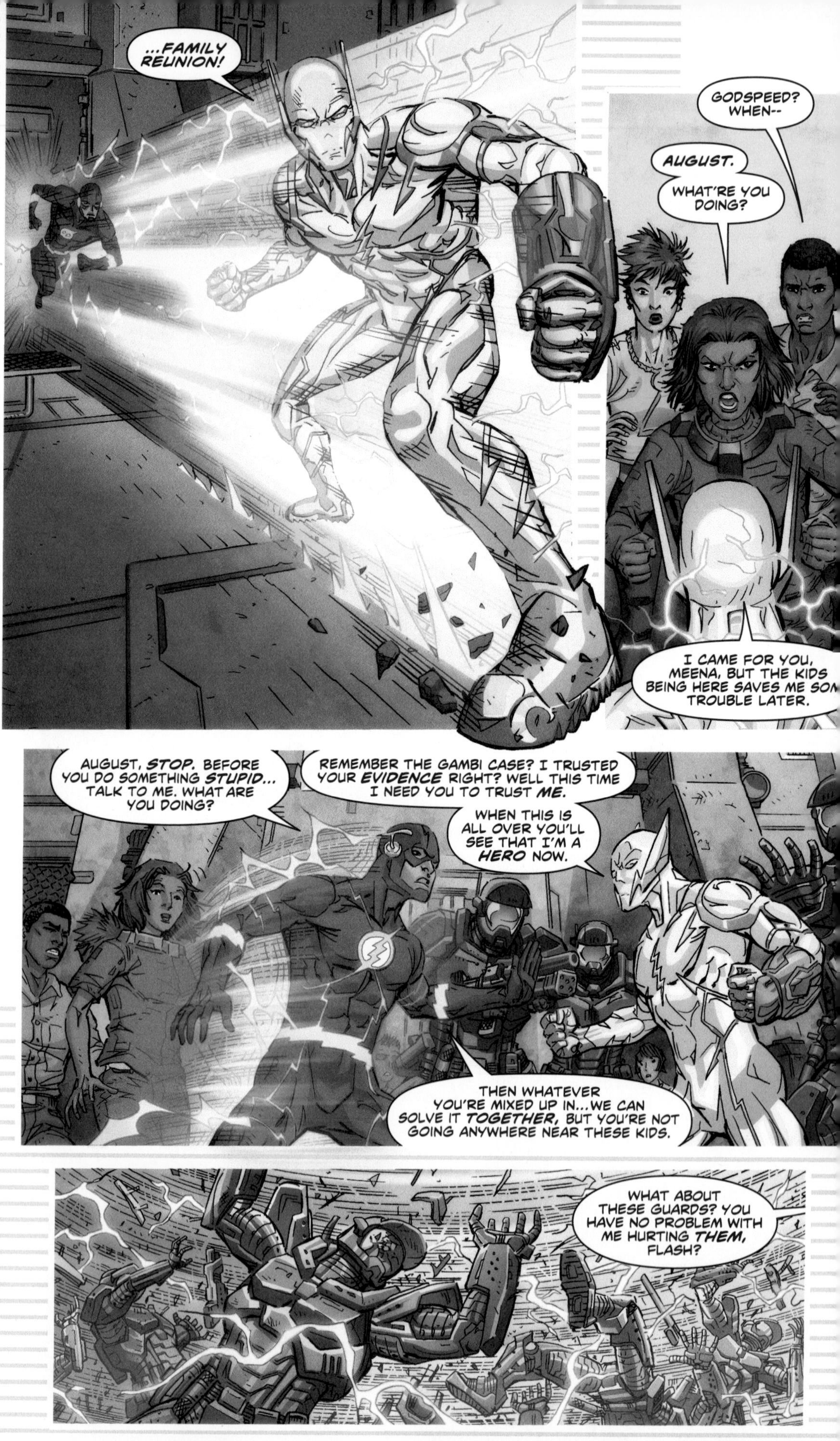
...FAMILY REUNION!
GODSPEED? WHEN--
AUGUST.
WHAT'RE YOU DOING?
I CAME FOR YOU, MEENA, BUT THE KIDS BEING HERE SAVES ME SOM TROUBLE LATER.
AUGUST, STOP. BEFORE YOU DO SOMETHING STUPID... TALK TO ME. WHAT ARE YOU DOING?
REMEMBER THE GAMBI CASE? I TRUSTED YOUR EVIDENCE RIGHT? WELL THIS TIME I NEED YOU TO TRUST ME.
WHEN THIS IS ALL OVER YOU'LL SEE THAT I'M A HERO NOW.
THEN WHATEVER YOU'RE MIXED UP IN...WE CAN SOLVE IT TOGETHER, BUT YOU'RE NOT GOING ANYWHERE NEAR THESE KIDS.
WHAT ABOUT THESE GUARDS? YOU HAVE NO PROBLEM WITH ME HURTING THEM, FLASH?

WHAT IS RONG WITH YOU?!

WALLACE, AVERY, RUN!

WAM

NO. STAY!

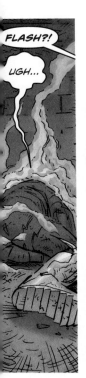

FLASH?!

UGH...

THE FLASH IS THE ONLY ONE WHO BELIEVED IN YOU, AUGUST.

IF I DIDN'T HAVE MY POWER INHIBITOR ON, I'D KICK YOUR ASS MYSELF, AUGUST.

IS THAT ANY WAY TO TALK TO AN OLD FRIEND?

YOU AND I WERE NEVER FRIENDS, BUT I'VE STUDIED THE SPEED FORCE AND I CAN SEE THERE'S SOMETHING WRONG WITH YOU.

IS SOMEONE IN YOUR HEAD?

I'VE NEVER BEEN MORE LUCID.

KKRACKK

I'M DOING THIS FOR YOUR OWN GOOD, MEENA.

AAHHHH!

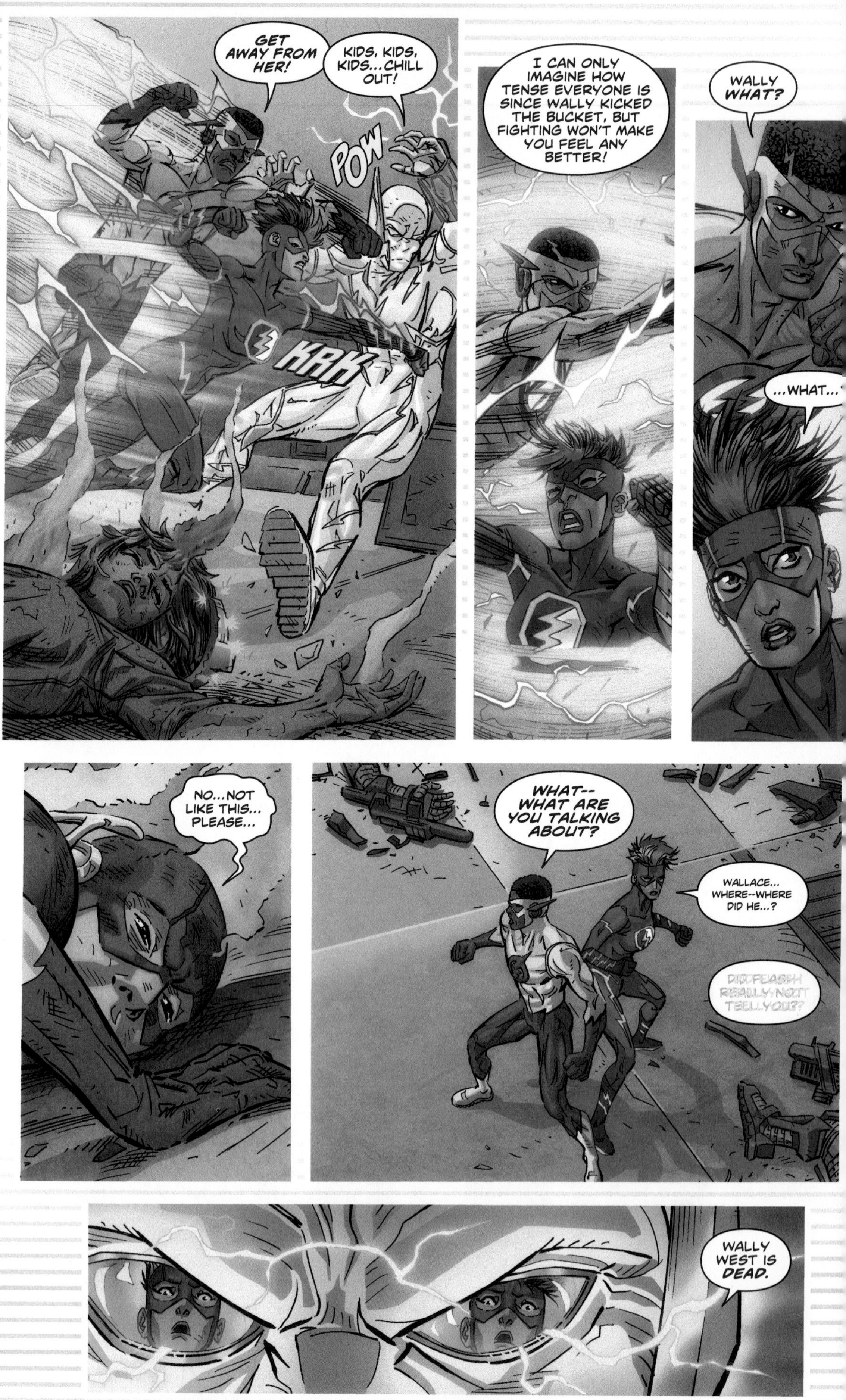
GET AWAY FROM HER!
KIDS, KIDS, KIDS...CHILL OUT!
POW
KRK
I CAN ONLY IMAGINE HOW TENSE EVERYONE IS SINCE WALLY KICKED THE BUCKET, BUT FIGHTING WON'T MAKE YOU FEEL ANY BETTER!
WALLY WHAT?
...WHAT...
NO...NOT LIKE THIS... PLEASE...
WHAT-- WHAT ARE YOU TALKING ABOUT?
WALLACE... WHERE--WHERE DID HE...?
DID FLASH REALLY NOT TELL YOU??
WALLY WEST IS DEAD.

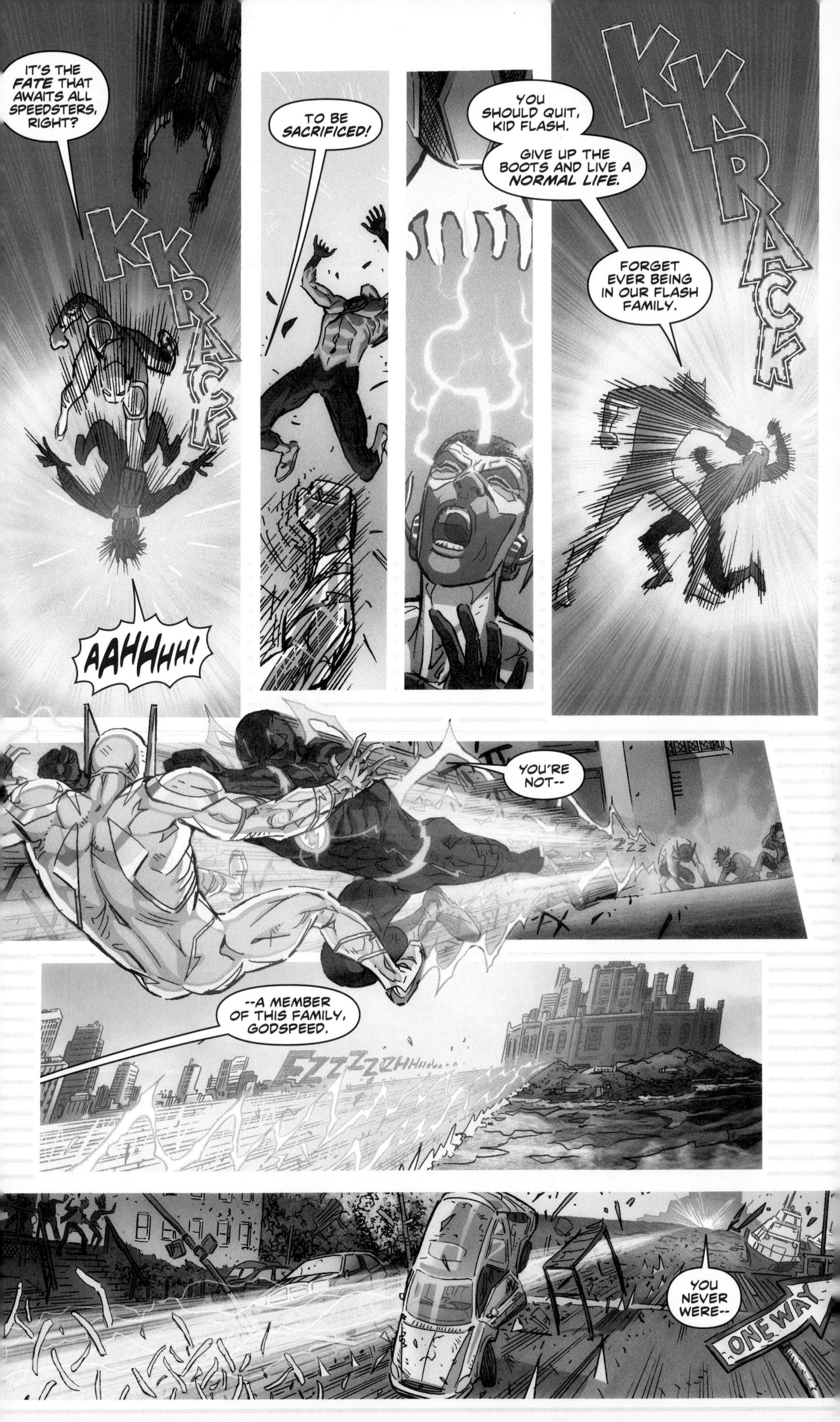
IT'S THE FATE THAT AWAITS ALL SPEEDSTERS, RIGHT?
KKRACK
AAHHHH!
TO BE SACRIFICED!
YOU SHOULD QUIT, KID FLASH.
GIVE UP THE BOOTS AND LIVE A NORMAL LIFE.
FORGET EVER BEING IN OUR FLASH FAMILY.
KKRACK
YOU'RE NOT--
ZZZ
--A MEMBER OF THIS FAMILY, GODSPEED.
EZZZZZHHHH...
YOU NEVER WERE--
ONE WAY

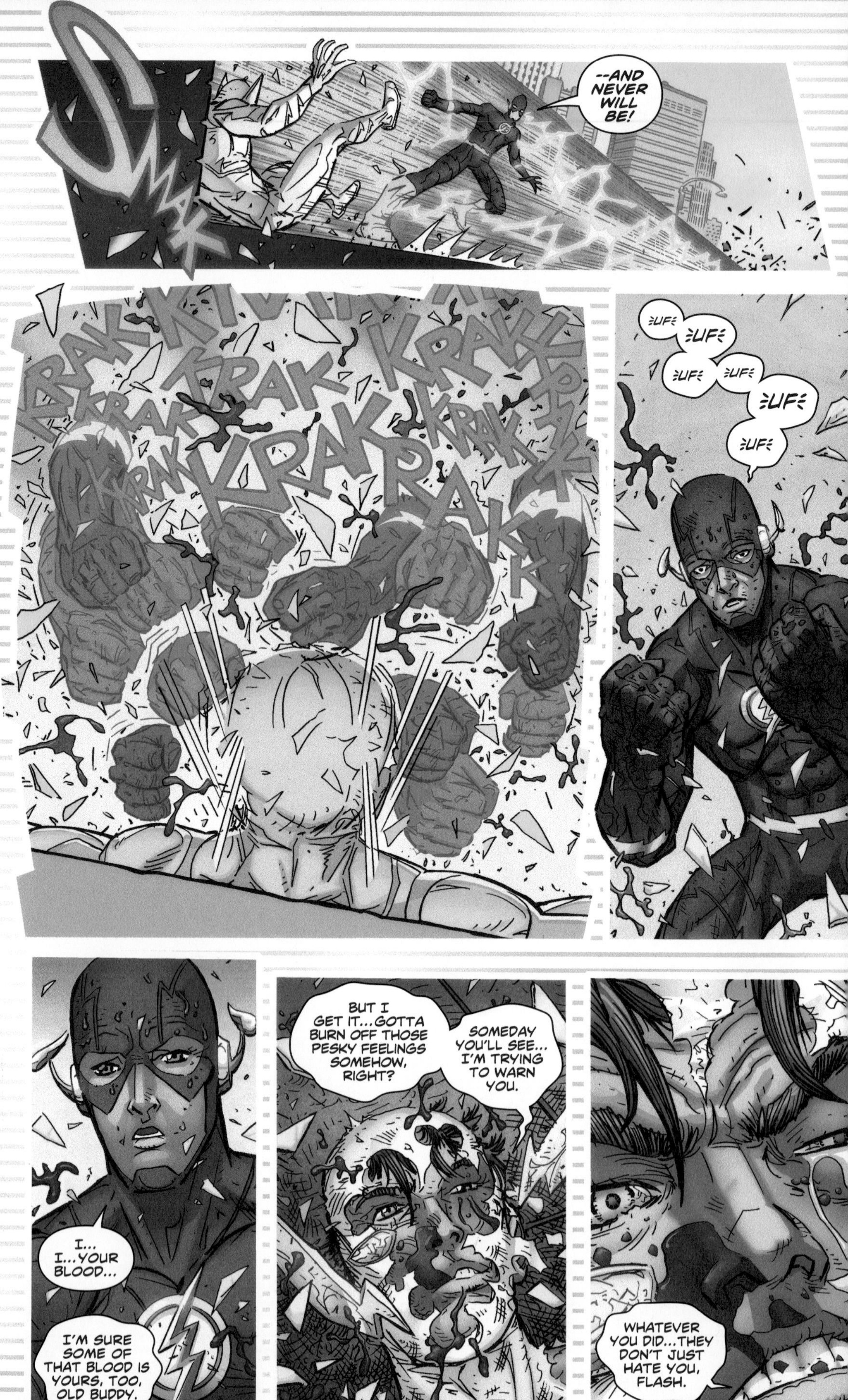
SMAK
--AND NEVER WILL BE!
KRAK KRAK KRAK KRAK KRAK KRAK KRAK KRAK
UF
UF
UF
UF
UF
UF
UF
I... I...YOUR BLOOD...
I'M SURE SOME OF THAT BLOOD IS YOURS, TOO, OLD BUDDY.
BUT I GET IT...GOTTA BURN OFF THOSE PESKY FEELINGS SOMEHOW, RIGHT?
SOMEDAY YOU'LL SEE... I'M TRYING TO WARN YOU.
WHATEVER YOU DID...THEY DON'T JUST HATE YOU, FLASH.

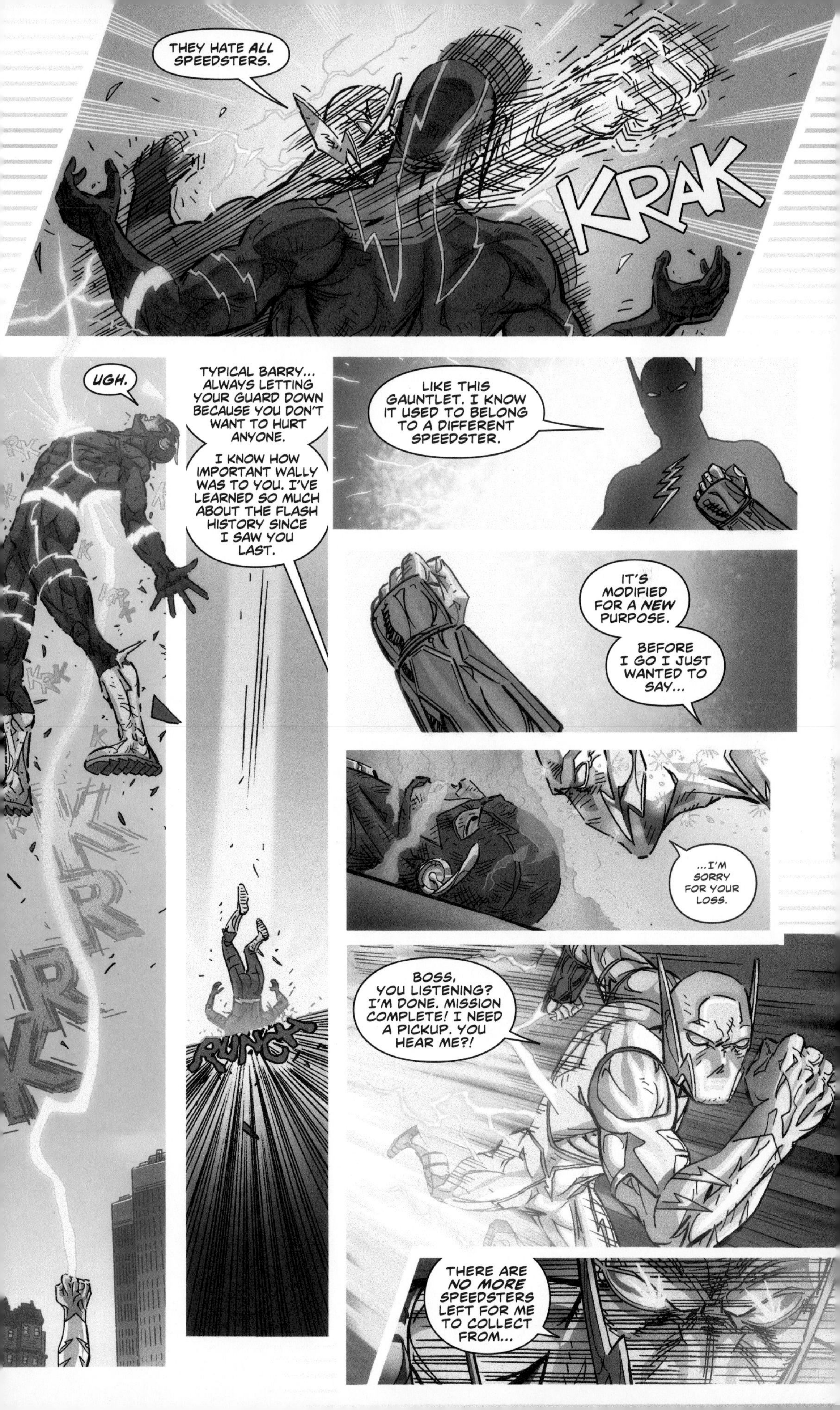
THEY HATE ALL SPEEDSTERS.
KRAK
UGH.
TYPICAL BARRY... ALWAYS LETTING YOUR GUARD DOWN BECAUSE YOU DON'T WANT TO HURT ANYONE.
I KNOW HOW IMPORTANT WALLY WAS TO YOU. I'VE LEARNED SO MUCH ABOUT THE FLASH HISTORY SINCE I SAW YOU LAST.
RUNCH
LIKE THIS GAUNTLET. I KNOW IT USED TO BELONG TO A DIFFERENT SPEEDSTER.
IT'S MODIFIED FOR A NEW PURPOSE.
BEFORE I GO I JUST WANTED TO SAY...
...I'M SORRY FOR YOUR LOSS.
BOSS, YOU LISTENING? I'M DONE. MISSION COMPLETE! I NEED A PICKUP. YOU HEAR ME?!
THERE ARE NO MORE SPEEDSTERS LEFT FOR ME TO COLLECT FROM...

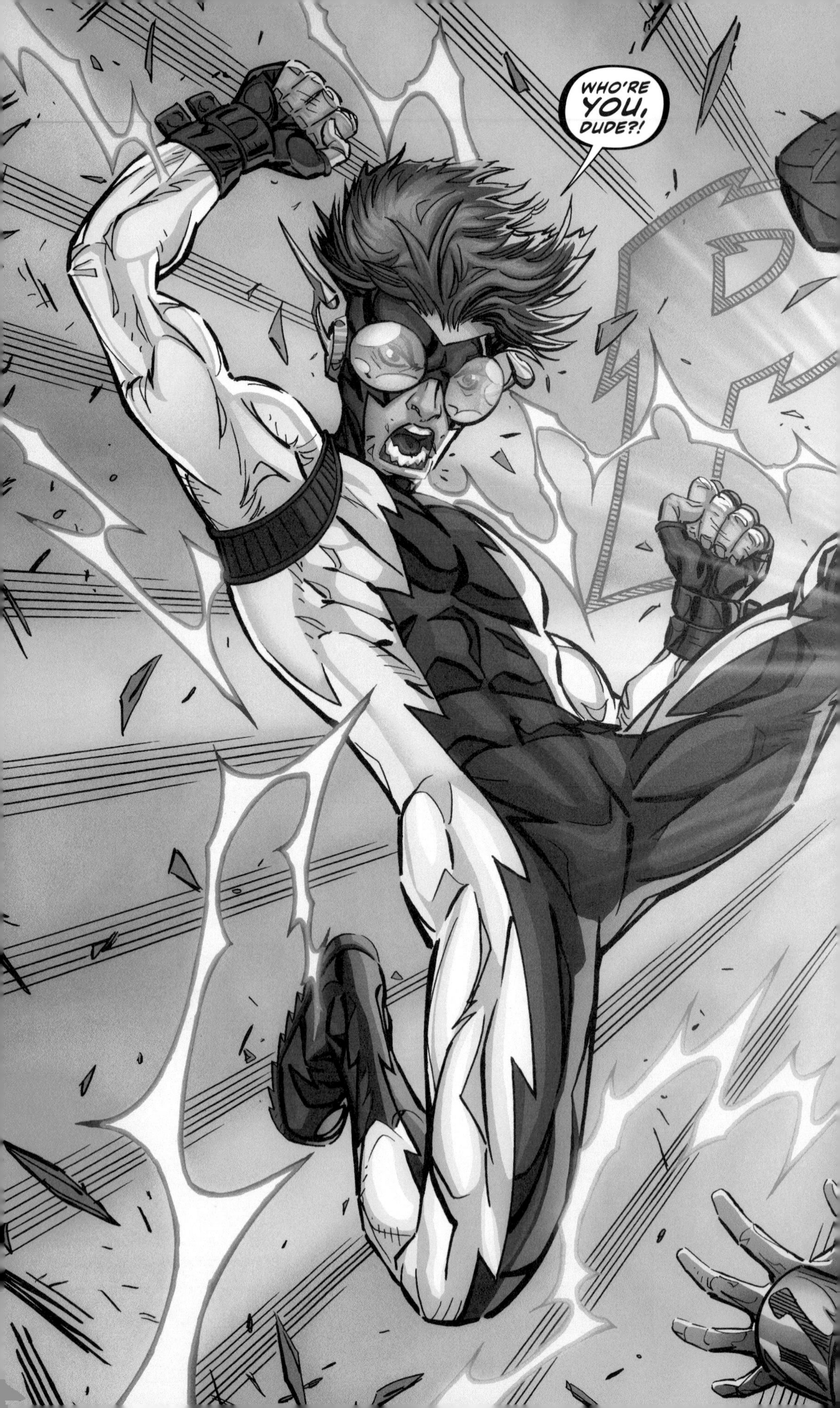
WHO'RE YOU, DUDE?!

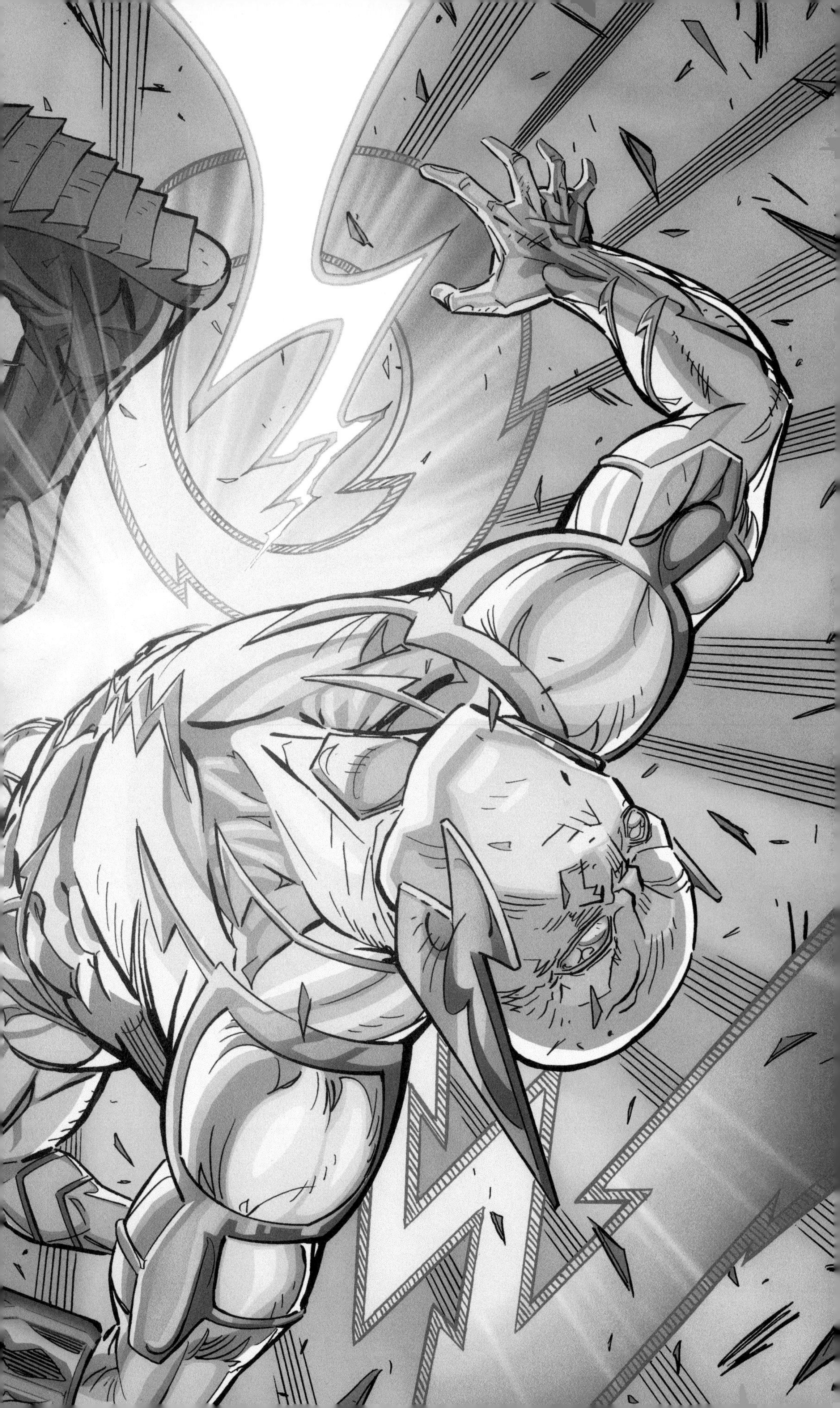

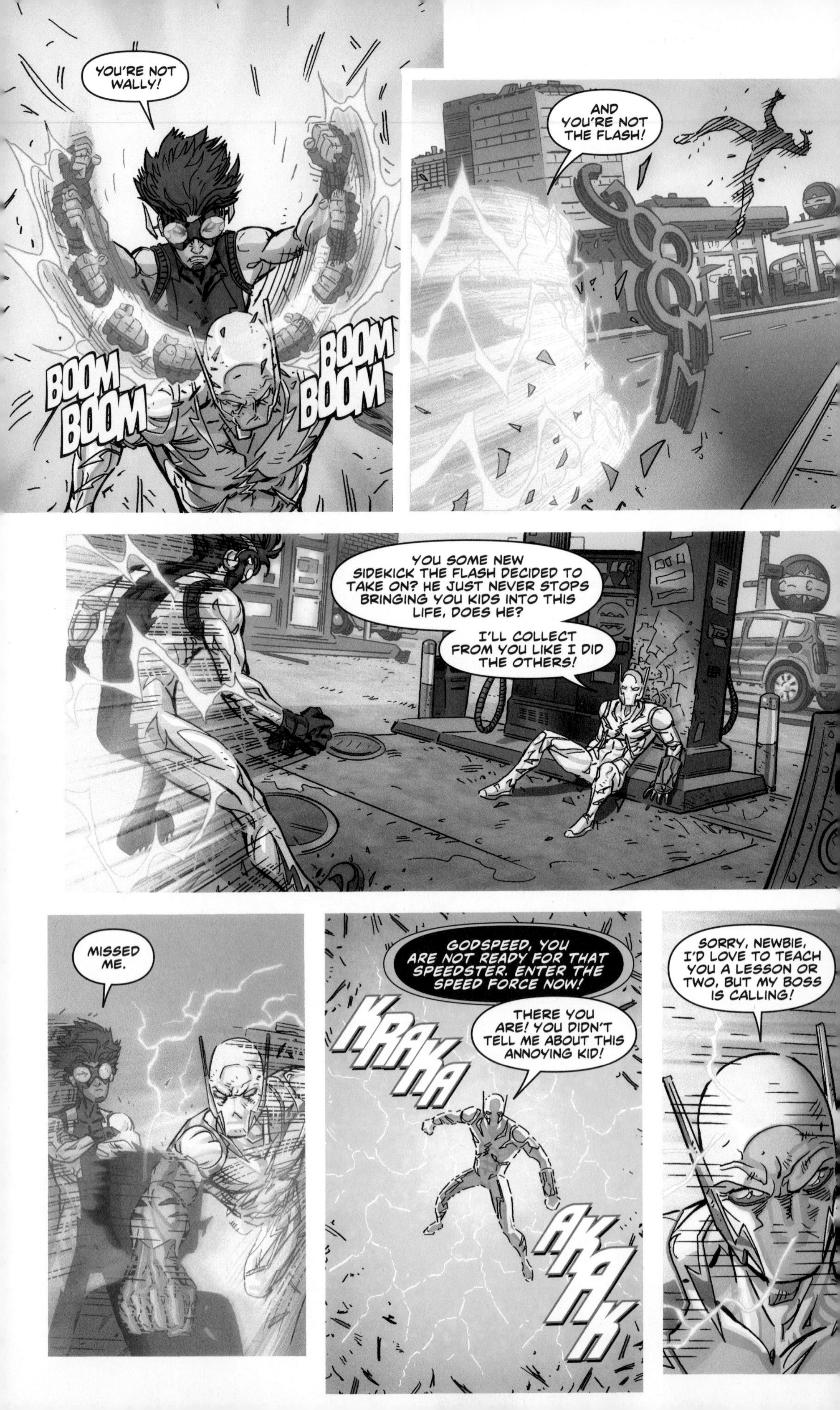
YOU'RE NOT WALLY!
BOOM BOOM
BOOM BOOM
AND YOU'RE NOT THE FLASH!
YOU SOME NEW SIDEKICK THE FLASH DECIDED TO TAKE ON? HE JUST NEVER STOPS BRINGING YOU KIDS INTO THIS LIFE, DOES HE?
I'LL COLLECT FROM YOU LIKE I DID THE OTHERS!
MISSED ME.
GODSPEED, YOU ARE NOT READY FOR THAT SPEEDSTER. ENTER THE SPEED FORCE NOW!
KRAKA
THERE YOU ARE! YOU DIDN'T TELL ME ABOUT THIS ANNOYING KID!
AKAK
SORRY, NEWBIE, I'D LOVE TO TEACH YOU A LESSON OR TWO, BUT MY BOSS IS CALLING!

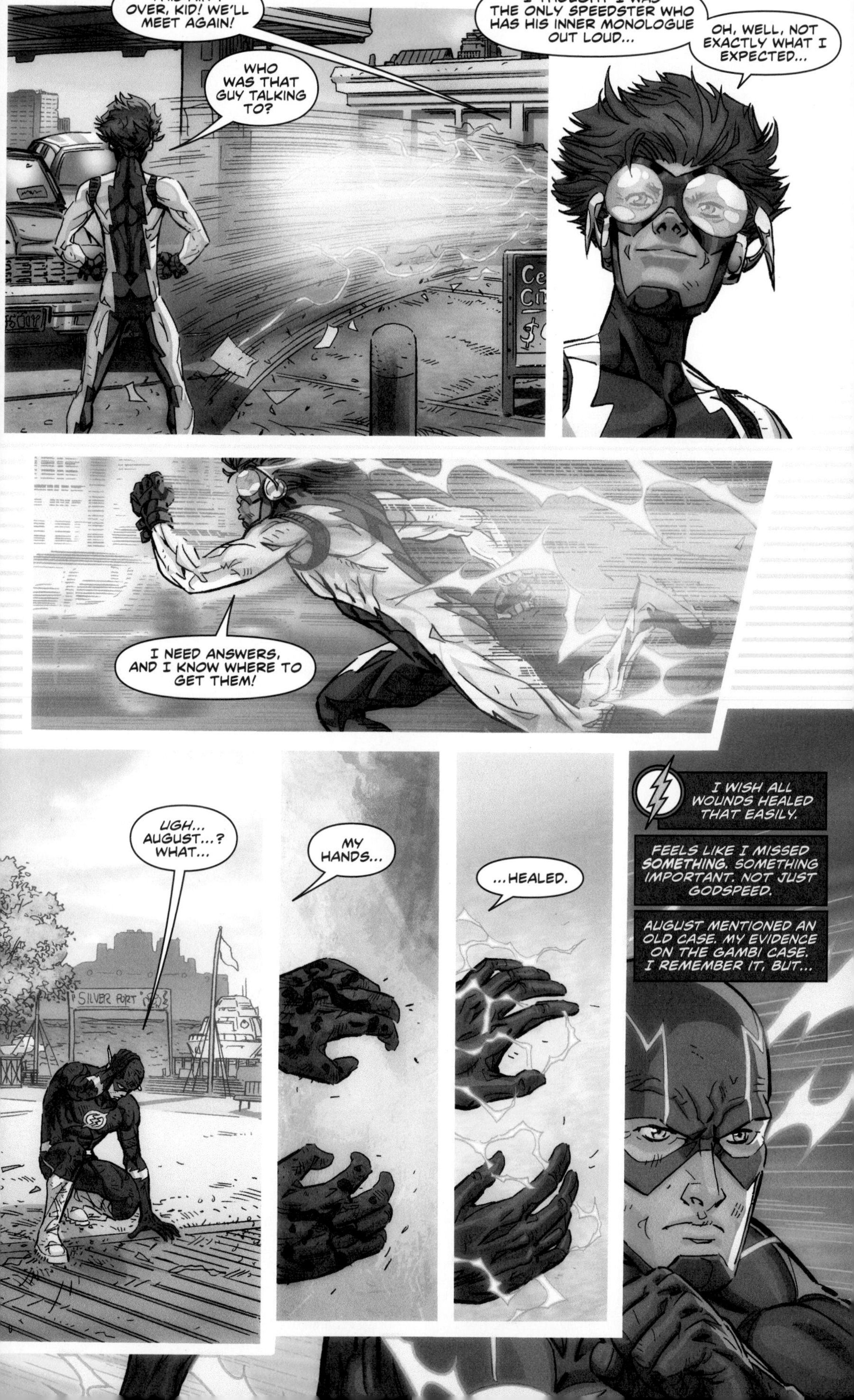

THIS AIN'T OVER, KID! WE'LL MEET AGAIN!
WHO WAS THAT GUY TALKING TO?
I THOUGHT I WAS THE ONLY SPEEDSTER WHO HAS HIS INNER MONOLOGUE OUT LOUD...
OH, WELL, NOT EXACTLY WHAT I EXPECTED...
I NEED ANSWERS, AND I KNOW WHERE TO GET THEM!
UGH... AUGUST...? WHAT...
SILVER PORT
MY HANDS...
...HEALED.
I WISH ALL WOUNDS HEALED THAT EASILY.
FEELS LIKE I MISSED SOMETHING. SOMETHING IMPORTANT. NOT JUST GODSPEED.
AUGUST MENTIONED AN OLD CASE. MY EVIDENCE ON THE GAMBI CASE. I REMEMBER IT, BUT...

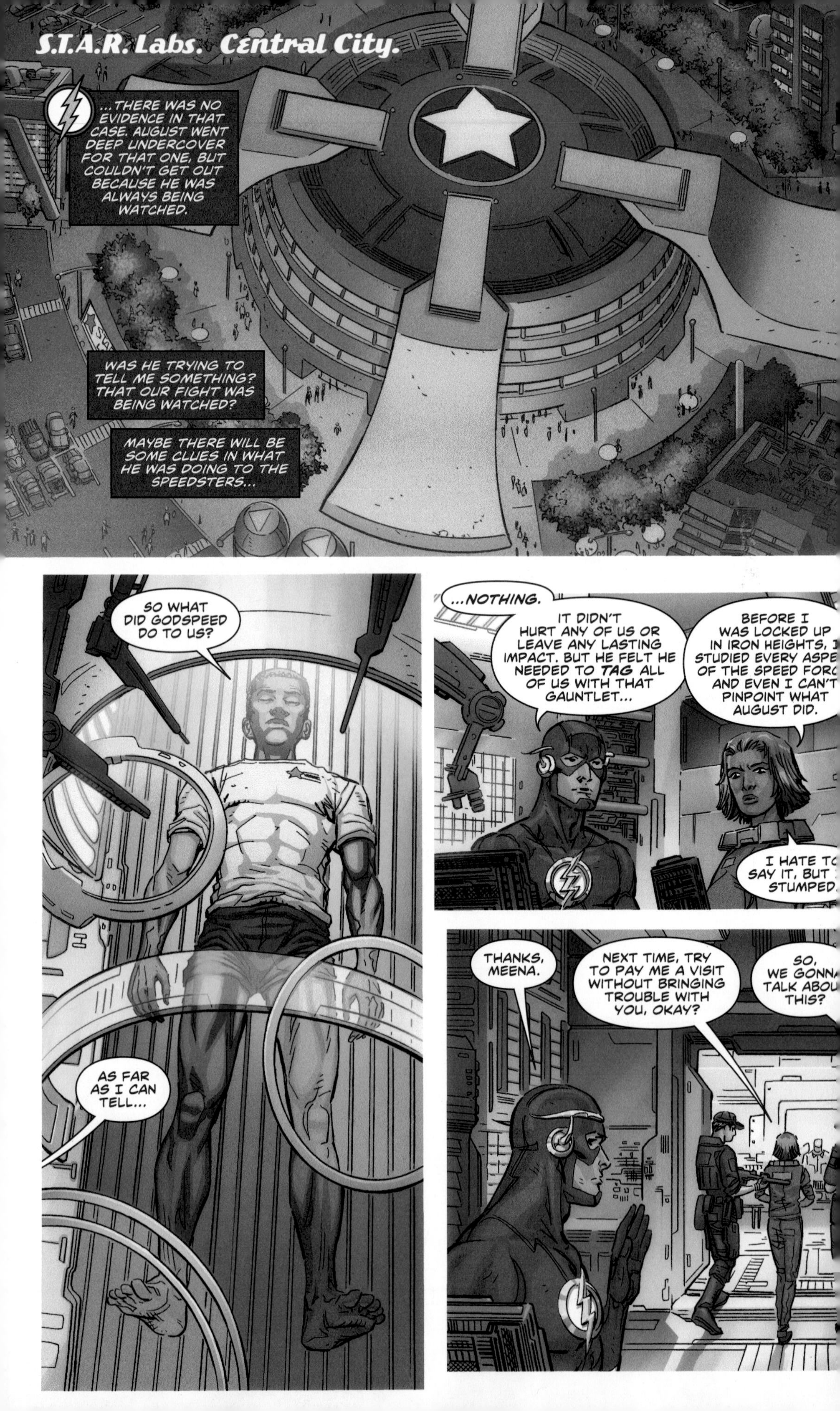
S.T.A.R. Labs. Central City.
...THERE WAS NO EVIDENCE IN THAT CASE. AUGUST WENT DEEP UNDERCOVER FOR THAT ONE, BUT COULDN'T GET OUT BECAUSE HE WAS ALWAYS BEING WATCHED.
WAS HE TRYING TO TELL ME SOMETHING? THAT OUR FIGHT WAS BEING WATCHED?
MAYBE THERE WILL BE SOME CLUES IN WHAT HE WAS DOING TO THE SPEEDSTERS...
SO WHAT DID GODSPEED DO TO US?
AS FAR AS I CAN TELL...
...NOTHING.
IT DIDN'T HURT ANY OF US OR LEAVE ANY LASTING IMPACT. BUT HE FELT HE NEEDED TO TAG ALL OF US WITH THAT GAUNTLET...
BEFORE I WAS LOCKED UP IN IRON HEIGHTS, I STUDIED EVERY ASPE OF THE SPEED FORC AND EVEN I CAN'T PINPOINT WHAT AUGUST DID.
I HATE T SAY IT, BUT STUMPED.
THANKS, MEENA.
NEXT TIME, TRY TO PAY ME A VISIT WITHOUT BRINGING TROUBLE WITH YOU, OKAY?
SO, WE GONN TALK ABOU THIS?

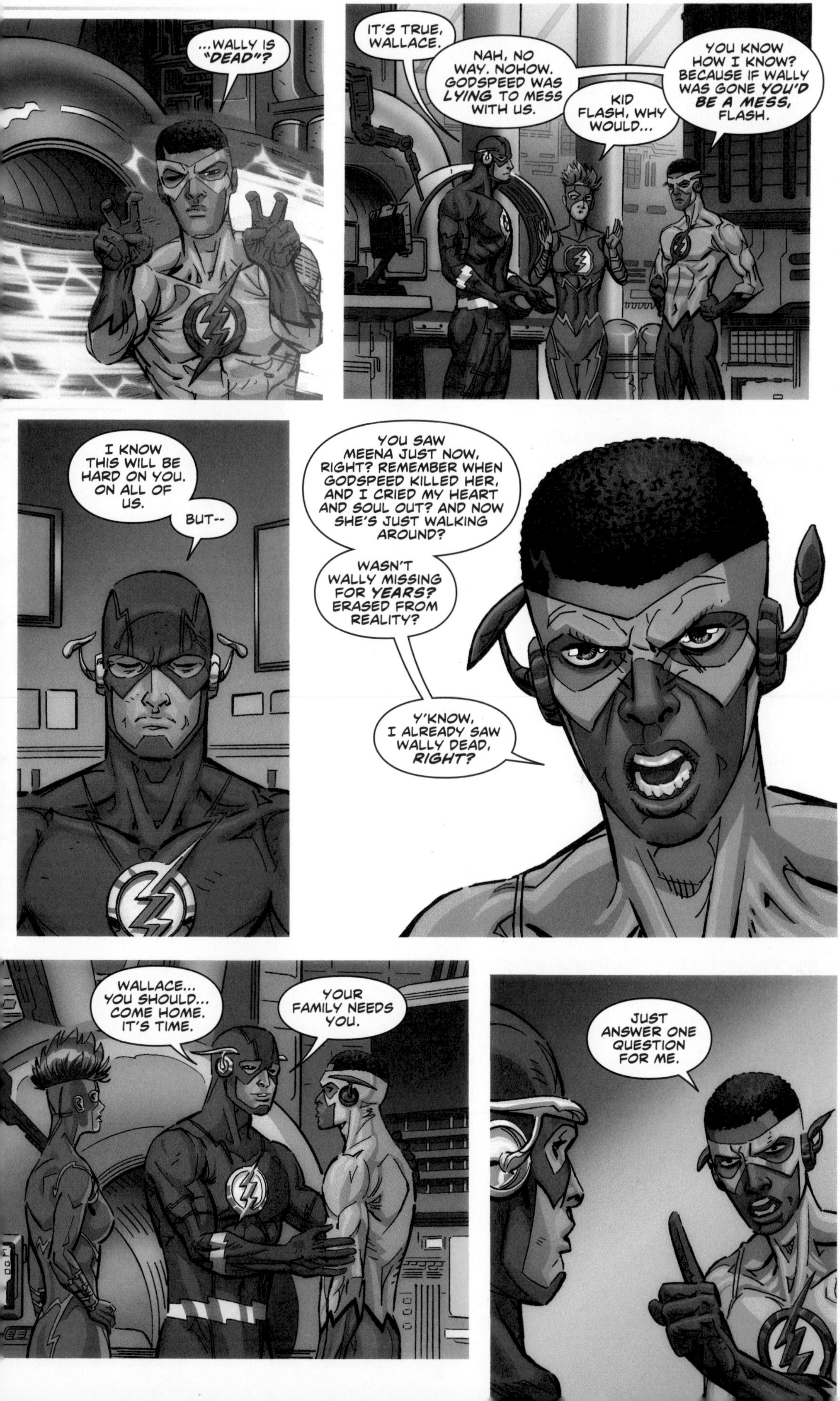
...WALLY IS "DEAD"?
IT'S TRUE, WALLACE.
NAH, NO WAY. NOHOW. GODSPEED WAS LYING TO MESS WITH US.
KID FLASH, WHY WOULD...
YOU KNOW HOW I KNOW? BECAUSE IF WALLY WAS GONE YOU'D BE A MESS, FLASH.
I KNOW THIS WILL BE HARD ON YOU. ON ALL OF US.
BUT--
YOU SAW MEENA JUST NOW, RIGHT? REMEMBER WHEN GODSPEED KILLED HER, AND I CRIED MY HEART AND SOUL OUT? AND NOW SHE'S JUST WALKING AROUND?
WASN'T WALLY MISSING FOR YEARS? ERASED FROM REALITY?
Y'KNOW, I ALREADY SAW WALLY DEAD, RIGHT?
WALLACE... YOU SHOULD... COME HOME. IT'S TIME.
YOUR FAMILY NEEDS YOU.
JUST ANSWER ONE QUESTION FOR ME.

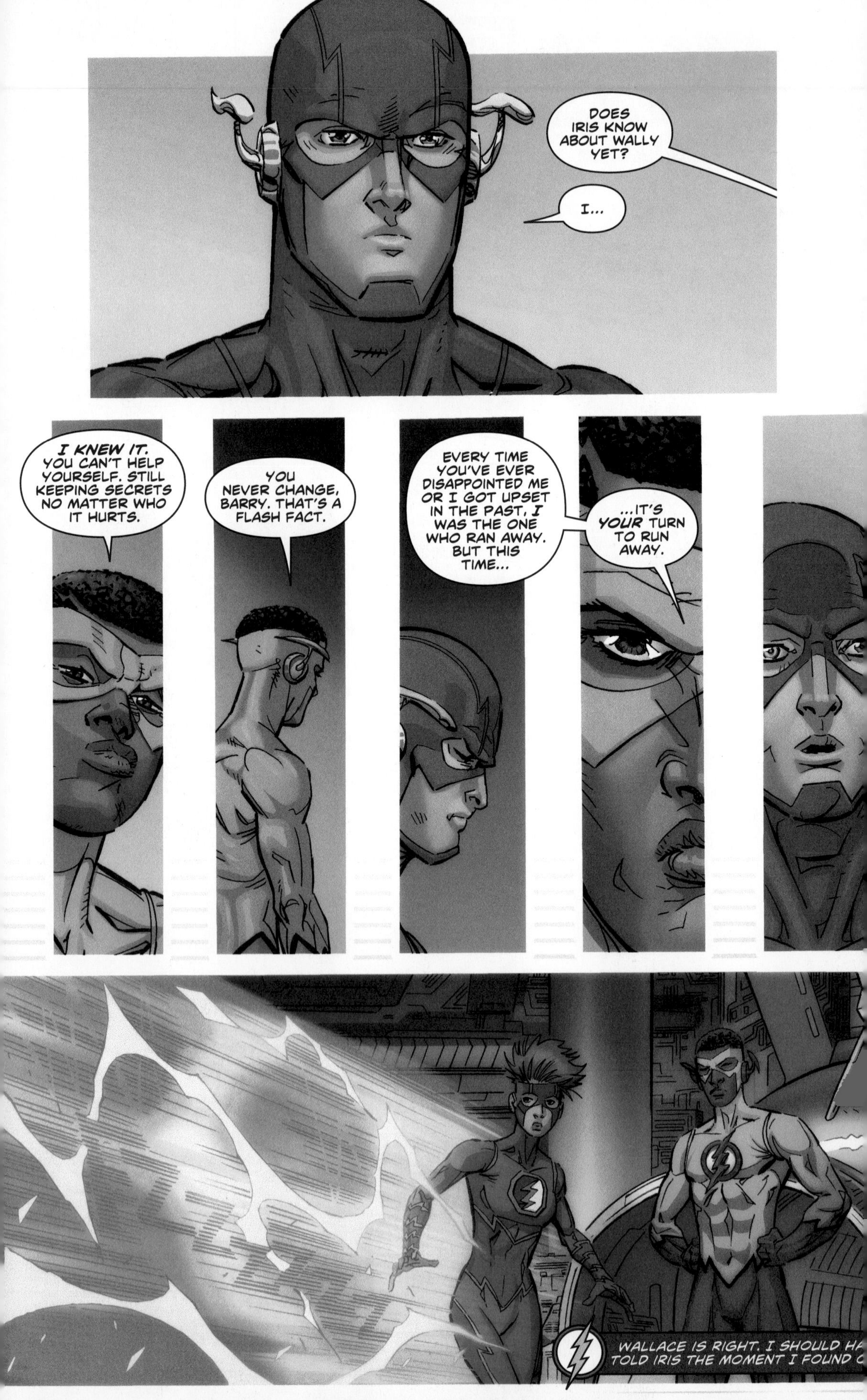
DOES IRIS KNOW ABOUT WALLY YET?
I...
I KNEW IT. YOU CAN'T HELP YOURSELF. STILL KEEPING SECRETS NO MATTER WHO IT HURTS.
YOU NEVER CHANGE, BARRY. THAT'S A FLASH FACT.
EVERY TIME YOU'VE EVER DISAPPOINTED ME OR I GOT UPSET IN THE PAST, I WAS THE ONE WHO RAN AWAY. BUT THIS TIME...
...IT'S YOUR TURN TO RUN AWAY.
WALLACE IS RIGHT. I SHOULD HA
TOLD IRIS THE MOMENT I FOUND

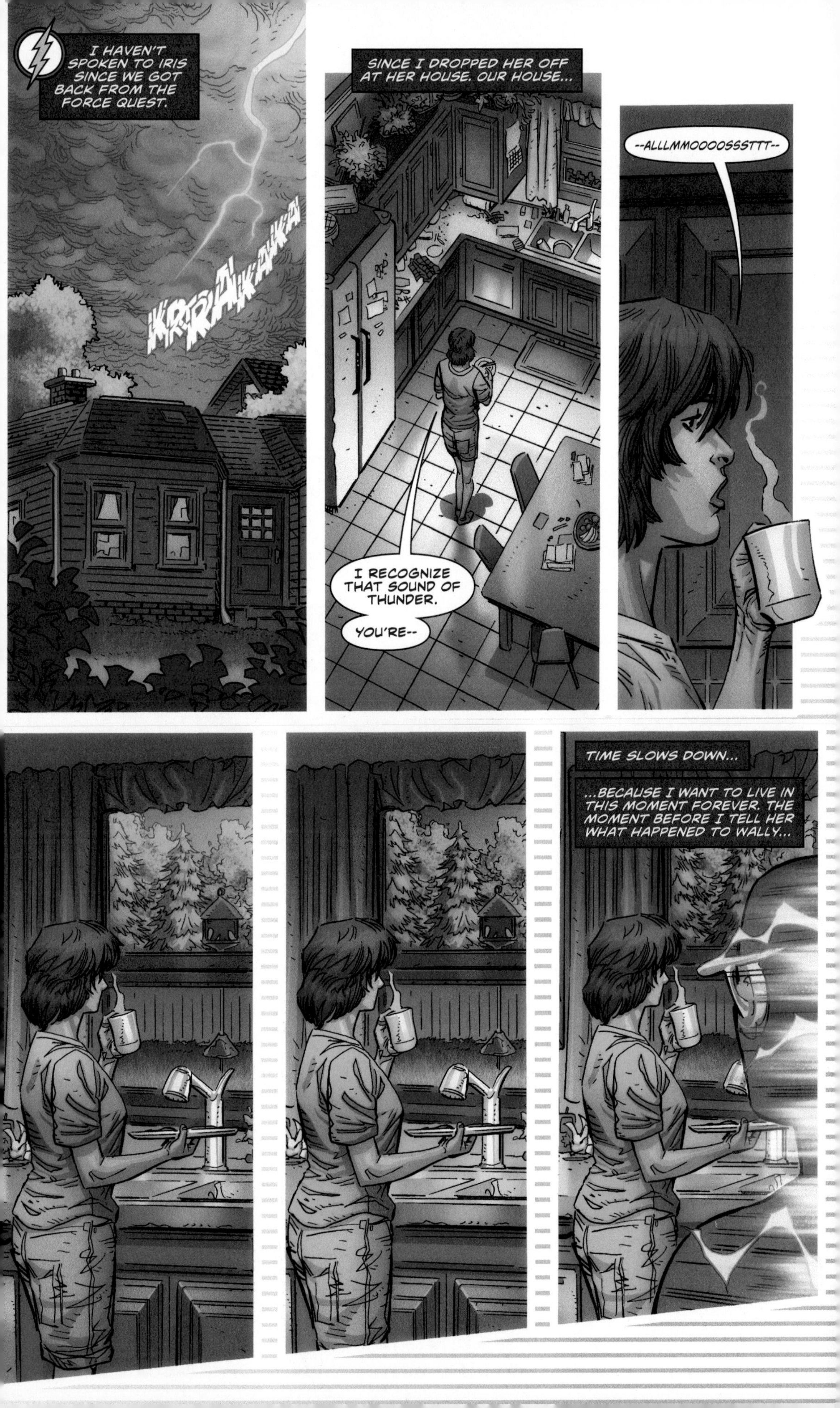
I HAVEN'T SPOKEN TO IRIS SINCE WE GOT BACK FROM THE FORCE QUEST.
KRAKAKAKA
SINCE I DROPPED HER OFF AT HER HOUSE. OUR HOUSE...
I RECOGNIZE THAT SOUND OF THUNDER.
YOU'RE--
--ALLLMMOOOOSSSTTT--
TIME SLOWS DOWN...
...BECAUSE I WANT TO LIVE IN THIS MOMENT FOREVER. THE MOMENT BEFORE I TELL HER WHAT HAPPENED TO WALLY...

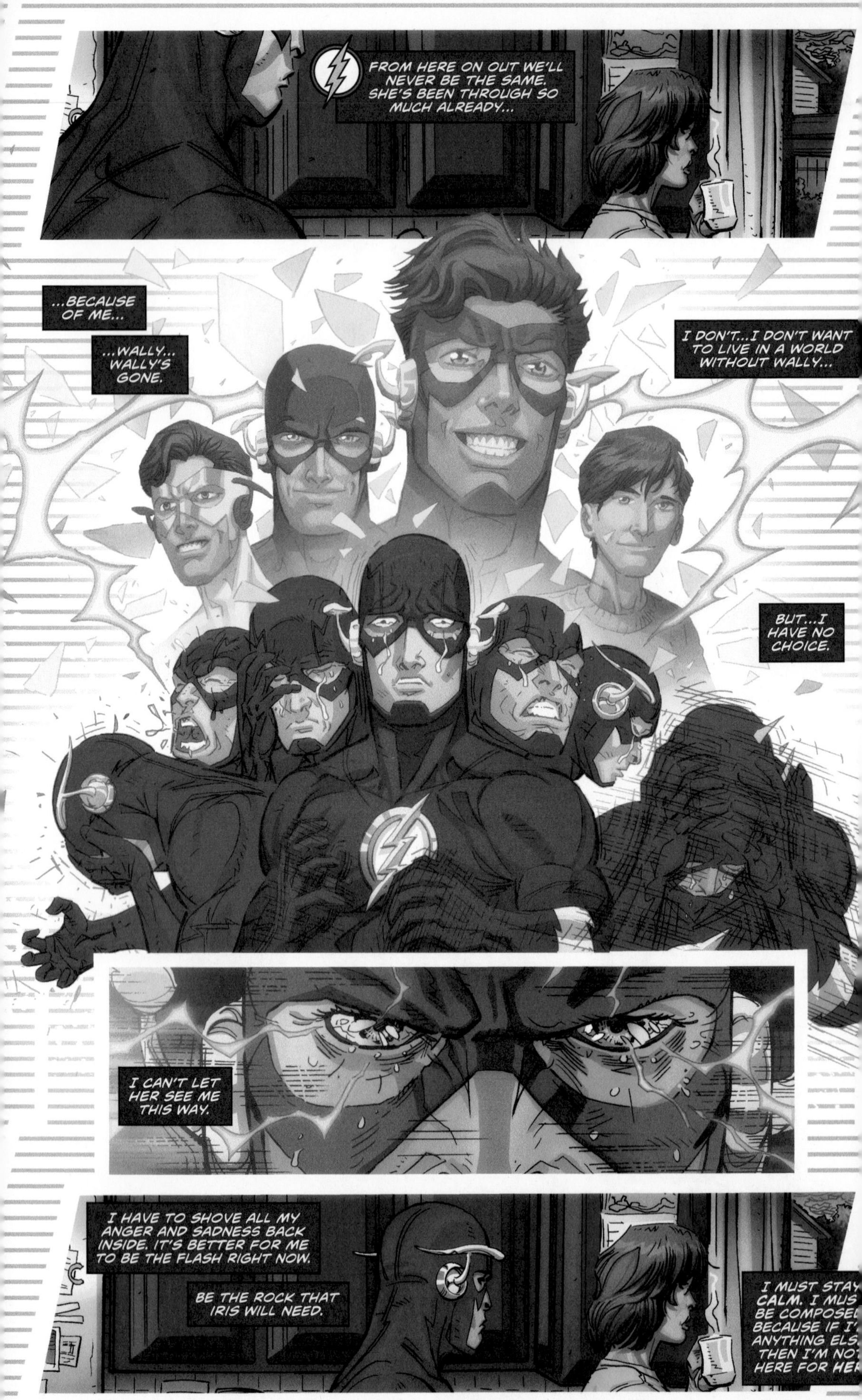

FROM HERE ON OUT WE'LL NEVER BE THE SAME. SHE'S BEEN THROUGH SO MUCH ALREADY...
...BECAUSE OF ME...
...WALLY... WALLY'S GONE.
I DON'T...I DON'T WANT TO LIVE IN A WORLD WITHOUT WALLY...
BUT...I HAVE NO CHOICE.
I CAN'T LET HER SEE ME THIS WAY.
I HAVE TO SHOVE ALL MY ANGER AND SADNESS BACK INSIDE. IT'S BETTER FOR ME TO BE THE FLASH RIGHT NOW.
BE THE ROCK THAT IRIS WILL NEED.

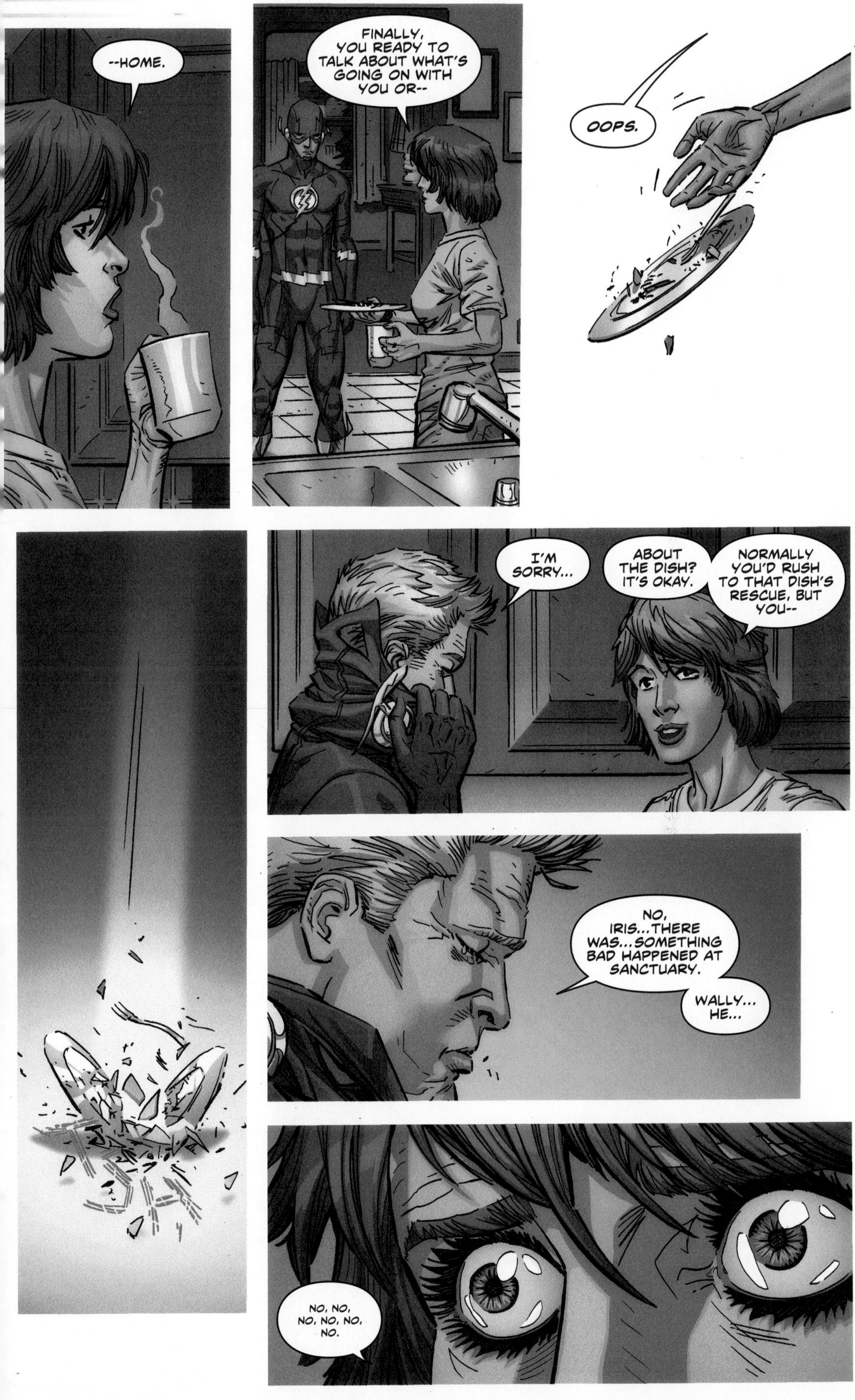
--HOME.
FINALLY, YOU READY TO TALK ABOUT WHAT'S GOING ON WITH YOU OR--
OOPS.
I'M SORRY...
ABOUT THE DISH? IT'S OKAY.
NORMALLY YOU'D RUSH TO THAT DISH'S RESCUE, BUT YOU--
NO, IRIS...THERE WAS...SOMETHING BAD HAPPENED AT SANCTUARY.
WALLY... HE...
NO, NO, NO, NO, NO, NO.

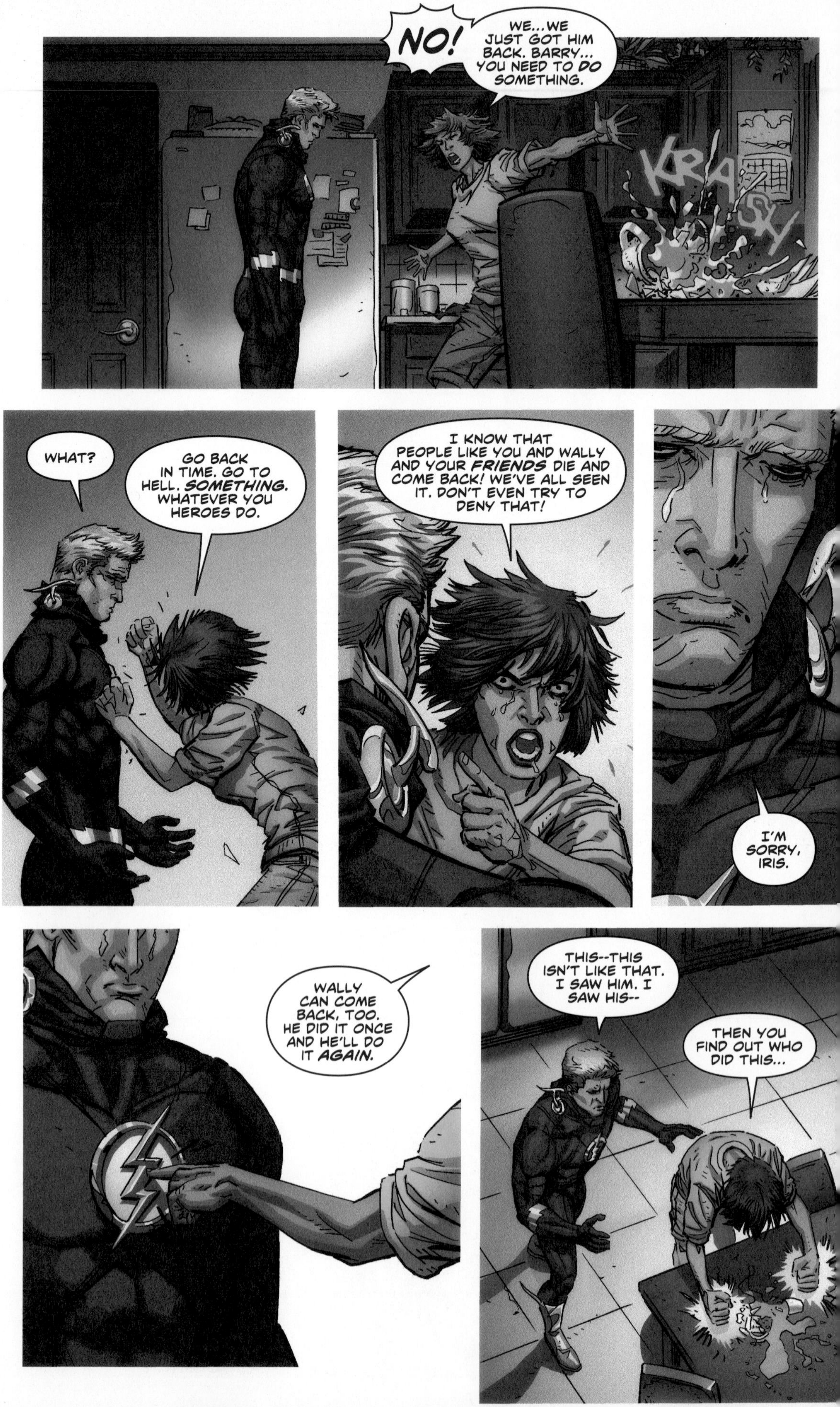

NO!
WE...WE JUST GOT HIM BACK. BARRY... YOU NEED TO DO SOMETHING.
KRASSH
WHAT?
GO BACK IN TIME. GO TO HELL. SOMETHING. WHATEVER YOU HEROES DO.
I KNOW THAT PEOPLE LIKE YOU AND WALLY AND YOUR FRIENDS DIE AND COME BACK! WE'VE ALL SEEN IT. DON'T EVEN TRY TO DENY THAT!
I'M SORRY, IRIS.
WALLY CAN COME BACK, TOO. HE DID IT ONCE AND HE'LL DO IT AGAIN.
THIS--THIS ISN'T LIKE THAT. I SAW HIM. I SAW HIS--
THEN YOU FIND OUT WHO DID THIS...

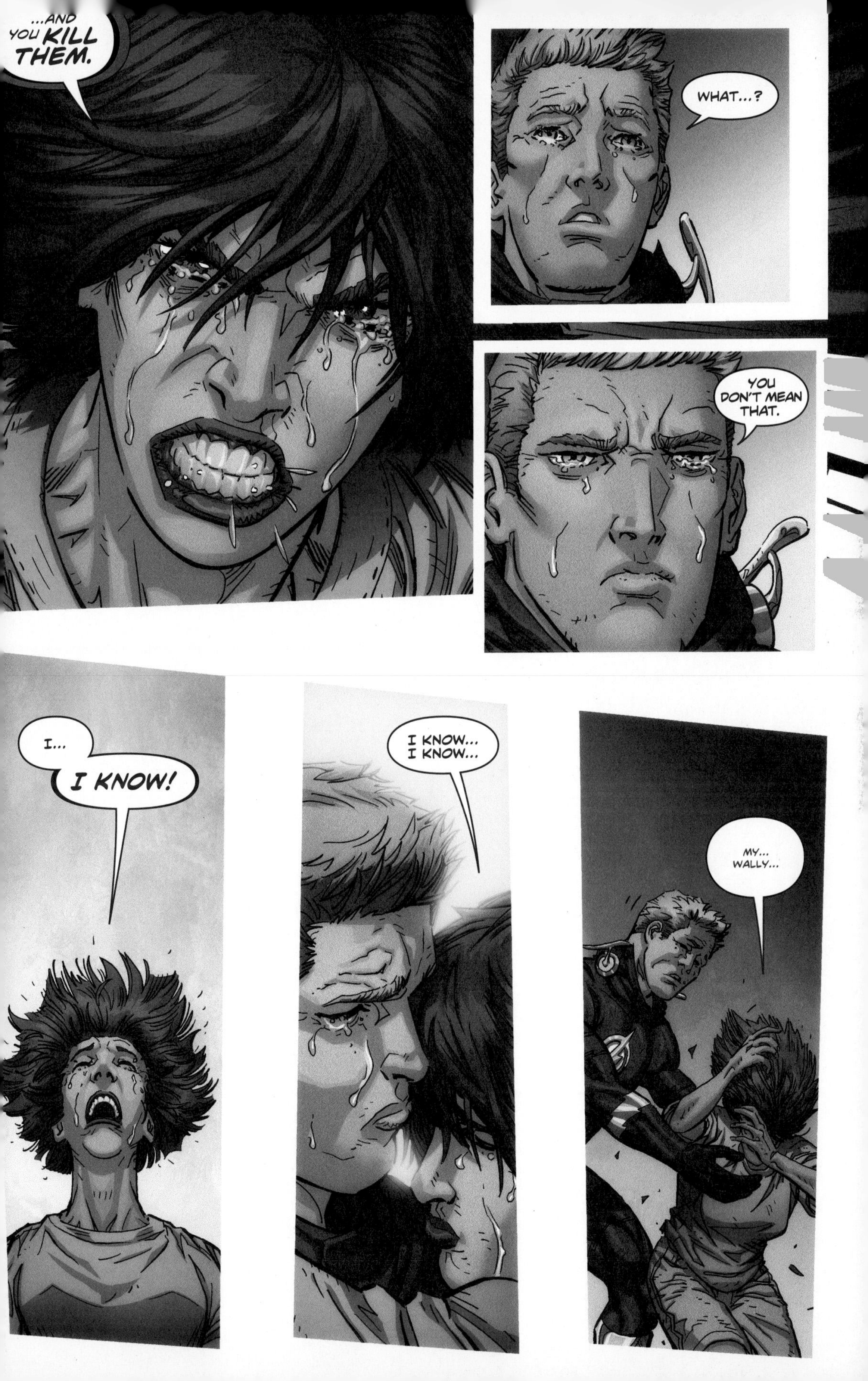
...AND YOU KILL THEM.
WHAT...?
YOU DON'T MEAN THAT.
I...
I KNOW!
I KNOW... I KNOW...
MY... WALLY...

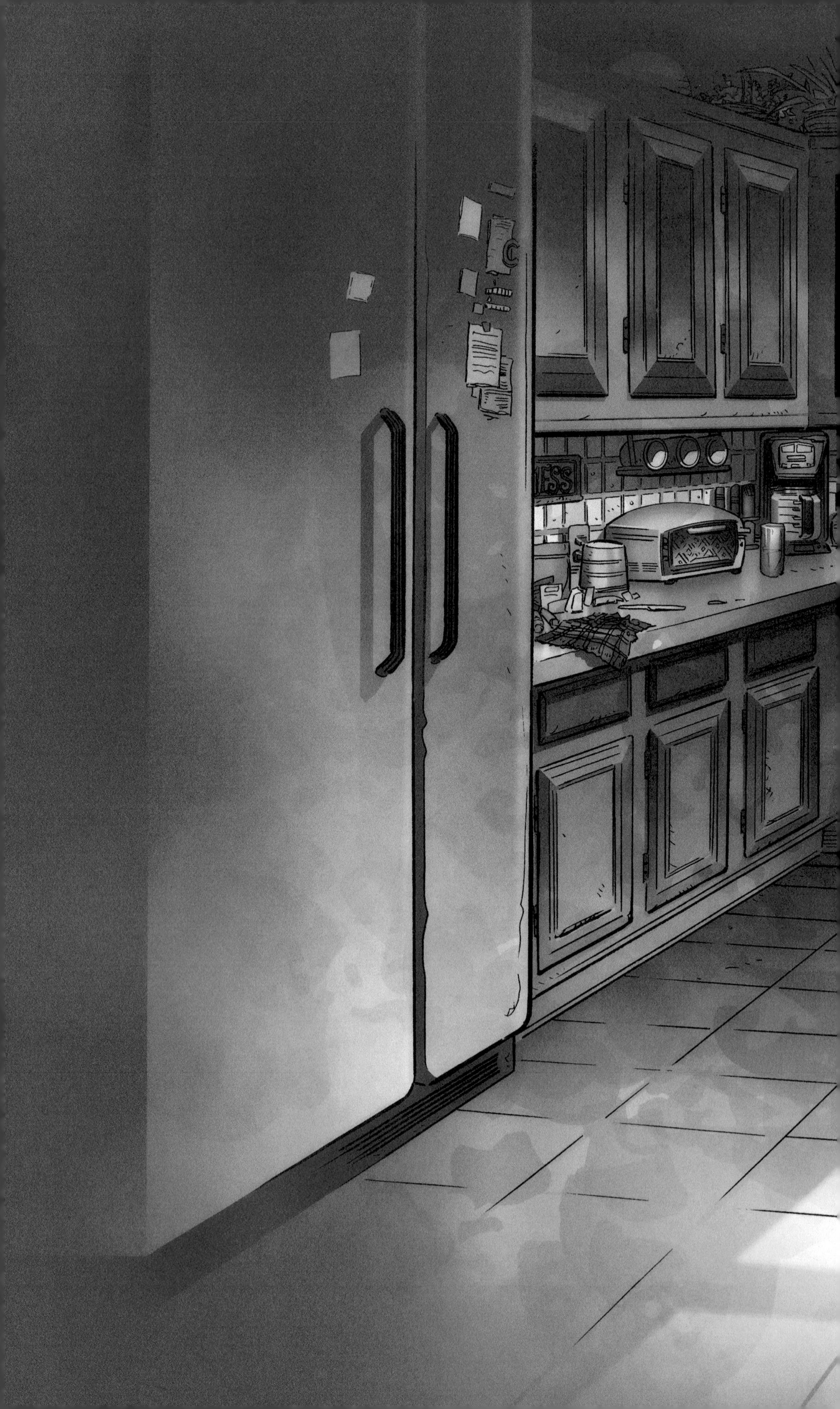

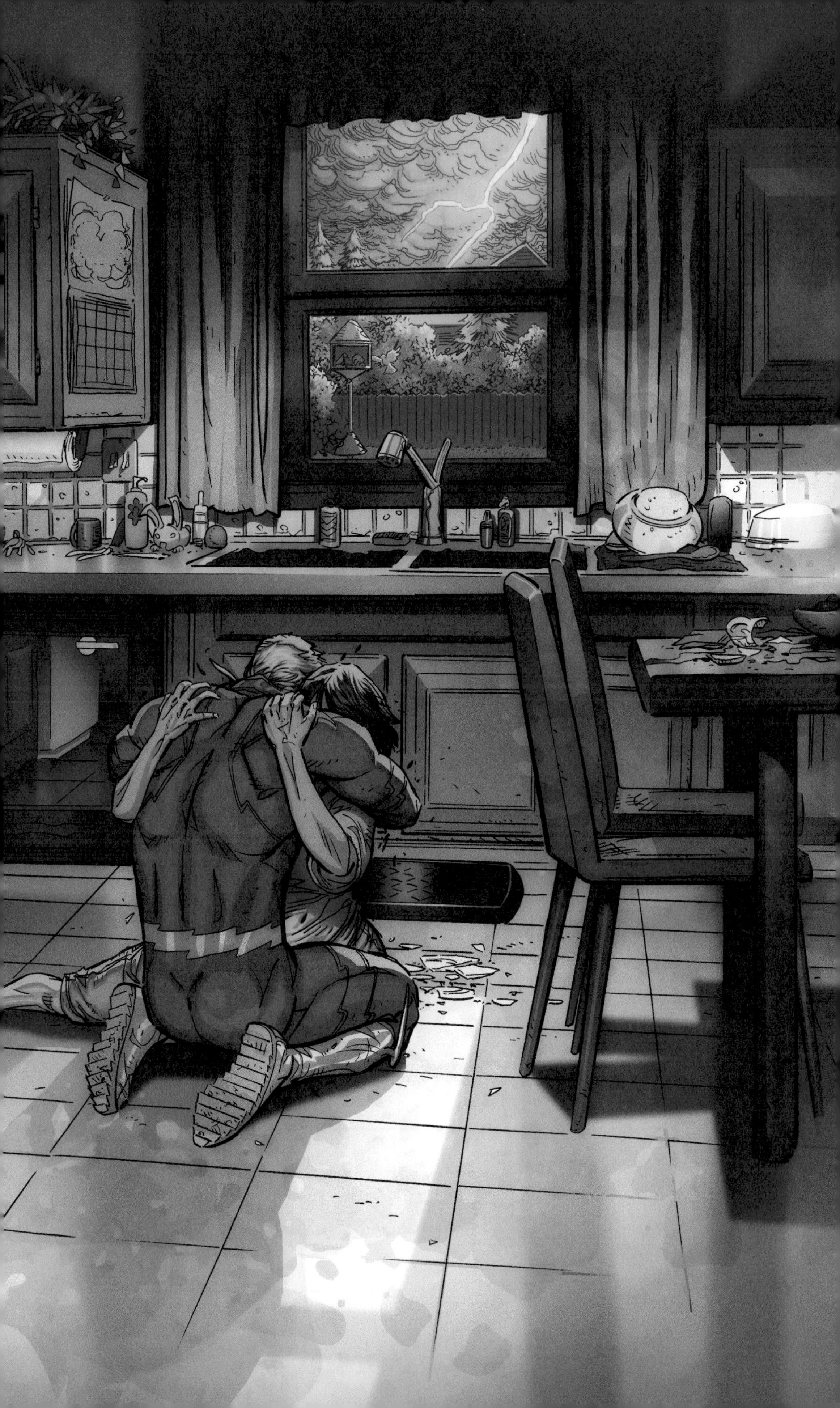

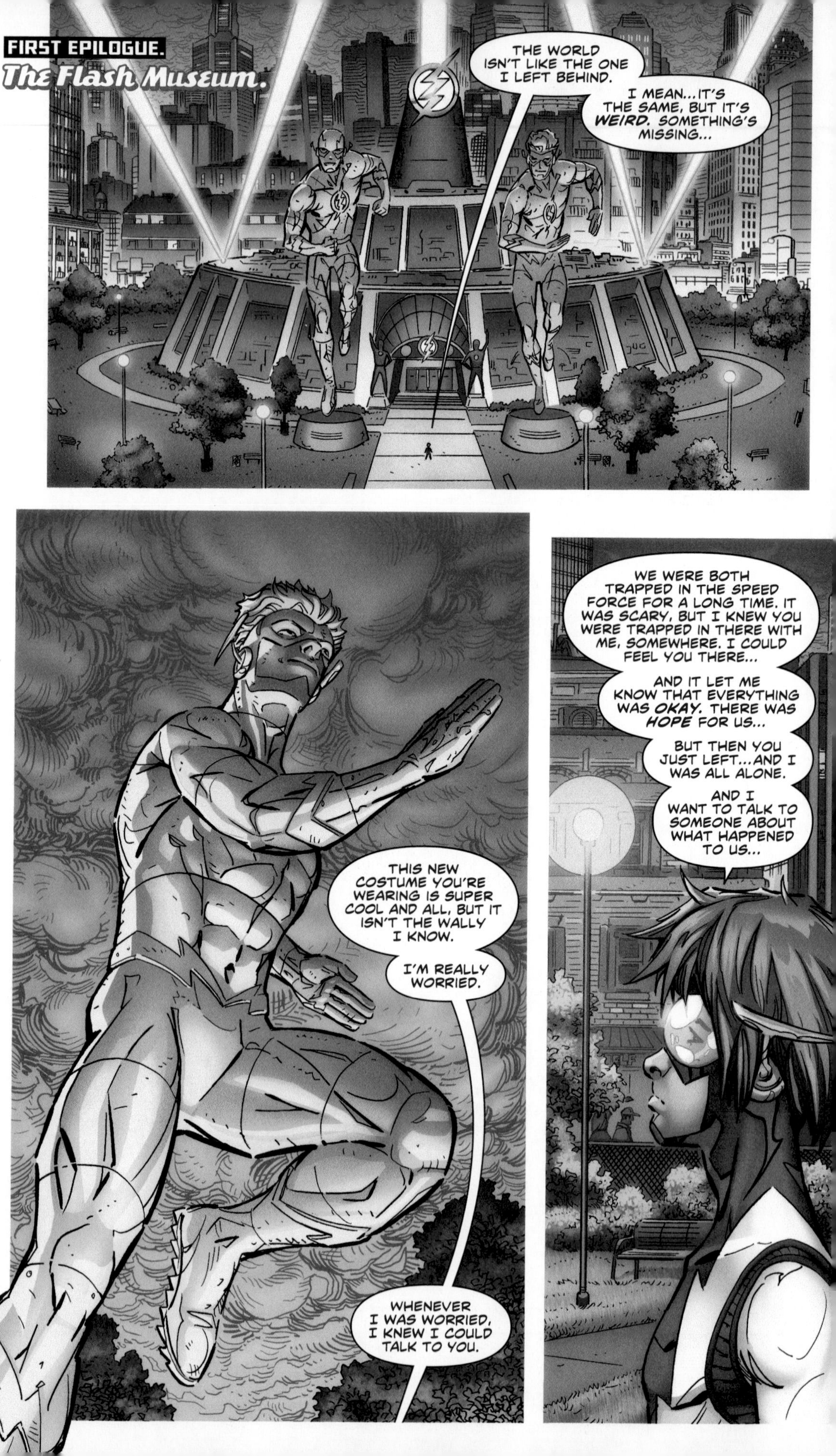

FIRST EPILOGUE.
The Flash Museum.
THE WORLD ISN'T LIKE THE ONE I LEFT BEHIND.
I MEAN...IT'S THE SAME, BUT IT'S WEIRD. SOMETHING'S MISSING...
THIS NEW COSTUME YOU'RE WEARING IS SUPER COOL AND ALL, BUT IT ISN'T THE WALLY I KNOW.
I'M REALLY WORRIED.
WHENEVER I WAS WORRIED, I KNEW I COULD TALK TO YOU.
WE WERE BOTH TRAPPED IN THE SPEED FORCE FOR A LONG TIME. IT WAS SCARY, BUT I KNEW YOU WERE TRAPPED IN THERE WITH ME, SOMEWHERE. I COULD FEEL YOU THERE...
AND IT LET ME KNOW THAT EVERYTHING WAS OKAY. THERE WAS HOPE FOR US...
BUT THEN YOU JUST LEFT...AND I WAS ALL ALONE.
AND I WANT TO TALK TO SOMEONE ABOUT WHAT HAPPENED TO US...

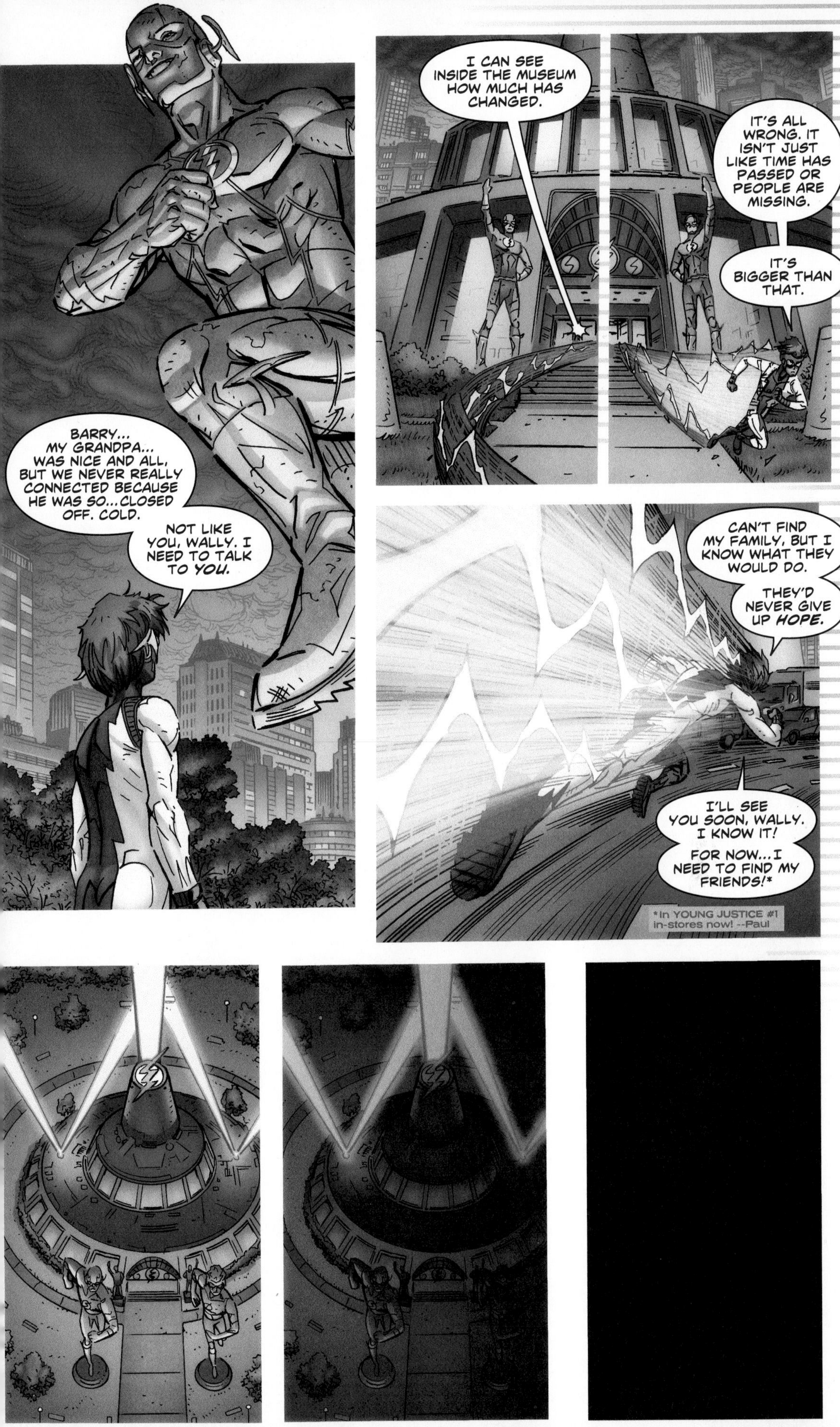

BARRY... MY GRANDPA... WAS NICE AND ALL, BUT WE NEVER REALLY CONNECTED BECAUSE HE WAS SO...CLOSED OFF. COLD.
NOT LIKE YOU, WALLY. I NEED TO TALK TO YOU.
I CAN SEE INSIDE THE MUSEUM HOW MUCH HAS CHANGED.
IT'S ALL WRONG. IT ISN'T JUST LIKE TIME HAS PASSED OR PEOPLE ARE MISSING.
IT'S BIGGER THAN THAT.
CAN'T FIND MY FAMILY, BUT I KNOW WHAT THEY WOULD DO.
THEY'D NEVER GIVE UP HOPE.
I'LL SEE YOU SOON, WALLY. I KNOW IT!
FOR NOW...I NEED TO FIND MY FRIENDS!*
*In YOUNG JUSTICE #1 in-stores now! --Paul

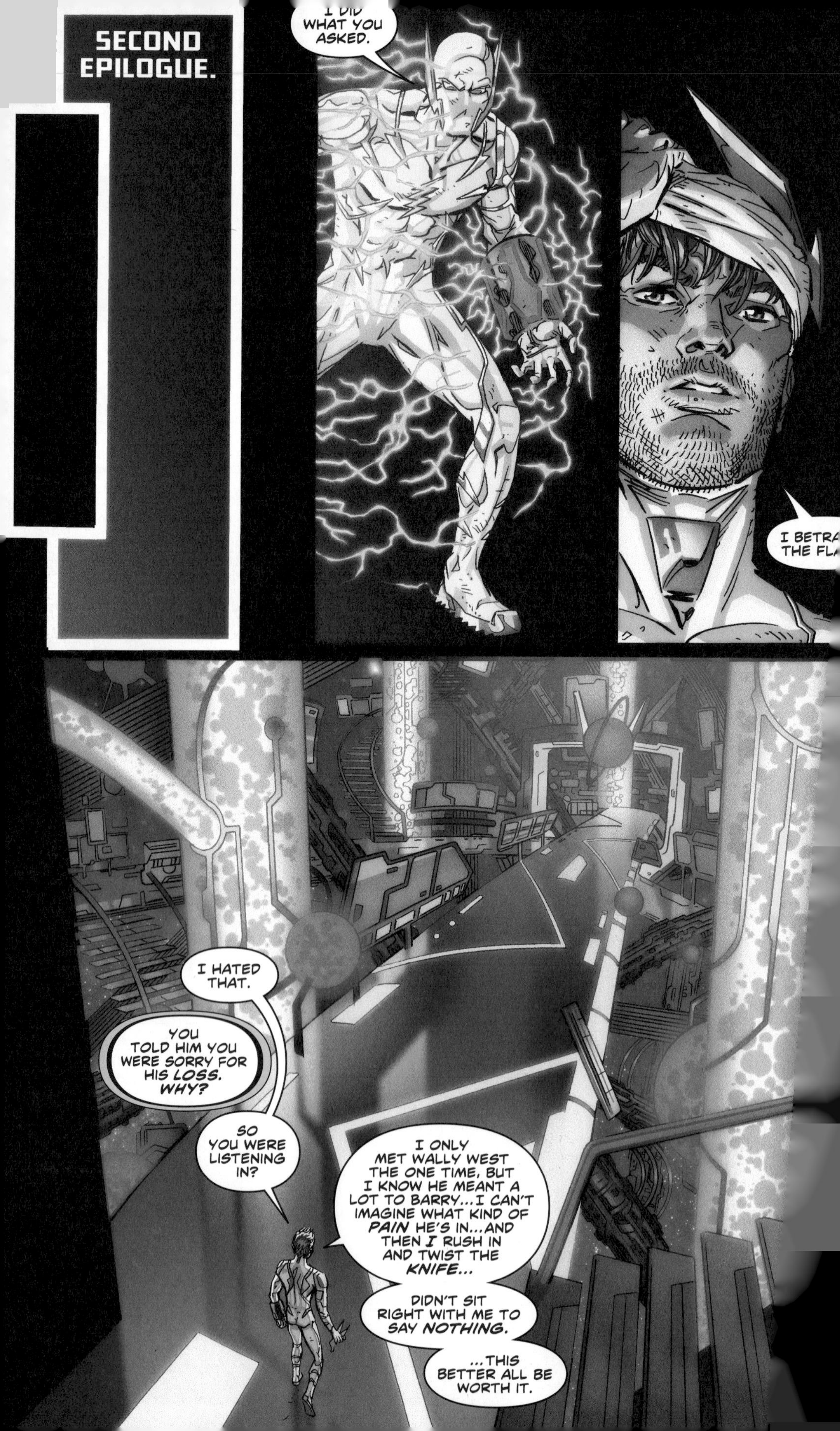
SECOND EPILOGUE.
I DID WHAT YOU ASKED.
I BETRA THE FLA
I HATED THAT.
YOU TOLD HIM YOU WERE SORRY FOR HIS LOSS. WHY?
SO YOU WERE LISTENING IN?
I ONLY MET WALLY WEST THE ONE TIME, BUT I KNOW HE MEANT A LOT TO BARRY...I CAN'T IMAGINE WHAT KIND OF PAIN HE'S IN...AND THEN I RUSH IN AND TWIST THE KNIFE...
DIDN'T SIT RIGHT WITH ME TO SAY NOTHING.
...THIS BETTER ALL BE WORTH IT.

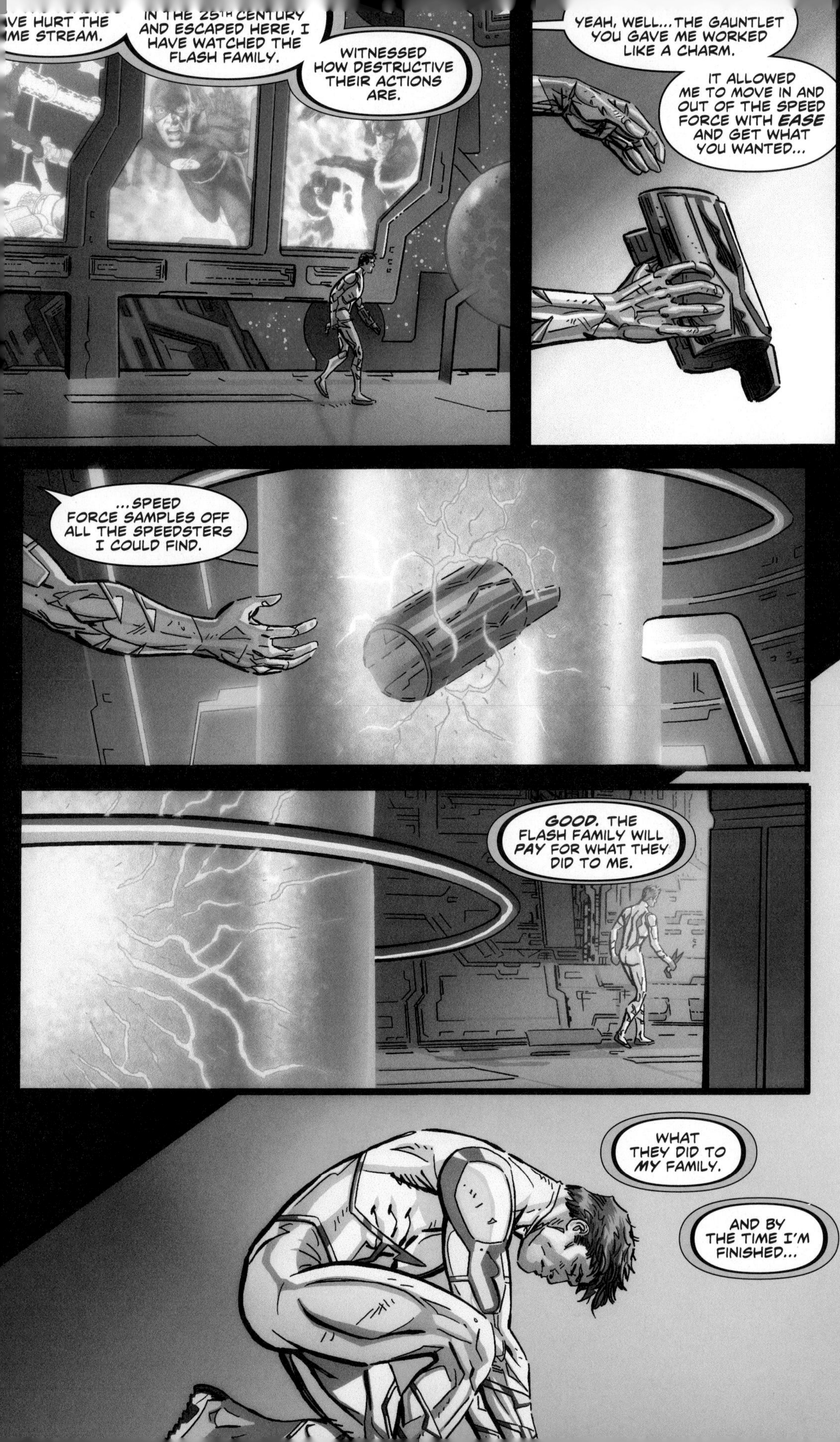
AVE HURT THE
ME STREAM.
IN THE 25TH CENTURY AND ESCAPED HERE, I HAVE WATCHED THE FLASH FAMILY.
WITNESSED HOW DESTRUCTIVE THEIR ACTIONS ARE.
YEAH, WELL...THE GAUNTLET YOU GAVE ME WORKED LIKE A CHARM.
IT ALLOWED ME TO MOVE IN AND OUT OF THE SPEED FORCE WITH *EASE* AND GET WHAT YOU WANTED...
...SPEED FORCE SAMPLES OFF ALL THE SPEEDSTERS I COULD FIND.
GOOD. THE FLASH FAMILY WILL *PAY* FOR WHAT THEY DID TO ME.
WHAT THEY DID TO *MY* FAMILY.
AND BY THE TIME I'M FINISHED...

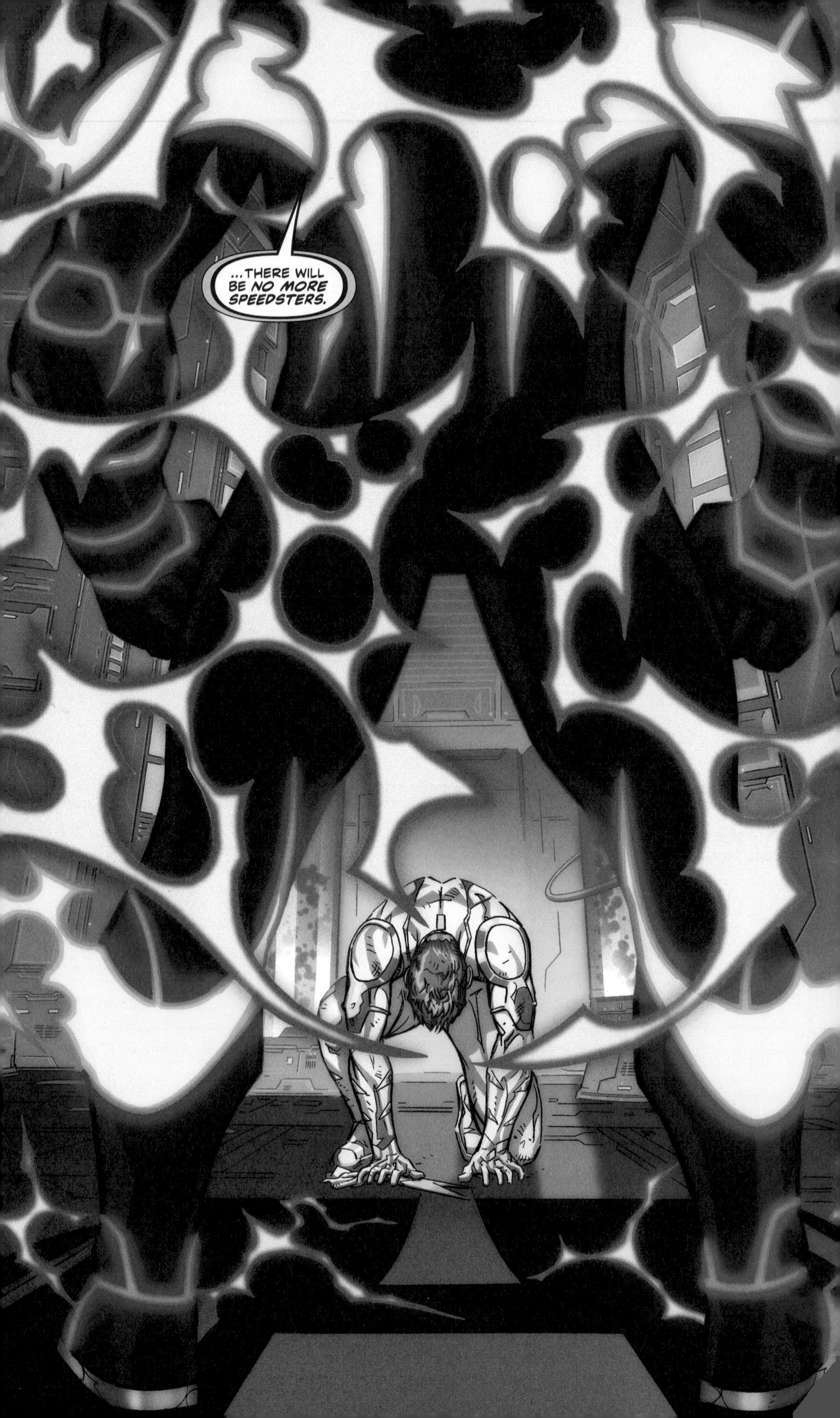
...THERE WILL BE NO MORE SPEEDSTERS.

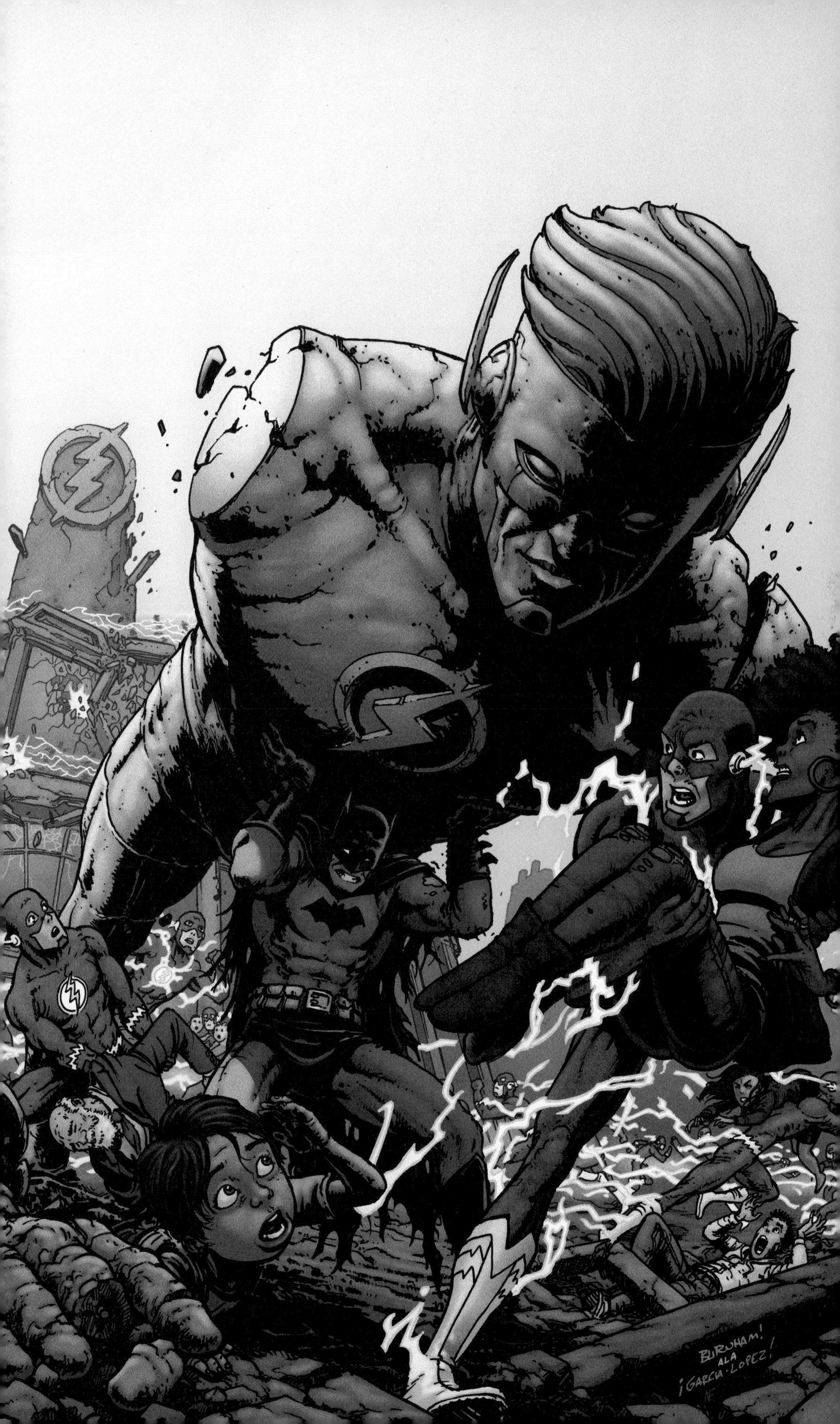
BURNHAM!
ALA
¡GARCIA-LOPEZ!

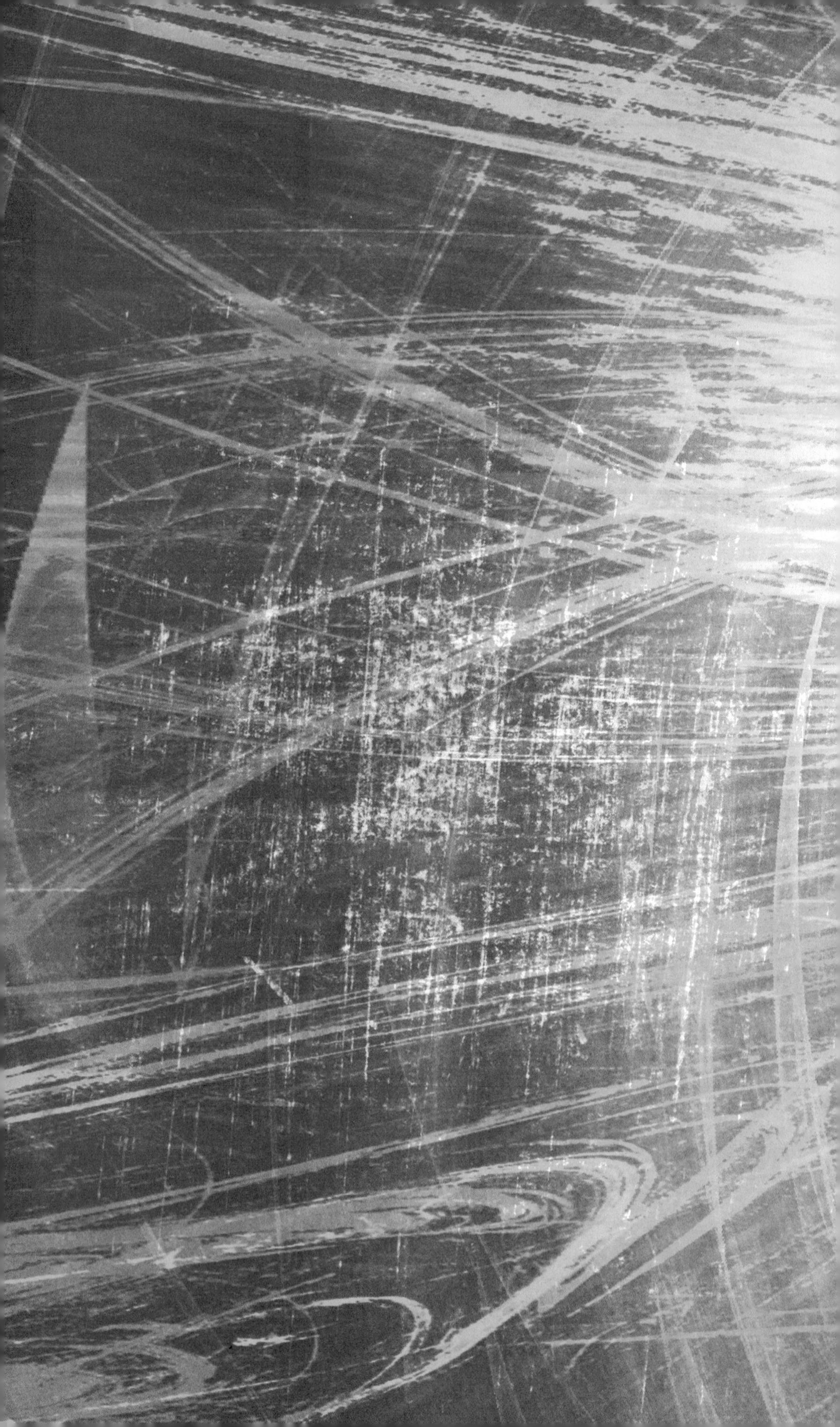

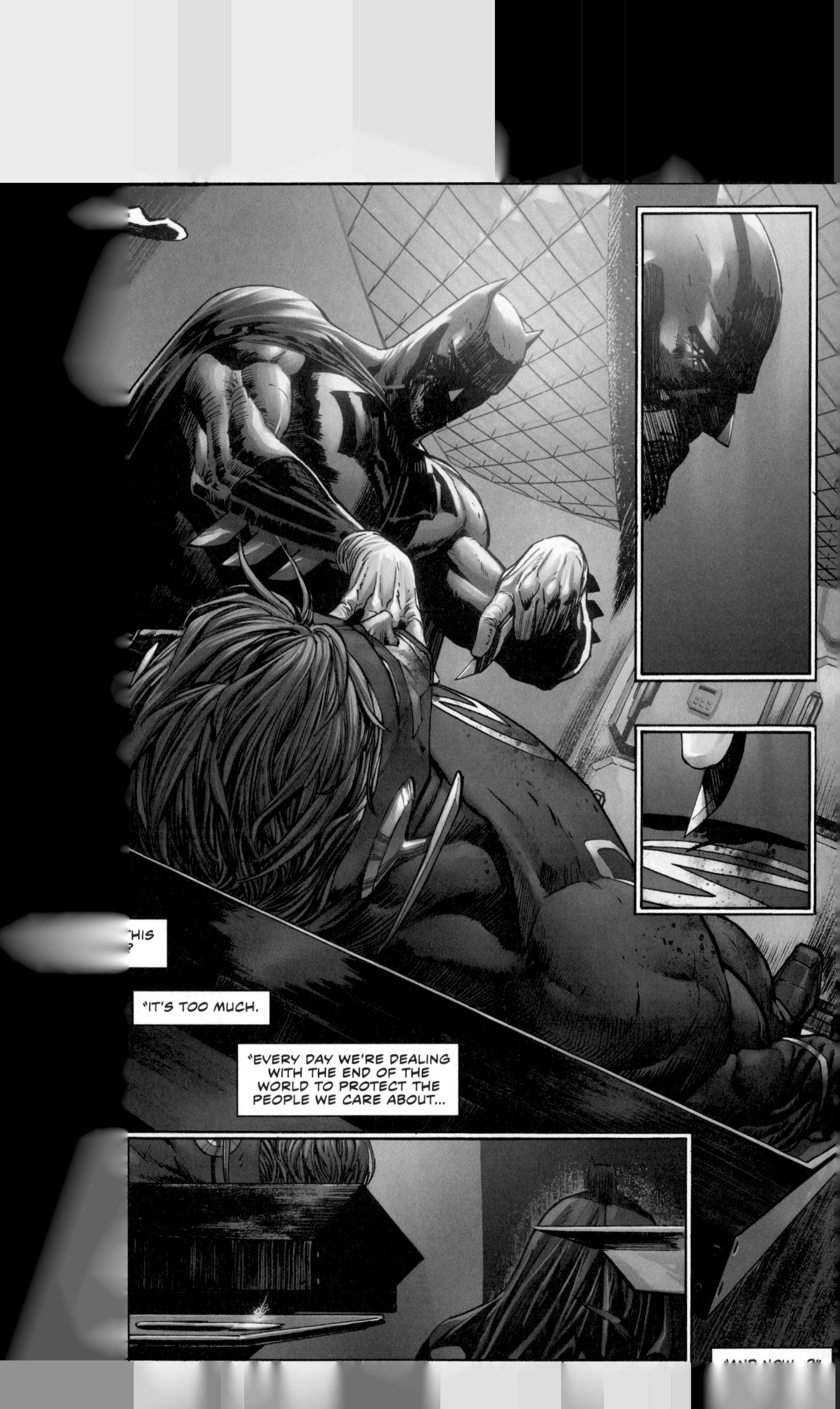
"IT'S TOO MUCH.
"EVERY DAY WE'RE DEALING WITH THE END OF THE WORLD TO PROTECT THE PEOPLE WE CARE ABOUT...

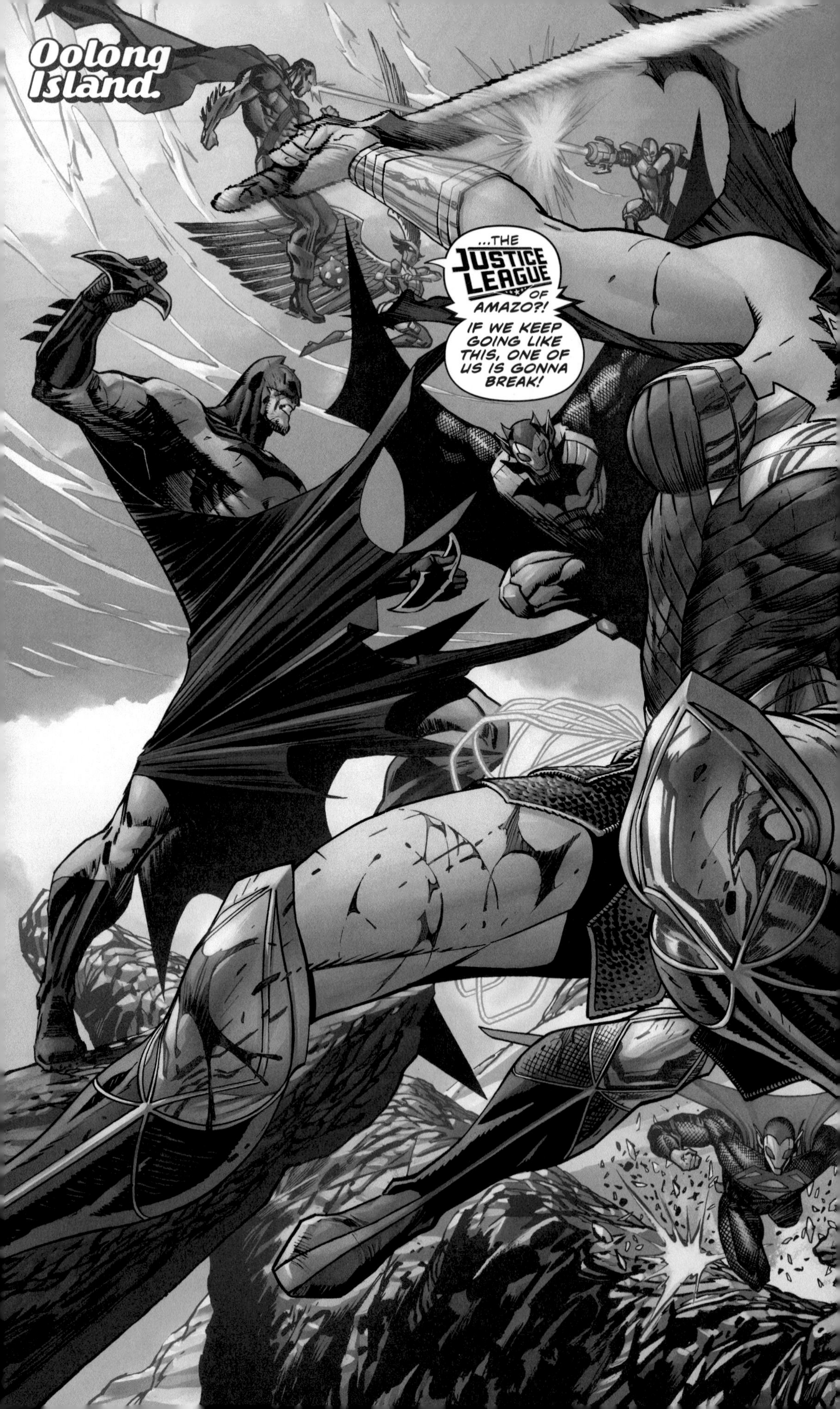
Oolong Island.
...THE JUSTICE LEAGUE OF AMAZO?!
IF WE KEEP GOING LIKE THIS, ONE OF US IS GONNA BREAK!

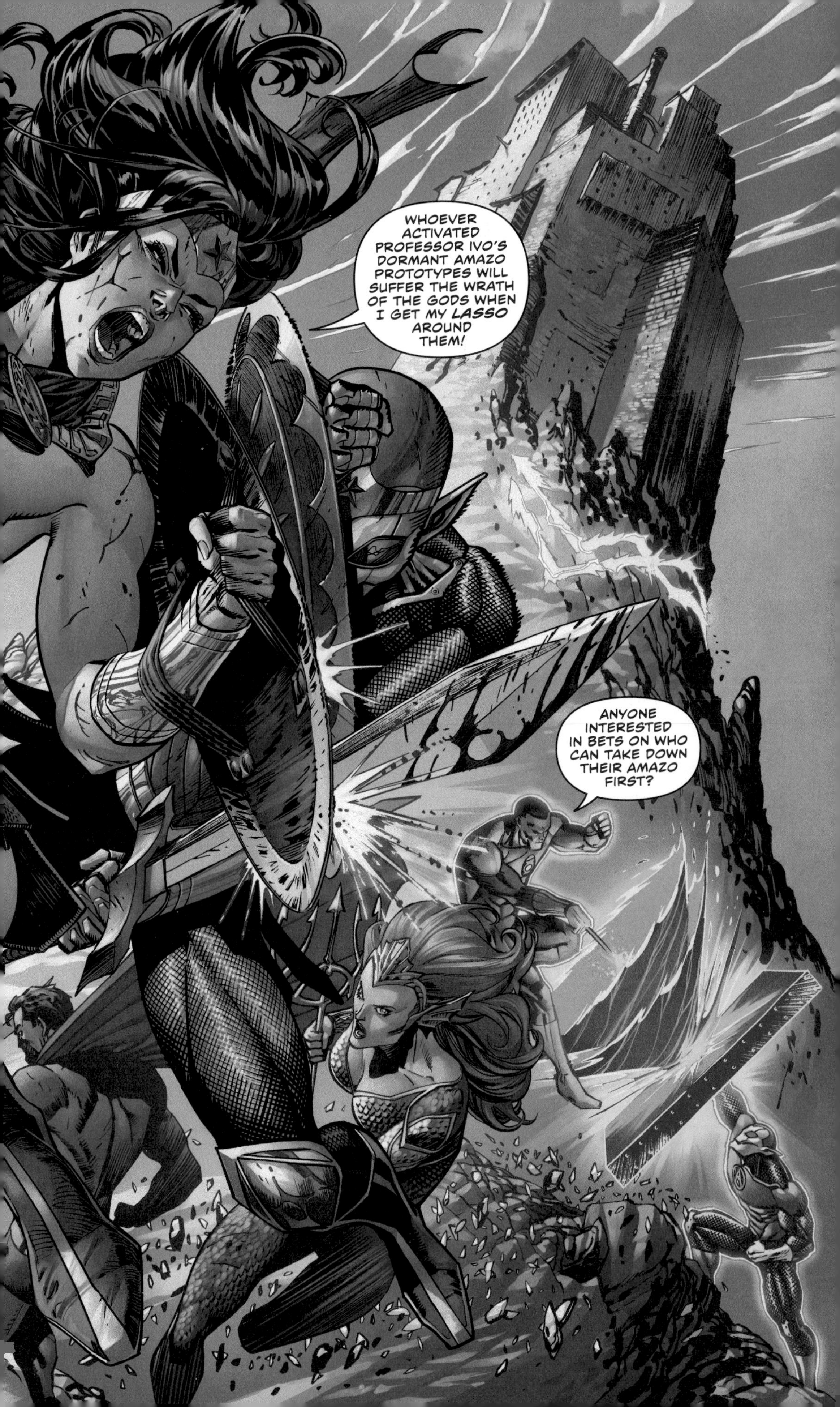
WHOEVER ACTIVATED PROFESSOR IVO'S DORMANT AMAZO PROTOTYPES WILL SUFFER THE WRATH OF THE GODS WHEN I GET MY *LASSO* AROUND THEM!
ANYONE INTERESTED IN BETS ON WHO CAN TAKE DOWN THEIR AMAZO FIRST?

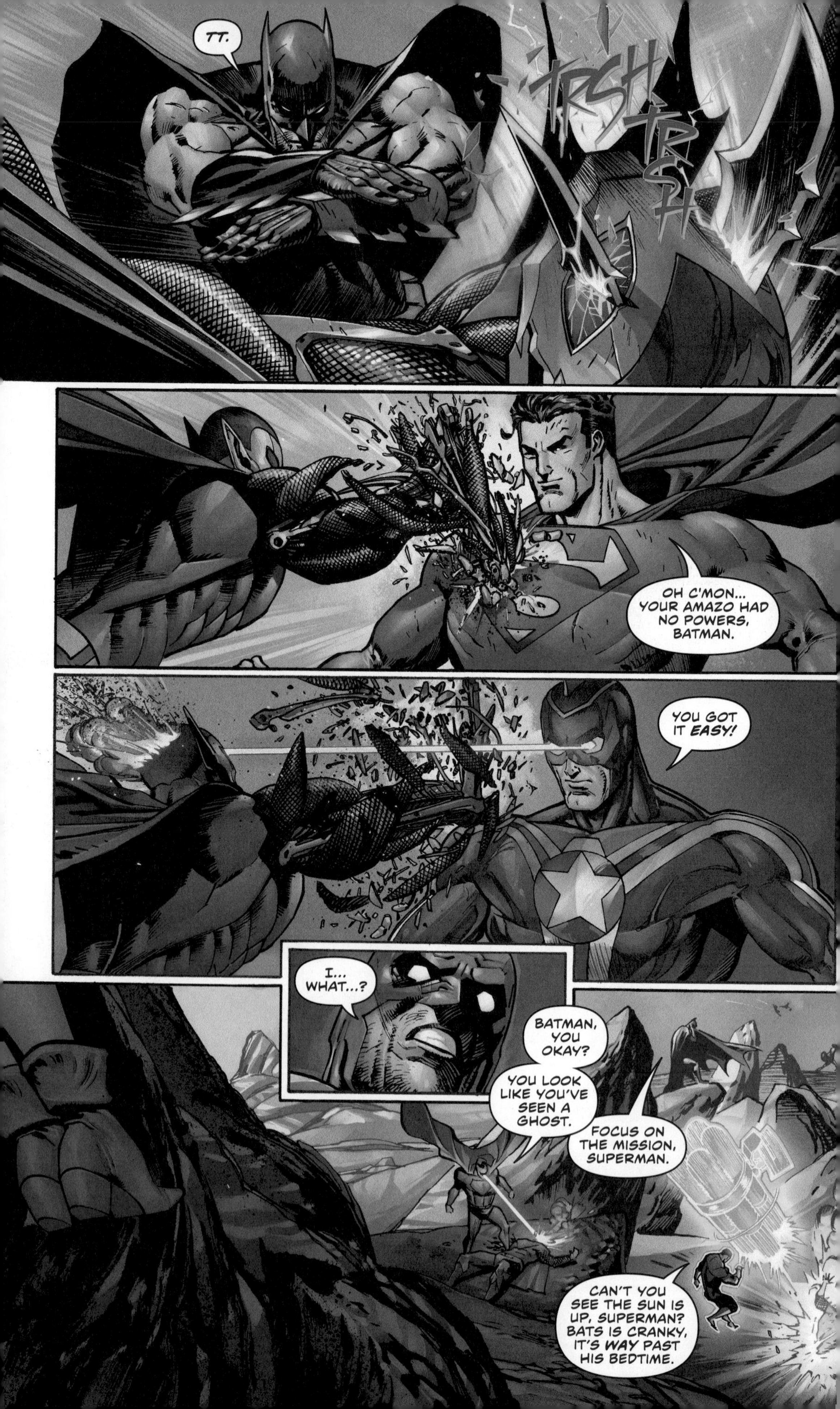
TT.
TRSH TRSH
OH C'MON... YOUR AMAZO HAD NO POWERS, BATMAN.
YOU GOT IT EASY!
I... WHAT...?
BATMAN, YOU OKAY?
YOU LOOK LIKE YOU'VE SEEN A GHOST.
FOCUS ON THE MISSION, SUPERMAN.
CAN'T YOU SEE THE SUN IS UP, SUPERMAN? BATS IS CRANKY, IT'S WAY PAST HIS BEDTIME.

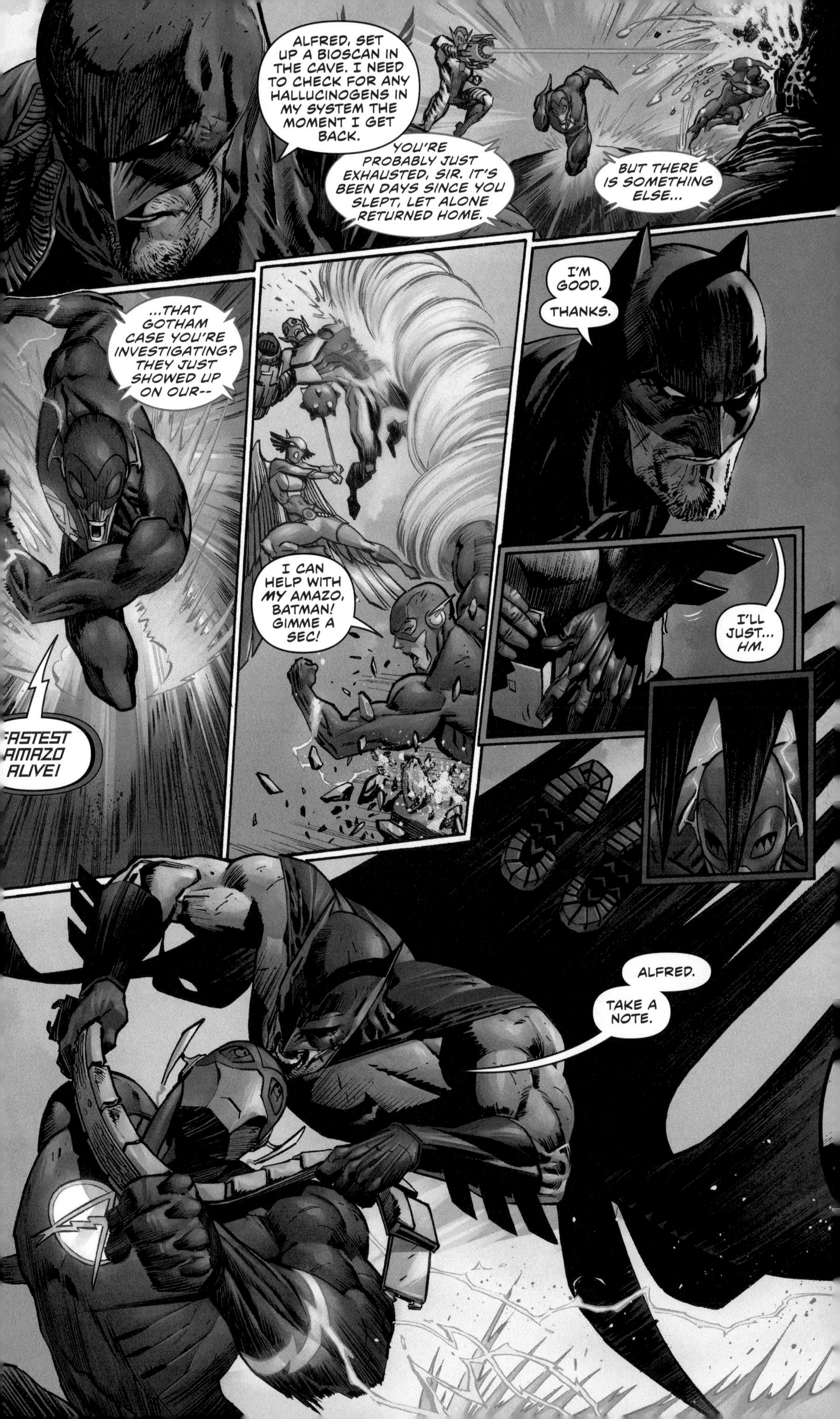

ALFRED, SET UP A BIOSCAN IN THE CAVE. I NEED TO CHECK FOR ANY HALLUCINOGENS IN MY SYSTEM THE MOMENT I GET BACK.
YOU'RE PROBABLY JUST EXHAUSTED, SIR. IT'S BEEN DAYS SINCE YOU SLEPT, LET ALONE RETURNED HOME.
BUT THERE IS SOMETHING ELSE...
...THAT GOTHAM CASE YOU'RE INVESTIGATING? THEY JUST SHOWED UP ON OUR--
FASTEST AMAZO ALIVE!
I CAN HELP WITH MY AMAZO, BATMAN! GIMME A SEC!
I'M GOOD.
THANKS.
I'LL JUST... HM.
ALFRED.
TAKE A NOTE.

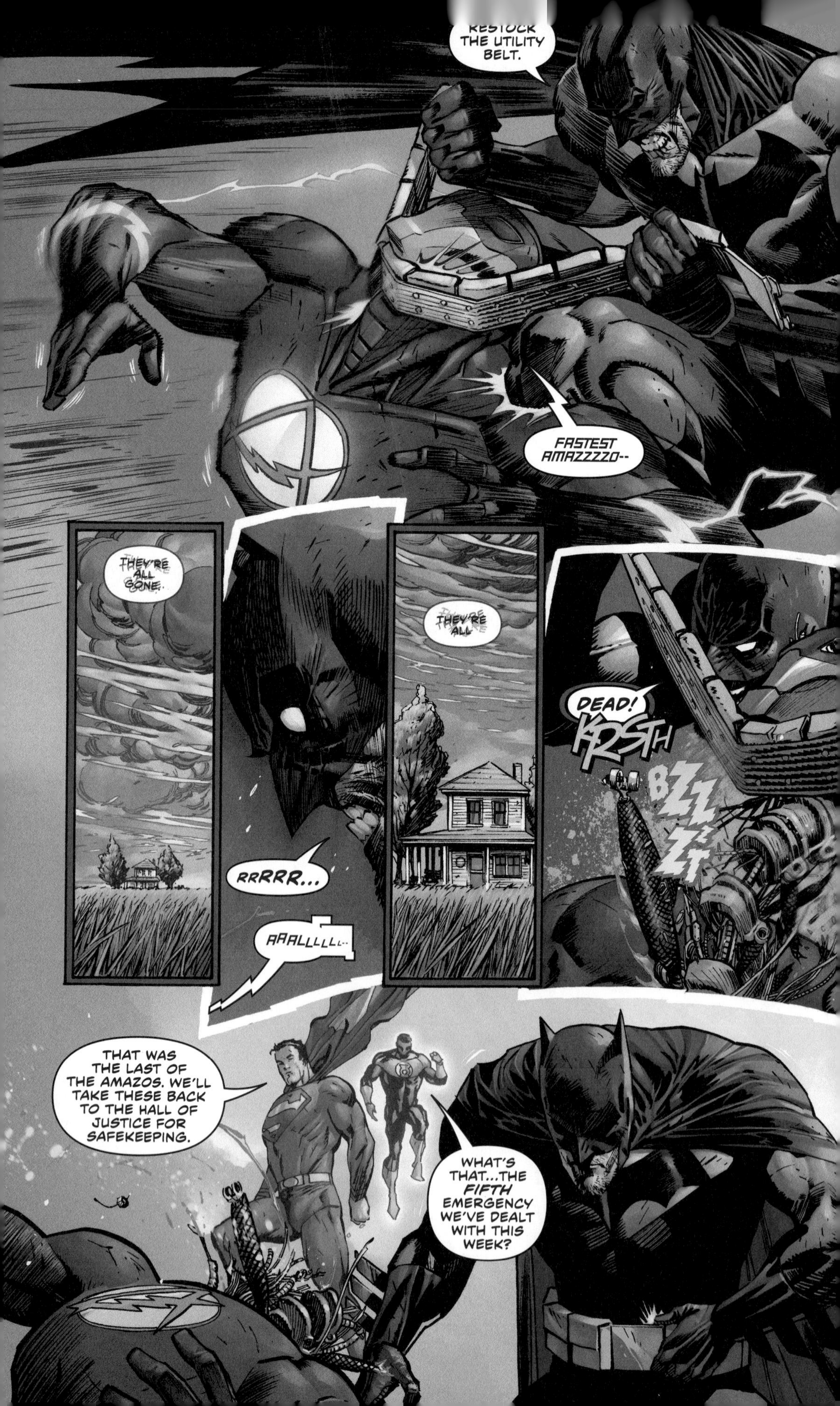

RESTOCK THE UTILITY BELT.
FASTEST AMAZZZZO--
THEY'RE ALL GONE.
RRRRR...
AAALLLLLL--
THEY'RE ALL
DEAD!
KRSTH
BZZZZT
THAT WAS THE LAST OF THE AMAZOS. WE'LL TAKE THESE BACK TO THE HALL OF JUSTICE FOR SAFEKEEPING.
WHAT'S THAT...THE *FIFTH* EMERGENCY WE'VE DEALT WITH THIS WEEK?

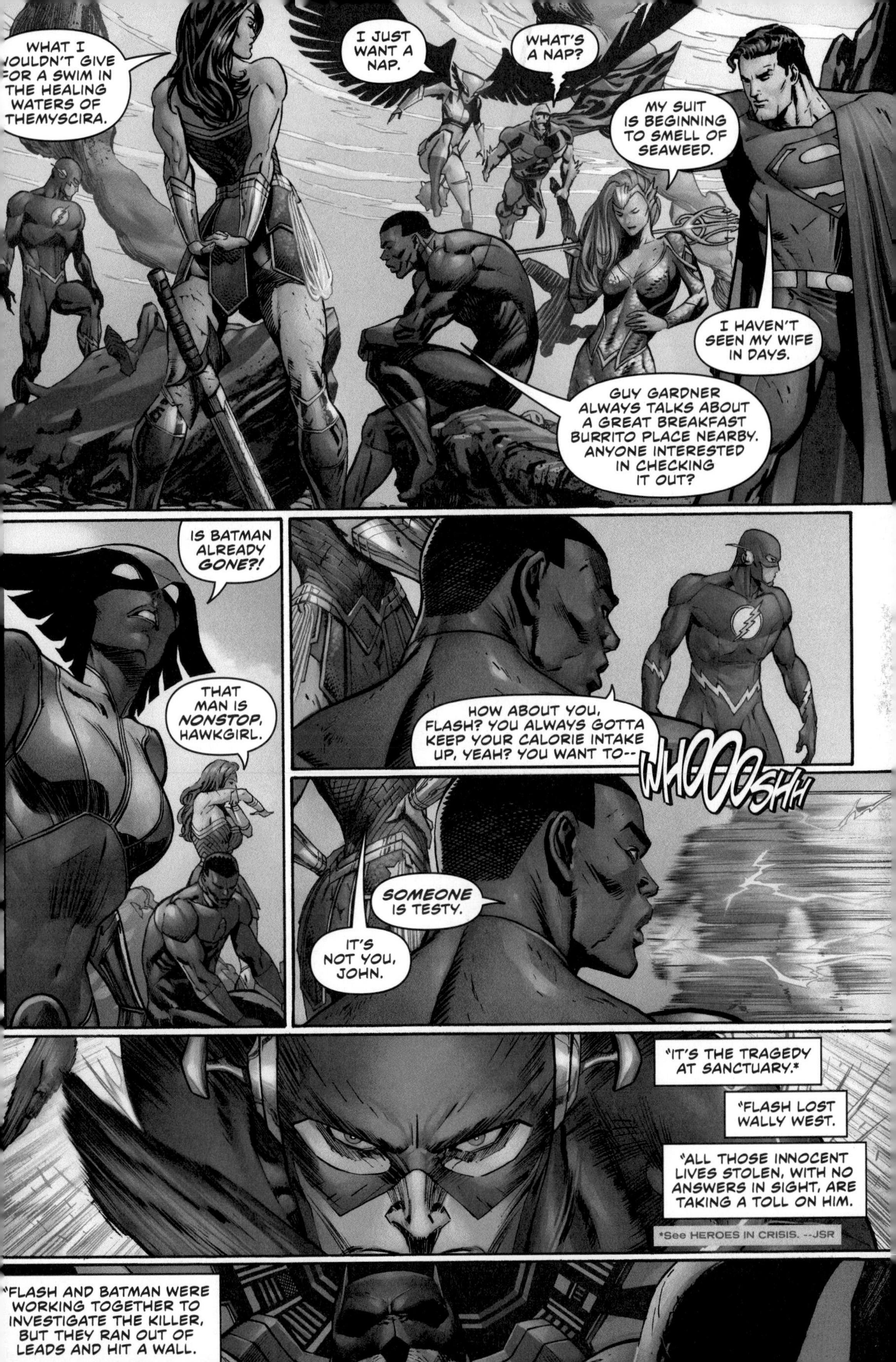

WHAT I WOULDN'T GIVE FOR A SWIM IN THE HEALING WATERS OF THEMYSCIRA.
I JUST WANT A NAP.
WHAT'S A NAP?
MY SUIT IS BEGINNING TO SMELL OF SEAWEED.
I HAVEN'T SEEN MY WIFE IN DAYS.
GUY GARDNER ALWAYS TALKS ABOUT A GREAT BREAKFAST BURRITO PLACE NEARBY. ANYONE INTERESTED IN CHECKING IT OUT?
IS BATMAN ALREADY GONE?!
THAT MAN IS NONSTOP, HAWKGIRL.
HOW ABOUT YOU, FLASH? YOU ALWAYS GOTTA KEEP YOUR CALORIE INTAKE UP, YEAH? YOU WANT TO--
WHOOOOSHH
SOMEONE IS TESTY.
IT'S NOT YOU, JOHN.
"IT'S THE TRAGEDY AT SANCTUARY.*
"FLASH LOST WALLY WEST.
"ALL THOSE INNOCENT LIVES STOLEN, WITH NO ANSWERS IN SIGHT, ARE TAKING A TOLL ON HIM.
*See HEROES IN CRISIS. --JSR
"FLASH AND BATMAN WERE WORKING TOGETHER TO INVESTIGATE THE KILLER, BUT THEY RAN OUT OF LEADS AND HIT A WALL.

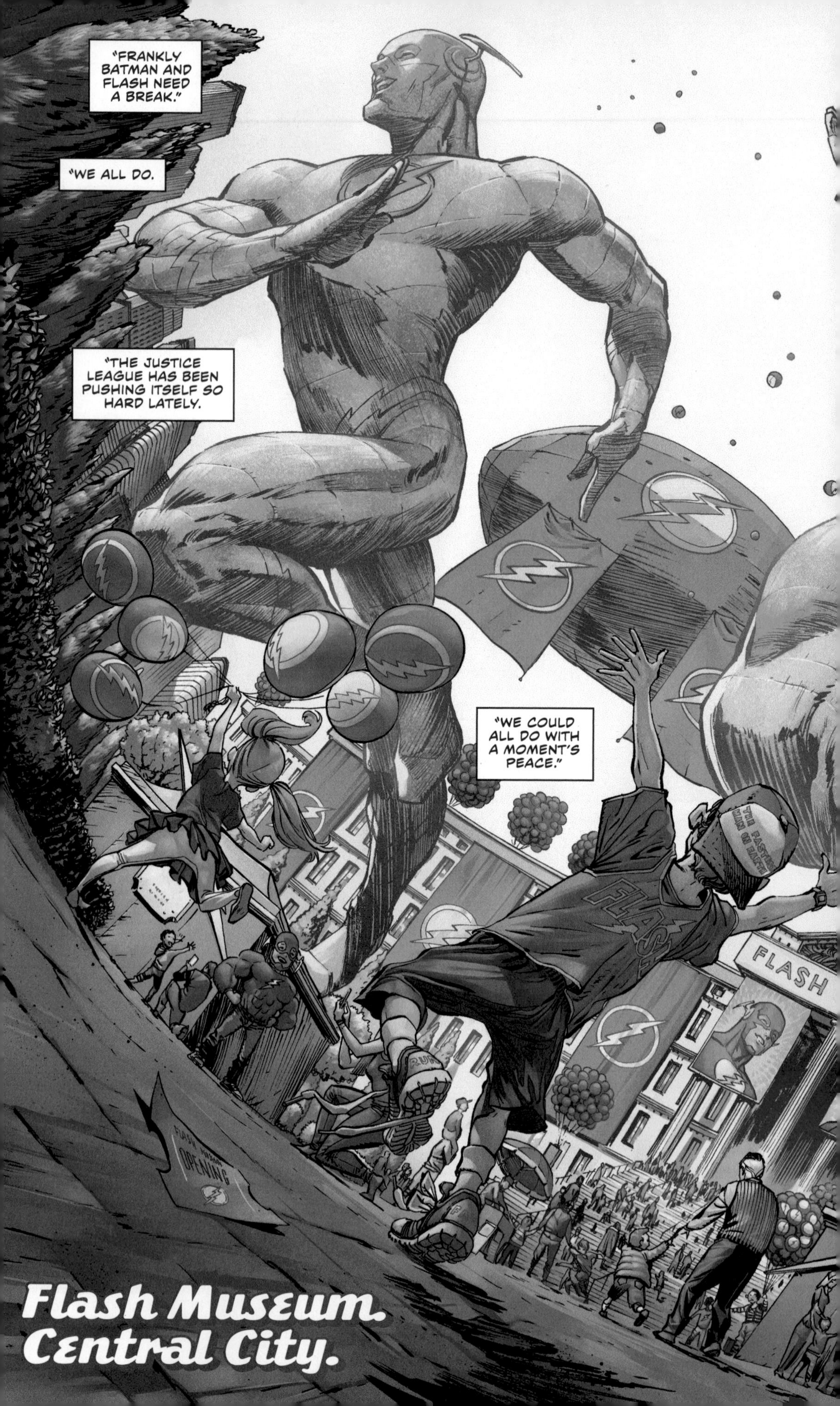
"FRANKLY BATMAN AND FLASH NEED A BREAK."
"WE ALL DO.
"THE JUSTICE LEAGUE HAS BEEN PUSHING ITSELF SO HARD LATELY.
"WE COULD ALL DO WITH A MOMENT'S PEACE."
FLASH
Flash Museum. Central City.

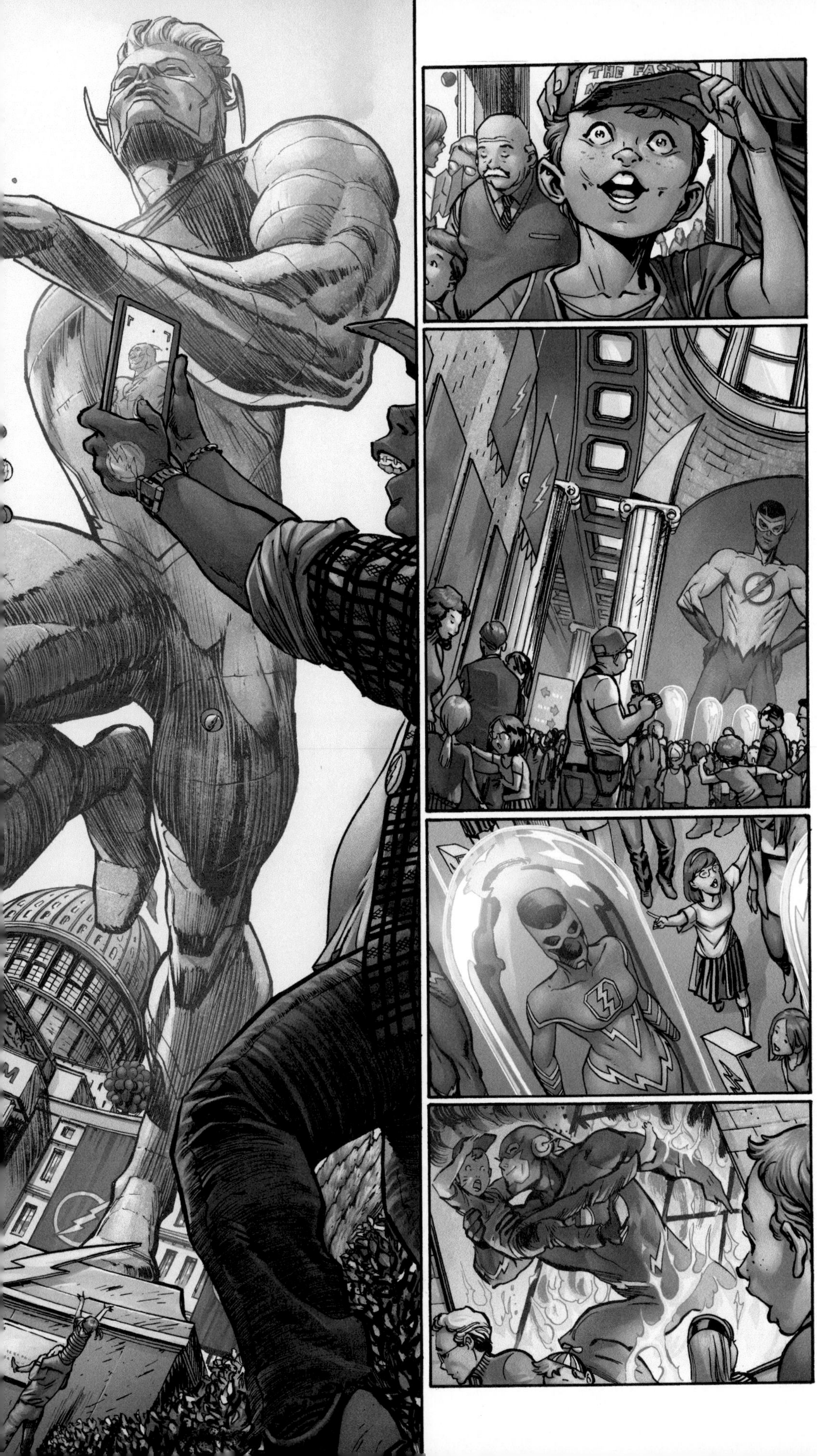

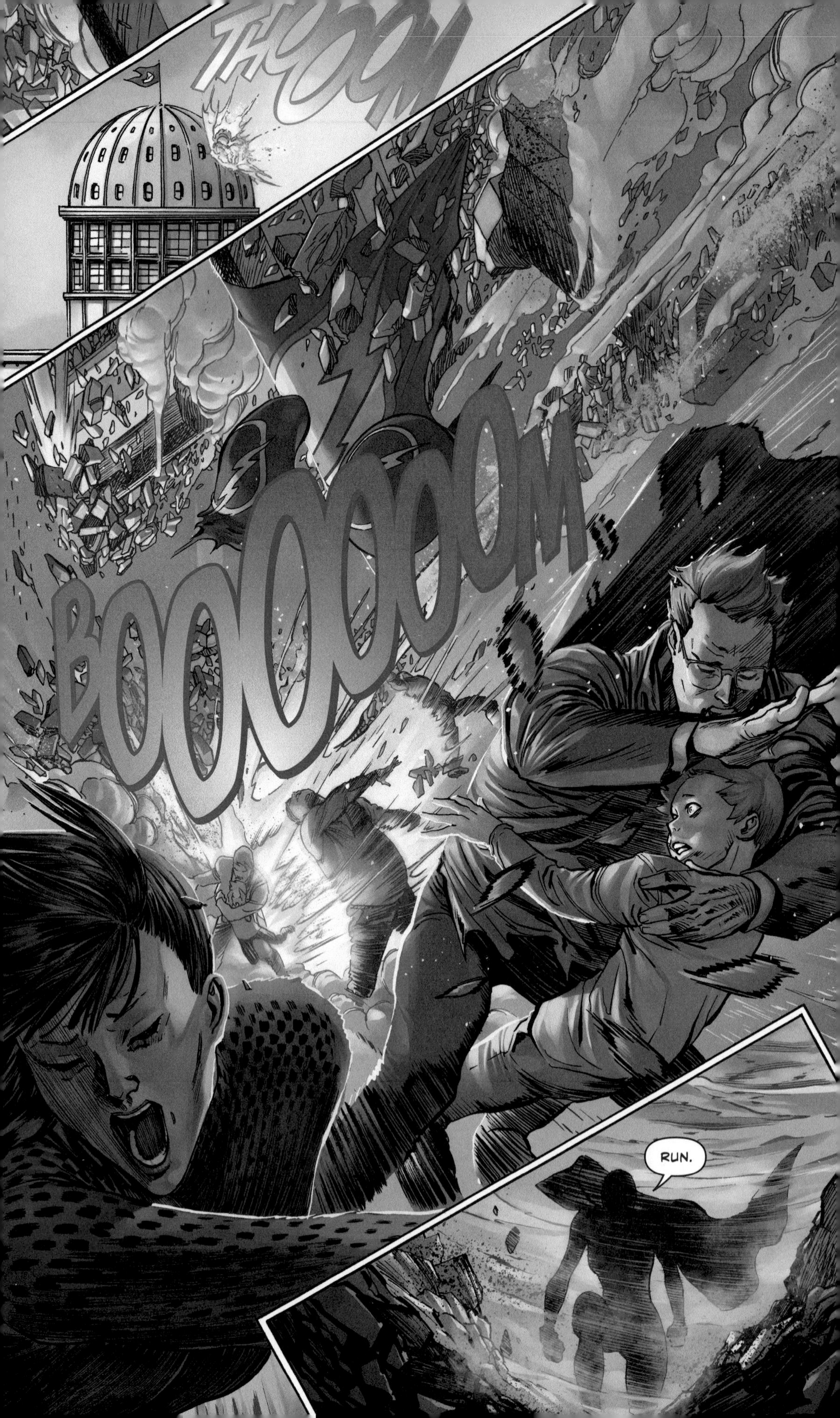
THOOM
BOOOOOOM
RUN.

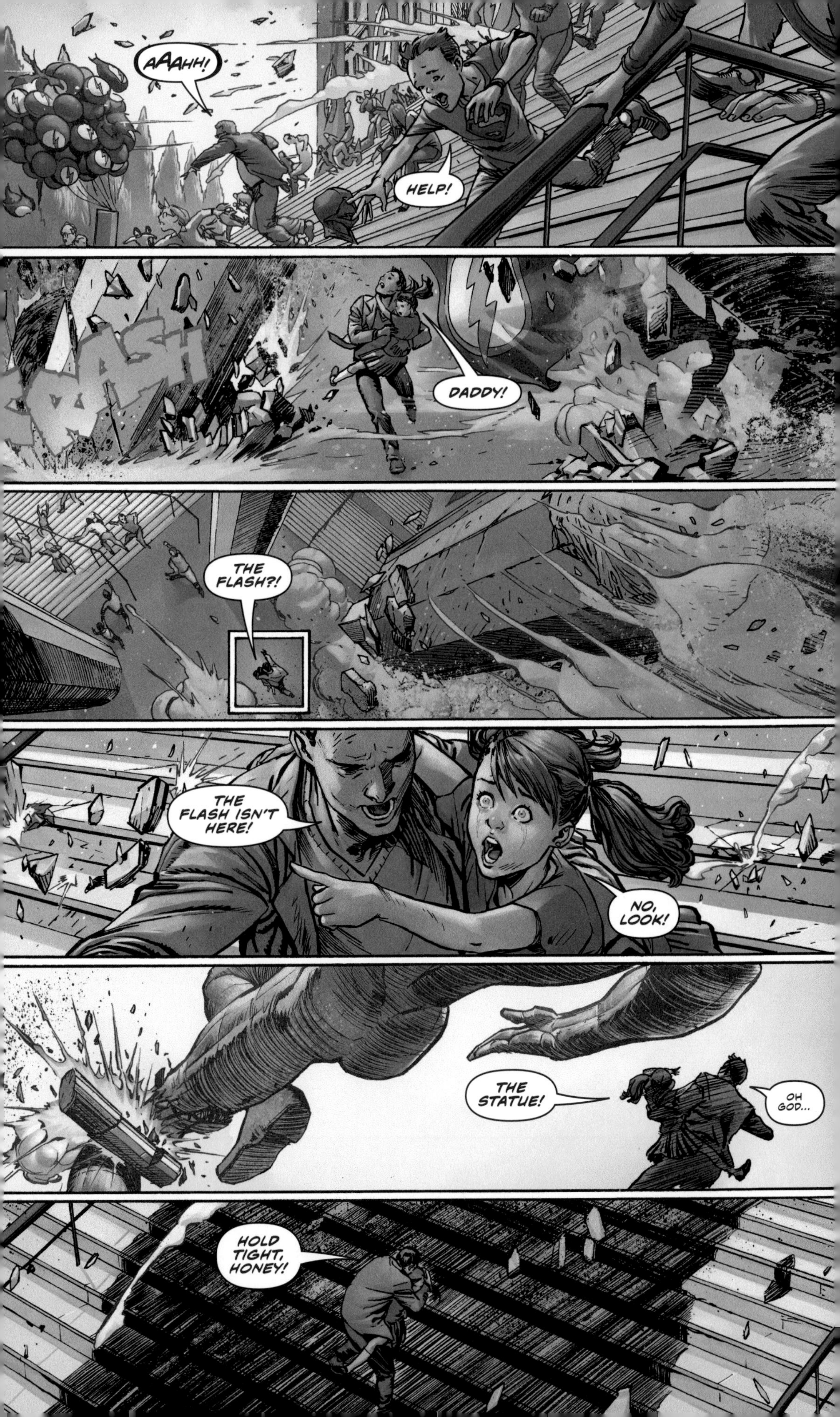
AAAHH!
HELP!
DADDY!
THE FLASH?!
THE FLASH ISN'T HERE!
NO, LOOK!
THE STATUE!
OH GOD...
HOLD TIGHT, HONEY!

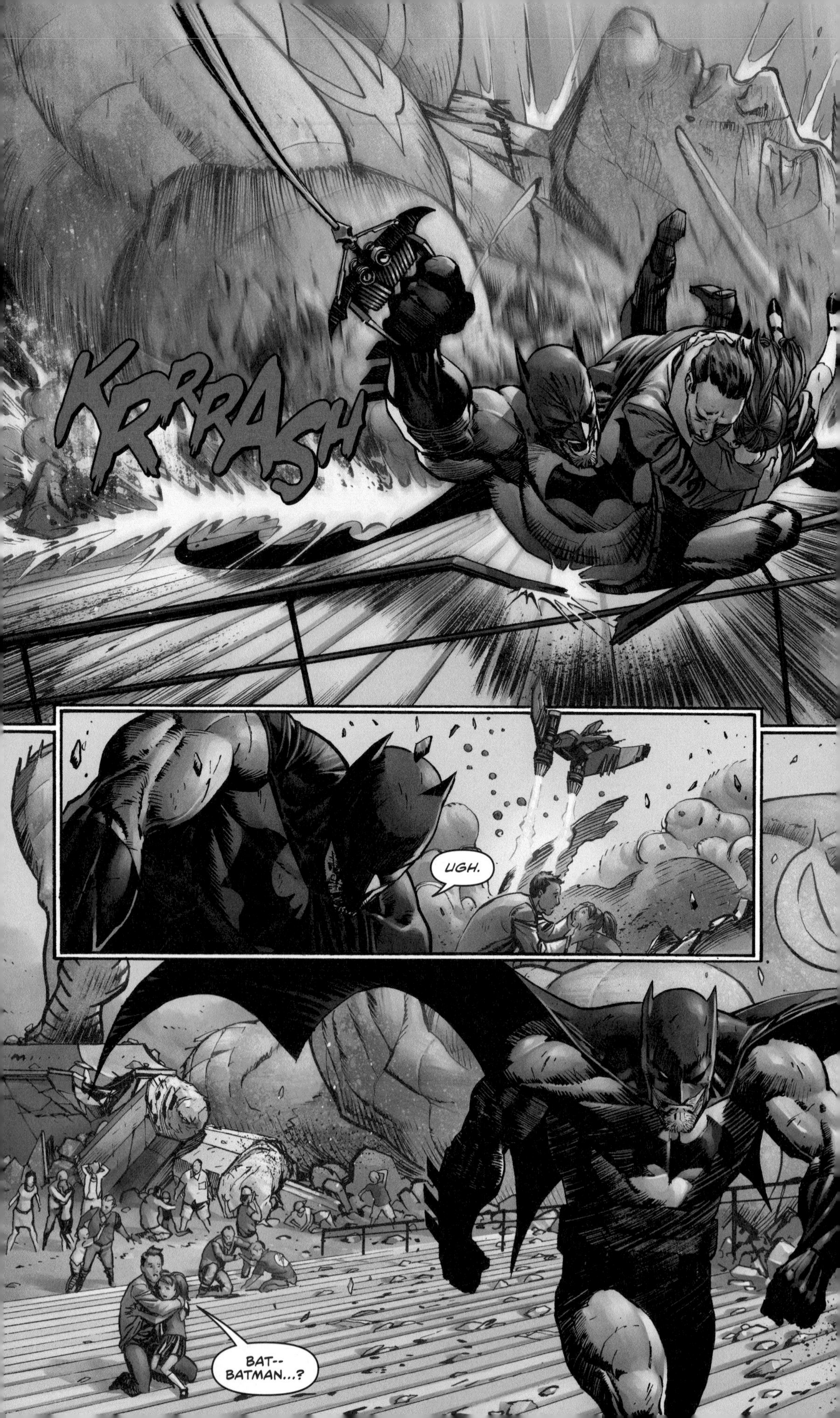
KRRRASH
UGH.
BAT--
BATMAN...?

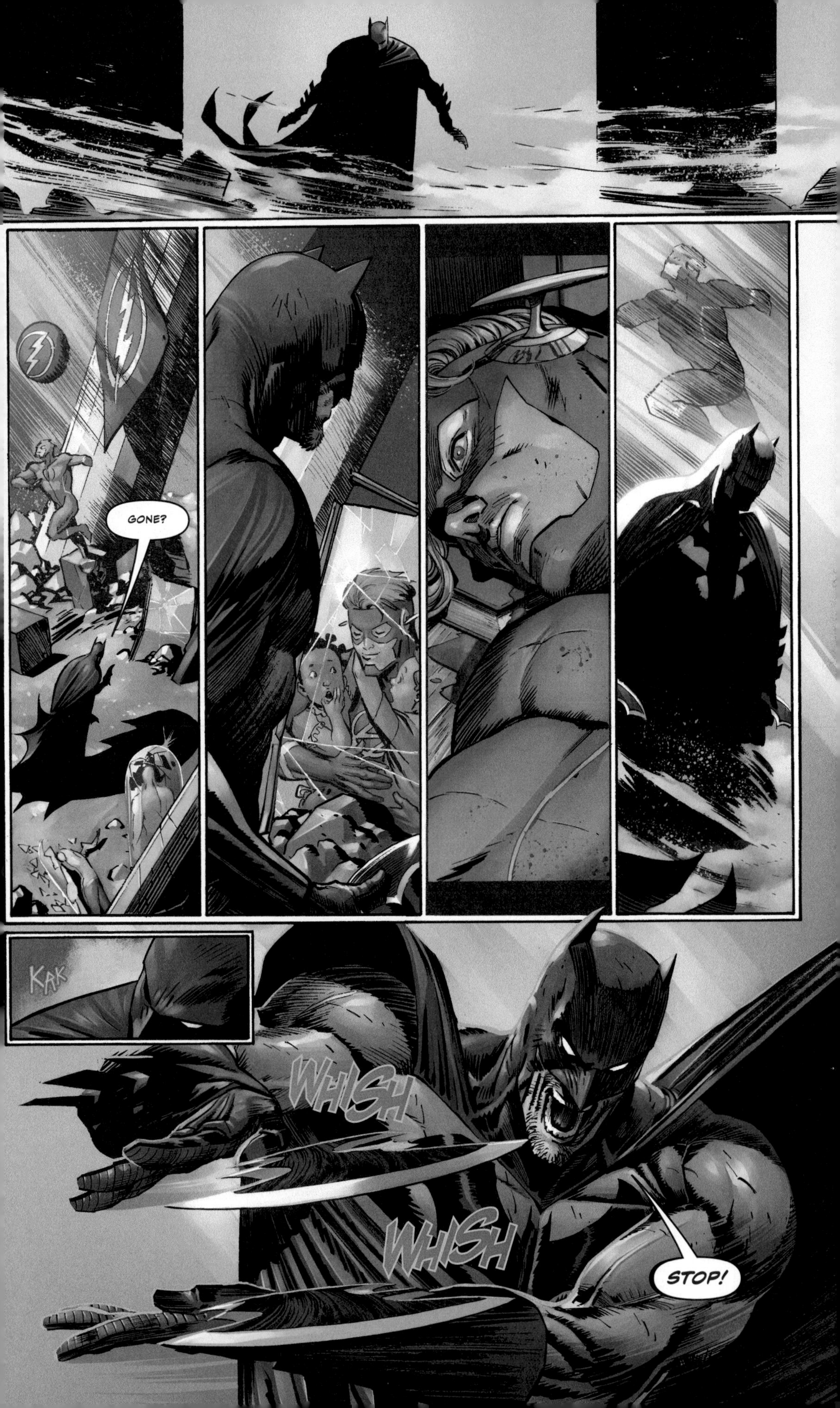
GONE?
KAK
WHISH
WHISH
STOP!

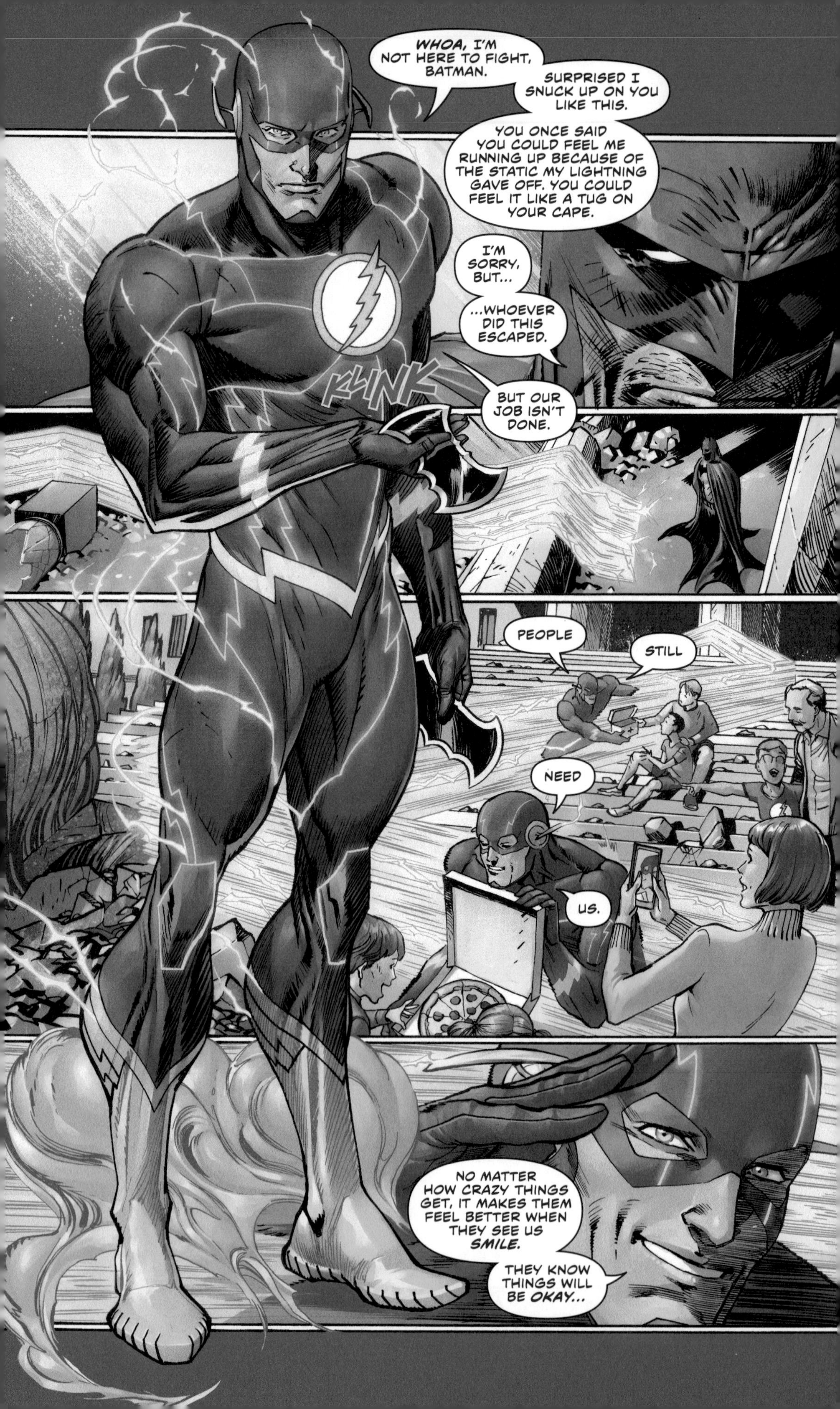
WHOA, I'M NOT HERE TO FIGHT, BATMAN.
SURPRISED I SNUCK UP ON YOU LIKE THIS.
YOU ONCE SAID YOU COULD FEEL ME RUNNING UP BECAUSE OF THE STATIC MY LIGHTNING GAVE OFF. YOU COULD FEEL IT LIKE A TUG ON YOUR CAPE.
I'M SORRY, BUT...
...WHOEVER DID THIS ESCAPED.
KLINK
BUT OUR JOB ISN'T DONE.
PEOPLE
STILL
NEED
US.
NO MATTER HOW CRAZY THINGS GET, IT MAKES THEM FEEL BETTER WHEN THEY SEE US SMILE.
THEY KNOW THINGS WILL BE OKAY...

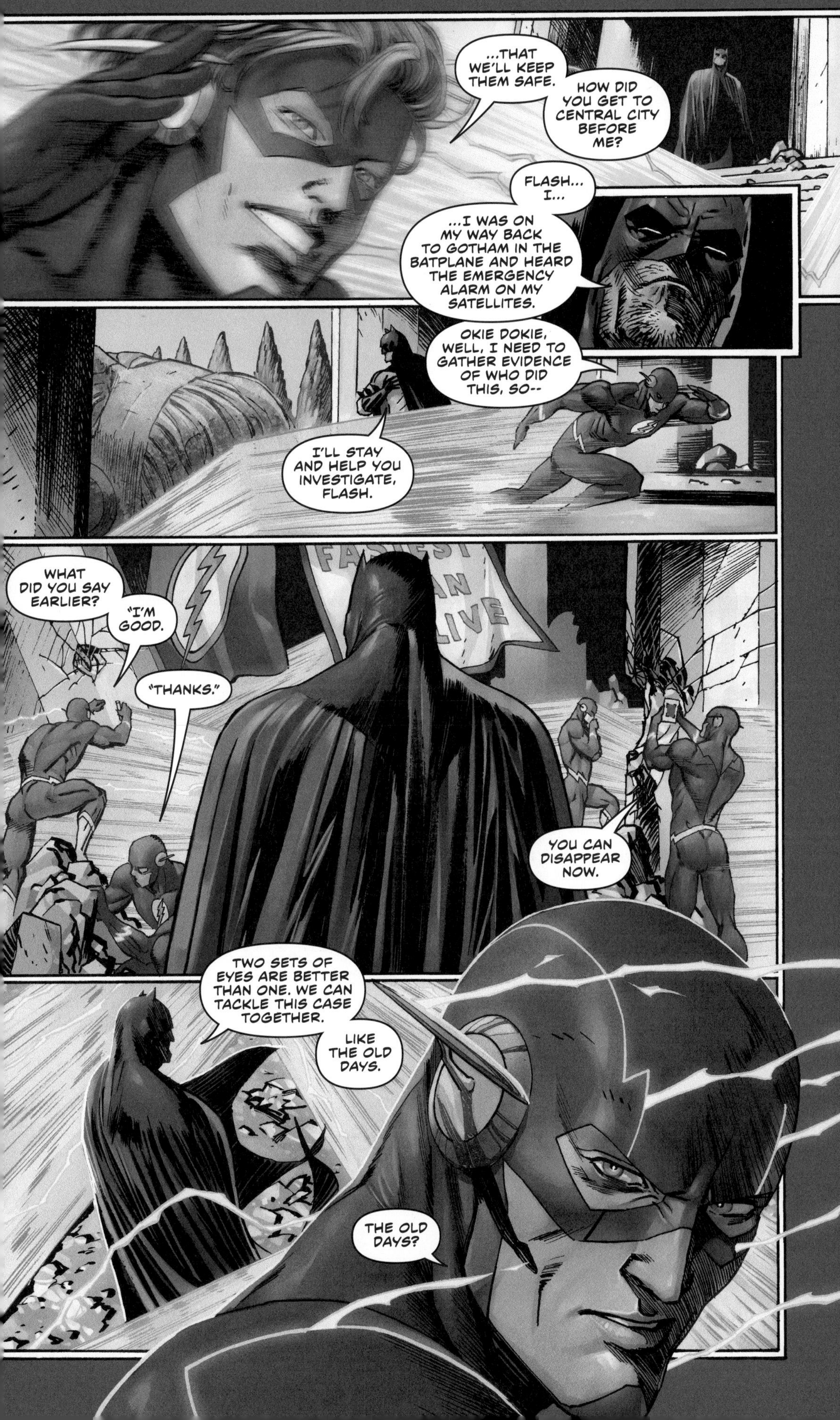
...THAT WE'LL KEEP THEM SAFE.
HOW DID YOU GET TO CENTRAL CITY BEFORE ME?
FLASH... I...
...I WAS ON MY WAY BACK TO GOTHAM IN THE BATPLANE AND HEARD THE EMERGENCY ALARM ON MY SATELLITES.
OKIE DOKIE, WELL, I NEED TO GATHER EVIDENCE OF WHO DID THIS, SO--
I'LL STAY AND HELP YOU INVESTIGATE, FLASH.
WHAT DID YOU SAY EARLIER?
"I'M GOOD.
"THANKS."
YOU CAN DISAPPEAR NOW.
TWO SETS OF EYES ARE BETTER THAN ONE. WE CAN TACKLE THIS CASE TOGETHER.
LIKE THE OLD DAYS.
THE OLD DAYS?

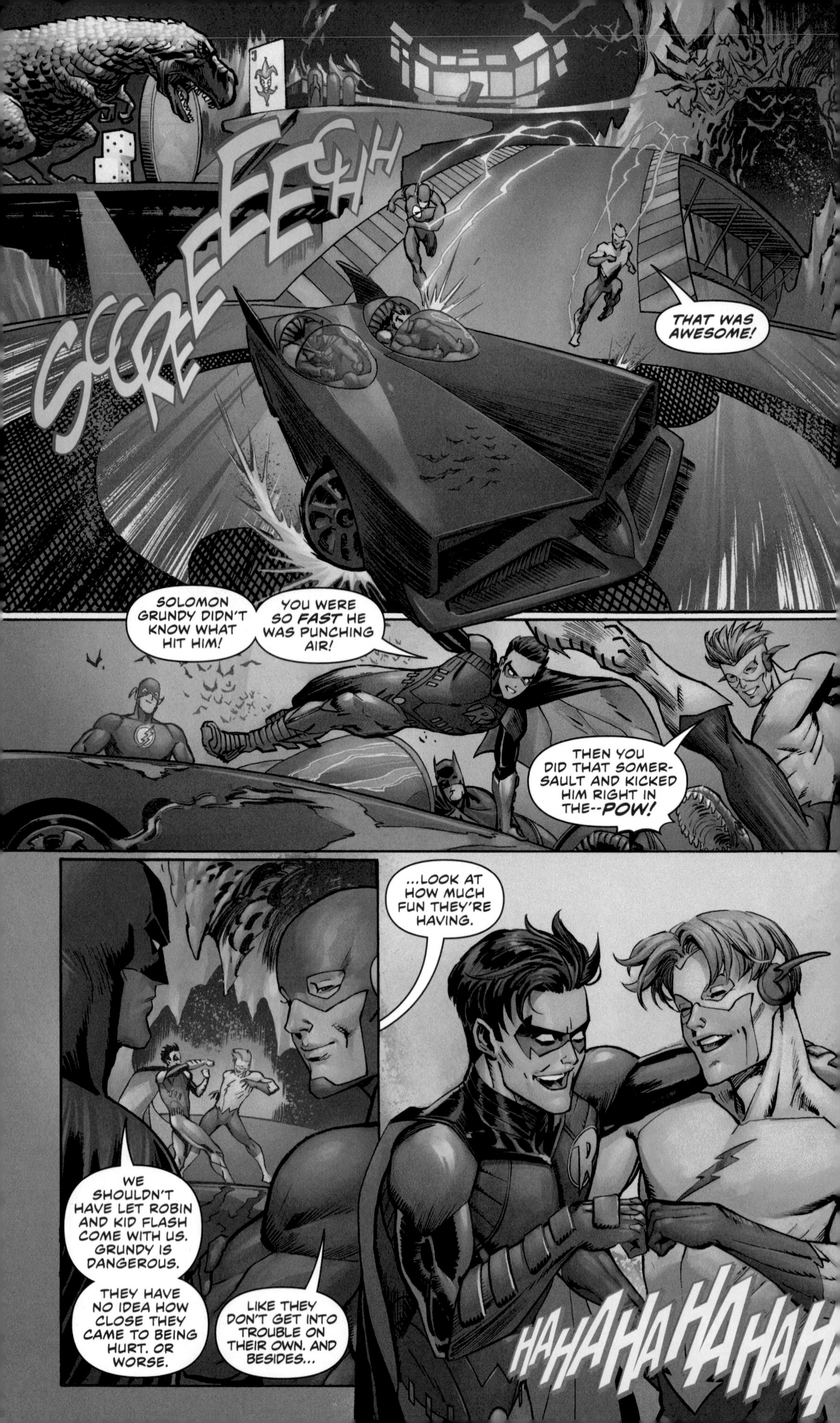
SCREEEEECHH
THAT WAS AWESOME!
SOLOMON GRUNDY DIDN'T KNOW WHAT HIT HIM!
YOU WERE SO FAST HE WAS PUNCHING AIR!
THEN YOU DID THAT SOMER-SAULT AND KICKED HIM RIGHT IN THE--POW!
WE SHOULDN'T HAVE LET ROBIN AND KID FLASH COME WITH US. GRUNDY IS DANGEROUS.
THEY HAVE NO IDEA HOW CLOSE THEY CAME TO BEING HURT. OR WORSE.
LIKE THEY DON'T GET INTO TROUBLE ON THEIR OWN. AND BESIDES...
...LOOK AT HOW MUCH FUN THEY'RE HAVING.
HAHAHAHAHAHAH

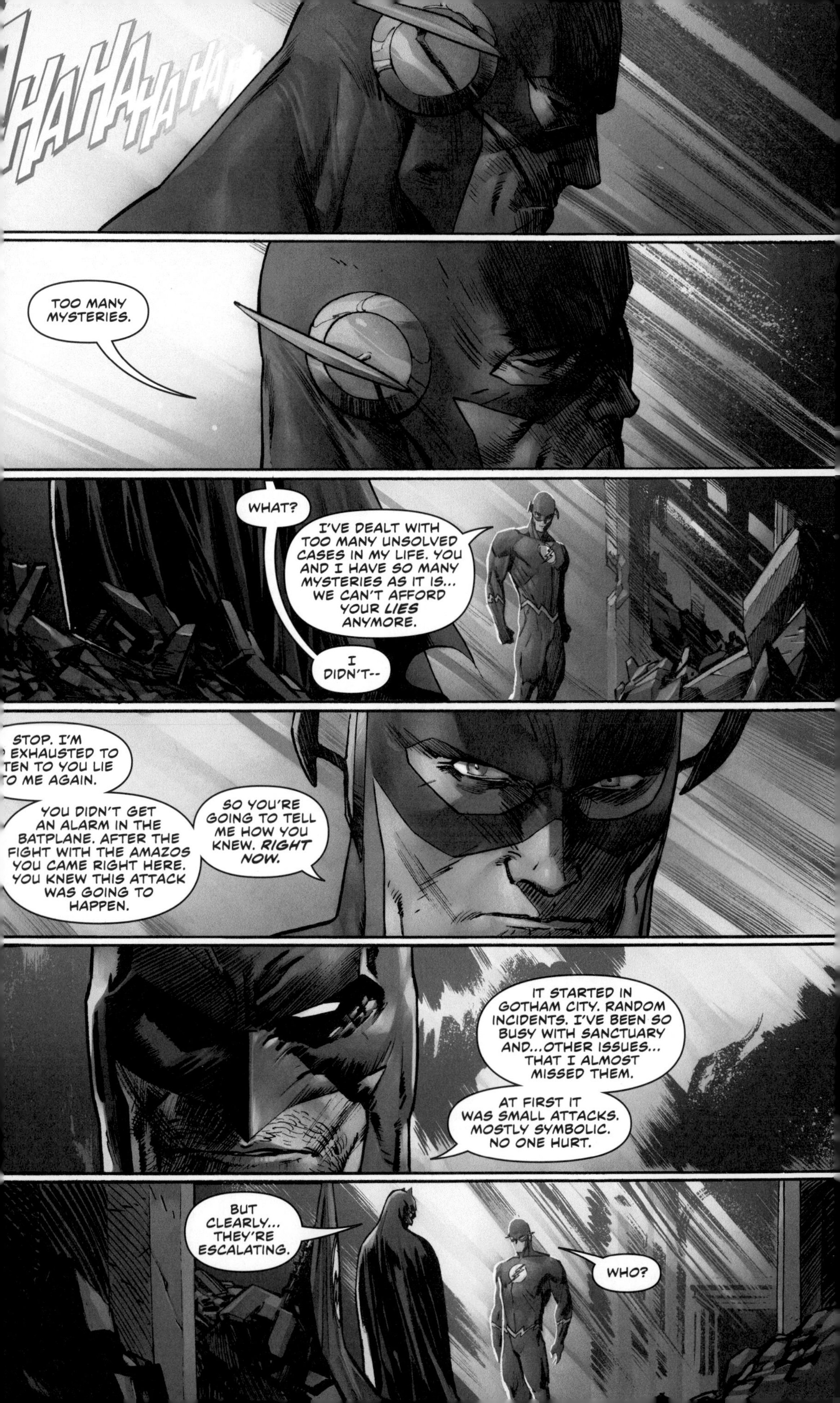
HAHAHAHAHA
TOO MANY MYSTERIES.
WHAT?
I'VE DEALT WITH TOO MANY UNSOLVED CASES IN MY LIFE. YOU AND I HAVE SO MANY MYSTERIES AS IT IS... WE CAN'T AFFORD YOUR *LIES* ANYMORE.
I DIDN'T--
STOP. I'M EXHAUSTED TO TEN TO YOU LIE TO ME AGAIN.
YOU DIDN'T GET AN ALARM IN THE BATPLANE. AFTER THE FIGHT WITH THE AMAZOS YOU CAME RIGHT HERE. YOU KNEW THIS ATTACK WAS GOING TO HAPPEN.
SO YOU'RE GOING TO TELL ME HOW YOU KNEW. *RIGHT NOW.*
IT STARTED IN GOTHAM CITY. RANDOM INCIDENTS. I'VE BEEN SO BUSY WITH SANCTUARY AND...OTHER ISSUES... THAT I ALMOST MISSED THEM.
AT FIRST IT WAS SMALL ATTACKS. MOSTLY SYMBOLIC. NO ONE HURT.
BUT CLEARLY... THEY'RE ESCALATING.
WHO?

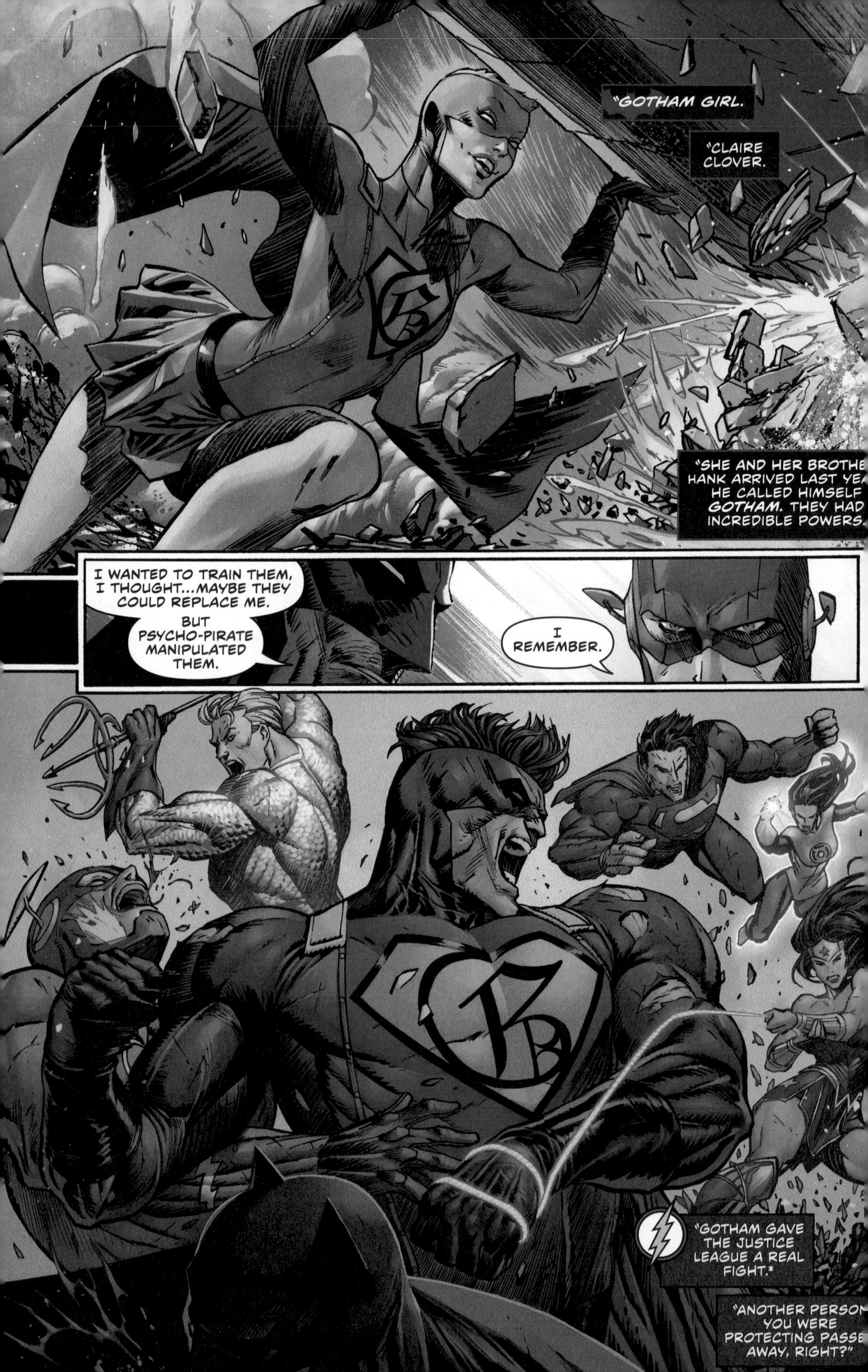
"GOTHAM GIRL.
"CLAIRE CLOVER.
"SHE AND HER BROTHE HANK ARRIVED LAST YEA HE CALLED HIMSELF GOTHAM. THEY HAD INCREDIBLE POWERS.
I WANTED TO TRAIN THEM, I THOUGHT...MAYBE THEY COULD REPLACE ME.
BUT PSYCHO-PIRATE MANIPULATED THEM.
I REMEMBER.
"GOTHAM GAVE THE JUSTICE LEAGUE A REAL FIGHT.*
"ANOTHER PERSON YOU WERE PROTECTING PASSE AWAY, RIGHT?"
*See BATMAN: I AM GOTH for the full story. --JSR

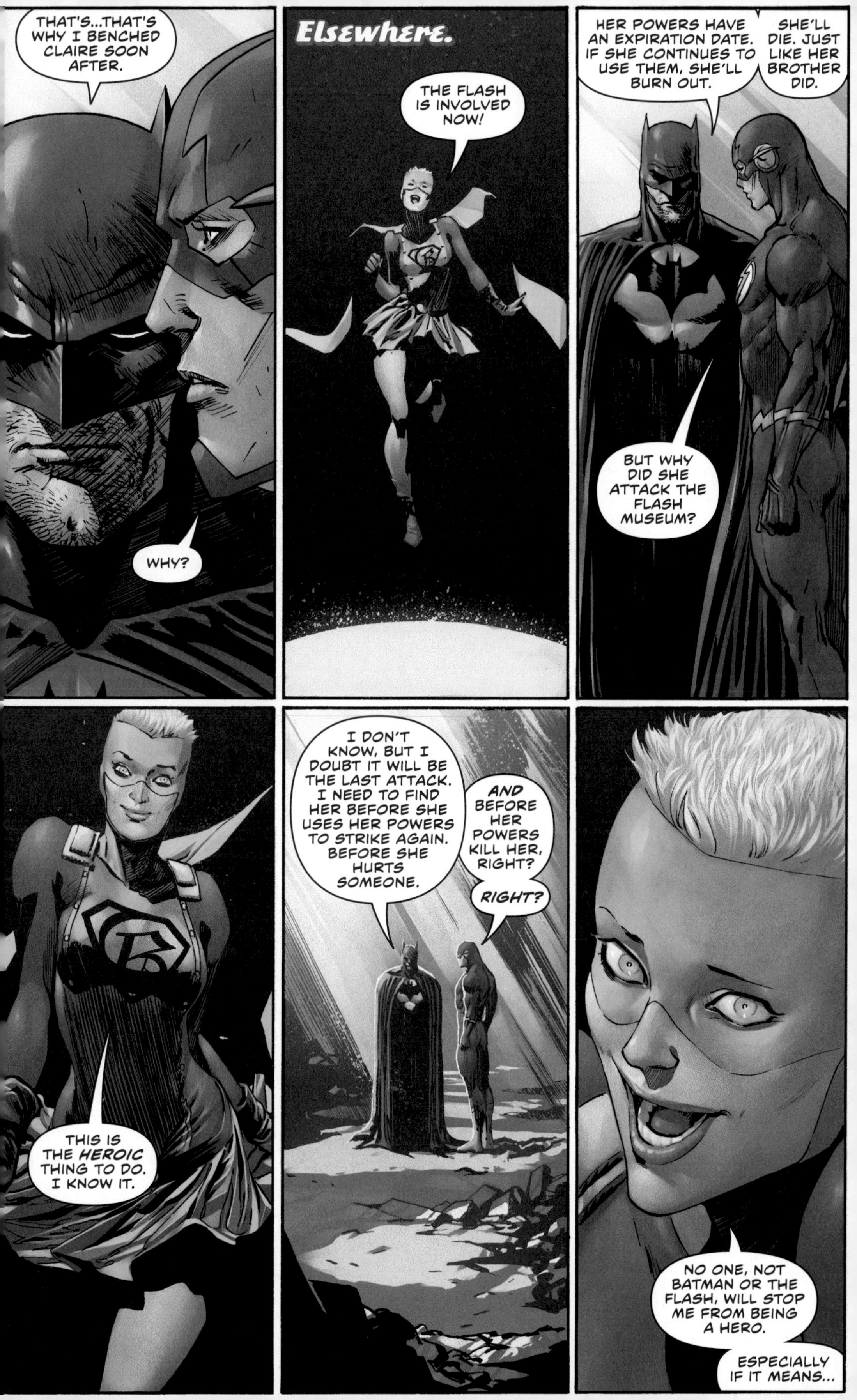
THAT'S...THAT'S WHY I BENCHED CLAIRE SOON AFTER.
WHY?
Elsewhere.
THE FLASH IS INVOLVED NOW!
HER POWERS HAVE AN EXPIRATION DATE. IF SHE CONTINUES TO USE THEM, SHE'LL BURN OUT.
SHE'LL DIE. JUST LIKE HER BROTHER DID.
BUT WHY DID SHE ATTACK THE FLASH MUSEUM?
THIS IS THE *HEROIC* THING TO DO. I KNOW IT.
I DON'T KNOW, BUT I DOUBT IT WILL BE THE LAST ATTACK. I NEED TO FIND HER BEFORE SHE USES HER POWERS TO STRIKE AGAIN. BEFORE SHE HURTS SOMEONE.
AND BEFORE HER POWERS KILL HER, RIGHT?
RIGHT?
NO ONE, NOT BATMAN OR THE FLASH, WILL STOP ME FROM BEING A HERO.
ESPECIALLY IF IT MEANS...

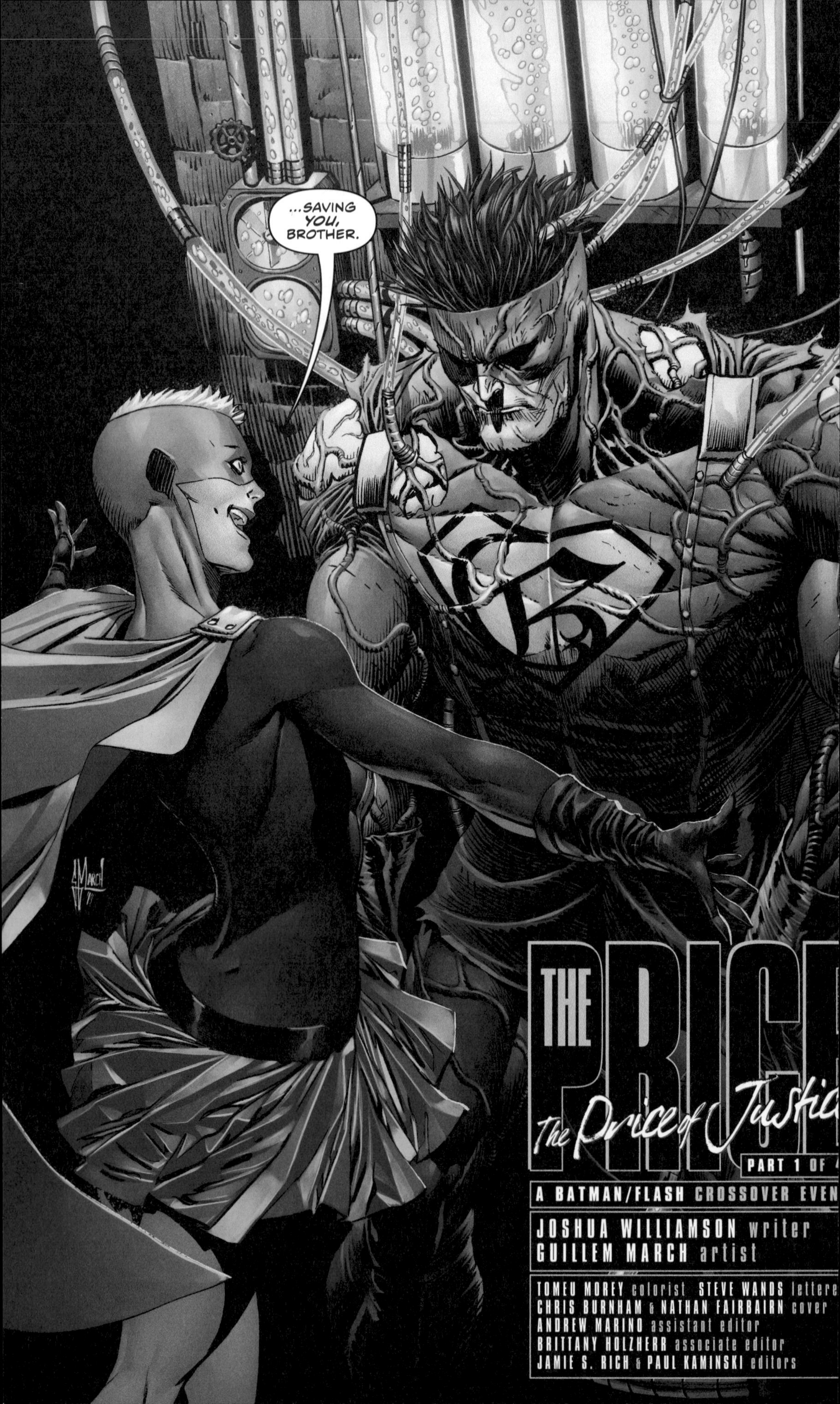
...SAVING YOU, BROTHER.
THE PRIC
The Price of Justic
PART 1 OF
A BATMAN/FLASH CROSSOVER EVEN
JOSHUA WILLIAMSON writer
GUILLEM MARCH artist
TOMEU MOREY colorist STEVE WANDS lettere
CHRIS BURNHAM & NATHAN FAIRBAIRN cover
ANDREW MARINO assistant editor
BRITTANY HOLZHERR associate editor
JAMIE S. RICH & PAUL KAMINSKI editors

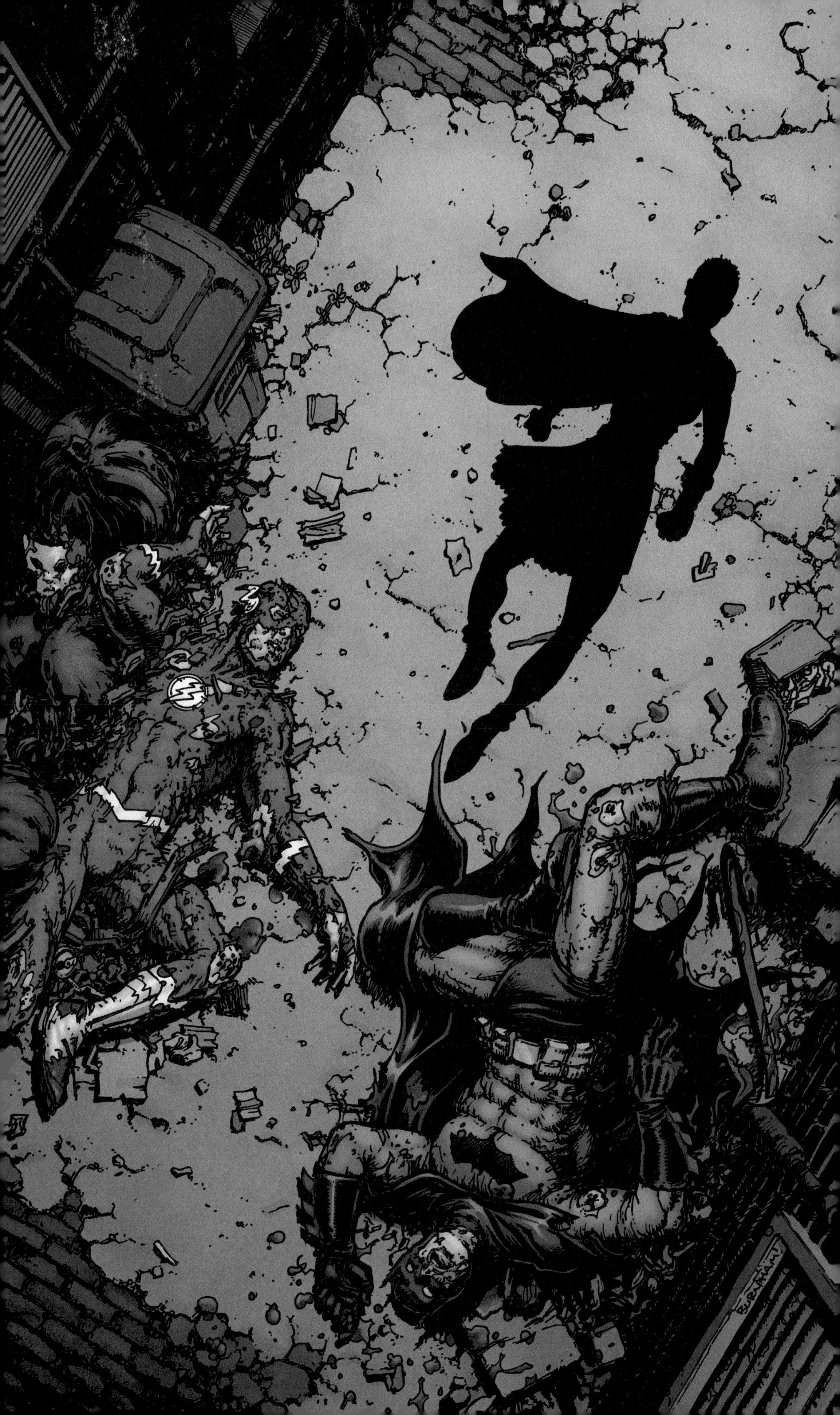
BURNHAM

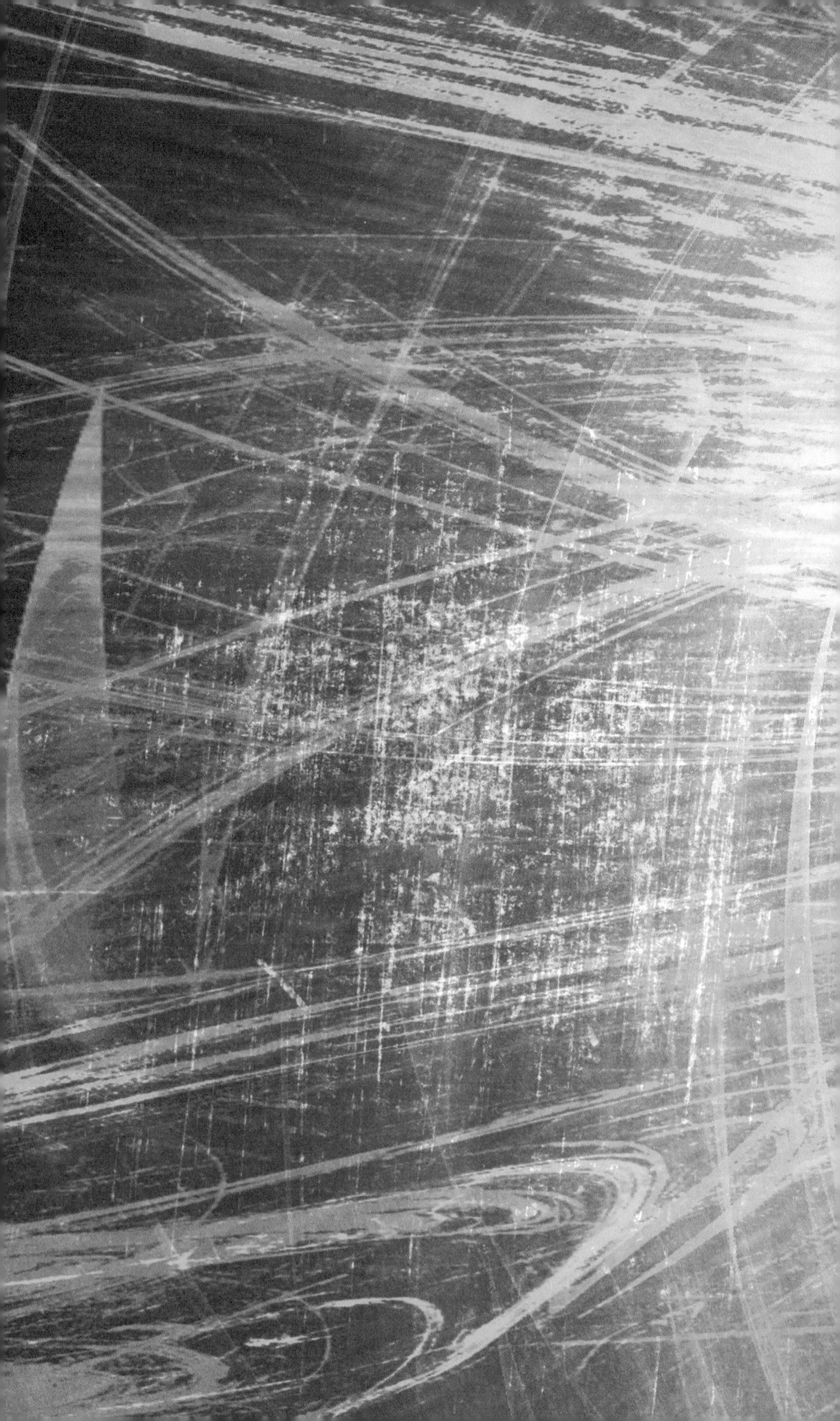

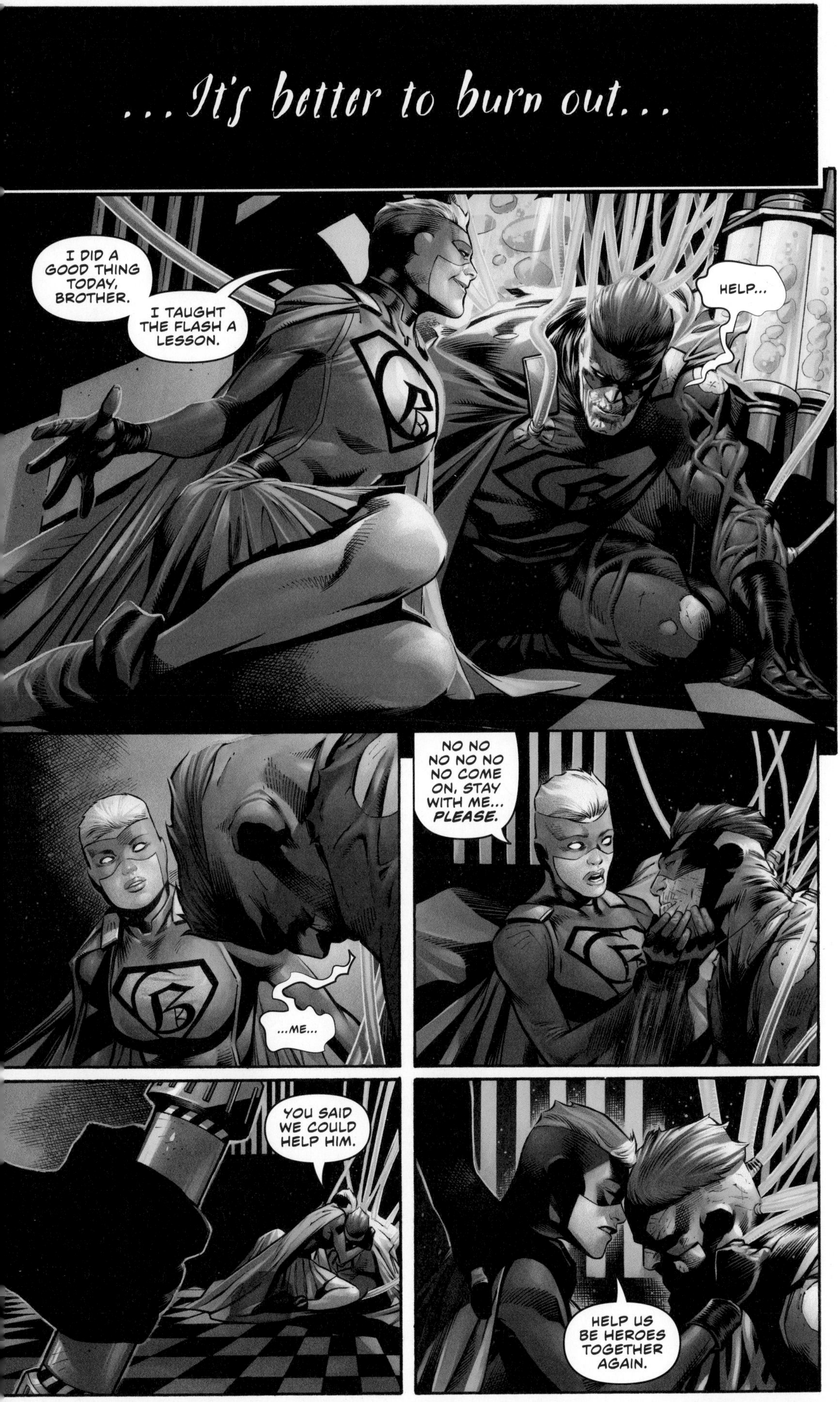
...It's better to burn out...
I DID A GOOD THING TODAY, BROTHER.
I TAUGHT THE FLASH A LESSON.
HELP...
...ME...
NO NO NO NO NO NO COME ON, STAY WITH ME... *PLEASE.*
YOU SAID WE COULD HELP HIM.
HELP US BE HEROES TOGETHER AGAIN.

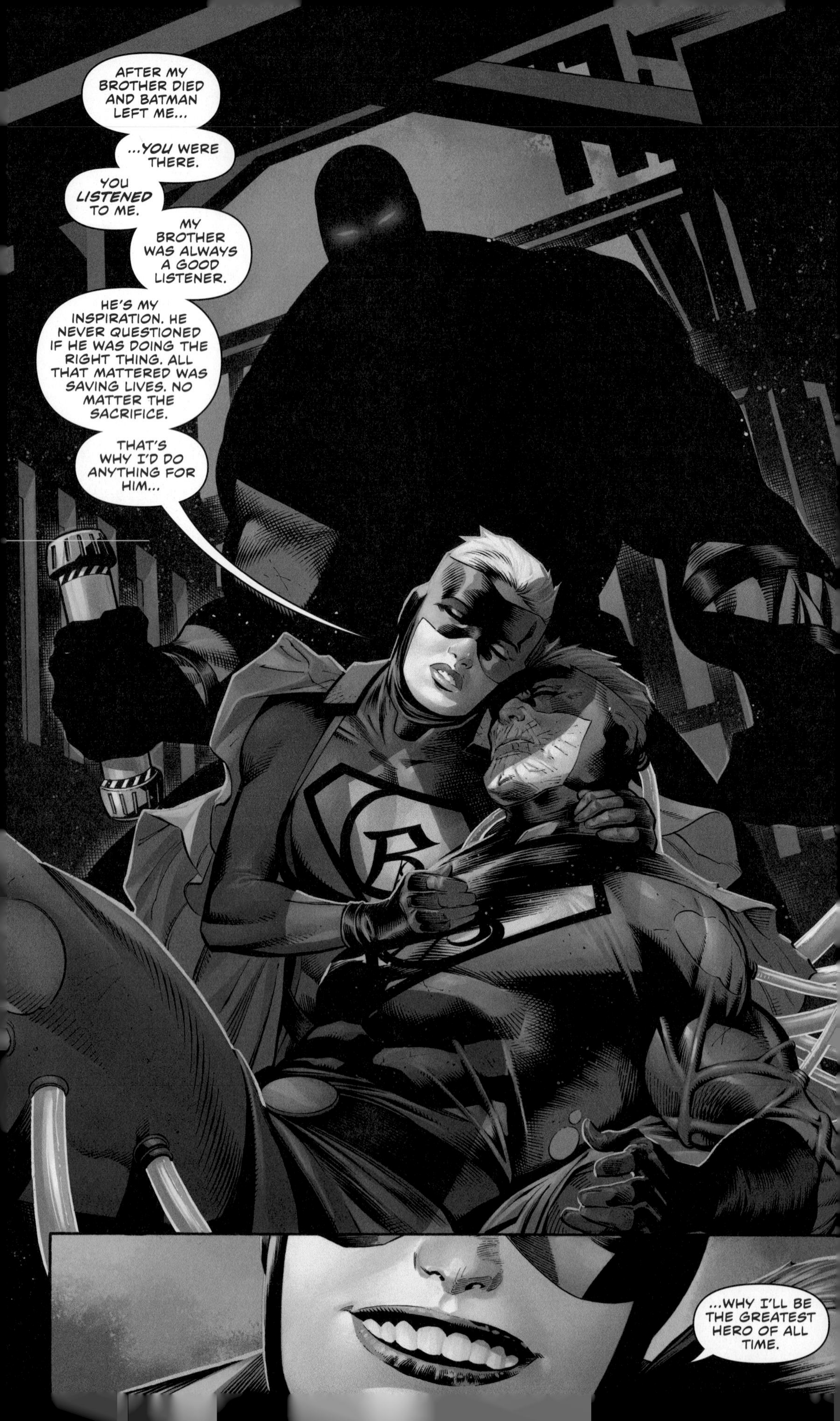
AFTER MY BROTHER DIED AND BATMAN LEFT ME...
...YOU WERE THERE.
YOU LISTENED TO ME.
MY BROTHER WAS ALWAYS A GOOD LISTENER.
HE'S MY INSPIRATION. HE NEVER QUESTIONED IF HE WAS DOING THE RIGHT THING. ALL THAT MATTERED WAS SAVING LIVES. NO MATTER THE SACRIFICE.
THAT'S WHY I'D DO ANYTHING FOR HIM...
...WHY I'LL BE THE GREATEST HERO OF ALL TIME.

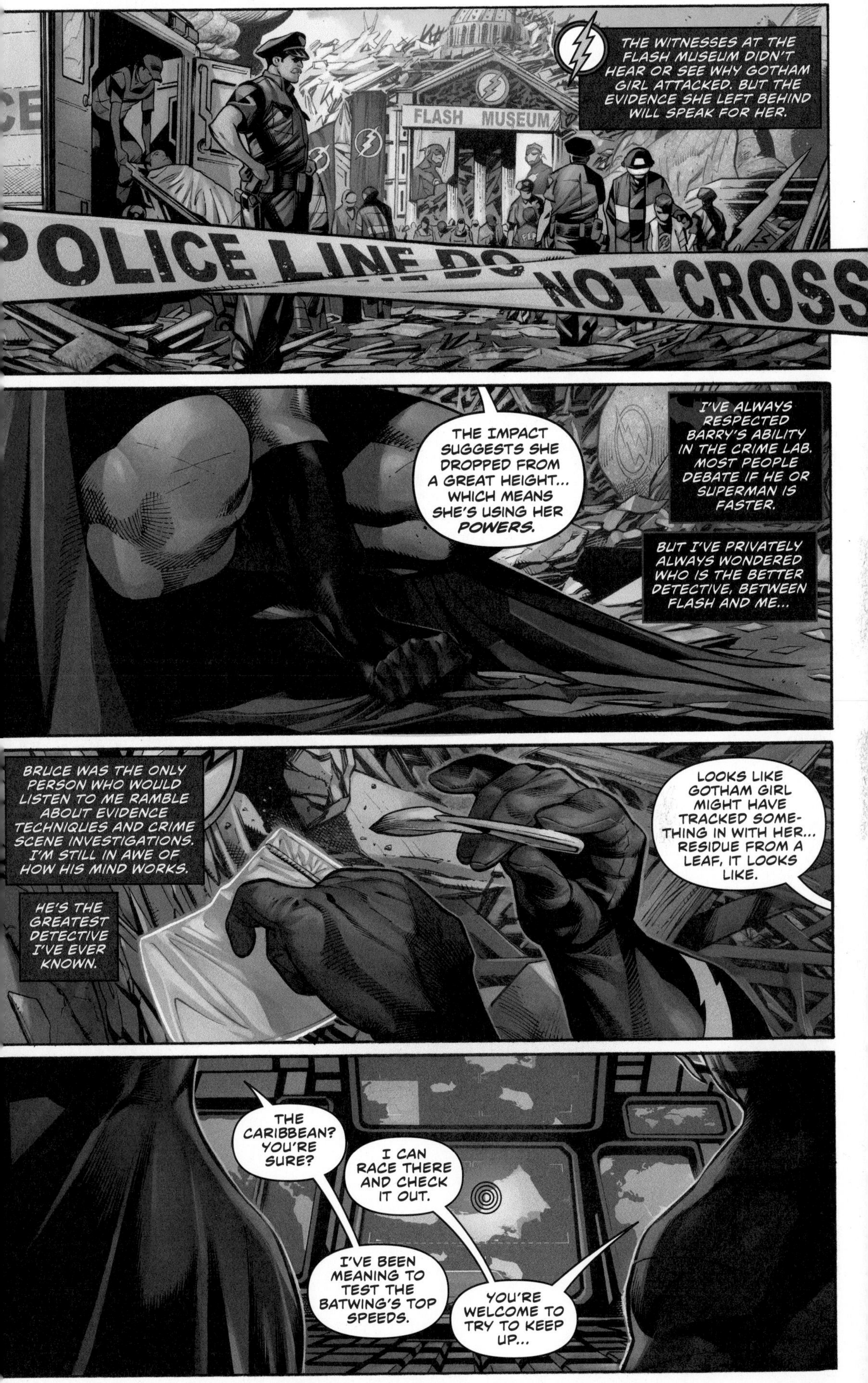
THE WITNESSES AT THE FLASH MUSEUM DIDN'T HEAR OR SEE WHY GOTHAM GIRL ATTACKED. BUT THE EVIDENCE SHE LEFT BEHIND WILL SPEAK FOR HER.
FLASH MUSEUM
POLICE LINE DO NOT CROSS
THE IMPACT SUGGESTS SHE DROPPED FROM A GREAT HEIGHT... WHICH MEANS SHE'S USING HER POWERS.
I'VE ALWAYS RESPECTED BARRY'S ABILITY IN THE CRIME LAB. MOST PEOPLE DEBATE IF HE OR SUPERMAN IS FASTER.
BUT I'VE PRIVATELY ALWAYS WONDERED WHO IS THE BETTER DETECTIVE, BETWEEN FLASH AND ME...
BRUCE WAS THE ONLY PERSON WHO WOULD LISTEN TO ME RAMBLE ABOUT EVIDENCE TECHNIQUES AND CRIME SCENE INVESTIGATIONS. I'M STILL IN AWE OF HOW HIS MIND WORKS.
HE'S THE GREATEST DETECTIVE I'VE EVER KNOWN.
LOOKS LIKE GOTHAM GIRL MIGHT HAVE TRACKED SOME-THING IN WITH HER... RESIDUE FROM A LEAF, IT LOOKS LIKE.
THE CARIBBEAN? YOU'RE SURE?
I CAN RACE THERE AND CHECK IT OUT.
I'VE BEEN MEANING TO TEST THE BATWING'S TOP SPEEDS.
YOU'RE WELCOME TO TRY TO KEEP UP...

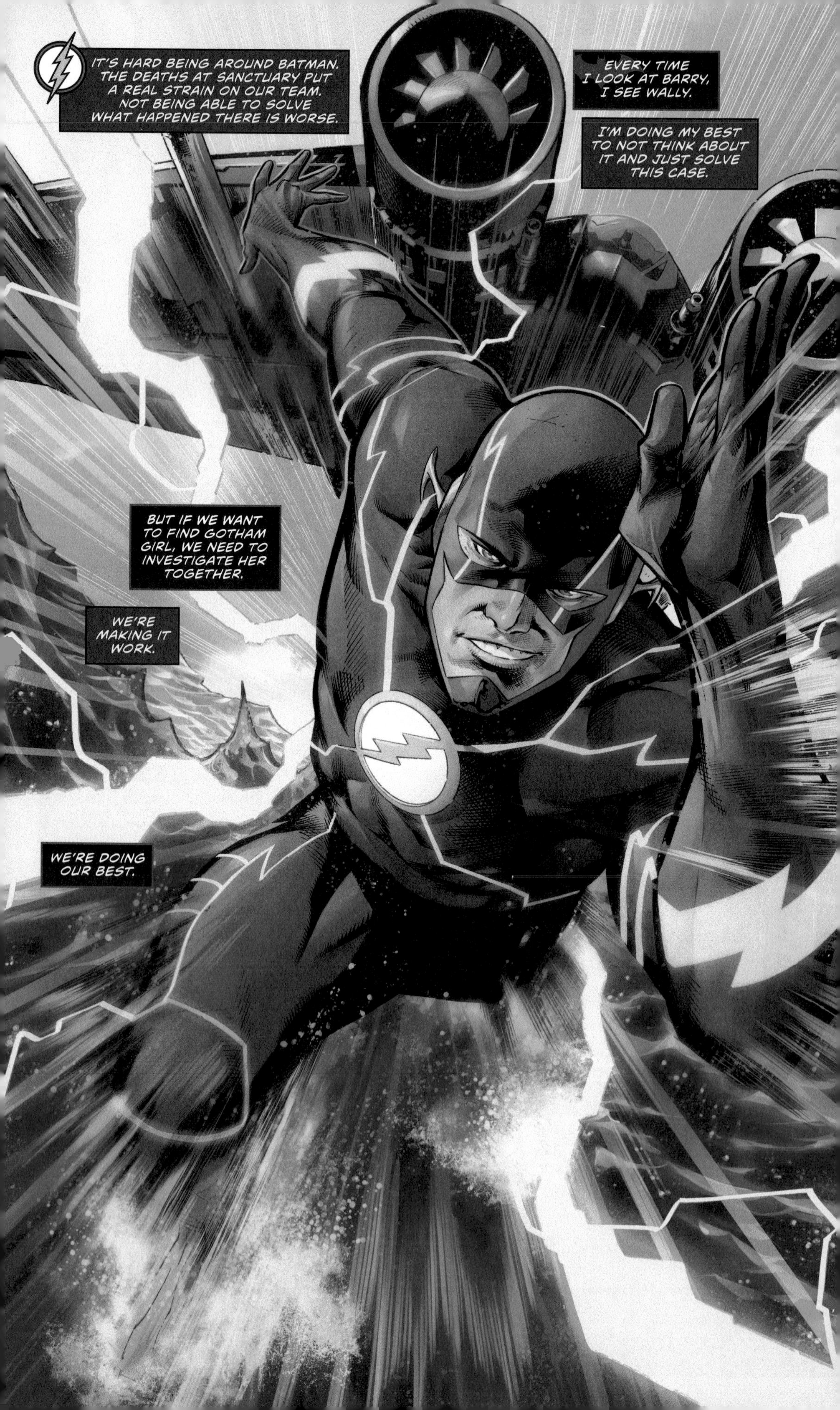
IT'S HARD BEING AROUND BATMAN. THE DEATHS AT SANCTUARY PUT A REAL STRAIN ON OUR TEAM. NOT BEING ABLE TO SOLVE WHAT HAPPENED THERE IS WORSE.
EVERY TIME I LOOK AT BARRY, I SEE WALLY.
I'M DOING MY BEST TO NOT THINK ABOUT IT AND JUST SOLVE THIS CASE.
BUT IF WE WANT TO FIND GOTHAM GIRL, WE NEED TO INVESTIGATE HER TOGETHER.
WE'RE MAKING IT WORK.
WE'RE DOING OUR BEST.

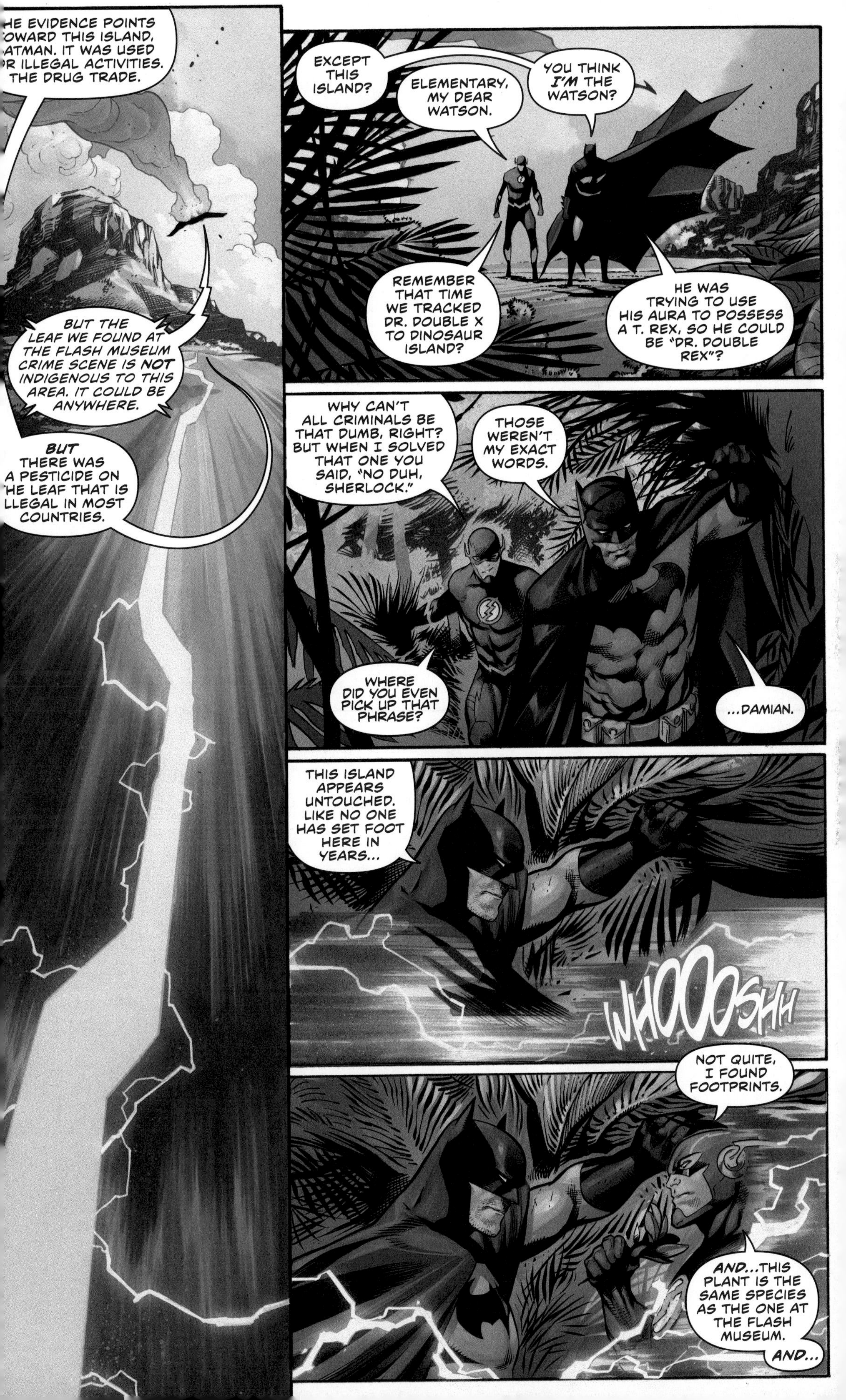

HE EVIDENCE POINTS TOWARD THIS ISLAND, ATMAN. IT WAS USED R ILLEGAL ACTIVITIES. THE DRUG TRADE.
BUT THE LEAF WE FOUND AT THE FLASH MUSEUM CRIME SCENE IS NOT INDIGENOUS TO THIS AREA. IT COULD BE ANYWHERE.
BUT THERE WAS A PESTICIDE ON HE LEAF THAT IS LLEGAL IN MOST COUNTRIES.
EXCEPT THIS ISLAND?
ELEMENTARY, MY DEAR WATSON.
YOU THINK I'M THE WATSON?
REMEMBER THAT TIME WE TRACKED DR. DOUBLE X TO DINOSAUR ISLAND?
HE WAS TRYING TO USE HIS AURA TO POSSESS A T. REX, SO HE COULD BE "DR. DOUBLE REX"?
WHY CAN'T ALL CRIMINALS BE THAT DUMB, RIGHT? BUT WHEN I SOLVED THAT ONE YOU SAID, "NO DUH, SHERLOCK."
THOSE WEREN'T MY EXACT WORDS.
WHERE DID YOU EVEN PICK UP THAT PHRASE?
...DAMIAN.
THIS ISLAND APPEARS UNTOUCHED. LIKE NO ONE HAS SET FOOT HERE IN YEARS...
WHOOOSHH
NOT QUITE, I FOUND FOOTPRINTS.
AND...THIS PLANT IS THE SAME SPECIES AS THE ONE AT THE FLASH MUSEUM.
AND...

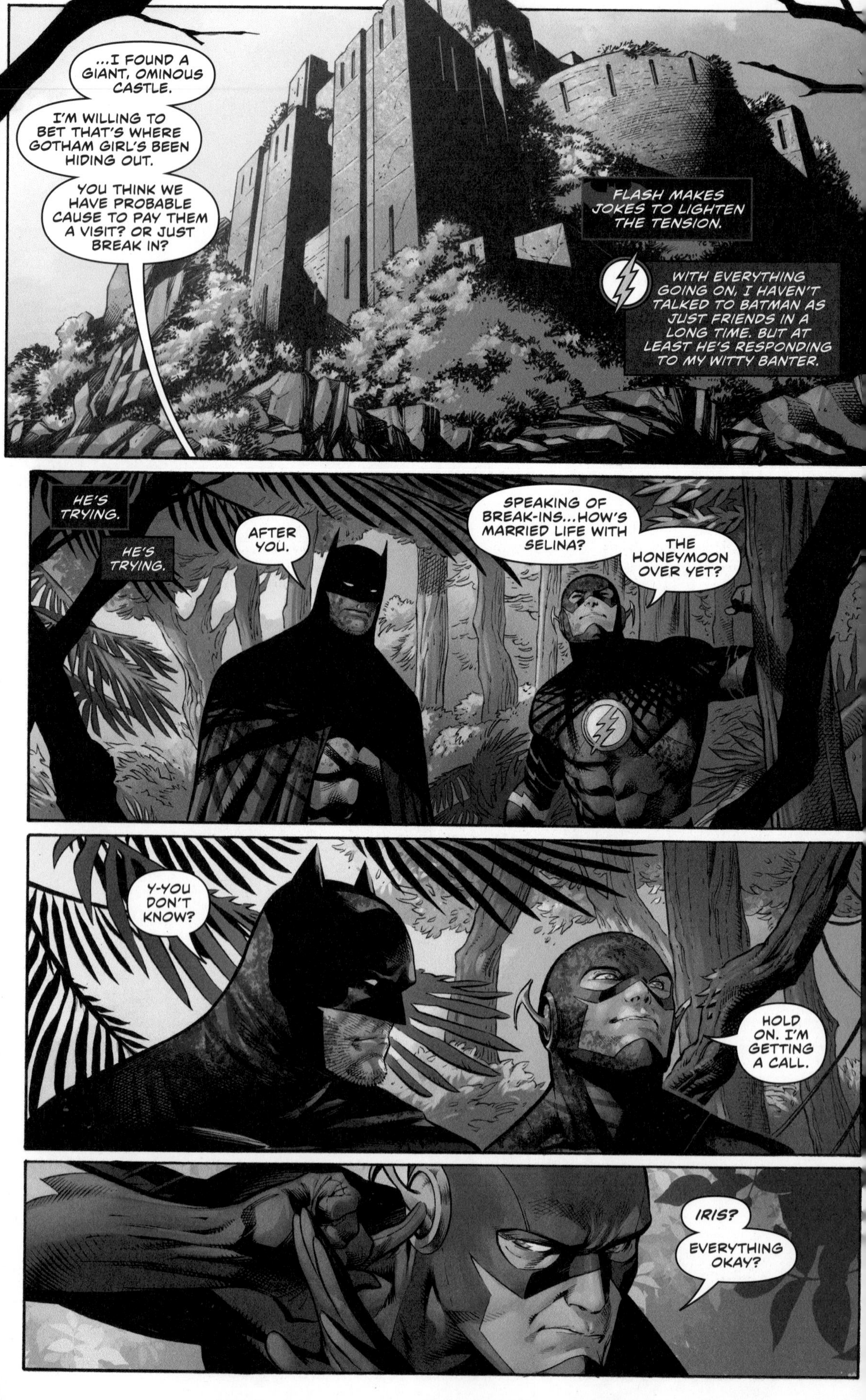
...I FOUND A GIANT, OMINOUS CASTLE.
I'M WILLING TO BET THAT'S WHERE GOTHAM GIRL'S BEEN HIDING OUT.
YOU THINK WE HAVE PROBABLE CAUSE TO PAY THEM A VISIT? OR JUST BREAK IN?
FLASH MAKES JOKES TO LIGHTEN THE TENSION.
WITH EVERYTHING GOING ON, I HAVEN'T TALKED TO BATMAN AS JUST FRIENDS IN A LONG TIME. BUT AT LEAST HE'S RESPONDING TO MY WITTY BANTER.
HE'S TRYING.
HE'S TRYING.
AFTER YOU.
SPEAKING OF BREAK-INS...HOW'S MARRIED LIFE WITH SELINA?
THE HONEYMOON OVER YET?
Y-YOU DON'T KNOW?
HOLD ON. I'M GETTING A CALL.
IRIS?
EVERYTHING OKAY?

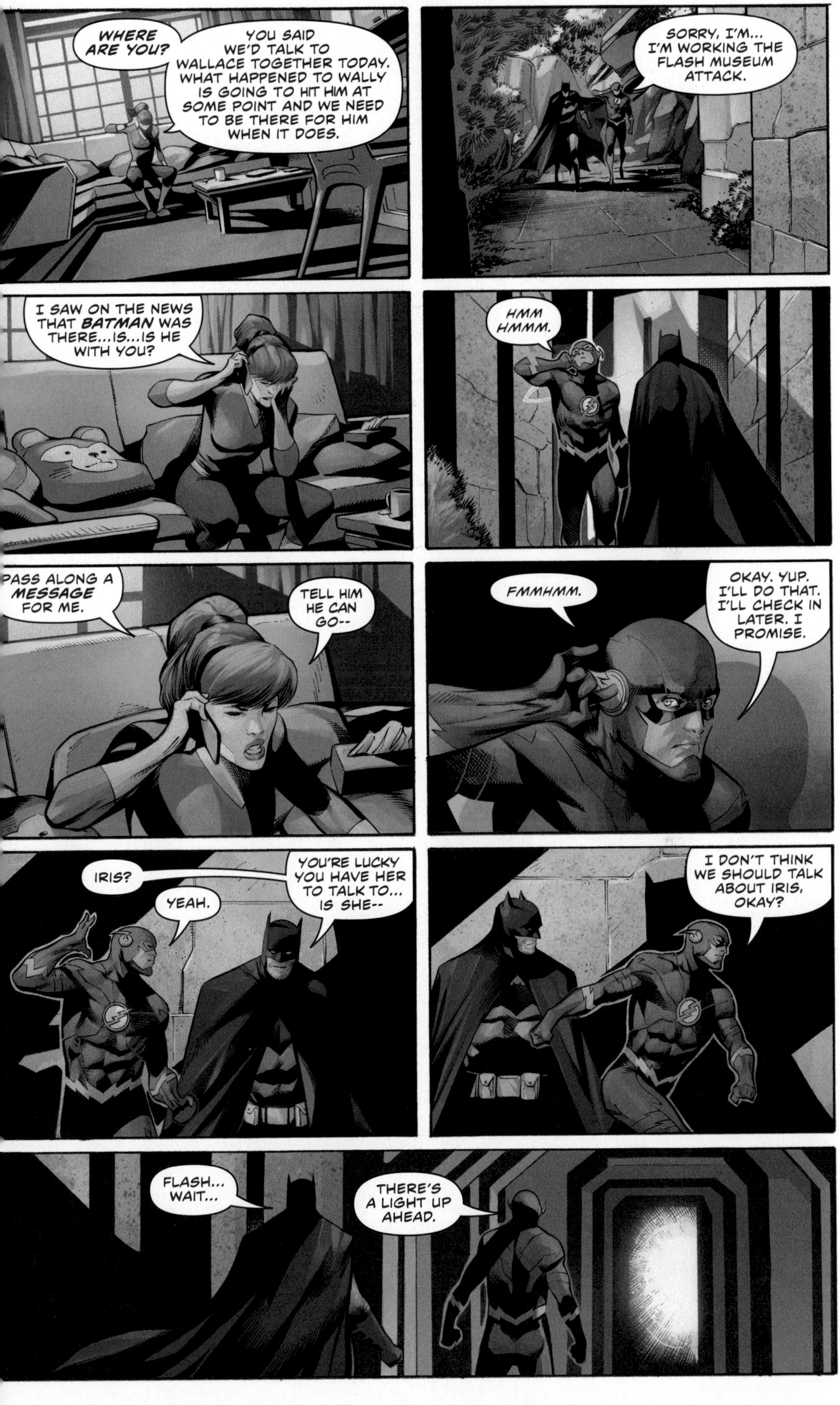
WHERE ARE YOU?
YOU SAID WE'D TALK TO WALLACE TOGETHER TODAY. WHAT HAPPENED TO WALLY IS GOING TO HIT HIM AT SOME POINT AND WE NEED TO BE THERE FOR HIM WHEN IT DOES.
SORRY, I'M... I'M WORKING THE FLASH MUSEUM ATTACK.
I SAW ON THE NEWS THAT BATMAN WAS THERE...IS...IS HE WITH YOU?
HMM HMMM.
PASS ALONG A MESSAGE FOR ME.
TELL HIM HE CAN GO--
FMMHMM.
OKAY. YUP. I'LL DO THAT. I'LL CHECK IN LATER. I PROMISE.
IRIS?
YEAH.
YOU'RE LUCKY YOU HAVE HER TO TALK TO... IS SHE--
I DON'T THINK WE SHOULD TALK ABOUT IRIS, OKAY?
FLASH... WAIT...
THERE'S A LIGHT UP AHEAD.

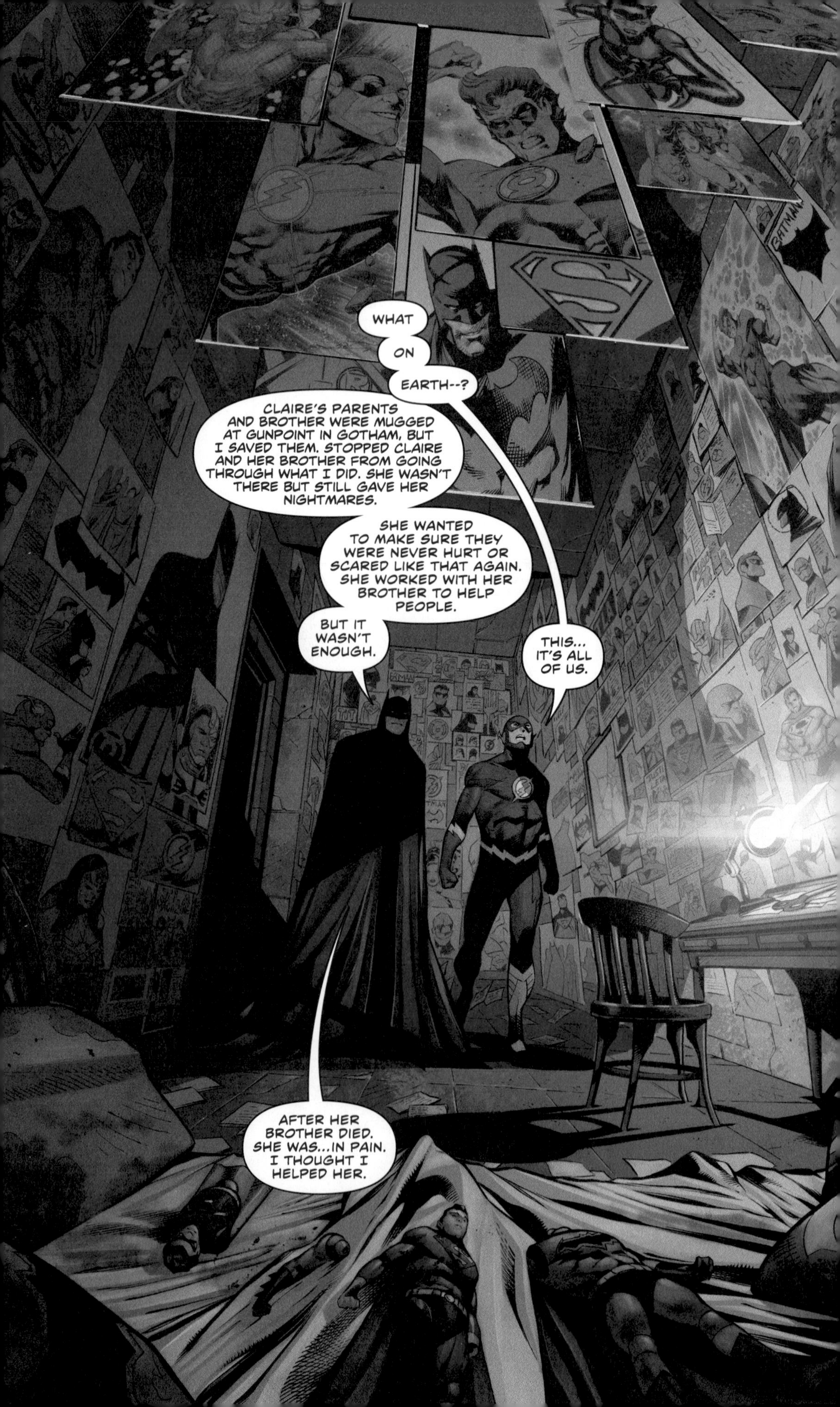
WHAT ON EARTH--?
CLAIRE'S PARENTS AND BROTHER WERE MUGGED AT GUNPOINT IN GOTHAM, BUT I SAVED THEM. STOPPED CLAIRE AND HER BROTHER FROM GOING THROUGH WHAT I DID. SHE WASN'T THERE BUT STILL GAVE HER NIGHTMARES.
SHE WANTED TO MAKE SURE THEY WERE NEVER HURT OR SCARED LIKE THAT AGAIN. SHE WORKED WITH HER BROTHER TO HELP PEOPLE.
BUT IT WASN'T ENOUGH.
THIS... IT'S ALL OF US.
AFTER HER BROTHER DIED. SHE WAS...IN PAIN. I THOUGHT I HELPED HER.

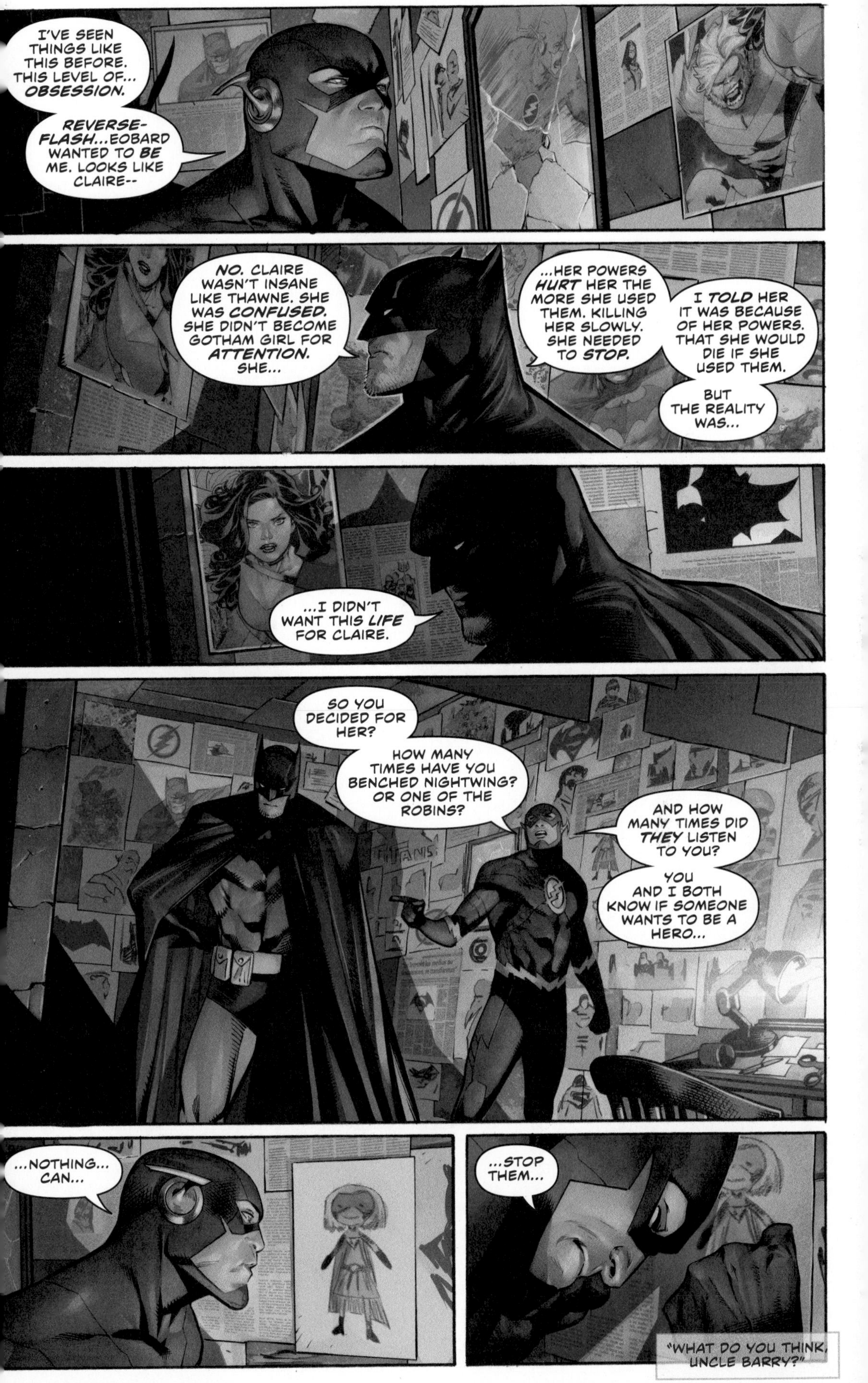
I'VE SEEN THINGS LIKE THIS BEFORE. THIS LEVEL OF... OBSESSION.
REVERSE-FLASH...EOBARD WANTED TO BE ME. LOOKS LIKE CLAIRE--
NO. CLAIRE WASN'T INSANE LIKE THAWNE. SHE WAS CONFUSED. SHE DIDN'T BECOME GOTHAM GIRL FOR ATTENTION. SHE...
...HER POWERS HURT HER THE MORE SHE USED THEM. KILLING HER SLOWLY. SHE NEEDED TO STOP.
I TOLD HER IT WAS BECAUSE OF HER POWERS. THAT SHE WOULD DIE IF SHE USED THEM.
BUT THE REALITY WAS...
...I DIDN'T WANT THIS LIFE FOR CLAIRE.
SO YOU DECIDED FOR HER?
HOW MANY TIMES HAVE YOU BENCHED NIGHTWING? OR ONE OF THE ROBINS?
AND HOW MANY TIMES DID THEY LISTEN TO YOU?
YOU AND I BOTH KNOW IF SOMEONE WANTS TO BE A HERO...
...NOTHING... CAN...
...STOP THEM...
"WHAT DO YOU THINK, UNCLE BARRY?"

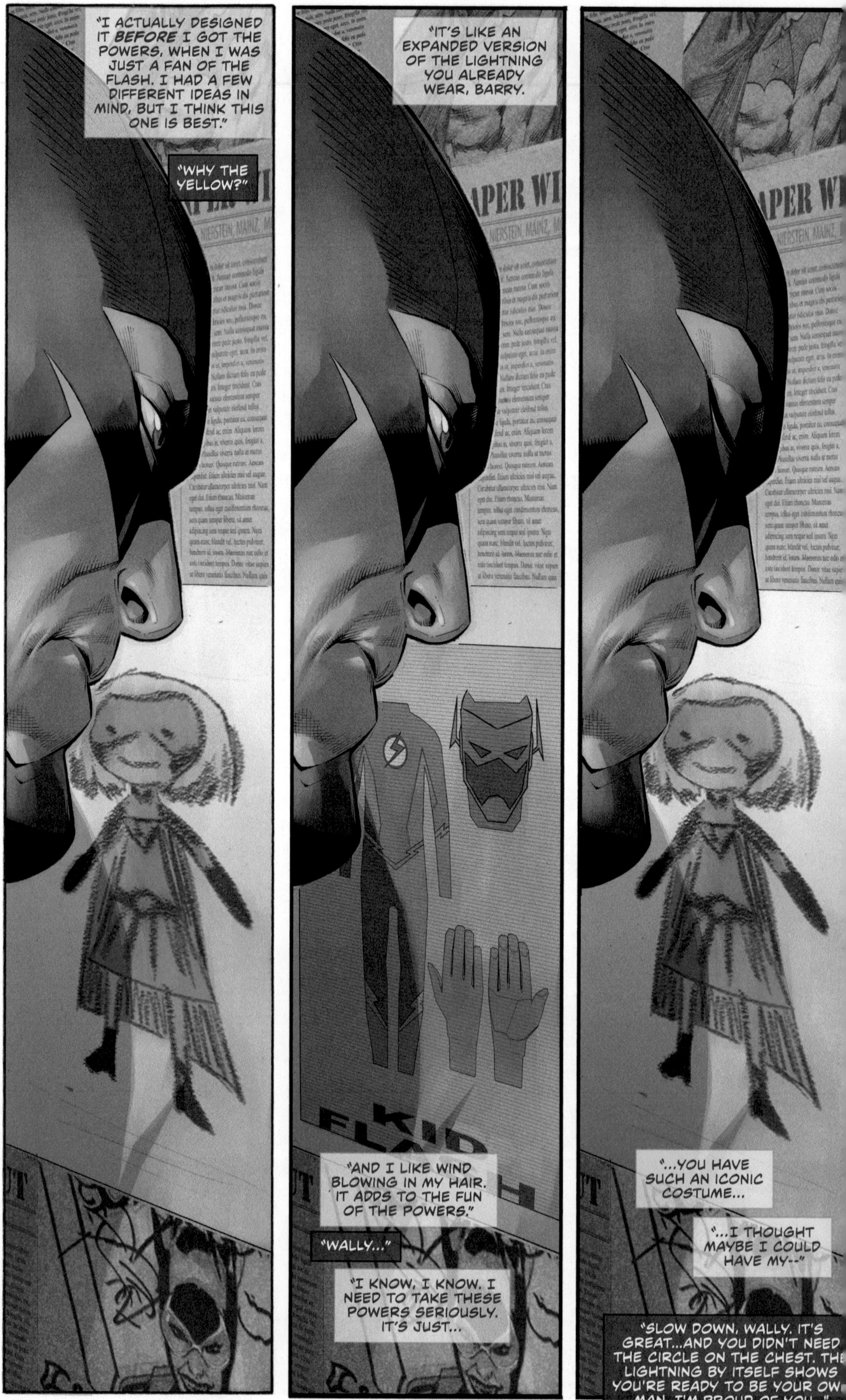
"I ACTUALLY DESIGNED IT BEFORE I GOT THE POWERS, WHEN I WAS JUST A FAN OF THE FLASH. I HAD A FEW DIFFERENT IDEAS IN MIND, BUT I THINK THIS ONE IS BEST."
"WHY THE YELLOW?"
"IT'S LIKE AN EXPANDED VERSION OF THE LIGHTNING YOU ALREADY WEAR, BARRY.
"AND I LIKE WIND BLOWING IN MY HAIR. IT ADDS TO THE FUN OF THE POWERS."
"WALLY..."
"I KNOW, I KNOW. I NEED TO TAKE THESE POWERS SERIOUSLY. IT'S JUST...
"...YOU HAVE SUCH AN ICONIC COSTUME...
"...I THOUGHT MAYBE I COULD HAVE MY--"
"SLOW DOWN, WALLY. IT'S GREAT...AND YOU DIDN'T NEED THE CIRCLE ON THE CHEST. THE LIGHTNING BY ITSELF SHOWS YOU'RE READY TO BE YOUR OWN MAN. I'M PROUD OF YOU..."

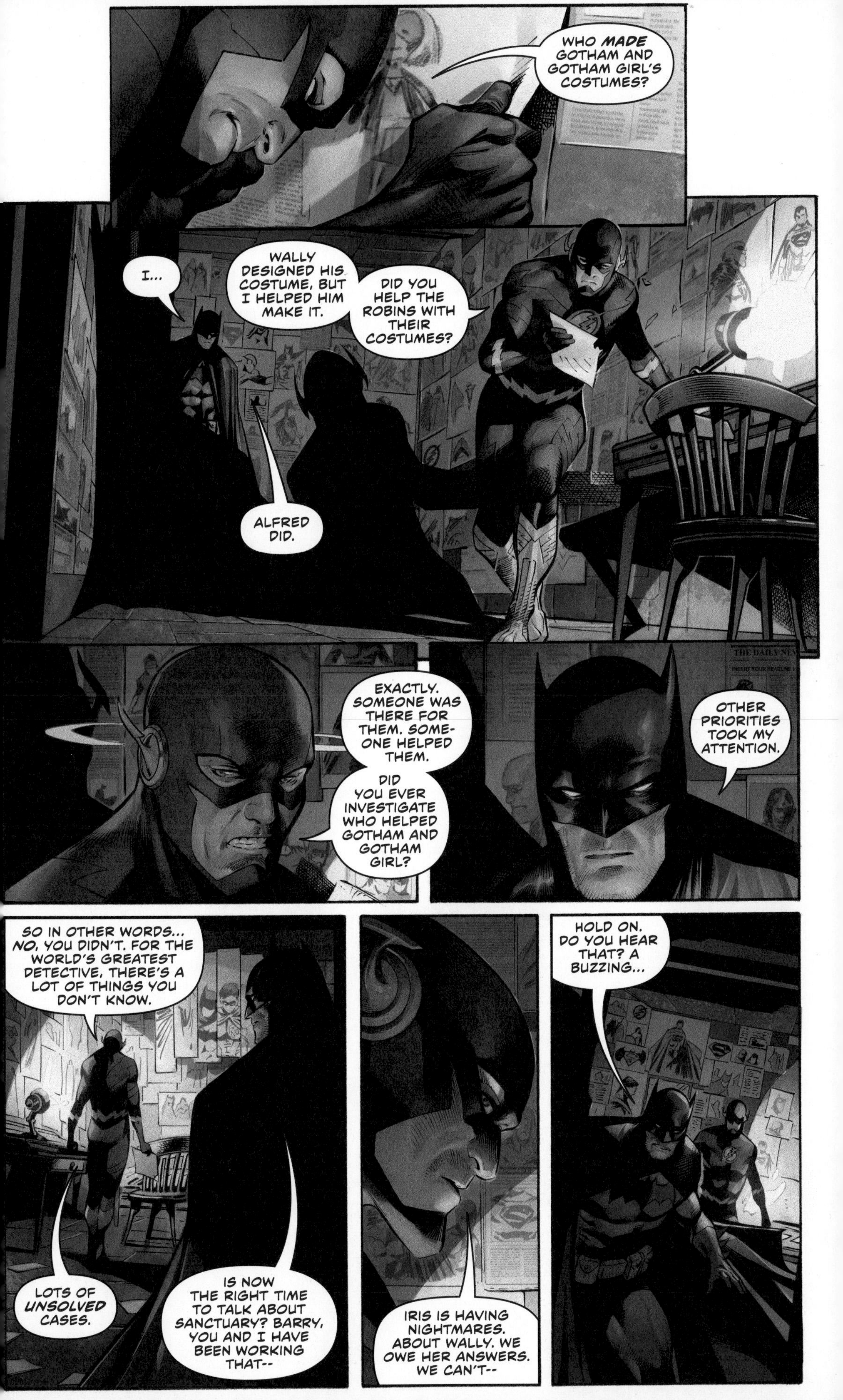
WHO *MADE* GOTHAM AND GOTHAM GIRL'S COSTUMES?
I...
WALLY DESIGNED HIS COSTUME, BUT I HELPED HIM MAKE IT.
DID YOU HELP THE ROBINS WITH THEIR COSTUMES?
ALFRED DID.
EXACTLY. SOMEONE WAS THERE FOR THEM. SOME-ONE HELPED THEM.
DID YOU EVER INVESTIGATE WHO HELPED GOTHAM AND GOTHAM GIRL?
OTHER PRIORITIES TOOK MY ATTENTION.
SO IN OTHER WORDS... *NO*, YOU DIDN'T. FOR THE WORLD'S GREATEST DETECTIVE, THERE'S A LOT OF THINGS YOU DON'T KNOW.
LOTS OF *UNSOLVED* CASES.
IS NOW THE RIGHT TIME TO TALK ABOUT SANCTUARY? BARRY, YOU AND I HAVE BEEN WORKING THAT--
IRIS IS HAVING NIGHTMARES. ABOUT WALLY. WE OWE HER ANSWERS. WE CAN'T--
HOLD ON. DO YOU HEAR THAT? A BUZZING...

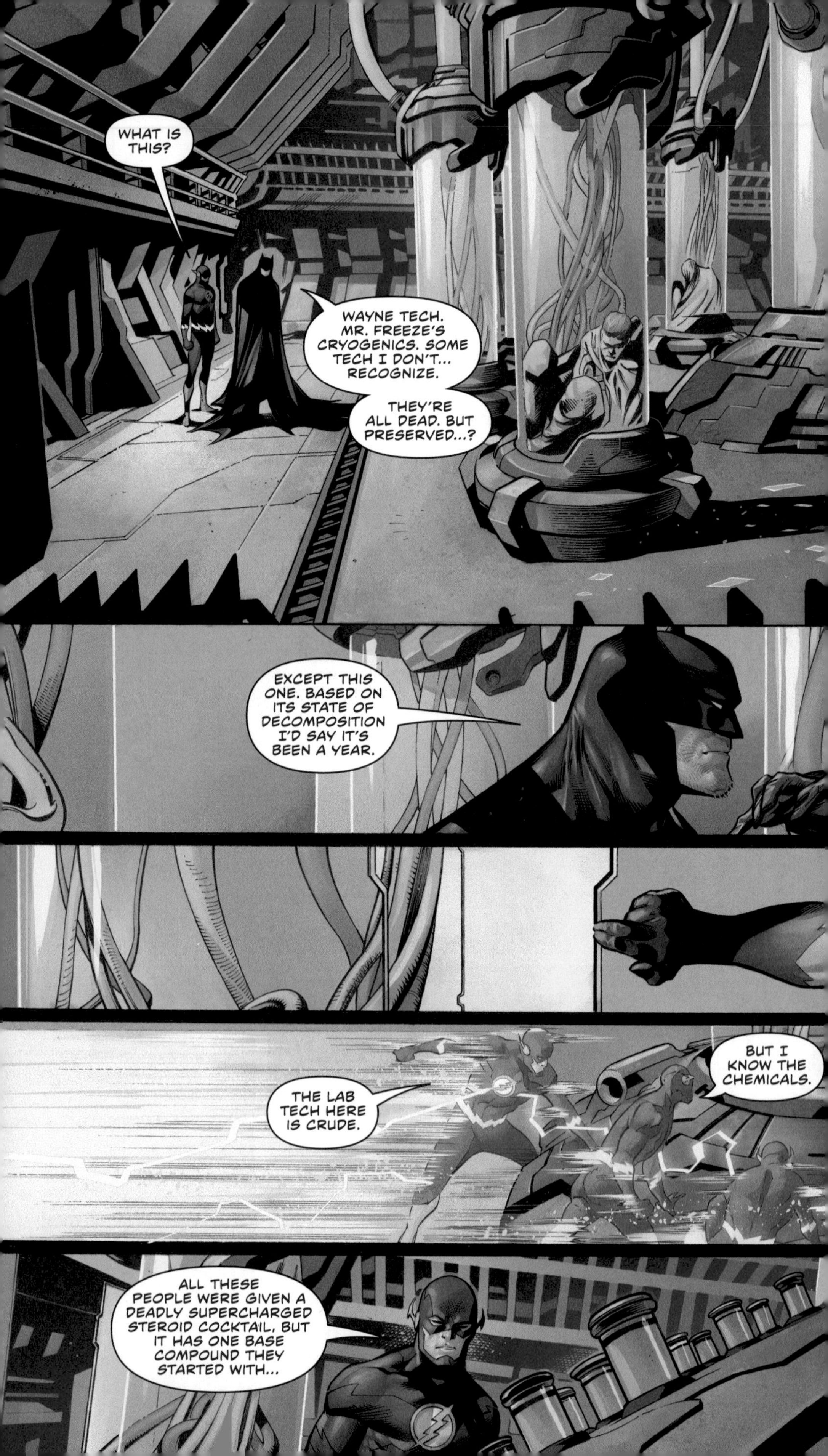
WHAT IS THIS?
WAYNE TECH. MR. FREEZE'S CRYOGENICS. SOME TECH I DON'T... RECOGNIZE.
THEY'RE ALL DEAD. BUT PRESERVED...?
EXCEPT THIS ONE. BASED ON ITS STATE OF DECOMPOSITION I'D SAY IT'S BEEN A YEAR.
THE LAB TECH HERE IS CRUDE.
BUT I KNOW THE CHEMICALS.
ALL THESE PEOPLE WERE GIVEN A DEADLY SUPERCHARGED STEROID COCKTAIL, BUT IT HAS ONE BASE COMPOUND THEY STARTED WITH...

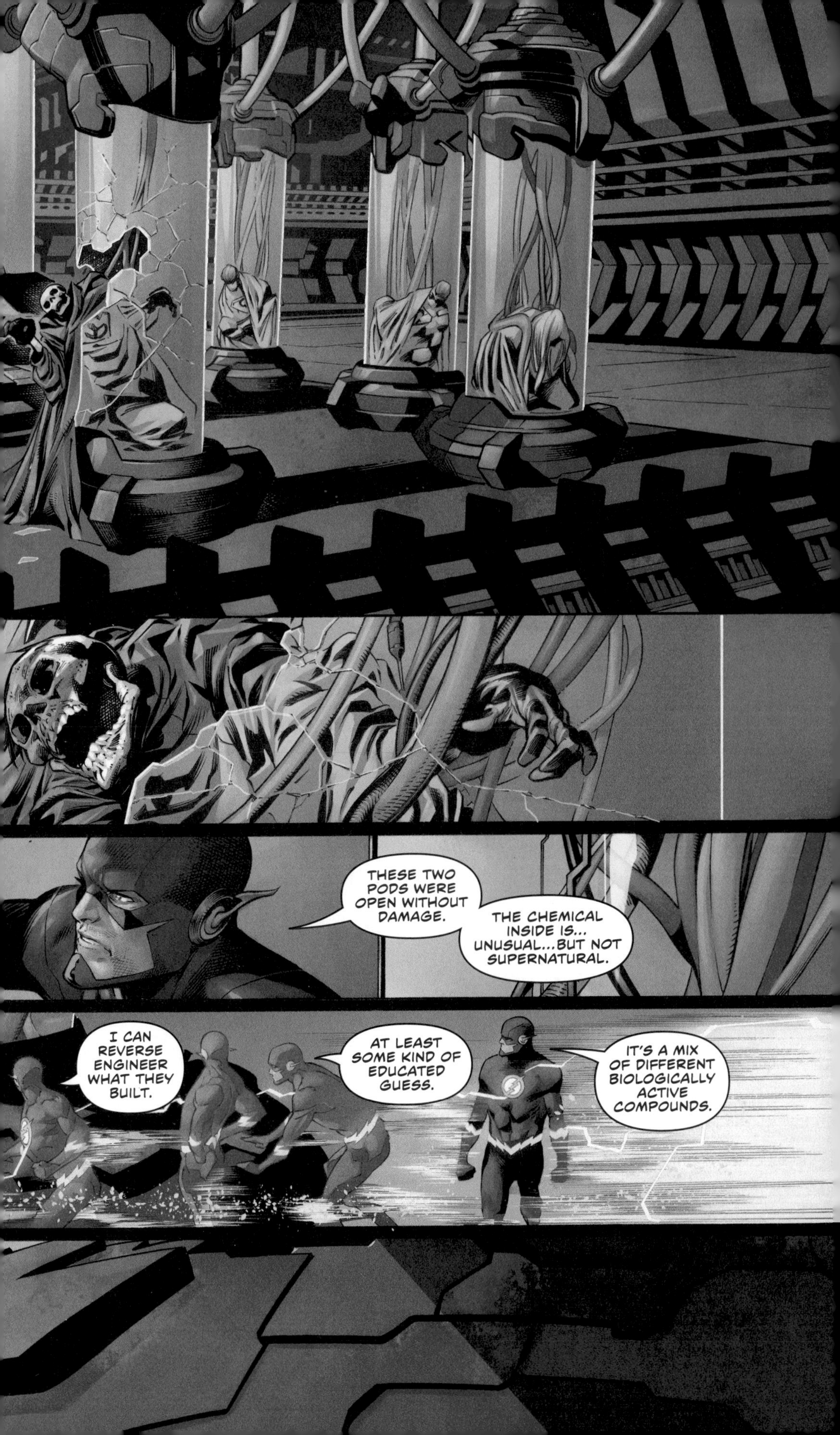
THESE TWO PODS WERE OPEN WITHOUT DAMAGE.
THE CHEMICAL INSIDE IS... UNUSUAL...BUT NOT SUPERNATURAL.
IT'S A MIX OF DIFFERENT BIOLOGICALLY ACTIVE COMPOUNDS.
AT LEAST SOME KIND OF EDUCATED GUESS.
I CAN REVERSE ENGINEER WHAT THEY BUILT.

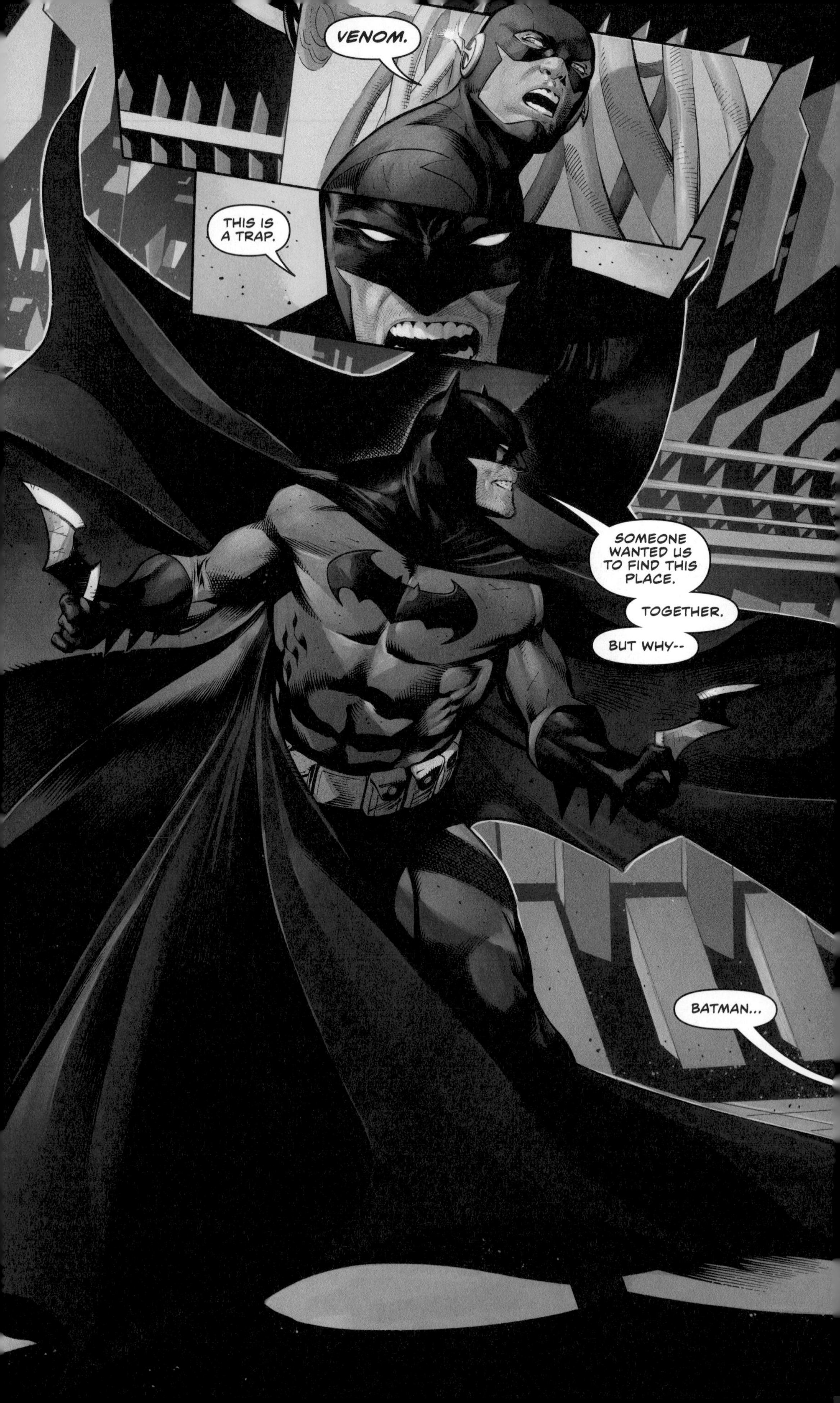
VENOM.
THIS IS A TRAP.
SOMEONE WANTED US TO FIND THIS PLACE.
TOGETHER.
BUT WHY--
BATMAN...

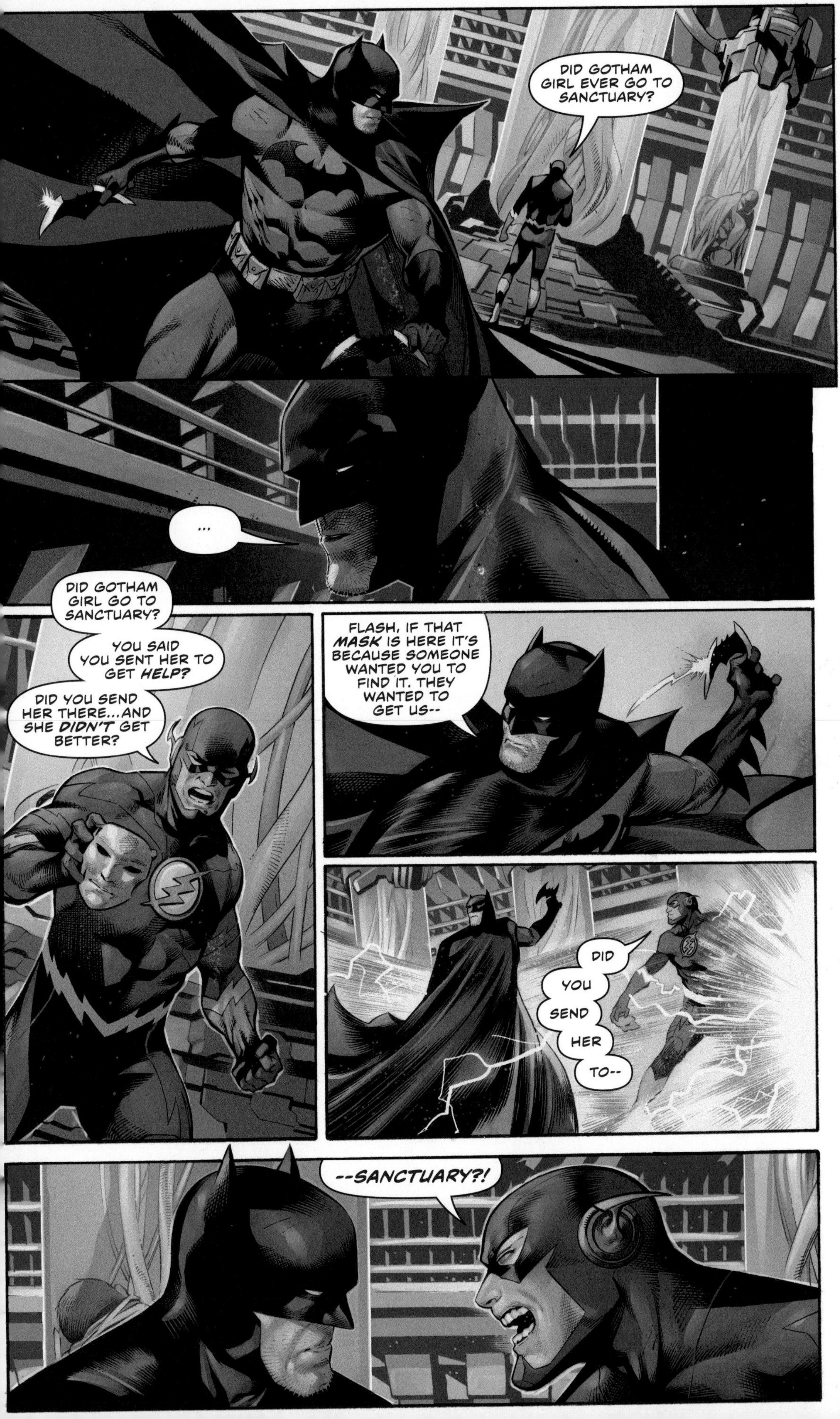
DID GOTHAM GIRL EVER GO TO SANCTUARY?
...
DID GOTHAM GIRL GO TO SANCTUARY?
YOU SAID YOU SENT HER TO GET *HELP*?
DID YOU SEND HER THERE...AND SHE *DIDN'T* GET BETTER?
FLASH, IF THAT *MASK* IS HERE IT'S BECAUSE SOMEONE WANTED YOU TO FIND IT. THEY WANTED TO GET US--
DID
YOU
SEND
HER
TO--
--SANCTUARY?!

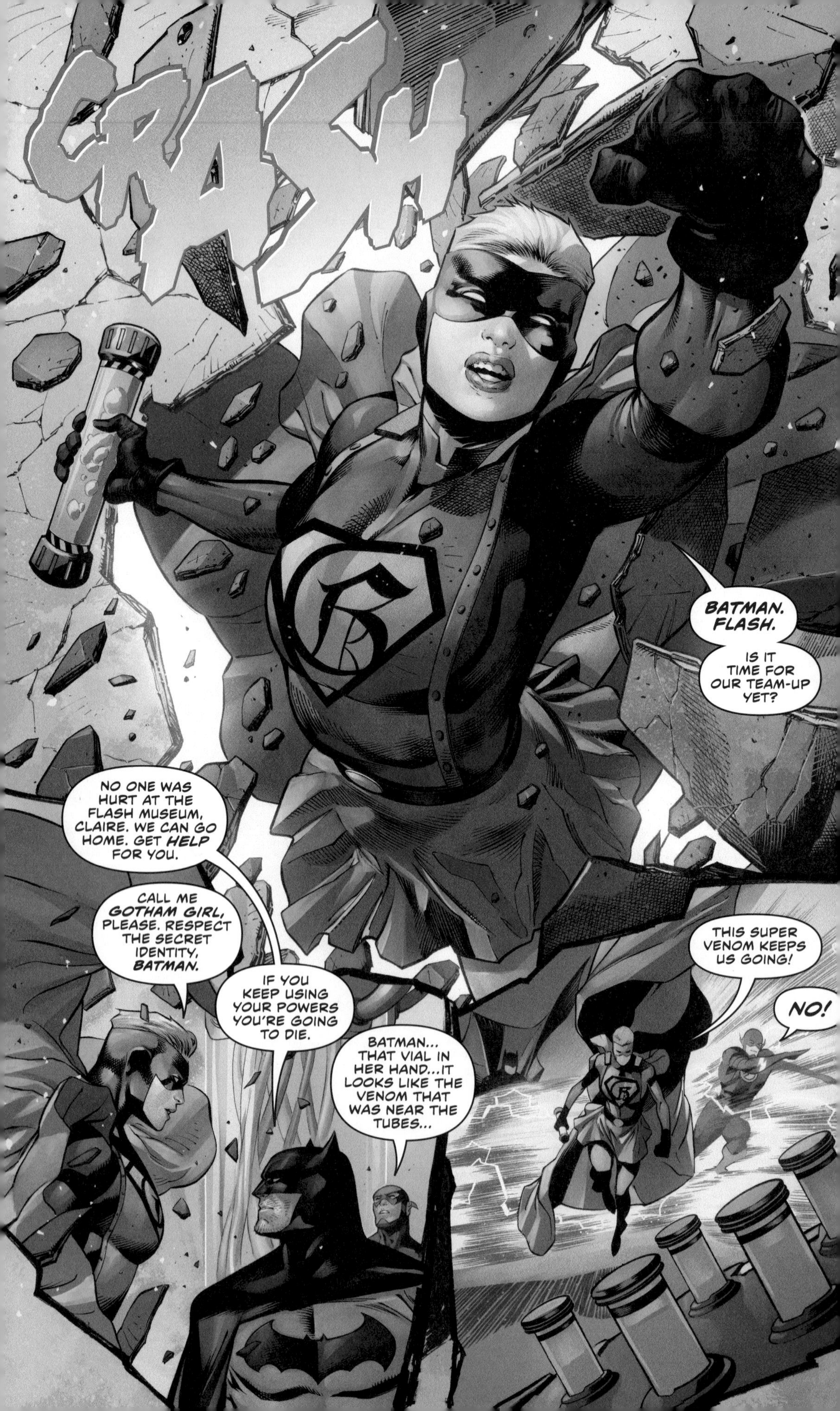
CRASH
BATMAN. FLASH.
IS IT TIME FOR OUR TEAM-UP YET?
NO ONE WAS HURT AT THE FLASH MUSEUM, CLAIRE. WE CAN GO HOME. GET HELP FOR YOU.
CALL ME GOTHAM GIRL, PLEASE. RESPECT THE SECRET IDENTITY, BATMAN.
IF YOU KEEP USING YOUR POWERS YOU'RE GOING TO DIE.
BATMAN... THAT VIAL IN HER HAND...IT LOOKS LIKE THE VENOM THAT WAS NEAR THE TUBES...
THIS SUPER VENOM KEEPS US GOING!
NO!

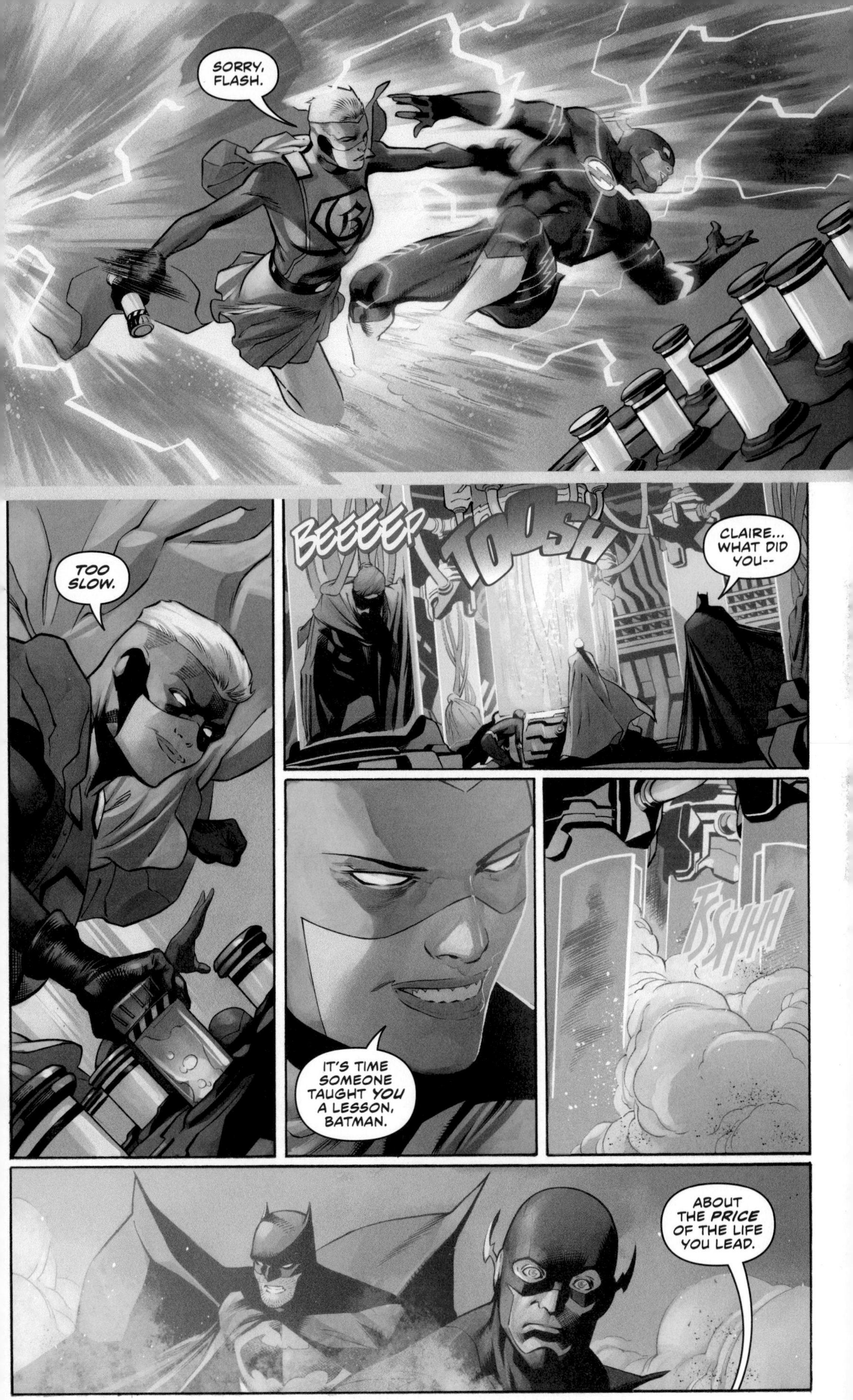

SORRY, FLASH.
TOO SLOW.
BEEEEP
TOOSH
CLAIRE... WHAT DID YOU--
IT'S TIME SOMEONE TAUGHT YOU A LESSON, BATMAN.
TSHHH
ABOUT THE PRICE OF THE LIFE YOU LEAD.

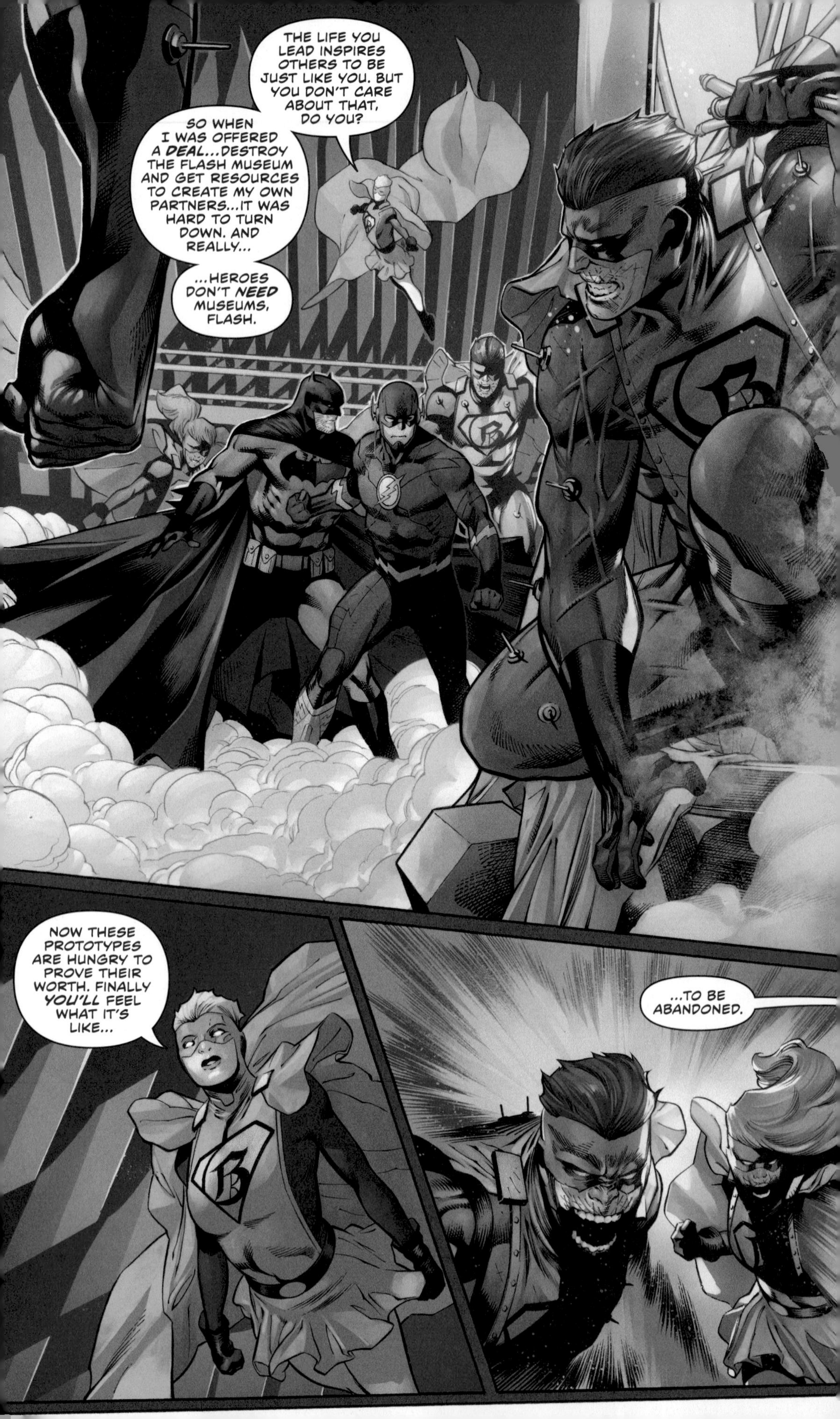
THE LIFE YOU LEAD INSPIRES OTHERS TO BE JUST LIKE YOU. BUT YOU DON'T CARE ABOUT THAT, DO YOU?
SO WHEN I WAS OFFERED A *DEAL*...DESTROY THE FLASH MUSEUM AND GET RESOURCES TO CREATE MY OWN PARTNERS...IT WAS HARD TO TURN DOWN. AND REALLY...
...HEROES DON'T *NEED* MUSEUMS, FLASH.
NOW THESE PROTOTYPES ARE HUNGRY TO PROVE THEIR WORTH. FINALLY *YOU'LL* FEEL WHAT IT'S LIKE...
...TO BE ABANDONED.

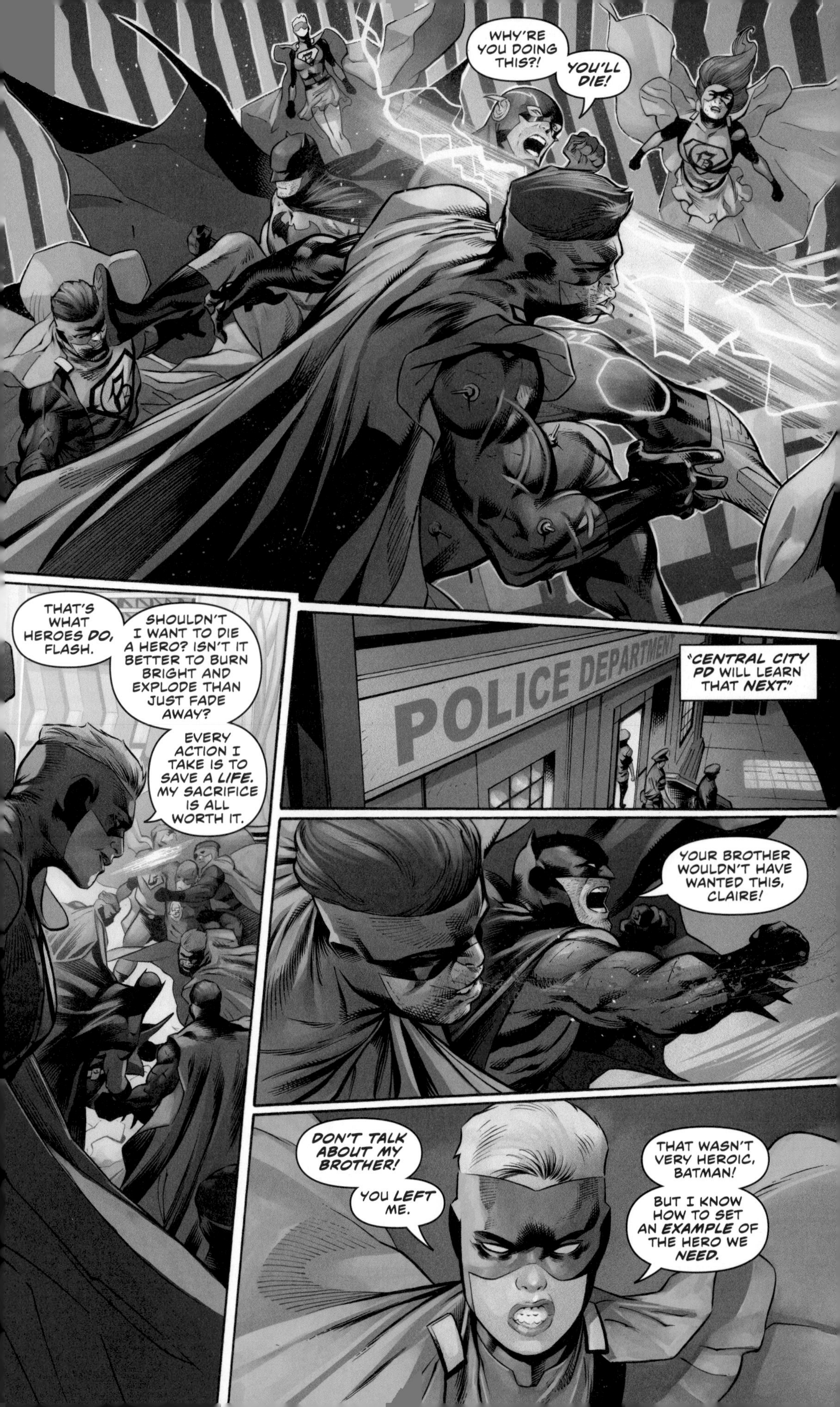

WHY'RE YOU DOING THIS?!
YOU'LL DIE!
THAT'S WHAT HEROES DO, FLASH.
SHOULDN'T I WANT TO DIE A HERO? ISN'T IT BETTER TO BURN BRIGHT AND EXPLODE THAN JUST FADE AWAY?
EVERY ACTION I TAKE IS TO SAVE A LIFE. MY SACRIFICE IS ALL WORTH IT.
POLICE DEPARTMENT
"CENTRAL CITY PD WILL LEARN THAT NEXT."
YOUR BROTHER WOULDN'T HAVE WANTED THIS, CLAIRE!
DON'T TALK ABOUT MY BROTHER!
YOU LEFT ME.
THAT WASN'T VERY HEROIC, BATMAN!
BUT I KNOW HOW TO SET AN EXAMPLE OF THE HERO WE NEED.

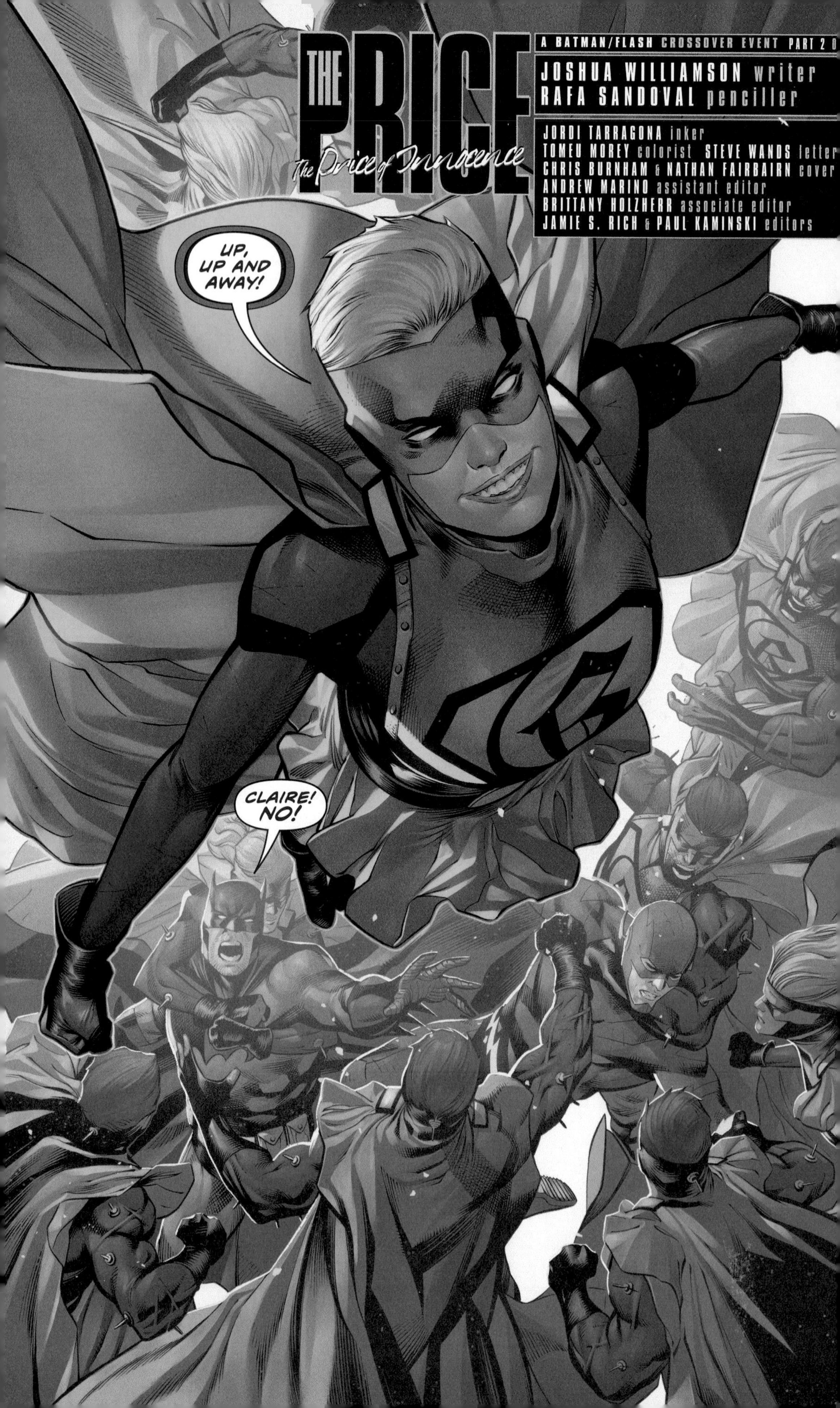
THE PRICE
The Price of Innocence
A BATMAN/FLASH CROSSOVER EVENT PART 2 O
JOSHUA WILLIAMSON writer
RAFA SANDOVAL penciller
JORDI TARRAGONA inker
TOMEU MOREY colorist STEVE WANDS letter
CHRIS BURNHAM & NATHAN FAIRBAIRN cover
ANDREW MARINO assistant editor
BRITTANY HOLZHERR associate editor
JAMIE S. RICH & PAUL KAMINSKI editors
UP, UP AND AWAY!
CLAIRE! NO!

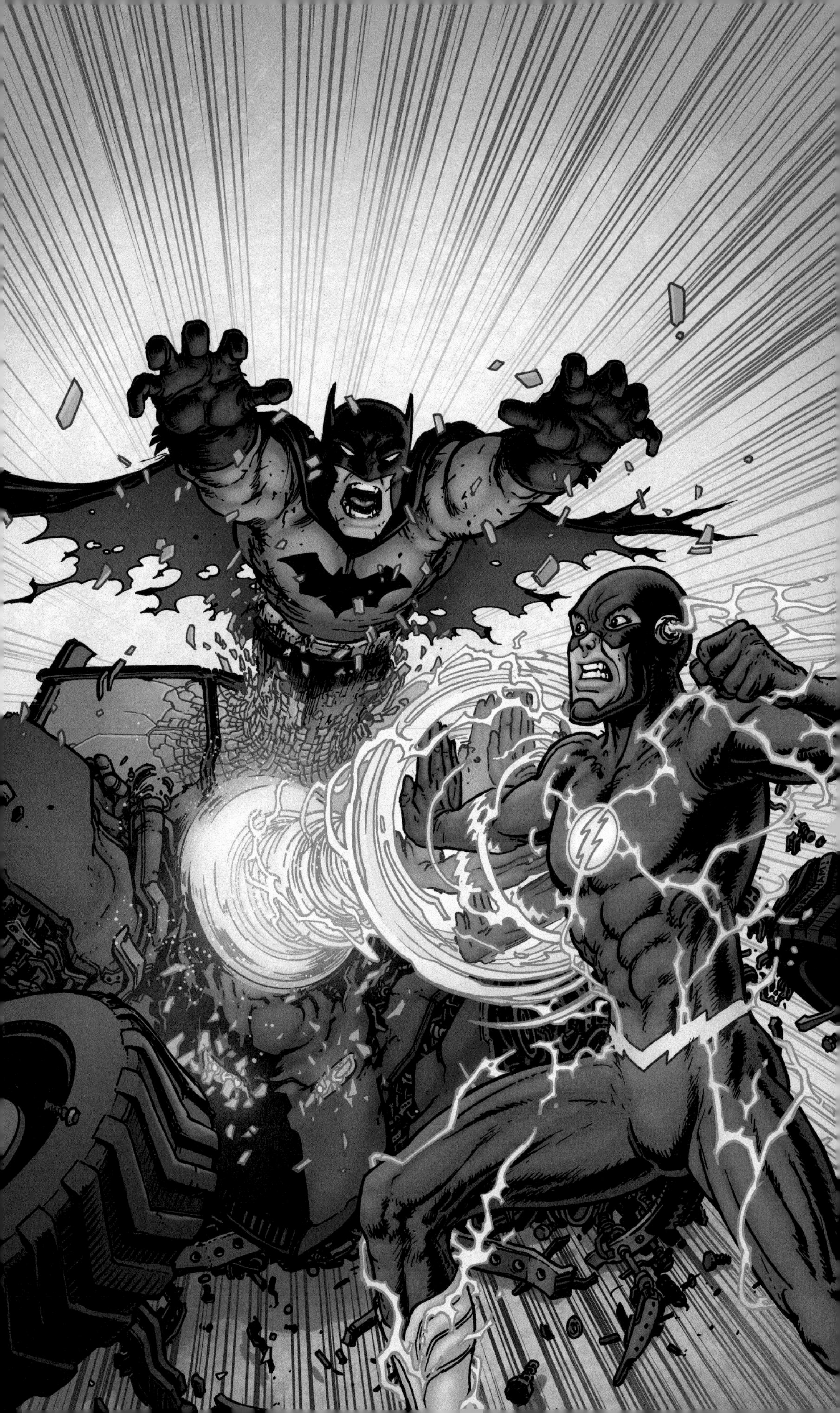

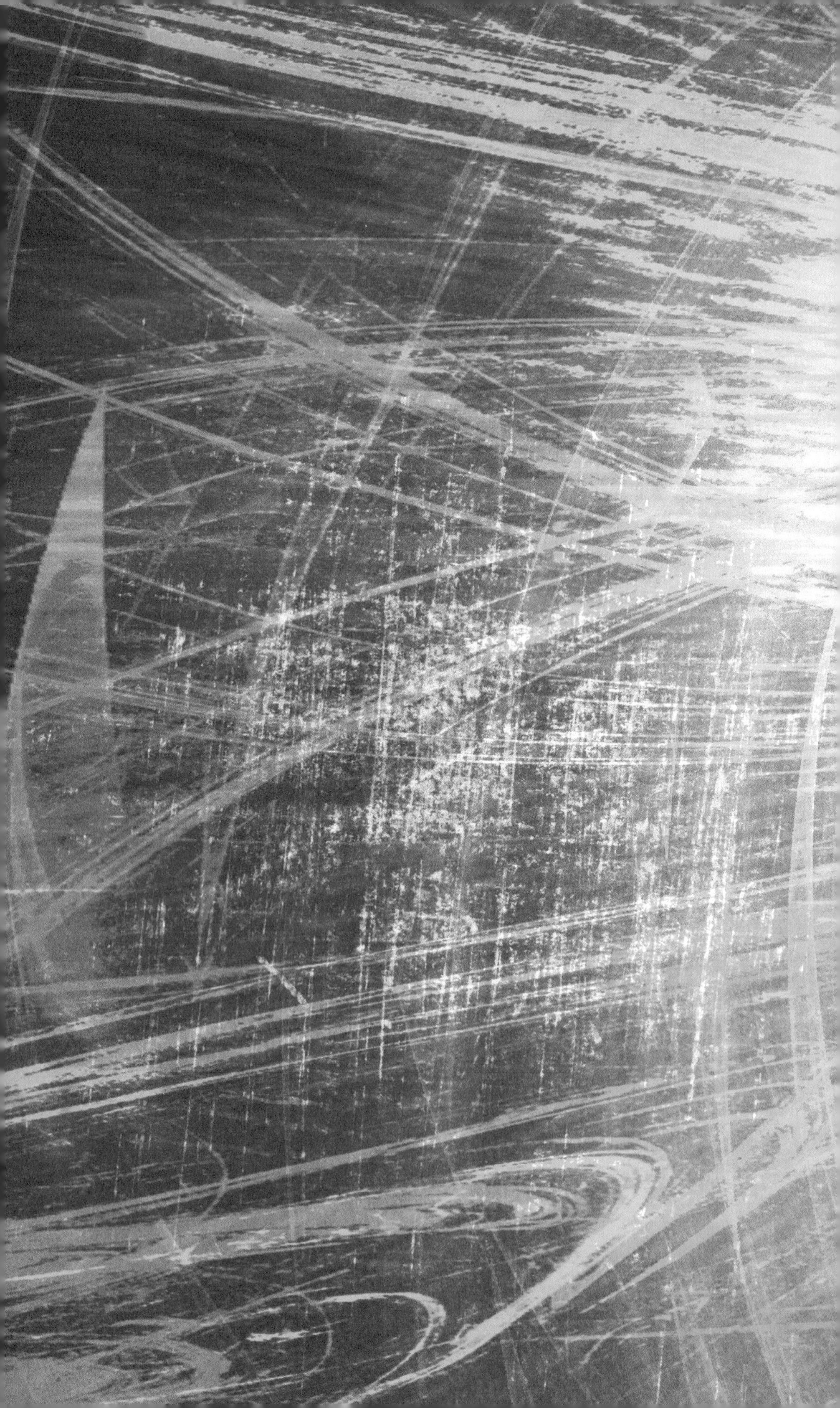

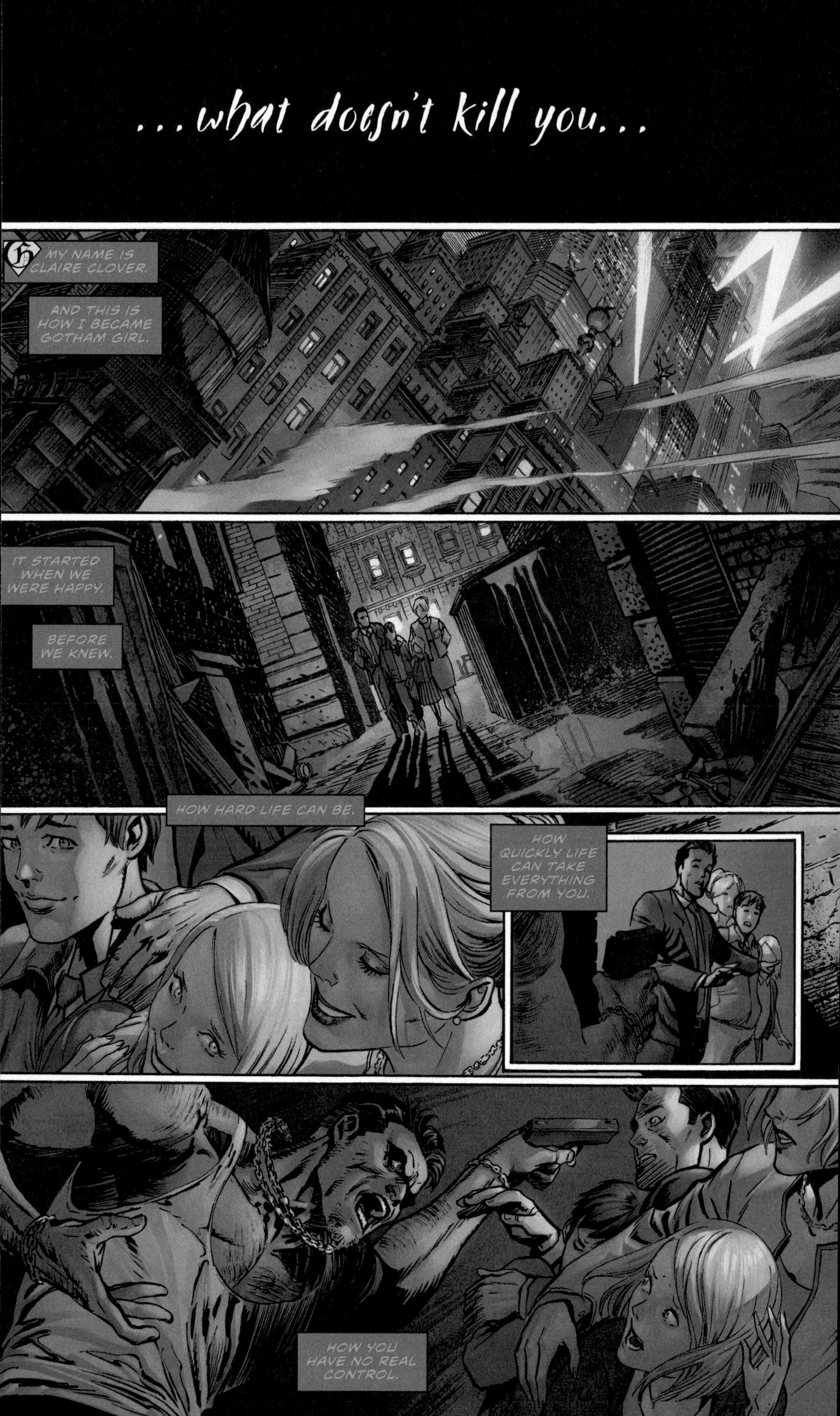
...what doesn't kill you...
MY NAME IS CLAIRE CLOVER.
AND THIS IS HOW I BECAME GOTHAM GIRL.
IT STARTED WHEN WE WERE HAPPY.
BEFORE WE KNEW.
HOW HARD LIFE CAN BE.
HOW QUICKLY LIFE CAN TAKE EVERYTHING FROM YOU.
HOW YOU HAVE NO REAL CONTROL.

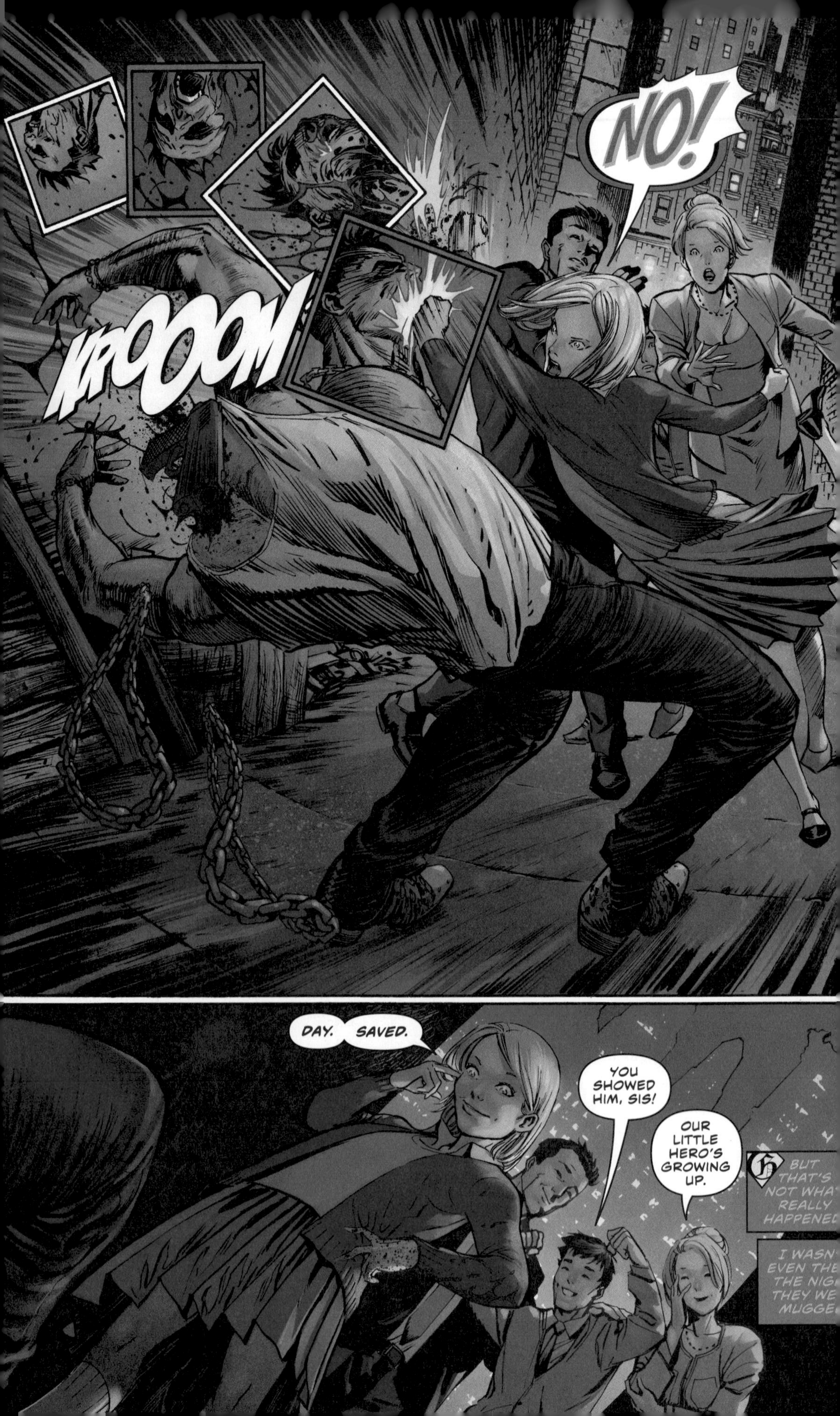
KROOOM
NO!
DAY. SAVED.
YOU SHOWED HIM, SIS!
OUR LITTLE HERO'S GROWING UP.
BUT THAT'S NOT WHA REALLY HAPPENED
I WASN EVEN THE THE NIG THEY WE MUGGE

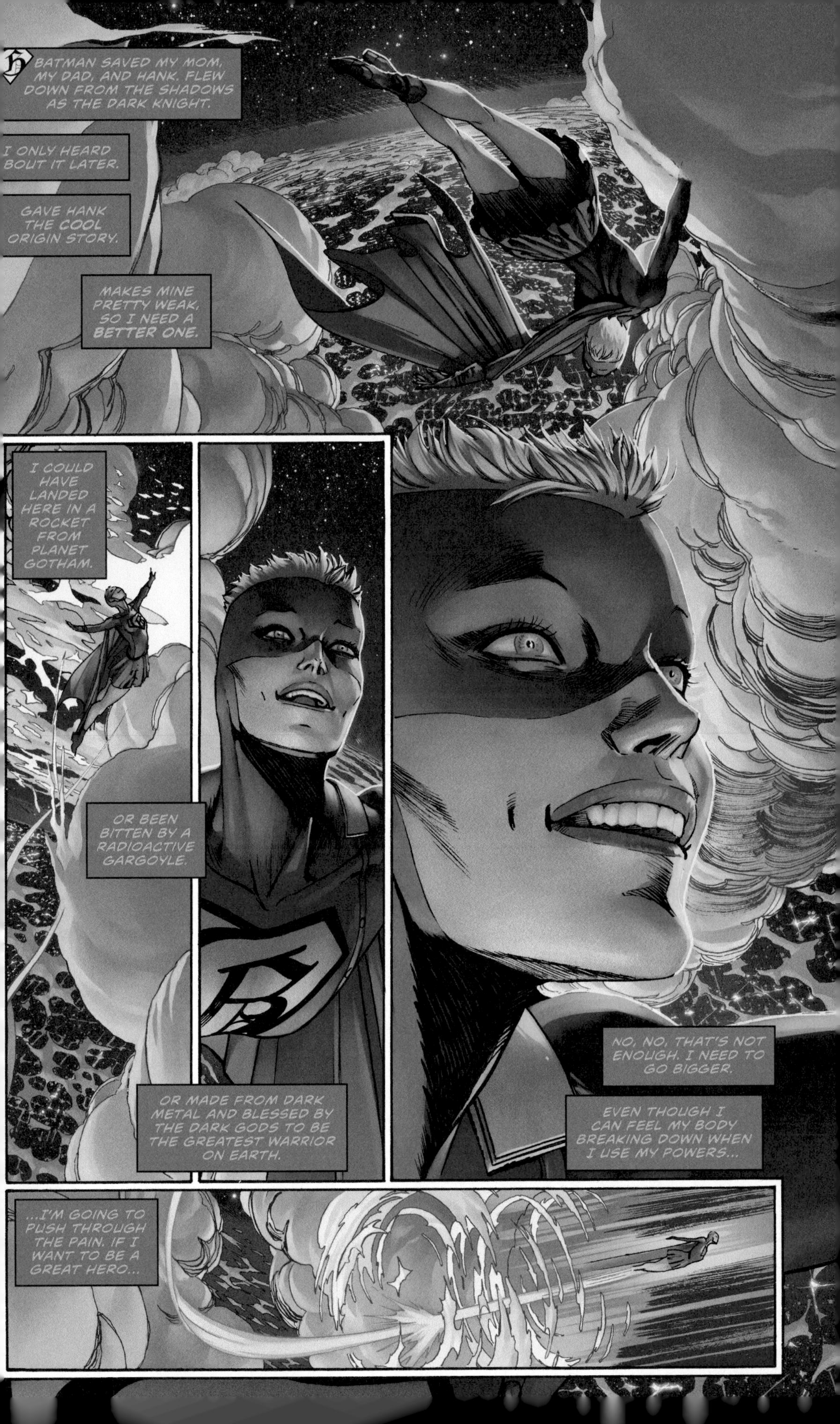
BATMAN SAVED MY MOM, MY DAD, AND HANK. FLEW DOWN FROM THE SHADOWS AS THE DARK KNIGHT.
I ONLY HEARD BOUT IT LATER.
GAVE HANK THE COOL ORIGIN STORY.
MAKES MINE PRETTY WEAK, SO I NEED A BETTER ONE.
I COULD HAVE LANDED HERE IN A ROCKET FROM PLANET GOTHAM.
OR BEEN BITTEN BY A RADIOACTIVE GARGOYLE.
OR MADE FROM DARK METAL AND BLESSED BY THE DARK GODS TO BE THE GREATEST WARRIOR ON EARTH.
NO, NO, THAT'S NOT ENOUGH. I NEED TO GO BIGGER.
EVEN THOUGH I CAN FEEL MY BODY BREAKING DOWN WHEN I USE MY POWERS...
...I'M GOING TO PUSH THROUGH THE PAIN. IF I WANT TO BE A GREAT HERO...

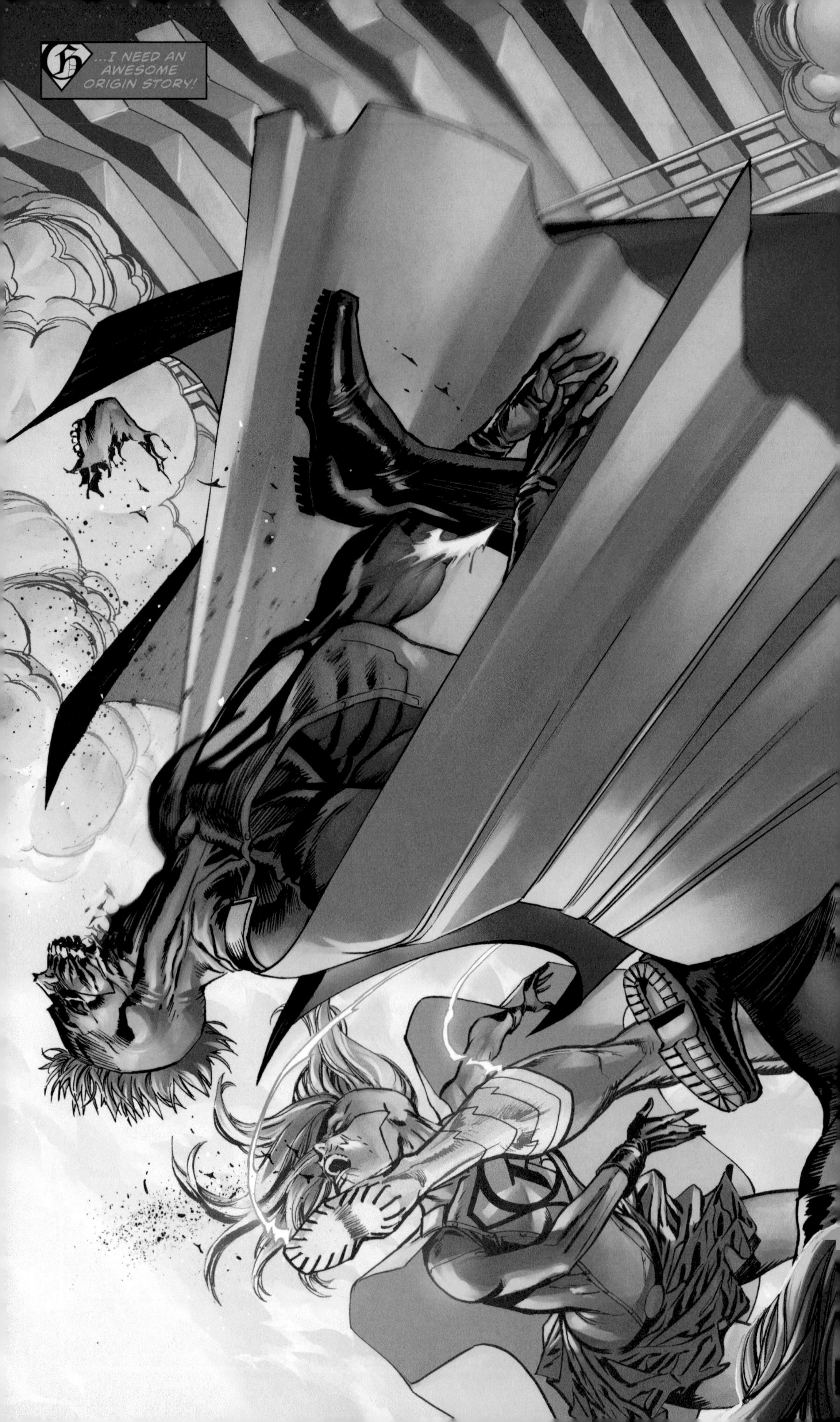
...I NEED AN AWESOME ORIGIN STORY!

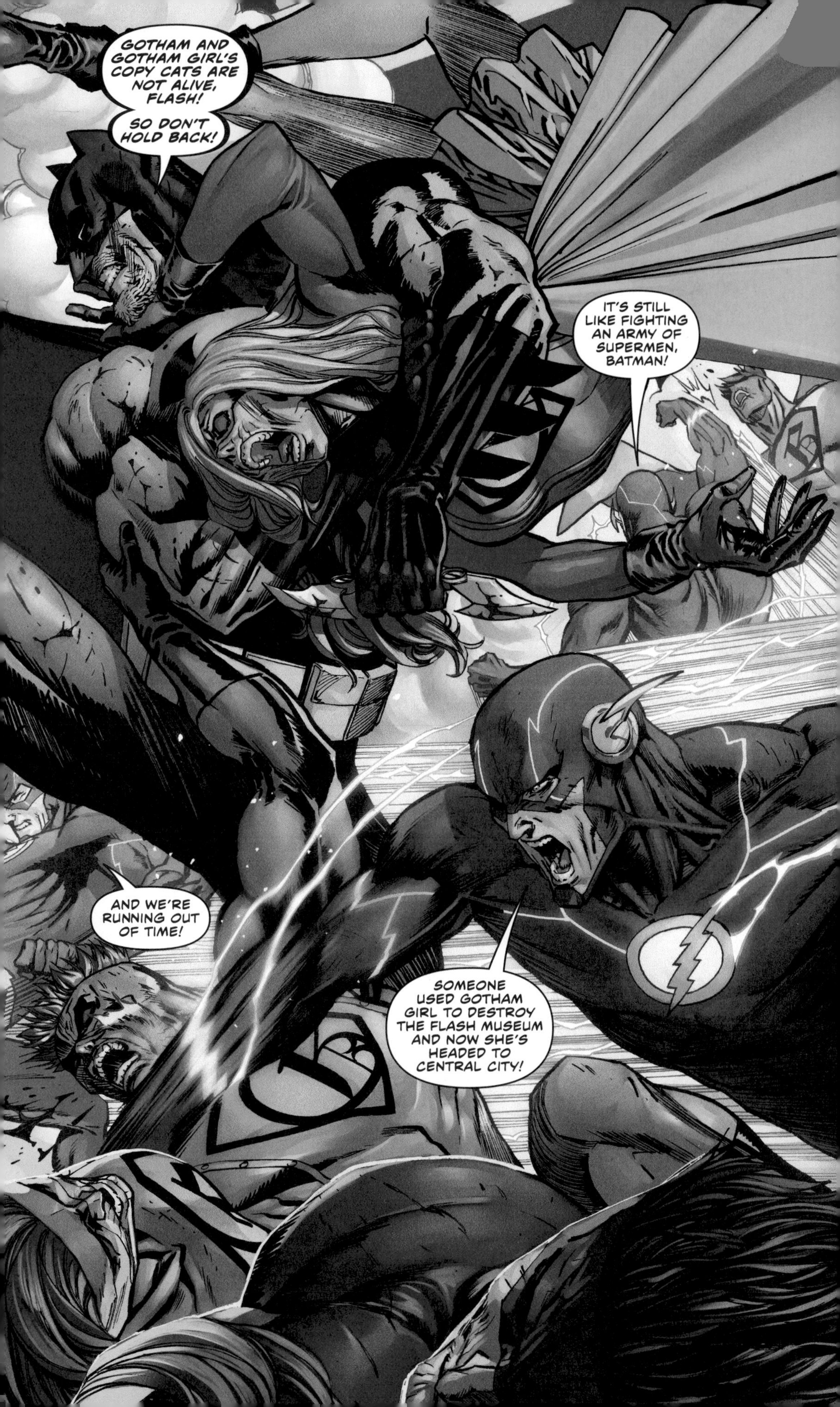
GOTHAM AND GOTHAM GIRL'S COPY CATS ARE NOT ALIVE, FLASH!
SO DON'T HOLD BACK!
IT'S STILL LIKE FIGHTING AN ARMY OF SUPERMEN, BATMAN!
AND WE'RE RUNNING OUT OF TIME!
SOMEONE USED GOTHAM GIRL TO DESTROY THE FLASH MUSEUM AND NOW SHE'S HEADED TO CENTRAL CITY!

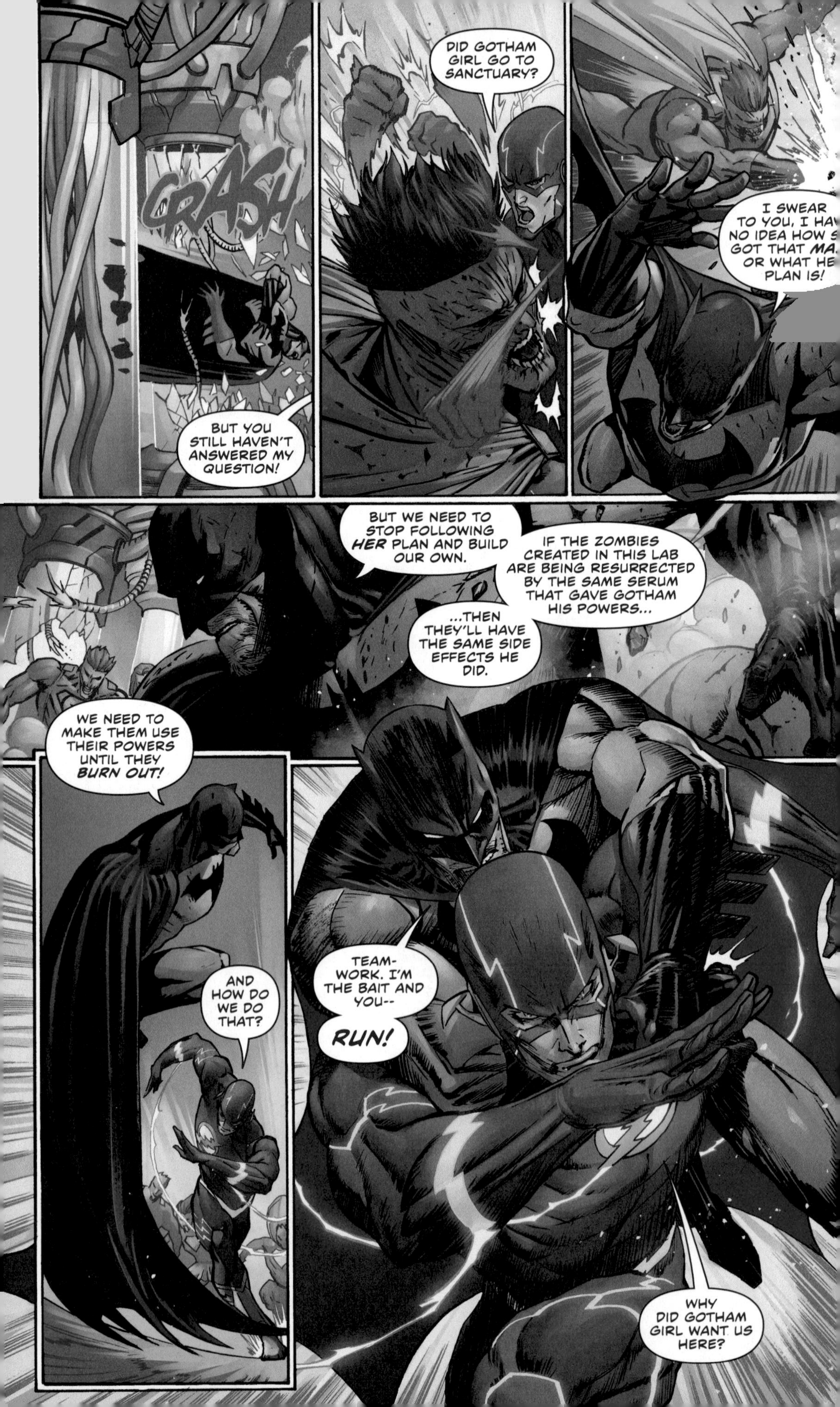
CRASH
BUT YOU STILL HAVEN'T ANSWERED MY QUESTION!
DID GOTHAM GIRL GO TO SANCTUARY?
I SWEAR TO YOU, I HA NO IDEA HOW S GOT THAT MA OR WHAT HE PLAN IS!
BUT WE NEED TO STOP FOLLOWING *HER* PLAN AND BUILD OUR OWN.
IF THE ZOMBIES CREATED IN THIS LAB ARE BEING RESURRECTED BY THE SAME SERUM THAT GAVE GOTHAM HIS POWERS...
...THEN THEY'LL HAVE THE SAME SIDE EFFECTS HE DID.
WE NEED TO MAKE THEM USE THEIR POWERS UNTIL THEY *BURN OUT!*
AND HOW DO WE DO THAT?
TEAM-WORK. I'M THE BAIT AND YOU--
RUN!
WHY DID GOTHAM GIRL WANT US HERE?

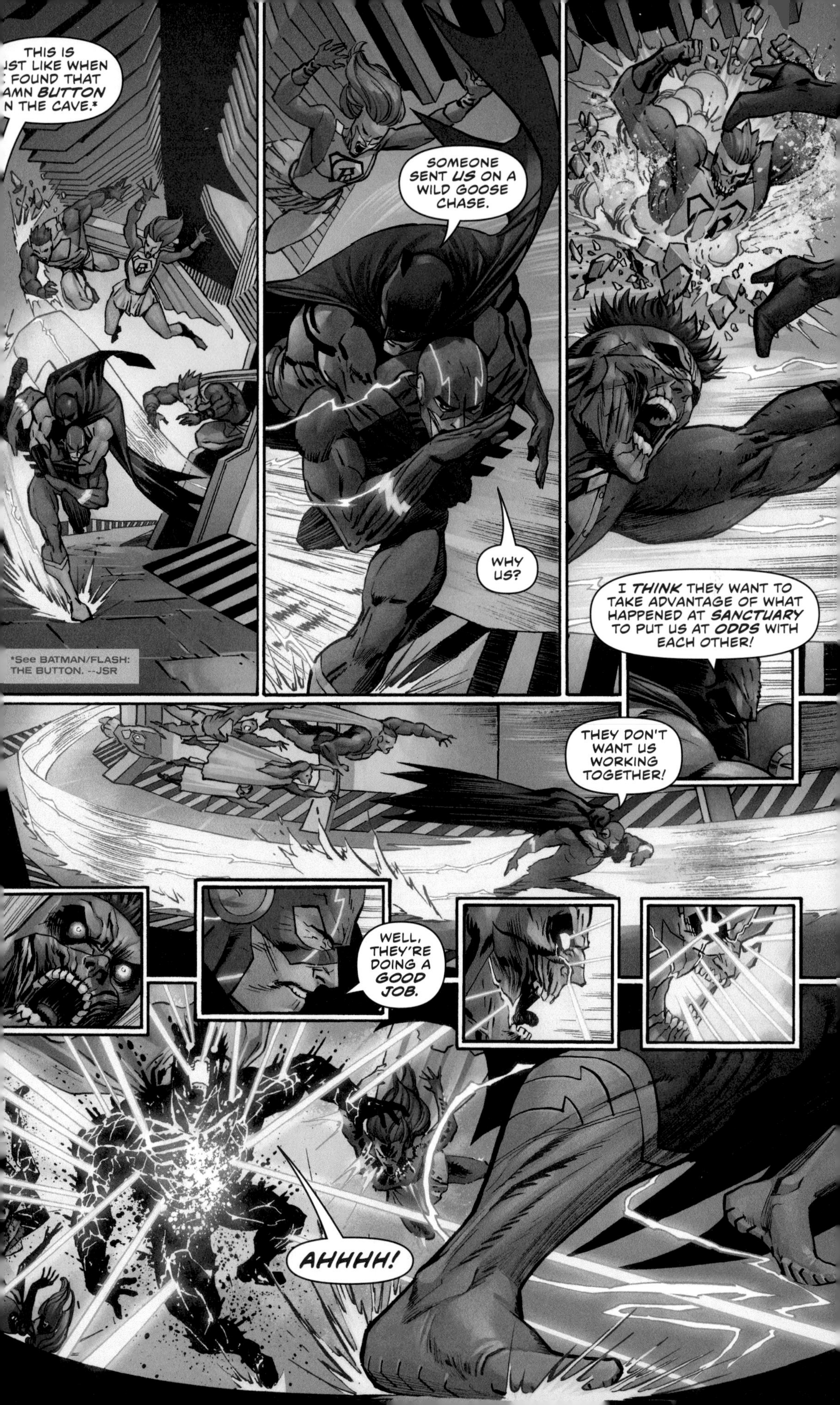

THIS IS
UST LIKE WHEN
FOUND THAT
AMN BUTTON
N THE CAVE.*
SOMEONE SENT US ON A WILD GOOSE CHASE.
WHY US?
*See BATMAN/FLASH: THE BUTTON. --JSR
I THINK THEY WANT TO TAKE ADVANTAGE OF WHAT HAPPENED AT SANCTUARY TO PUT US AT ODDS WITH EACH OTHER!
THEY DON'T WANT US WORKING TOGETHER!
WELL, THEY'RE DOING A GOOD JOB.
AHHHH!

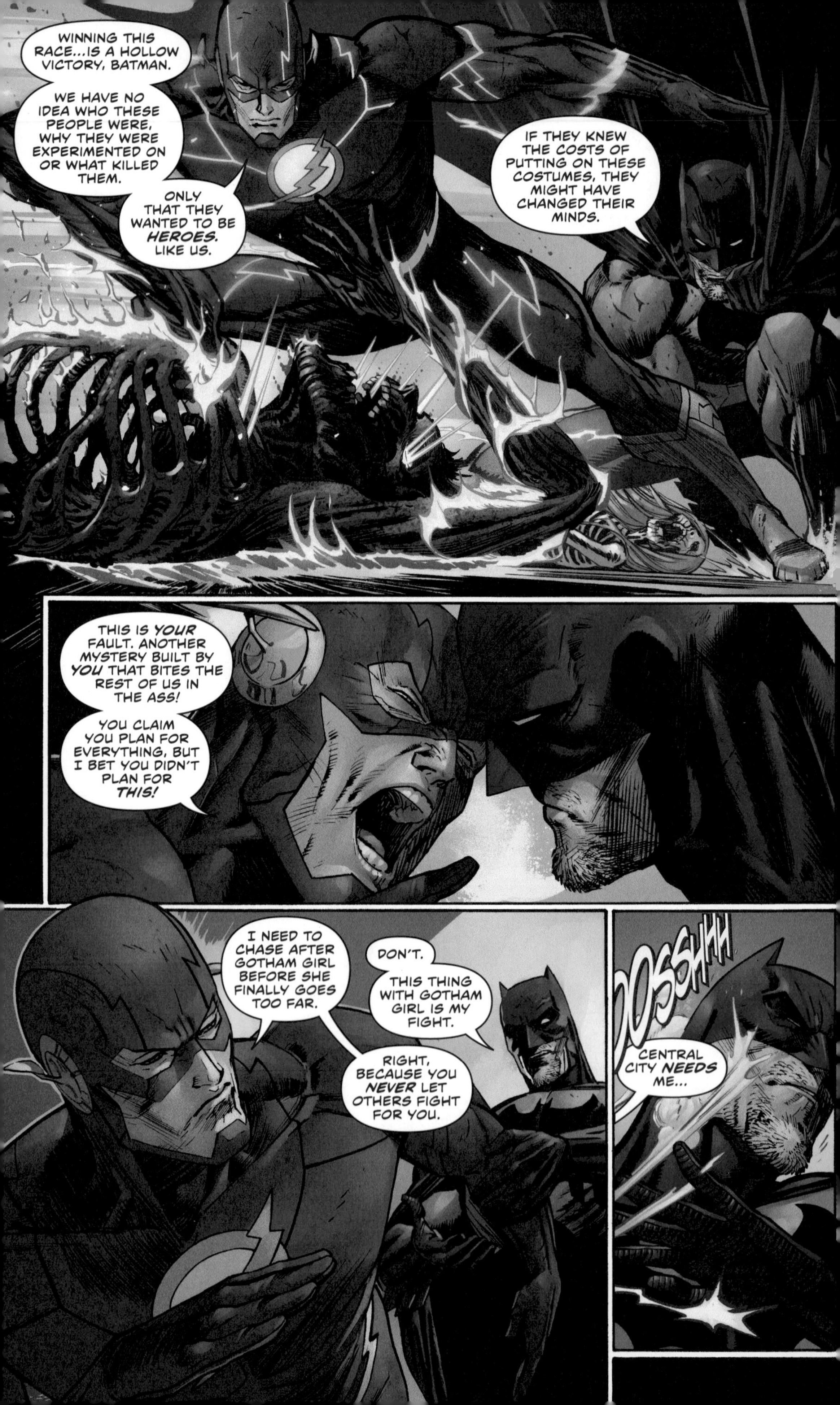
WINNING THIS RACE...IS A HOLLOW VICTORY, BATMAN.
WE HAVE NO IDEA WHO THESE PEOPLE WERE, WHY THEY WERE EXPERIMENTED ON OR WHAT KILLED THEM.
ONLY THAT THEY WANTED TO BE *HEROES.* LIKE US.
IF THEY KNEW THE COSTS OF PUTTING ON THESE COSTUMES, THEY MIGHT HAVE CHANGED THEIR MINDS.
THIS IS *YOUR* FAULT. ANOTHER MYSTERY BUILT BY *YOU* THAT BITES THE REST OF US IN THE ASS!
YOU CLAIM YOU PLAN FOR EVERYTHING, BUT I BET YOU DIDN'T PLAN FOR *THIS!*
I NEED TO CHASE AFTER GOTHAM GIRL BEFORE SHE FINALLY GOES TOO FAR.
DON'T.
THIS THING WITH GOTHAM GIRL IS MY FIGHT.
RIGHT, BECAUSE YOU *NEVER* LET OTHERS FIGHT FOR YOU.
OOSSHHH
CENTRAL CITY *NEEDS* ME...

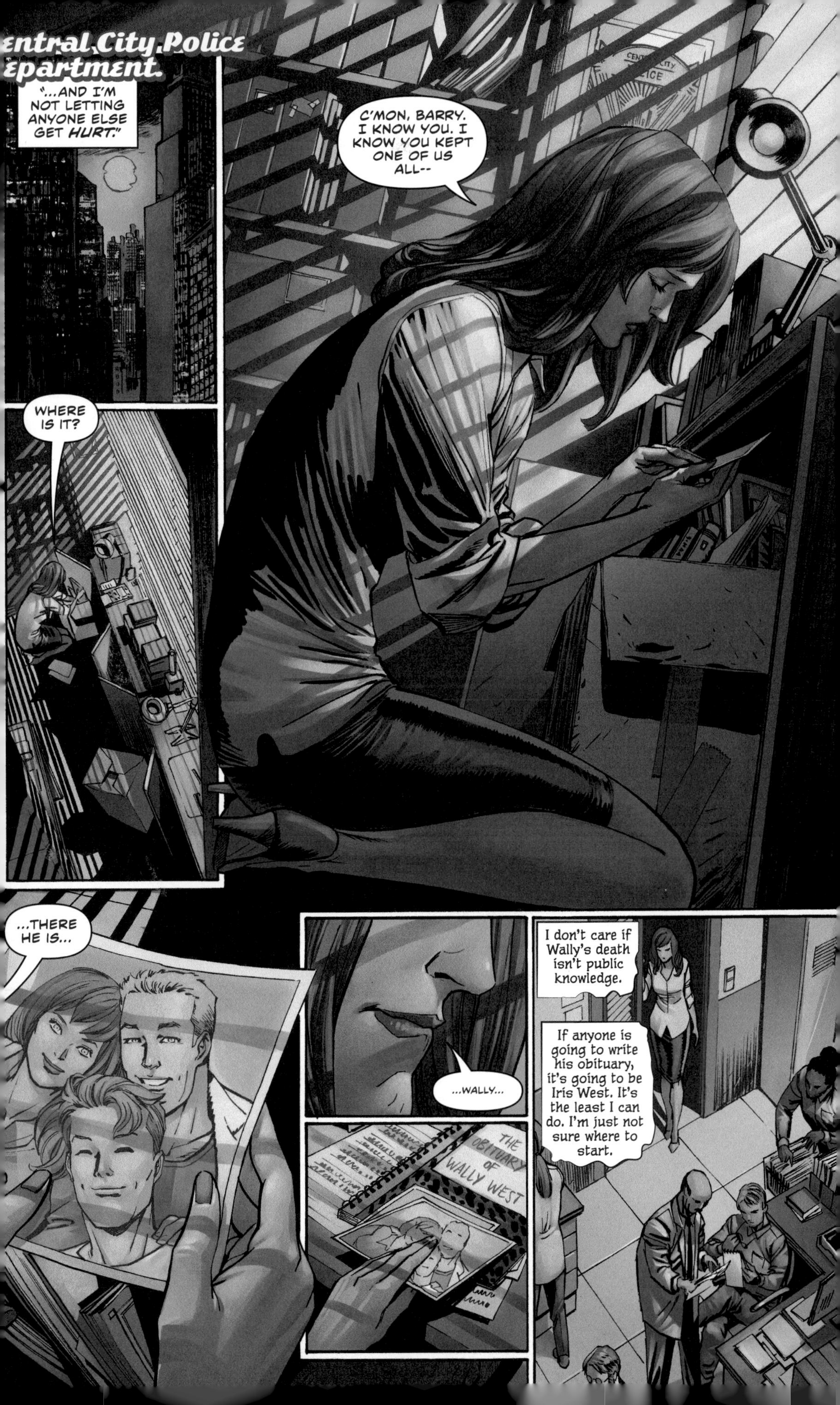
entral City Police
epartment.
"...AND I'M NOT LETTING ANYONE ELSE GET HURT."
C'MON, BARRY. I KNOW YOU. I KNOW YOU KEPT ONE OF US ALL--
WHERE IS IT?
...THERE HE IS...
...WALLY...
THE OBITUARY OF WALLY WEST
I don't care if Wally's death isn't public knowledge.
If anyone is going to write his obituary, it's going to be Iris West. It's the least I can do. I'm just not sure where to start.

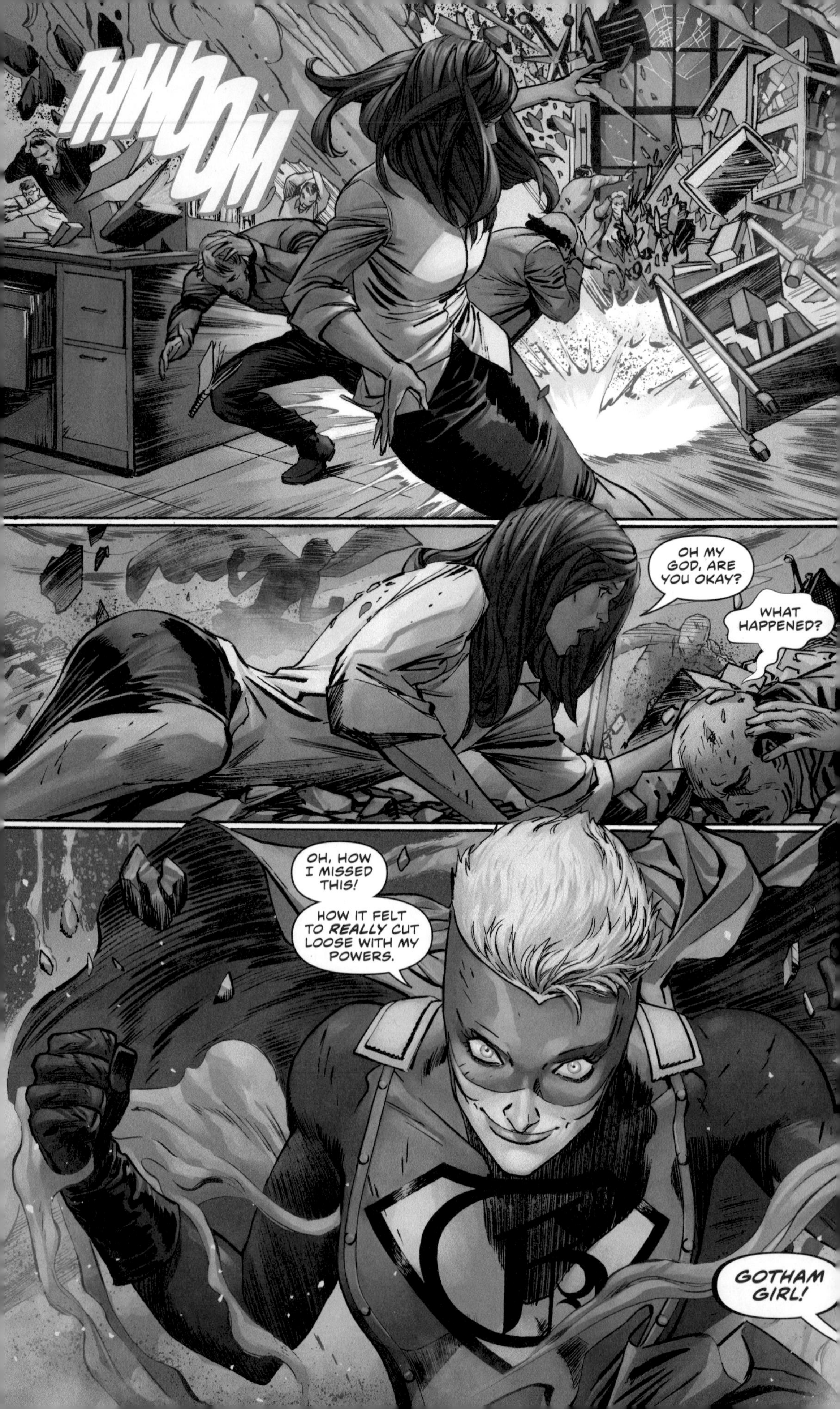
THWOOM
OH MY GOD, ARE YOU OKAY?
WHAT HAPPENED?
OH, HOW I MISSED THIS!
HOW IT FELT TO *REALLY* CUT LOOSE WITH MY POWERS.
GOTHAM GIRL!

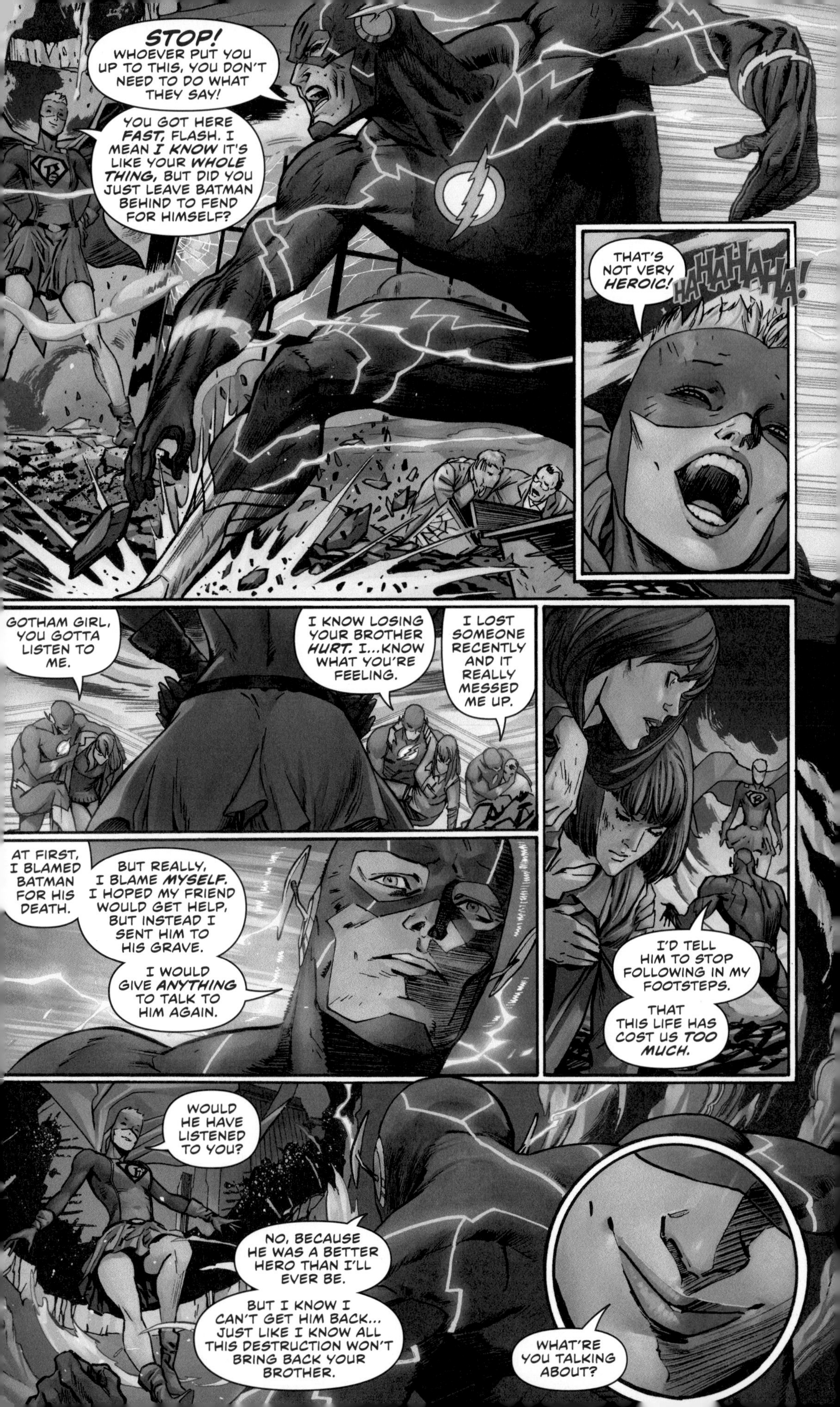

STOP! WHOEVER PUT YOU UP TO THIS, YOU DON'T NEED TO DO WHAT THEY SAY!
YOU GOT HERE FAST, FLASH. I MEAN I KNOW IT'S LIKE YOUR WHOLE THING, BUT DID YOU JUST LEAVE BATMAN BEHIND TO FEND FOR HIMSELF?
THAT'S NOT VERY HEROIC!
HAHAHAHA!
GOTHAM GIRL, YOU GOTTA LISTEN TO ME.
I KNOW LOSING YOUR BROTHER HURT. I...KNOW WHAT YOU'RE FEELING.
I LOST SOMEONE RECENTLY AND IT REALLY MESSED ME UP.
AT FIRST, I BLAMED BATMAN FOR HIS DEATH.
BUT REALLY, I BLAME MYSELF. I HOPED MY FRIEND WOULD GET HELP, BUT INSTEAD I SENT HIM TO HIS GRAVE.
I WOULD GIVE ANYTHING TO TALK TO HIM AGAIN.
I'D TELL HIM TO STOP FOLLOWING IN MY FOOTSTEPS.
THAT THIS LIFE HAS COST US TOO MUCH.
WOULD HE HAVE LISTENED TO YOU?
NO, BECAUSE HE WAS A BETTER HERO THAN I'LL EVER BE.
BUT I KNOW I CAN'T GET HIM BACK... JUST LIKE I KNOW ALL THIS DESTRUCTION WON'T BRING BACK YOUR BROTHER.
WHAT'RE YOU TALKING ABOUT?

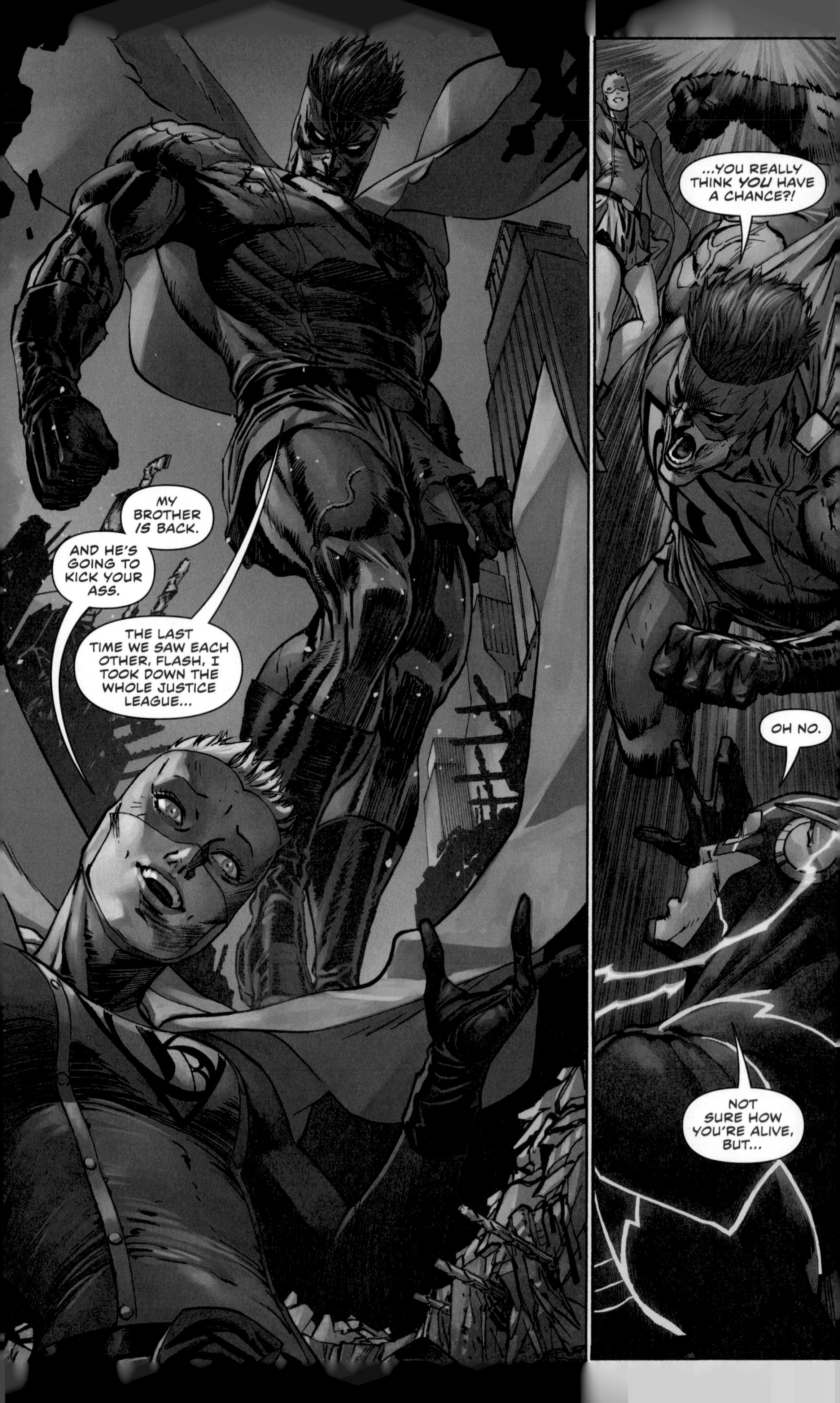
THE LAST TIME WE SAW EACH OTHER, FLASH, I TOOK DOWN THE WHOLE JUSTICE LEAGUE...
MY BROTHER IS BACK.
AND HE'S GOING TO KICK YOUR ASS.
...YOU REALLY THINK YOU HAVE A CHANCE?!
OH NO.
NOT SURE HOW YOU'RE ALIVE, BUT...

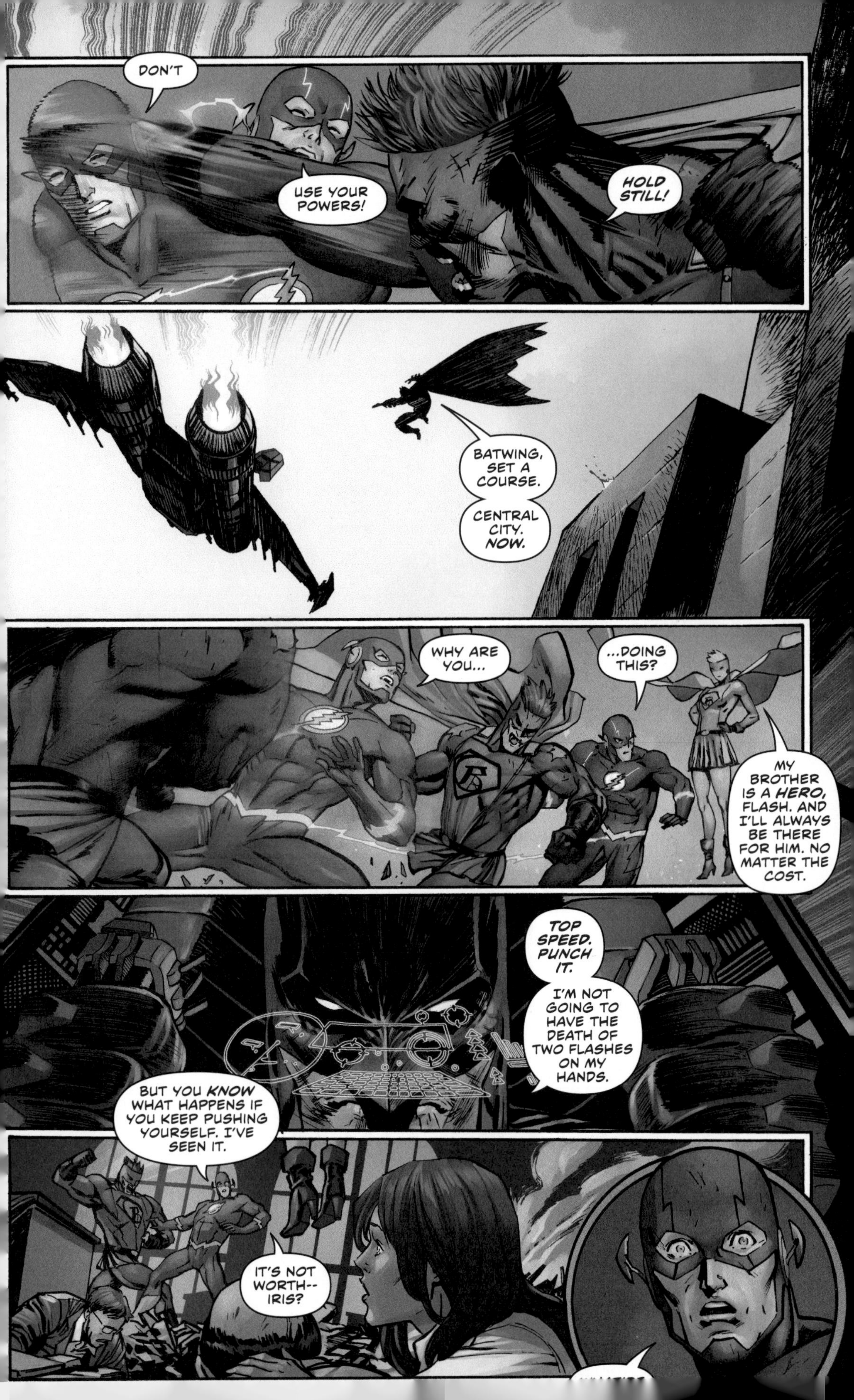
DON'T
USE YOUR POWERS!
HOLD STILL!
BATWING, SET A COURSE.
CENTRAL CITY. NOW.
WHY ARE YOU...
...DOING THIS?
MY BROTHER IS A HERO, FLASH. AND I'LL ALWAYS BE THERE FOR HIM. NO MATTER THE COST.
TOP SPEED. PUNCH IT.
I'M NOT GOING TO HAVE THE DEATH OF TWO FLASHES ON MY HANDS.
BUT YOU KNOW WHAT HAPPENS IF YOU KEEP PUSHING YOURSELF. I'VE SEEN IT.
IT'S NOT WORTH-- IRIS?

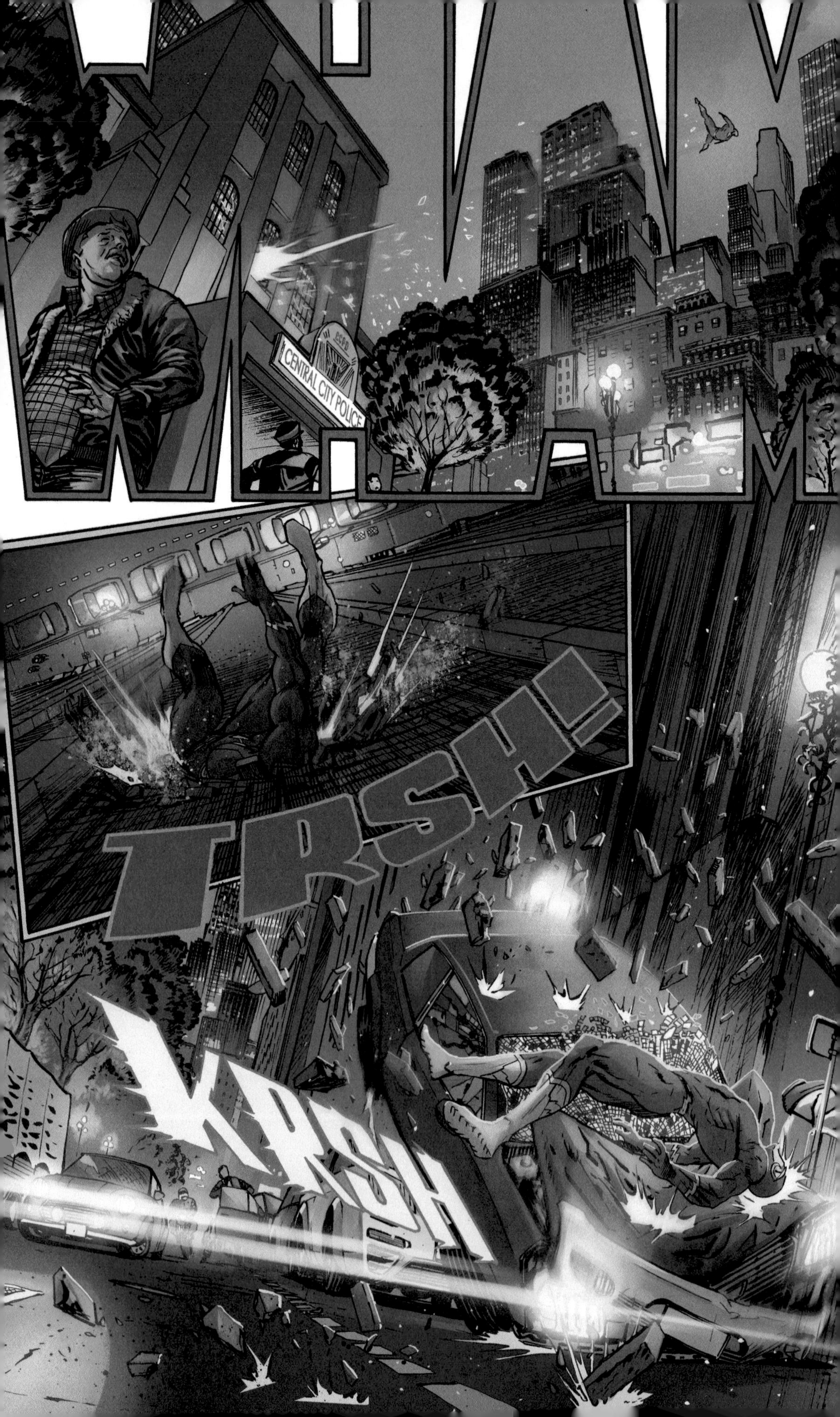
CCPD
CENTRAL CITY POLICE
TRSH!!
KRSH

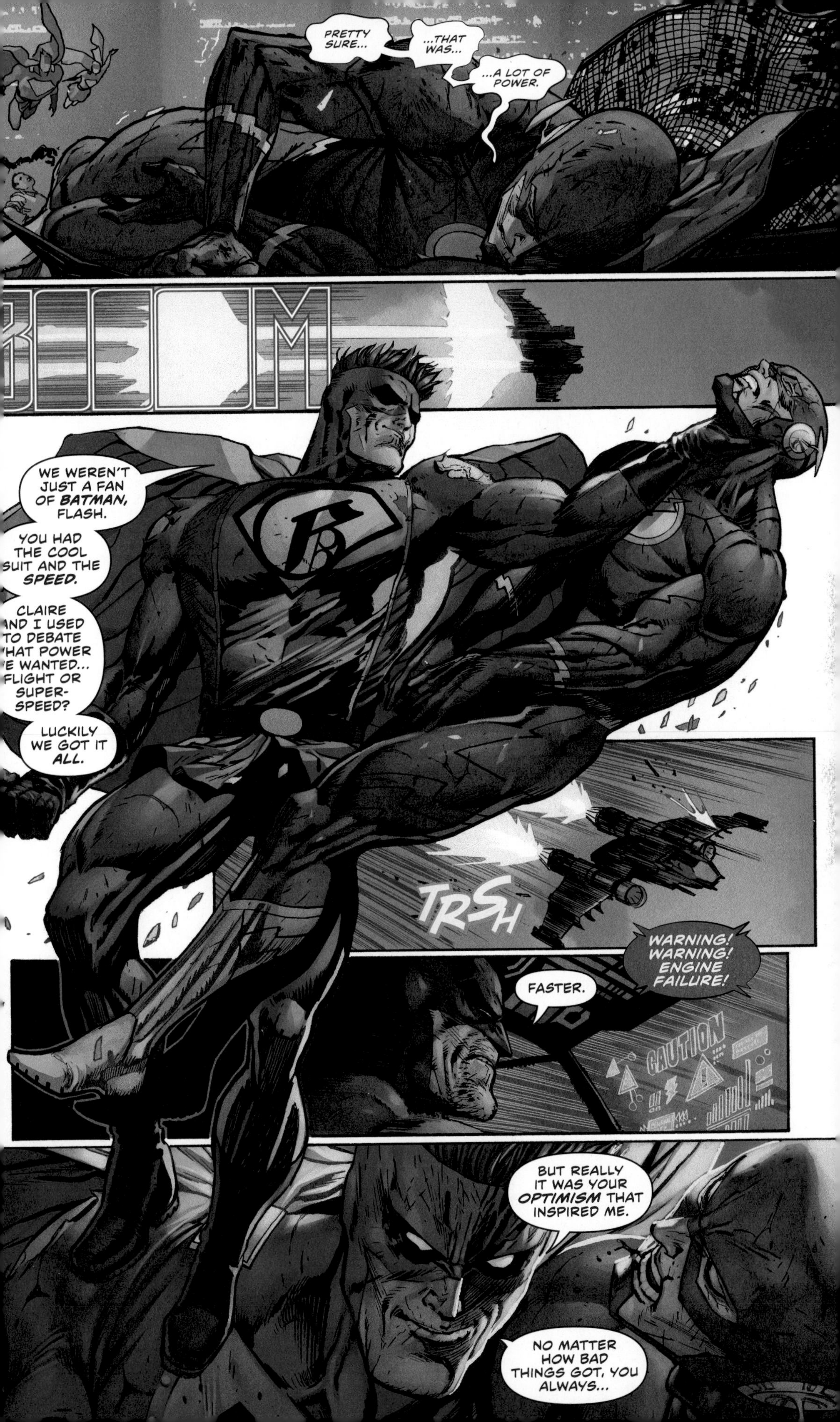
PRETTY SURE...
...THAT WAS...
...A LOT OF POWER.
BOOM
WE WEREN'T JUST A FAN OF *BATMAN,* FLASH.
YOU HAD THE COOL SUIT AND THE *SPEED.*
CLAIRE AND I USED TO DEBATE WHAT POWER WE WANTED... FLIGHT OR SUPER-SPEED?
LUCKILY WE GOT IT *ALL.*
TRSH
WARNING! WARNING! ENGINE FAILURE!
FASTER.
CAUTION
BUT REALLY IT WAS YOUR *OPTIMISM* THAT INSPIRED ME.
NO MATTER HOW BAD THINGS GOT, YOU ALWAYS...

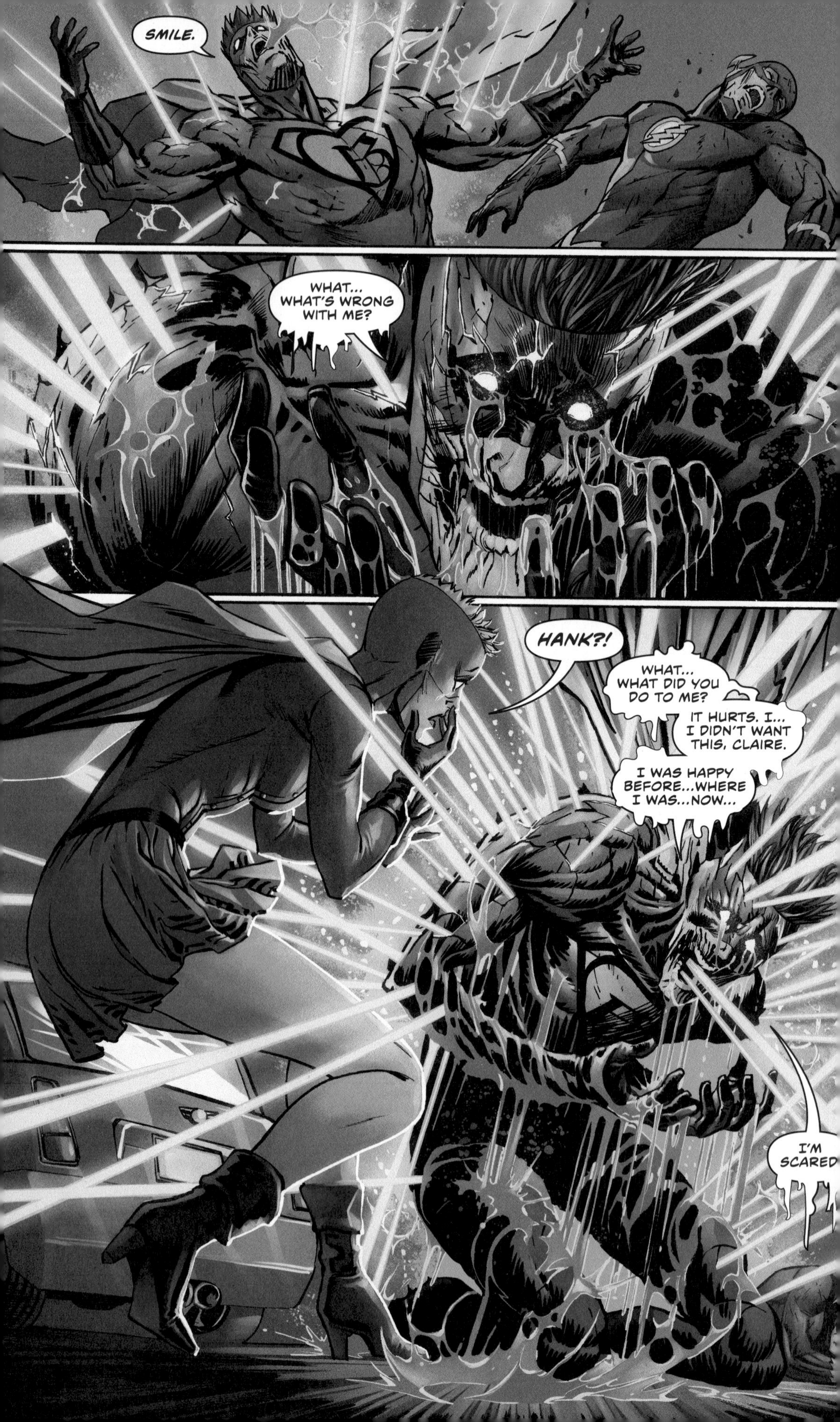
SMILE.
WHAT... WHAT'S WRONG WITH ME?
HANK?!
WHAT... WHAT DID YOU DO TO ME?
IT HURTS. I... I DIDN'T WANT THIS, CLAIRE.
I WAS HAPPY BEFORE...WHERE I WAS...NOW...
I'M SCARED

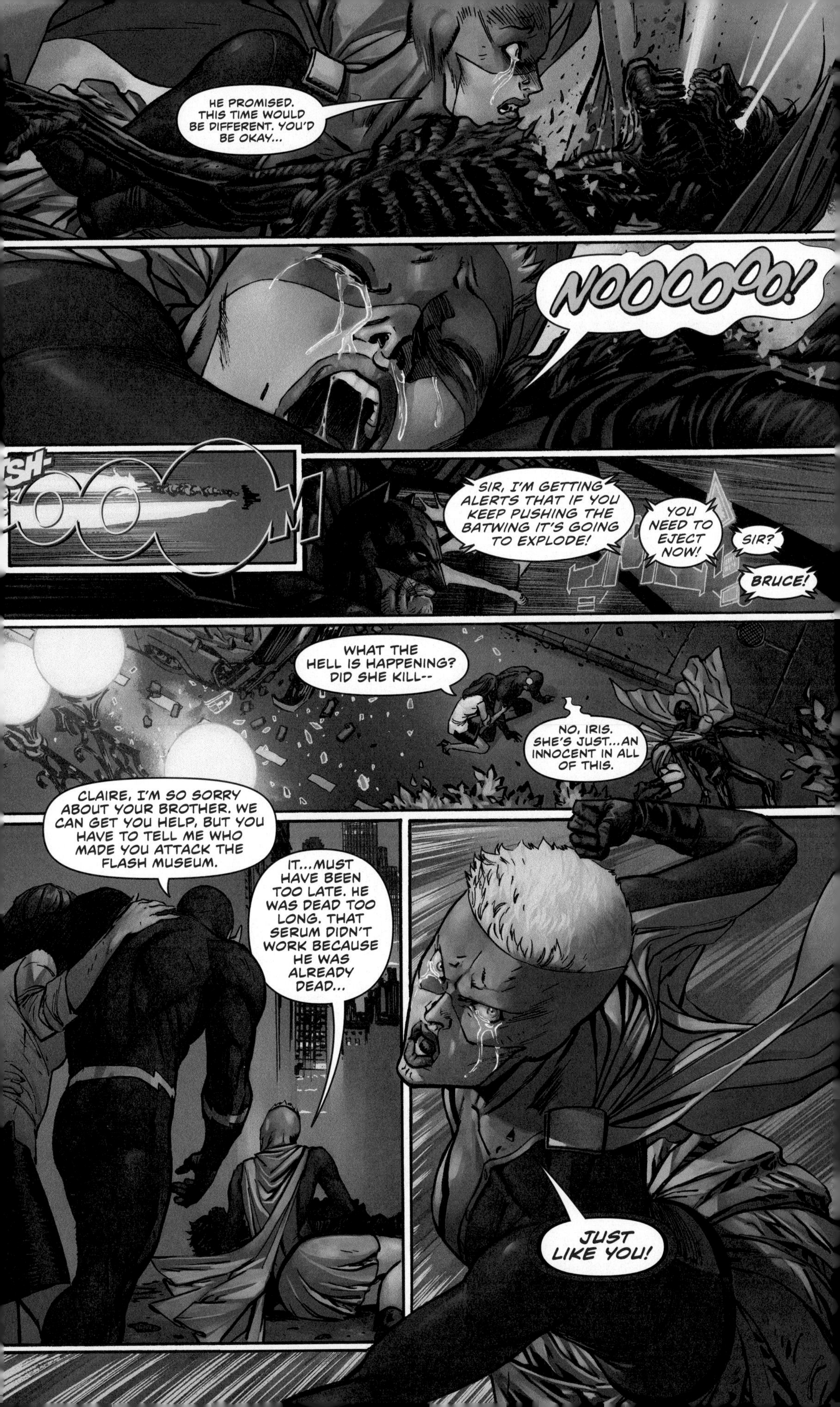
HE PROMISED. THIS TIME WOULD BE DIFFERENT. YOU'D BE OKAY...
NOOOOOOO!
SH-BOOOOM
SIR, I'M GETTING ALERTS THAT IF YOU KEEP PUSHING THE BATWING IT'S GOING TO EXPLODE!
YOU NEED TO EJECT NOW!
SIR?
BRUCE!
WHAT THE HELL IS HAPPENING? DID SHE KILL--
NO, IRIS. SHE'S JUST...AN INNOCENT IN ALL OF THIS.
CLAIRE, I'M SO SORRY ABOUT YOUR BROTHER. WE CAN GET YOU HELP, BUT YOU HAVE TO TELL ME WHO MADE YOU ATTACK THE FLASH MUSEUM.
IT...MUST HAVE BEEN TOO LATE. HE WAS DEAD TOO LONG. THAT SERUM DIDN'T WORK BECAUSE HE WAS ALREADY DEAD...
JUST LIKE YOU!

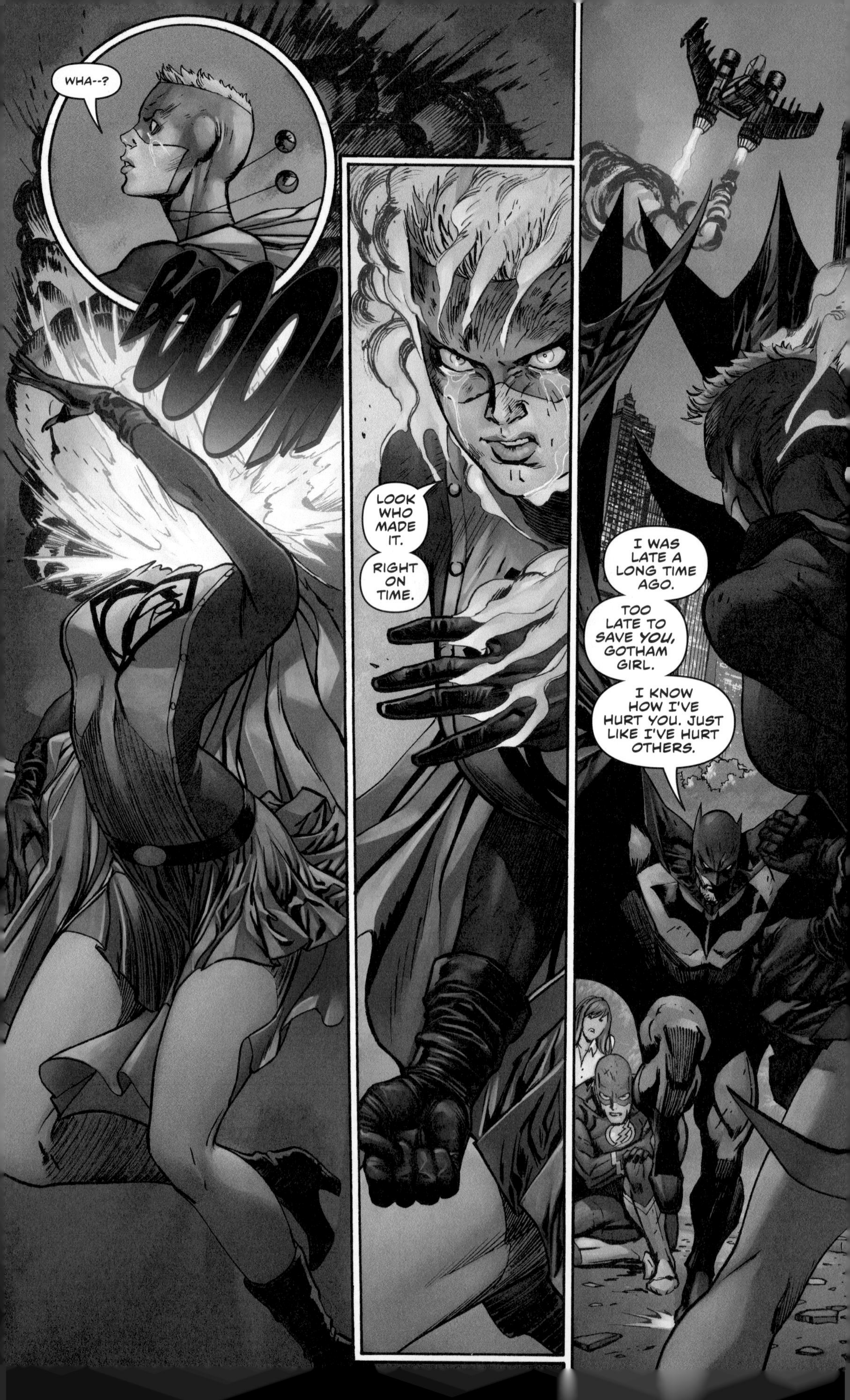

WHA--?
LOOK WHO MADE IT.
RIGHT ON TIME.
I WAS LATE A LONG TIME AGO.
TOO LATE TO SAVE YOU, GOTHAM GIRL.
I KNOW HOW I'VE HURT YOU. JUST LIKE I'VE HURT OTHERS.

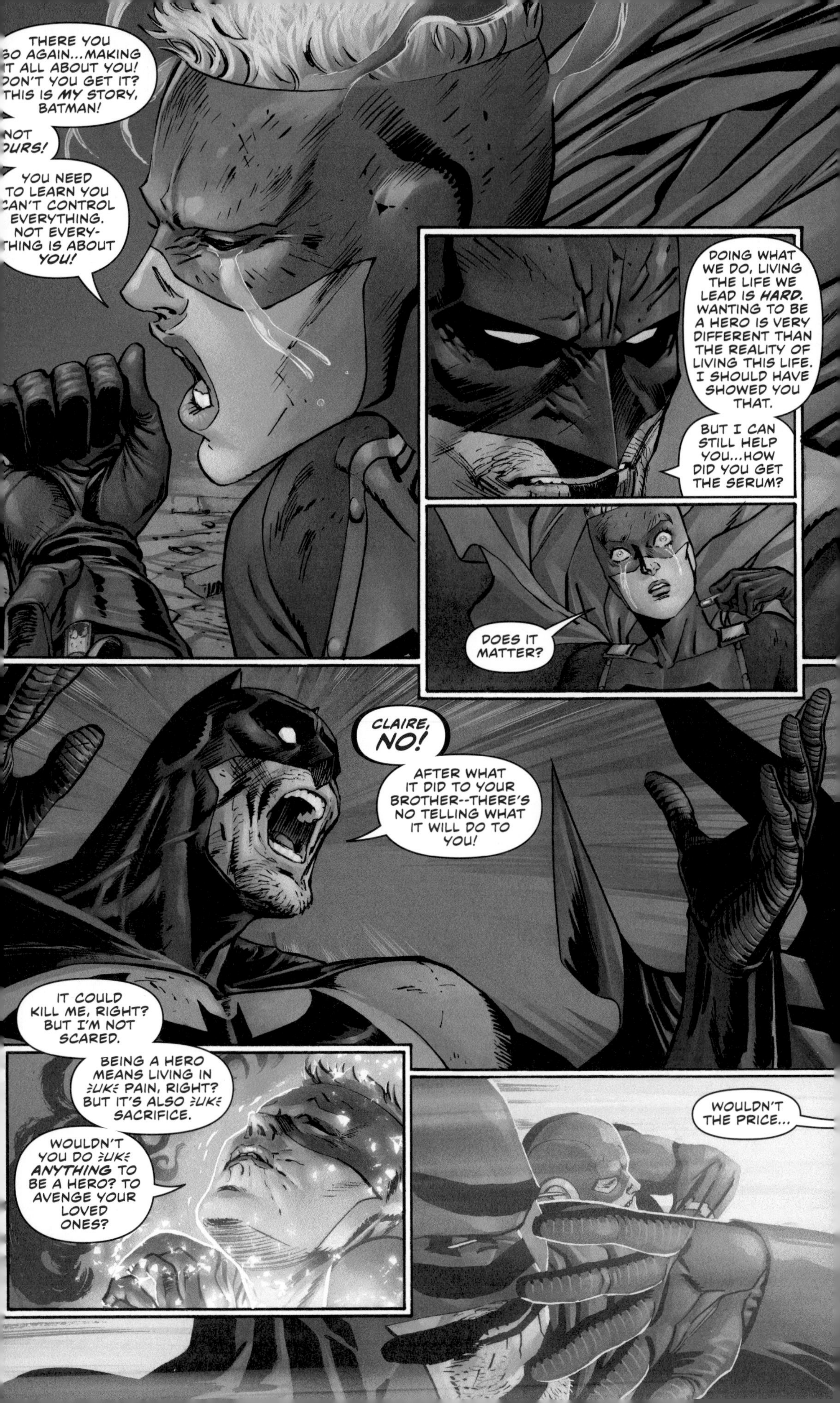

THERE YOU GO AGAIN...MAKING IT ALL ABOUT YOU! DON'T YOU GET IT? THIS IS *MY* STORY, BATMAN!
NOT YOURS!
YOU NEED TO LEARN YOU CAN'T CONTROL EVERYTHING. NOT EVERYTHING IS ABOUT *YOU!*
DOING WHAT WE DO, LIVING THE LIFE WE LEAD IS *HARD.* WANTING TO BE A HERO IS VERY DIFFERENT THAN THE REALITY OF LIVING THIS LIFE. I SHOULD HAVE SHOWED YOU THAT.
BUT I CAN STILL HELP YOU...HOW DID YOU GET THE SERUM?
DOES IT MATTER?
CLAIRE, NO!
AFTER WHAT IT DID TO YOUR BROTHER--THERE'S NO TELLING WHAT IT WILL DO TO YOU!
IT COULD KILL ME, RIGHT? BUT I'M NOT SCARED.
BEING A HERO MEANS LIVING IN *UK* PAIN, RIGHT? BUT IT'S ALSO *UK* SACRIFICE.
WOULDN'T YOU DO *UK* *ANYTHING* TO BE A HERO? TO AVENGE YOUR LOVED ONES?
WOULDN'T THE PRICE...

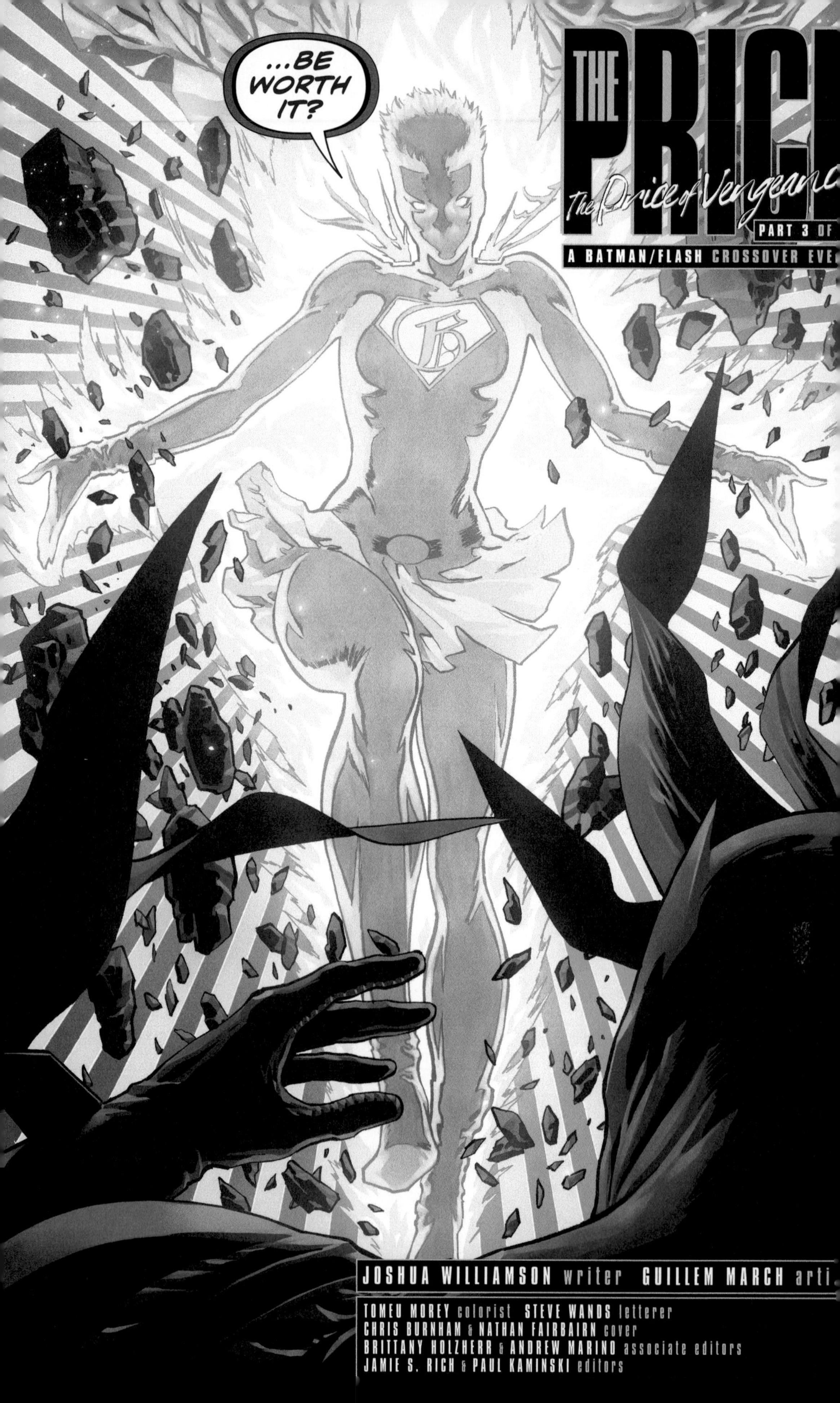

...BE WORTH IT?
THE PRIC
The Price of Vengeanc
PART 3 OF
A BATMAN/FLASH CROSSOVER EVE
JOSHUA WILLIAMSON writer GUILLEM MARCH arti
TOMEU MOREY colorist STEVE WANDS letterer
CHRIS BURNHAM & NATHAN FAIRBAIRN cover
BRITTANY HOLZHERR & ANDREW MARINO associate editors
JAMIE S. RICH & PAUL KAMINSKI editors

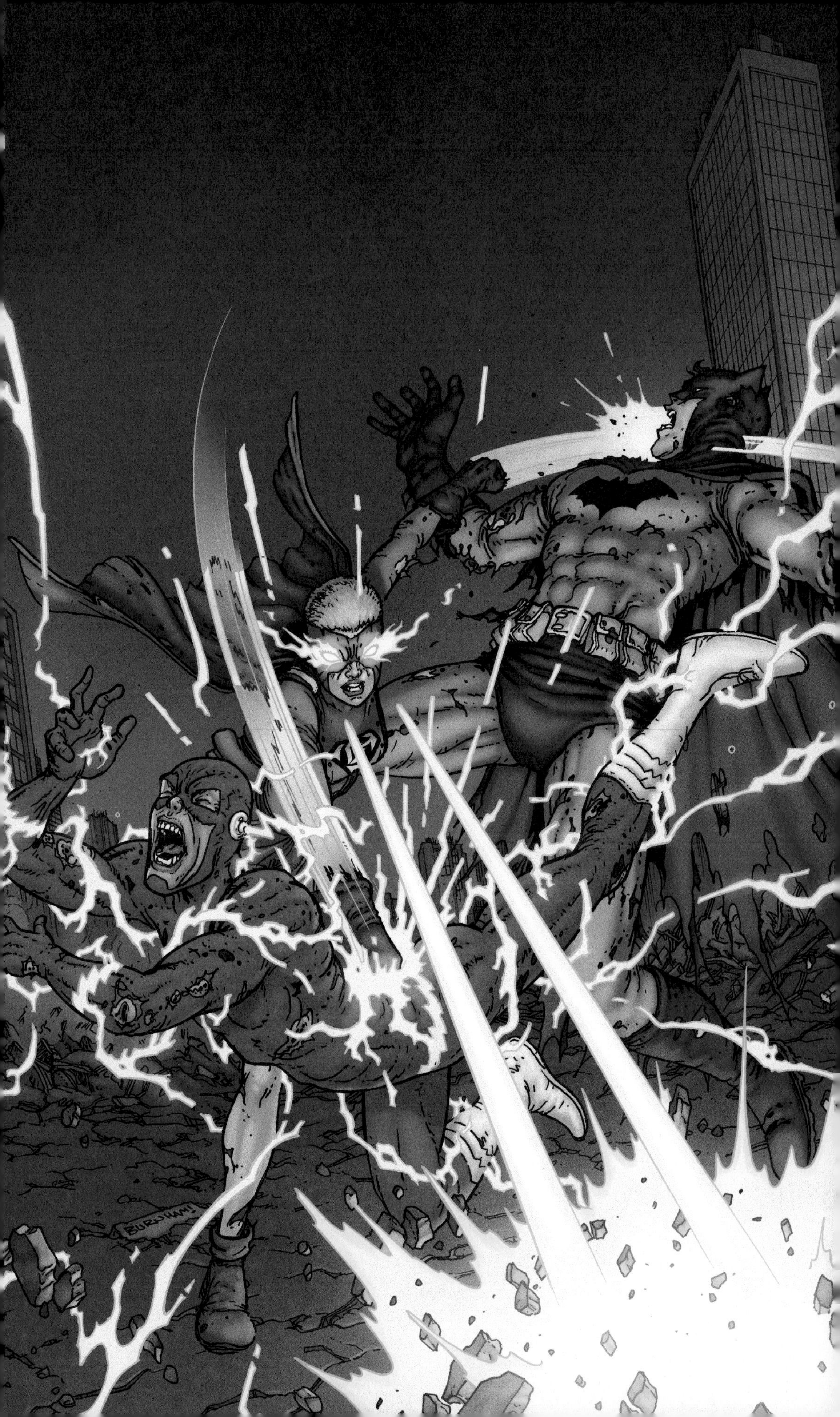

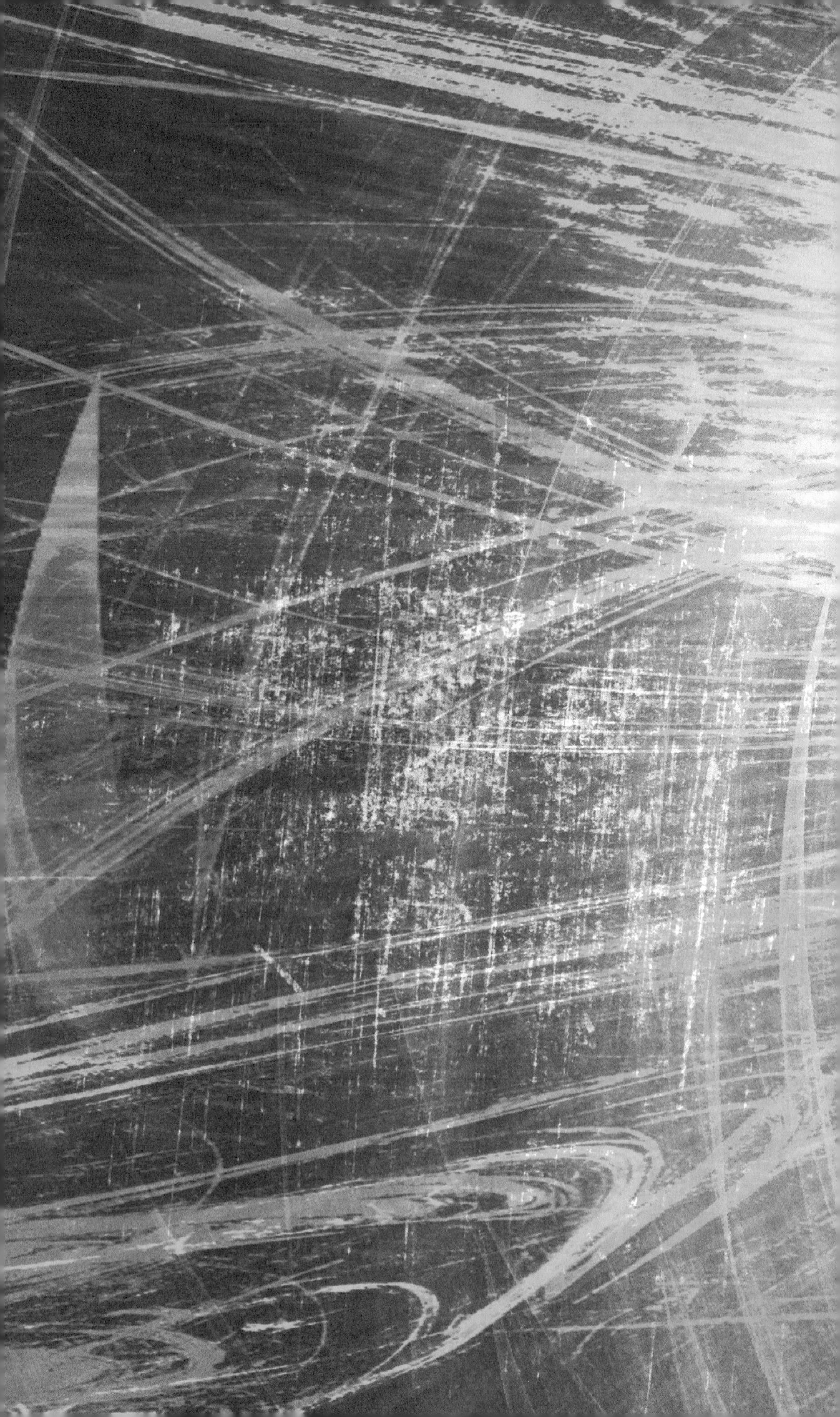

...at what cost...

EVERY STEP I TOOK BROUGHT ME CLOSER TO MY WORST NIGHTMARE.

BOOSTER GOLD SAID WALLY WAS DEAD. I DIDN'T WANT TO BELIEVE HIM.

HE WAS INSIDE SANCTUARY AND IT WAS MY FAULT HE WAS THERE.

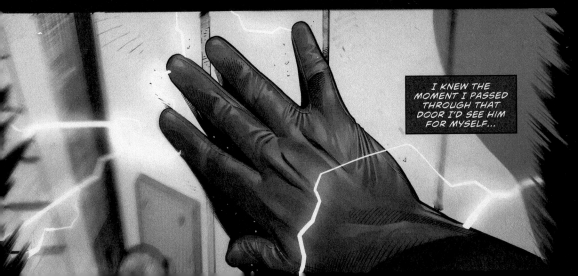

I KNEW THE MOMENT I PASSED THROUGH THAT DOOR I'D SEE HIM FOR MYSELF...

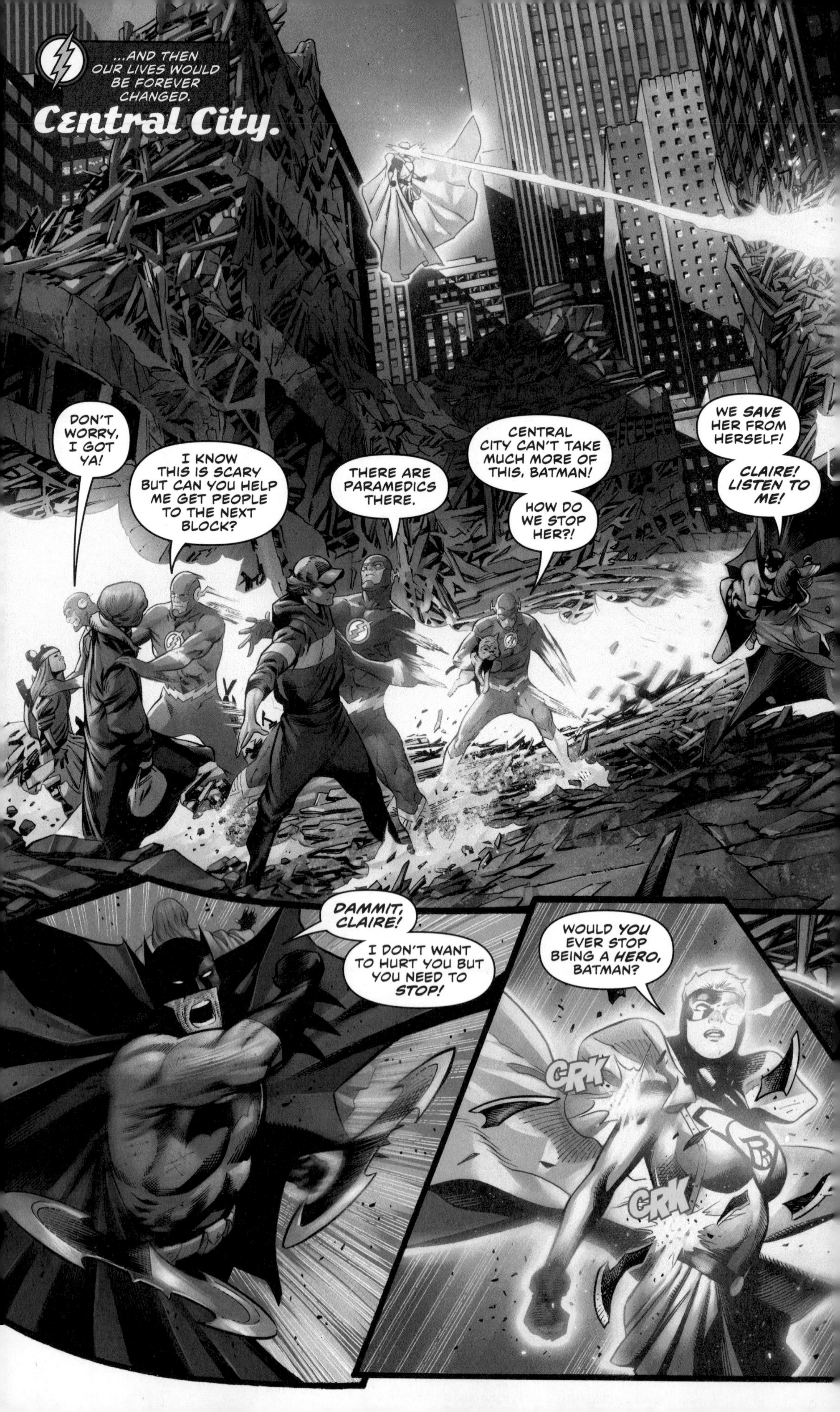
...AND THEN OUR LIVES WOULD BE FOREVER CHANGED.
Central City.
DON'T WORRY, I GOT YA!
I KNOW THIS IS SCARY BUT CAN YOU HELP ME GET PEOPLE TO THE NEXT BLOCK?
THERE ARE PARAMEDICS THERE.
CENTRAL CITY CAN'T TAKE MUCH MORE OF THIS, BATMAN!
HOW DO WE STOP HER?!
WE SAVE HER FROM HERSELF!
CLAIRE! LISTEN TO ME!
DAMMIT, CLAIRE!
I DON'T WANT TO HURT YOU BUT YOU NEED TO STOP!
WOULD YOU EVER STOP BEING A HERO, BATMAN?
GRK
GRK

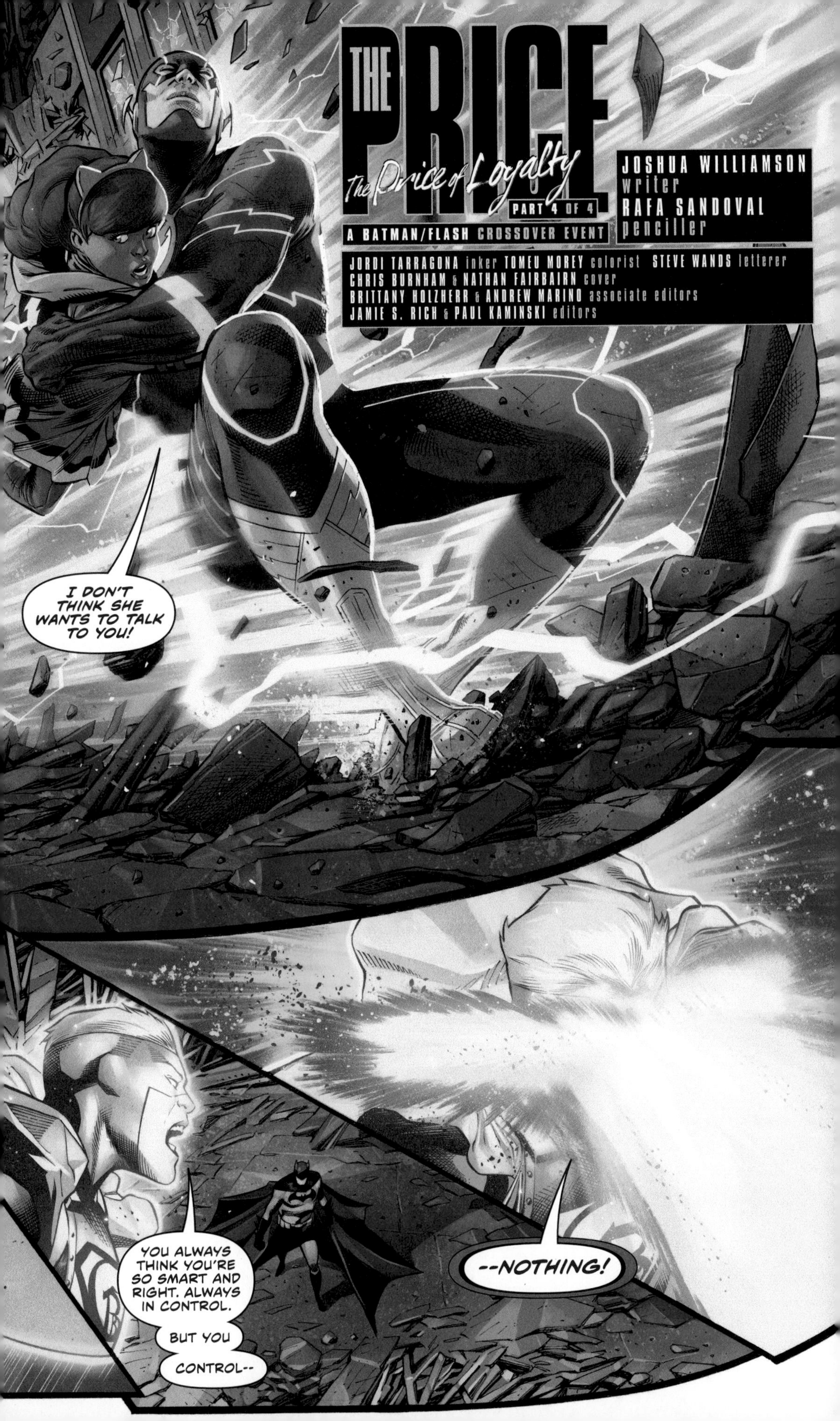

THE PRICE
The Price of Loyalty
PART 4 OF 4
A BATMAN/FLASH CROSSOVER EVENT
JOSHUA WILLIAMSON writer
RAFA SANDOVAL penciller
JORDI TARRAGONA inker TOMEU MOREY colorist STEVE WANDS letterer
CHRIS BURNHAM & NATHAN FAIRBAIRN cover
BRITTANY HOLZHERR & ANDREW MARINO associate editors
JAMIE S. RICH & PAUL KAMINSKI editors
I DON'T THINK SHE WANTS TO TALK TO YOU!
YOU ALWAYS THINK YOU'RE SO SMART AND RIGHT. ALWAYS IN CONTROL.
BUT YOU
CONTROL--
--NOTHING!

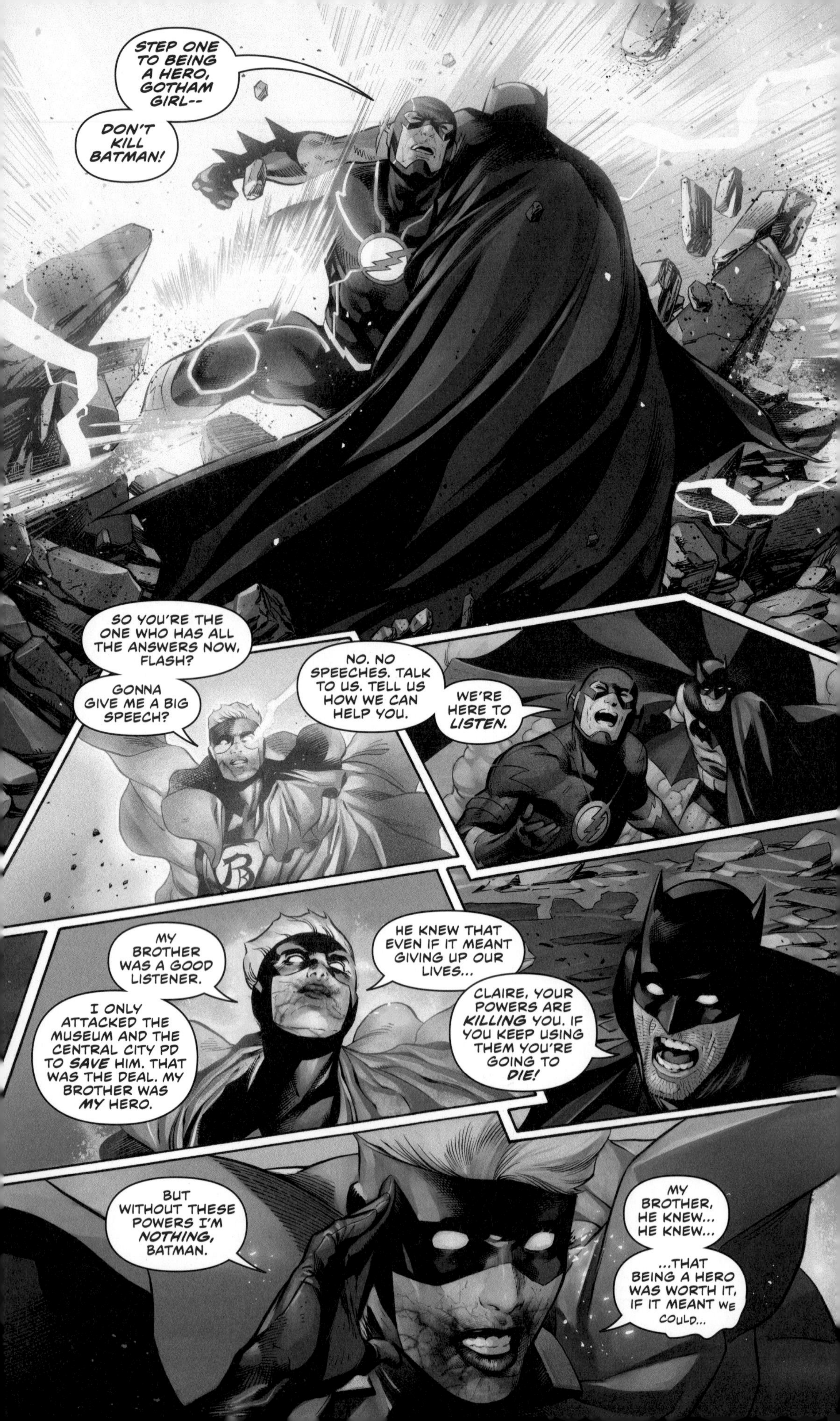
STEP ONE TO BEING A HERO, GOTHAM GIRL--
DON'T KILL BATMAN!
SO YOU'RE THE ONE WHO HAS ALL THE ANSWERS NOW, FLASH?
GONNA GIVE ME A BIG SPEECH?
NO. NO SPEECHES. TALK TO US. TELL US HOW WE CAN HELP YOU.
WE'RE HERE TO LISTEN.
MY BROTHER WAS A GOOD LISTENER.
I ONLY ATTACKED THE MUSEUM AND THE CENTRAL CITY PD TO SAVE HIM. THAT WAS THE DEAL. MY BROTHER WAS MY HERO.
HE KNEW THAT EVEN IF IT MEANT GIVING UP OUR LIVES...
CLAIRE, YOUR POWERS ARE KILLING YOU. IF YOU KEEP USING THEM YOU'RE GOING TO DIE!
BUT WITHOUT THESE POWERS I'M NOTHING, BATMAN.
MY BROTHER, HE KNEW... HE KNEW...
...THAT BEING A HERO WAS WORTH IT, IF IT MEANT WE COULD...

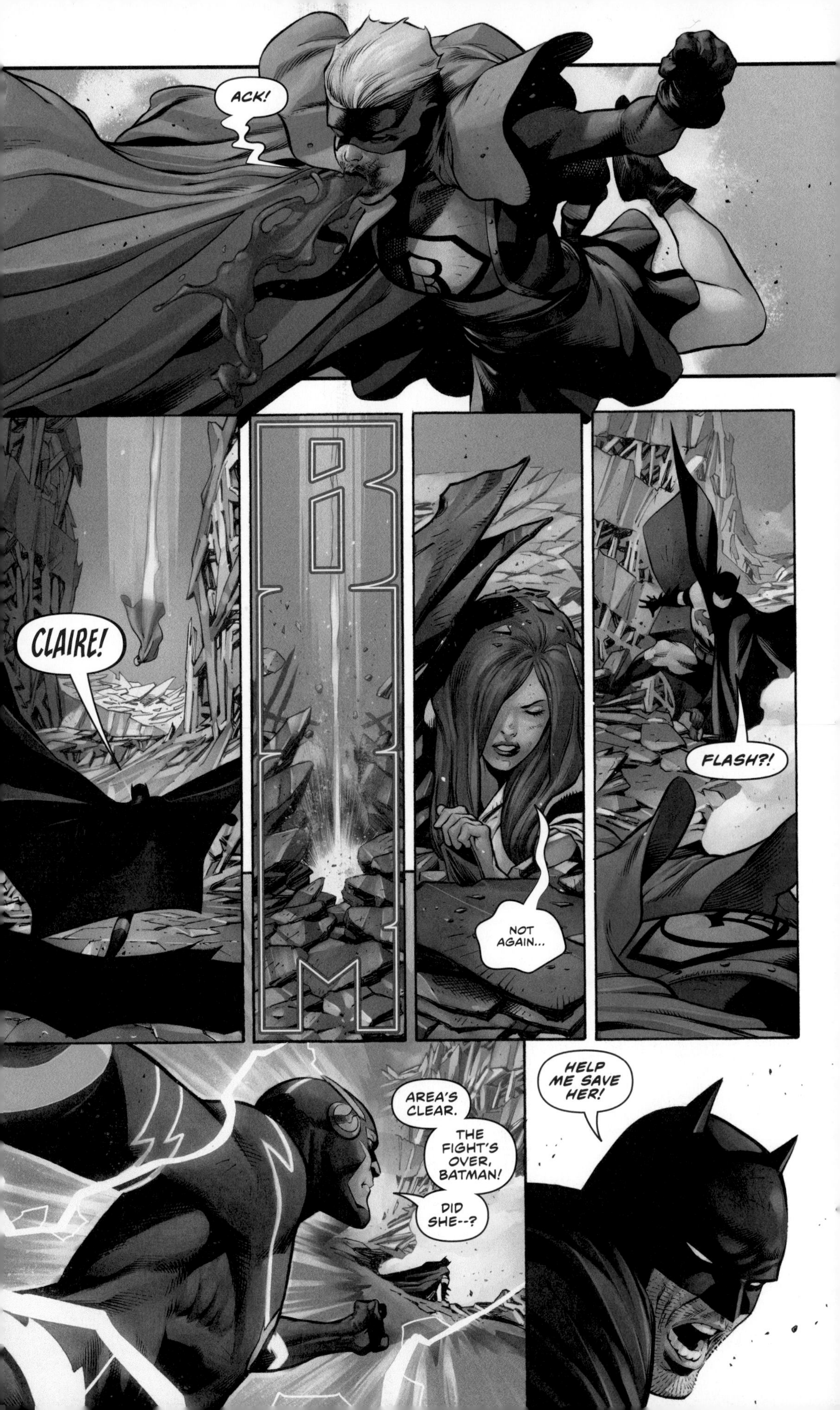
ACK!
CLAIRE!
BOOM
NOT AGAIN...
FLASH?!
AREA'S CLEAR.
THE FIGHT'S OVER, BATMAN!
DID SHE--?
HELP ME SAVE HER!

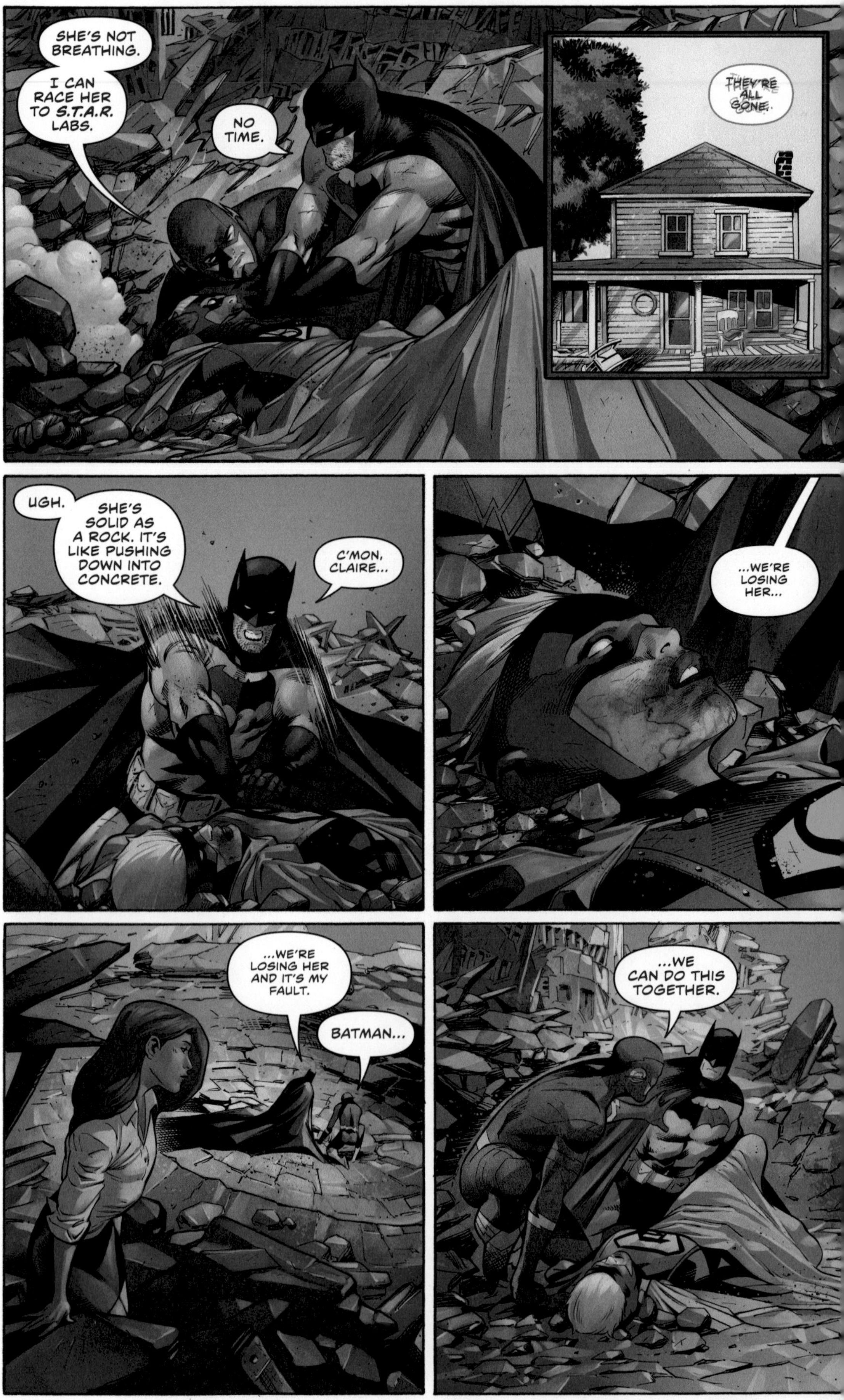
SHE'S NOT BREATHING.
I CAN RACE HER TO S.T.A.R. LABS.
NO TIME.
THEY'RE ALL GONE.
UGH.
SHE'S SOLID AS A ROCK. IT'S LIKE PUSHING DOWN INTO CONCRETE.
C'MON, CLAIRE...
...WE'RE LOSING HER...
...WE'RE LOSING HER AND IT'S MY FAULT.
BATMAN...
...WE CAN DO THIS TOGETHER.

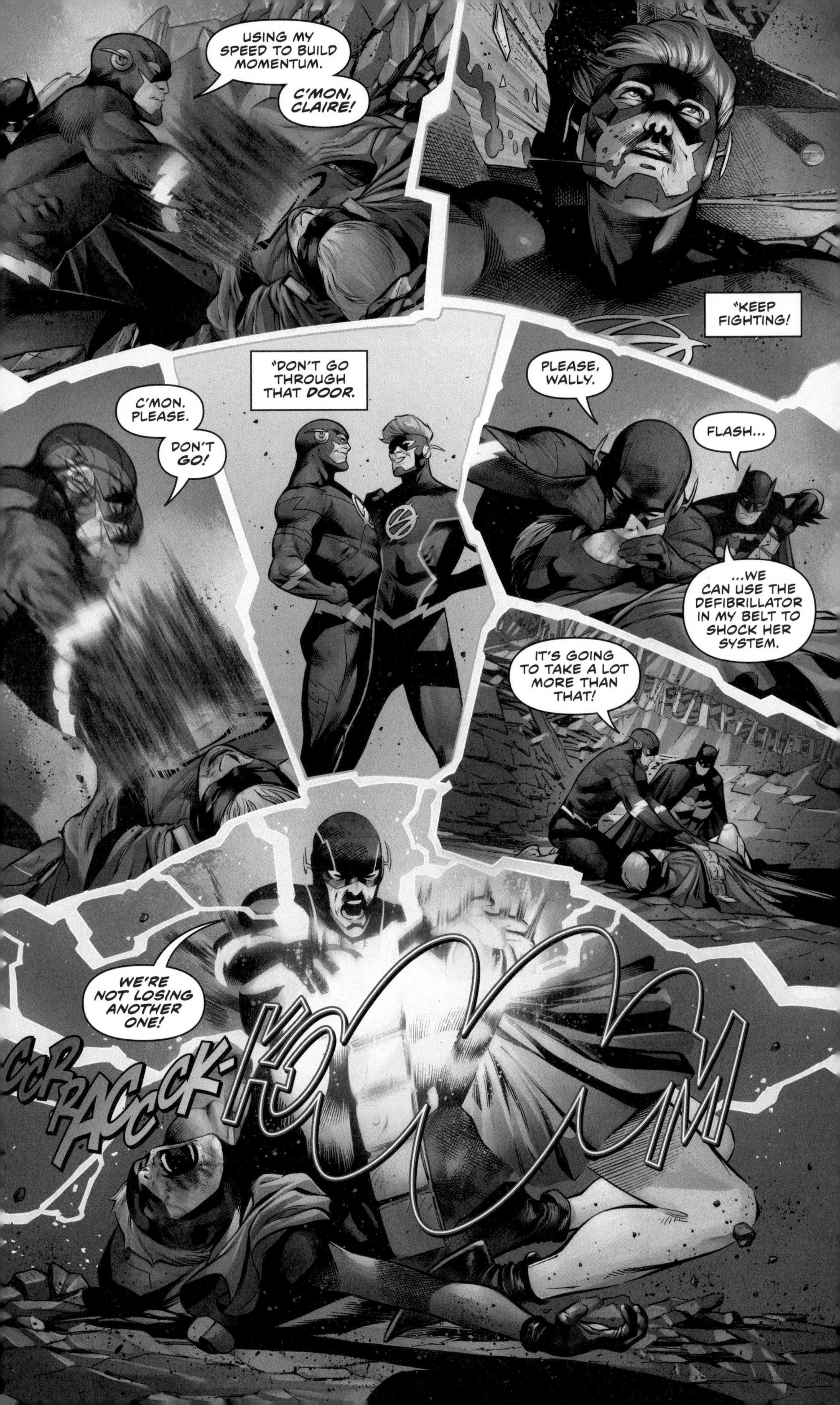
USING MY SPEED TO BUILD MOMENTUM.
C'MON, CLAIRE!
"KEEP FIGHTING!
C'MON. PLEASE.
DON'T GO!
"DON'T GO THROUGH THAT DOOR.
PLEASE, WALLY.
FLASH...
...WE CAN USE THE DEFIBRILLATOR IN MY BELT TO SHOCK HER SYSTEM.
IT'S GOING TO TAKE A LOT MORE THAN THAT!
WE'RE NOT LOSING ANOTHER ONE!
CCRACCCK-KOOOM

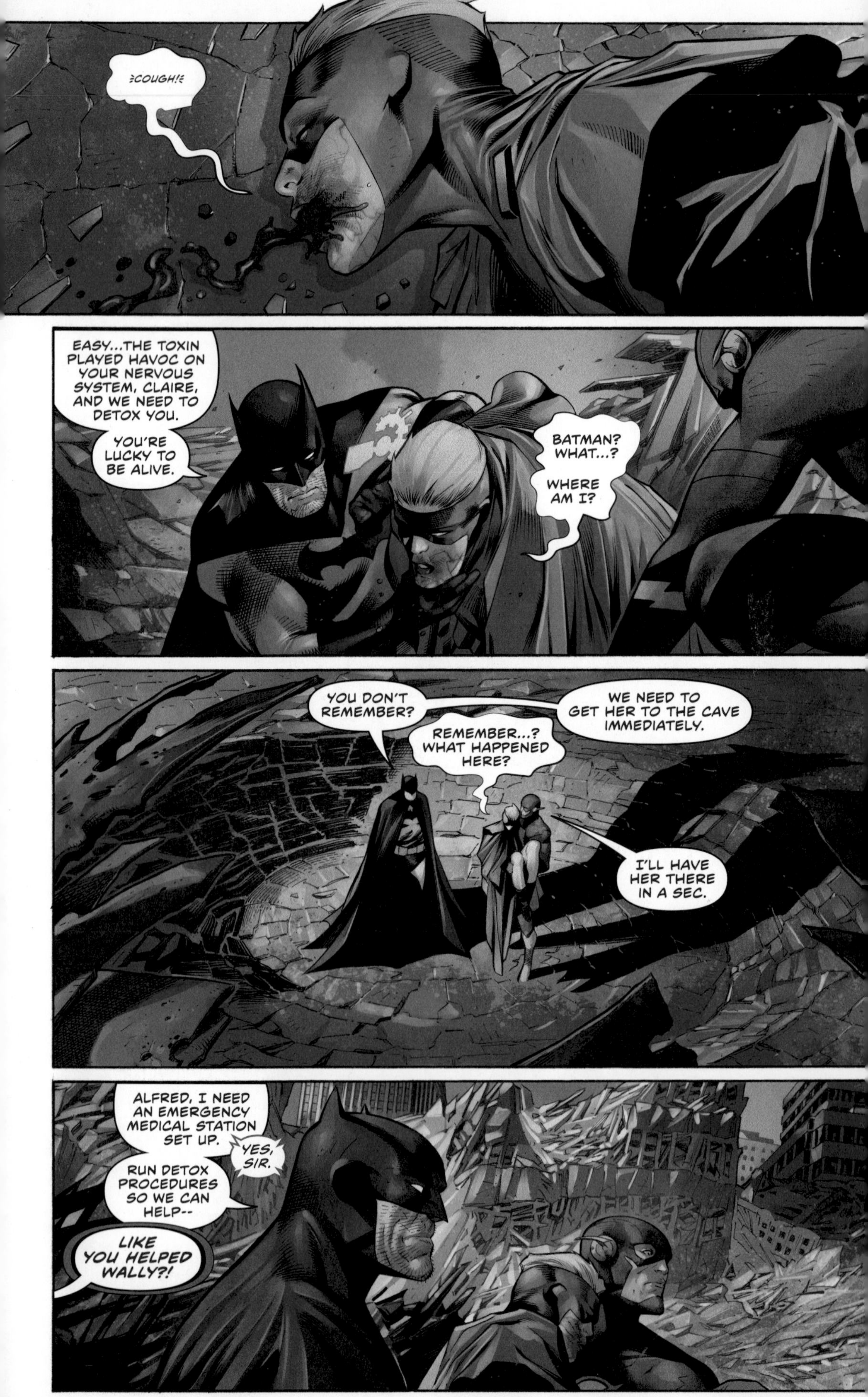
COUGH!
EASY...THE TOXIN PLAYED HAVOC ON YOUR NERVOUS SYSTEM, CLAIRE, AND WE NEED TO DETOX YOU.
YOU'RE LUCKY TO BE ALIVE.
BATMAN? WHAT...?
WHERE AM I?
YOU DON'T REMEMBER?
REMEMBER...? WHAT HAPPENED HERE?
WE NEED TO GET HER TO THE CAVE IMMEDIATELY.
I'LL HAVE HER THERE IN A SEC.
ALFRED, I NEED AN EMERGENCY MEDICAL STATION SET UP.
YES, SIR.
RUN DETOX PROCEDURES SO WE CAN HELP--
LIKE YOU HELPED WALLY?!

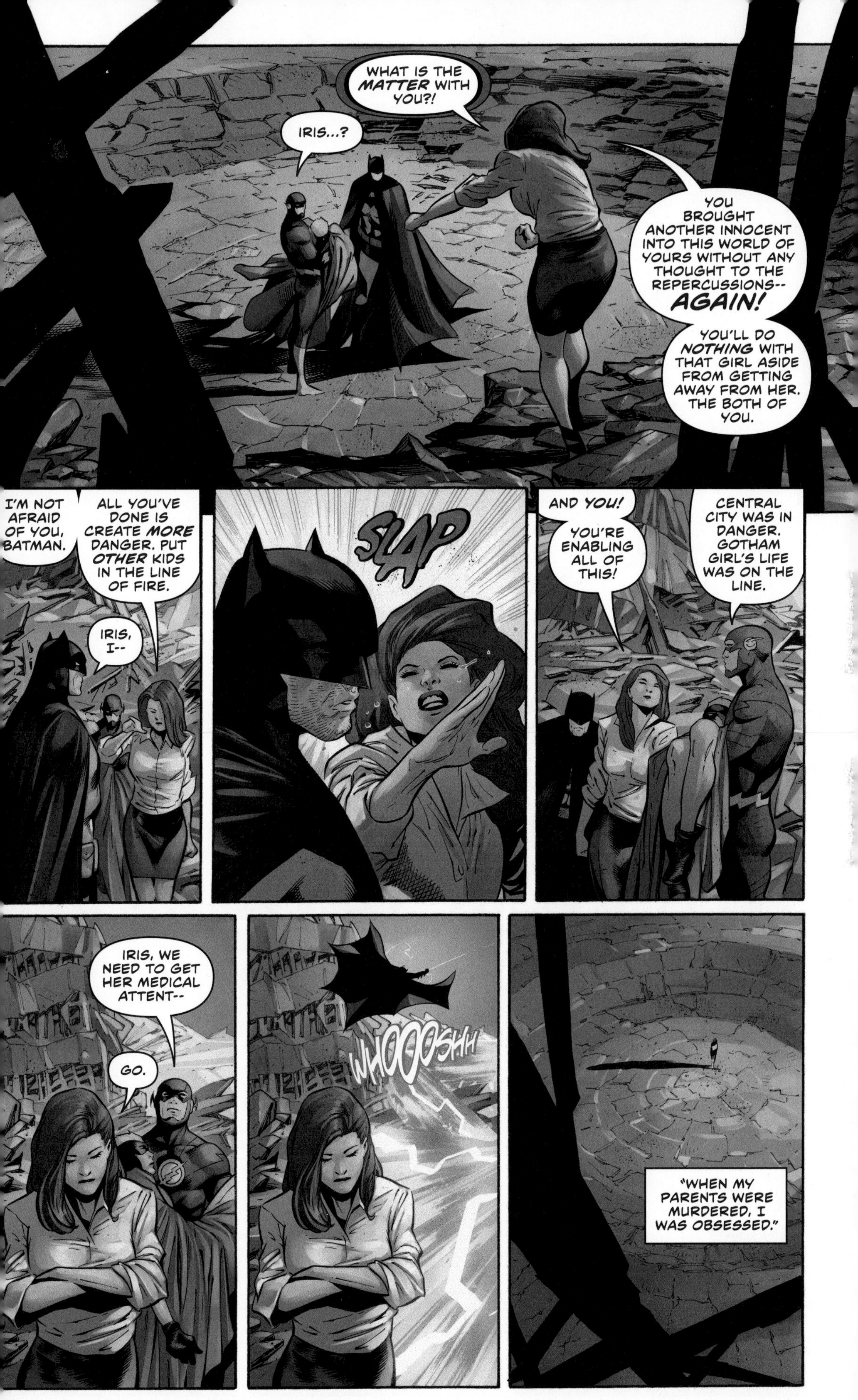

IRIS...?
WHAT IS THE MATTER WITH YOU?!
YOU BROUGHT ANOTHER INNOCENT INTO THIS WORLD OF YOURS WITHOUT ANY THOUGHT TO THE REPERCUSSIONS-- AGAIN!
YOU'LL DO NOTHING WITH THAT GIRL ASIDE FROM GETTING AWAY FROM HER. THE BOTH OF YOU.
I'M NOT AFRAID OF YOU, BATMAN.
ALL YOU'VE DONE IS CREATE MORE DANGER. PUT OTHER KIDS IN THE LINE OF FIRE.
IRIS, I--
SLAP
AND YOU!
YOU'RE ENABLING ALL OF THIS!
CENTRAL CITY WAS IN DANGER. GOTHAM GIRL'S LIFE WAS ON THE LINE.
IRIS, WE NEED TO GET HER MEDICAL ATTENT--
GO.
WHOOOSHH
"WHEN MY PARENTS WERE MURDERED, I WAS OBSESSED."

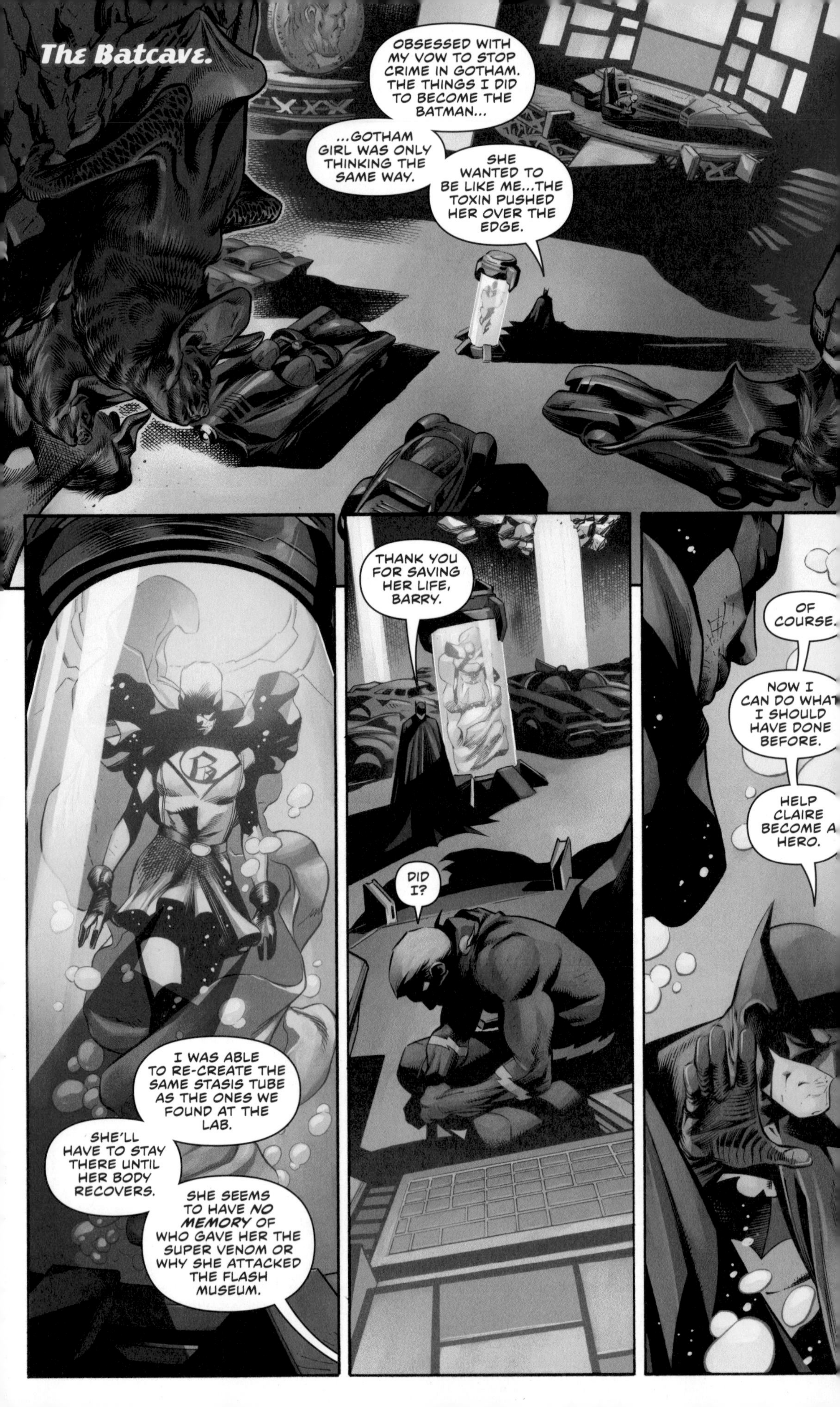

The Batcave.
OBSESSED WITH MY VOW TO STOP CRIME IN GOTHAM. THE THINGS I DID TO BECOME THE BATMAN...
...GOTHAM GIRL WAS ONLY THINKING THE SAME WAY.
SHE WANTED TO BE LIKE ME...THE TOXIN PUSHED HER OVER THE EDGE.
I WAS ABLE TO RE-CREATE THE SAME STASIS TUBE AS THE ONES WE FOUND AT THE LAB.
SHE'LL HAVE TO STAY THERE UNTIL HER BODY RECOVERS.
SHE SEEMS TO HAVE NO MEMORY OF WHO GAVE HER THE SUPER VENOM OR WHY SHE ATTACKED THE FLASH MUSEUM.
THANK YOU FOR SAVING HER LIFE, BARRY.
DID I?
OF COURSE.
NOW I CAN DO WHAT I SHOULD HAVE DONE BEFORE.
HELP CLAIRE BECOME A HERO.

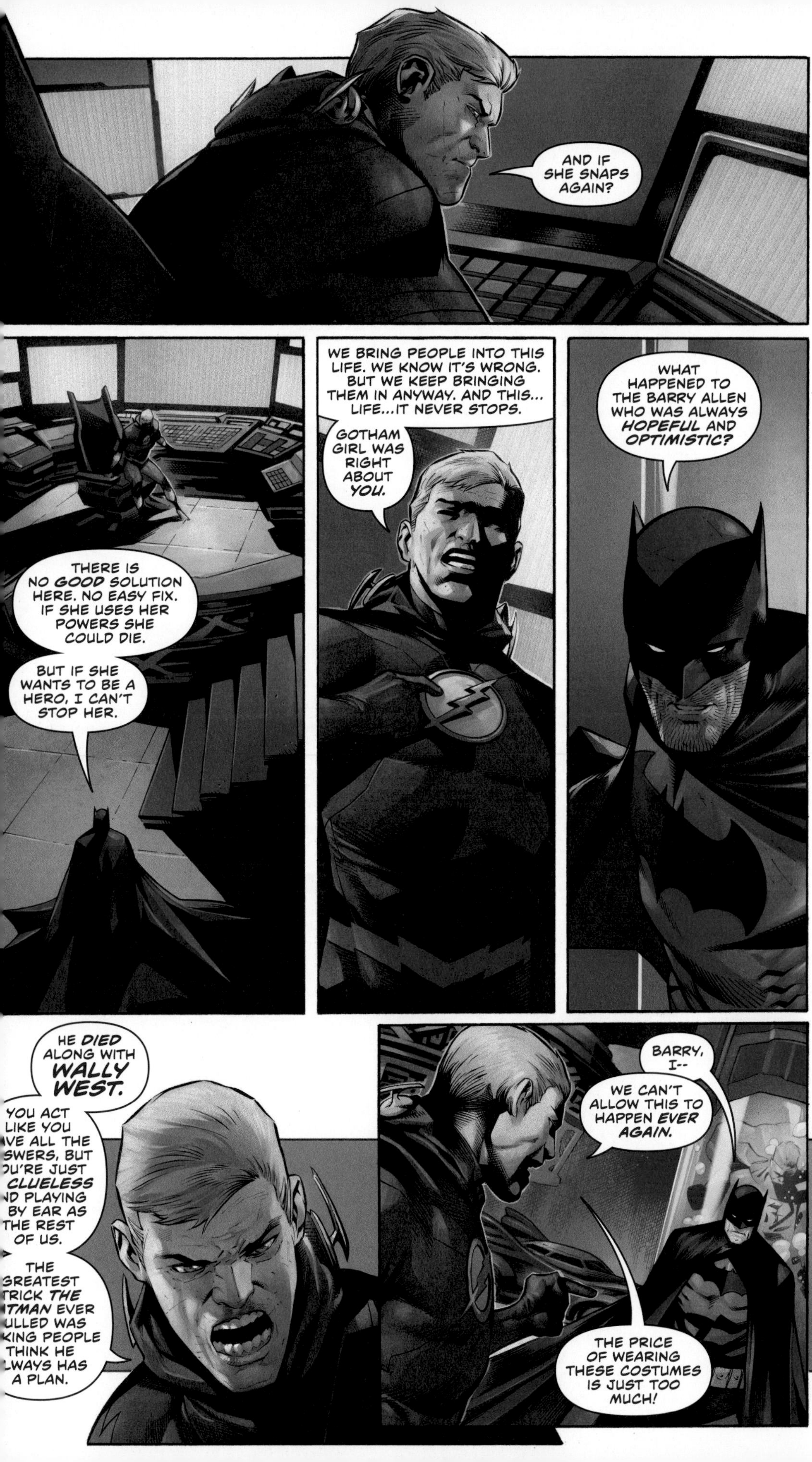
AND IF SHE SNAPS AGAIN?
THERE IS NO GOOD SOLUTION HERE. NO EASY FIX. IF SHE USES HER POWERS SHE COULD DIE.
BUT IF SHE WANTS TO BE A HERO, I CAN'T STOP HER.
WE BRING PEOPLE INTO THIS LIFE. WE KNOW IT'S WRONG. BUT WE KEEP BRINGING THEM IN ANYWAY. AND THIS... LIFE...IT NEVER STOPS.
GOTHAM GIRL WAS RIGHT ABOUT YOU.
WHAT HAPPENED TO THE BARRY ALLEN WHO WAS ALWAYS HOPEFUL AND OPTIMISTIC?
HE DIED ALONG WITH WALLY WEST.
YOU ACT LIKE YOU VE ALL THE SWERS, BUT U'RE JUST CLUELESS D PLAYING BY EAR AS THE REST OF US.
THE GREATEST TRICK THE TMAN EVER ULLED WAS KING PEOPLE THINK HE LWAYS HAS A PLAN.
BARRY, I--
WE CAN'T ALLOW THIS TO HAPPEN EVER AGAIN.
THE PRICE OF WEARING THESE COSTUMES IS JUST TOO MUCH!

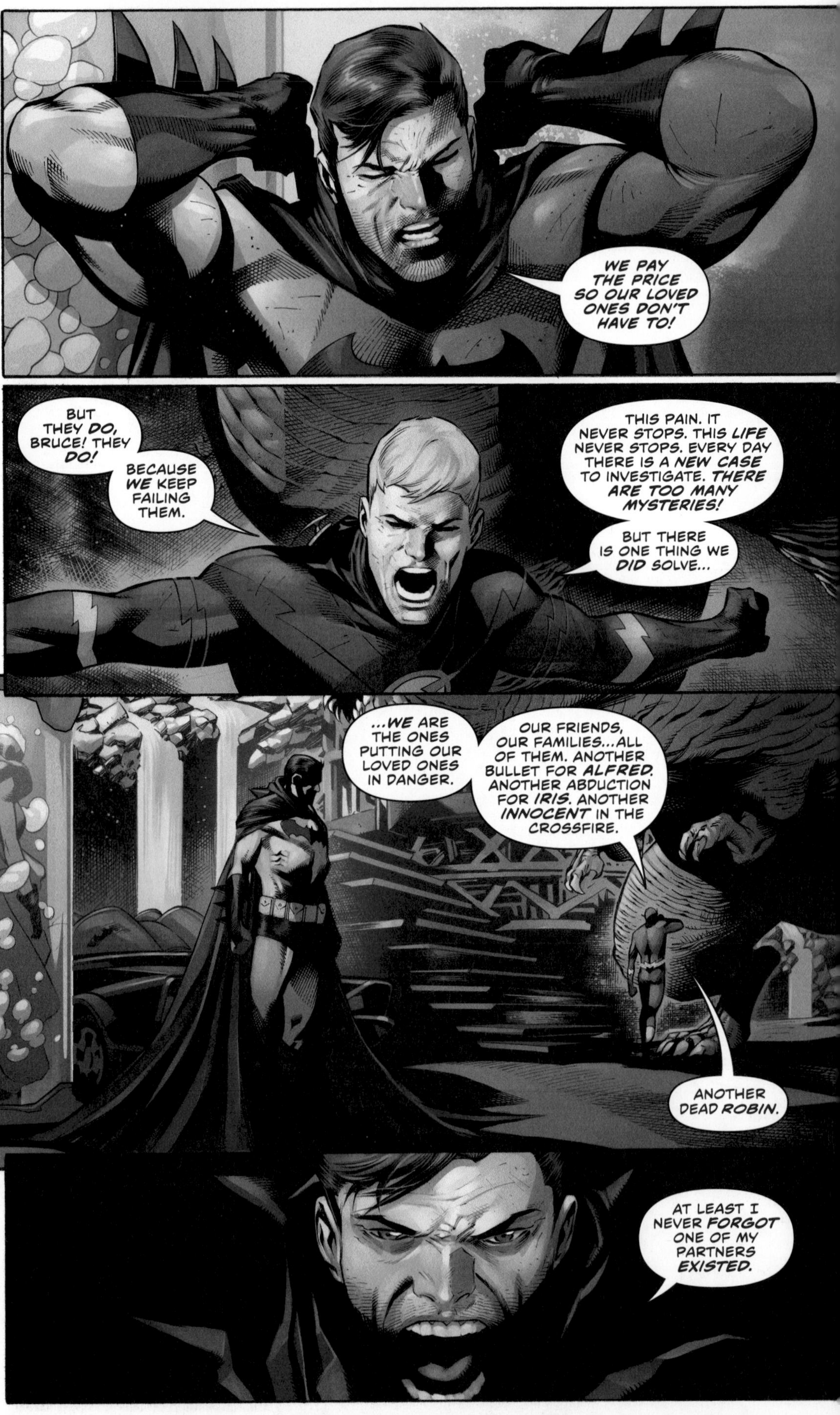
WE PAY THE PRICE SO OUR LOVED ONES DON'T HAVE TO!
BUT THEY DO, BRUCE! THEY DO!
BECAUSE WE KEEP FAILING THEM.
THIS PAIN. IT NEVER STOPS. THIS LIFE NEVER STOPS. EVERY DAY THERE IS A NEW CASE TO INVESTIGATE. THERE ARE TOO MANY MYSTERIES!
BUT THERE IS ONE THING WE DID SOLVE...
...WE ARE THE ONES PUTTING OUR LOVED ONES IN DANGER.
OUR FRIENDS, OUR FAMILIES...ALL OF THEM. ANOTHER BULLET FOR ALFRED. ANOTHER ABDUCTION FOR IRIS. ANOTHER INNOCENT IN THE CROSSFIRE.
ANOTHER DEAD ROBIN.
AT LEAST I NEVER FORGOT ONE OF MY PARTNERS EXISTED.

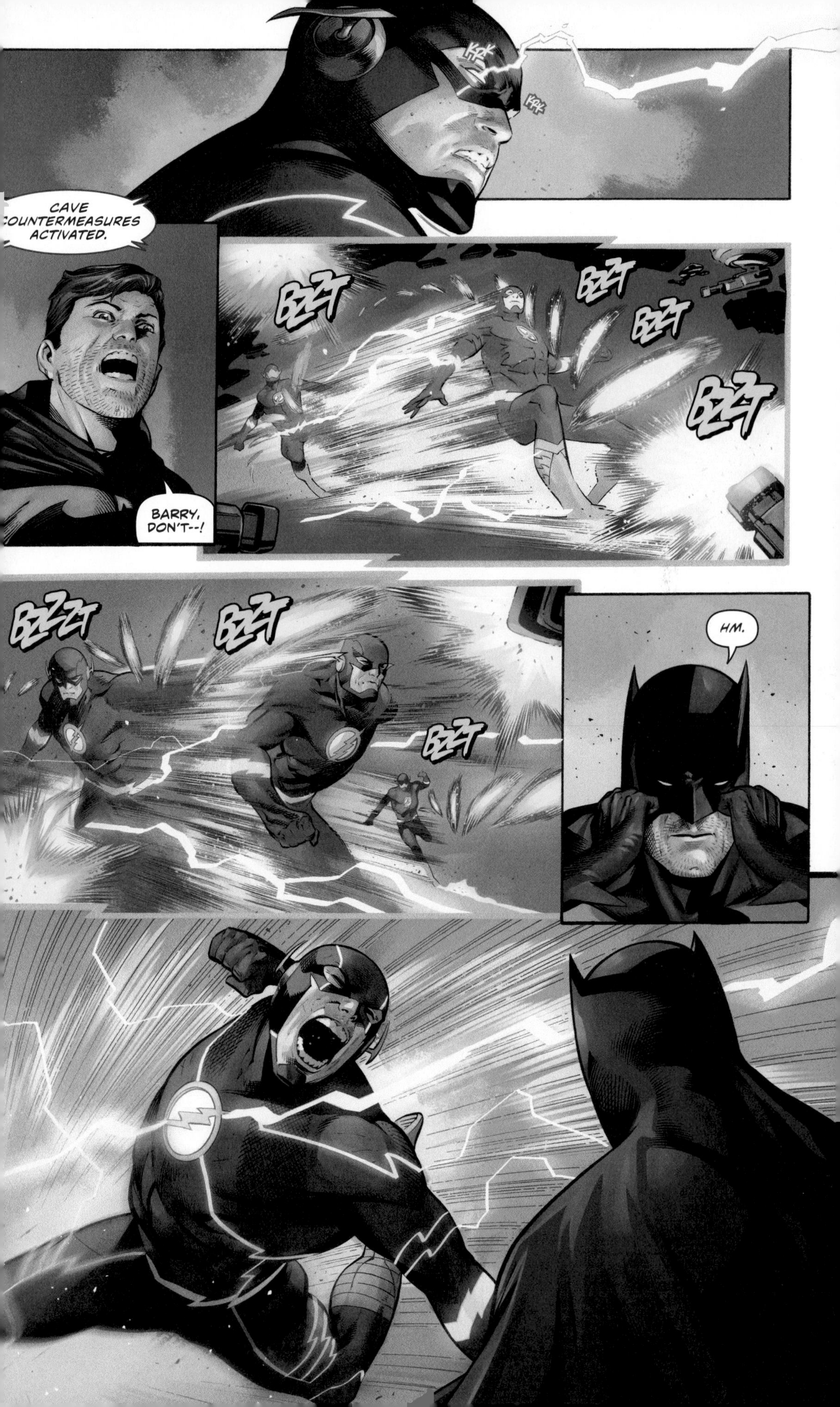
KRK
KRK
CAVE COUNTERMEASURES ACTIVATED.
BARRY, DON'T--!
BZZT
BZZT
BZZT
BZZT
BZZZT
BZZT
BZZT
HM.

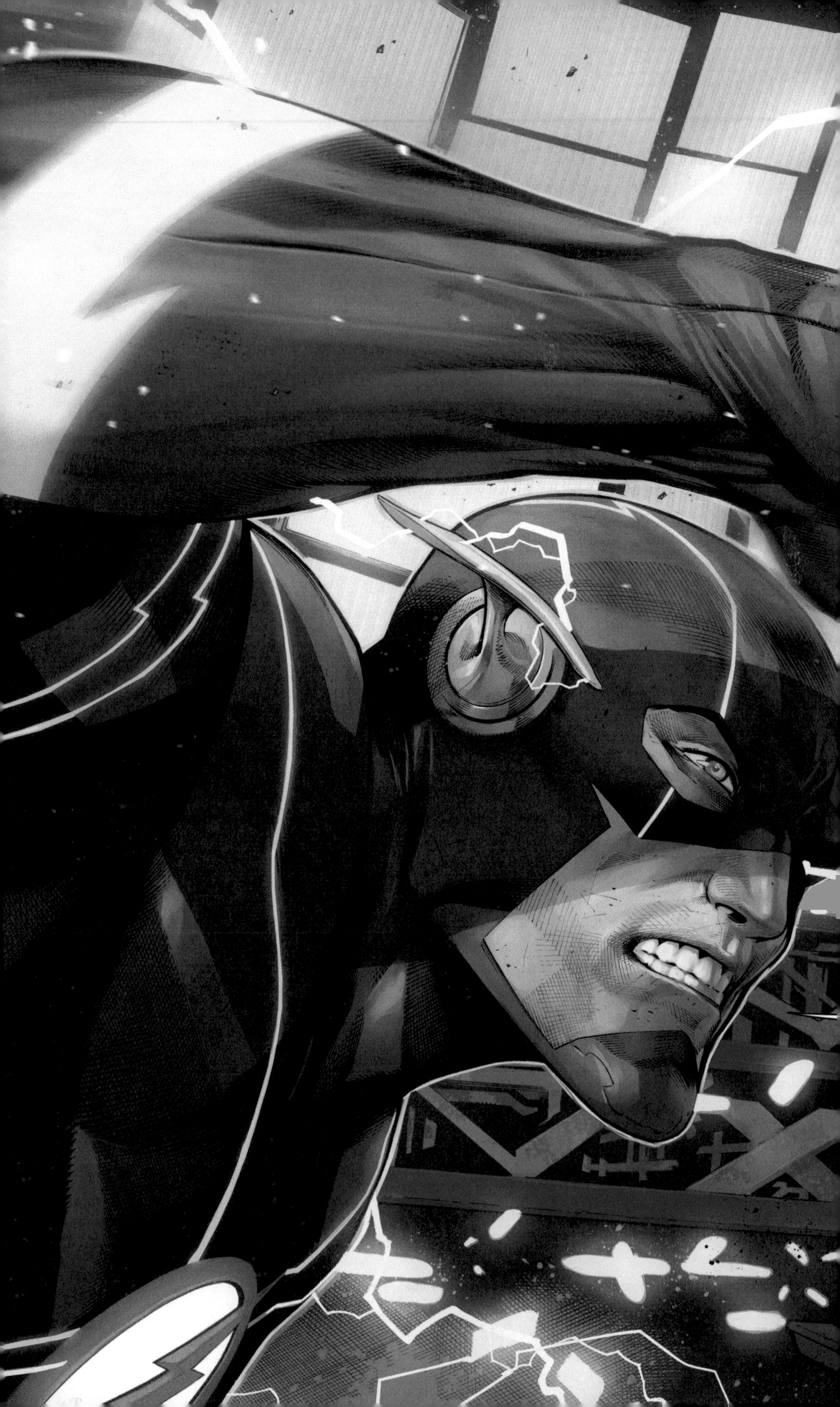

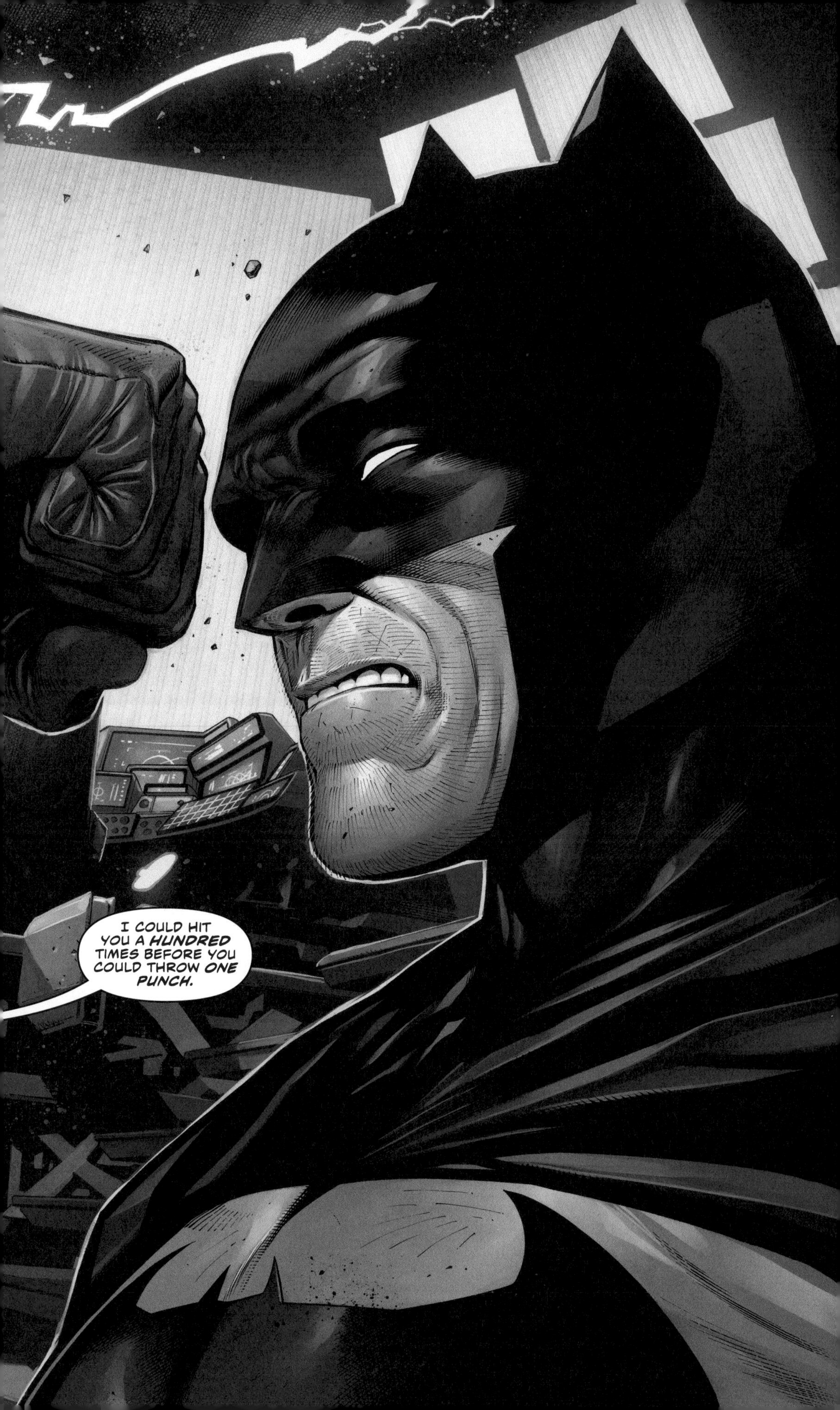
I COULD HIT YOU A *HUNDRED* TIMES BEFORE YOU COULD THROW *ONE PUNCH.*

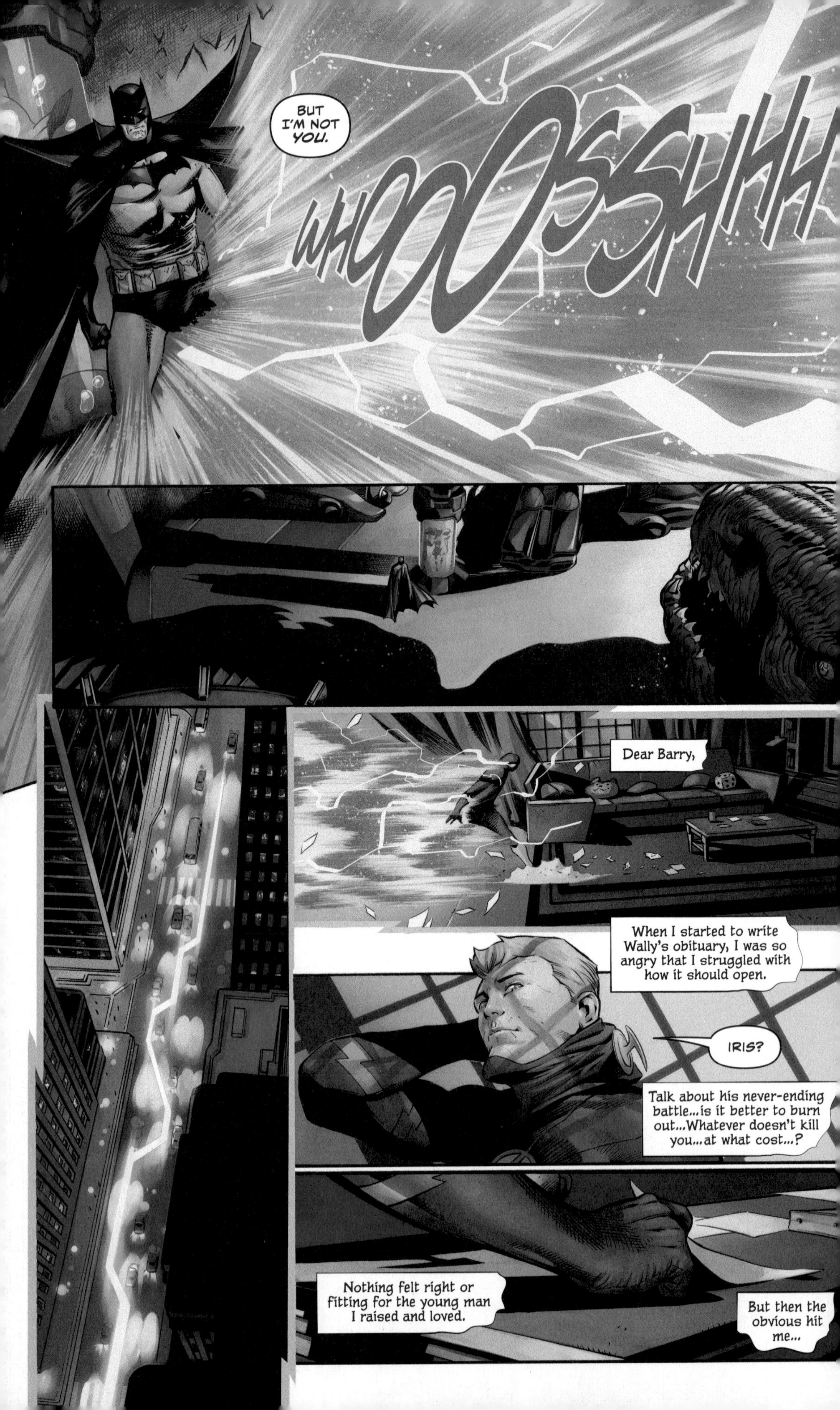

BUT I'M NOT YOU.
WHOOOSSHHH
Dear Barry,
When I started to write Wally's obituary, I was so angry that I struggled with how it should open.
IRIS?
Talk about his never-ending battle...is it better to burn out...Whatever doesn't kill you...at what cost...?
Nothing felt right or fitting for the young man I raised and loved.
But then the obvious hit me...

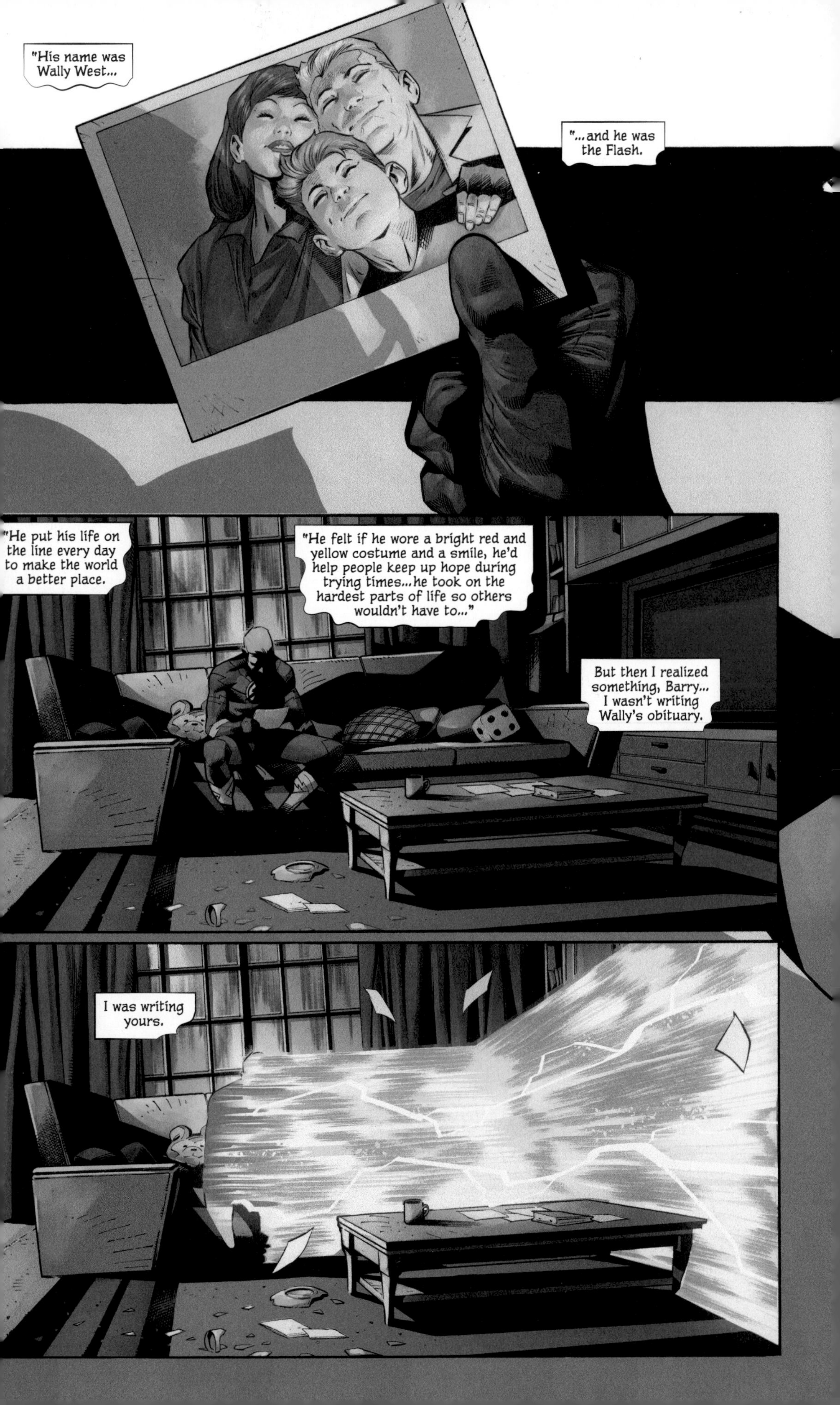
"His name was Wally West...
"...and he was the Flash.
"He put his life on the line every day to make the world a better place.
"He felt if he wore a bright red and yellow costume and a smile, he'd help people keep up hope during trying times...he took on the hardest parts of life so others wouldn't have to..."
But then I realized something, Barry... I wasn't writing Wally's obituary.
I was writing yours.

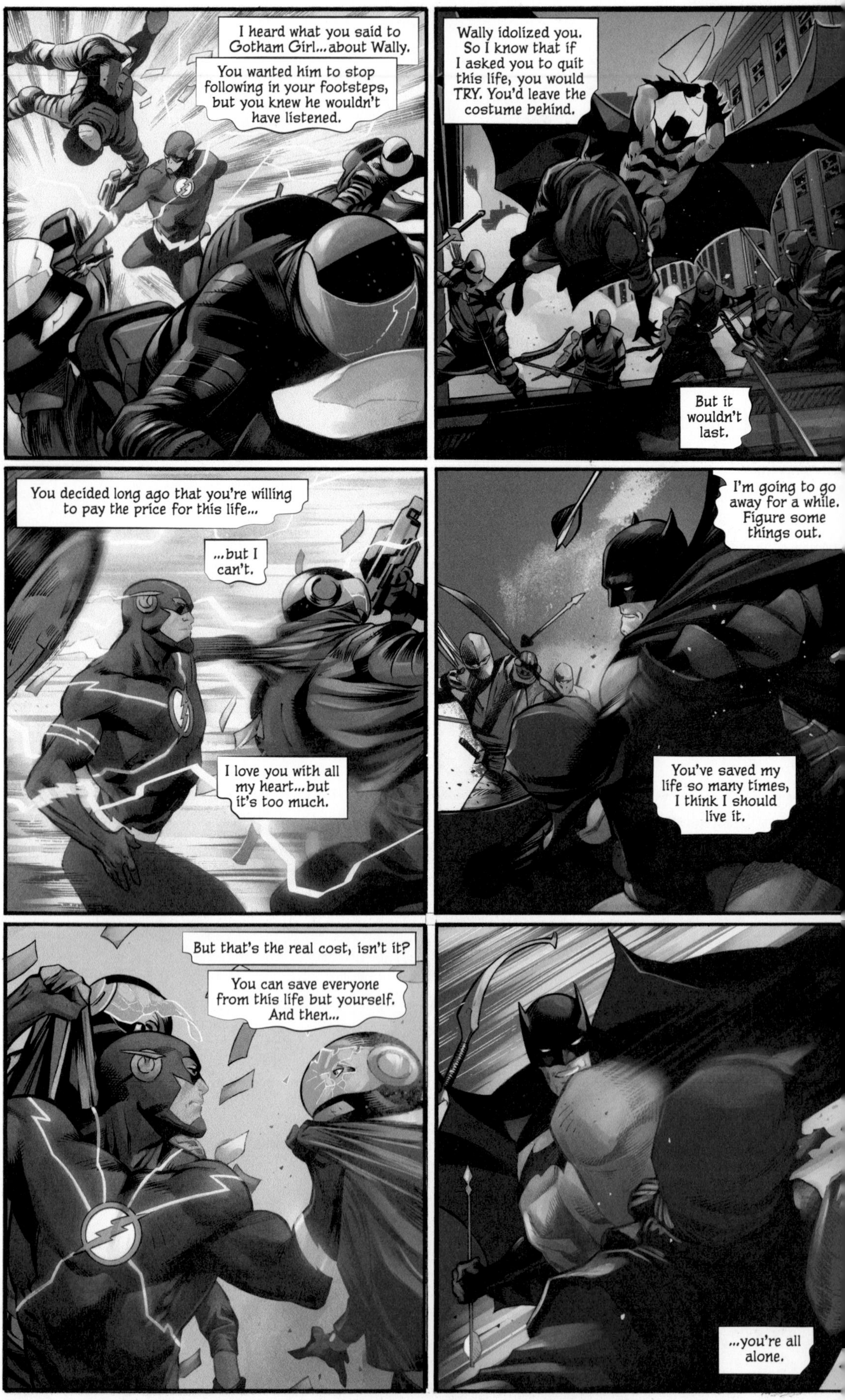
I heard what you said to Gotham Girl... about Wally.
You wanted him to stop following in your footsteps, but you knew he wouldn't have listened.
Wally idolized you. So I know that if I asked you to quit this life, you would TRY. You'd leave the costume behind.
But it wouldn't last.
You decided long ago that you're willing to pay the price for this life...
...but I can't.
I love you with all my heart... but it's too much.
I'm going to go away for a while. Figure some things out.
You've saved my life so many times, I think I should live it.
But that's the real cost, isn't it?
You can save everyone from this life but yourself. And then...
...you're all alone.

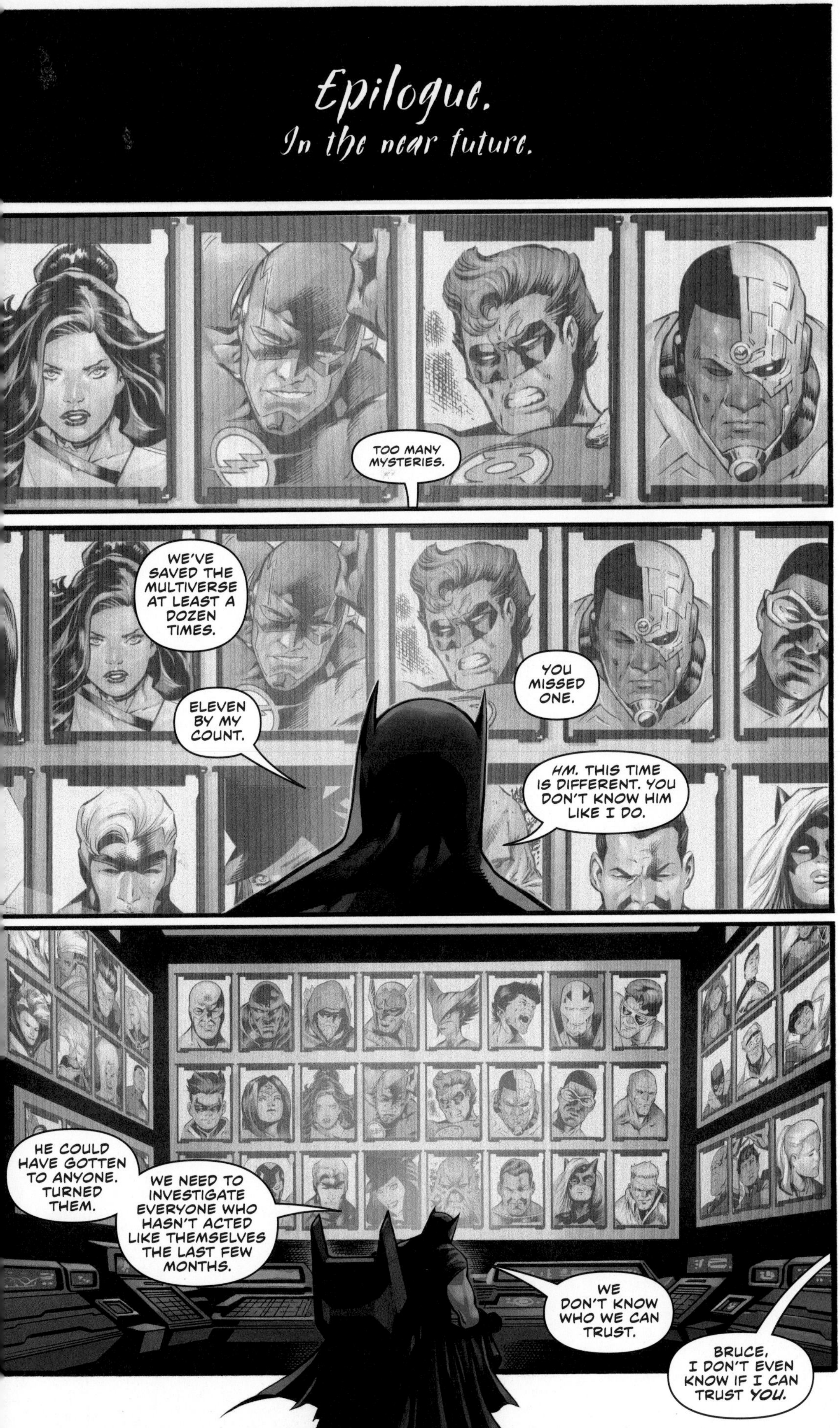
Epilogue.
In the near future.
TOO MANY MYSTERIES.
WE'VE SAVED THE MULTIVERSE AT LEAST A DOZEN TIMES.
ELEVEN BY MY COUNT.
YOU MISSED ONE.
HM. THIS TIME IS DIFFERENT. YOU DON'T KNOW HIM LIKE I DO.
HE COULD HAVE GOTTEN TO ANYONE. TURNED THEM.
WE NEED TO INVESTIGATE EVERYONE WHO HASN'T ACTED LIKE THEMSELVES THE LAST FEW MONTHS.
WE DON'T KNOW WHO WE CAN TRUST.
BRUCE, I DON'T EVEN KNOW IF I CAN TRUST *YOU*.

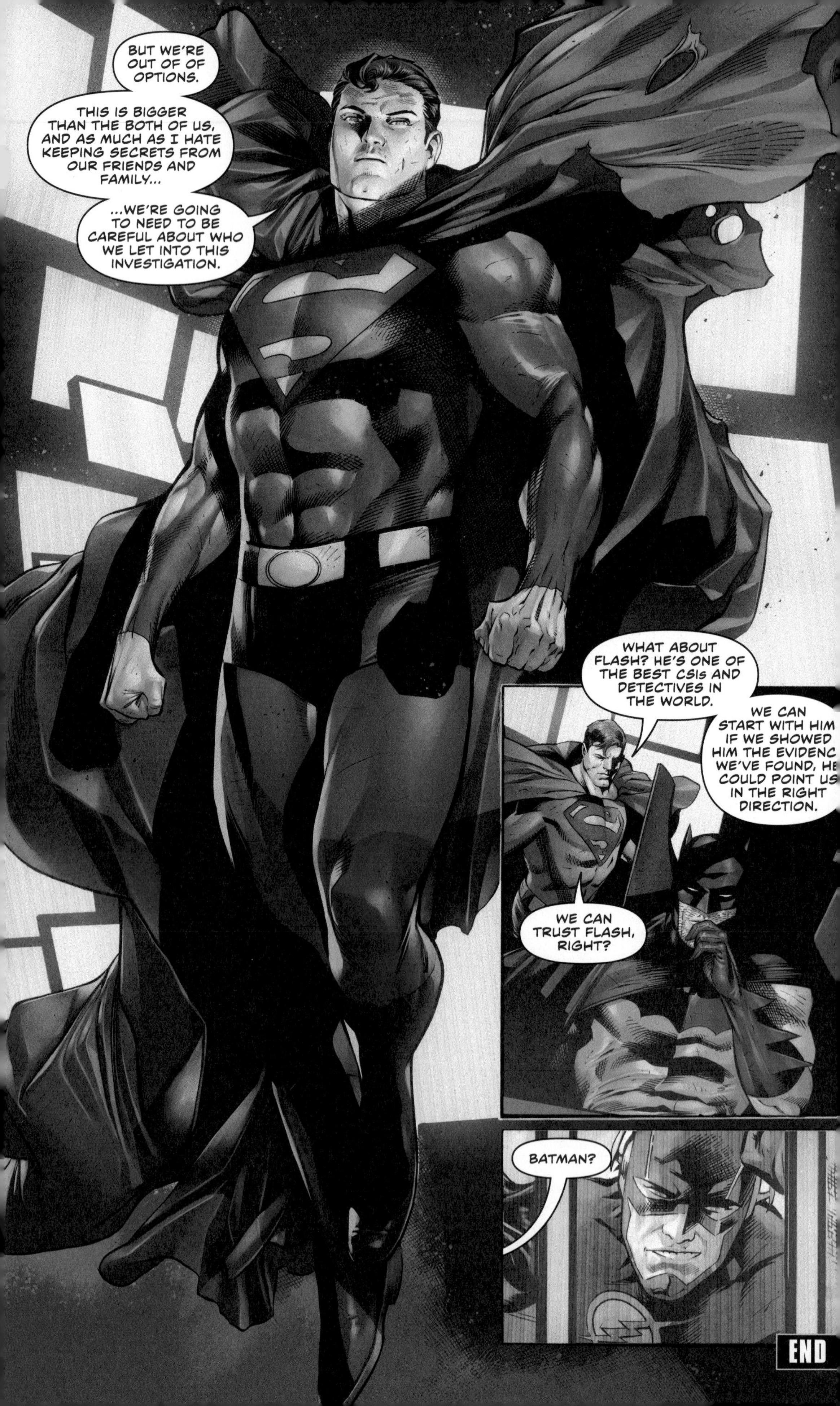
BUT WE'RE OUT OF OF OPTIONS.
THIS IS BIGGER THAN THE BOTH OF US, AND AS MUCH AS I HATE KEEPING SECRETS FROM OUR FRIENDS AND FAMILY...
...WE'RE GOING TO NEED TO BE CAREFUL ABOUT WHO WE LET INTO THIS INVESTIGATION.
WHAT ABOUT FLASH? HE'S ONE OF THE BEST CSIs AND DETECTIVES IN THE WORLD.
WE CAN START WITH HIM IF WE SHOWED HIM THE EVIDENC WE'VE FOUND, HE COULD POINT US IN THE RIGHT DIRECTION.
WE CAN TRUST FLASH, RIGHT?
BATMAN?
END

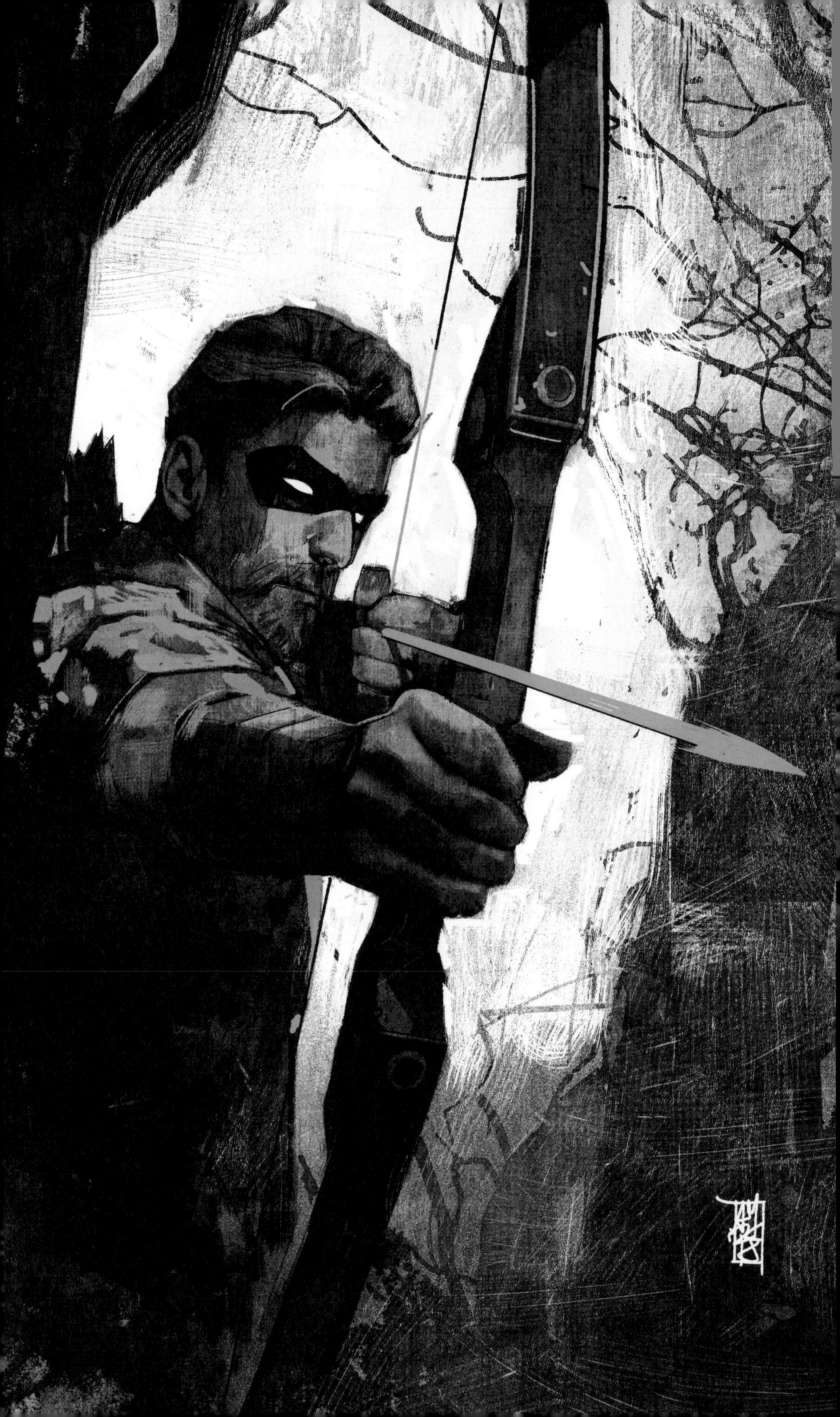

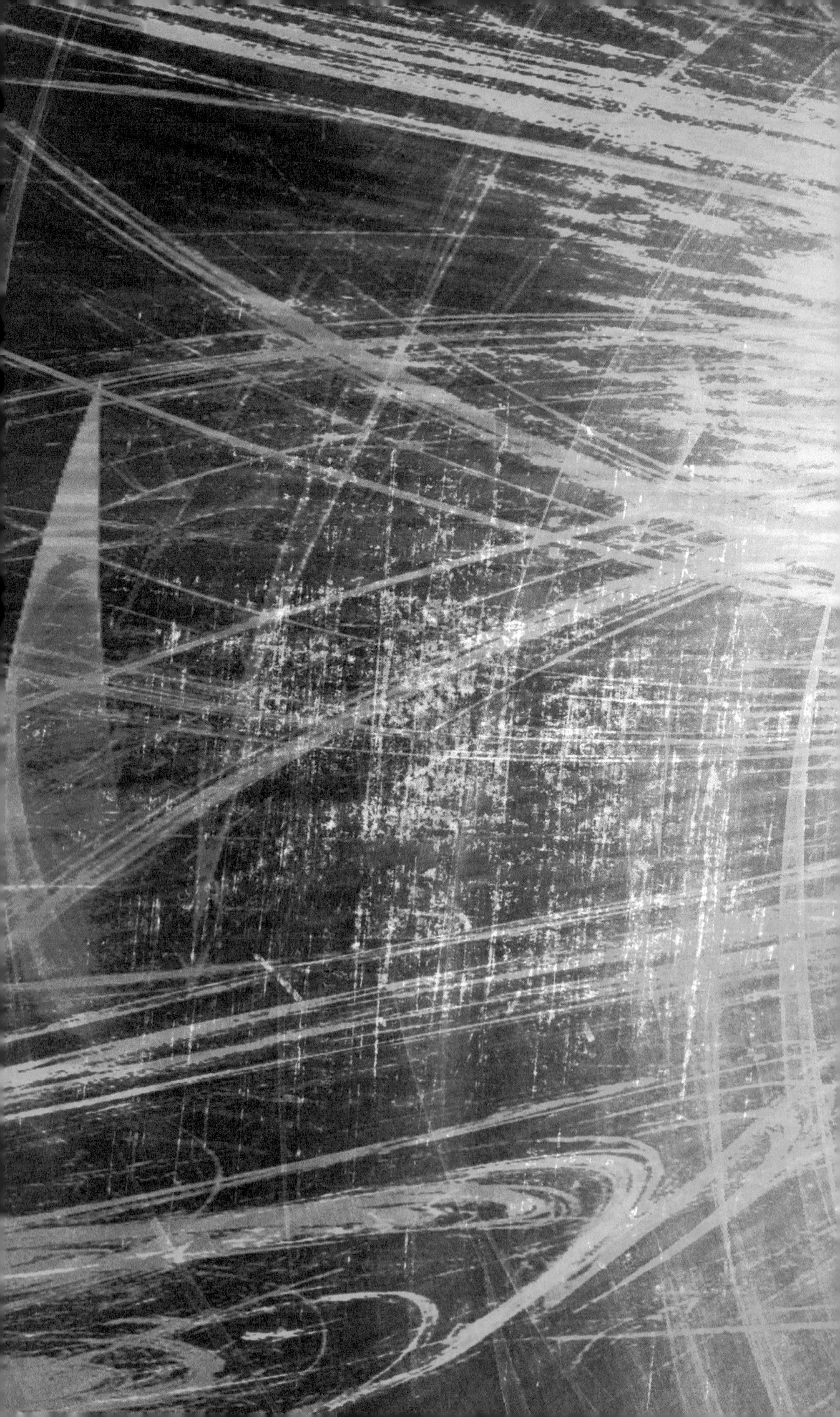

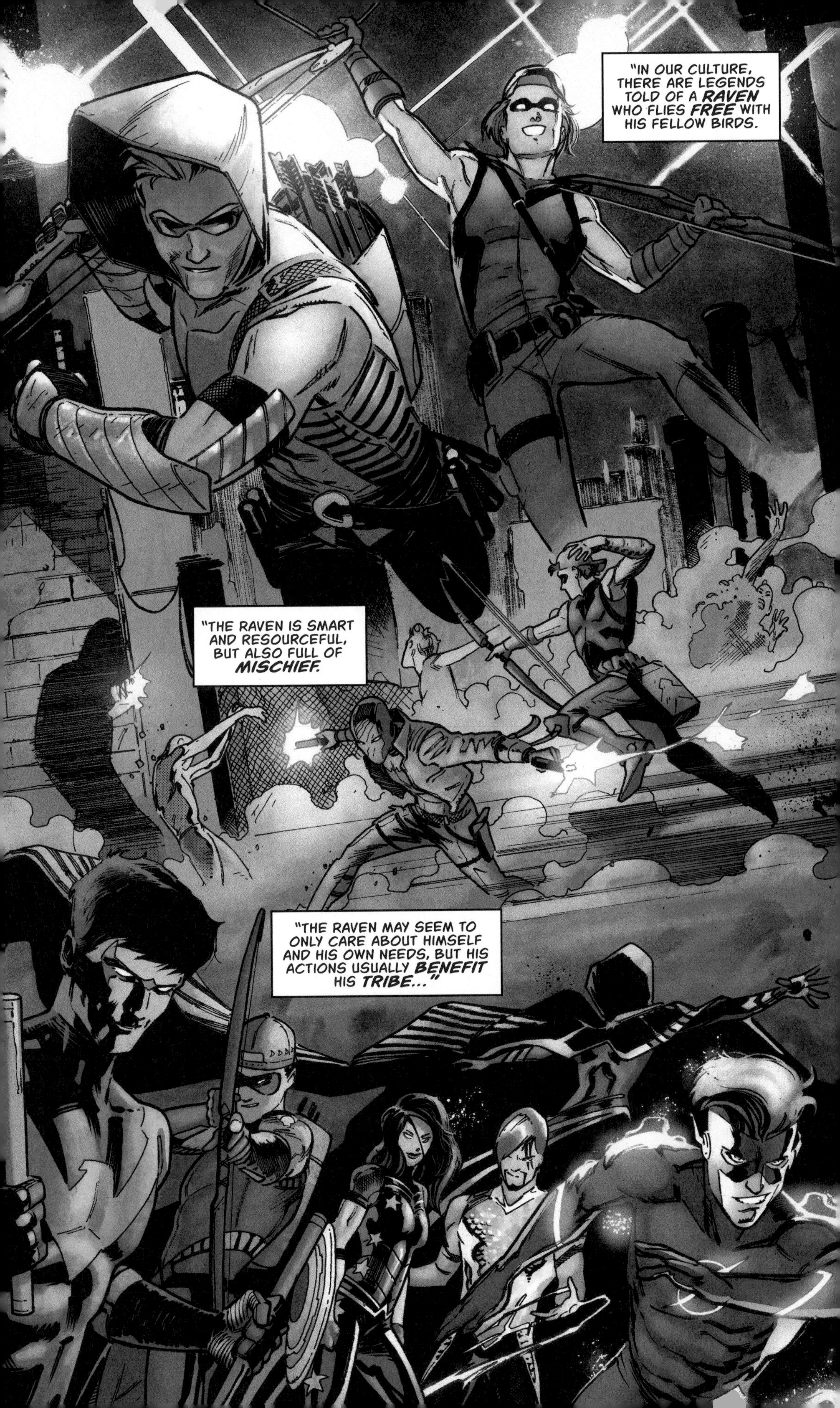
"IN OUR CULTURE, THERE ARE LEGENDS TOLD OF A RAVEN WHO FLIES FREE WITH HIS FELLOW BIRDS.
"THE RAVEN IS SMART AND RESOURCEFUL, BUT ALSO FULL OF MISCHIEF.
"THE RAVEN MAY SEEM TO ONLY CARE ABOUT HIMSELF AND HIS OWN NEEDS, BUT HIS ACTIONS USUALLY BENEFIT HIS TRIBE..."

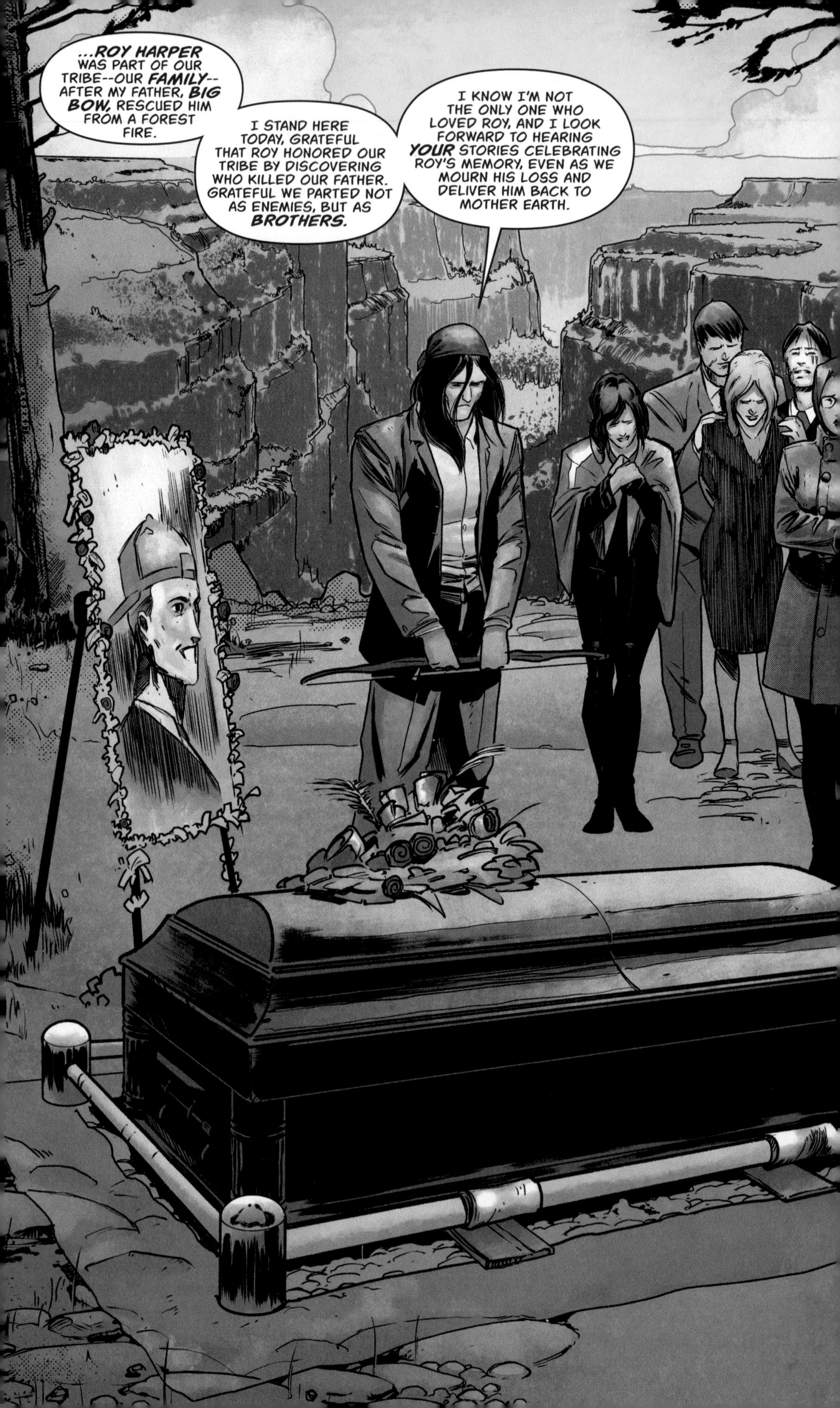
...ROY HARPER WAS PART OF OUR TRIBE--OUR FAMILY--AFTER MY FATHER, BIG BOW, RESCUED HIM FROM A FOREST FIRE.
I STAND HERE TODAY, GRATEFUL THAT ROY HONORED OUR TRIBE BY DISCOVERING WHO KILLED OUR FATHER. GRATEFUL WE PARTED NOT AS ENEMIES, BUT AS BROTHERS.
I KNOW I'M NOT THE ONLY ONE WHO LOVED ROY, AND I LOOK FORWARD TO HEARING YOUR STORIES CELEBRATING ROY'S MEMORY, EVEN AS WE MOURN HIS LOSS AND DELIVER HIM BACK TO MOTHER EARTH.

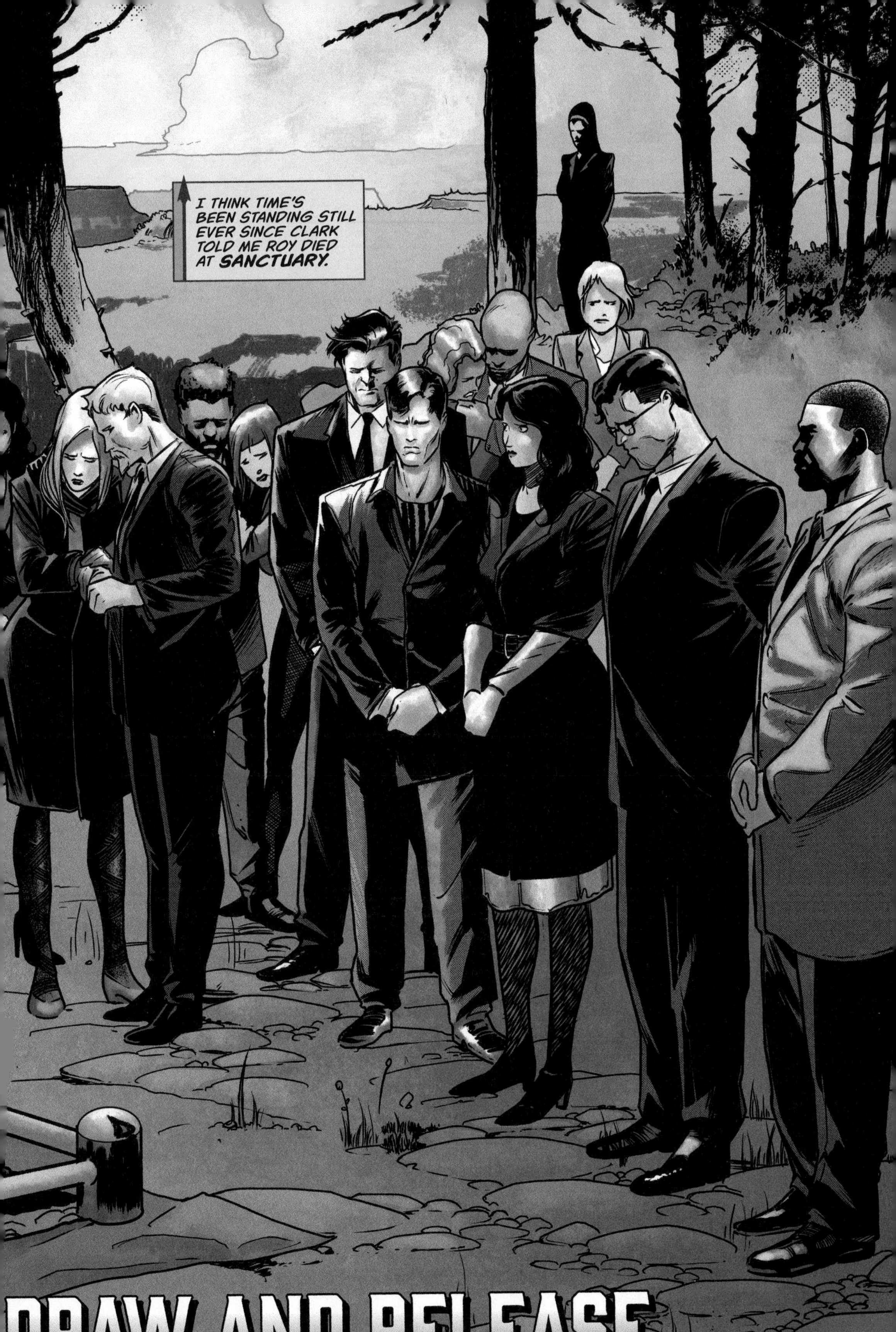
I THINK TIME'S BEEN STANDING STILL EVER SINCE CLARK TOLD ME ROY DIED AT SANCTUARY.

DRAW AND RELEASE

JULIE BENSON & SHAWNA BENSON Writers • JAVIER FERNANDEZ Artist
JOHN KALISZ Colors • DERON BENNETT Letters • ALEX MALEEV Cover
DAVE WIELGOSZ Asst. Editor • KATIE KUBERT Editor • JAMIE S. RICH Group Editor

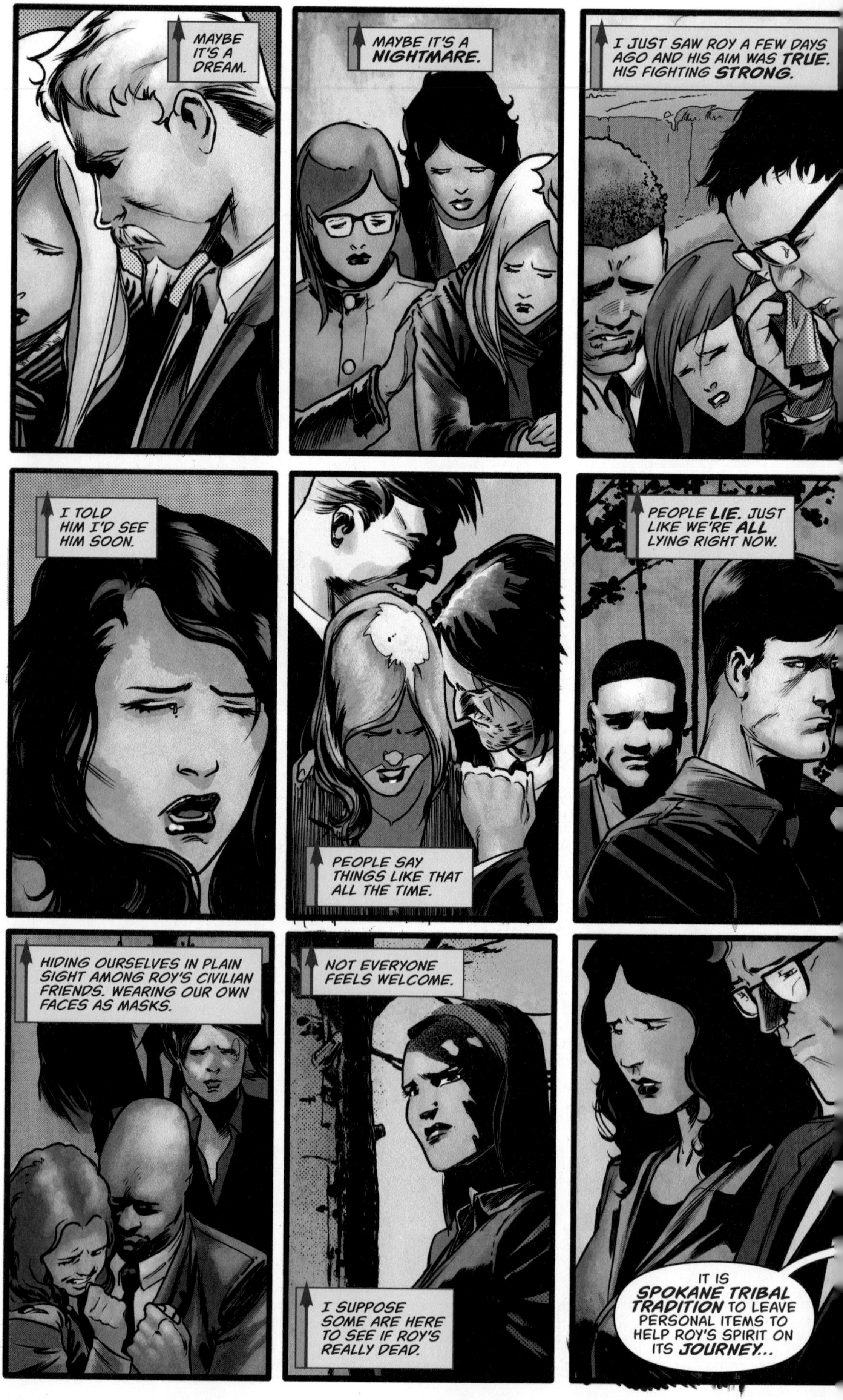
MAYBE IT'S A DREAM.
MAYBE IT'S A NIGHTMARE.
I JUST SAW ROY A FEW DAYS AGO AND HIS AIM WAS TRUE. HIS FIGHTING STRONG.
I TOLD HIM I'D SEE HIM SOON.
PEOPLE SAY THINGS LIKE THAT ALL THE TIME.
PEOPLE LIE. JUST LIKE WE'RE ALL LYING RIGHT NOW.
HIDING OURSELVES IN PLAIN SIGHT AMONG ROY'S CIVILIAN FRIENDS. WEARING OUR OWN FACES AS MASKS.
NOT EVERYONE FEELS WELCOME.
I SUPPOSE SOME ARE HERE TO SEE IF ROY'S REALLY DEAD.
IT IS SPOKANE TRIBAL TRADITION TO LEAVE PERSONAL ITEMS TO HELP ROY'S SPIRIT ON ITS JOURNEY...

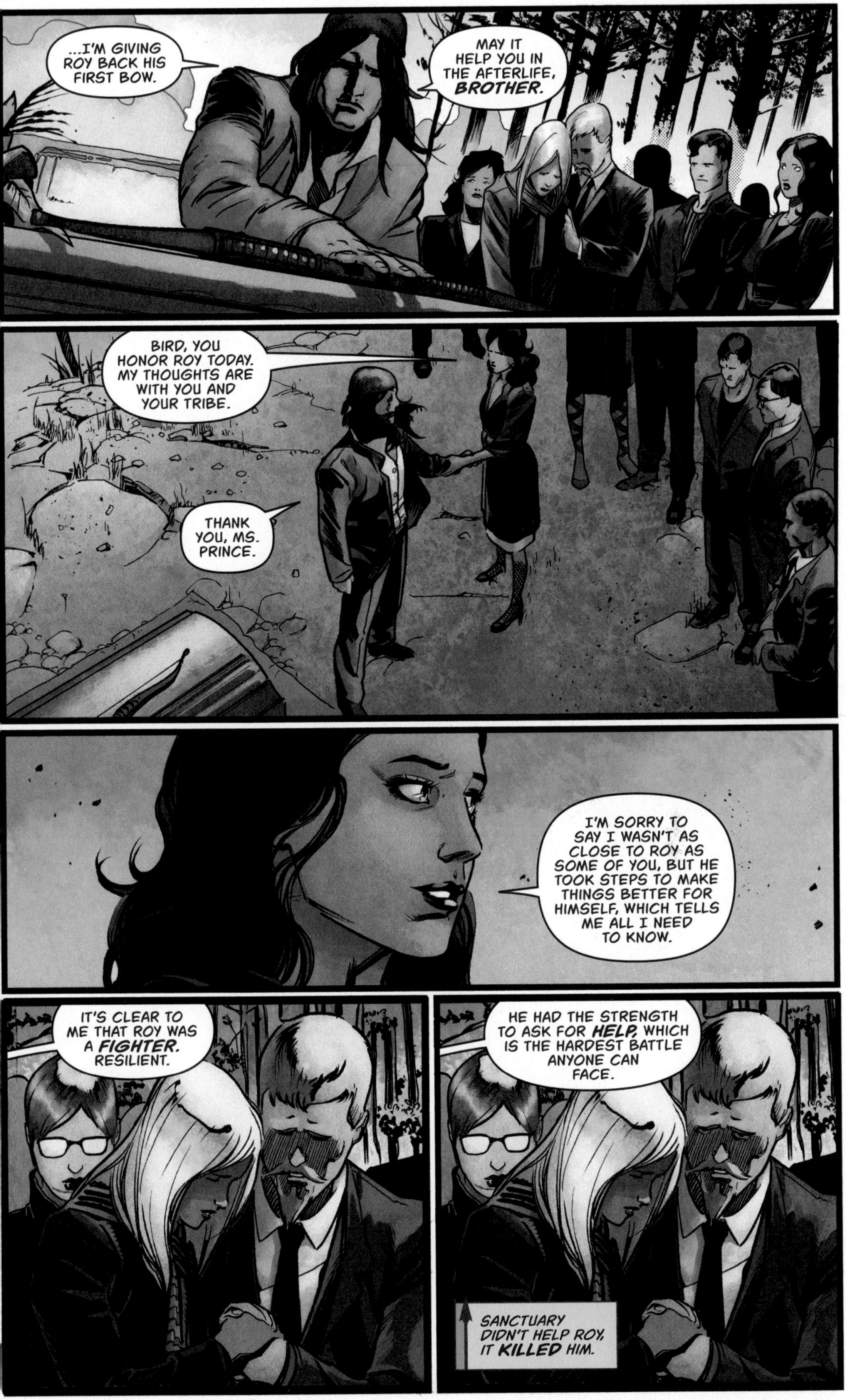

...I'M GIVING ROY BACK HIS FIRST BOW.
MAY IT HELP YOU IN THE AFTERLIFE, BROTHER.
BIRD, YOU HONOR ROY TODAY. MY THOUGHTS ARE WITH YOU AND YOUR TRIBE.
THANK YOU, MS. PRINCE.
I'M SORRY TO SAY I WASN'T AS CLOSE TO ROY AS SOME OF YOU, BUT HE TOOK STEPS TO MAKE THINGS BETTER FOR HIMSELF, WHICH TELLS ME ALL I NEED TO KNOW.
IT'S CLEAR TO ME THAT ROY WAS A FIGHTER. RESILIENT.
HE HAD THE STRENGTH TO ASK FOR HELP, WHICH IS THE HARDEST BATTLE ANYONE CAN FACE.
SANCTUARY DIDN'T HELP ROY, IT KILLED HIM.

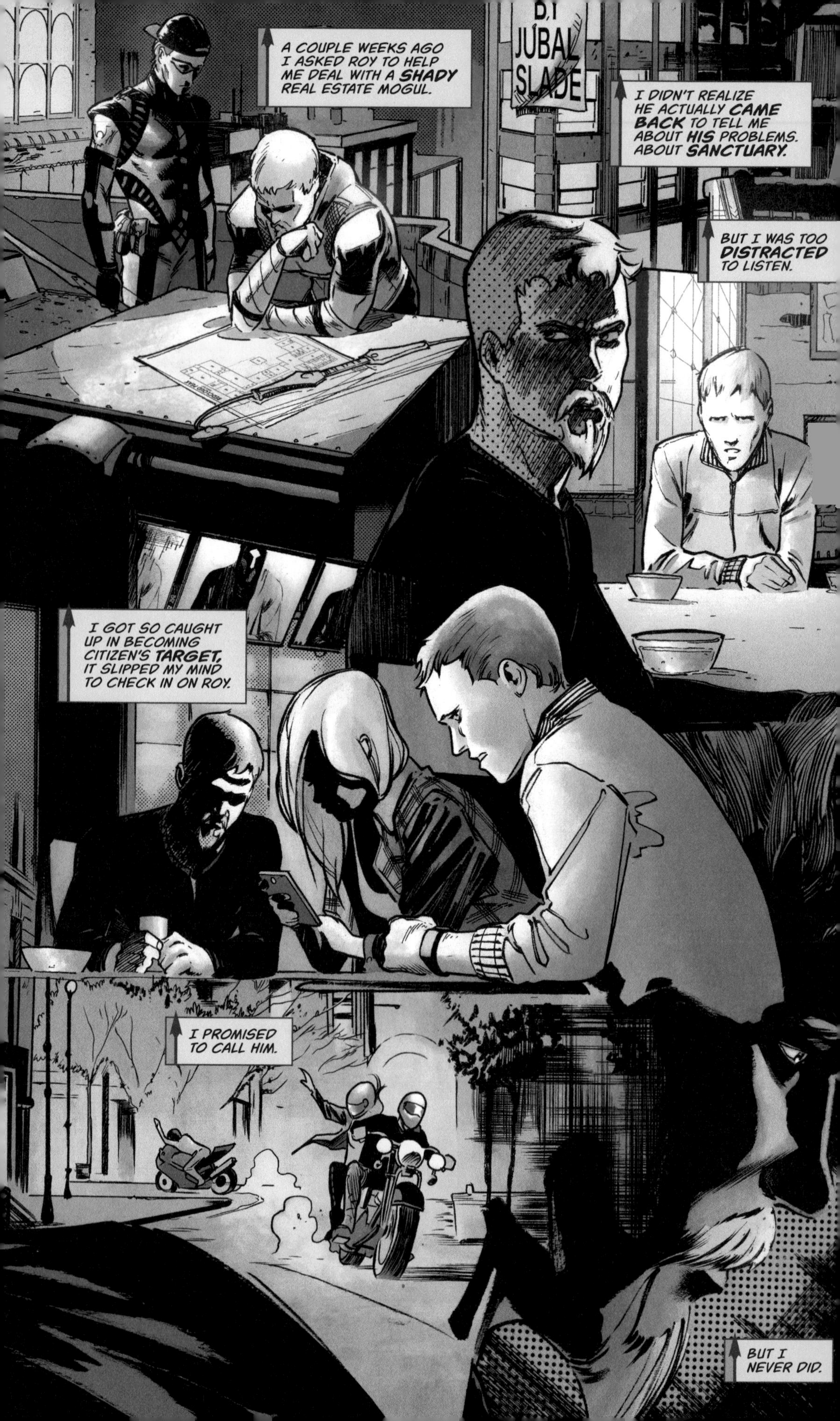

D.I
JUBAL
SLADE
A COUPLE WEEKS AGO I ASKED ROY TO HELP ME DEAL WITH A **SHADY** REAL ESTATE MOGUL.
I DIDN'T REALIZE HE ACTUALLY **CAME BACK** TO TELL ME ABOUT **HIS** PROBLEMS. ABOUT **SANCTUARY.**
BUT I WAS TOO **DISTRACTED** TO LISTEN.
I GOT SO CAUGHT UP IN BECOMING CITIZEN'S **TARGET,** IT SLIPPED MY MIND TO CHECK IN ON ROY.
I PROMISED TO CALL HIM.
BUT I NEVER DID.

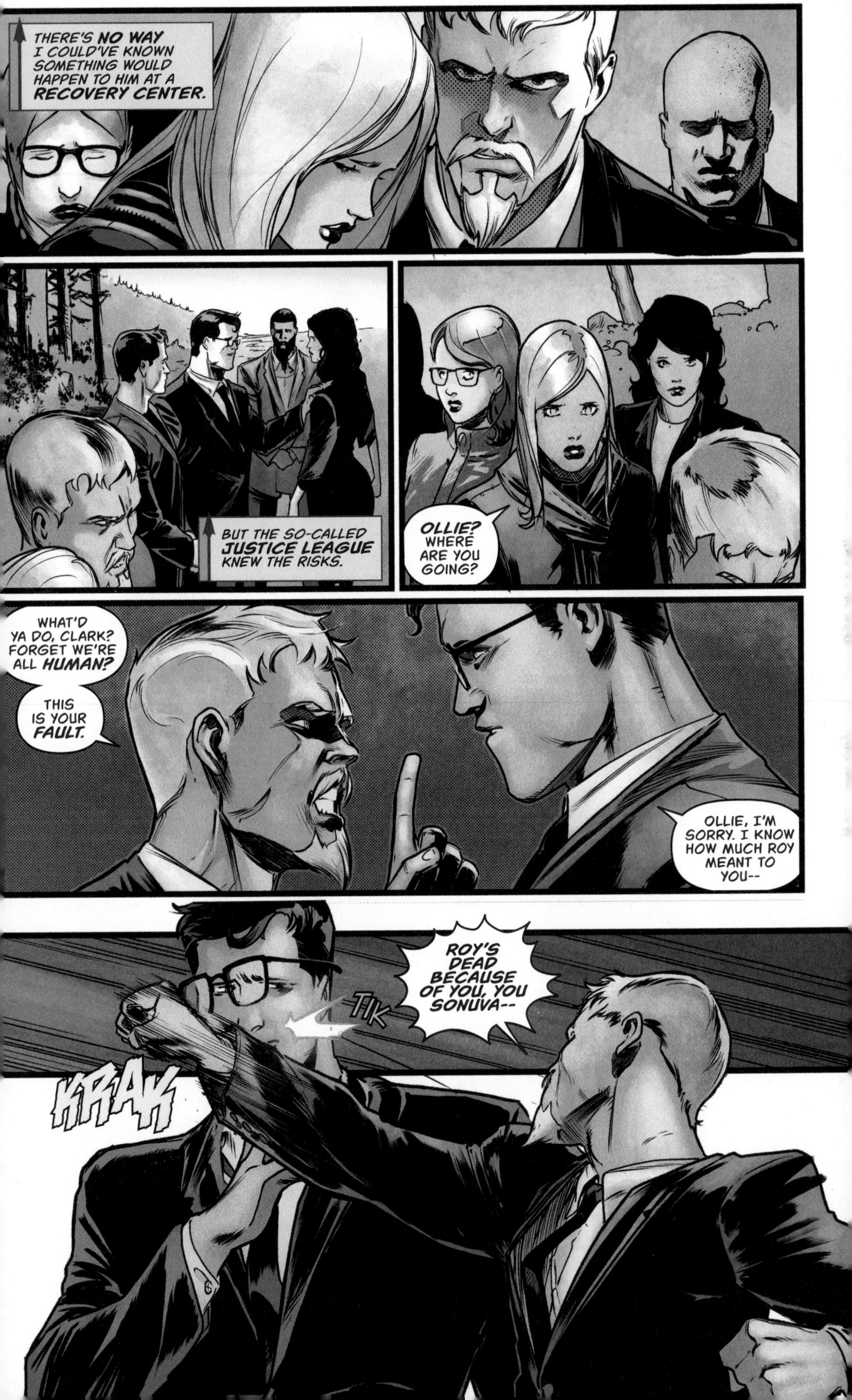
THERE'S NO WAY I COULD'VE KNOWN SOMETHING WOULD HAPPEN TO HIM AT A RECOVERY CENTER.
BUT THE SO-CALLED JUSTICE LEAGUE KNEW THE RISKS.
OLLIE? WHERE ARE YOU GOING?
WHAT'D YA DO, CLARK? FORGET WE'RE ALL HUMAN?
THIS IS YOUR FAULT.
OLLIE, I'M SORRY. I KNOW HOW MUCH ROY MEANT TO YOU--
ROY'S DEAD BECAUSE OF YOU, YOU SONUVA--
TIK
KRAK

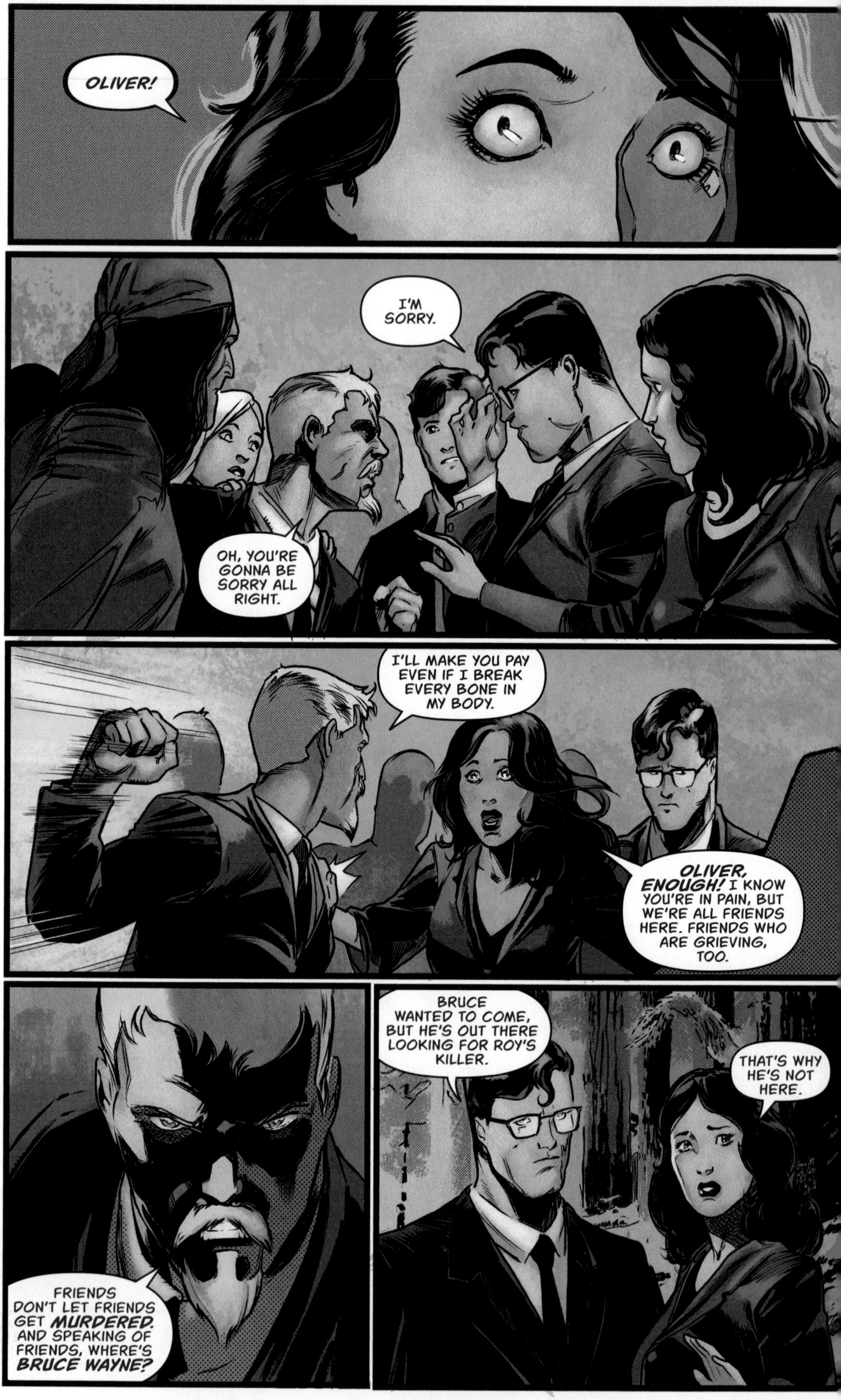
OLIVER!
I'M SORRY.
OH, YOU'RE GONNA BE SORRY ALL RIGHT.
I'LL MAKE YOU PAY EVEN IF I BREAK EVERY BONE IN MY BODY.
OLIVER, ENOUGH! I KNOW YOU'RE IN PAIN, BUT WE'RE ALL FRIENDS HERE. FRIENDS WHO ARE GRIEVING, TOO.
FRIENDS DON'T LET FRIENDS GET MURDERED. AND SPEAKING OF FRIENDS, WHERE'S BRUCE WAYNE?
BRUCE WANTED TO COME, BUT HE'S OUT THERE LOOKING FOR ROY'S KILLER.
THAT'S WHY HE'S NOT HERE.

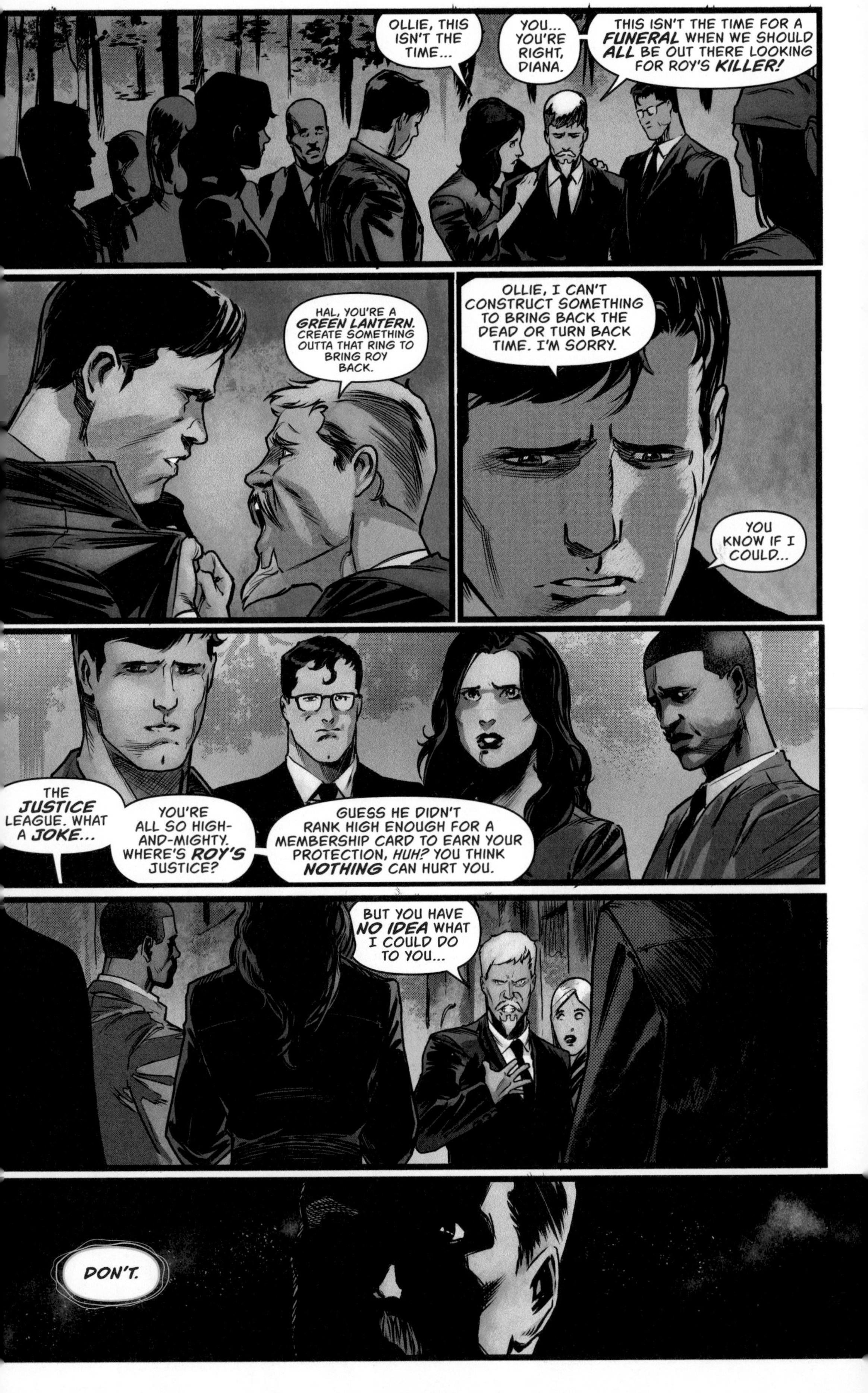

OLLIE, THIS ISN'T THE TIME...
YOU... YOU'RE RIGHT, DIANA.
THIS ISN'T THE TIME FOR A FUNERAL WHEN WE SHOULD ALL BE OUT THERE LOOKING FOR ROY'S KILLER!
HAL, YOU'RE A GREEN LANTERN. CREATE SOMETHING OUTTA THAT RING TO BRING ROY BACK.
OLLIE, I CAN'T CONSTRUCT SOMETHING TO BRING BACK THE DEAD OR TURN BACK TIME. I'M SORRY.
YOU KNOW IF I COULD...
THE JUSTICE LEAGUE. WHAT A JOKE...
YOU'RE ALL SO HIGH-AND-MIGHTY. WHERE'S ROY'S JUSTICE?
GUESS HE DIDN'T RANK HIGH ENOUGH FOR A MEMBERSHIP CARD TO EARN YOUR PROTECTION, HUH? YOU THINK NOTHING CAN HURT YOU.
BUT YOU HAVE NO IDEA WHAT I COULD DO TO YOU...
DON'T.

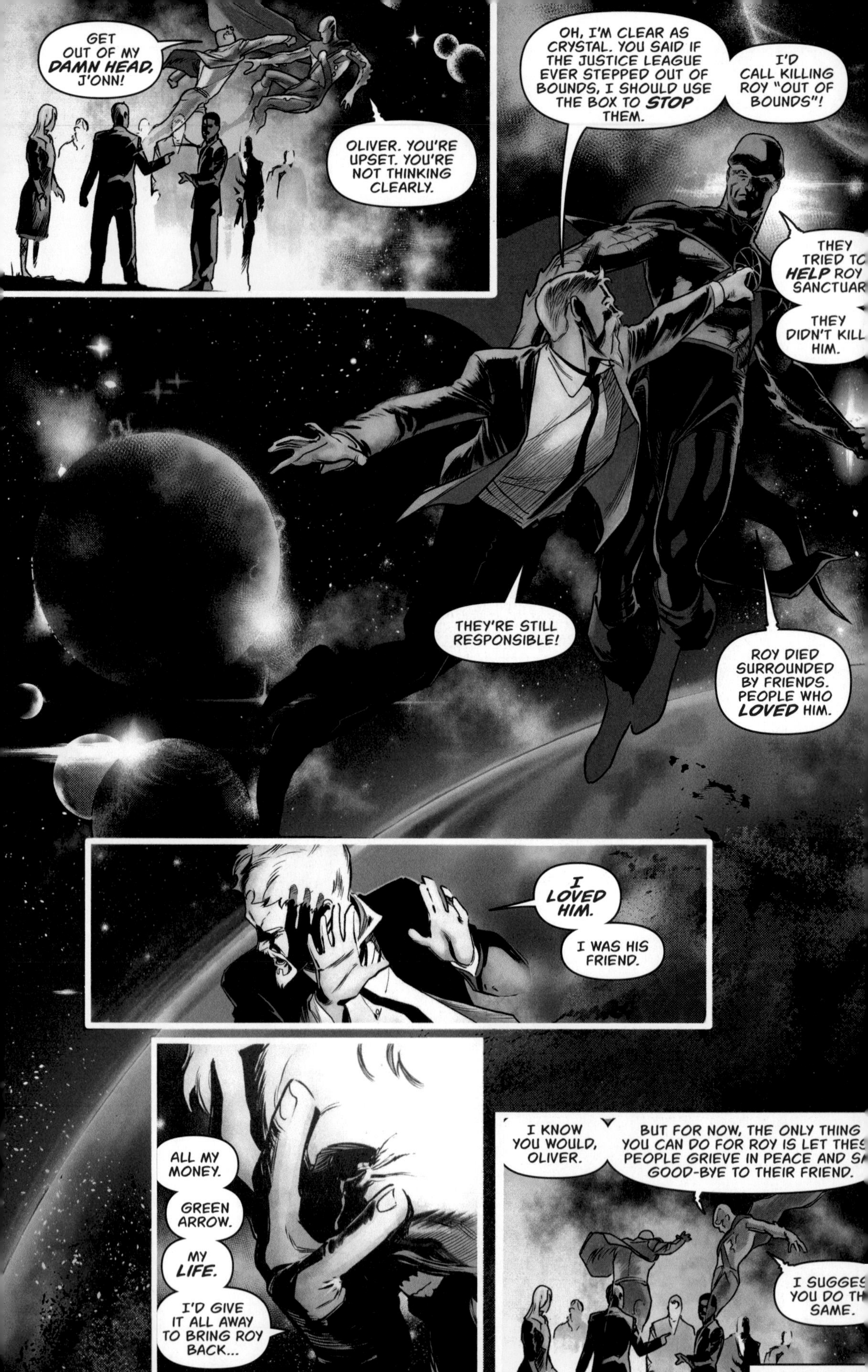
GET OUT OF MY DAMN HEAD, J'ONN!
OLIVER. YOU'RE UPSET. YOU'RE NOT THINKING CLEARLY.
OH, I'M CLEAR AS CRYSTAL. YOU SAID IF THE JUSTICE LEAGUE EVER STEPPED OUT OF BOUNDS, I SHOULD USE THE BOX TO STOP THEM.
I'D CALL KILLING ROY "OUT OF BOUNDS"!
THEY TRIED TO HELP ROY SANCTUAR
THEY DIDN'T KILL HIM.
THEY'RE STILL RESPONSIBLE!
ROY DIED SURROUNDED BY FRIENDS. PEOPLE WHO LOVED HIM.
I LOVED HIM.
I WAS HIS FRIEND.
ALL MY MONEY.
GREEN ARROW.
MY LIFE.
I'D GIVE IT ALL AWAY TO BRING ROY BACK...
I KNOW YOU WOULD, OLIVER.
BUT FOR NOW, THE ONLY THING YOU CAN DO FOR ROY IS LET THES PEOPLE GRIEVE IN PEACE AND S GOOD-BYE TO THEIR FRIEND.
I SUGGES YOU DO TH SAME.
"DONNA TROY WILL NOW SAY

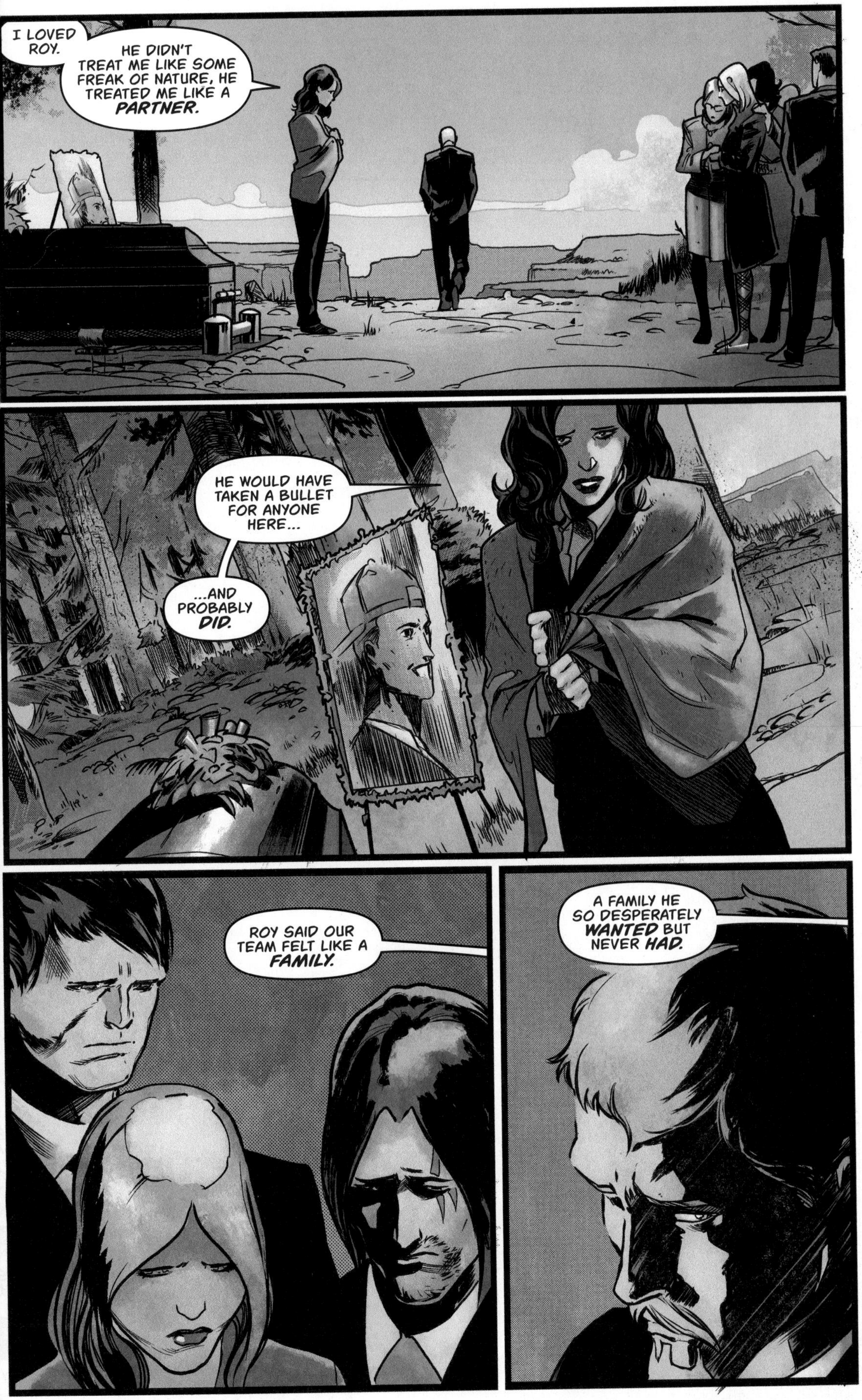
I LOVED ROY.
HE DIDN'T TREAT ME LIKE SOME FREAK OF NATURE, HE TREATED ME LIKE A PARTNER.
HE WOULD HAVE TAKEN A BULLET FOR ANYONE HERE...
...AND PROBABLY DID.
ROY SAID OUR TEAM FELT LIKE A FAMILY.
A FAMILY HE SO DESPERATELY WANTED BUT NEVER HAD.

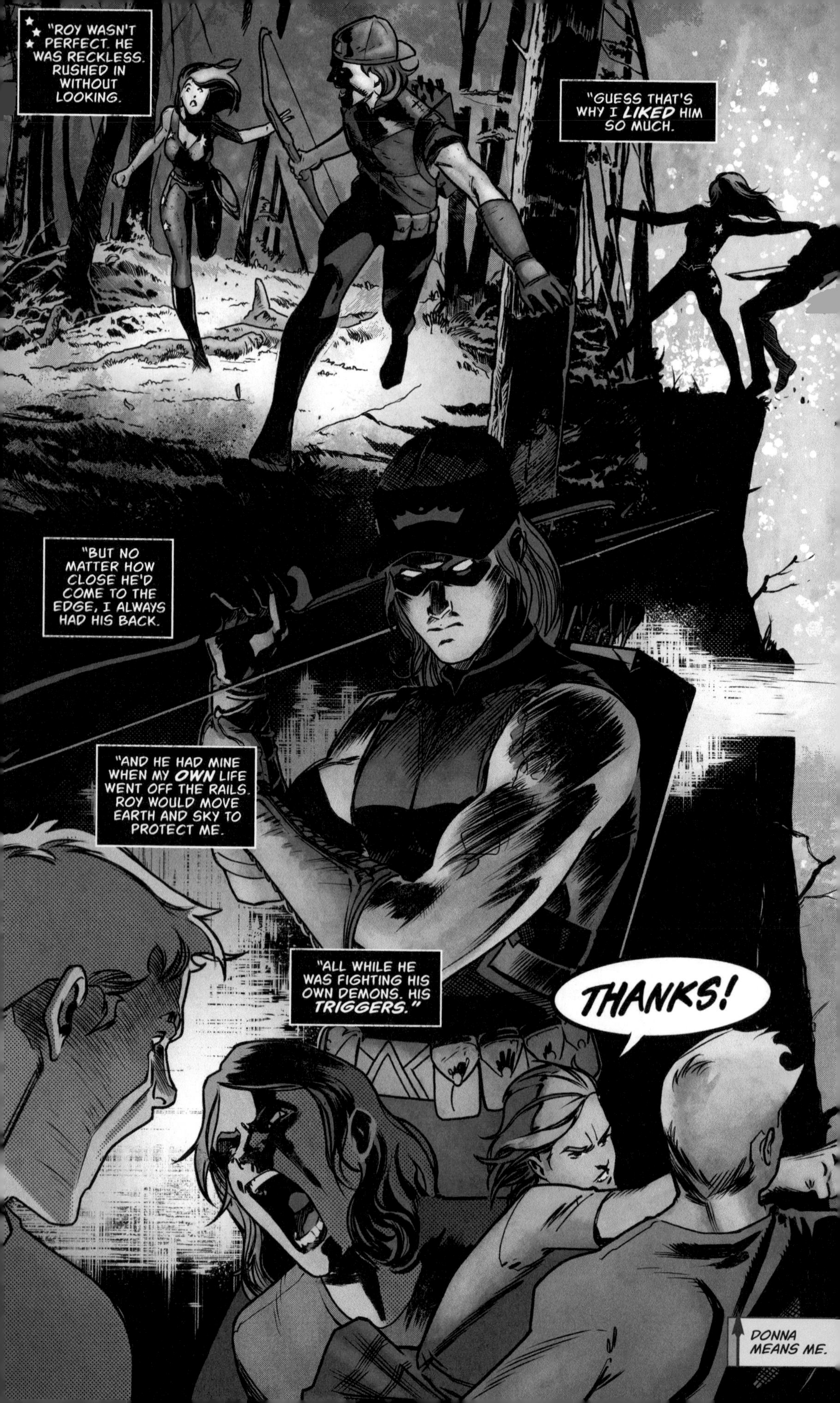
"ROY WASN'T PERFECT. HE WAS RECKLESS. RUSHED IN WITHOUT LOOKING.
"GUESS THAT'S WHY I LIKED HIM SO MUCH.
"BUT NO MATTER HOW CLOSE HE'D COME TO THE EDGE, I ALWAYS HAD HIS BACK.
"AND HE HAD MINE WHEN MY OWN LIFE WENT OFF THE RAILS. ROY WOULD MOVE EARTH AND SKY TO PROTECT ME.
"ALL WHILE HE WAS FIGHTING HIS OWN DEMONS. HIS TRIGGERS."
THANKS!
DONNA MEANS ME.

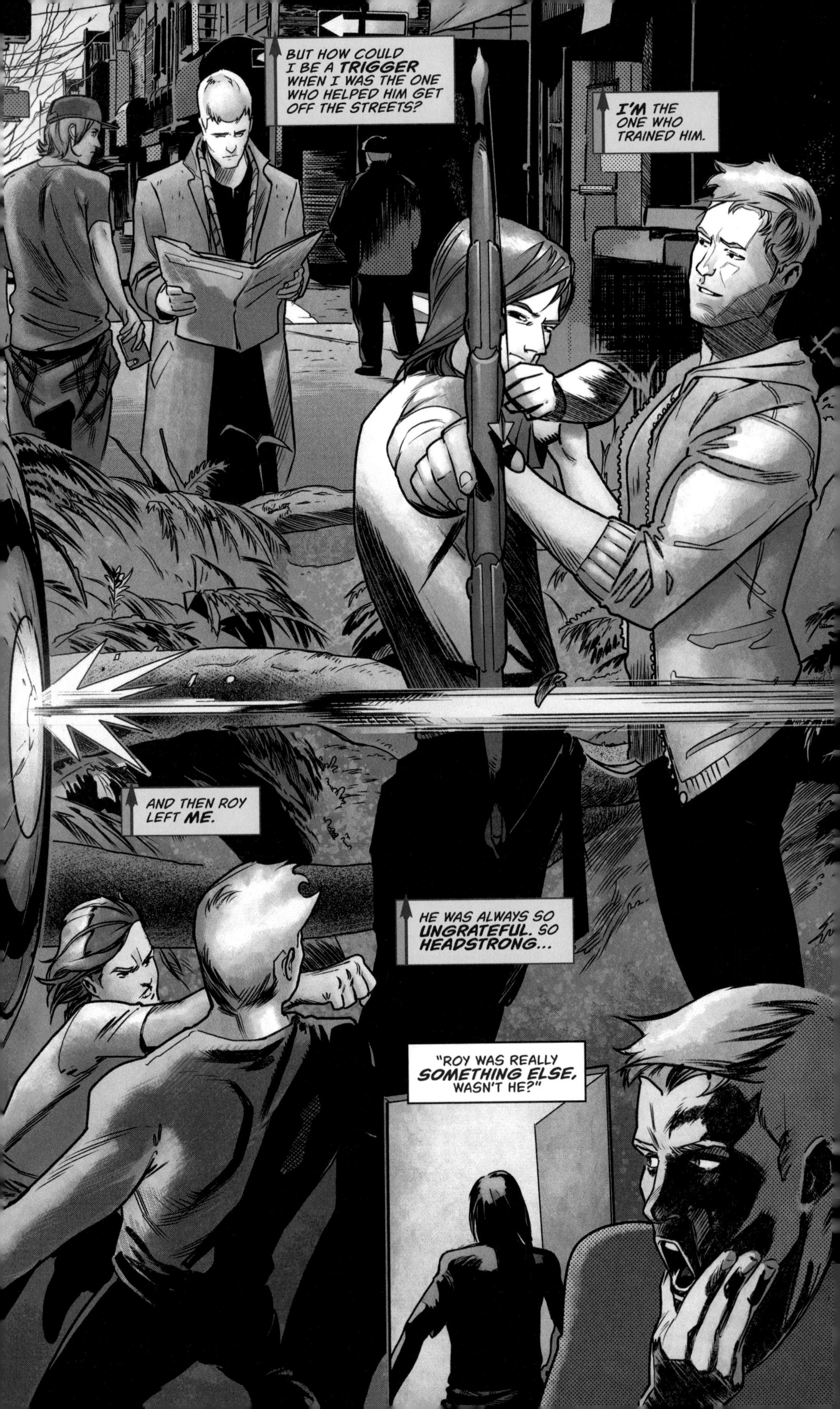
BUT HOW COULD I BE A TRIGGER WHEN I WAS THE ONE WHO HELPED HIM GET OFF THE STREETS?
I'M THE ONE WHO TRAINED HIM.
AND THEN ROY LEFT ME.
HE WAS ALWAYS SO UNGRATEFUL. SO HEADSTRONG...
"ROY WAS REALLY SOMETHING ELSE, WASN'T HE?"

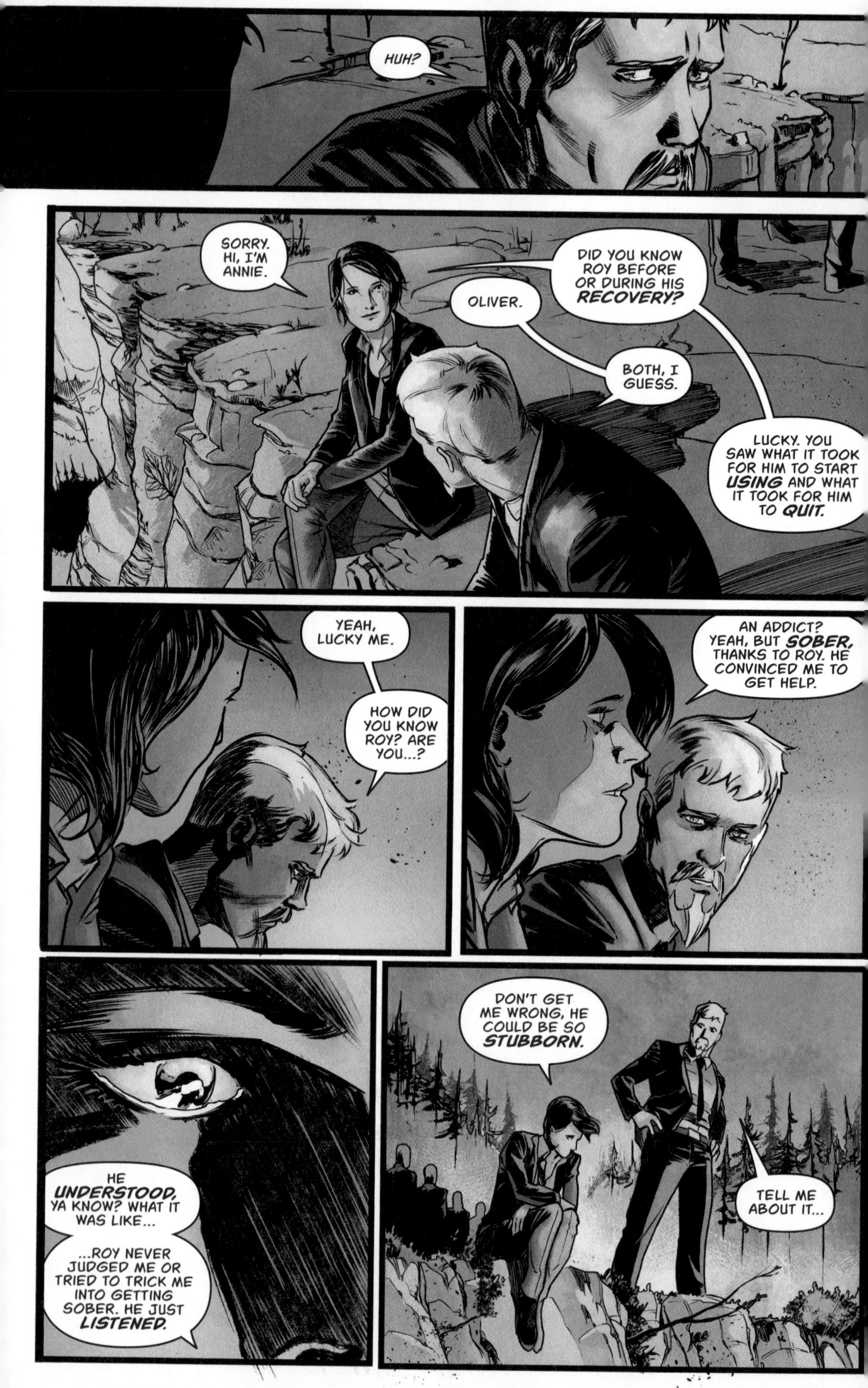
HUH?
SORRY. HI, I'M ANNIE.
OLIVER.
DID YOU KNOW ROY BEFORE OR DURING HIS RECOVERY?
BOTH, I GUESS.
LUCKY. YOU SAW WHAT IT TOOK FOR HIM TO START USING AND WHAT IT TOOK FOR HIM TO QUIT.
YEAH, LUCKY ME.
HOW DID YOU KNOW ROY? ARE YOU...?
AN ADDICT? YEAH, BUT SOBER, THANKS TO ROY. HE CONVINCED ME TO GET HELP.
HE UNDERSTOOD, YA KNOW? WHAT IT WAS LIKE...
...ROY NEVER JUDGED ME OR TRIED TO TRICK ME INTO GETTING SOBER. HE JUST LISTENED.
DON'T GET ME WRONG, HE COULD BE SO STUBBORN.
TELL ME ABOUT IT...

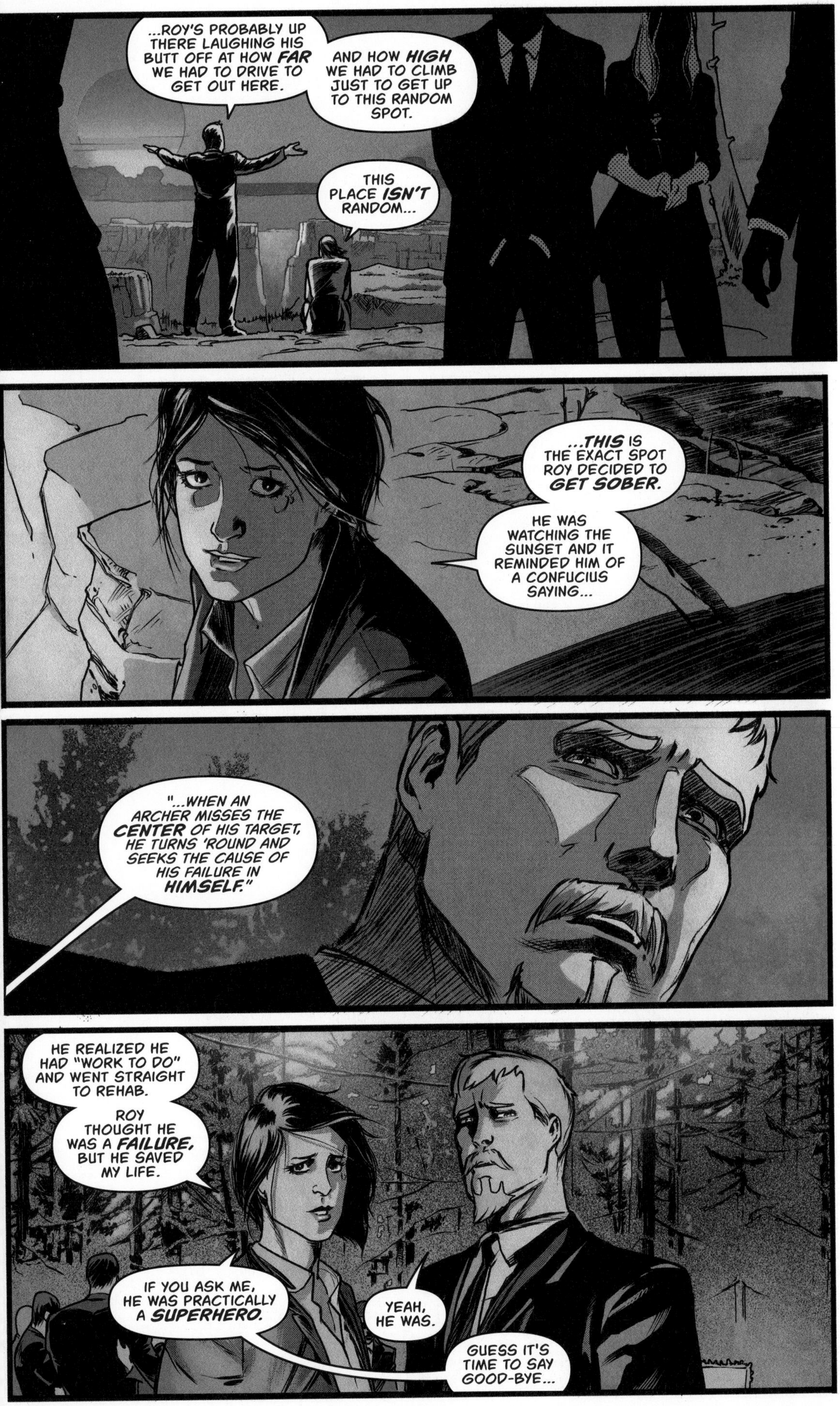
...ROY'S PROBABLY UP THERE LAUGHING HIS BUTT OFF AT HOW **FAR** WE HAD TO DRIVE TO GET OUT HERE.
AND HOW **HIGH** WE HAD TO CLIMB JUST TO GET UP TO THIS RANDOM SPOT.
THIS PLACE **ISN'T** RANDOM...
...THIS IS THE EXACT SPOT ROY DECIDED TO **GET SOBER.**
HE WAS WATCHING THE SUNSET AND IT REMINDED HIM OF A CONFUCIUS SAYING...
"...WHEN AN ARCHER MISSES THE **CENTER** OF HIS TARGET, HE TURNS 'ROUND AND SEEKS THE CAUSE OF HIS FAILURE IN **HIMSELF.**"
HE REALIZED HE HAD "WORK TO DO" AND WENT STRAIGHT TO REHAB.
ROY THOUGHT HE WAS A **FAILURE,** BUT HE SAVED MY LIFE.
IF YOU ASK ME, HE WAS PRACTICALLY A **SUPERHERO.**
YEAH, HE WAS.
GUESS IT'S TIME TO SAY GOOD-BYE...

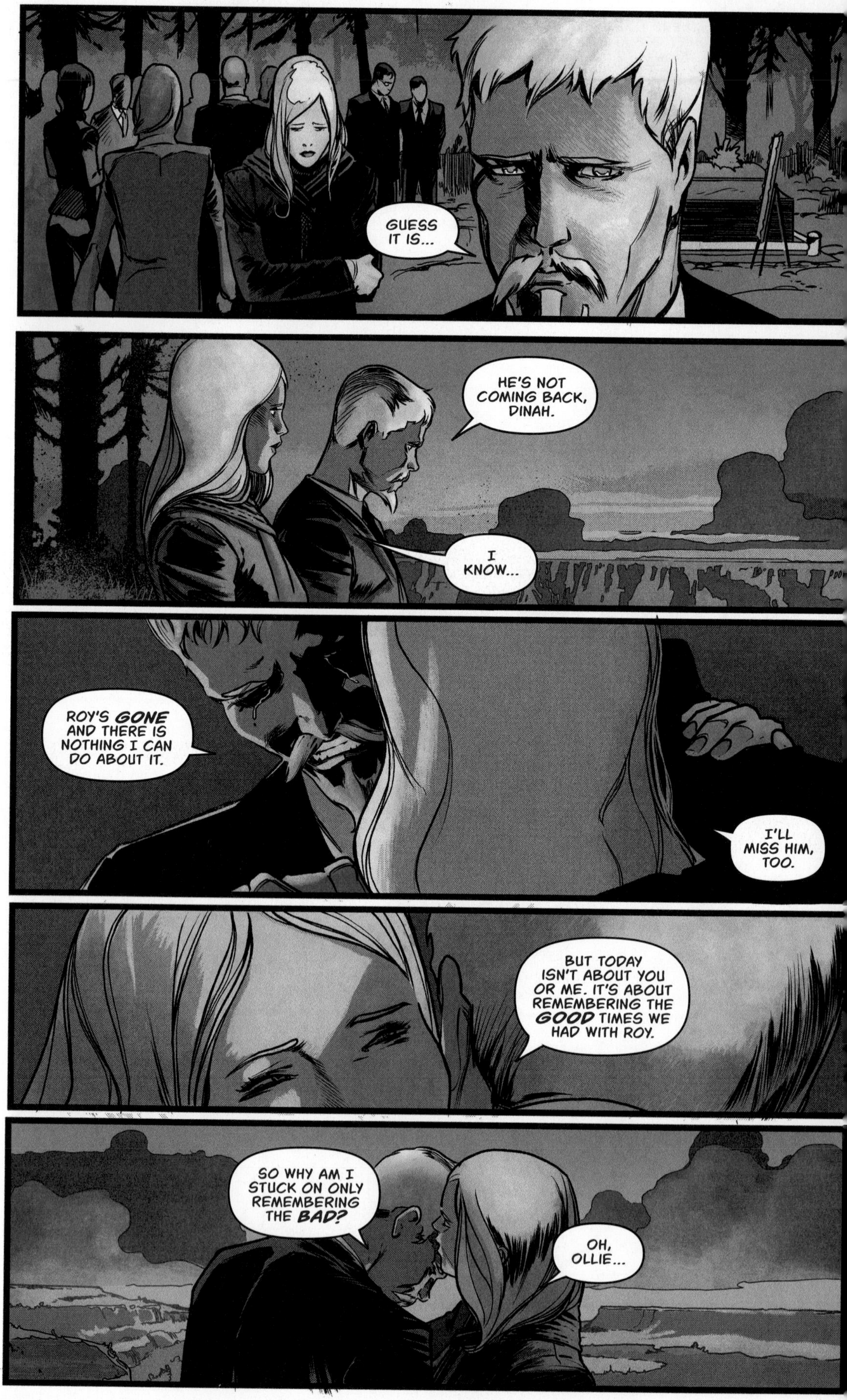
GUESS IT IS...
HE'S NOT COMING BACK, DINAH.
I KNOW...
ROY'S GONE AND THERE IS NOTHING I CAN DO ABOUT IT.
I'LL MISS HIM, TOO.
BUT TODAY ISN'T ABOUT YOU OR ME. IT'S ABOUT REMEMBERING THE GOOD TIMES WE HAD WITH ROY.
SO WHY AM I STUCK ON ONLY REMEMBERING THE BAD?
OH, OLLIE...

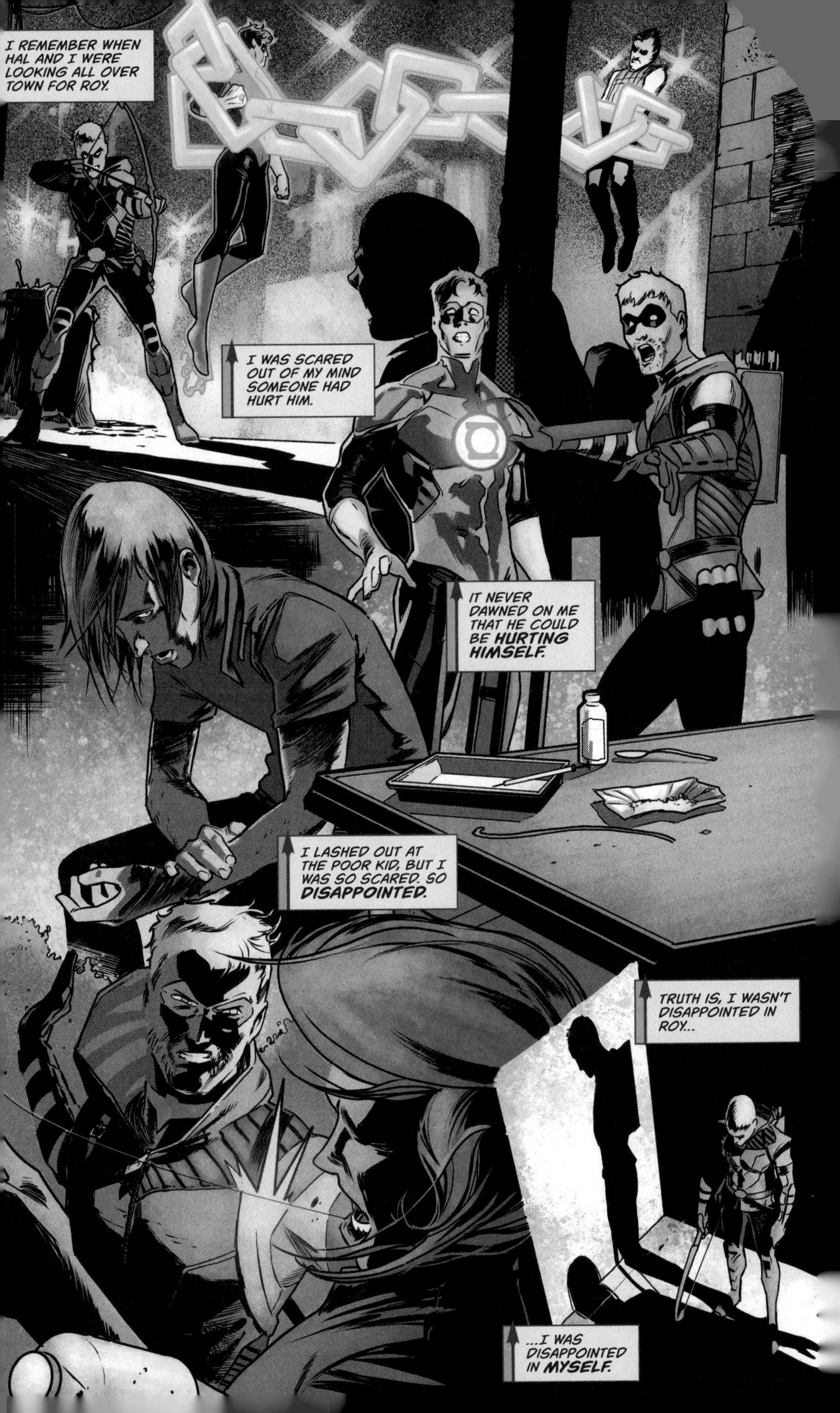

I REMEMBER WHEN HAL AND I WERE LOOKING ALL OVER TOWN FOR ROY.
I WAS SCARED OUT OF MY MIND SOMEONE HAD HURT HIM.
IT NEVER DAWNED ON ME THAT HE COULD BE **HURTING HIMSELF.**
I LASHED OUT AT THE POOR KID, BUT I WAS SO SCARED. SO **DISAPPOINTED.**
TRUTH IS, I WASN'T DISAPPOINTED IN ROY...
...I WAS DISAPPOINTED IN **MYSELF.**

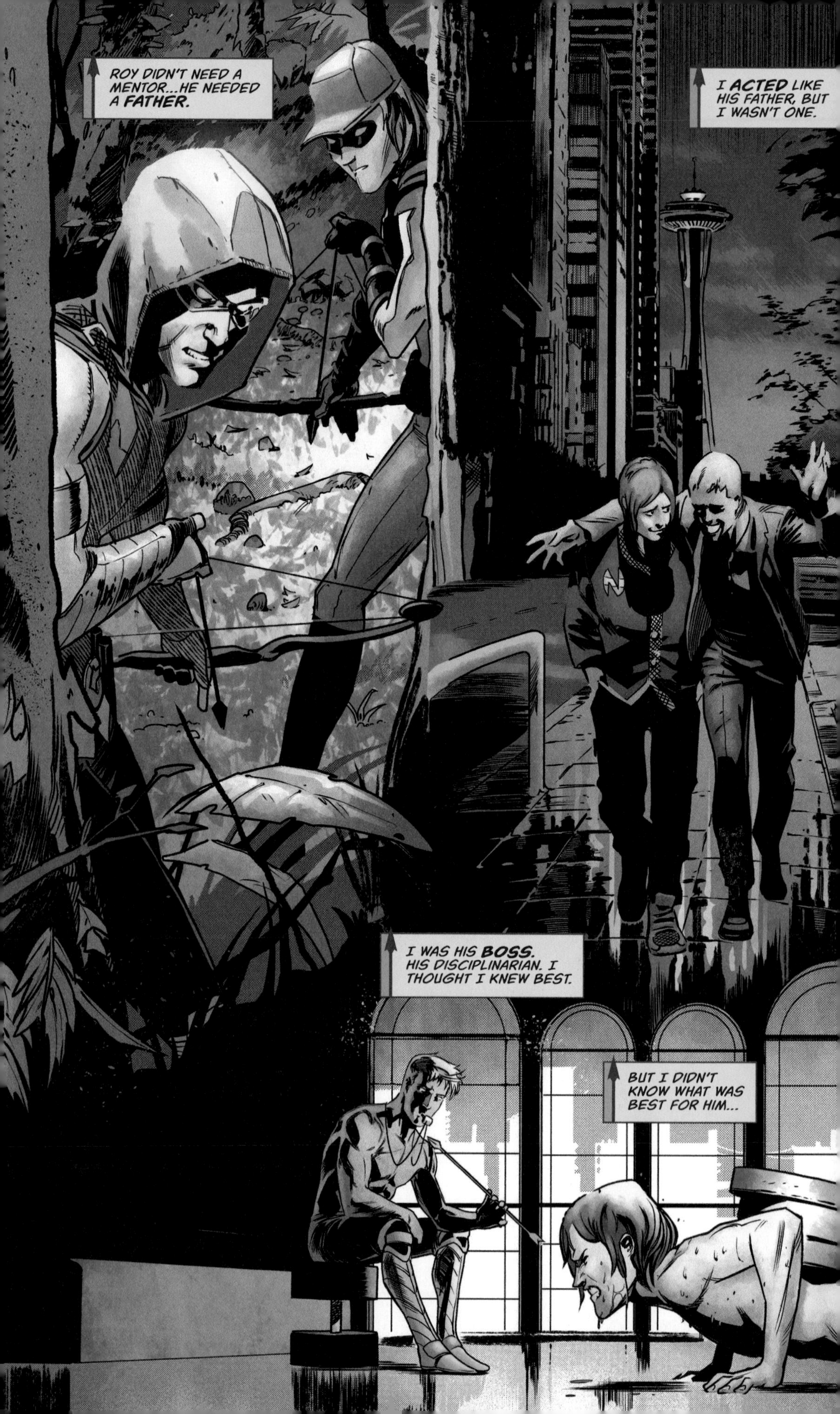
ROY DIDN'T NEED A MENTOR...HE NEEDED A **FATHER.**
I **ACTED** LIKE HIS FATHER, BUT I WASN'T ONE.
I WAS HIS **BOSS.** HIS DISCIPLINARIAN. I THOUGHT I KNEW BEST.
BUT I DIDN'T KNOW WHAT WAS BEST FOR HIM...

...AND NOW I'VE GOT TO LIVE WITH THAT.

SEE YOU ON THE OTHER SIDE, HARPER.

TINK

AND NOW IT'S MY TURN TO SAY GOOD-BYE AND I DON'T EVEN KNOW WHOM TO SAY GOOD-BYE TO.

SPEEDY? RED ARROW? ARSENAL?

ANNIE LEFT ROY'S FIRST SOBER COIN.

HEARD HIM RECITE THAT SERENITY PRAYER SO MANY TIMES, I GOT IT MEMORIZED.

GOD GRANT ME THE SERENITY TO ACCEPT THE THINGS I CANNOT CHANGE...

...THE COURAGE TO CHANGE THE THINGS I CAN...

...AND THE WISDOM TO KNOW THE DIFFERENCE.

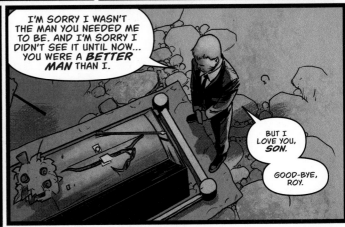

I'M SORRY I WASN'T THE MAN YOU NEEDED ME TO BE. AND I'M SORRY I DIDN'T SEE IT UNTIL NOW... YOU WERE A BETTER MAN THAN I.

BUT I LOVE YOU, SON.

GOOD-BYE, ROY.

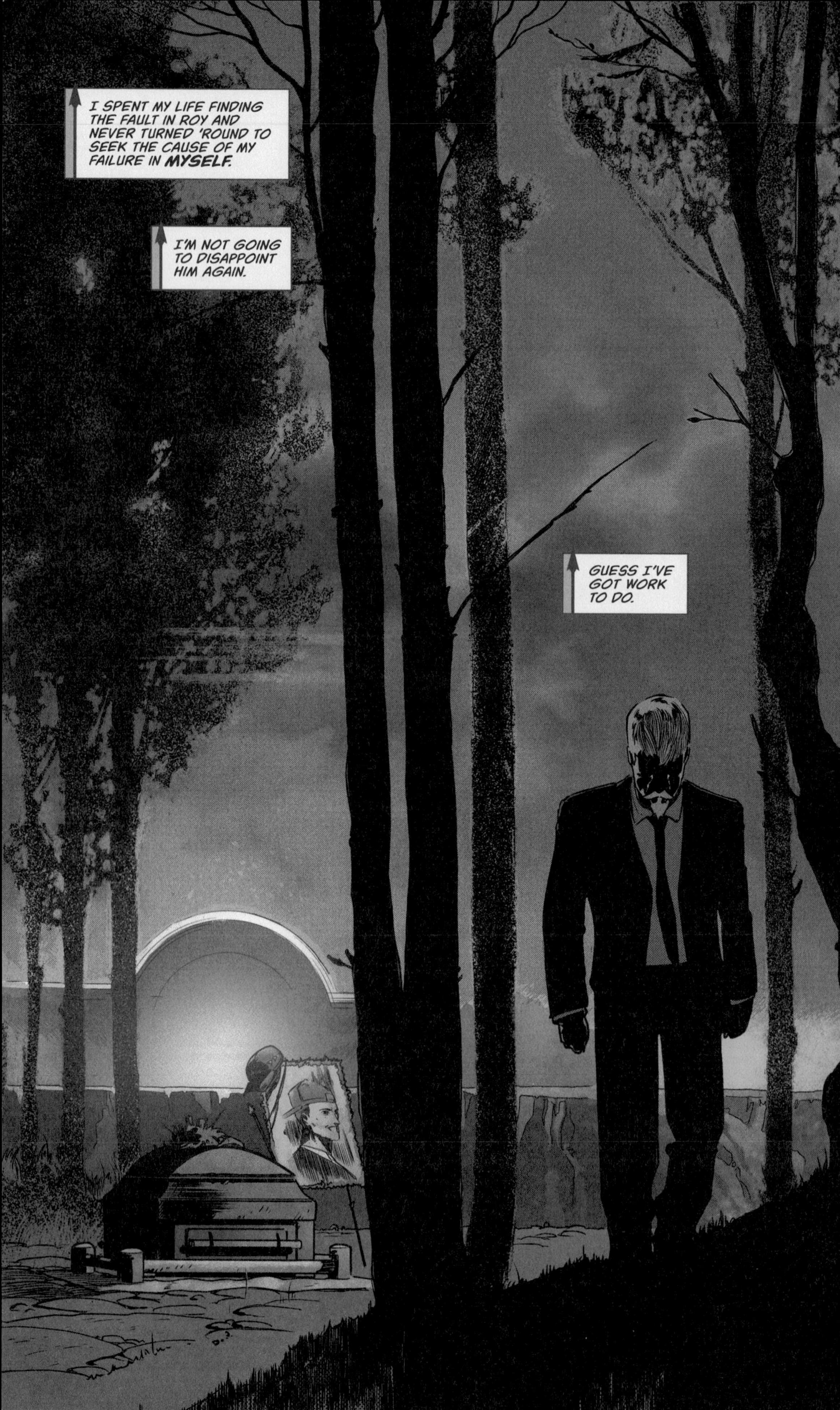

I SPENT MY LIFE FINDING THE FAULT IN ROY AND NEVER TURNED 'ROUND TO SEEK THE CAUSE OF MY FAILURE IN MYSELF.
I'M NOT GOING TO DISAPPOINT HIM AGAIN.
GUESS I'VE GOT WORK TO DO.

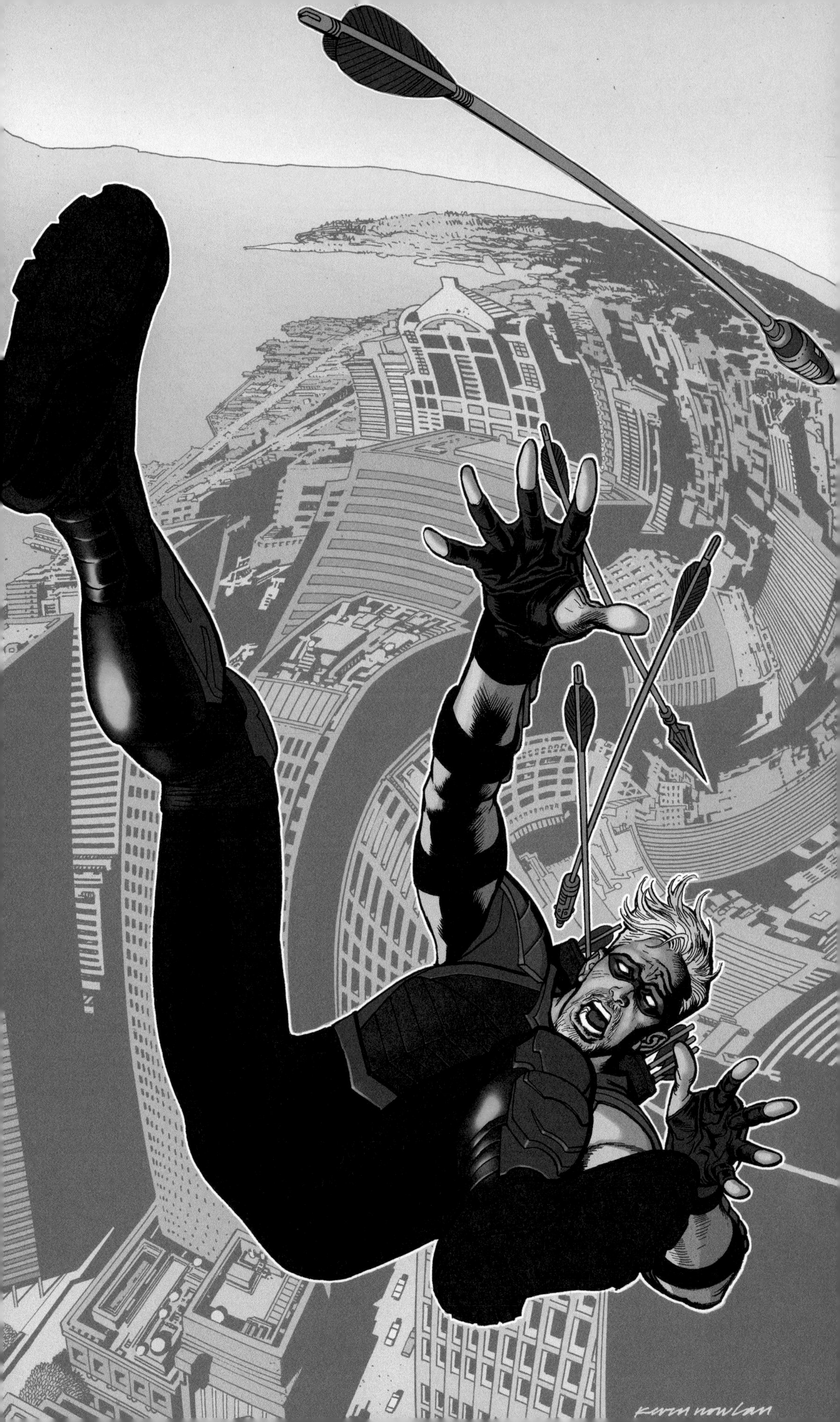
kevin nowlan

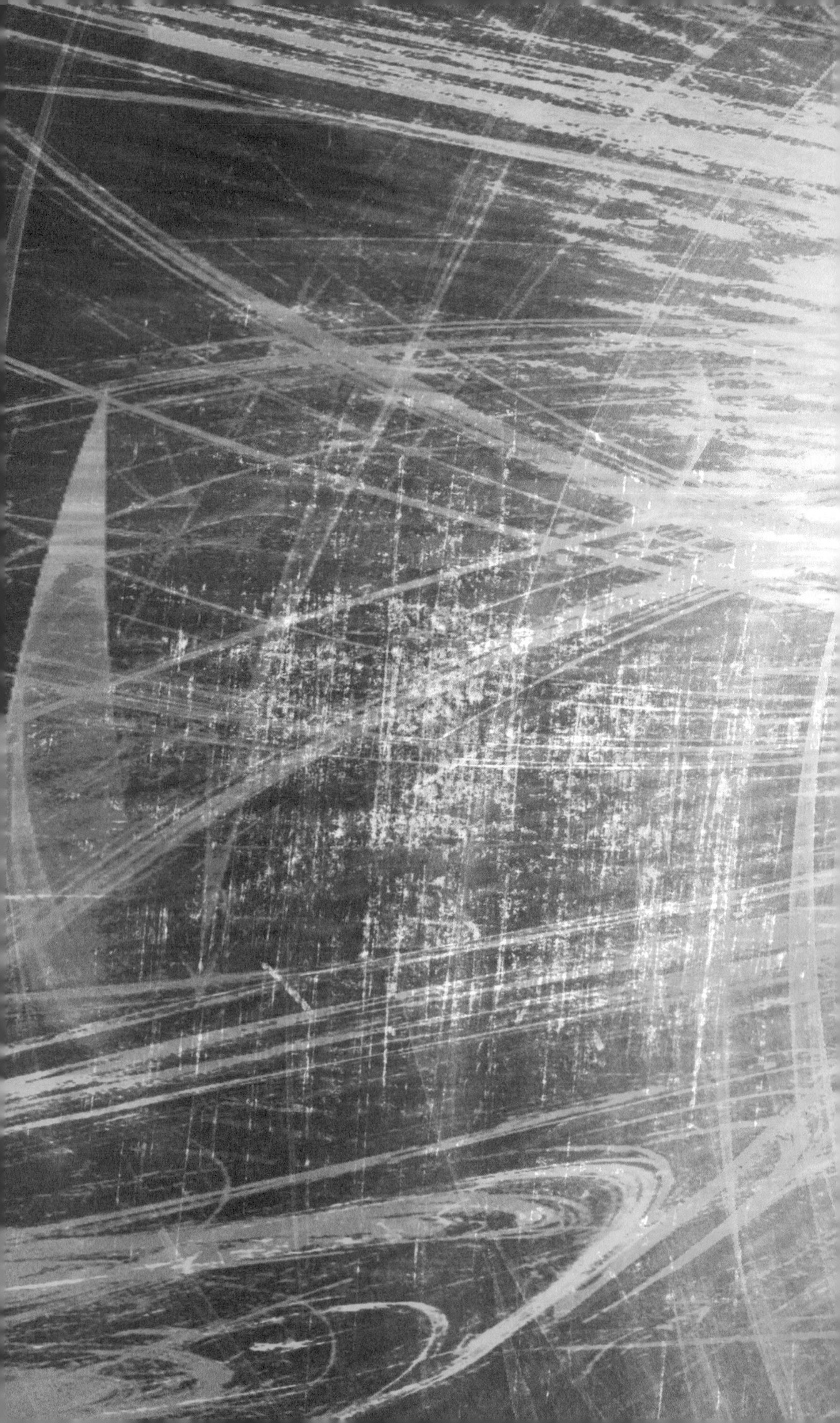

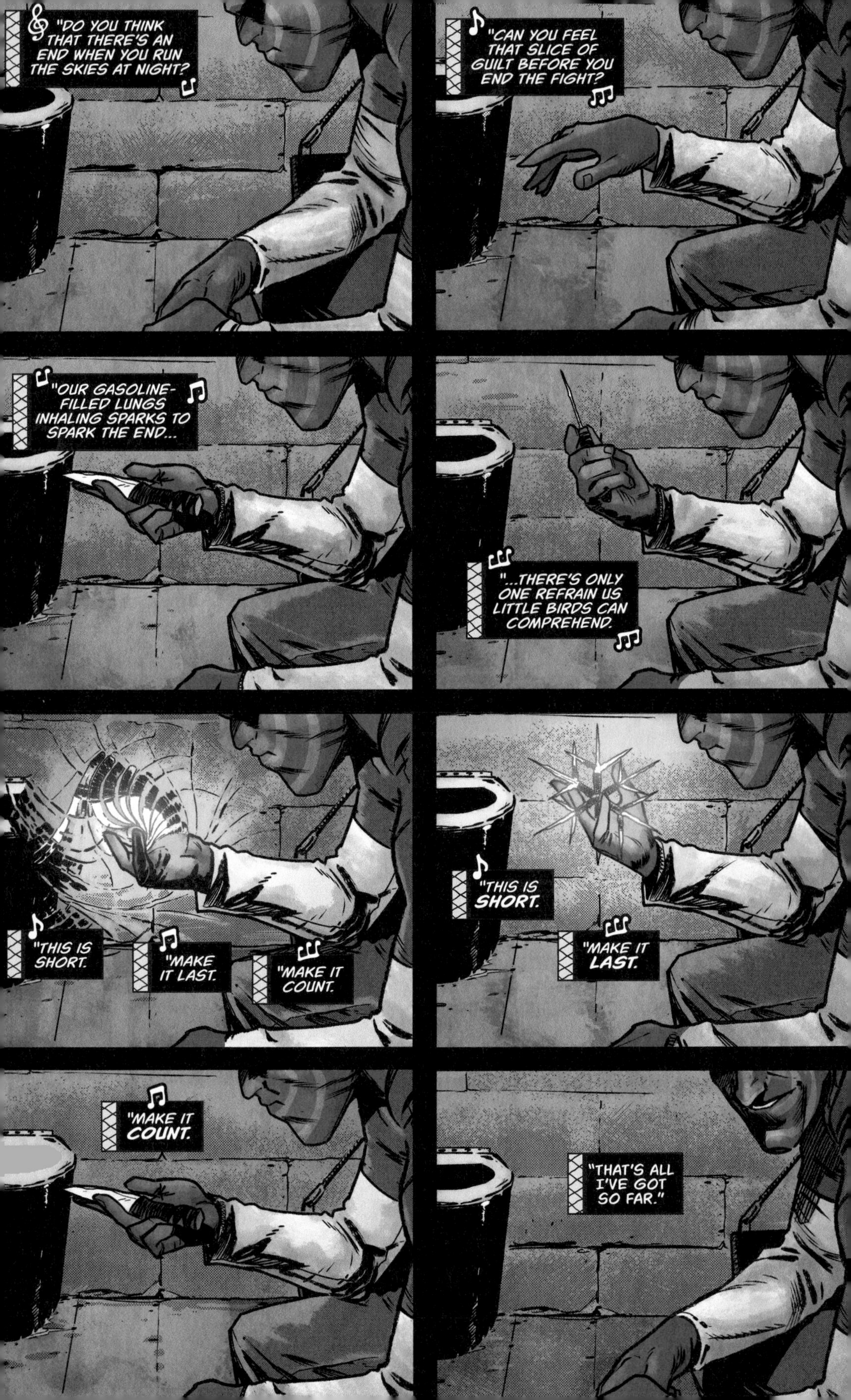
"DO YOU THINK THAT THERE'S AN END WHEN YOU RUN THE SKIES AT NIGHT?
"CAN YOU FEEL THAT SLICE OF GUILT BEFORE YOU END THE FIGHT?
"OUR GASOLINE-FILLED LUNGS INHALING SPARKS TO SPARK THE END...
"...THERE'S ONLY ONE REFRAIN US LITTLE BIRDS CAN COMPREHEND.
"THIS IS SHORT.
"MAKE IT LAST.
"MAKE IT COUNT.
"THIS IS SHORT.
"MAKE IT LAST.
"MAKE IT COUNT.
"THAT'S ALL I'VE GOT SO FAR."

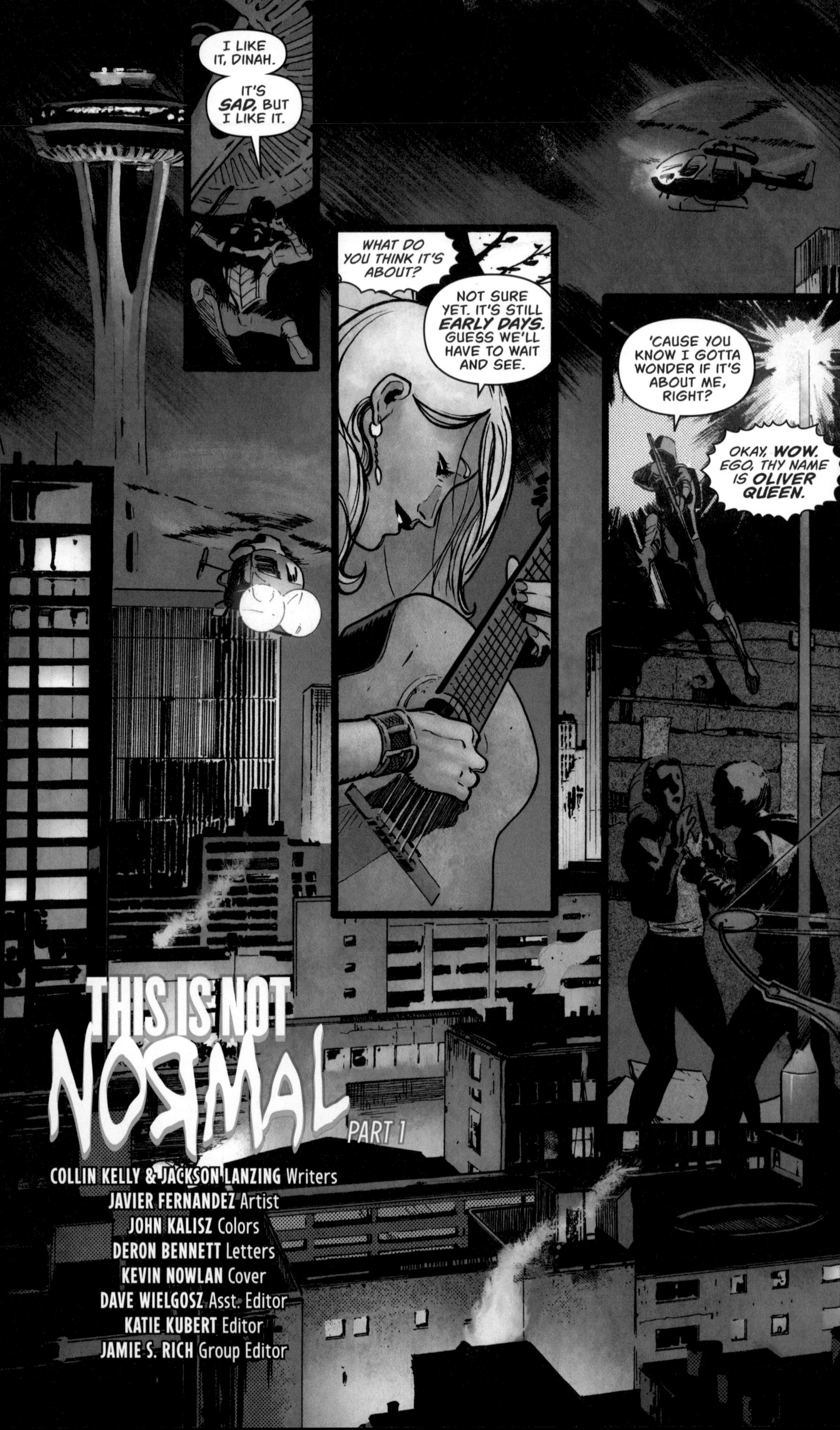
I LIKE IT, DINAH.
IT'S SAD, BUT I LIKE IT.
WHAT DO YOU THINK IT'S ABOUT?
NOT SURE YET. IT'S STILL EARLY DAYS. GUESS WE'LL HAVE TO WAIT AND SEE.
'CAUSE YOU KNOW I GOTTA WONDER IF IT'S ABOUT ME, RIGHT?
OKAY, WOW. EGO, THY NAME IS OLIVER QUEEN.
THIS IS NOT NORMAL PART 1
COLLIN KELLY & JACKSON LANZING Writers
JAVIER FERNANDEZ Artist
JOHN KALISZ Colors
DERON BENNETT Letters
KEVIN NOWLAN Cover
DAVE WIELGOSZ Asst. Editor
KATIE KUBERT Editor
JAMIE S. RICH Group Editor

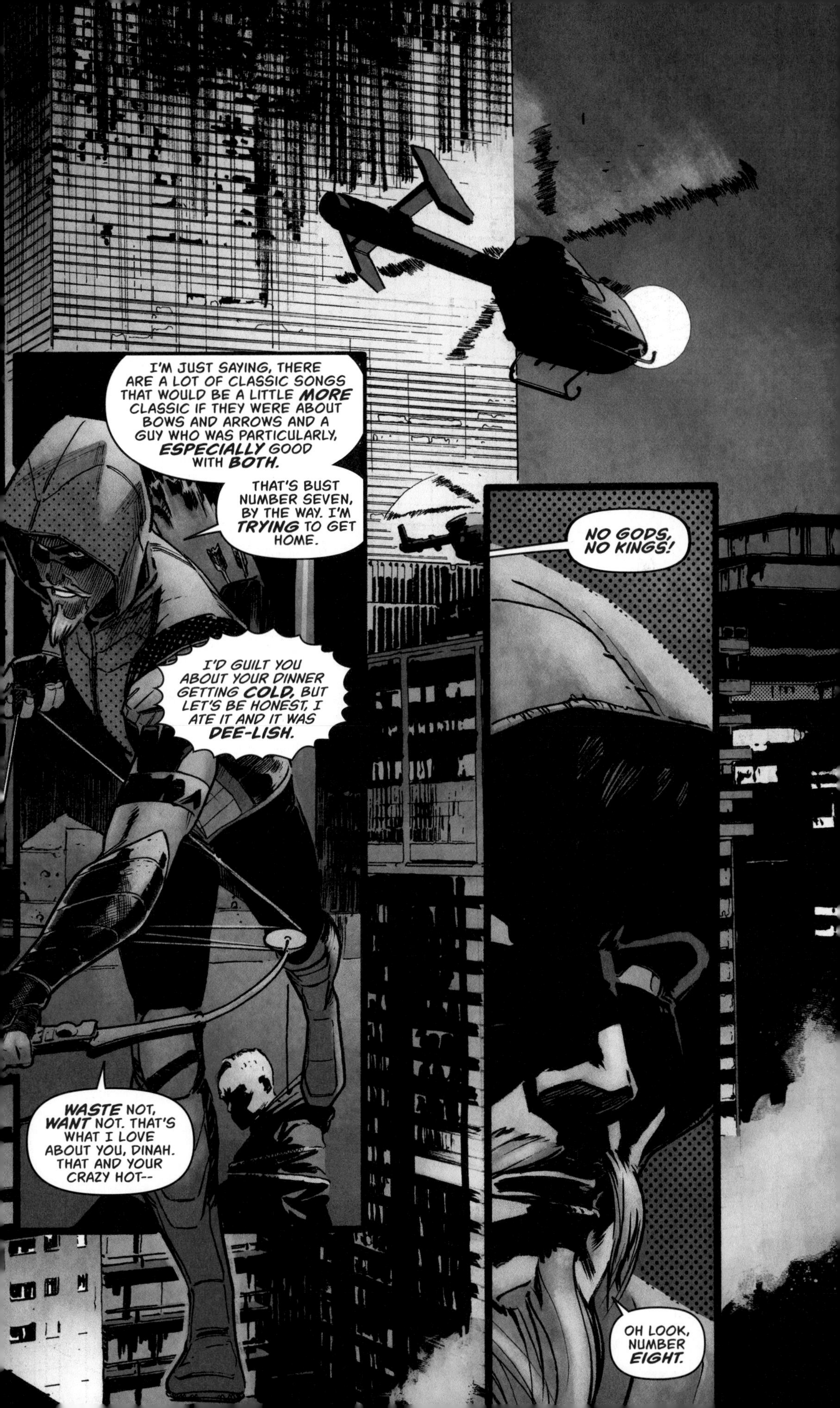
I'M JUST SAYING, THERE ARE A LOT OF CLASSIC SONGS THAT WOULD BE A LITTLE MORE CLASSIC IF THEY WERE ABOUT BOWS AND ARROWS AND A GUY WHO WAS PARTICULARLY, ESPECIALLY GOOD WITH BOTH.
THAT'S BUST NUMBER SEVEN, BY THE WAY. I'M TRYING TO GET HOME.
I'D GUILT YOU ABOUT YOUR DINNER GETTING COLD, BUT LET'S BE HONEST, I ATE IT AND IT WAS DEE-LISH.
WASTE NOT, WANT NOT. THAT'S WHAT I LOVE ABOUT YOU, DINAH. THAT AND YOUR CRAZY HOT--
NO GODS, NO KINGS!
OH LOOK, NUMBER EIGHT.

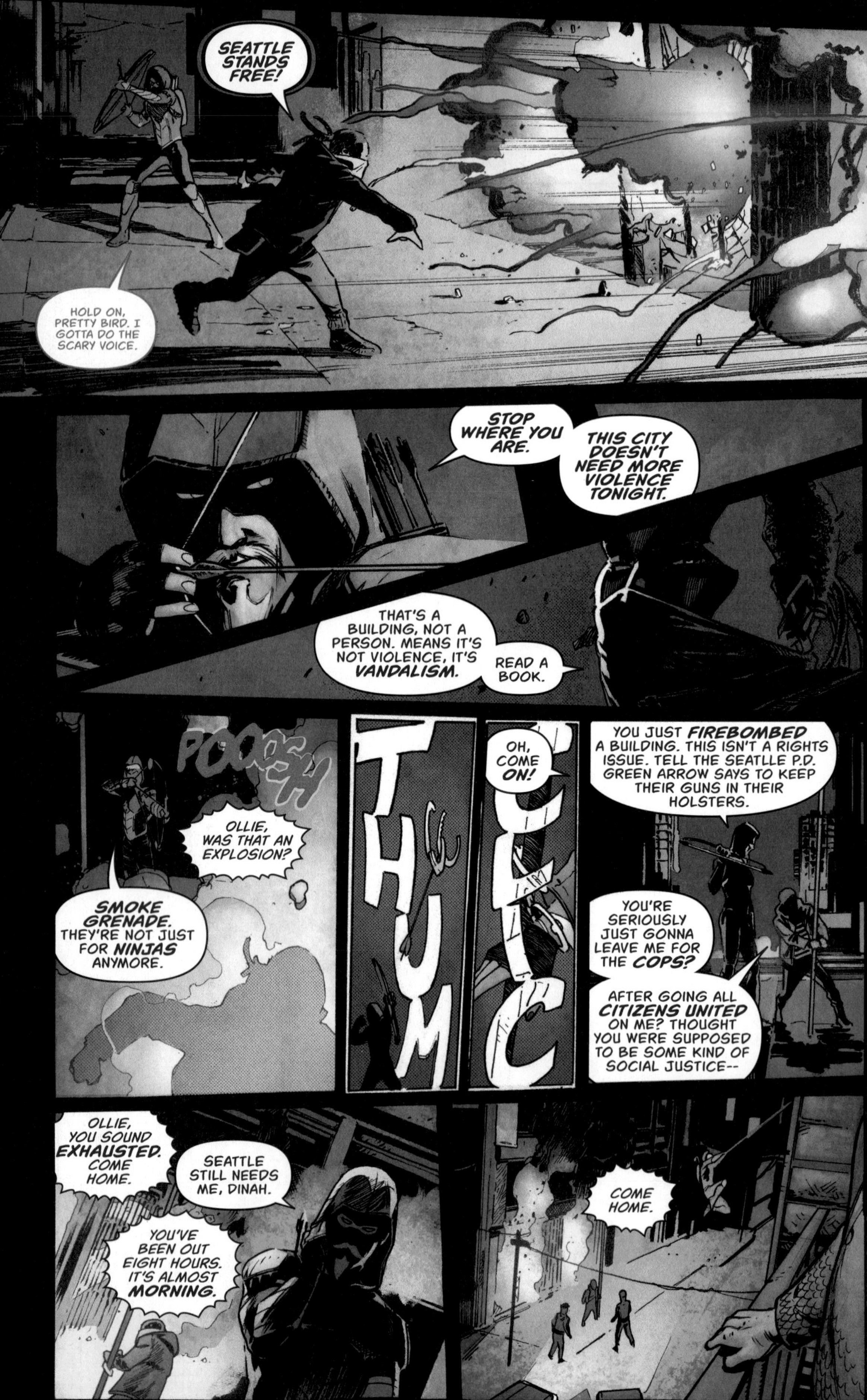
SEATTLE STANDS FREE!
HOLD ON, PRETTY BIRD. I GOTTA DO THE SCARY VOICE.
STOP WHERE YOU ARE.
THIS CITY DOESN'T NEED MORE VIOLENCE TONIGHT.
THAT'S A BUILDING, NOT A PERSON. MEANS IT'S NOT VIOLENCE, IT'S VANDALISM.
READ A BOOK.
POOOSH
OLLIE, WAS THAT AN EXPLOSION?
SMOKE GRENADE. THEY'RE NOT JUST FOR NINJAS ANYMORE.
THUM
OH, COME ON!
CLIC
YOU JUST FIREBOMBED A BUILDING. THIS ISN'T A RIGHTS ISSUE. TELL THE SEATTLE P.D. GREEN ARROW SAYS TO KEEP THEIR GUNS IN THEIR HOLSTERS.
YOU'RE SERIOUSLY JUST GONNA LEAVE ME FOR THE COPS?
AFTER GOING ALL CITIZENS UNITED ON ME? THOUGHT YOU WERE SUPPOSED TO BE SOME KIND OF SOCIAL JUSTICE--
OLLIE, YOU SOUND EXHAUSTED. COME HOME.
SEATTLE STILL NEEDS ME, DINAH.
YOU'VE BEEN OUT EIGHT HOURS. IT'S ALMOST MORNING.
COME HOME.

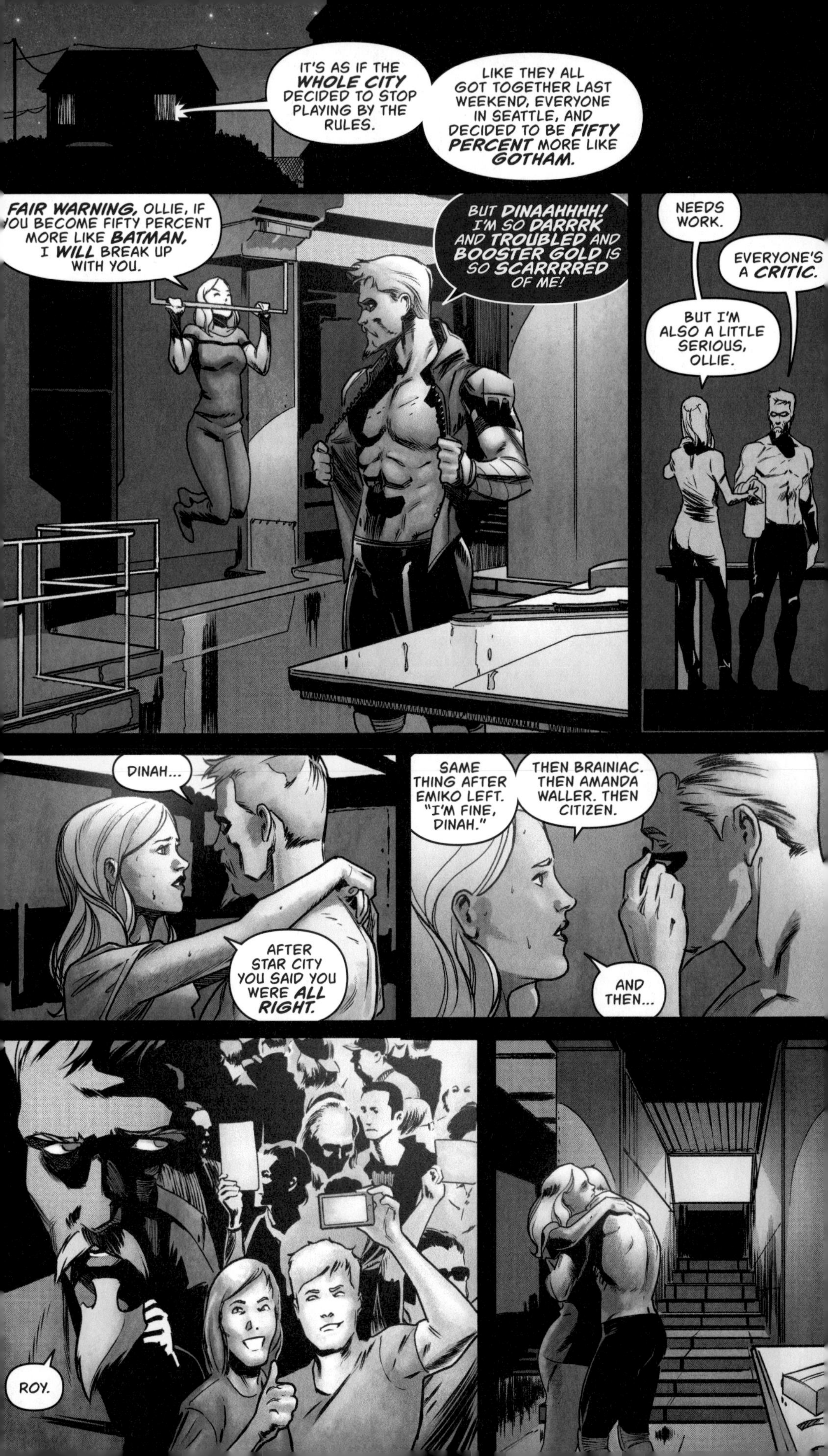
IT'S AS IF THE WHOLE CITY DECIDED TO STOP PLAYING BY THE RULES.
LIKE THEY ALL GOT TOGETHER LAST WEEKEND, EVERYONE IN SEATTLE, AND DECIDED TO BE FIFTY PERCENT MORE LIKE GOTHAM.
FAIR WARNING, OLLIE, IF YOU BECOME FIFTY PERCENT MORE LIKE BATMAN, I WILL BREAK UP WITH YOU.
BUT DINAAHHHH! I'M SO DARRRK AND TROUBLED AND BOOSTER GOLD IS SO SCARRRRED OF ME!
NEEDS WORK.
EVERYONE'S A CRITIC.
BUT I'M ALSO A LITTLE SERIOUS, OLLIE.
DINAH...
AFTER STAR CITY YOU SAID YOU WERE ALL RIGHT.
SAME THING AFTER EMIKO LEFT. "I'M FINE, DINAH."
THEN BRAINIAC. THEN AMANDA WALLER. THEN CITIZEN.
AND THEN...
ROY.

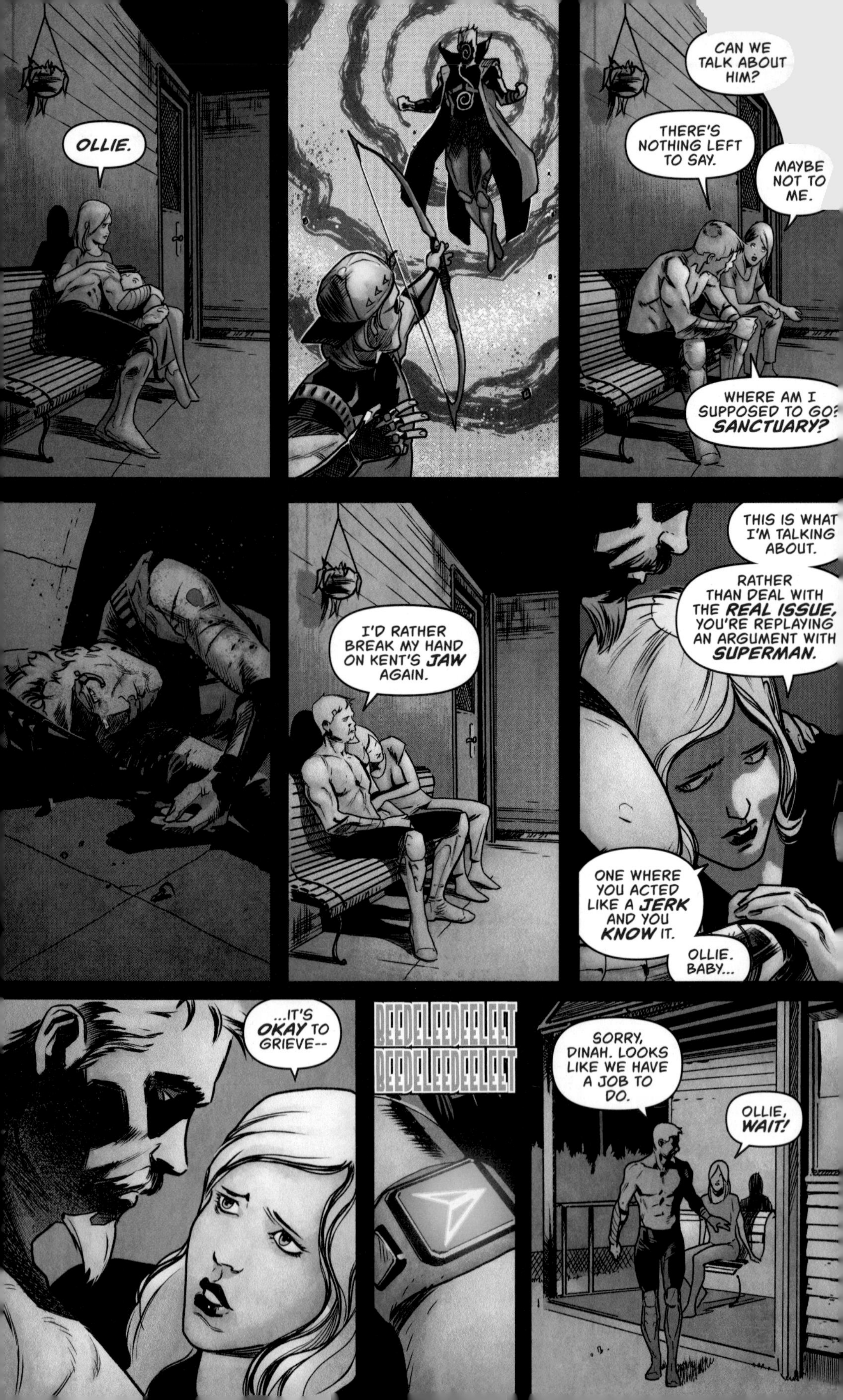
OLLIE.
CAN WE TALK ABOUT HIM?
THERE'S NOTHING LEFT TO SAY.
MAYBE NOT TO ME.
WHERE AM I SUPPOSED TO GO? SANCTUARY?
I'D RATHER BREAK MY HAND ON KENT'S JAW AGAIN.
THIS IS WHAT I'M TALKING ABOUT.
RATHER THAN DEAL WITH THE REAL ISSUE, YOU'RE REPLAYING AN ARGUMENT WITH SUPERMAN.
ONE WHERE YOU ACTED LIKE A JERK AND YOU KNOW IT.
OLLIE. BABY...
...IT'S OKAY TO GRIEVE--
BEEDELEEDEELEET
BEEDELEEDEELEET
SORRY, DINAH. LOOKS LIKE WE HAVE A JOB TO DO.
OLLIE, WAIT!

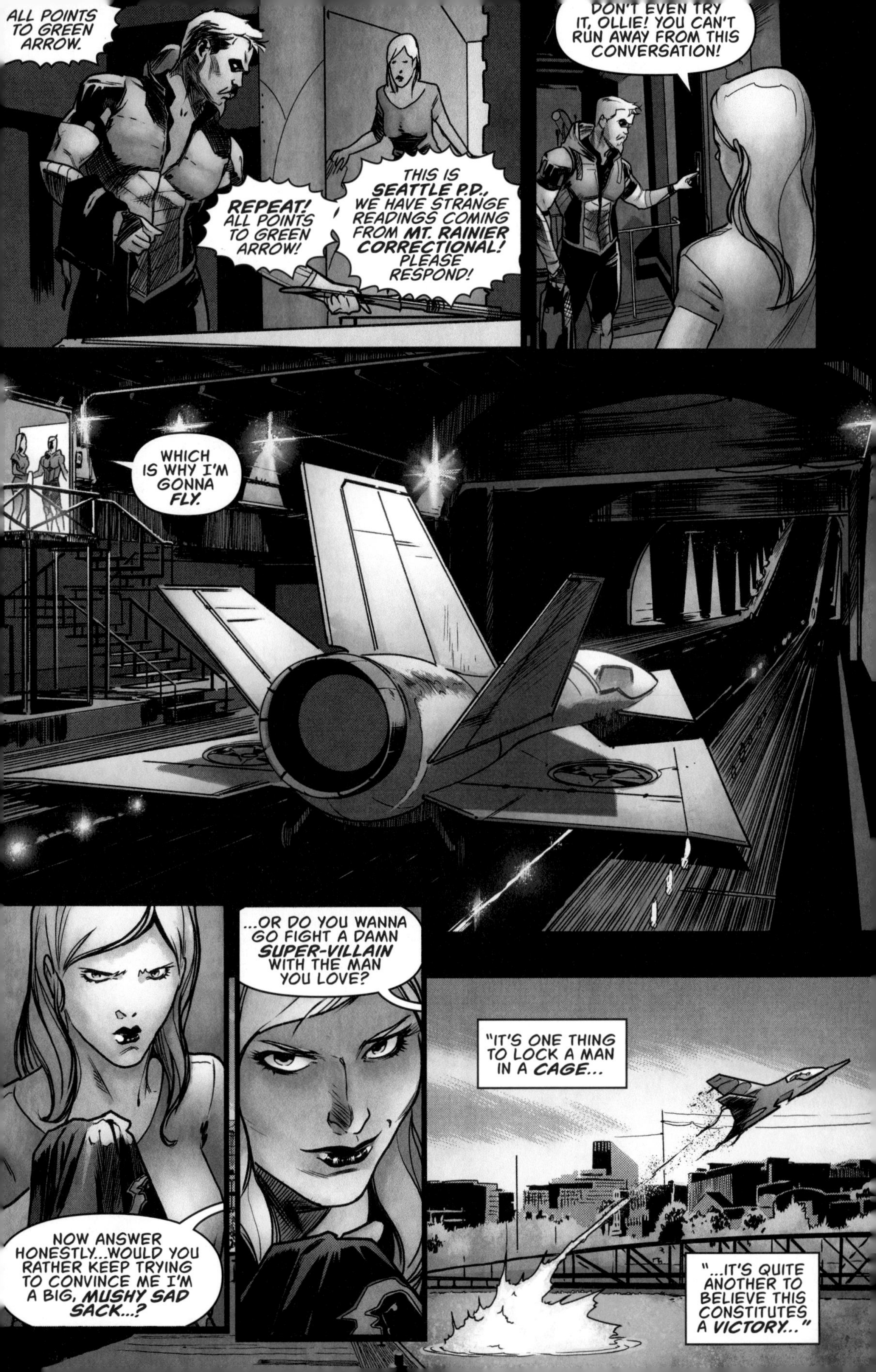
ALL POINTS TO GREEN ARROW.
REPEAT! ALL POINTS TO GREEN ARROW!
THIS IS SEATTLE P.D., WE HAVE STRANGE READINGS COMING FROM MT. RAINIER CORRECTIONAL! PLEASE RESPOND!
DON'T EVEN TRY IT, OLLIE! YOU CAN'T RUN AWAY FROM THIS CONVERSATION!
WHICH IS WHY I'M GONNA FLY.
NOW ANSWER HONESTLY...WOULD YOU RATHER KEEP TRYING TO CONVINCE ME I'M A BIG, MUSHY SAD SACK...?
...OR DO YOU WANNA GO FIGHT A DAMN SUPER-VILLAIN WITH THE MAN YOU LOVE?
"IT'S ONE THING TO LOCK A MAN IN A CAGE...
"...IT'S QUITE ANOTHER TO BELIEVE THIS CONSTITUTES A VICTORY..."

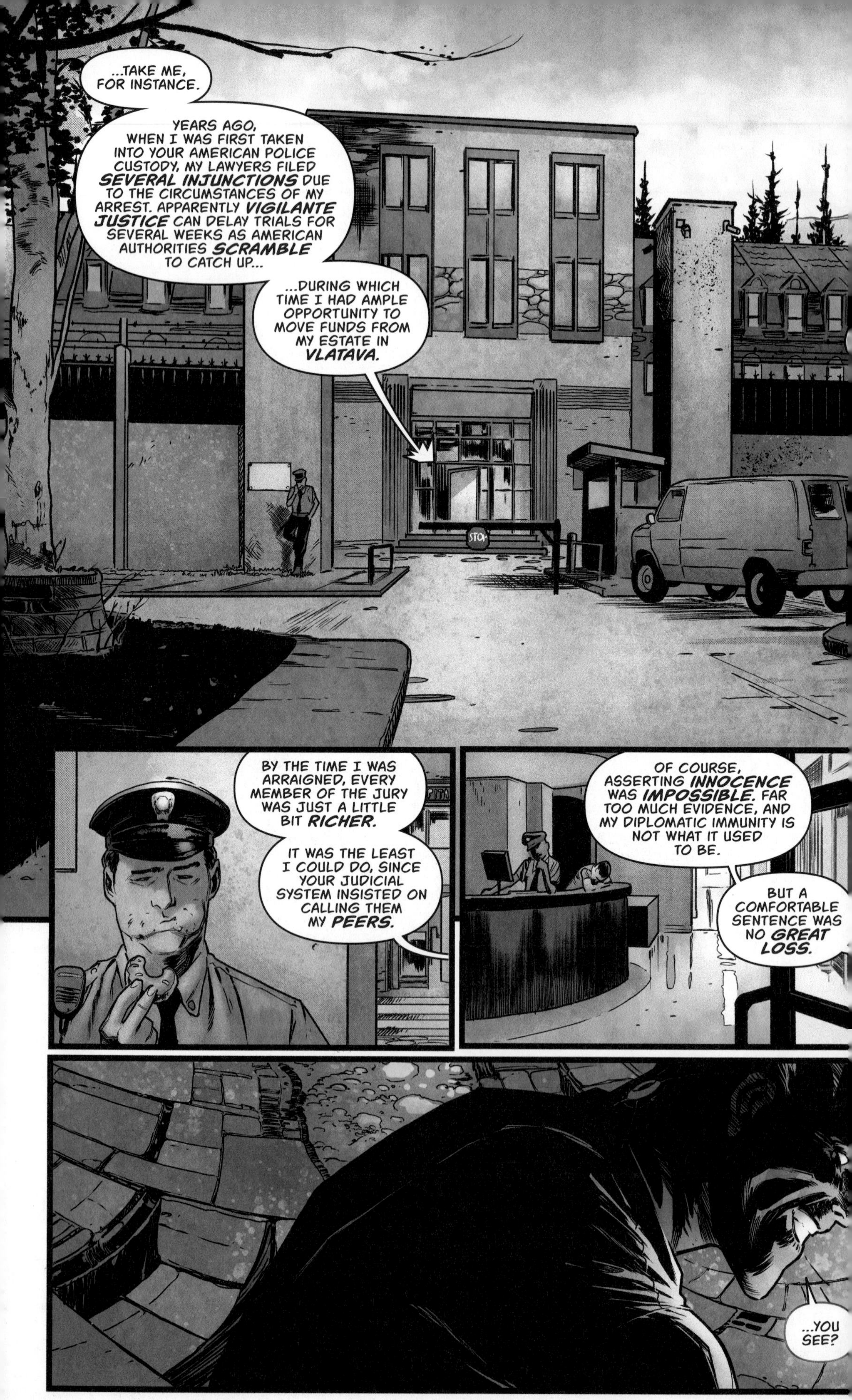

...TAKE ME, FOR INSTANCE.
YEARS AGO, WHEN I WAS FIRST TAKEN INTO YOUR AMERICAN POLICE CUSTODY, MY LAWYERS FILED SEVERAL INJUNCTIONS DUE TO THE CIRCUMSTANCES OF MY ARREST. APPARENTLY VIGILANTE JUSTICE CAN DELAY TRIALS FOR SEVERAL WEEKS AS AMERICAN AUTHORITIES SCRAMBLE TO CATCH UP...
...DURING WHICH TIME I HAD AMPLE OPPORTUNITY TO MOVE FUNDS FROM MY ESTATE IN VLATAVA.
STOP
BY THE TIME I WAS ARRAIGNED, EVERY MEMBER OF THE JURY WAS JUST A LITTLE BIT RICHER.
IT WAS THE LEAST I COULD DO, SINCE YOUR JUDICIAL SYSTEM INSISTED ON CALLING THEM MY PEERS.
OF COURSE, ASSERTING INNOCENCE WAS IMPOSSIBLE. FAR TOO MUCH EVIDENCE, AND MY DIPLOMATIC IMMUNITY IS NOT WHAT IT USED TO BE.
BUT A COMFORTABLE SENTENCE WAS NO GREAT LOSS.
...YOU SEE?

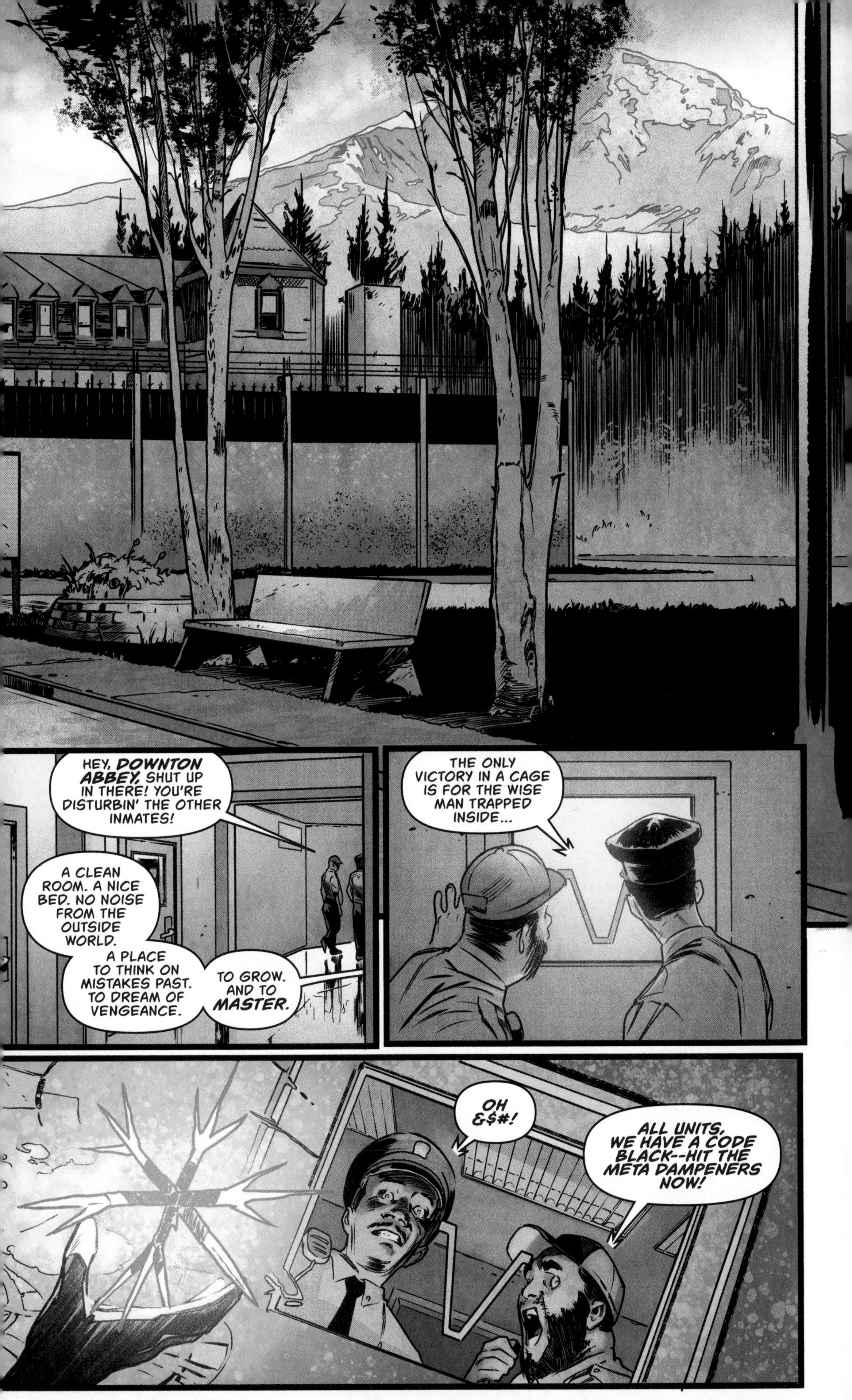
HEY, DOWNTON ABBEY, SHUT UP IN THERE! YOU'RE DISTURBIN' THE OTHER INMATES!
A CLEAN ROOM. A NICE BED. NO NOISE FROM THE OUTSIDE WORLD.
A PLACE TO THINK ON MISTAKES PAST. TO DREAM OF VENGEANCE.
TO GROW. AND TO MASTER.
THE ONLY VICTORY IN A CAGE IS FOR THE WISE MAN TRAPPED INSIDE...
OH &$#!
ALL UNITS, WE HAVE A CODE BLACK--HIT THE META DAMPENERS NOW!

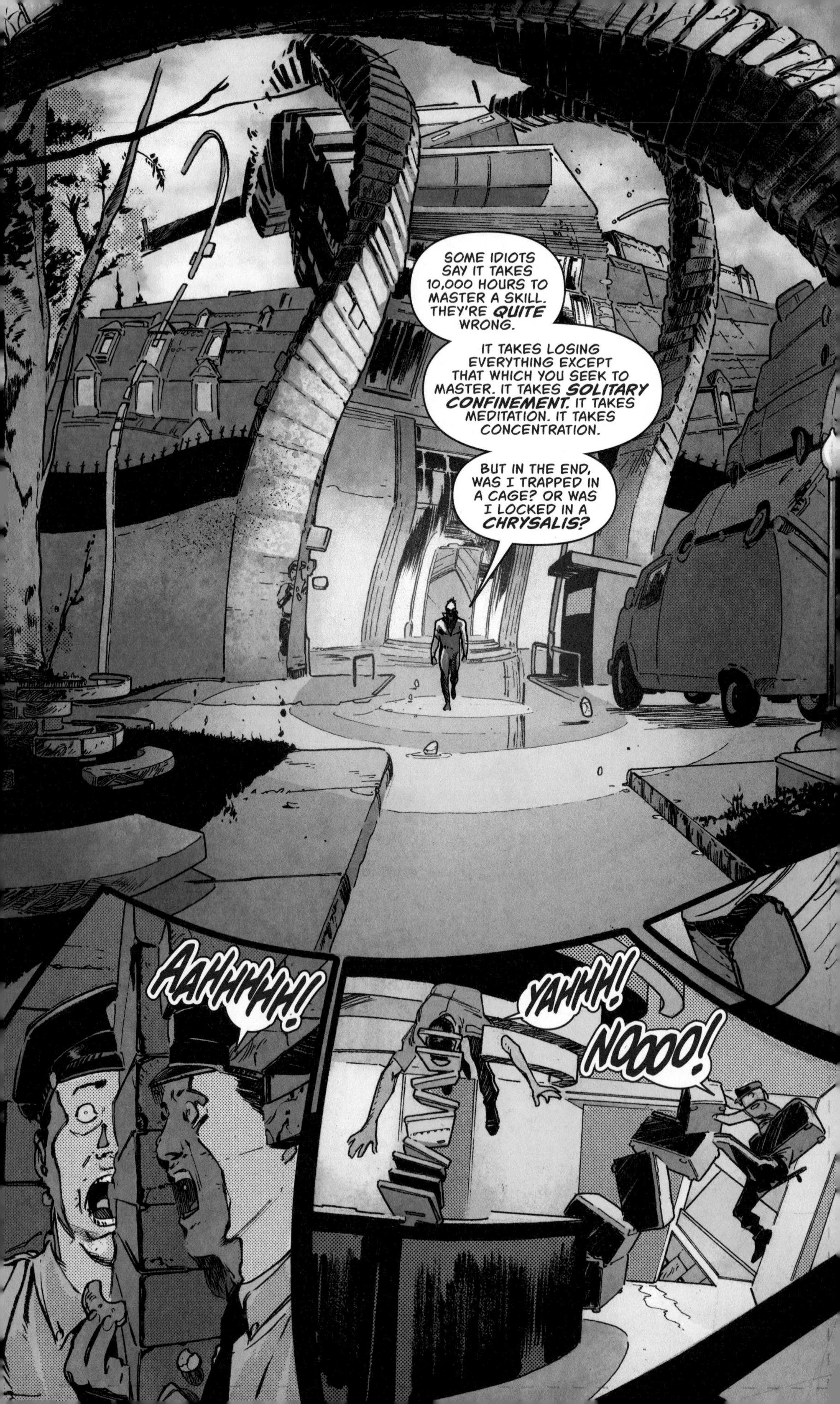
SOME IDIOTS SAY IT TAKES 10,000 HOURS TO MASTER A SKILL. THEY'RE *QUITE* WRONG.
IT TAKES LOSING EVERYTHING EXCEPT THAT WHICH YOU SEEK TO MASTER. IT TAKES *SOLITARY CONFINEMENT.* IT TAKES MEDITATION. IT TAKES CONCENTRATION.
BUT IN THE END, WAS I TRAPPED IN A CAGE? OR WAS I LOCKED IN A *CHRYSALIS?*
AAHHHHH!
YAHHH!
NOOOO!

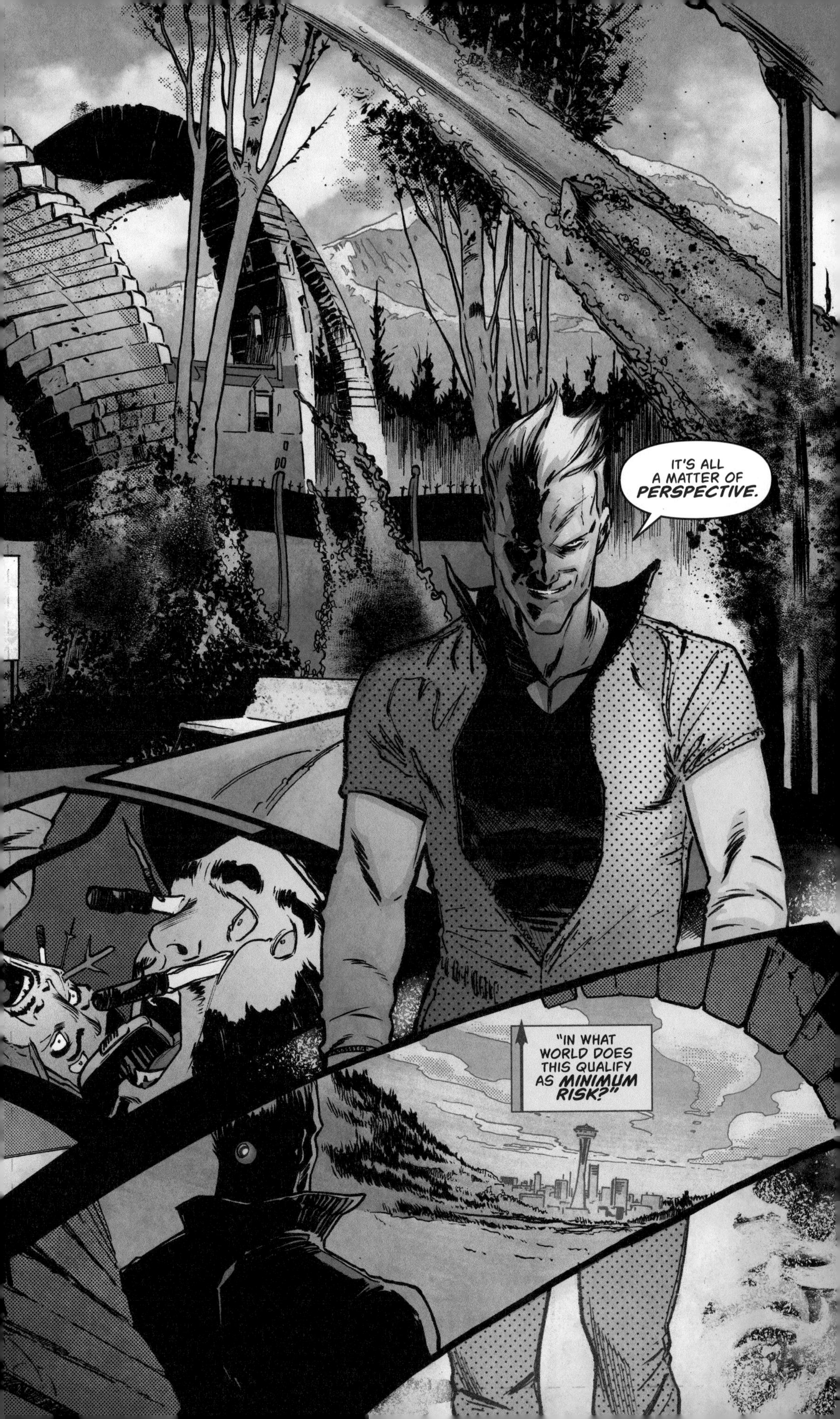
IT'S ALL A MATTER OF PERSPECTIVE.
"IN WHAT WORLD DOES THIS QUALIFY AS MINIMUM RISK?"

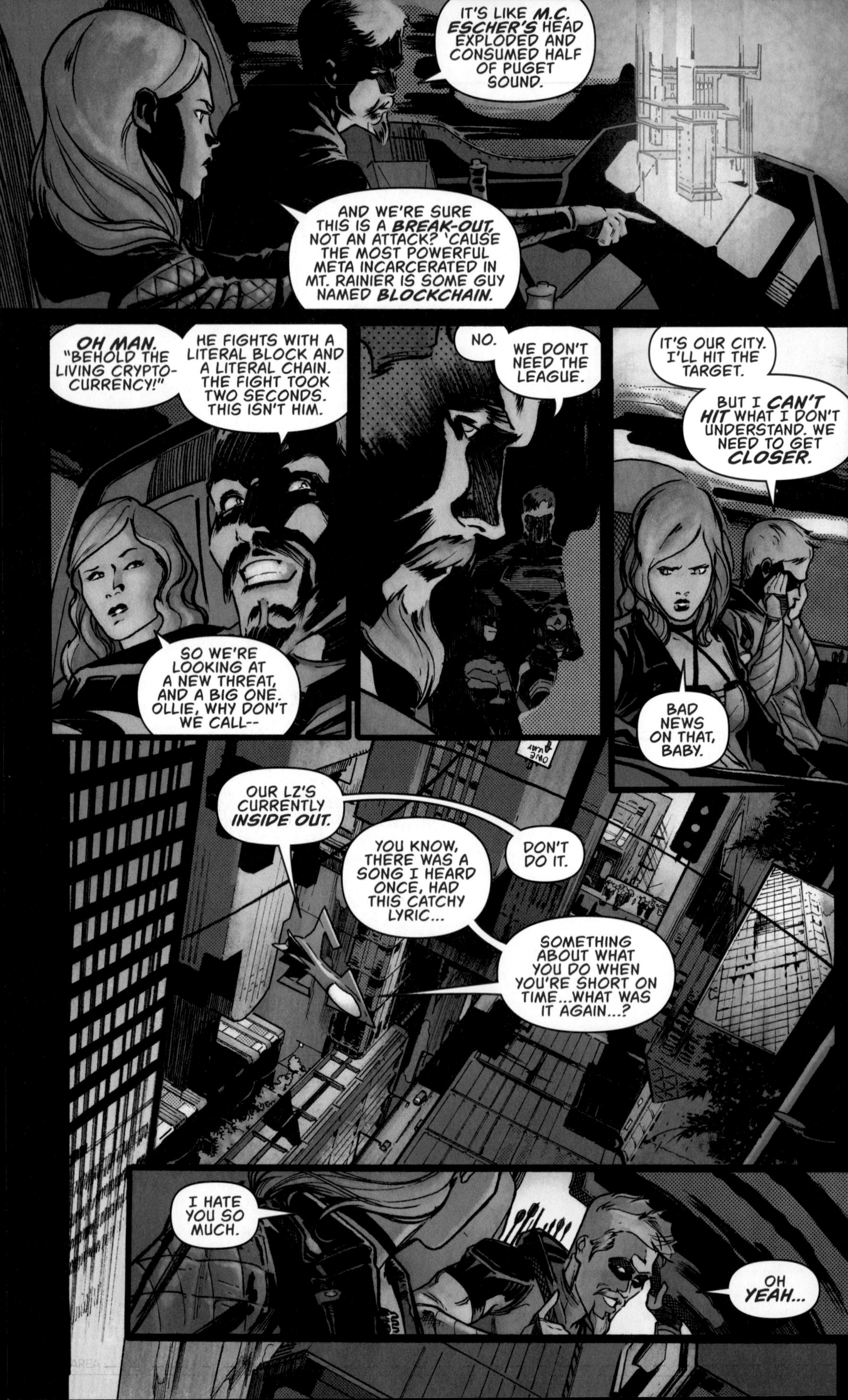
IT'S LIKE M.C. ESCHER'S HEAD EXPLODED AND CONSUMED HALF OF PUGET SOUND.
AND WE'RE SURE THIS IS A BREAK-OUT, NOT AN ATTACK? 'CAUSE THE MOST POWERFUL META INCARCERATED IN MT. RAINIER IS SOME GUY NAMED BLOCKCHAIN.
OH MAN. "BEHOLD THE LIVING CRYPTO-CURRENCY!"
HE FIGHTS WITH A LITERAL BLOCK AND A LITERAL CHAIN. THE FIGHT TOOK TWO SECONDS. THIS ISN'T HIM.
SO WE'RE LOOKING AT A NEW THREAT, AND A BIG ONE. OLLIE, WHY DON'T WE CALL--
NO.
WE DON'T NEED THE LEAGUE.
IT'S OUR CITY. I'LL HIT THE TARGET.
BUT I CAN'T HIT WHAT I DON'T UNDERSTAND. WE NEED TO GET CLOSER.
BAD NEWS ON THAT, BABY.
OUR LZ'S CURRENTLY INSIDE OUT.
YOU KNOW, THERE WAS A SONG I HEARD ONCE, HAD THIS CATCHY LYRIC...
DON'T DO IT.
SOMETHING ABOUT WHAT YOU DO WHEN YOU'RE SHORT ON TIME...WHAT WAS IT AGAIN...?
I HATE YOU SO MUCH.
OH YEAH...

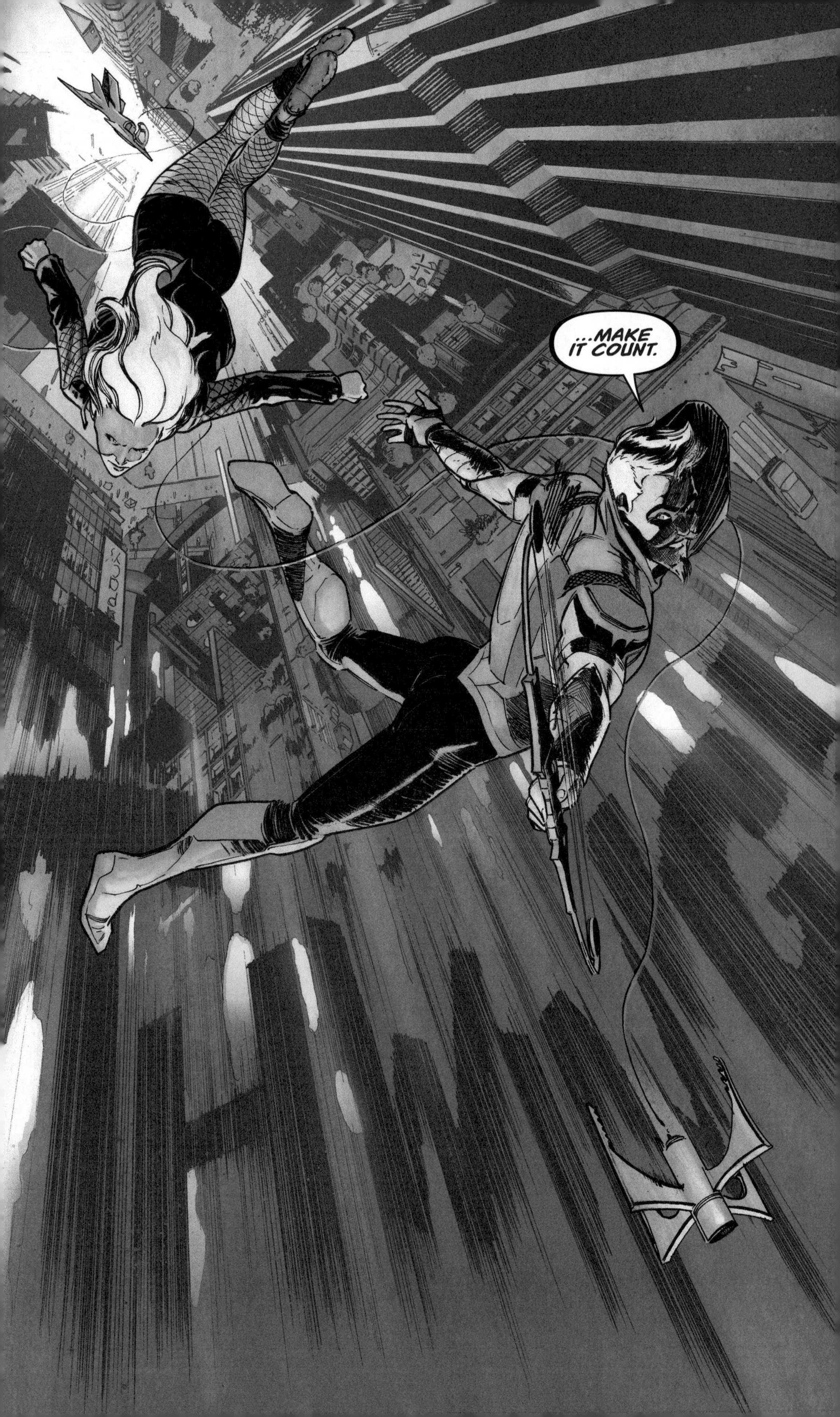
...MAKE IT COUNT.

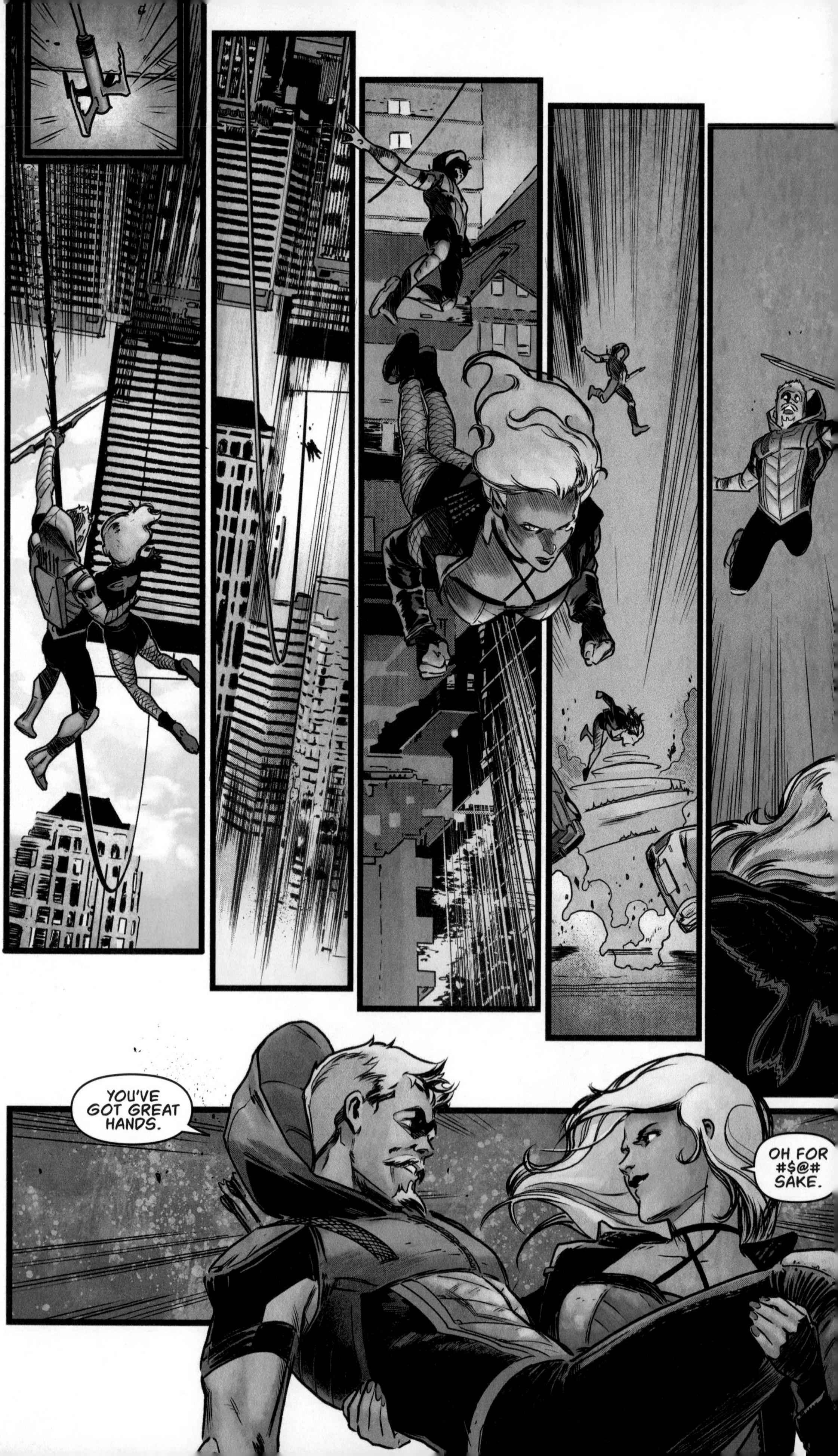
YOU'VE GOT GREAT HANDS.
OH FOR #$@# SAKE.

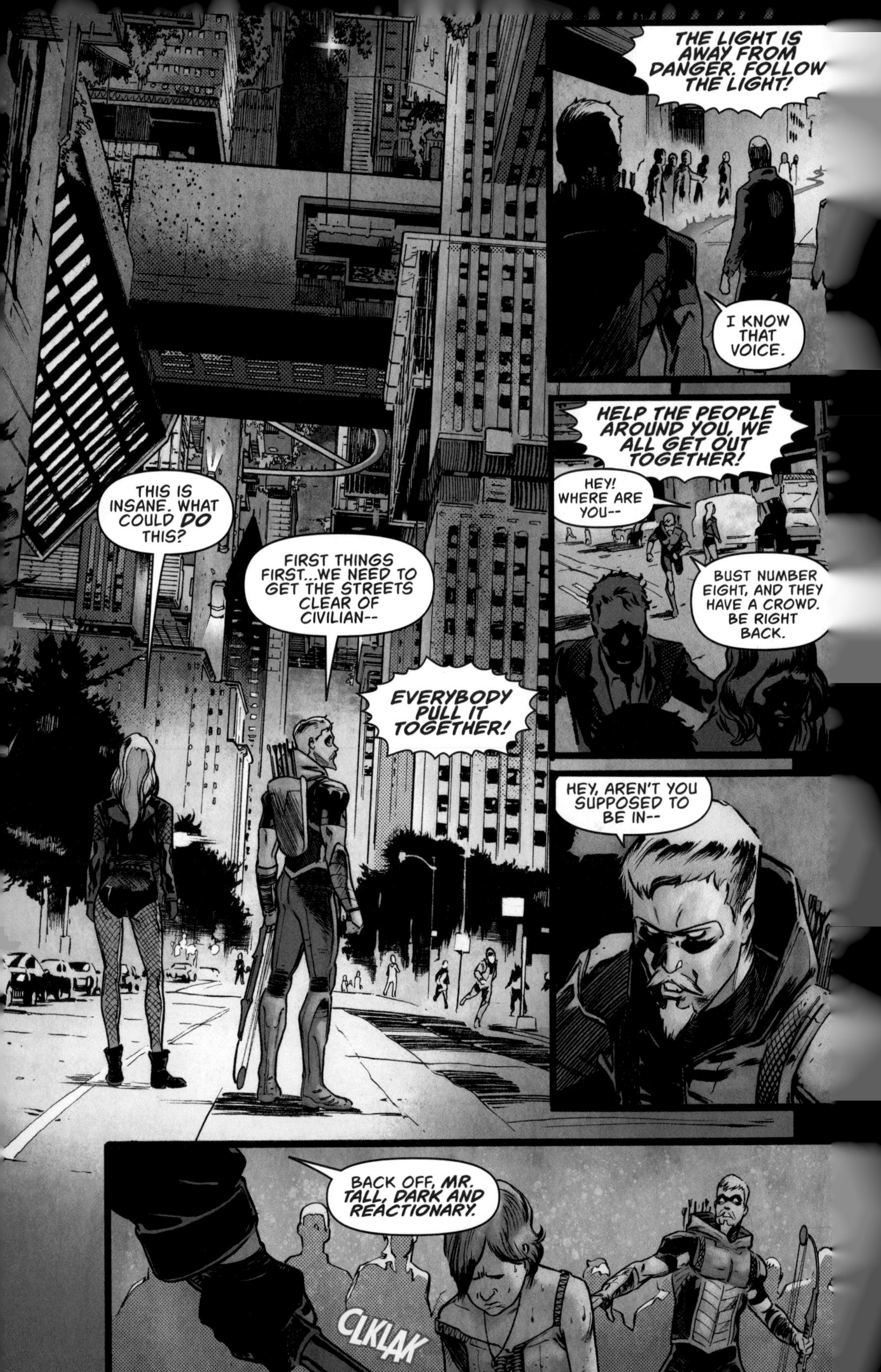
THE LIGHT IS AWAY FROM DANGER. FOLLOW THE LIGHT!
I KNOW THAT VOICE.
THIS IS INSANE. WHAT COULD DO THIS?
FIRST THINGS FIRST...WE NEED TO GET THE STREETS CLEAR OF CIVILIAN--
EVERYBODY PULL IT TOGETHER!
HELP THE PEOPLE AROUND YOU, WE ALL GET OUT TOGETHER!
HEY! WHERE ARE YOU--
BUST NUMBER EIGHT, AND THEY HAVE A CROWD. BE RIGHT BACK.
HEY, AREN'T YOU SUPPOSED TO BE IN--
BACK OFF, MR. TALL, DARK AND REACTIONARY.
CLKLAK

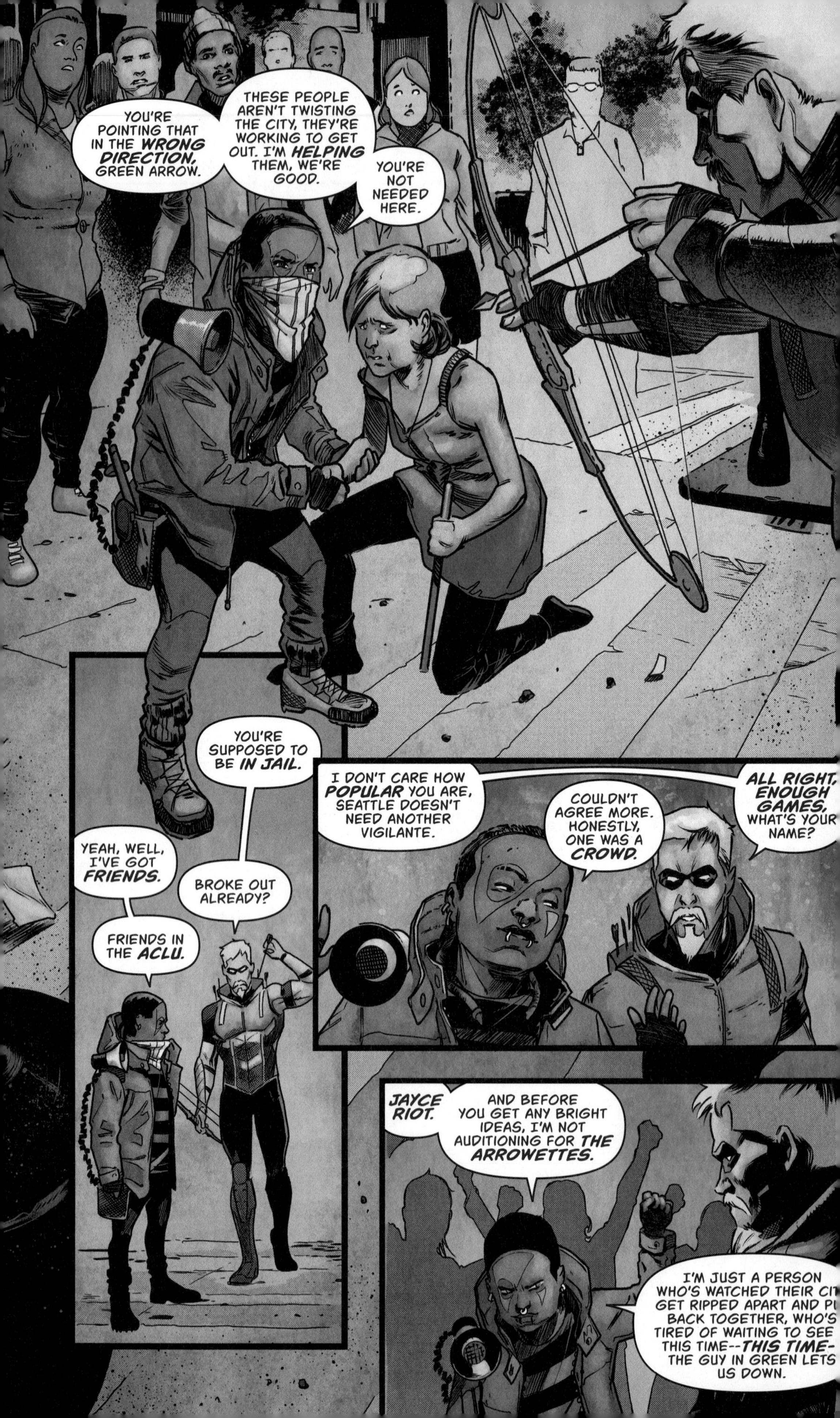
YOU'RE POINTING THAT IN THE WRONG DIRECTION, GREEN ARROW.
THESE PEOPLE AREN'T TWISTING THE CITY, THEY'RE WORKING TO GET OUT. I'M HELPING THEM, WE'RE GOOD.
YOU'RE NOT NEEDED HERE.
YOU'RE SUPPOSED TO BE IN JAIL.
YEAH, WELL, I'VE GOT FRIENDS.
BROKE OUT ALREADY?
FRIENDS IN THE ACLU.
I DON'T CARE HOW POPULAR YOU ARE, SEATTLE DOESN'T NEED ANOTHER VIGILANTE.
COULDN'T AGREE MORE. HONESTLY, ONE WAS A CROWD.
ALL RIGHT. ENOUGH GAMES. WHAT'S YOUR NAME?
JAYCE RIOT.
AND BEFORE YOU GET ANY BRIGHT IDEAS, I'M NOT AUDITIONING FOR THE ARROWETTES.
I'M JUST A PERSON WHO'S WATCHED THEIR CI GET RIPPED APART AND P BACK TOGETHER, WHO'S TIRED OF WAITING TO SEE THIS TIME--THIS TIME- THE GUY IN GREEN LETS US DOWN.

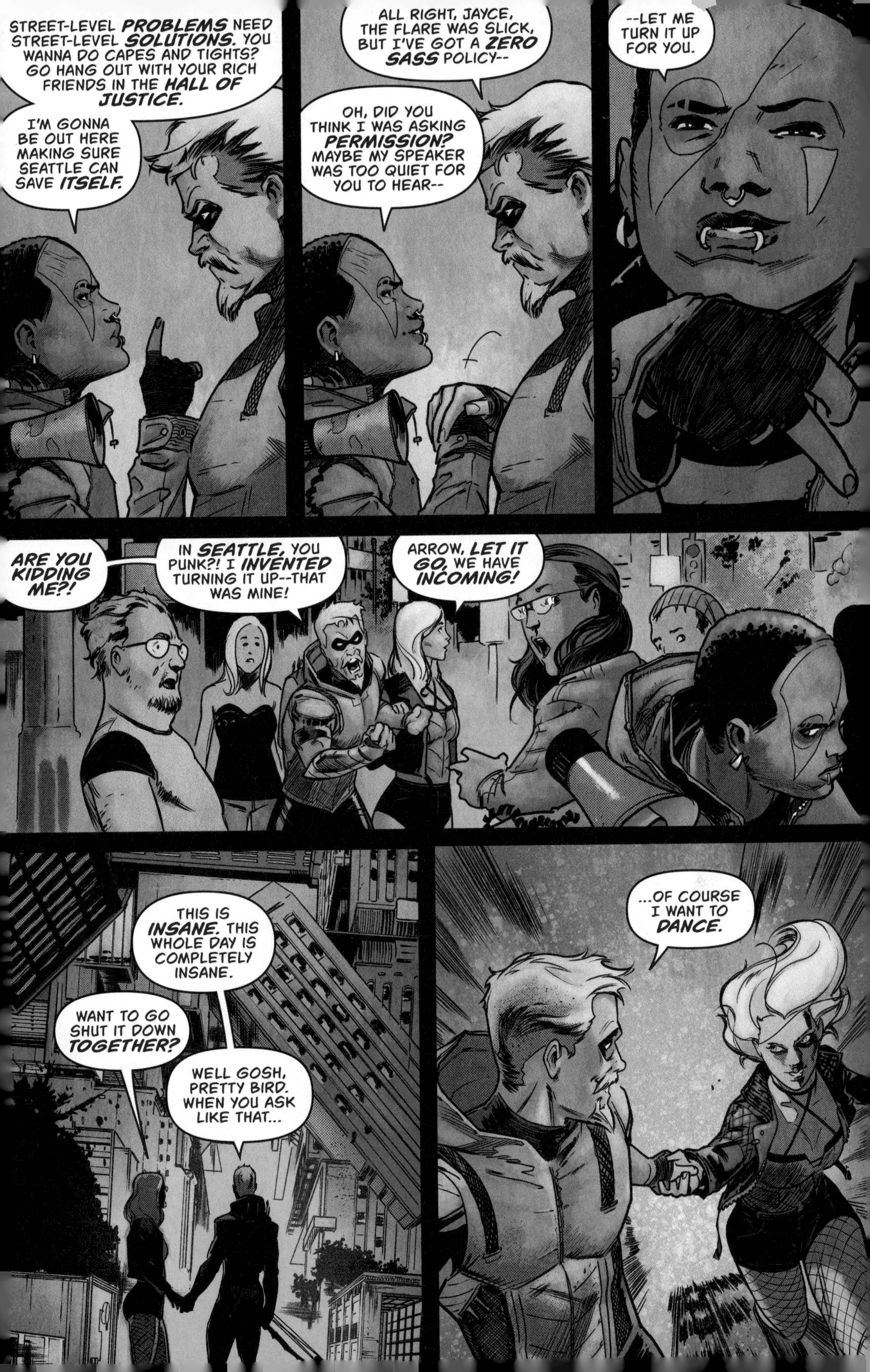
STREET-LEVEL PROBLEMS NEED STREET-LEVEL SOLUTIONS. YOU WANNA DO CAPES AND TIGHTS? GO HANG OUT WITH YOUR RICH FRIENDS IN THE HALL OF JUSTICE.
I'M GONNA BE OUT HERE MAKING SURE SEATTLE CAN SAVE ITSELF.
ALL RIGHT, JAYCE, THE FLARE WAS SLICK, BUT I'VE GOT A ZERO SASS POLICY--
OH, DID YOU THINK I WAS ASKING PERMISSION? MAYBE MY SPEAKER WAS TOO QUIET FOR YOU TO HEAR--
--LET ME TURN IT UP FOR YOU.
ARE YOU KIDDING ME?!
IN SEATTLE, YOU PUNK?! I INVENTED TURNING IT UP--THAT WAS MINE!
ARROW, LET IT GO, WE HAVE INCOMING!
THIS IS INSANE. THIS WHOLE DAY IS COMPLETELY INSANE.
WANT TO GO SHUT IT DOWN TOGETHER?
WELL GOSH, PRETTY BIRD. WHEN YOU ASK LIKE THAT...
...OF COURSE I WANT TO DANCE.

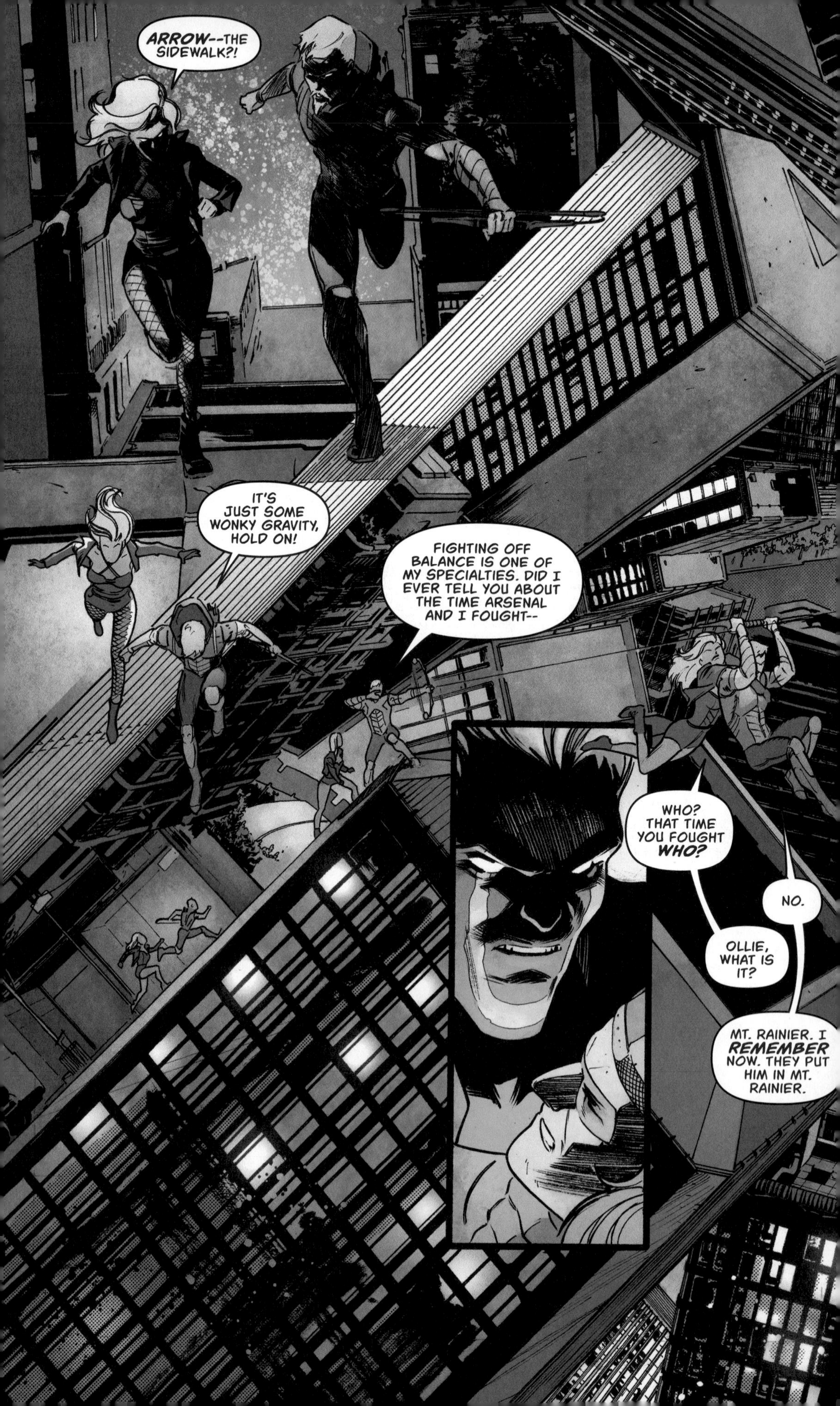
ARROW--THE SIDEWALK?!
IT'S JUST SOME WONKY GRAVITY, HOLD ON!
FIGHTING OFF BALANCE IS ONE OF MY SPECIALTIES. DID I EVER TELL YOU ABOUT THE TIME ARSENAL AND I FOUGHT--
WHO? THAT TIME YOU FOUGHT WHO?
NO.
OLLIE, WHAT IS IT?
MT. RAINIER. I REMEMBER NOW. THEY PUT HIM IN MT. RAINIER.

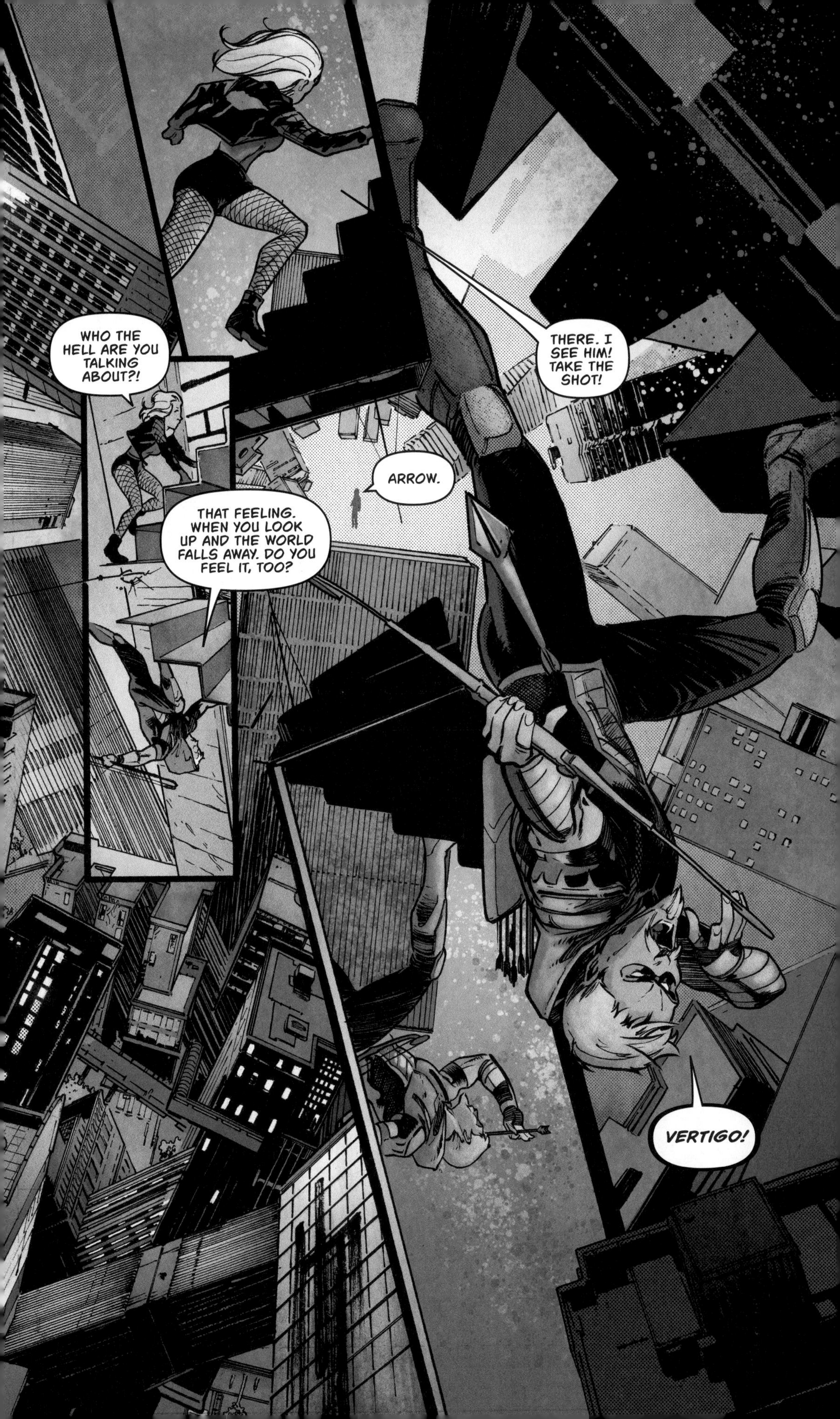
WHO THE HELL ARE YOU TALKING ABOUT?!
THERE. I SEE HIM! TAKE THE SHOT!
ARROW.
THAT FEELING. WHEN YOU LOOK UP AND THE WORLD FALLS AWAY. DO YOU FEEL IT, TOO?
VERTIGO!

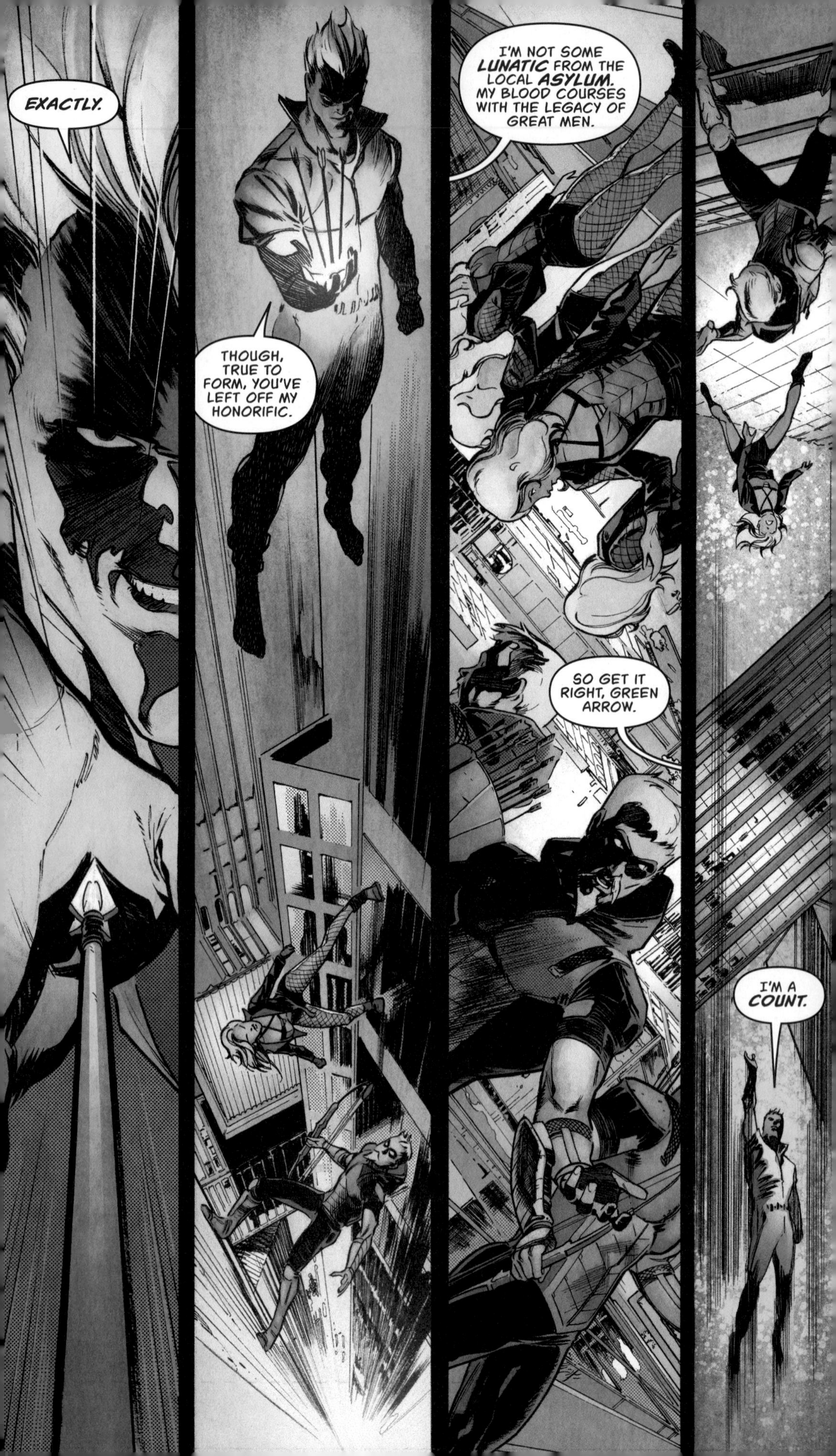
EXACTLY.
THOUGH, TRUE TO FORM, YOU'VE LEFT OFF MY HONORIFIC.
I'M NOT SOME LUNATIC FROM THE LOCAL ASYLUM. MY BLOOD COURSES WITH THE LEGACY OF GREAT MEN.
SO GET IT RIGHT, GREEN ARROW.
I'M A COUNT.

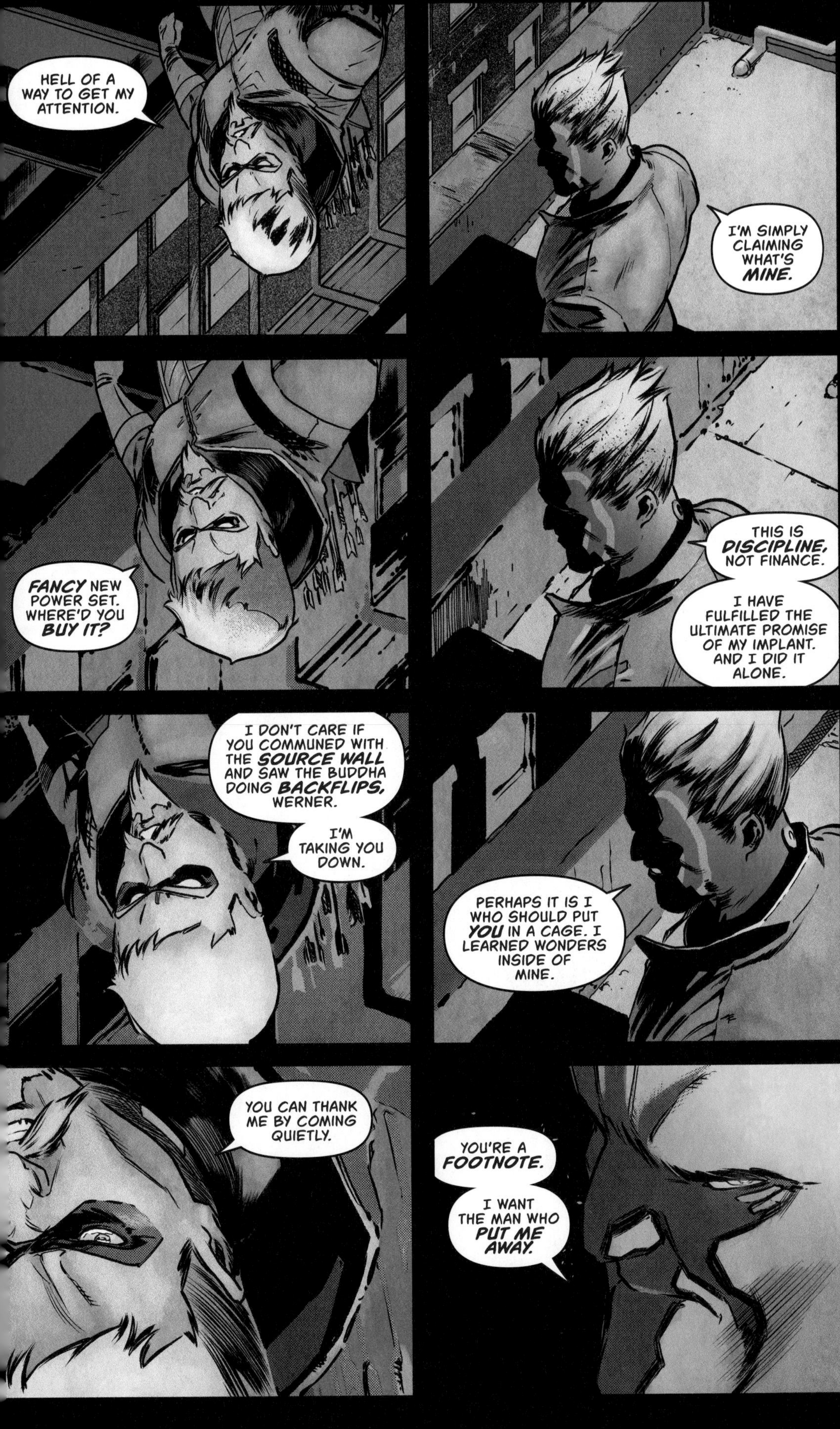
HELL OF A WAY TO GET MY ATTENTION.
I'M SIMPLY CLAIMING WHAT'S MINE.
FANCY NEW POWER SET. WHERE'D YOU BUY IT?
THIS IS DISCIPLINE, NOT FINANCE.
I HAVE FULFILLED THE ULTIMATE PROMISE OF MY IMPLANT. AND I DID IT ALONE.
I DON'T CARE IF YOU COMMUNED WITH THE SOURCE WALL AND SAW THE BUDDHA DOING BACKFLIPS, WERNER.
I'M TAKING YOU DOWN.
PERHAPS IT IS I WHO SHOULD PUT YOU IN A CAGE. I LEARNED WONDERS INSIDE OF MINE.
YOU CAN THANK ME BY COMING QUIETLY.
YOU'RE A FOOTNOTE.
I WANT THE MAN WHO PUT ME AWAY.

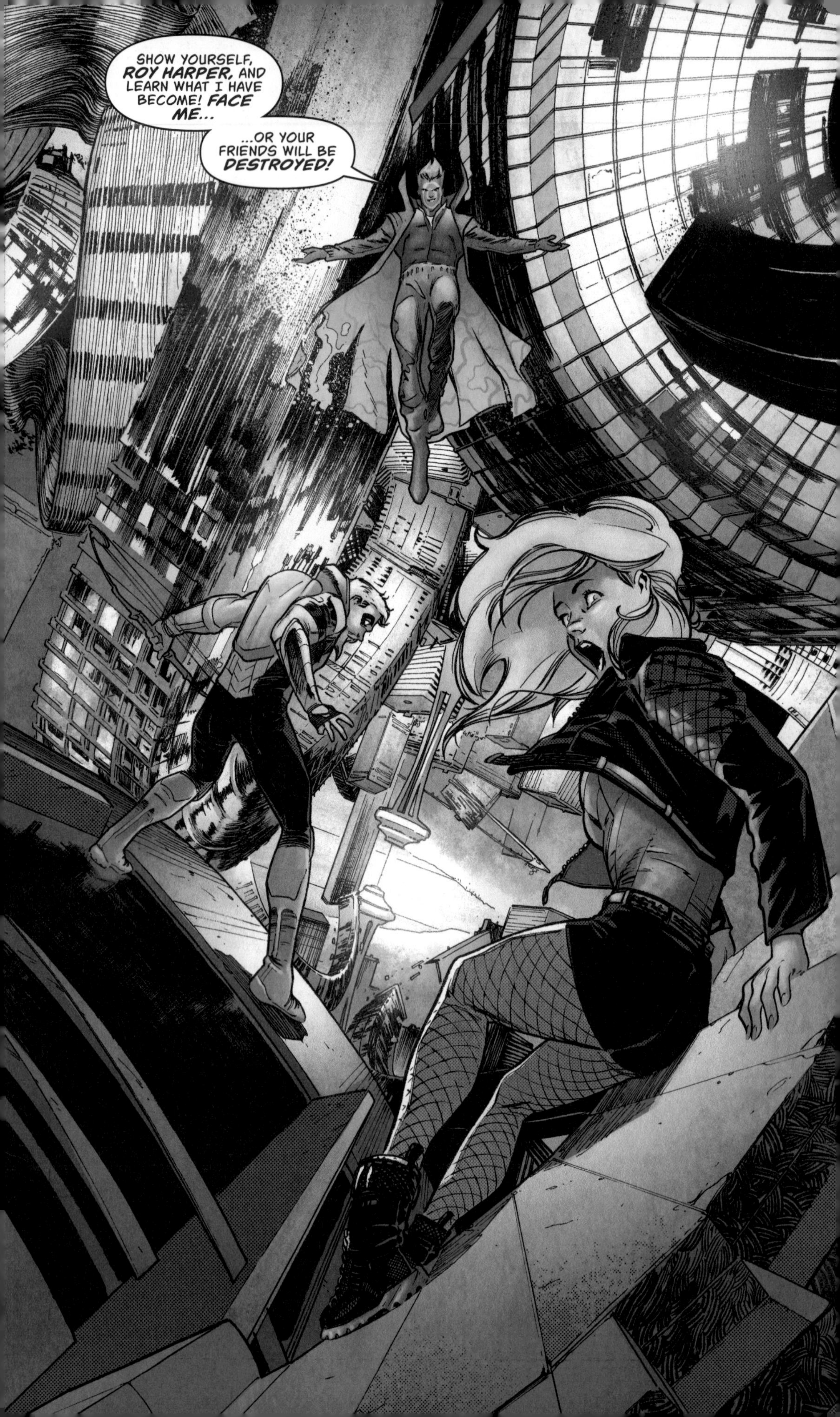
SHOW YOURSELF, **ROY HARPER,** AND LEARN WHAT I HAVE BECOME! ***FACE ME...***
...OR YOUR FRIENDS WILL BE ***DESTROYED!***

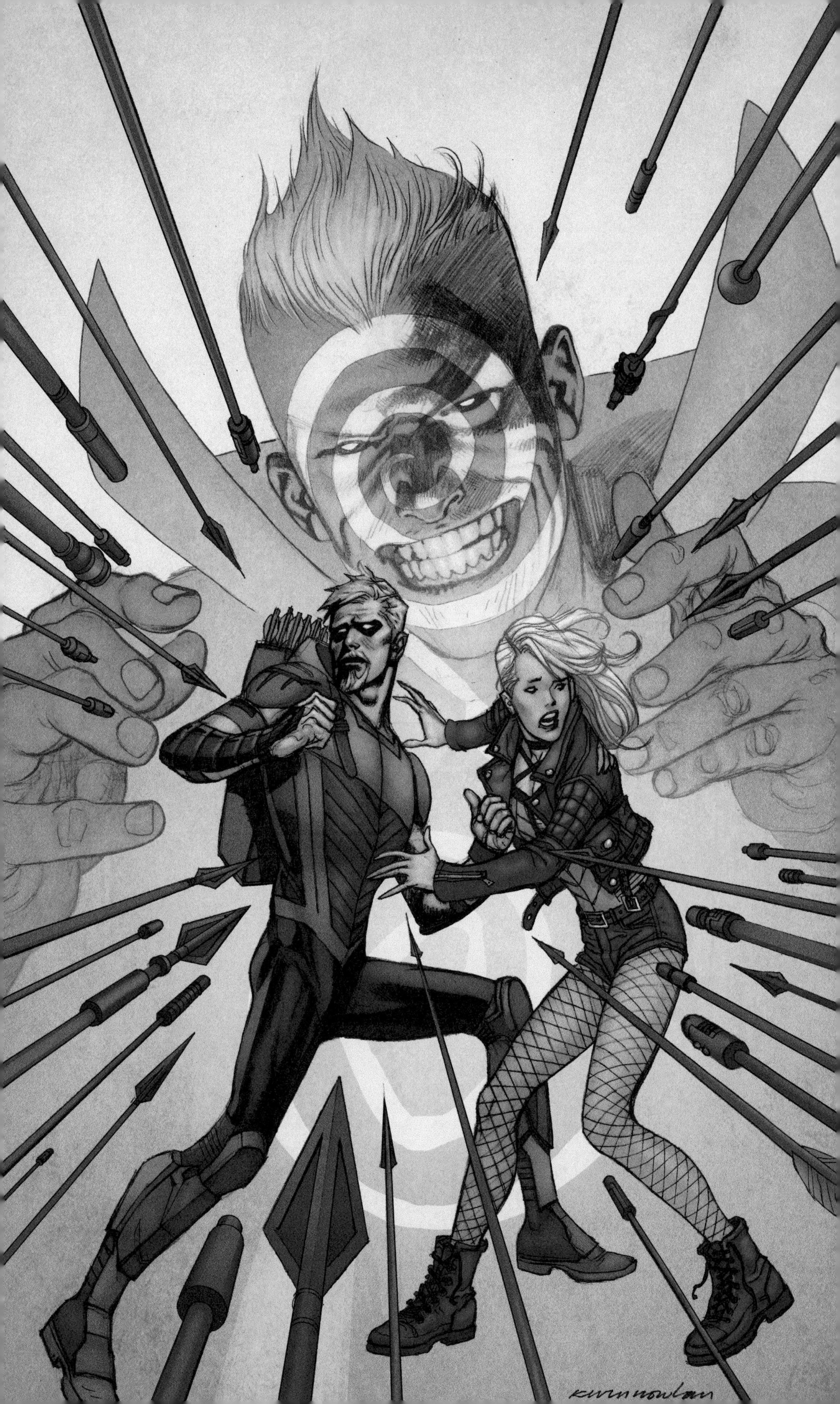
kevinnowlan

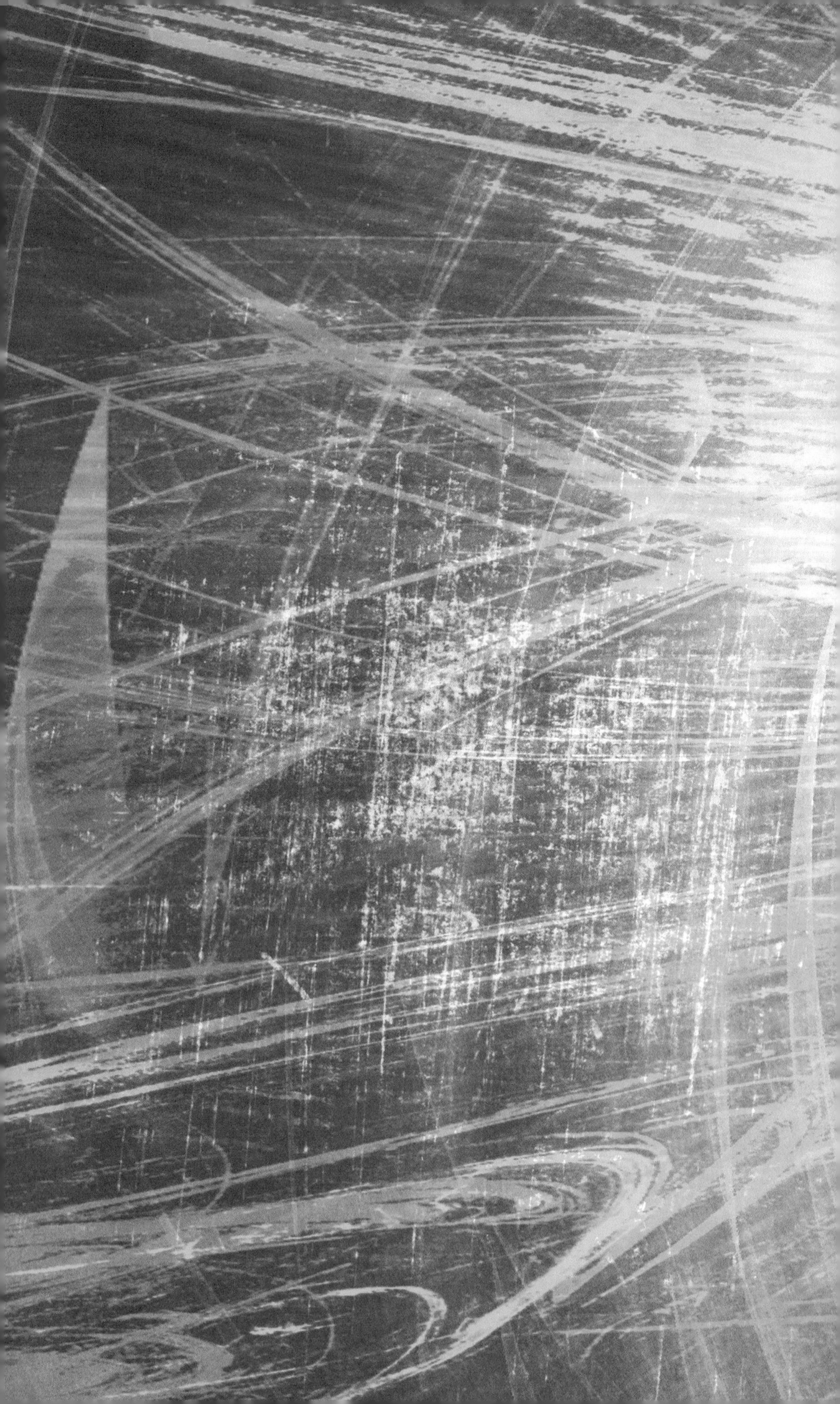

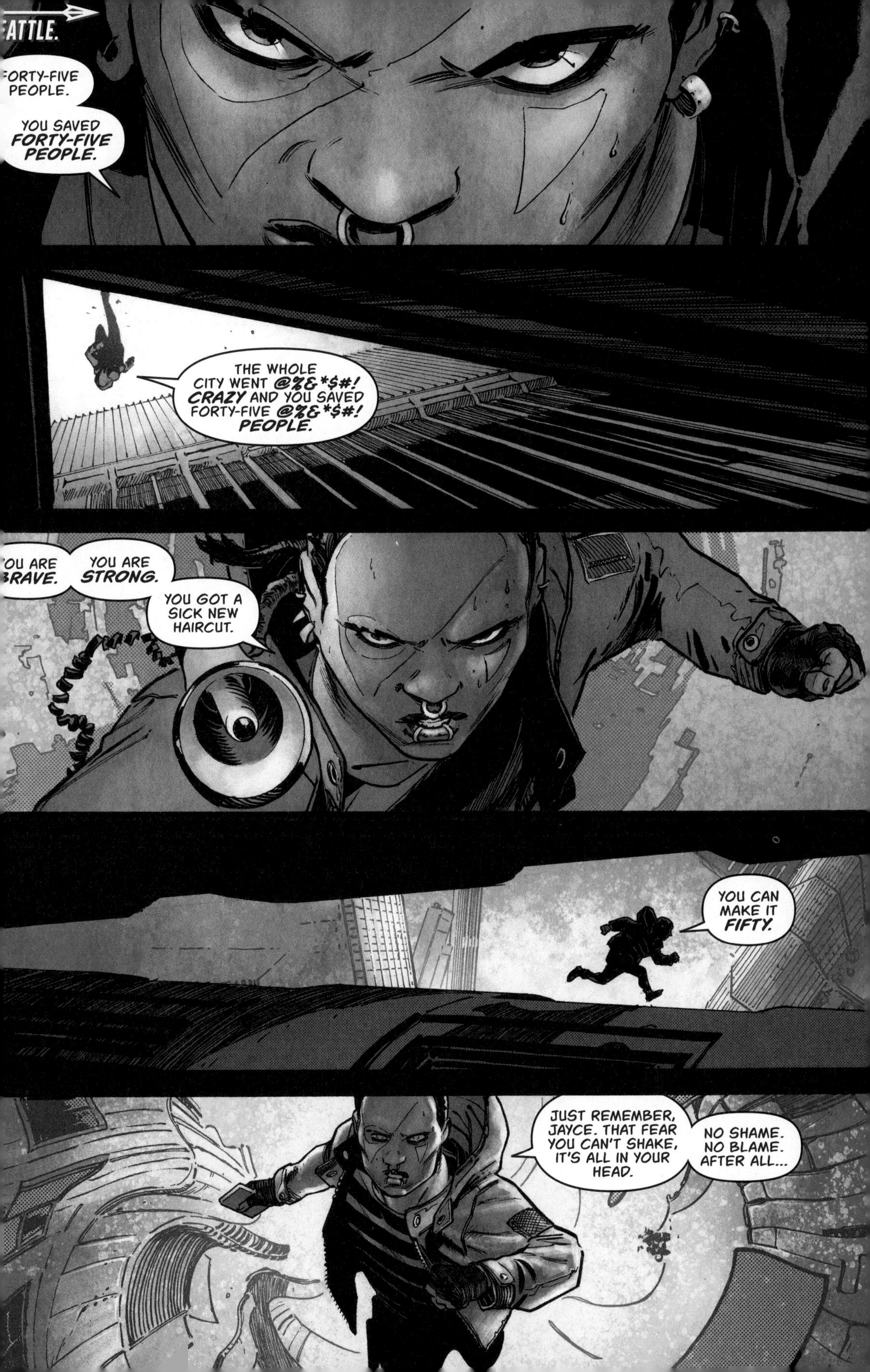

EATTLE.
FORTY-FIVE PEOPLE.
YOU SAVED FORTY-FIVE PEOPLE.
THE WHOLE CITY WENT @%&*$#! CRAZY AND YOU SAVED FORTY-FIVE @%&*$#! PEOPLE.
YOU ARE BRAVE.
YOU ARE STRONG.
YOU GOT A SICK NEW HAIRCUT.
YOU CAN MAKE IT FIFTY.
JUST REMEMBER, JAYCE. THAT FEAR YOU CAN'T SHAKE, IT'S ALL IN YOUR HEAD.
NO SHAME. NO BLAME. AFTER ALL...

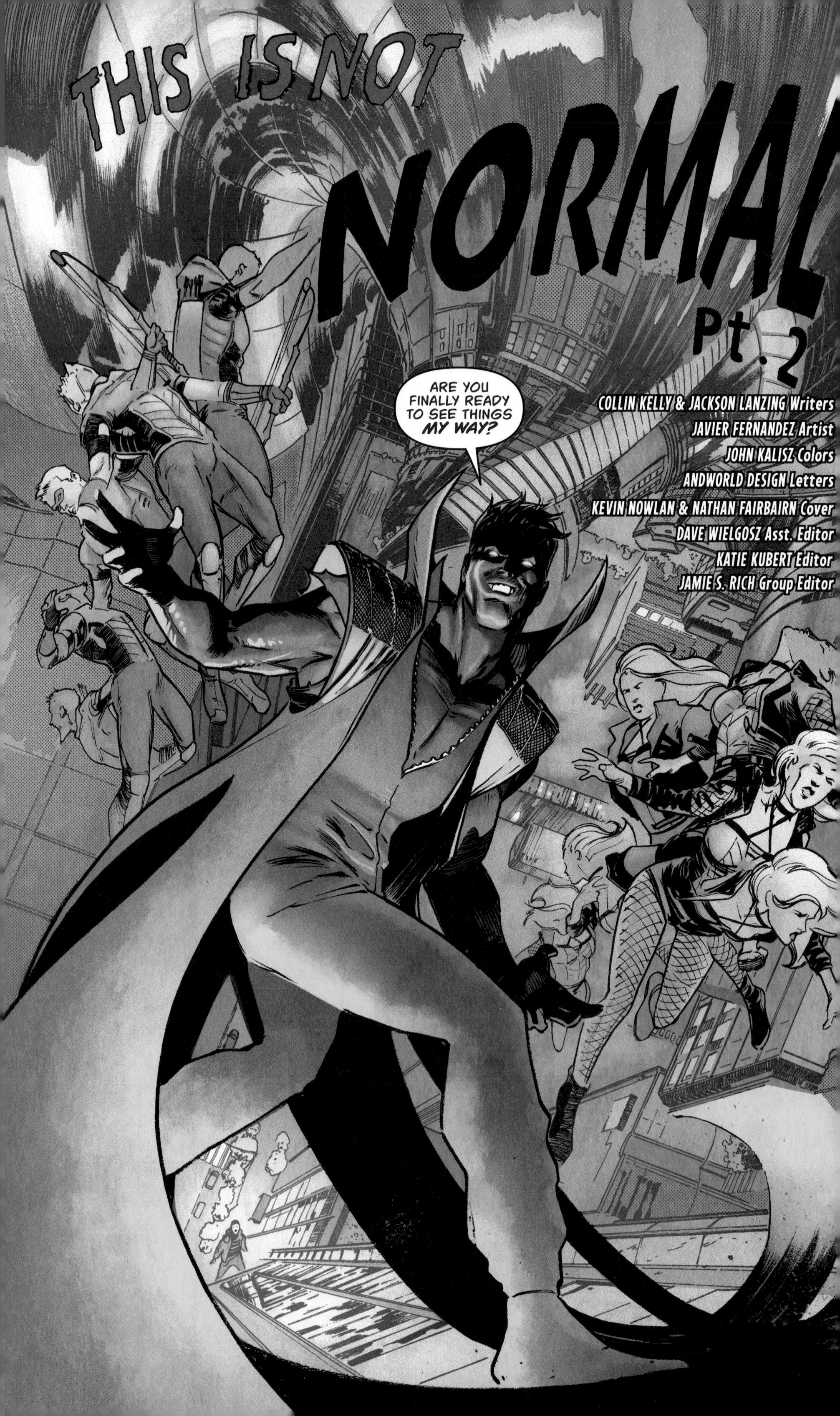
THIS IS NOT NORMAL Pt. 2
ARE YOU FINALLY READY TO SEE THINGS MY WAY?
COLLIN KELLY & JACKSON LANZING Writers
JAVIER FERNANDEZ Artist
JOHN KALISZ Colors
ANDWORLD DESIGN Letters
KEVIN NOWLAN & NATHAN FAIRBAIRN Cover
DAVE WIELGOSZ Asst. Editor
KATIE KUBERT Editor
JAMIE S. RICH Group Editor

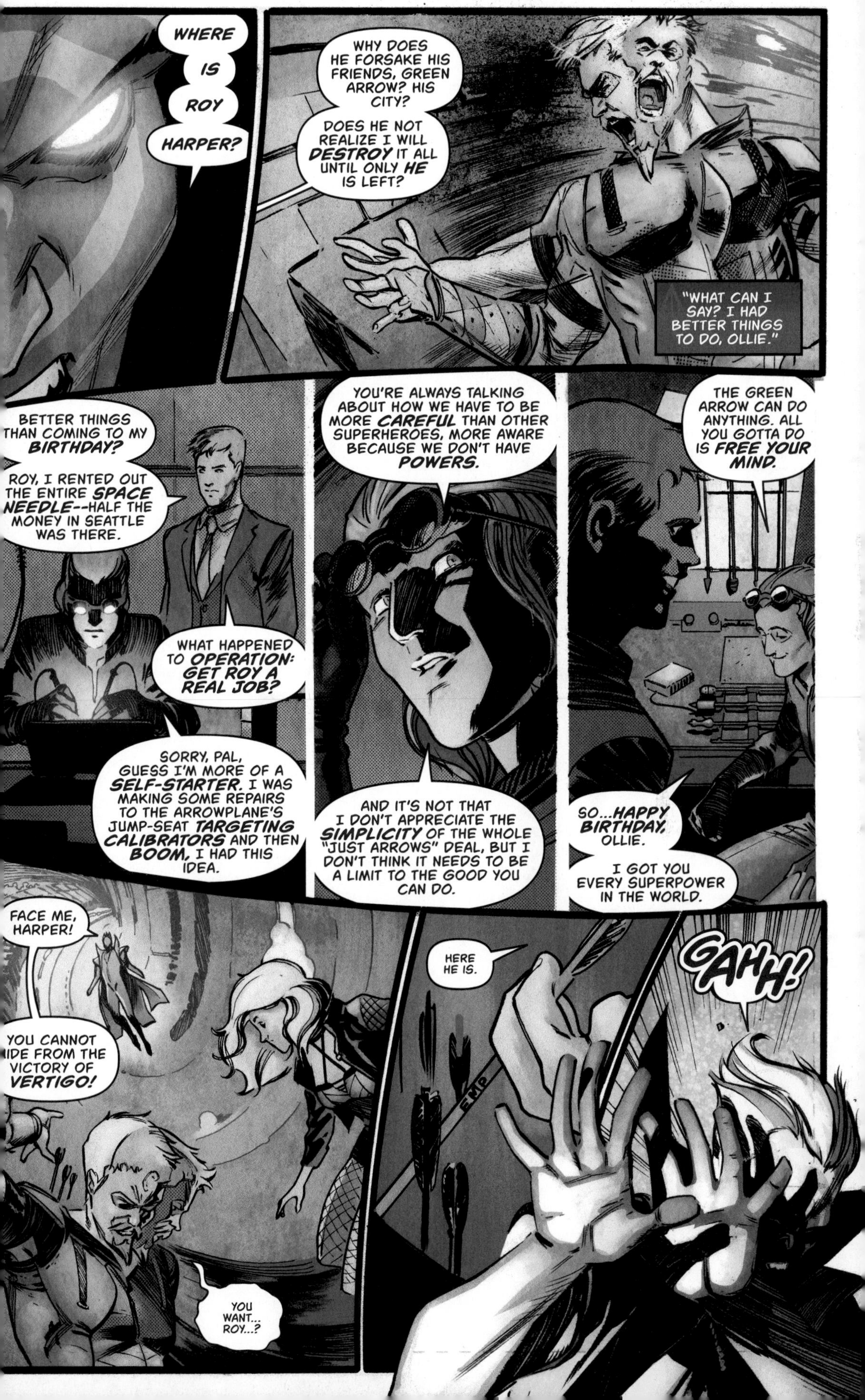
WHERE IS ROY HARPER?
WHY DOES HE FORSAKE HIS FRIENDS, GREEN ARROW? HIS CITY?
DOES HE NOT REALIZE I WILL DESTROY IT ALL UNTIL ONLY HE IS LEFT?
"WHAT CAN I SAY? I HAD BETTER THINGS TO DO, OLLIE."
BETTER THINGS THAN COMING TO MY BIRTHDAY?
ROY, I RENTED OUT THE ENTIRE SPACE NEEDLE--HALF THE MONEY IN SEATTLE WAS THERE.
WHAT HAPPENED TO OPERATION: GET ROY A REAL JOB?
SORRY, PAL, GUESS I'M MORE OF A SELF-STARTER. I WAS MAKING SOME REPAIRS TO THE ARROWPLANE'S JUMP-SEAT TARGETING CALIBRATORS AND THEN BOOM, I HAD THIS IDEA.
YOU'RE ALWAYS TALKING ABOUT HOW WE HAVE TO BE MORE CAREFUL THAN OTHER SUPERHEROES, MORE AWARE BECAUSE WE DON'T HAVE POWERS.
AND IT'S NOT THAT I DON'T APPRECIATE THE SIMPLICITY OF THE WHOLE "JUST ARROWS" DEAL, BUT I DON'T THINK IT NEEDS TO BE A LIMIT TO THE GOOD YOU CAN DO.
THE GREEN ARROW CAN DO ANYTHING. ALL YOU GOTTA DO IS FREE YOUR MIND.
SO...HAPPY BIRTHDAY, OLLIE.
I GOT YOU EVERY SUPERPOWER IN THE WORLD.
FACE ME, HARPER!
YOU CANNOT HIDE FROM THE VICTORY OF VERTIGO!
YOU WANT... ROY...?
HERE HE IS.
EMP
GAHH!

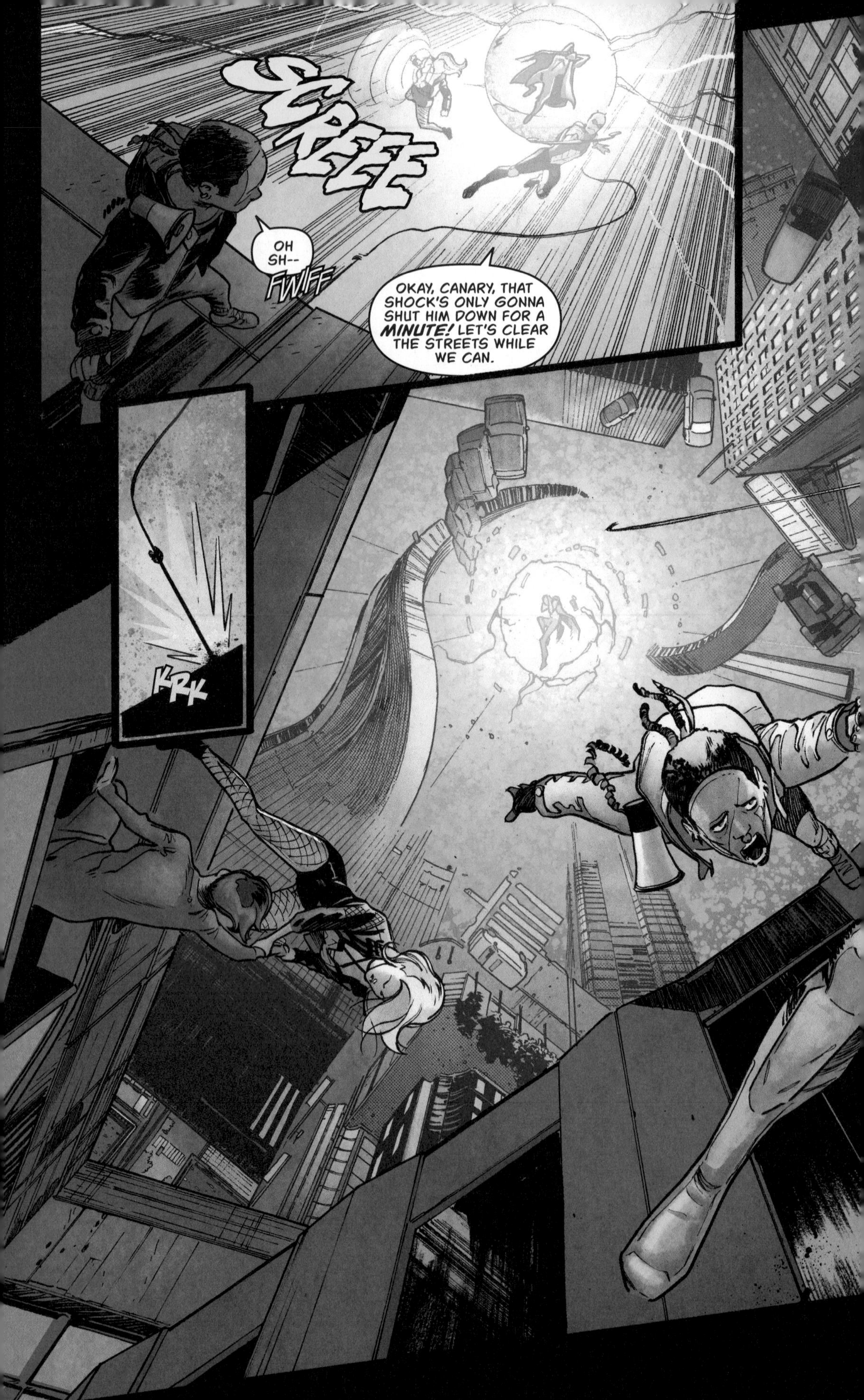
SCREEE
OH SH--
FWIFF
OKAY, CANARY, THAT SHOCK'S ONLY GONNA SHUT HIM DOWN FOR A MINUTE! LET'S CLEAR THE STREETS WHILE WE CAN.
KRK

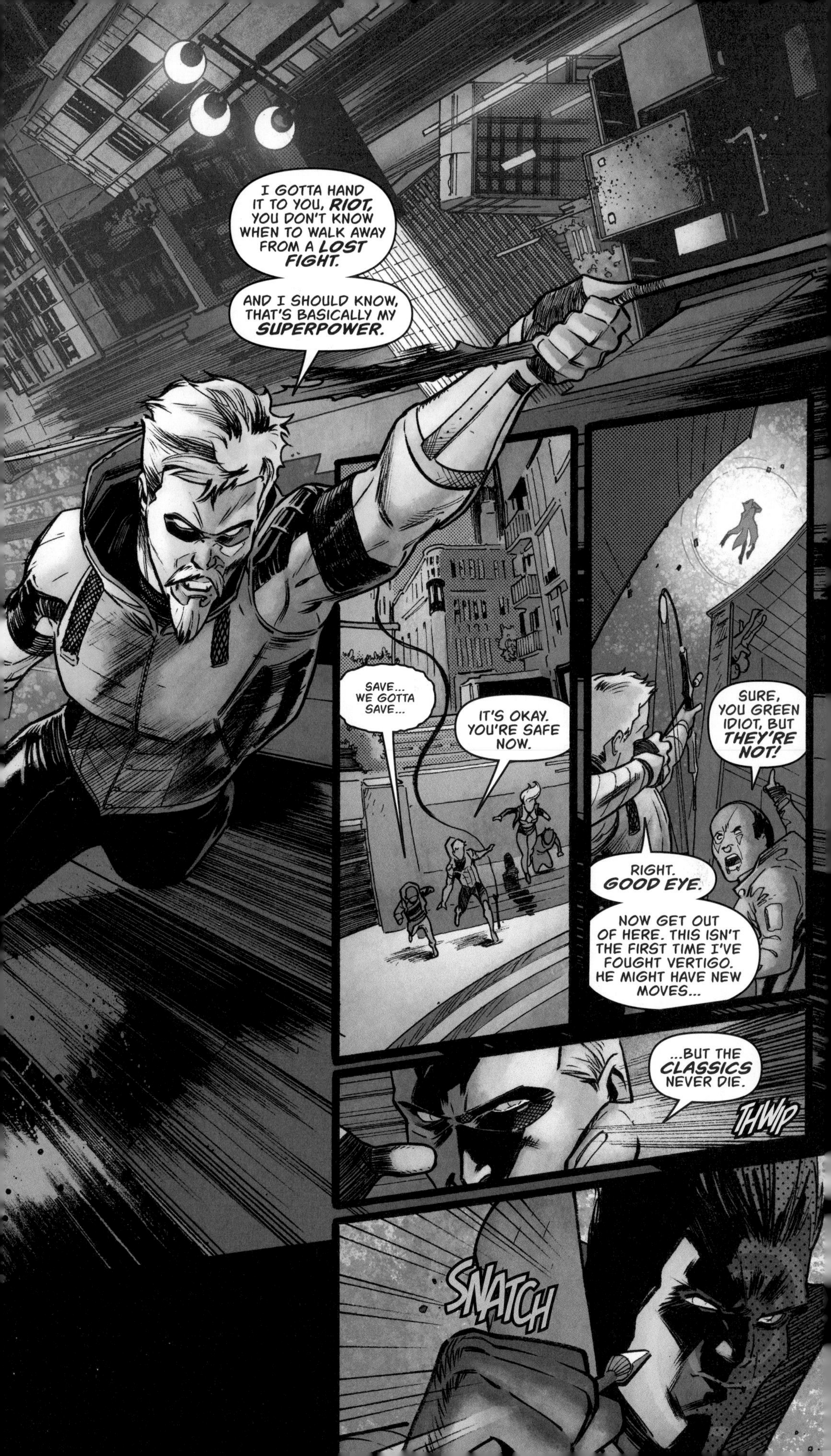
I GOTTA HAND IT TO YOU, RIOT, YOU DON'T KNOW WHEN TO WALK AWAY FROM A LOST FIGHT.
AND I SHOULD KNOW, THAT'S BASICALLY MY SUPERPOWER.
SAVE... WE GOTTA SAVE...
IT'S OKAY. YOU'RE SAFE NOW.
SURE, YOU GREEN IDIOT, BUT THEY'RE NOT!
RIGHT. GOOD EYE.
NOW GET OUT OF HERE. THIS ISN'T THE FIRST TIME I'VE FOUGHT VERTIGO. HE MIGHT HAVE NEW MOVES...
...BUT THE CLASSICS NEVER DIE.
THWIP
SNATCH

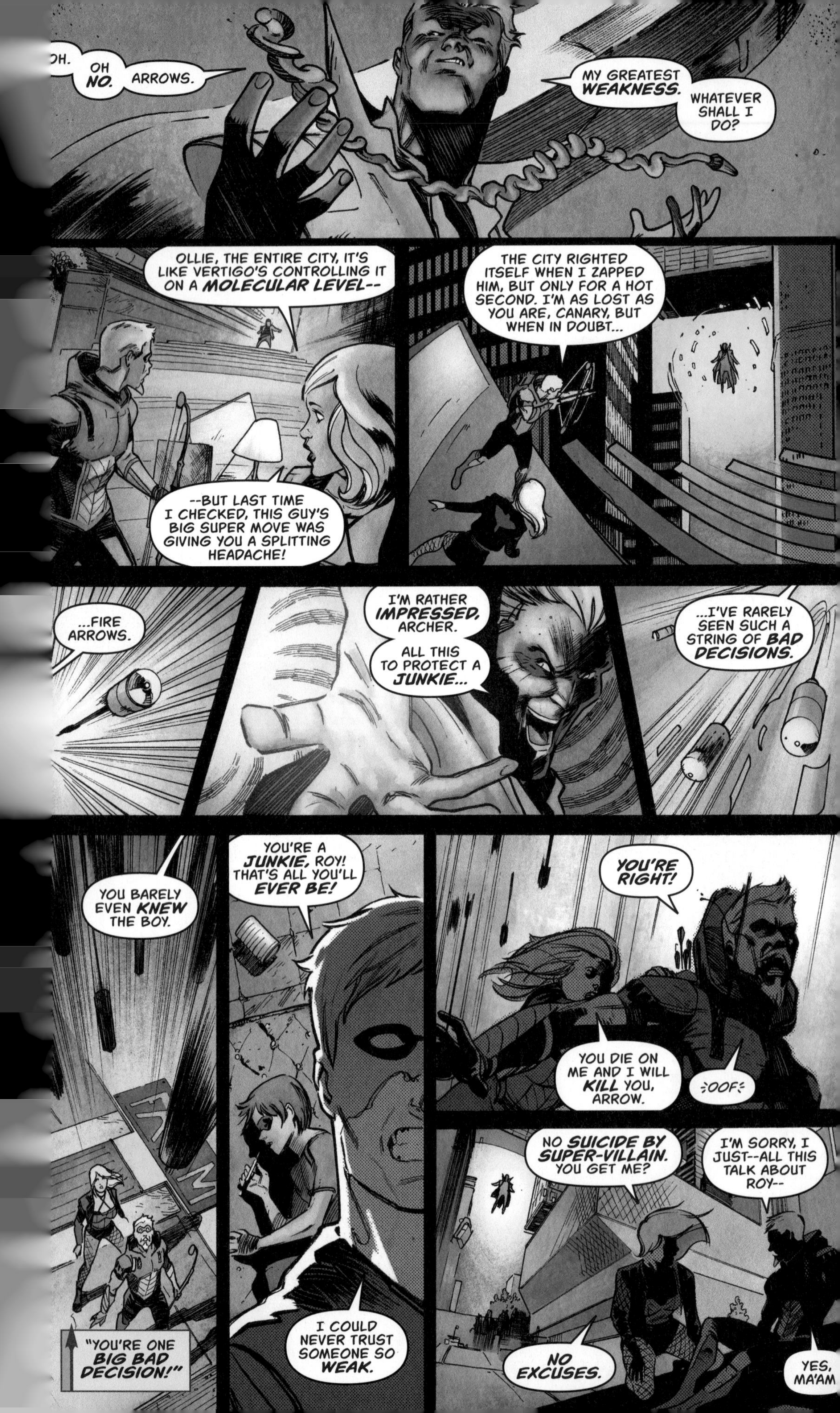
OH. OH NO. ARROWS.
MY GREATEST WEAKNESS.
WHATEVER SHALL I DO?
OLLIE, THE ENTIRE CITY, IT'S LIKE VERTIGO'S CONTROLLING IT ON A MOLECULAR LEVEL--
--BUT LAST TIME I CHECKED, THIS GUY'S BIG SUPER MOVE WAS GIVING YOU A SPLITTING HEADACHE!
THE CITY RIGHTED ITSELF WHEN I ZAPPED HIM, BUT ONLY FOR A HOT SECOND. I'M AS LOST AS YOU ARE, CANARY, BUT WHEN IN DOUBT...
...FIRE ARROWS.
I'M RATHER IMPRESSED, ARCHER.
ALL THIS TO PROTECT A JUNKIE...
...I'VE RARELY SEEN SUCH A STRING OF BAD DECISIONS.
YOU BARELY EVEN KNEW THE BOY.
"YOU'RE ONE BIG BAD DECISION!"
YOU'RE A JUNKIE, ROY! THAT'S ALL YOU'LL EVER BE!
I COULD NEVER TRUST SOMEONE SO WEAK.
YOU'RE RIGHT!
YOU DIE ON ME AND I WILL KILL YOU, ARROW.
OOF
NO SUICIDE BY SUPER-VILLAIN. YOU GET ME?
I'M SORRY, I JUST--ALL THIS TALK ABOUT ROY--
NO EXCUSES.
YES, MA'AM

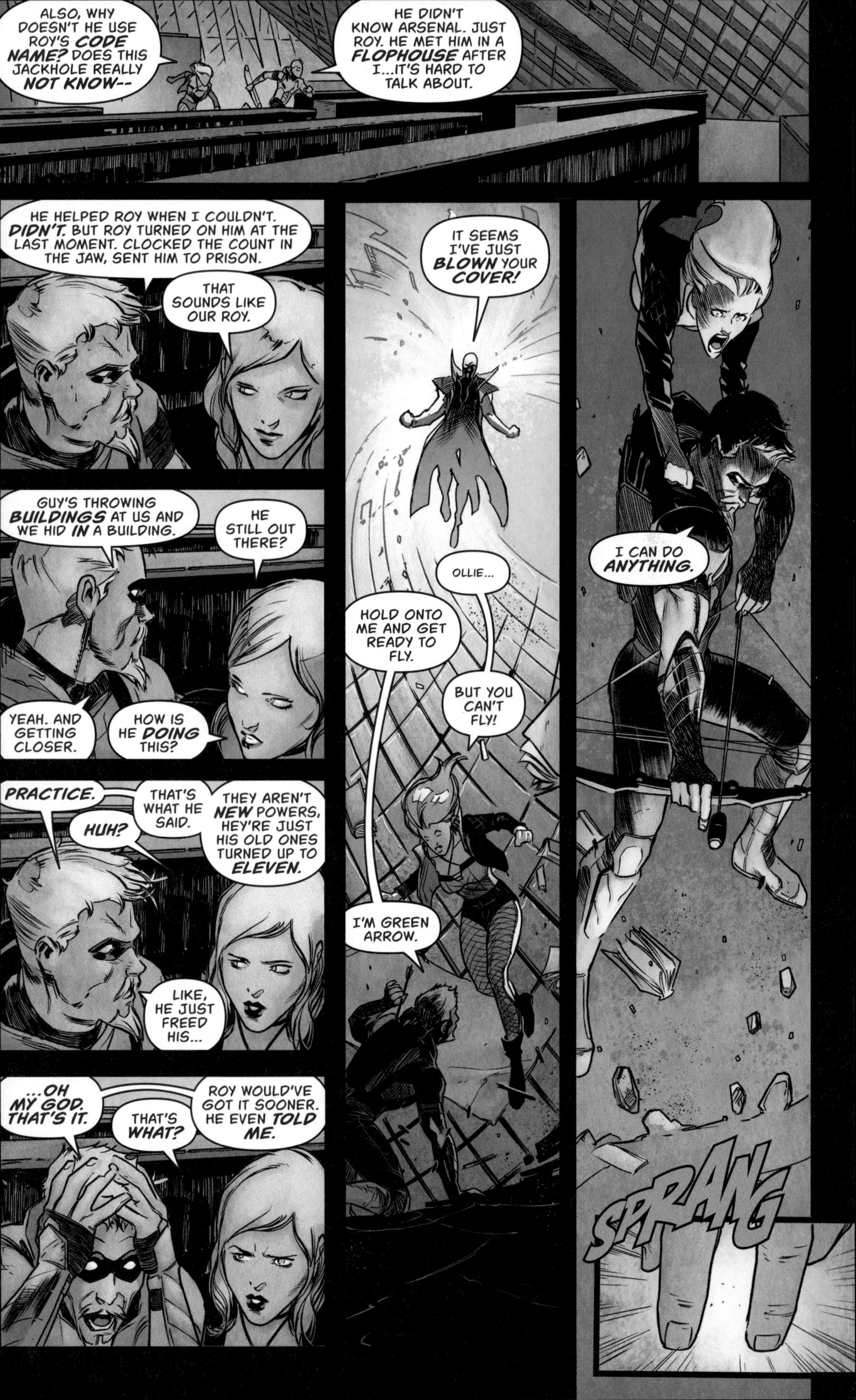
ALSO, WHY DOESN'T HE USE ROY'S CODE NAME? DOES THIS JACKHOLE REALLY NOT KNOW--
HE DIDN'T KNOW ARSENAL. JUST ROY. HE MET HIM IN A FLOPHOUSE AFTER I...IT'S HARD TO TALK ABOUT.
HE HELPED ROY WHEN I COULDN'T. DIDN'T. BUT ROY TURNED ON HIM AT THE LAST MOMENT. CLOCKED THE COUNT IN THE JAW, SENT HIM TO PRISON.
THAT SOUNDS LIKE OUR ROY.
GUY'S THROWING BUILDINGS AT US AND WE HID IN A BUILDING.
HE STILL OUT THERE?
YEAH. AND GETTING CLOSER.
HOW IS HE DOING THIS?
PRACTICE.
HUH?
THAT'S WHAT HE SAID.
THEY AREN'T NEW POWERS, HEY'RE JUST HIS OLD ONES TURNED UP TO ELEVEN.
LIKE, HE JUST FREED HIS...
...OH MY GOD. THAT'S IT.
THAT'S WHAT?
ROY WOULD'VE GOT IT SOONER. HE EVEN TOLD ME.
IT SEEMS I'VE JUST BLOWN YOUR COVER!
OLLIE...
HOLD ONTO ME AND GET READY TO FLY.
BUT YOU CAN'T FLY!
I'M GREEN ARROW.
I CAN DO ANYTHING.
SPRANG

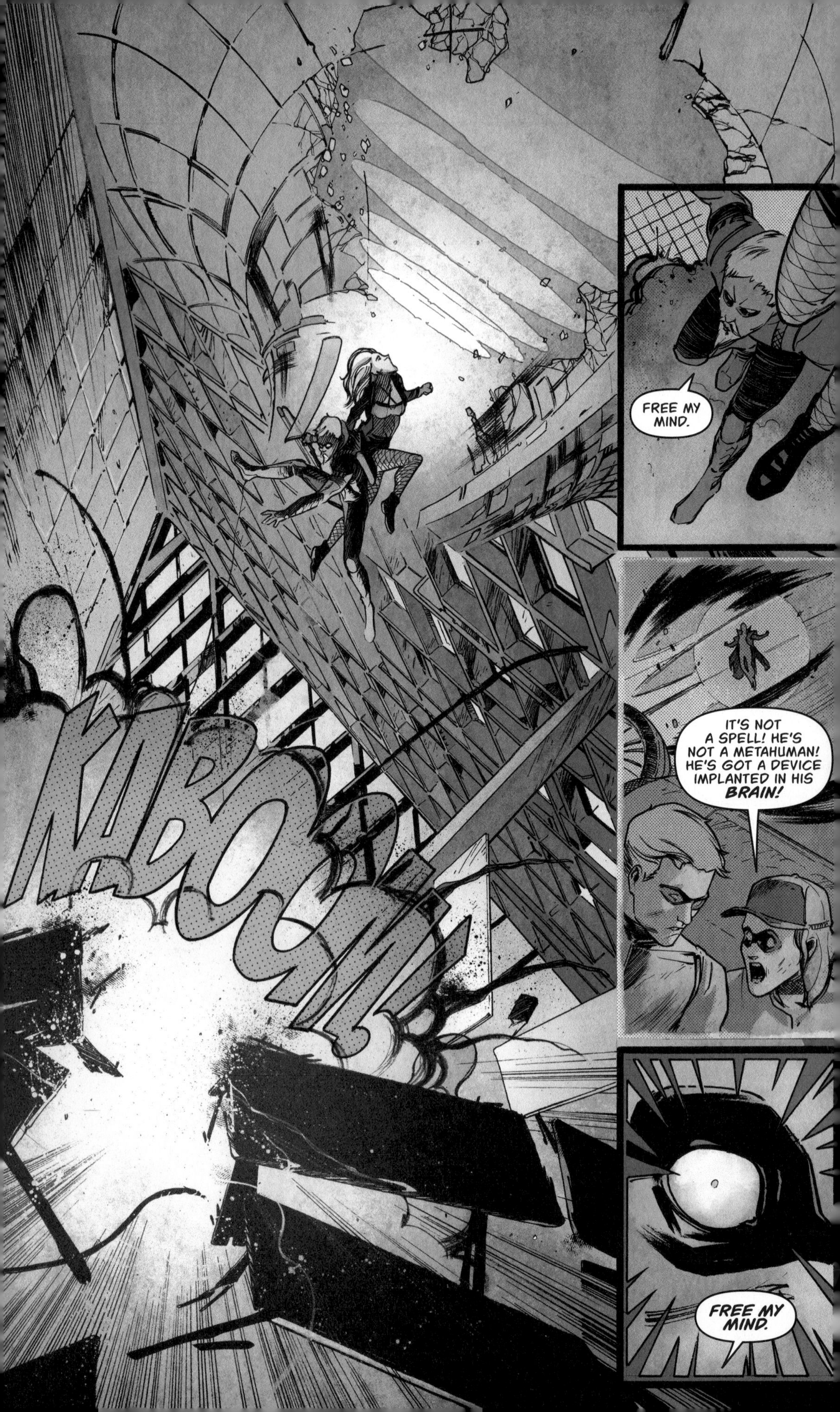
KABOOM!
FREE MY MIND.
IT'S NOT A SPELL! HE'S NOT A METAHUMAN! HE'S GOT A DEVICE IMPLANTED IN HIS BRAIN!
FREE MY MIND.

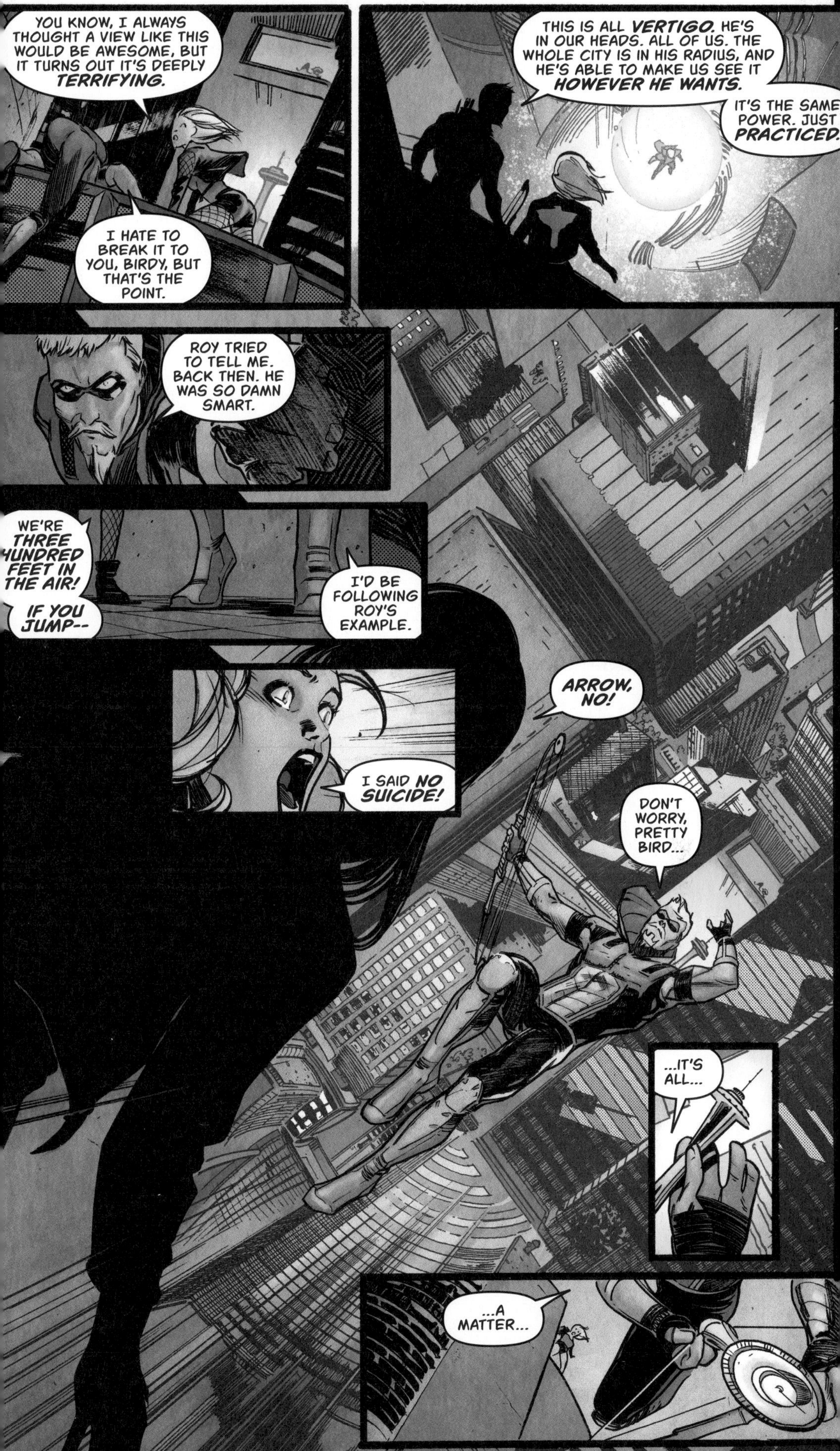

YOU KNOW, I ALWAYS THOUGHT A VIEW LIKE THIS WOULD BE AWESOME, BUT IT TURNS OUT IT'S DEEPLY TERRIFYING.
I HATE TO BREAK IT TO YOU, BIRDY, BUT THAT'S THE POINT.
THIS IS ALL VERTIGO. HE'S IN OUR HEADS. ALL OF US. THE WHOLE CITY IS IN HIS RADIUS, AND HE'S ABLE TO MAKE US SEE IT HOWEVER HE WANTS.
IT'S THE SAME POWER. JUST PRACTICED.
ROY TRIED TO TELL ME. BACK THEN. HE WAS SO DAMN SMART.
WE'RE THREE HUNDRED FEET IN THE AIR!
IF YOU JUMP--
I'D BE FOLLOWING ROY'S EXAMPLE.
ARROW, NO!
I SAID NO SUICIDE!
DON'T WORRY, PRETTY BIRD...
...IT'S ALL...
...A MATTER...

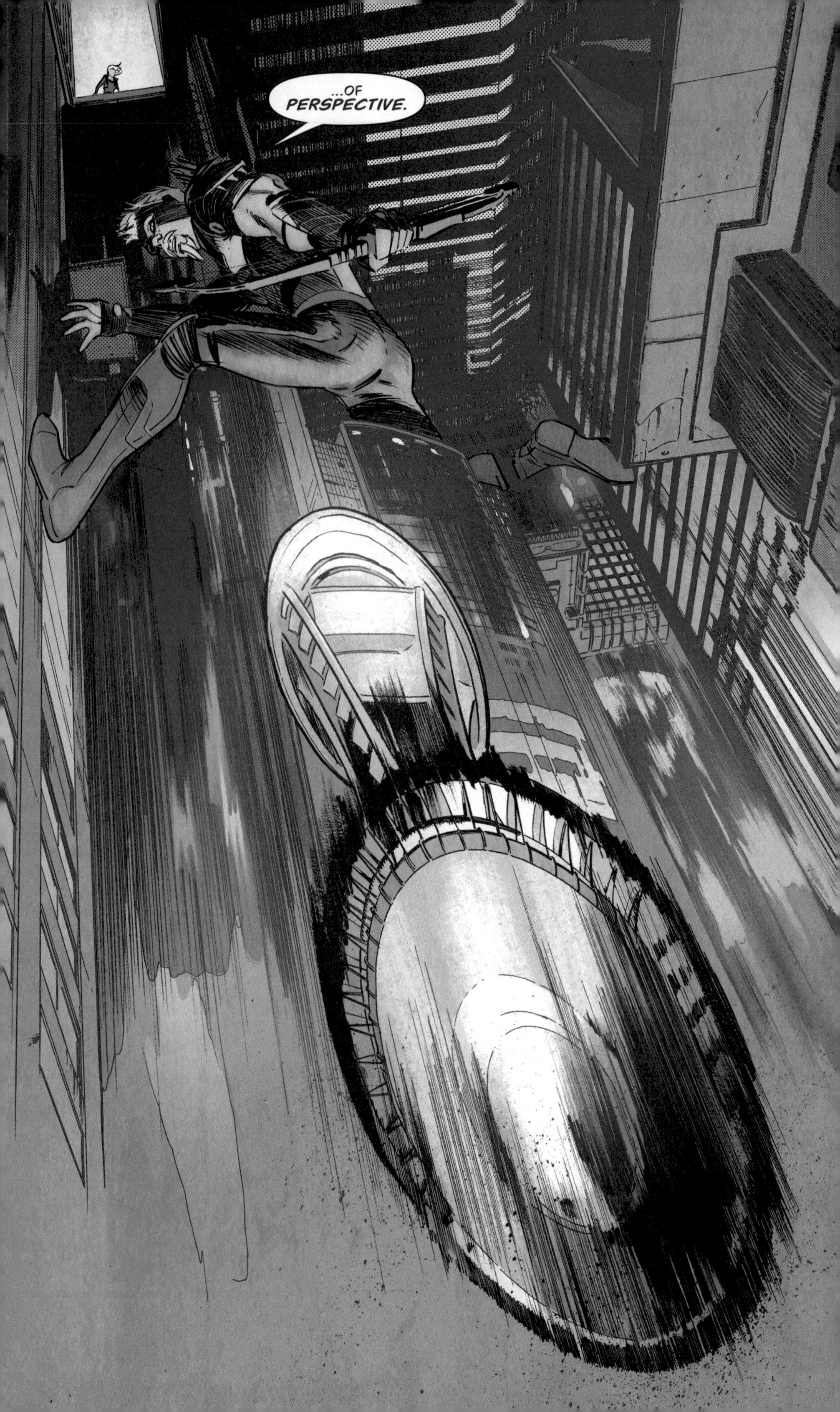
...OF PERSPECTIVE.

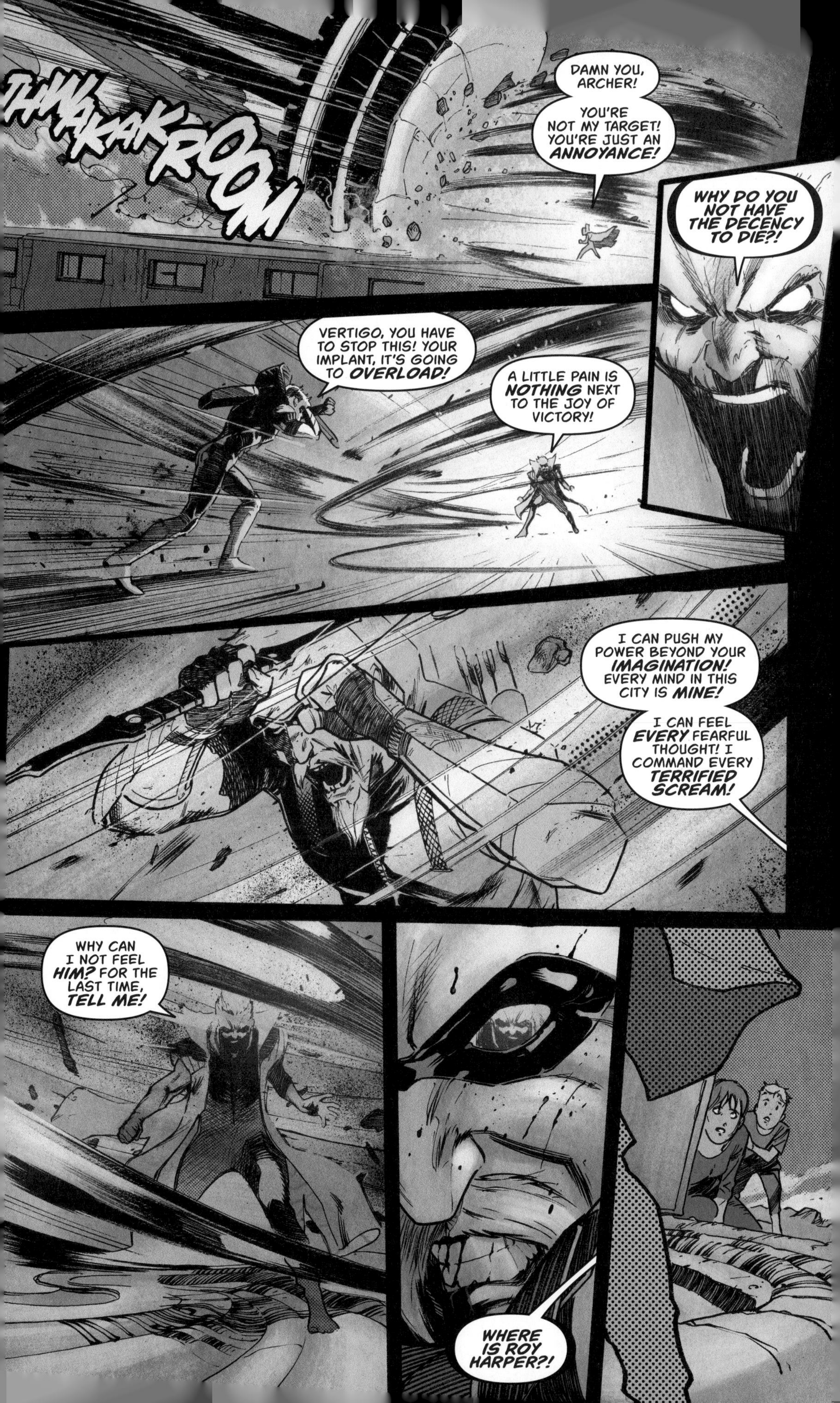
THWAKAKAKROOM
DAMN YOU, ARCHER!
YOU'RE NOT MY TARGET! YOU'RE JUST AN ANNOYANCE!
WHY DO YOU NOT HAVE THE DECENCY TO DIE?!
VERTIGO, YOU HAVE TO STOP THIS! YOUR IMPLANT, IT'S GOING TO OVERLOAD!
A LITTLE PAIN IS NOTHING NEXT TO THE JOY OF VICTORY!
I CAN PUSH MY POWER BEYOND YOUR IMAGINATION! EVERY MIND IN THIS CITY IS MINE!
I CAN FEEL EVERY FEARFUL THOUGHT! I COMMAND EVERY TERRIFIED SCREAM!
WHY CAN I NOT FEEL HIM? FOR THE LAST TIME, TELL ME!
WHERE IS ROY HARPER?!

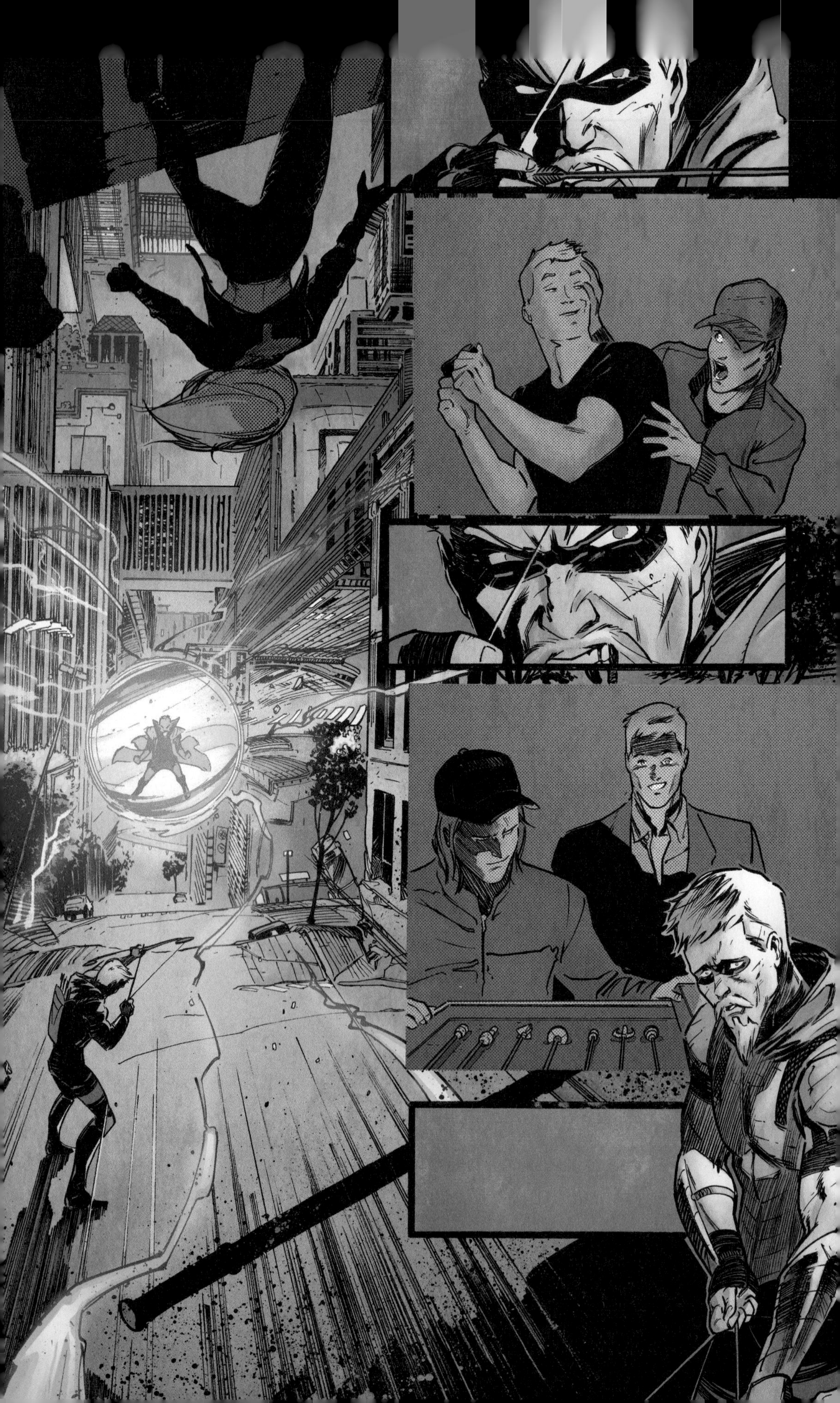

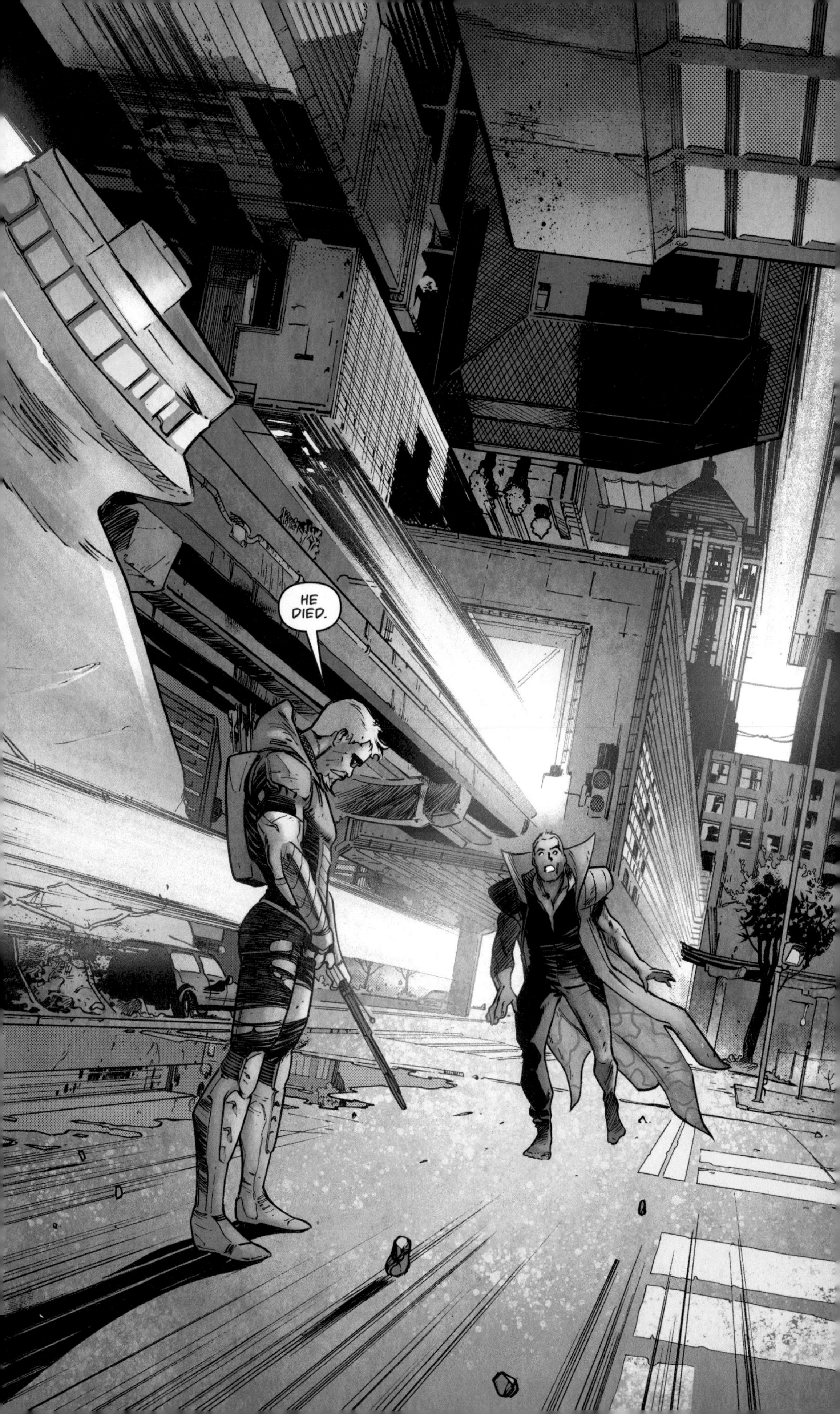
HE DIED.

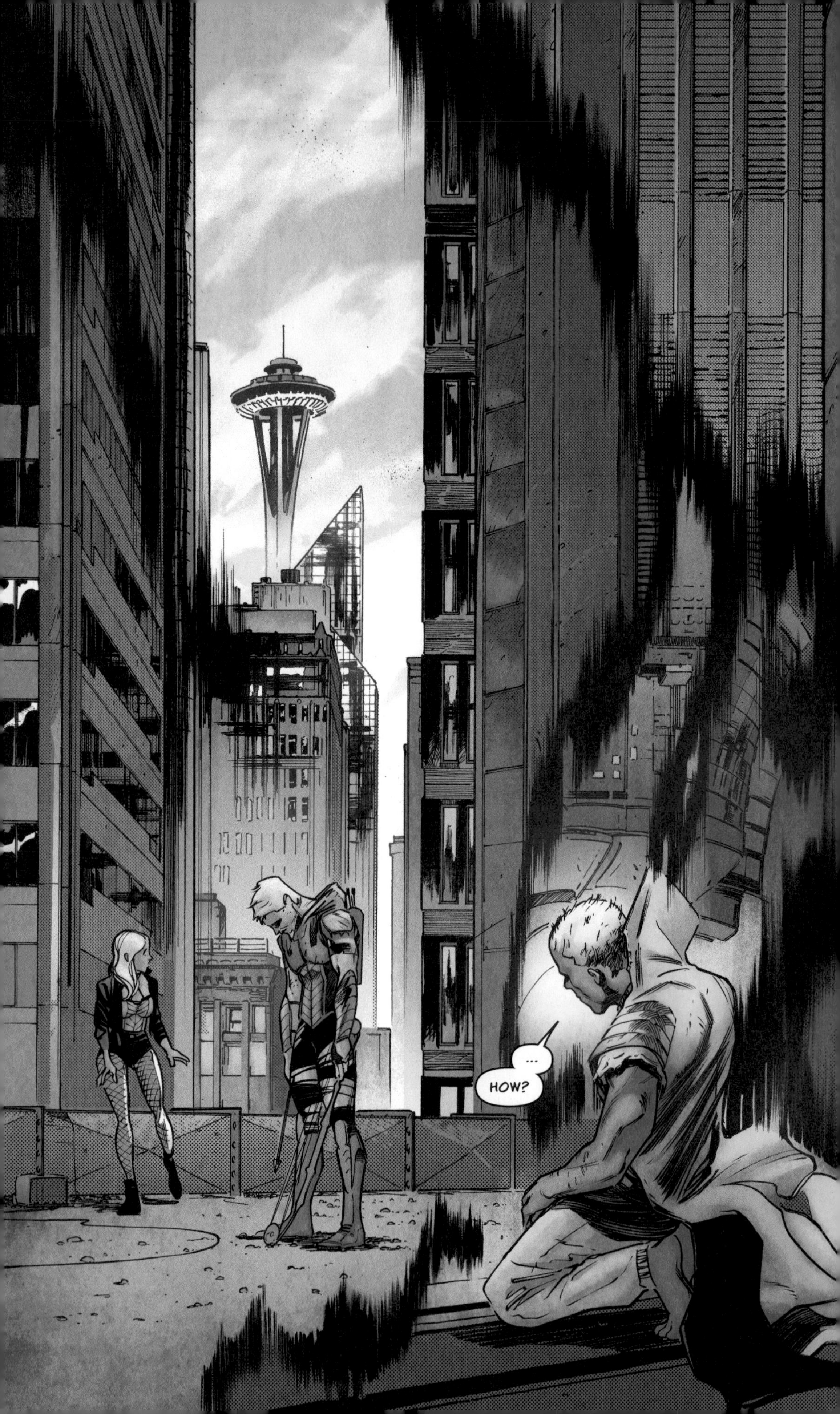
...
HOW?

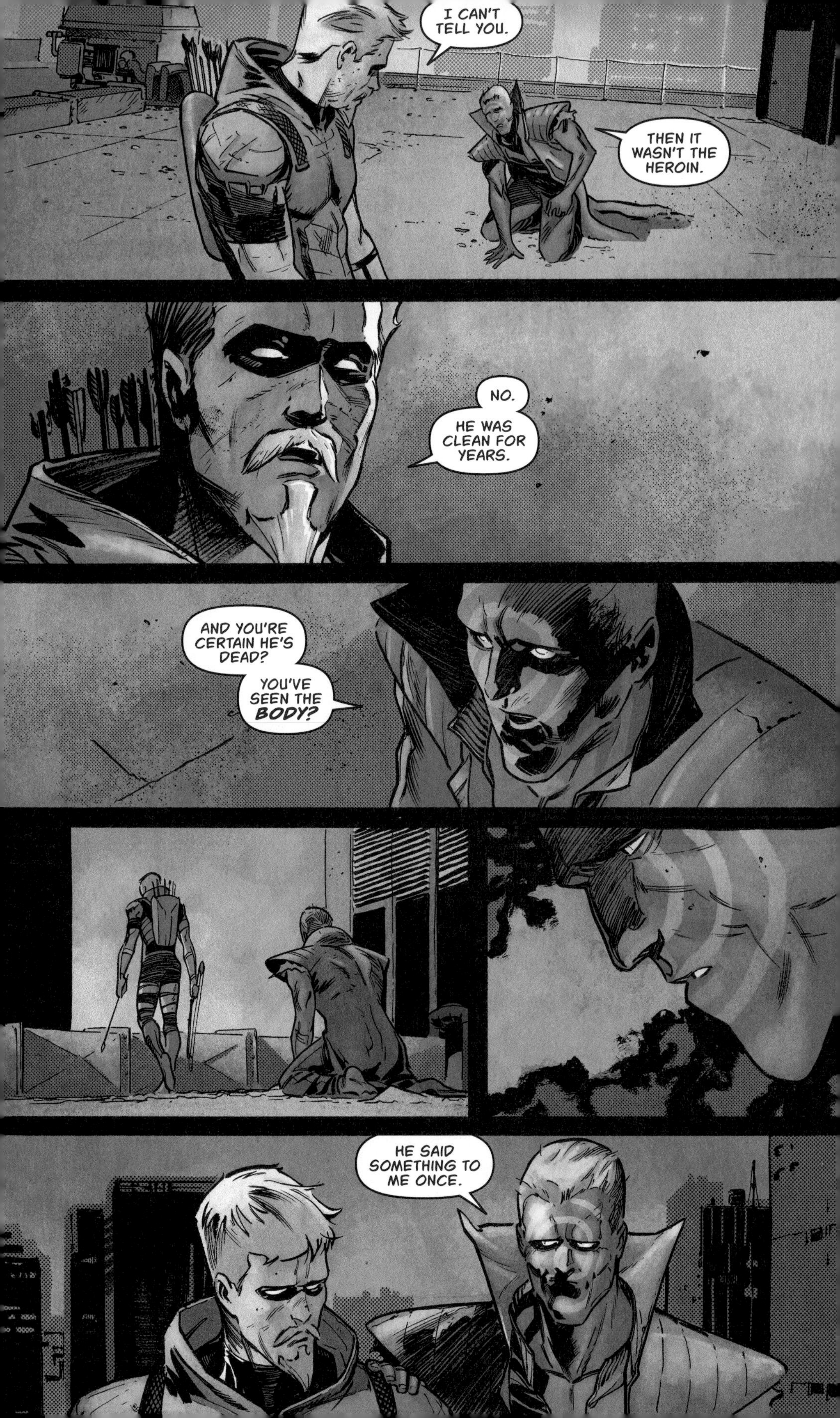
I CAN'T TELL YOU.
THEN IT WASN'T THE HEROIN.
NO.
HE WAS CLEAN FOR YEARS.
AND YOU'RE CERTAIN HE'S DEAD?
YOU'VE SEEN THE *BODY?*
HE SAID SOMETHING TO ME ONCE.

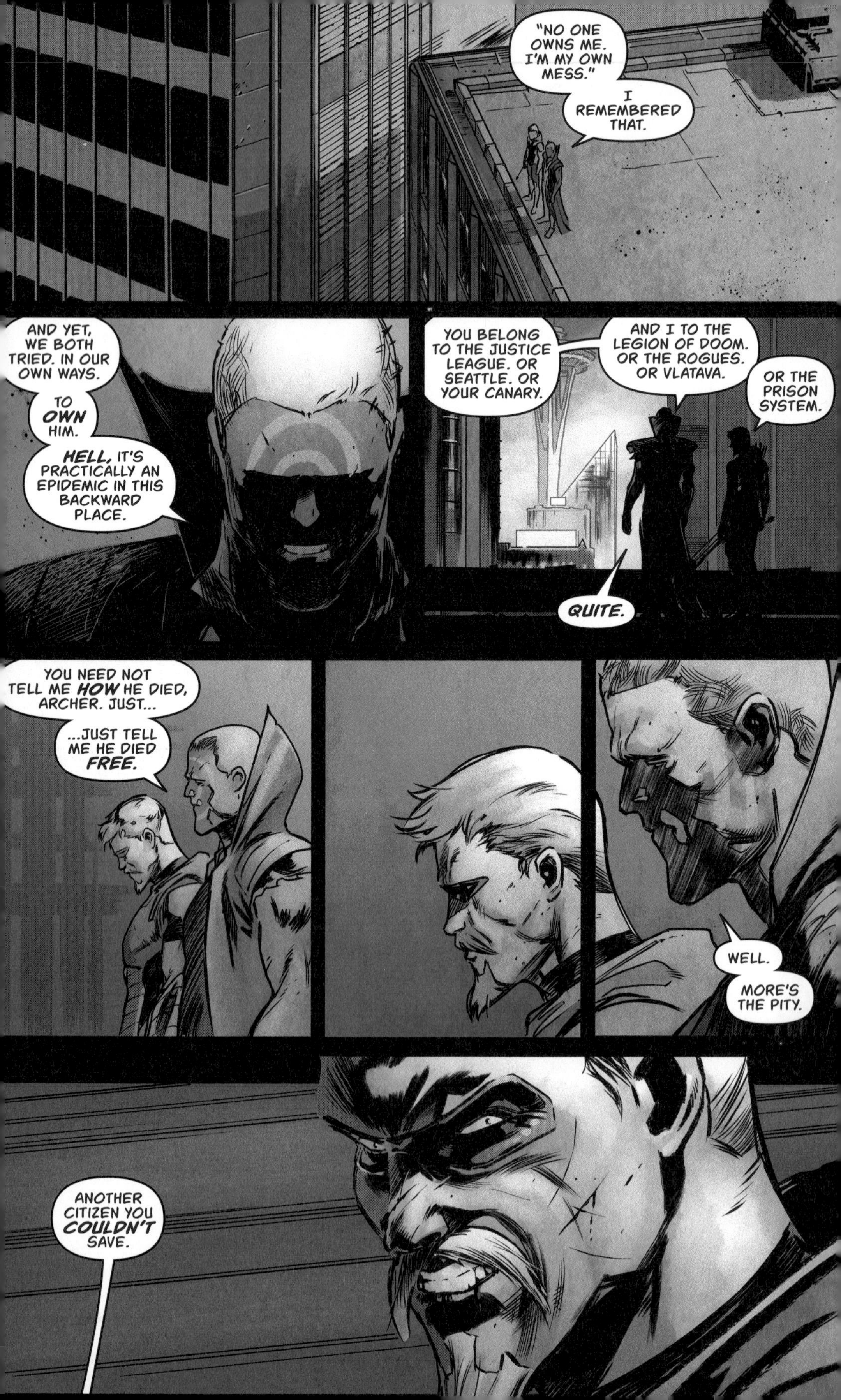
"NO ONE OWNS ME. I'M MY OWN MESS."
I REMEMBERED THAT.
AND YET, WE BOTH TRIED. IN OUR OWN WAYS.
TO OWN HIM.
HELL, IT'S PRACTICALLY AN EPIDEMIC IN THIS BACKWARD PLACE.
YOU BELONG TO THE JUSTICE LEAGUE. OR SEATTLE. OR YOUR CANARY.
AND I TO THE LEGION OF DOOM. OR THE ROGUES. OR VLATAVA.
OR THE PRISON SYSTEM.
QUITE.
YOU NEED NOT TELL ME HOW HE DIED, ARCHER. JUST...
...JUST TELL ME HE DIED FREE.
WELL.
MORE'S THE PITY.
ANOTHER CITIZEN YOU COULDN'T SAVE.

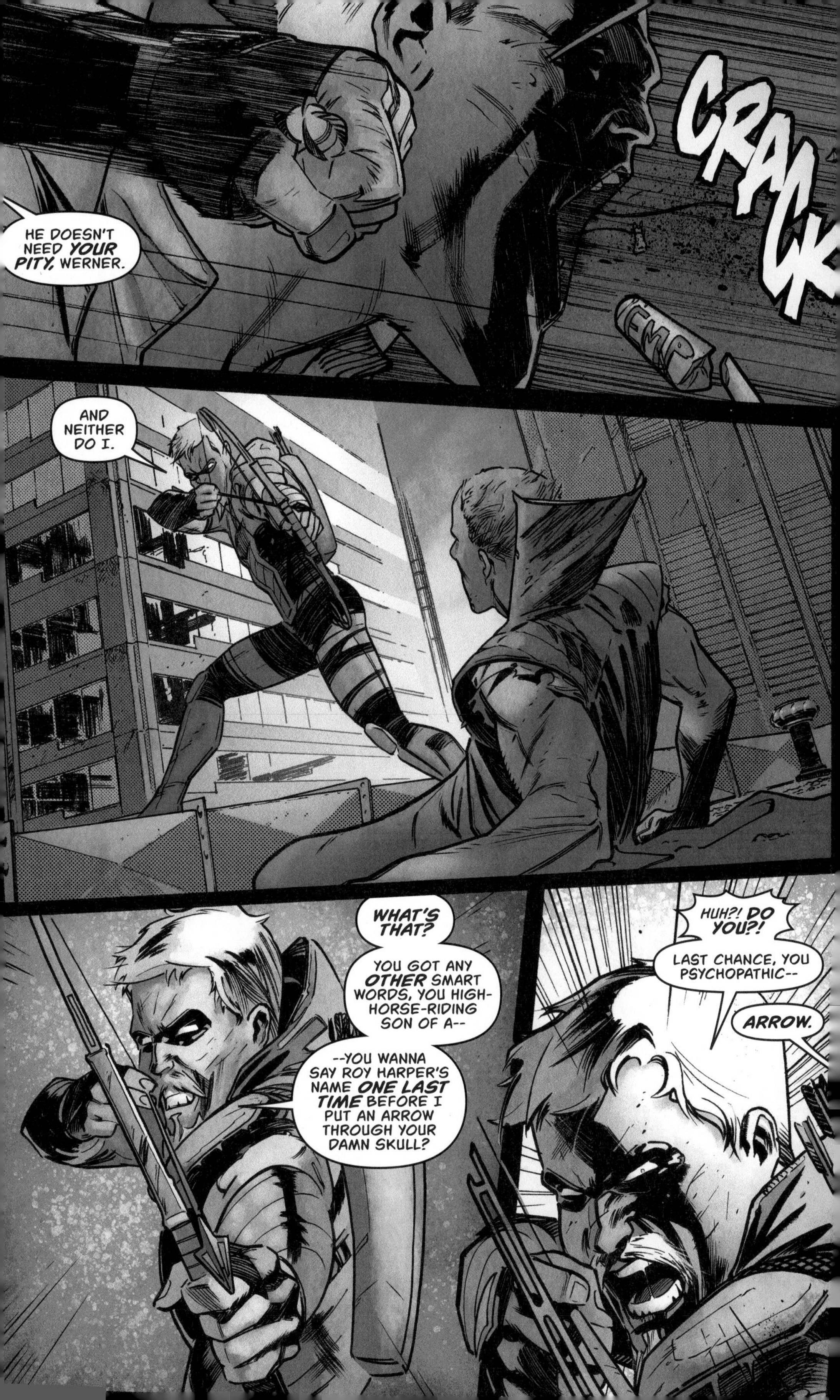
HE DOESN'T NEED YOUR PITY, WERNER.
CRACK
EMP
AND NEITHER DO I.
WHAT'S THAT?
YOU GOT ANY OTHER SMART WORDS, YOU HIGH-HORSE-RIDING SON OF A--
--YOU WANNA SAY ROY HARPER'S NAME ONE LAST TIME BEFORE I PUT AN ARROW THROUGH YOUR DAMN SKULL?
HUH?! DO YOU?!
LAST CHANCE, YOU PSYCHOPATHIC--
ARROW.

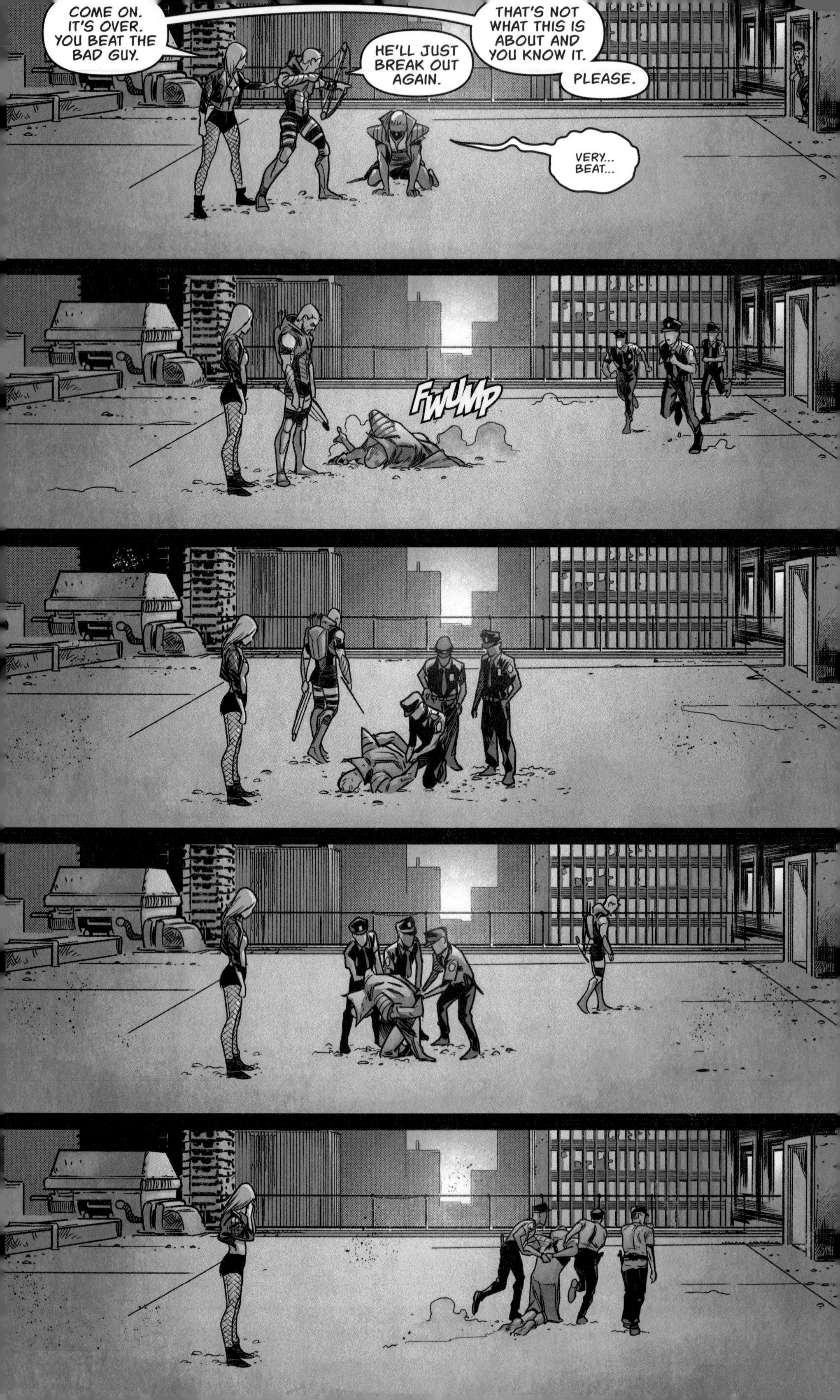
COME ON. IT'S OVER. YOU BEAT THE BAD GUY.
HE'LL JUST BREAK OUT AGAIN.
THAT'S NOT WHAT THIS IS ABOUT AND YOU KNOW IT.
PLEASE.
VERY... BEAT...
FWUMP

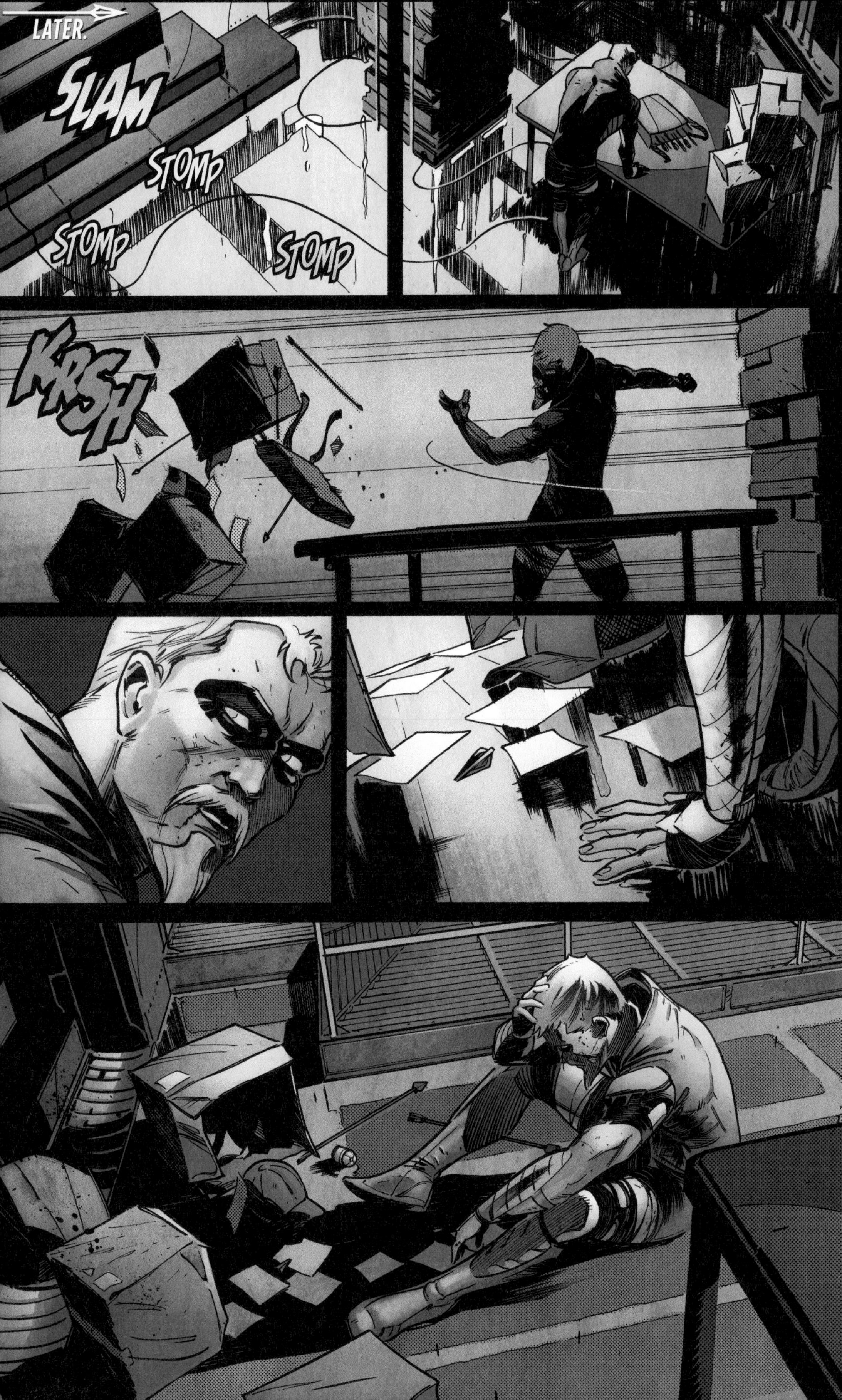

LATER.
SLAM
STOMP
STOMP
STOMP
KRSH

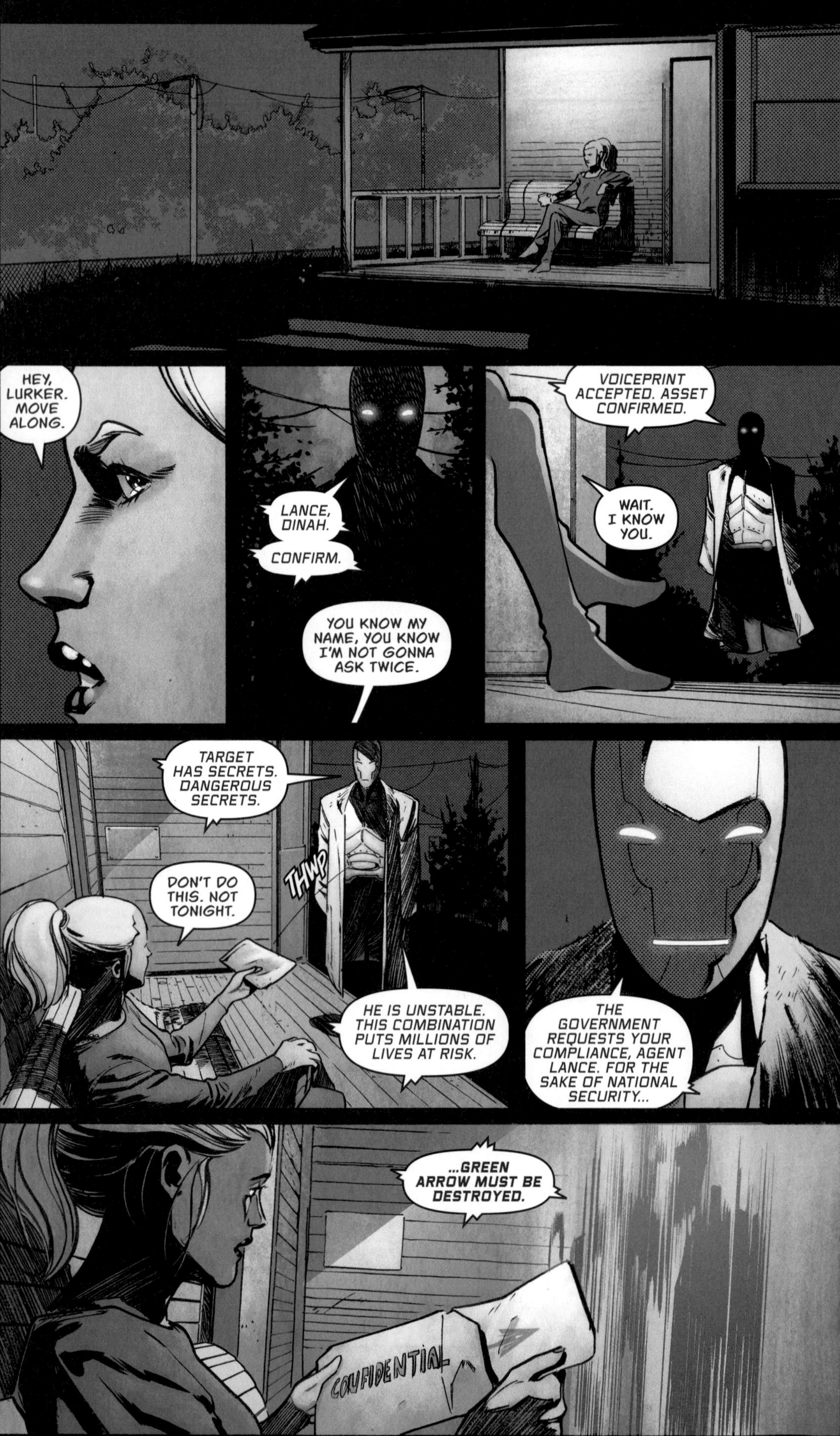
HEY, LURKER. MOVE ALONG.
LANCE, DINAH.
CONFIRM.
YOU KNOW MY NAME, YOU KNOW I'M NOT GONNA ASK TWICE.
VOICEPRINT ACCEPTED. ASSET CONFIRMED.
WAIT. I KNOW YOU.
TARGET HAS SECRETS. DANGEROUS SECRETS.
THWP
DON'T DO THIS. NOT TONIGHT.
HE IS UNSTABLE. THIS COMBINATION PUTS MILLIONS OF LIVES AT RISK.
THE GOVERNMENT REQUESTS YOUR COMPLIANCE, AGENT LANCE. FOR THE SAKE OF NATIONAL SECURITY...
...GREEN ARROW MUST BE DESTROYED.
CONFIDENTIAL

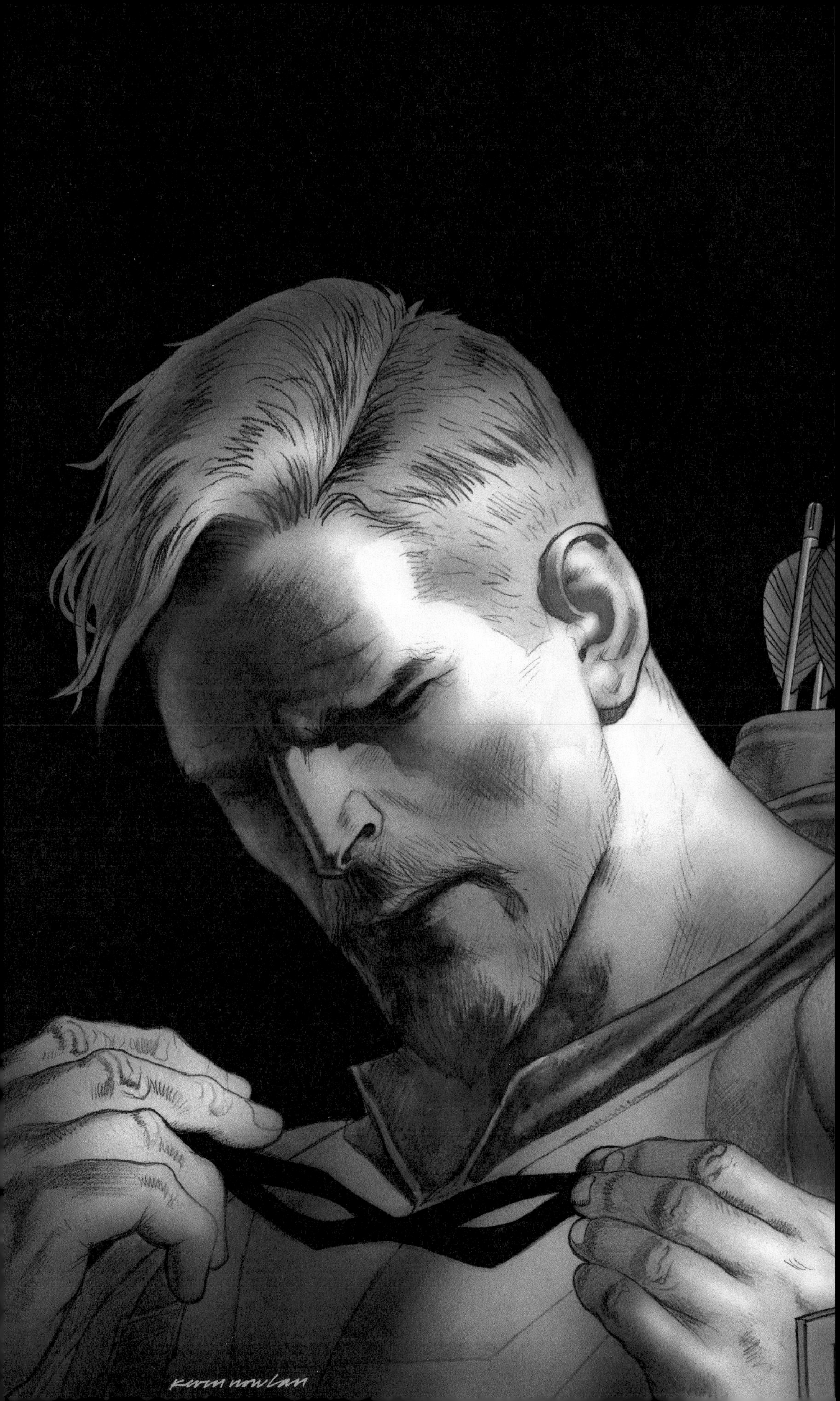
kevin nowlan

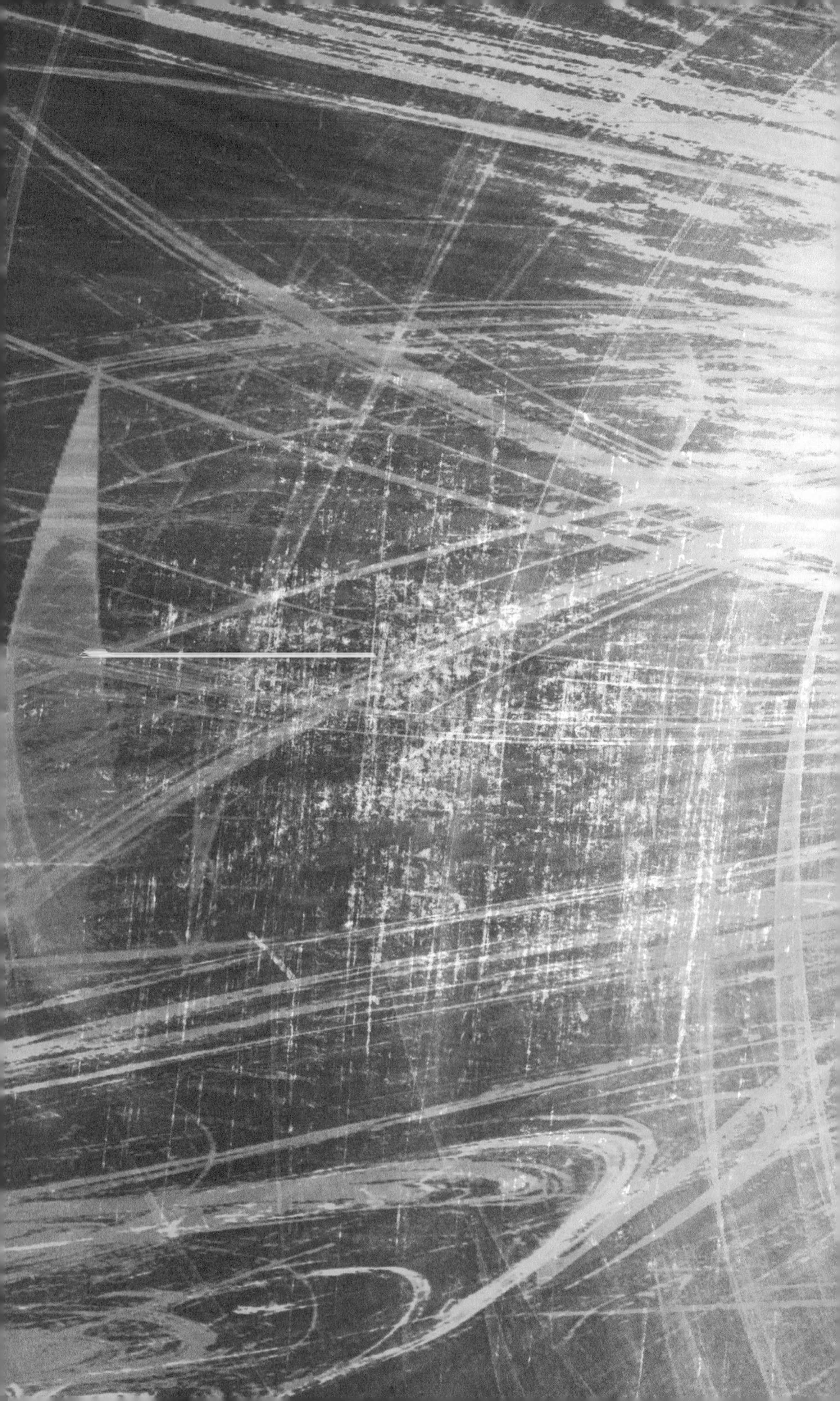

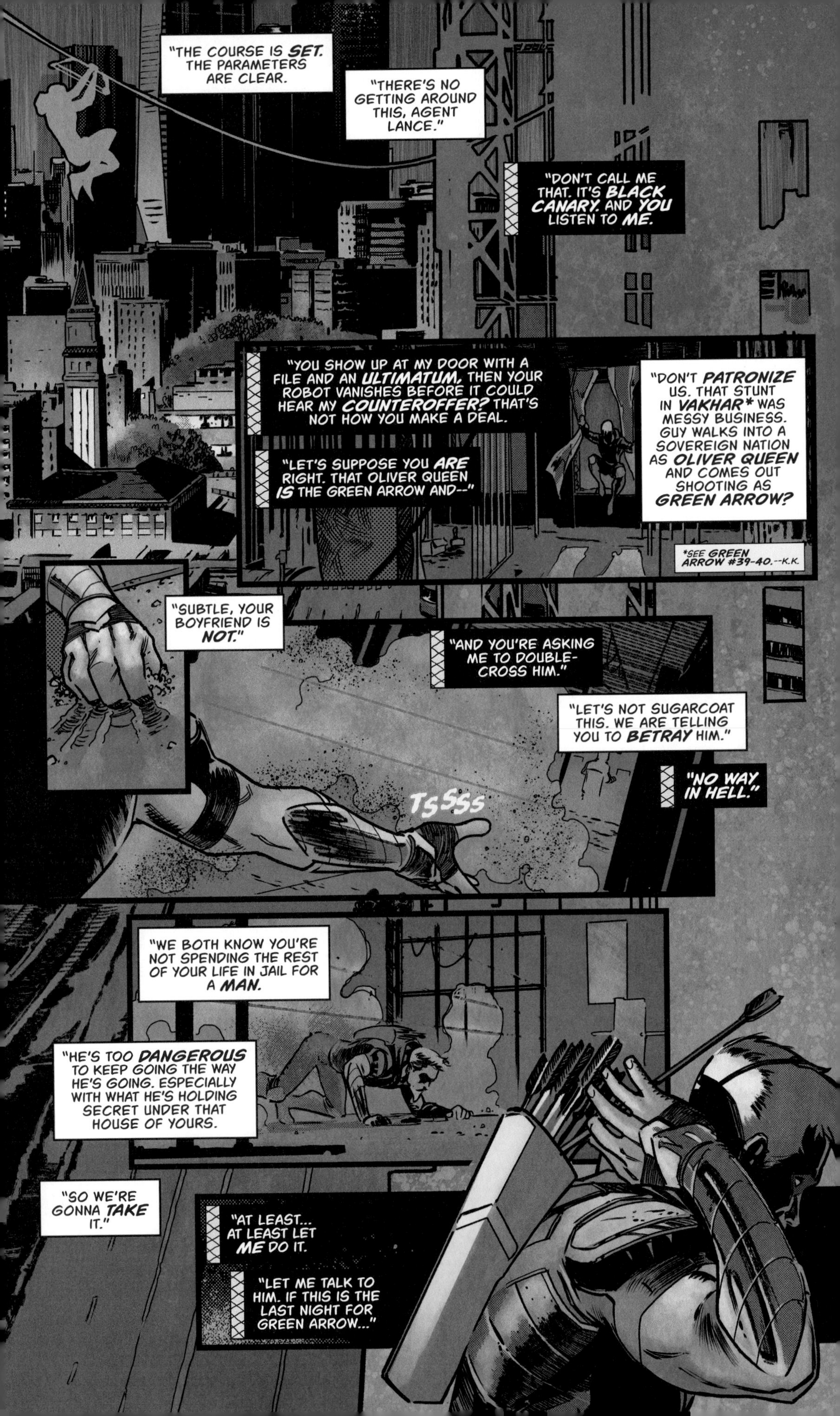
"THE COURSE IS SET. THE PARAMETERS ARE CLEAR.
"THERE'S NO GETTING AROUND THIS, AGENT LANCE."
"DON'T CALL ME THAT. IT'S BLACK CANARY. AND YOU LISTEN TO ME.
"YOU SHOW UP AT MY DOOR WITH A FILE AND AN ULTIMATUM, THEN YOUR ROBOT VANISHES BEFORE IT COULD HEAR MY COUNTEROFFER? THAT'S NOT HOW YOU MAKE A DEAL.
"LET'S SUPPOSE YOU ARE RIGHT. THAT OLIVER QUEEN IS THE GREEN ARROW AND--"
"DON'T PATRONIZE US. THAT STUNT IN VAKHAR* WAS MESSY BUSINESS. GUY WALKS INTO A SOVEREIGN NATION AS OLIVER QUEEN AND COMES OUT SHOOTING AS GREEN ARROW?
*SEE GREEN ARROW #39-40.--K.K.
"SUBTLE, YOUR BOYFRIEND IS NOT."
"AND YOU'RE ASKING ME TO DOUBLE-CROSS HIM."
"LET'S NOT SUGARCOAT THIS. WE ARE TELLING YOU TO BETRAY HIM."
"NO WAY IN HELL."
TSSSS
"WE BOTH KNOW YOU'RE NOT SPENDING THE REST OF YOUR LIFE IN JAIL FOR A MAN.
"HE'S TOO DANGEROUS TO KEEP GOING THE WAY HE'S GOING. ESPECIALLY WITH WHAT HE'S HOLDING SECRET UNDER THAT HOUSE OF YOURS.
"SO WE'RE GONNA TAKE IT."
"AT LEAST... AT LEAST LET ME DO IT.
"LET ME TALK TO HIM. IF THIS IS THE LAST NIGHT FOR GREEN ARROW..."

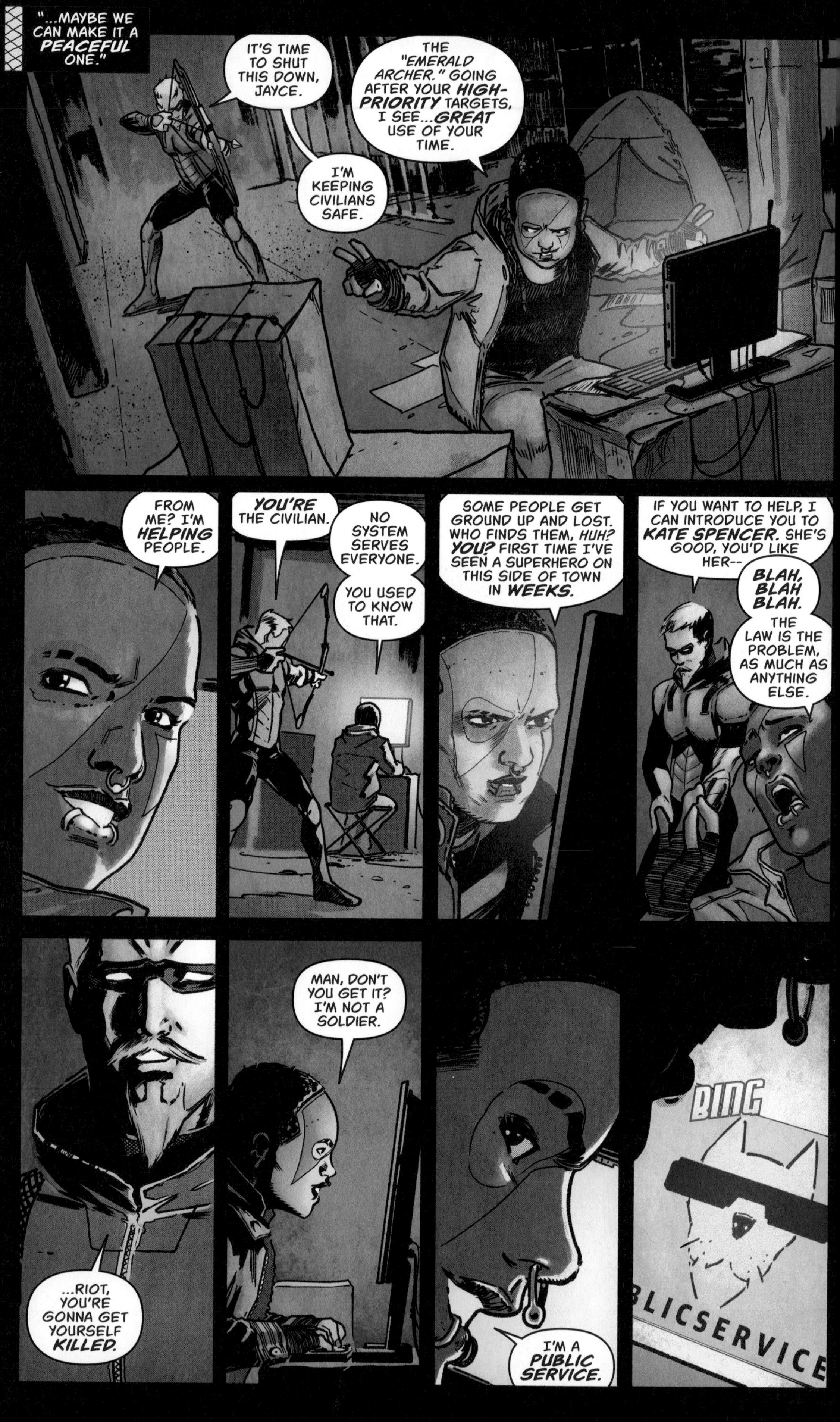
"...MAYBE WE CAN MAKE IT A PEACEFUL ONE."
IT'S TIME TO SHUT THIS DOWN, JAYCE.
THE "EMERALD ARCHER." GOING AFTER YOUR HIGH-PRIORITY TARGETS, I SEE...GREAT USE OF YOUR TIME.
I'M KEEPING CIVILIANS SAFE.
FROM ME? I'M HELPING PEOPLE.
YOU'RE THE CIVILIAN.
NO SYSTEM SERVES EVERYONE.
YOU USED TO KNOW THAT.
SOME PEOPLE GET GROUND UP AND LOST. WHO FINDS THEM, HUH? YOU? FIRST TIME I'VE SEEN A SUPERHERO ON THIS SIDE OF TOWN IN WEEKS.
IF YOU WANT TO HELP, I CAN INTRODUCE YOU TO KATE SPENCER. SHE'S GOOD, YOU'D LIKE HER--
BLAH, BLAH BLAH.
THE LAW IS THE PROBLEM, AS MUCH AS ANYTHING ELSE.
...RIOT, YOU'RE GONNA GET YOURSELF KILLED.
MAN, DON'T YOU GET IT? I'M NOT A SOLDIER.
I'M A PUBLIC SERVICE.
BING
LICSERVICE

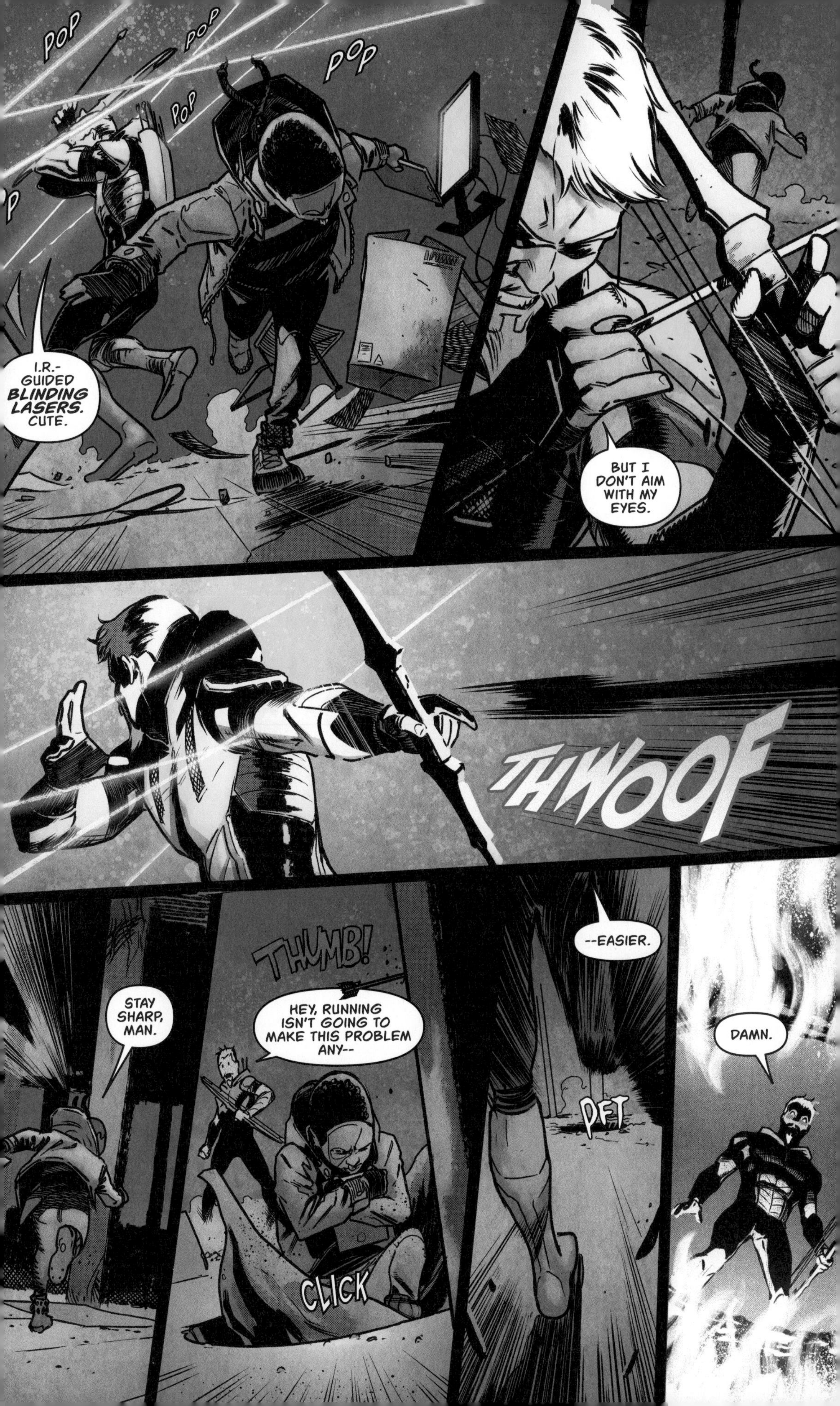
POP
POP
POP
POP
P
I.R.-GUIDED BLINDING LASERS. CUTE.
BUT I DON'T AIM WITH MY EYES.
THWOOF
STAY SHARP, MAN.
THUMB!
HEY, RUNNING ISN'T GOING TO MAKE THIS PROBLEM ANY--
CLICK
--EASIER.
PFT
DAMN.

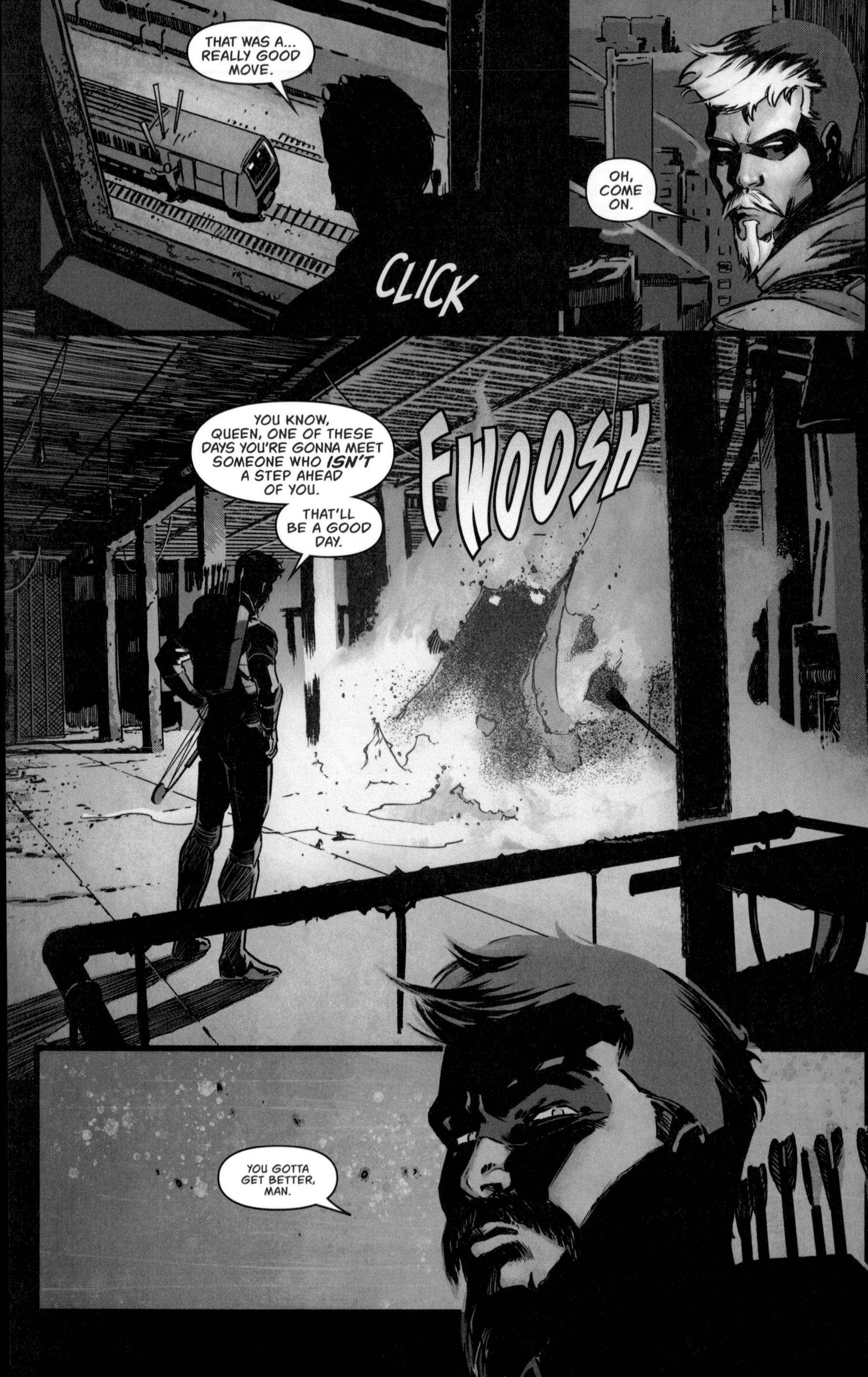
THAT WAS A... REALLY GOOD MOVE.
CLICK
OH, COME ON.
YOU KNOW, QUEEN, ONE OF THESE DAYS YOU'RE GONNA MEET SOMEONE WHO *ISN'T* A STEP AHEAD OF YOU.
THAT'LL BE A GOOD DAY.
FWOOSH
YOU GOTTA GET BETTER, MAN.

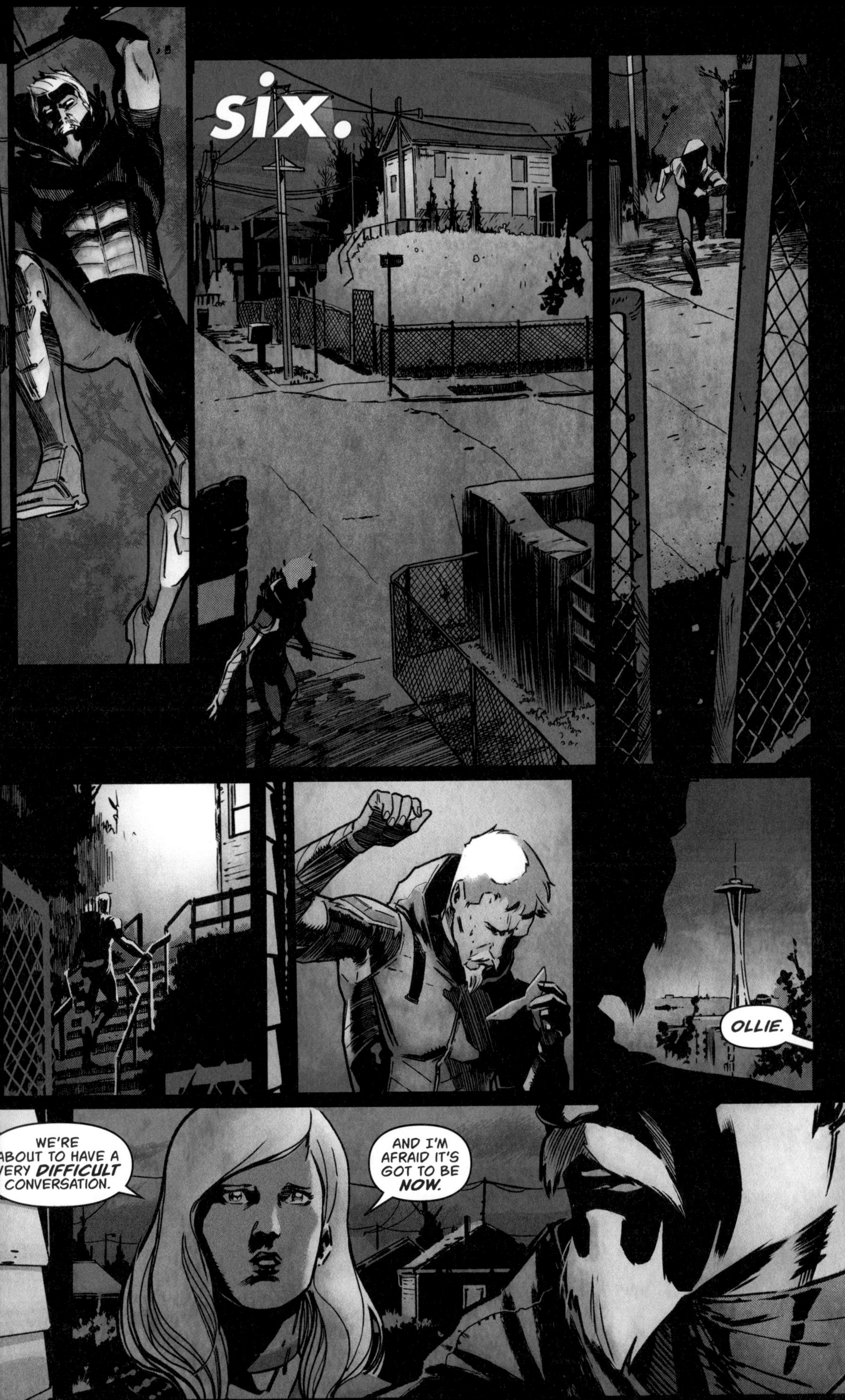
six.
OLLIE.
WE'RE ABOUT TO HAVE A VERY DIFFICULT CONVERSATION.
AND I'M AFRAID IT'S GOT TO BE NOW.

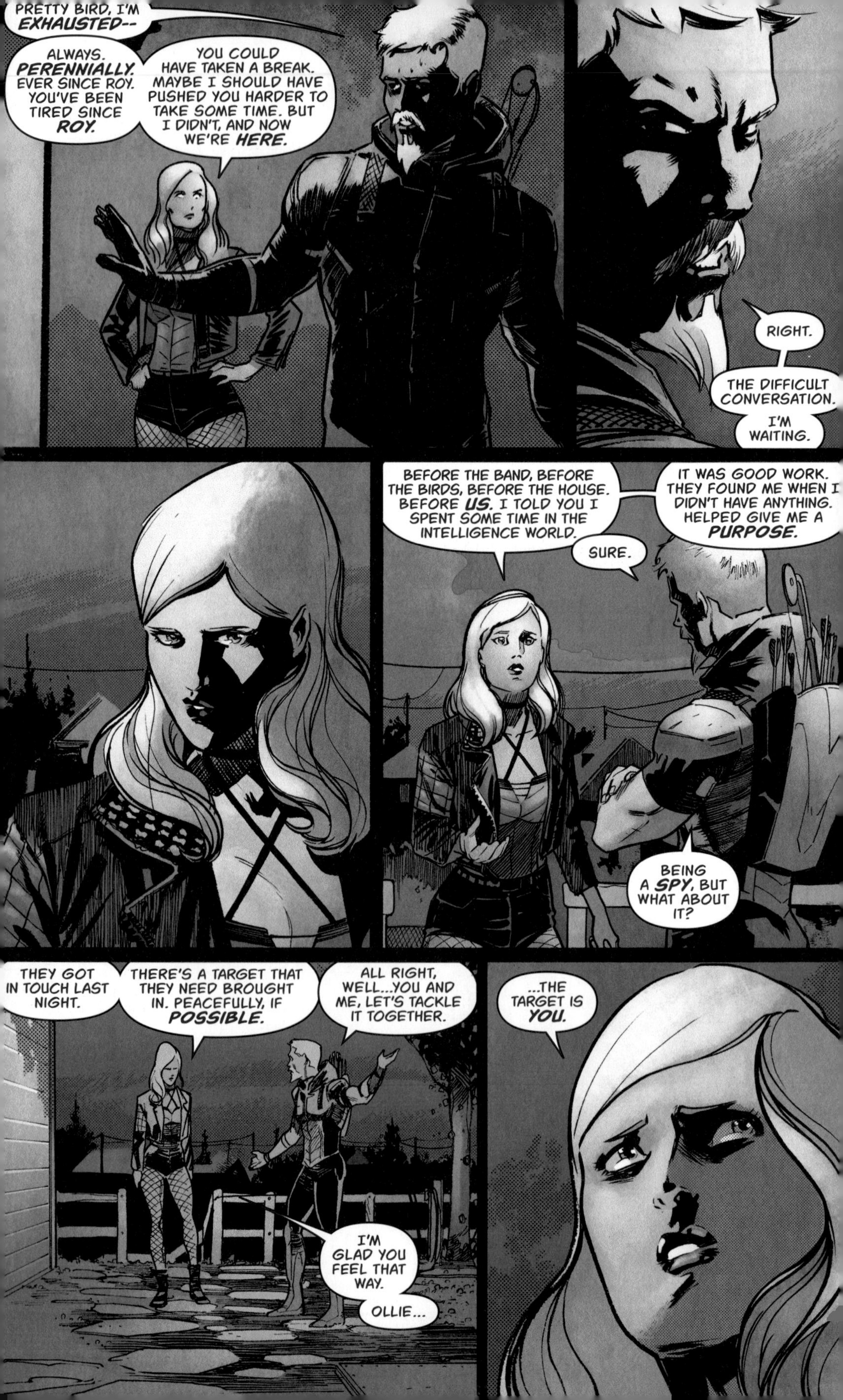
PRETTY BIRD, I'M EXHAUSTED--
ALWAYS. PERENNIALLY. EVER SINCE ROY. YOU'VE BEEN TIRED SINCE ROY.
YOU COULD HAVE TAKEN A BREAK. MAYBE I SHOULD HAVE PUSHED YOU HARDER TO TAKE SOME TIME. BUT I DIDN'T, AND NOW WE'RE HERE.
RIGHT.
THE DIFFICULT CONVERSATION.
I'M WAITING.
BEFORE THE BAND, BEFORE THE BIRDS, BEFORE THE HOUSE. BEFORE US. I TOLD YOU I SPENT SOME TIME IN THE INTELLIGENCE WORLD.
SURE.
IT WAS GOOD WORK. THEY FOUND ME WHEN I DIDN'T HAVE ANYTHING. HELPED GIVE ME A PURPOSE.
BEING A SPY, BUT WHAT ABOUT IT?
THEY GOT IN TOUCH LAST NIGHT.
THERE'S A TARGET THAT THEY NEED BROUGHT IN. PEACEFULLY, IF POSSIBLE.
ALL RIGHT, WELL...YOU AND ME, LET'S TACKLE IT TOGETHER.
I'M GLAD YOU FEEL THAT WAY.
OLLIE...
...THE TARGET IS YOU.

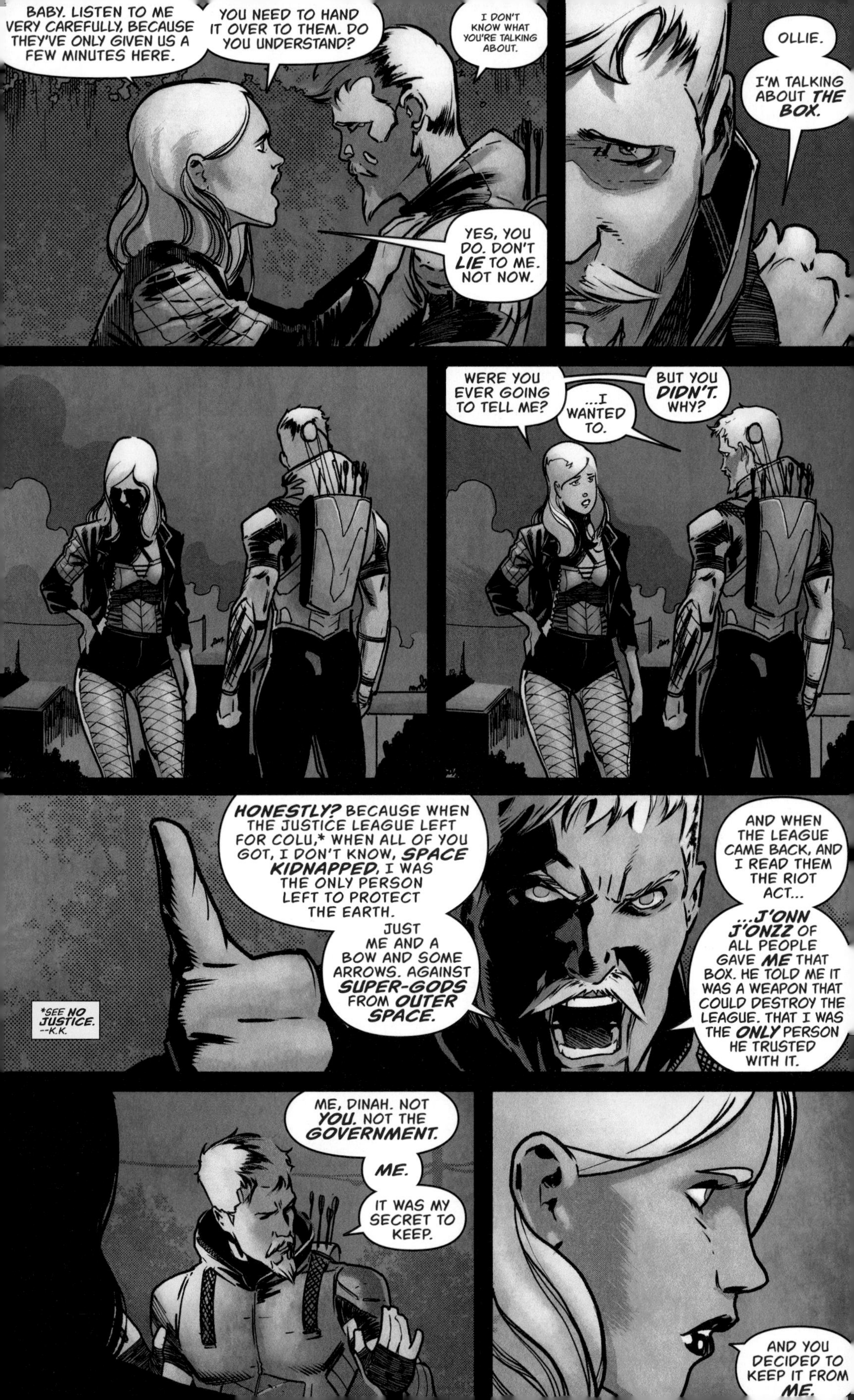

BABY. LISTEN TO ME VERY CAREFULLY, BECAUSE THEY'VE ONLY GIVEN US A FEW MINUTES HERE.
YOU NEED TO HAND IT OVER TO THEM. DO YOU UNDERSTAND?
I DON'T KNOW WHAT YOU'RE TALKING ABOUT.
YES, YOU DO. DON'T LIE TO ME. NOT NOW.
OLLIE.
I'M TALKING ABOUT THE BOX.
WERE YOU EVER GOING TO TELL ME?
...I WANTED TO.
BUT YOU DIDN'T. WHY?
HONESTLY? BECAUSE WHEN THE JUSTICE LEAGUE LEFT FOR COLU,* WHEN ALL OF YOU GOT, I DON'T KNOW, SPACE KIDNAPPED, I WAS THE ONLY PERSON LEFT TO PROTECT THE EARTH.
JUST ME AND A BOW AND SOME ARROWS. AGAINST SUPER-GODS FROM OUTER SPACE.
*SEE NO JUSTICE. --K.K.
AND WHEN THE LEAGUE CAME BACK, AND I READ THEM THE RIOT ACT...
...J'ONN J'ONZZ OF ALL PEOPLE GAVE ME THAT BOX. HE TOLD ME IT WAS A WEAPON THAT COULD DESTROY THE LEAGUE. THAT I WAS THE ONLY PERSON HE TRUSTED WITH IT.
ME, DINAH. NOT YOU. NOT THE GOVERNMENT.
ME.
IT WAS MY SECRET TO KEEP.
AND YOU DECIDED TO KEEP IT FROM ME.

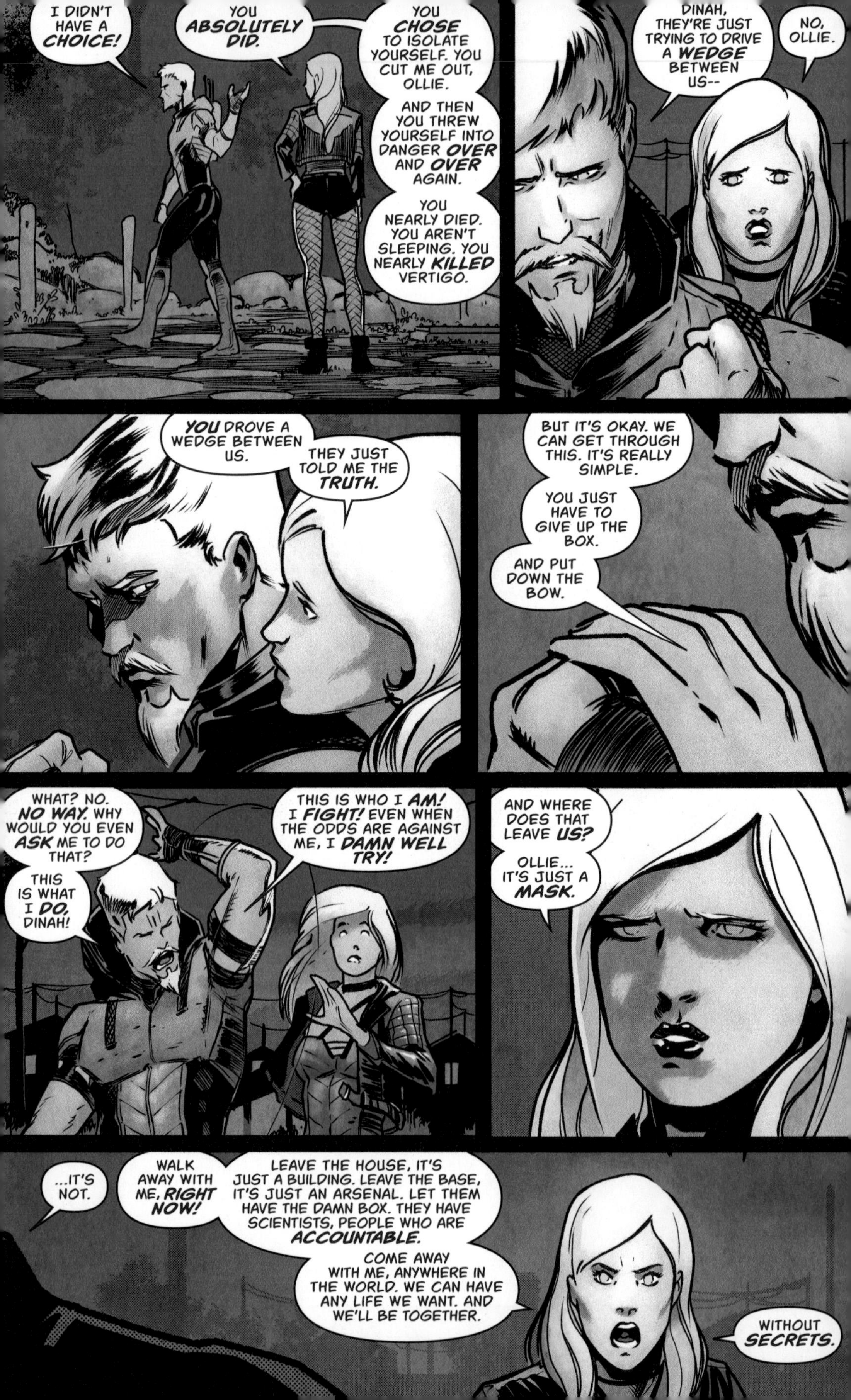
I DIDN'T HAVE A **CHOICE!**
YOU **ABSOLUTELY DID.**
YOU **CHOSE** TO ISOLATE YOURSELF. YOU CUT ME OUT, OLLIE.
AND THEN YOU THREW YOURSELF INTO DANGER **OVER** AND **OVER** AGAIN.
YOU NEARLY DIED. YOU AREN'T SLEEPING. YOU NEARLY **KILLED** VERTIGO.
DINAH, THEY'RE JUST TRYING TO DRIVE A **WEDGE** BETWEEN US--
NO, OLLIE.
YOU DROVE A WEDGE BETWEEN US.
THEY JUST TOLD ME THE **TRUTH.**
BUT IT'S OKAY. WE CAN GET THROUGH THIS. IT'S REALLY SIMPLE.
YOU JUST HAVE TO GIVE UP THE BOX.
AND PUT DOWN THE BOW.
WHAT? NO. **NO WAY.** WHY WOULD YOU EVEN **ASK** ME TO DO THAT?
THIS IS WHAT I **DO,** DINAH!
THIS IS WHO I **AM!** I **FIGHT!** EVEN WHEN THE ODDS ARE AGAINST ME, I **DAMN WELL TRY!**
AND WHERE DOES THAT LEAVE **US?**
OLLIE... IT'S JUST A **MASK.**
...IT'S NOT.
WALK AWAY WITH ME, **RIGHT NOW!**
LEAVE THE HOUSE, IT'S JUST A BUILDING. LEAVE THE BASE, IT'S JUST AN ARSENAL. LET THEM HAVE THE DAMN BOX. THEY HAVE SCIENTISTS, PEOPLE WHO ARE **ACCOUNTABLE.**
COME AWAY WITH ME, ANYWHERE IN THE WORLD. WE CAN HAVE ANY LIFE WE WANT. AND WE'LL BE TOGETHER.
WITHOUT **SECRETS.**

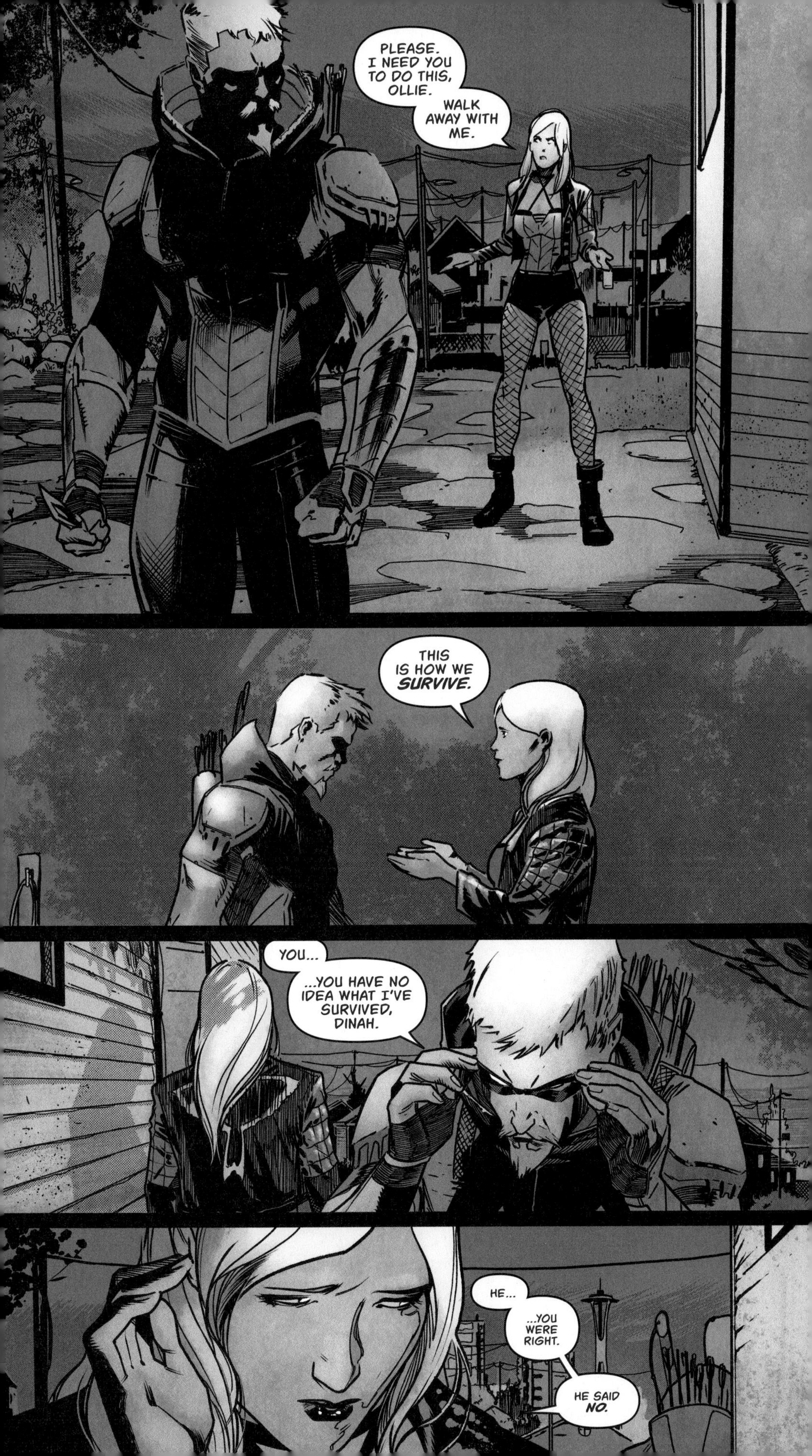
PLEASE. I NEED YOU TO DO THIS, OLLIE.
WALK AWAY WITH ME.
THIS IS HOW WE SURVIVE.
YOU...
...YOU HAVE NO IDEA WHAT I'VE SURVIVED, DINAH.
HE...
...YOU WERE RIGHT.
HE SAID NO.

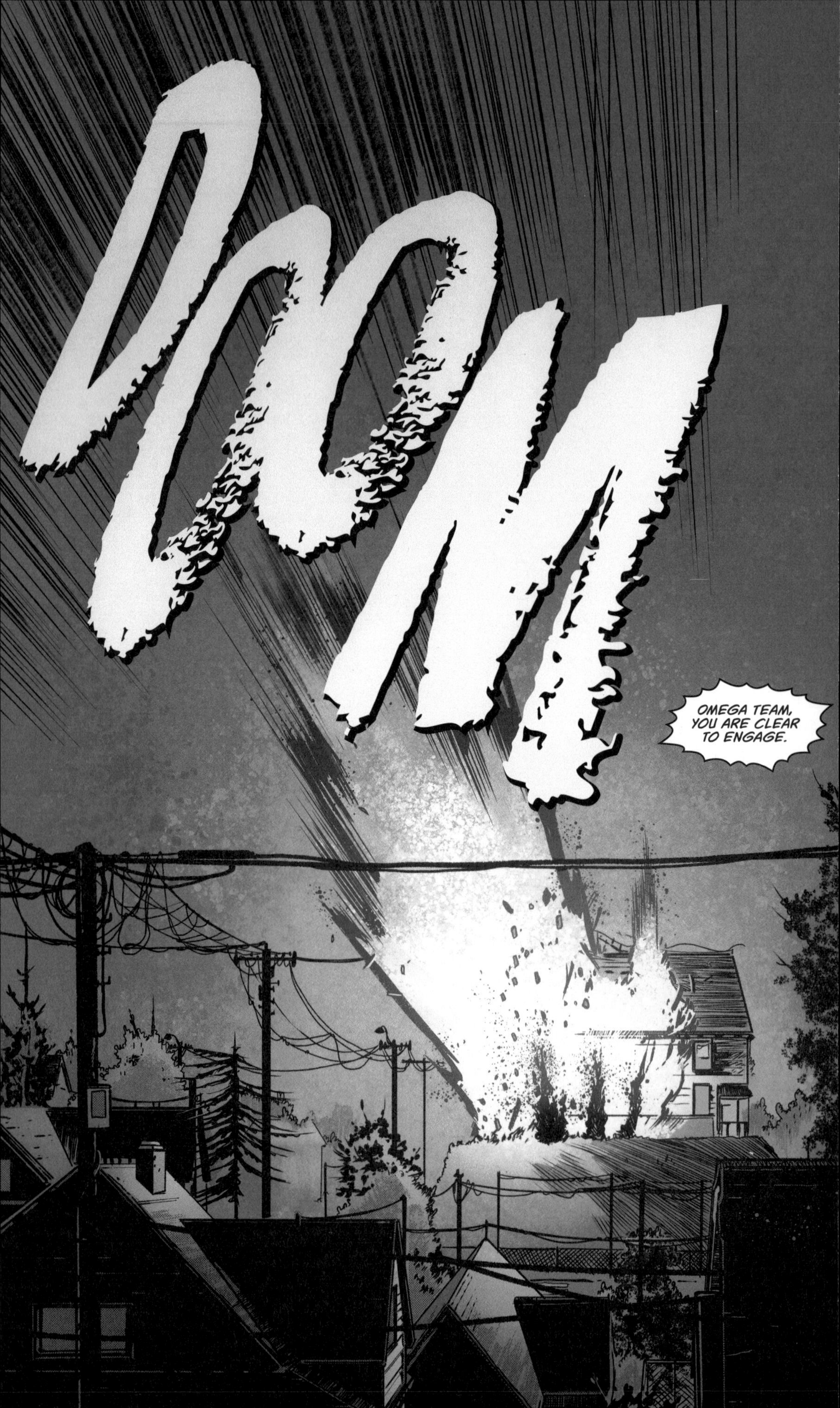
OMEGA TEAM, YOU ARE CLEAR TO ENGAGE.

five.

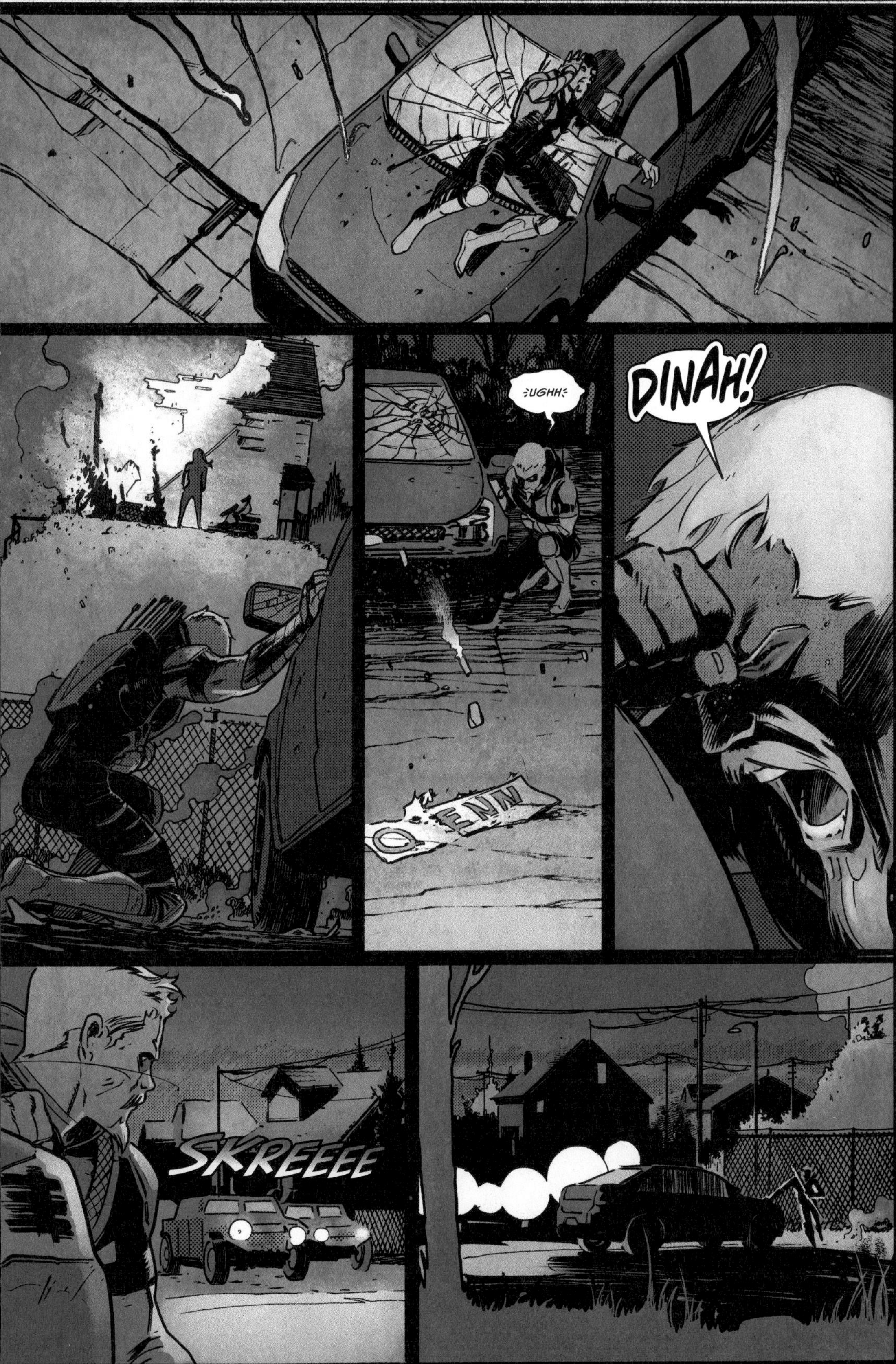
UGHH
DINAH!
SKREEEE

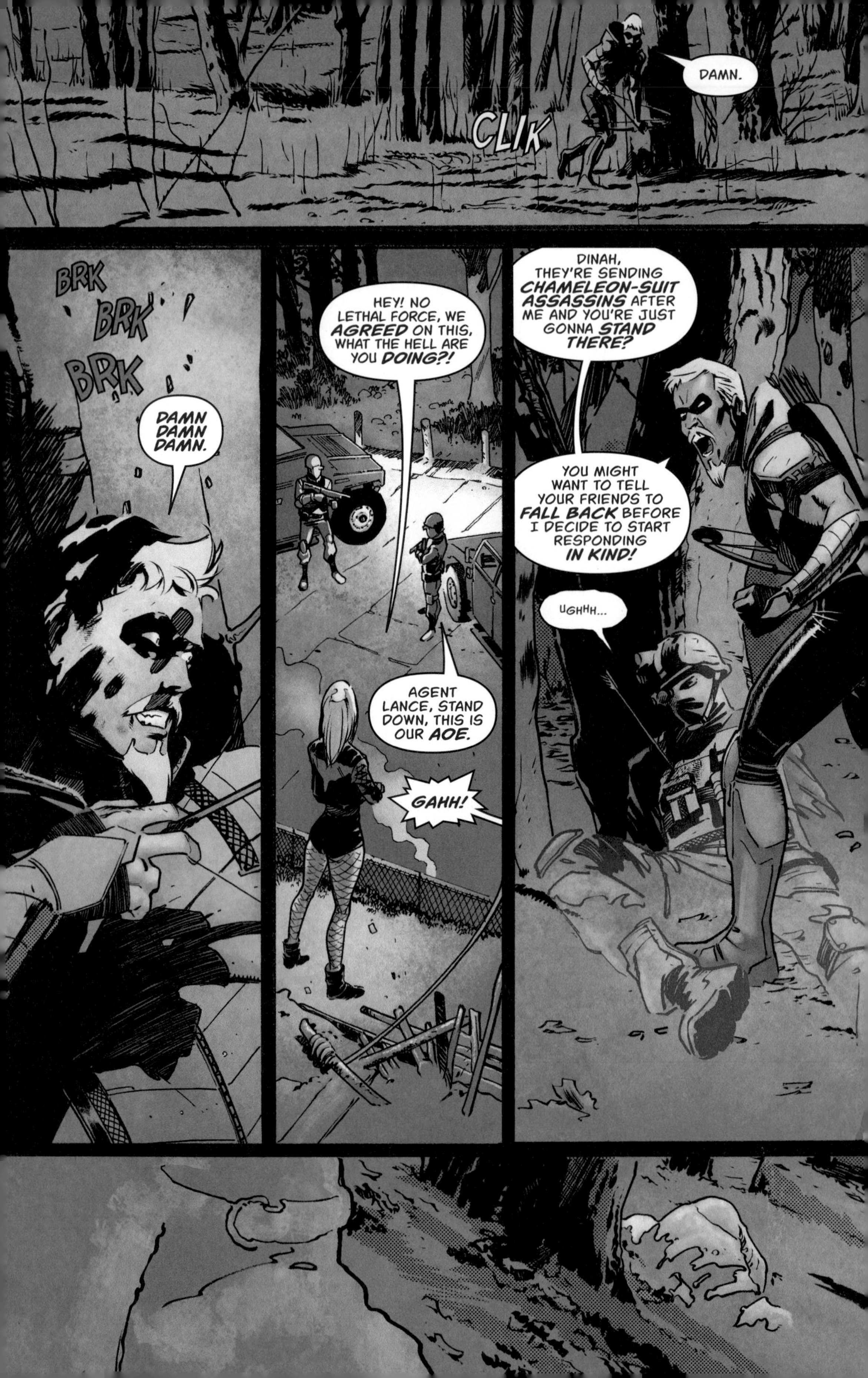

DAMN.
CLIK
BRK
BRK
BRK
DAMN DAMN DAMN.
HEY! NO LETHAL FORCE, WE AGREED ON THIS, WHAT THE HELL ARE YOU DOING?!
AGENT LANCE, STAND DOWN, THIS IS OUR AOE.
GAHH!
DINAH, THEY'RE SENDING CHAMELEON-SUIT ASSASSINS AFTER ME AND YOU'RE JUST GONNA STAND THERE?
YOU MIGHT WANT TO TELL YOUR FRIENDS TO FALL BACK BEFORE I DECIDE TO START RESPONDING IN KIND!
UGHHH...

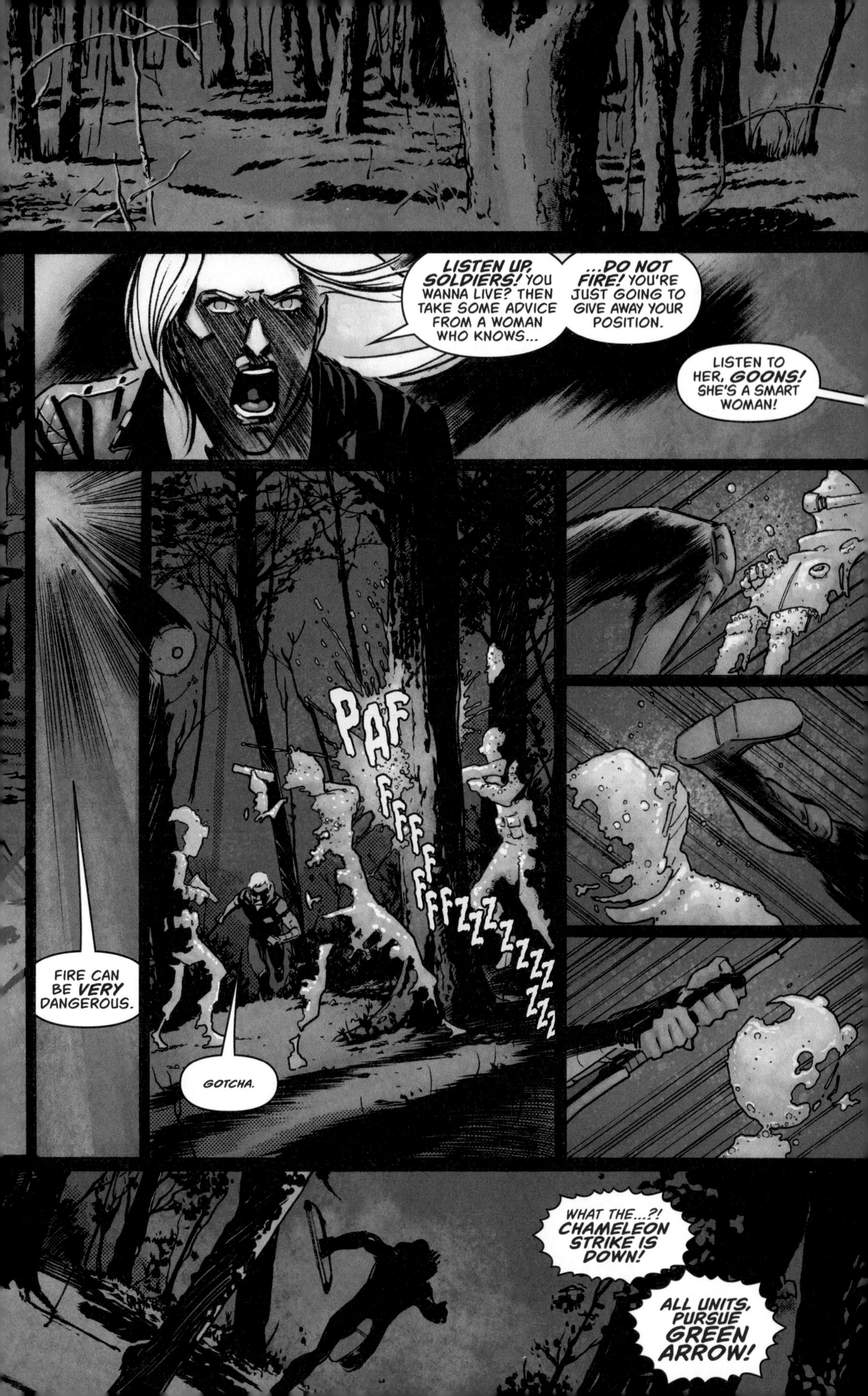
LISTEN UP, SOLDIERS! YOU WANNA LIVE? THEN TAKE SOME ADVICE FROM A WOMAN WHO KNOWS...
...DO NOT FIRE! YOU'RE JUST GOING TO GIVE AWAY YOUR POSITION.
LISTEN TO HER, GOONS! SHE'S A SMART WOMAN!
FIRE CAN BE VERY DANGEROUS.
PAFFFFFFFZZZZZZZZZ
GOTCHA.
WHAT THE...?! CHAMELEON STRIKE IS DOWN!
ALL UNITS, PURSUE GREEN ARROW!

THEY'RE AFTER ME. THAT'S GOOD.
THEY DON'T HAVE THE BOX IF THEY'RE AFTER ME.
WHICH MEANS I'VE GOT TO GET TO THE BOX.
HOW AM I GOING TO GET TO THE BOX...
...OH.
THIS IS DUMB.
THIS IS A VERY DUMB IDEA.

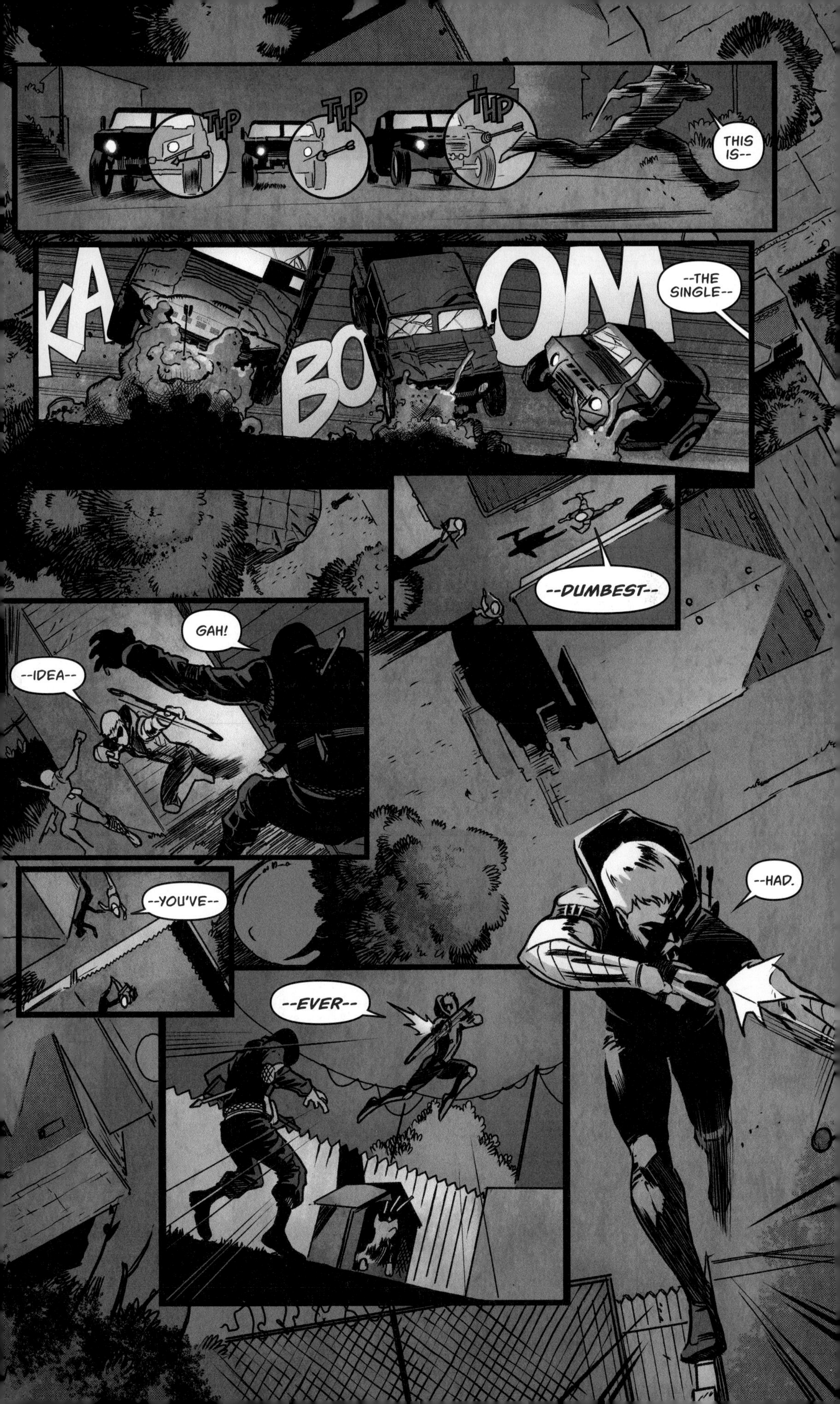

THP
THP
THP
THIS IS--
KA BOOM
--THE SINGLE--
--DUMBEST--
GAH!
--IDEA--
--YOU'VE--
--EVER--
--HAD.

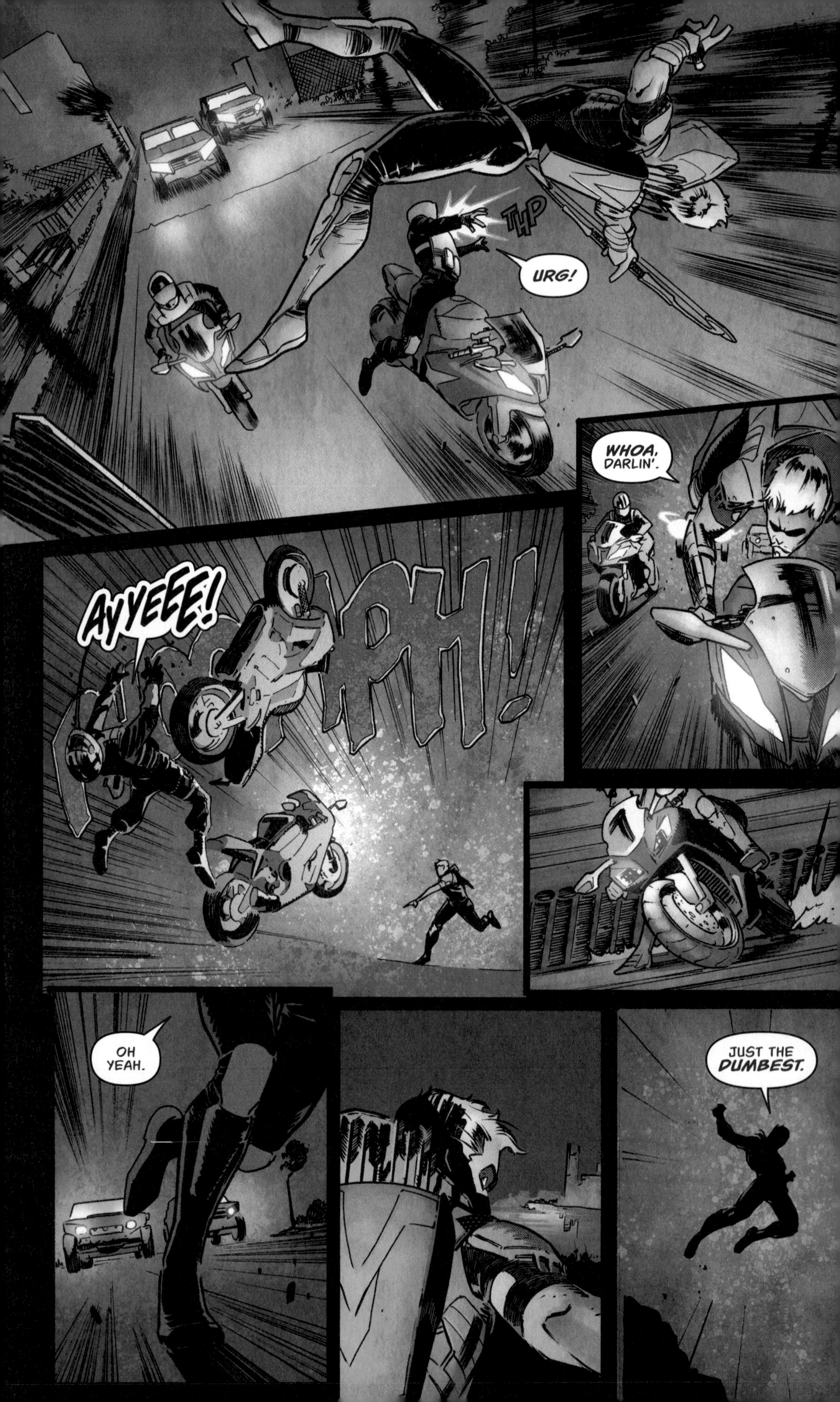
THP
URG!
WHOA, DARLIN'.
AyYEEE!
OH YEAH.
JUST THE DUMBEST.

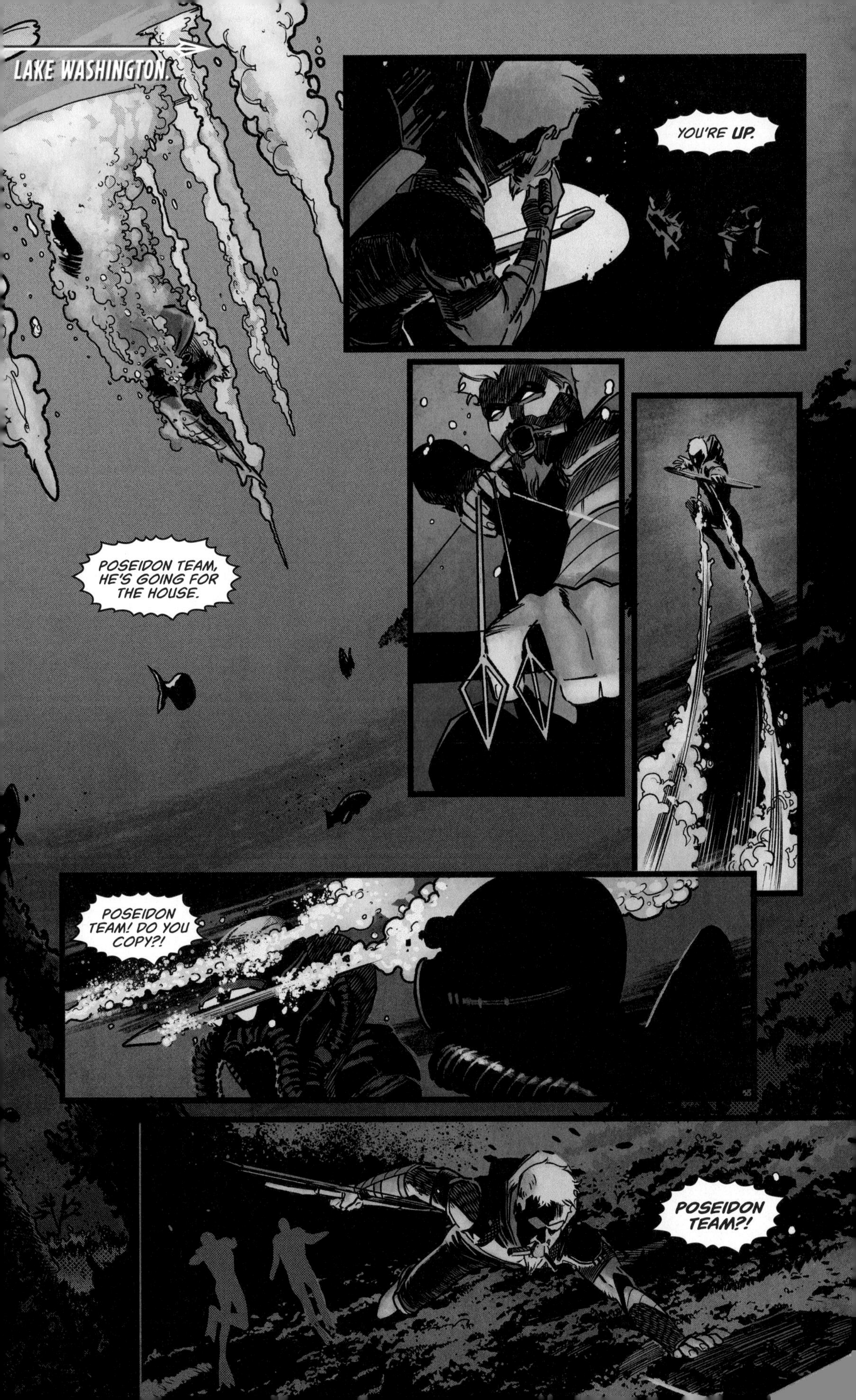
LAKE WASHINGTON.
YOU'RE UP.
POSEIDON TEAM, HE'S GOING FOR THE HOUSE.
POSEIDON TEAM! DO YOU COPY?!
POSEIDON TEAM?!

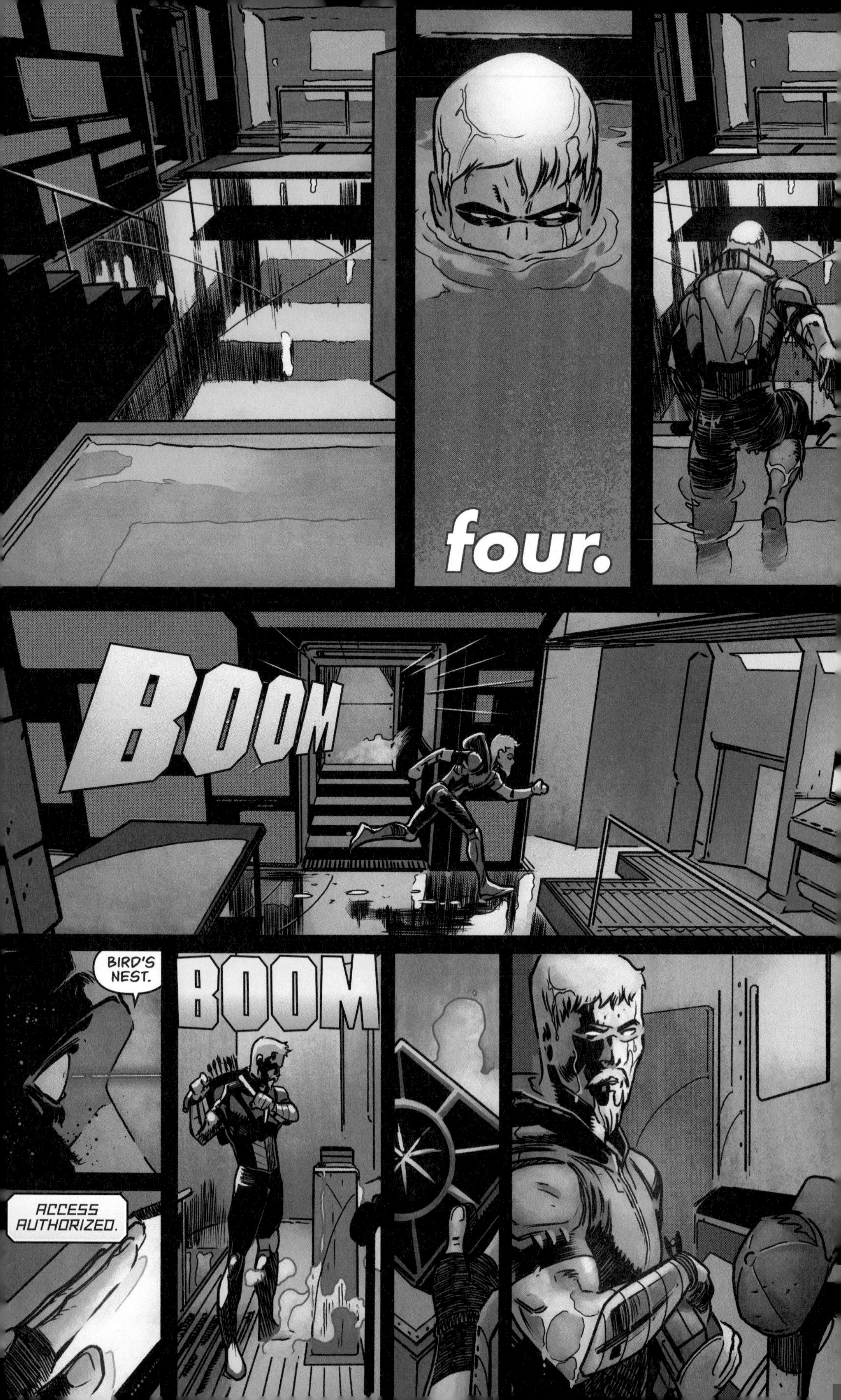
four.
BOOM
BIRD'S NEST.
ACCESS AUTHORIZED.
BOOM

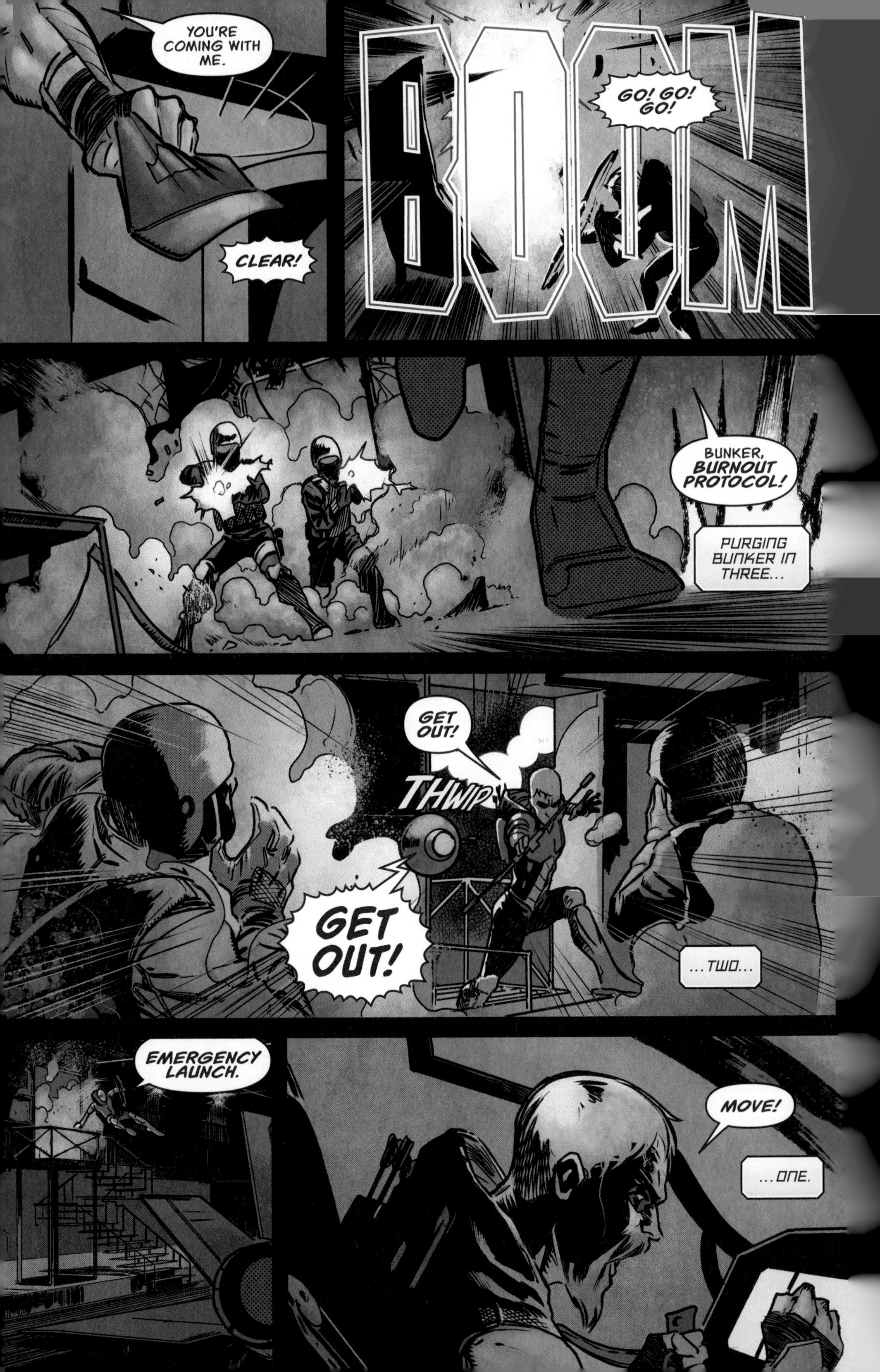

YOU'RE COMING WITH ME.
CLEAR!
BOOM
GO! GO! GO!
BUNKER, BURNOUT PROTOCOL!
PURGING BUNKER IN THREE...
GET OUT!
THWIP
GET OUT!
...TWO...
EMERGENCY LAUNCH.
MOVE!
...ONE.

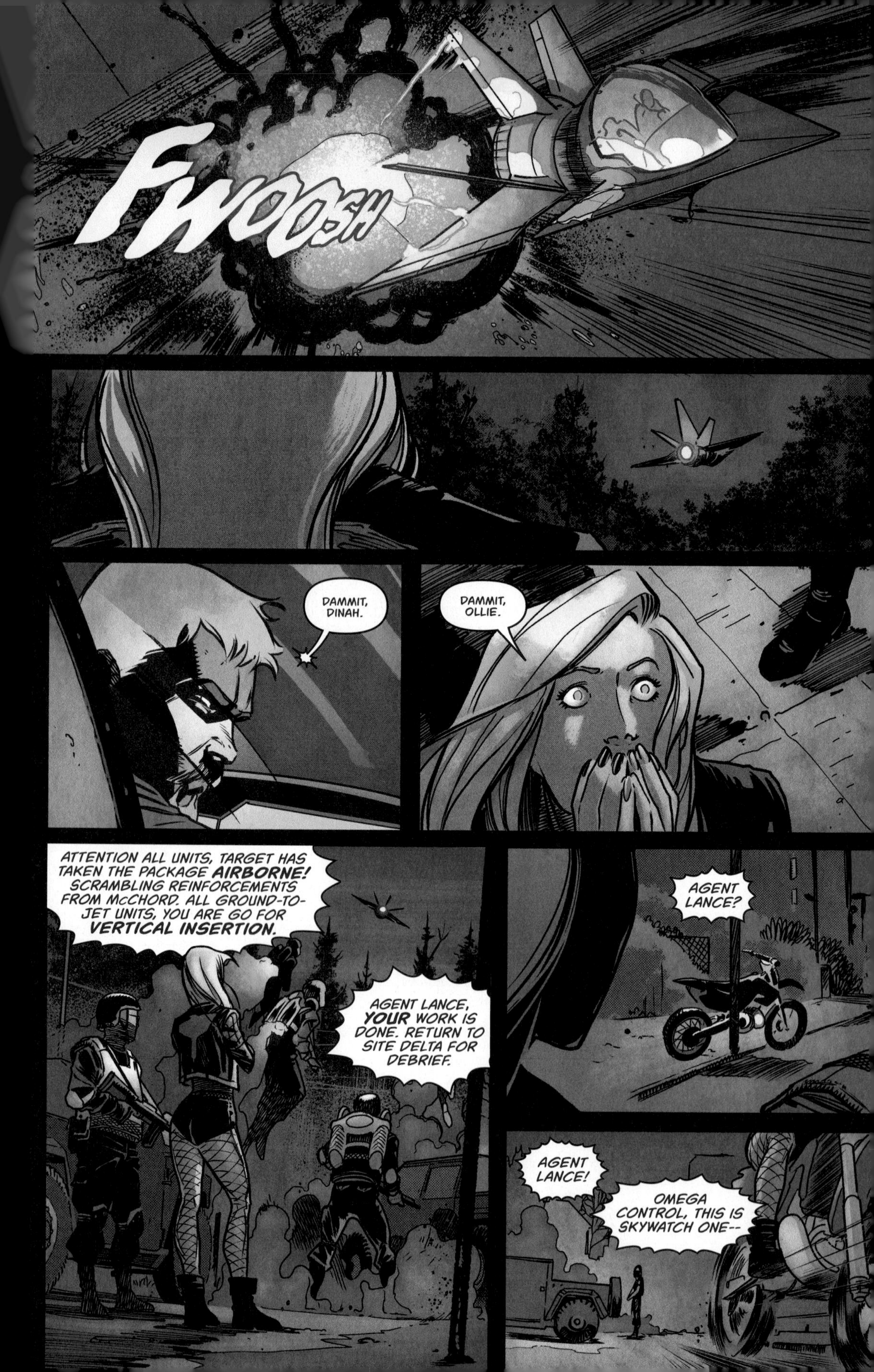
FWOOSH
DAMMIT, DINAH.
DAMMIT, OLLIE.
ATTENTION ALL UNITS, TARGET HAS TAKEN THE PACKAGE AIRBORNE! SCRAMBLING REINFORCEMENTS FROM McCHORD. ALL GROUND-TO-JET UNITS, YOU ARE GO FOR VERTICAL INSERTION.
AGENT LANCE, YOUR WORK IS DONE. RETURN TO SITE DELTA FOR DEBRIEF.
AGENT LANCE?
AGENT LANCE!
OMEGA CONTROL, THIS IS SKYWATCH ONE--

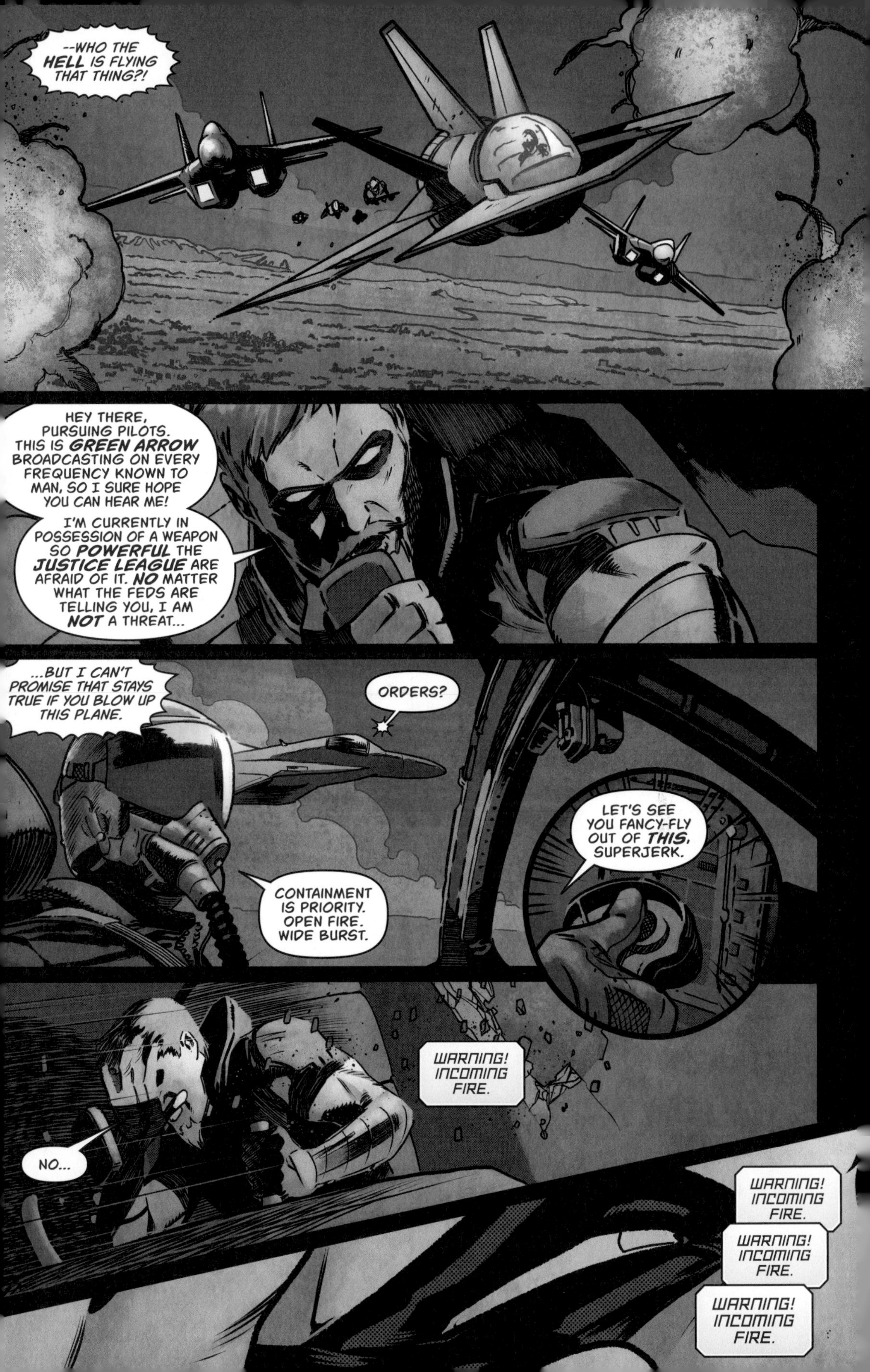
--WHO THE HELL IS FLYING THAT THING?!
HEY THERE, PURSUING PILOTS. THIS IS GREEN ARROW BROADCASTING ON EVERY FREQUENCY KNOWN TO MAN, SO I SURE HOPE YOU CAN HEAR ME!
I'M CURRENTLY IN POSSESSION OF A WEAPON SO POWERFUL THE JUSTICE LEAGUE ARE AFRAID OF IT. NO MATTER WHAT THE FEDS ARE TELLING YOU, I AM NOT A THREAT...
...BUT I CAN'T PROMISE THAT STAYS TRUE IF YOU BLOW UP THIS PLANE.
ORDERS?
CONTAINMENT IS PRIORITY. OPEN FIRE. WIDE BURST.
LET'S SEE YOU FANCY-FLY OUT OF THIS, SUPERJERK.
WARNING! INCOMING FIRE.
NO...
WARNING! INCOMING FIRE.
WARNING! INCOMING FIRE.
WARNING! INCOMING FIRE.

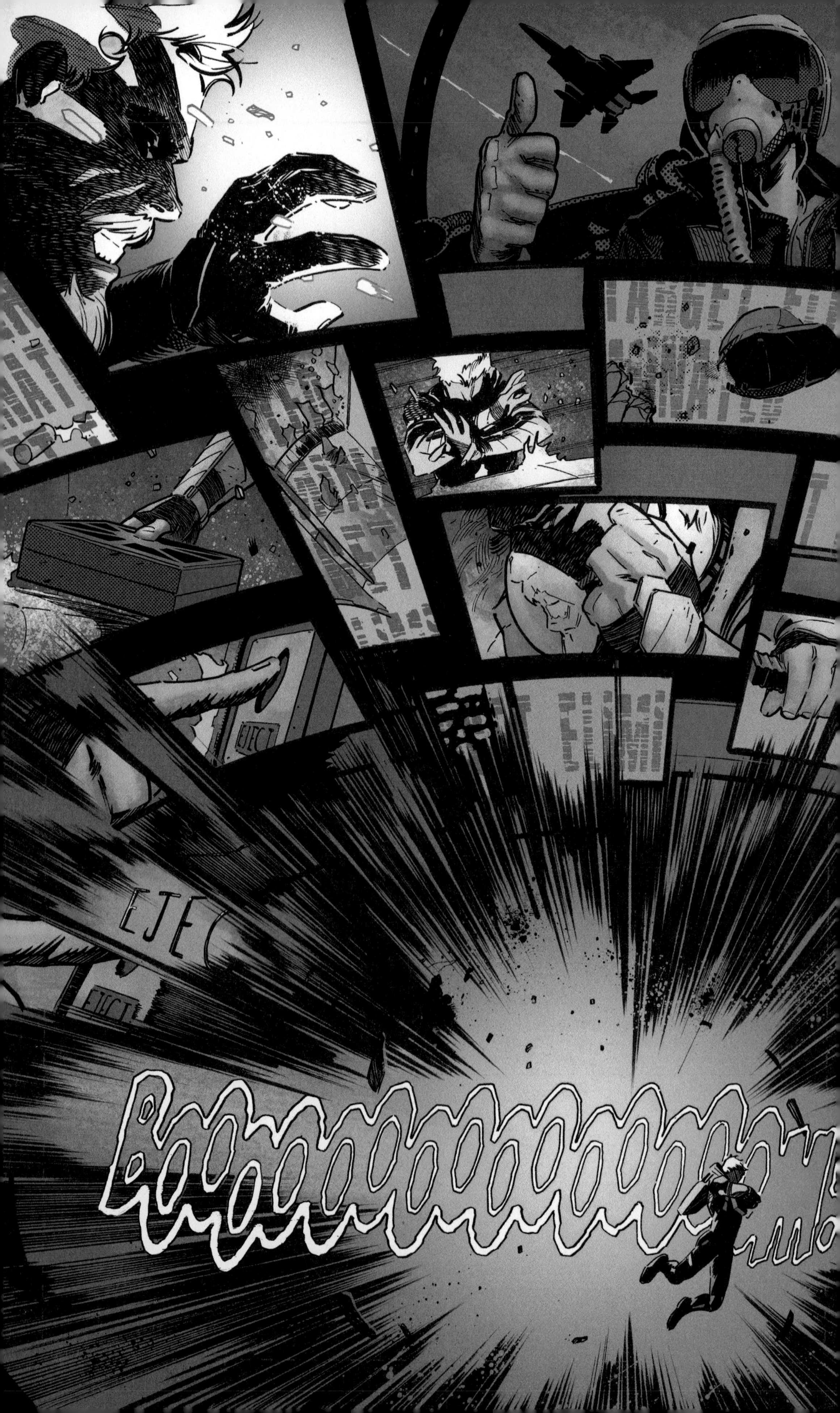
EJECT
EJEC

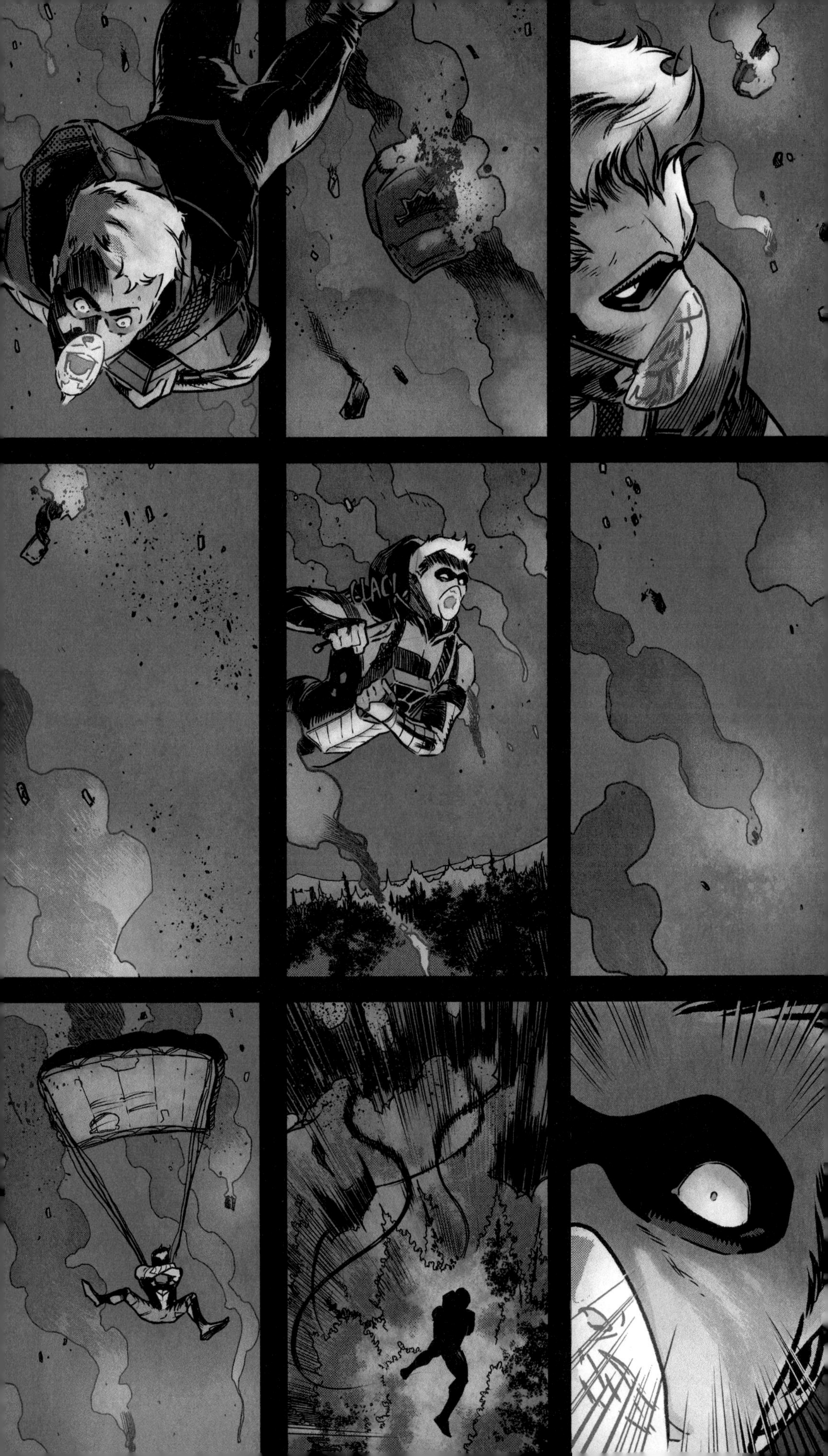
CLAC!

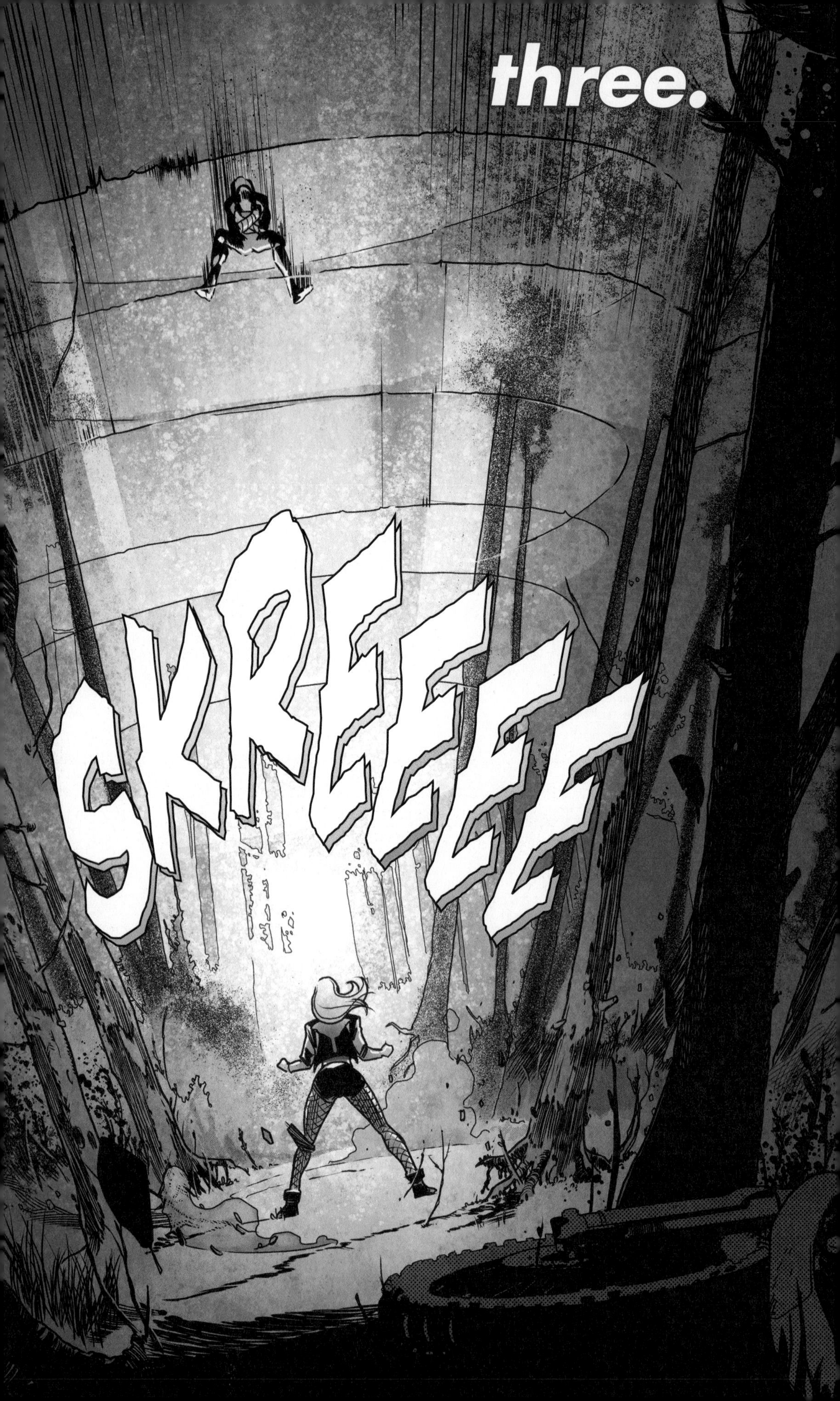
three.
SKREEEEE

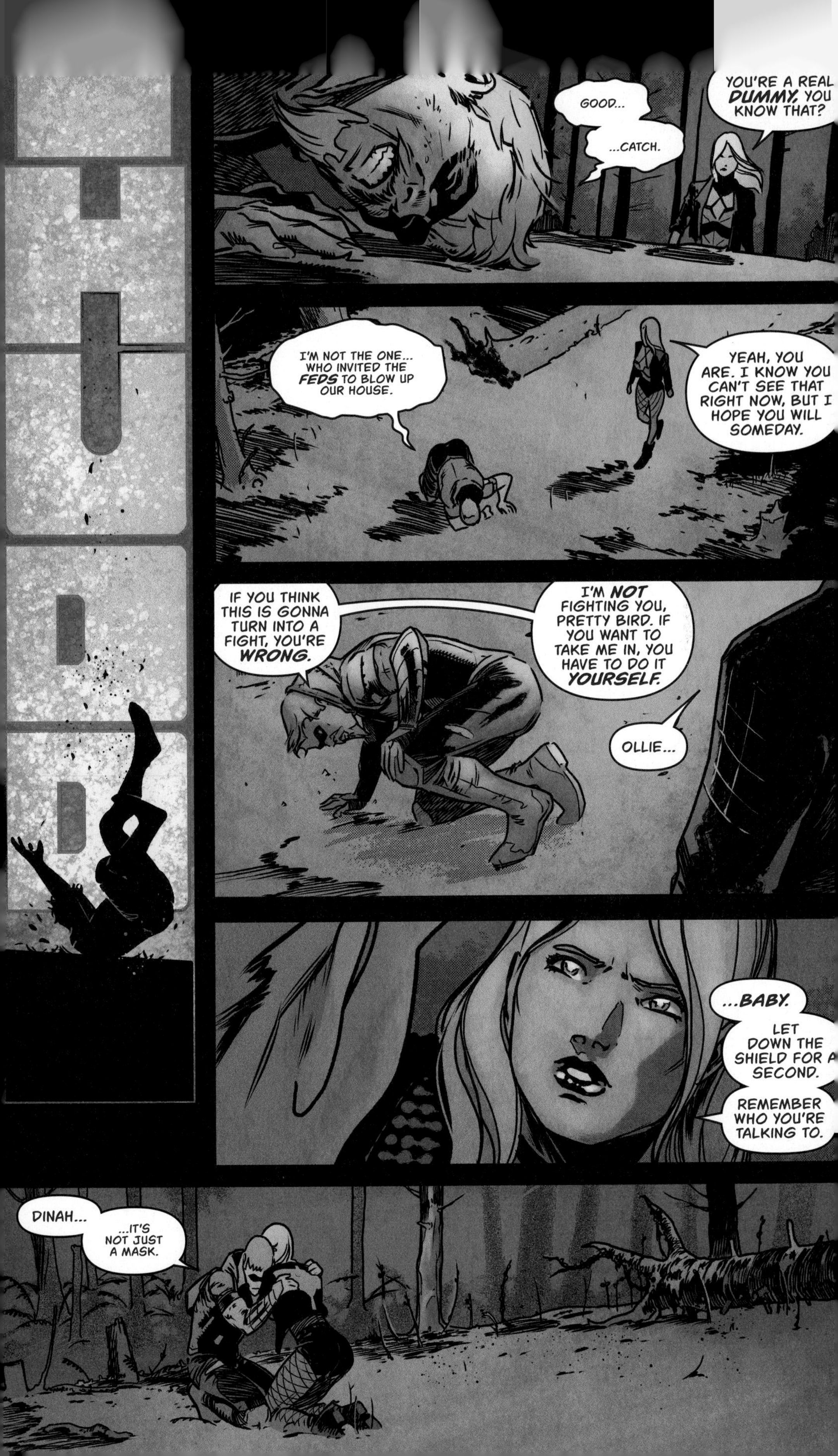
GOOD...
...CATCH.
YOU'RE A REAL DUMMY, YOU KNOW THAT?
I'M NOT THE ONE... WHO INVITED THE FEDS TO BLOW UP OUR HOUSE.
YEAH, YOU ARE. I KNOW YOU CAN'T SEE THAT RIGHT NOW, BUT I HOPE YOU WILL SOMEDAY.
IF YOU THINK THIS IS GONNA TURN INTO A FIGHT, YOU'RE WRONG.
I'M NOT FIGHTING YOU, PRETTY BIRD. IF YOU WANT TO TAKE ME IN, YOU HAVE TO DO IT YOURSELF.
OLLIE...
...BABY.
LET DOWN THE SHIELD FOR A SECOND.
REMEMBER WHO YOU'RE TALKING TO.
DINAH...
...IT'S NOT JUST A MASK.

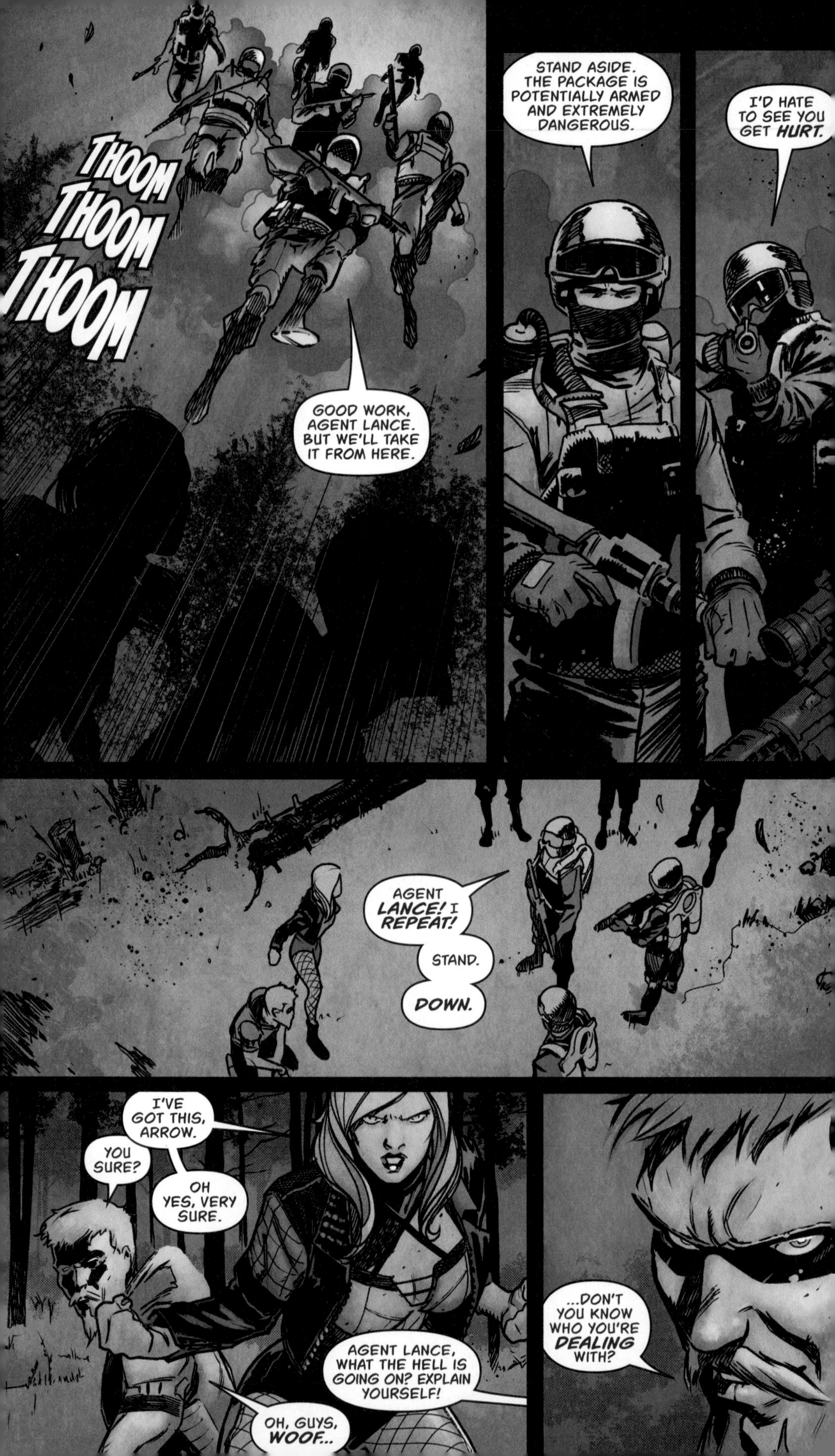
THOOM THOOM THOOM
GOOD WORK, AGENT LANCE. BUT WE'LL TAKE IT FROM HERE.
STAND ASIDE. THE PACKAGE IS POTENTIALLY ARMED AND EXTREMELY DANGEROUS.
I'D HATE TO SEE YOU GET HURT.
AGENT LANCE! I REPEAT!
STAND.
DOWN.
I'VE GOT THIS, ARROW.
YOU SURE?
OH YES, VERY SURE.
AGENT LANCE, WHAT THE HELL IS GOING ON? EXPLAIN YOURSELF!
OH, GUYS, WOOF...
...DON'T YOU KNOW WHO YOU'RE DEALING WITH?

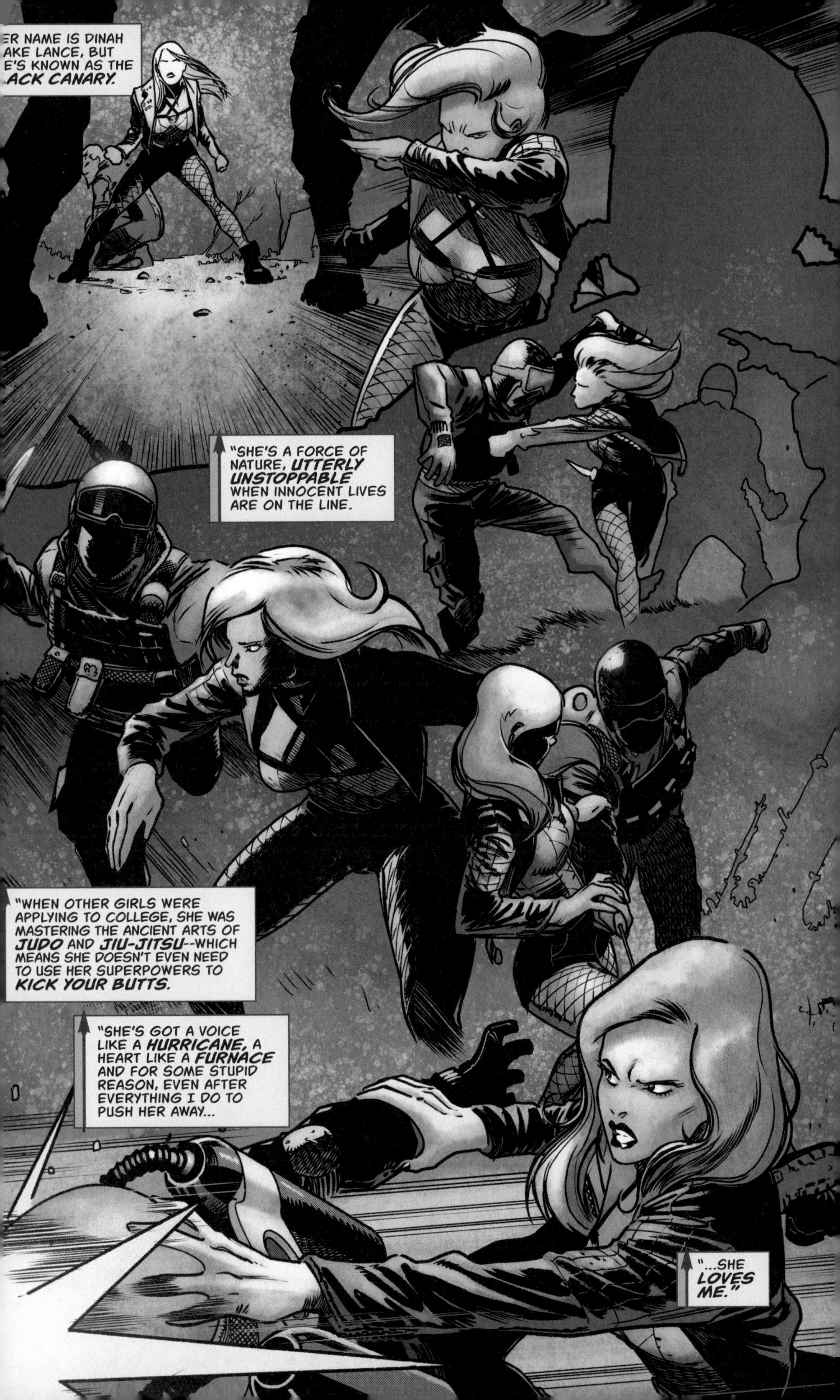
ER NAME IS DINAH ...AKE LANCE, BUT ...E'S KNOWN AS THE ...ACK CANARY.
"SHE'S A FORCE OF NATURE, UTTERLY UNSTOPPABLE WHEN INNOCENT LIVES ARE ON THE LINE.
"WHEN OTHER GIRLS WERE APPLYING TO COLLEGE, SHE WAS MASTERING THE ANCIENT ARTS OF JUDO AND JIU-JITSU--WHICH MEANS SHE DOESN'T EVEN NEED TO USE HER SUPERPOWERS TO KICK YOUR BUTTS.
"SHE'S GOT A VOICE LIKE A HURRICANE, A HEART LIKE A FURNACE AND FOR SOME STUPID REASON, EVEN AFTER EVERYTHING I DO TO PUSH HER AWAY...
"...SHE LOVES ME."

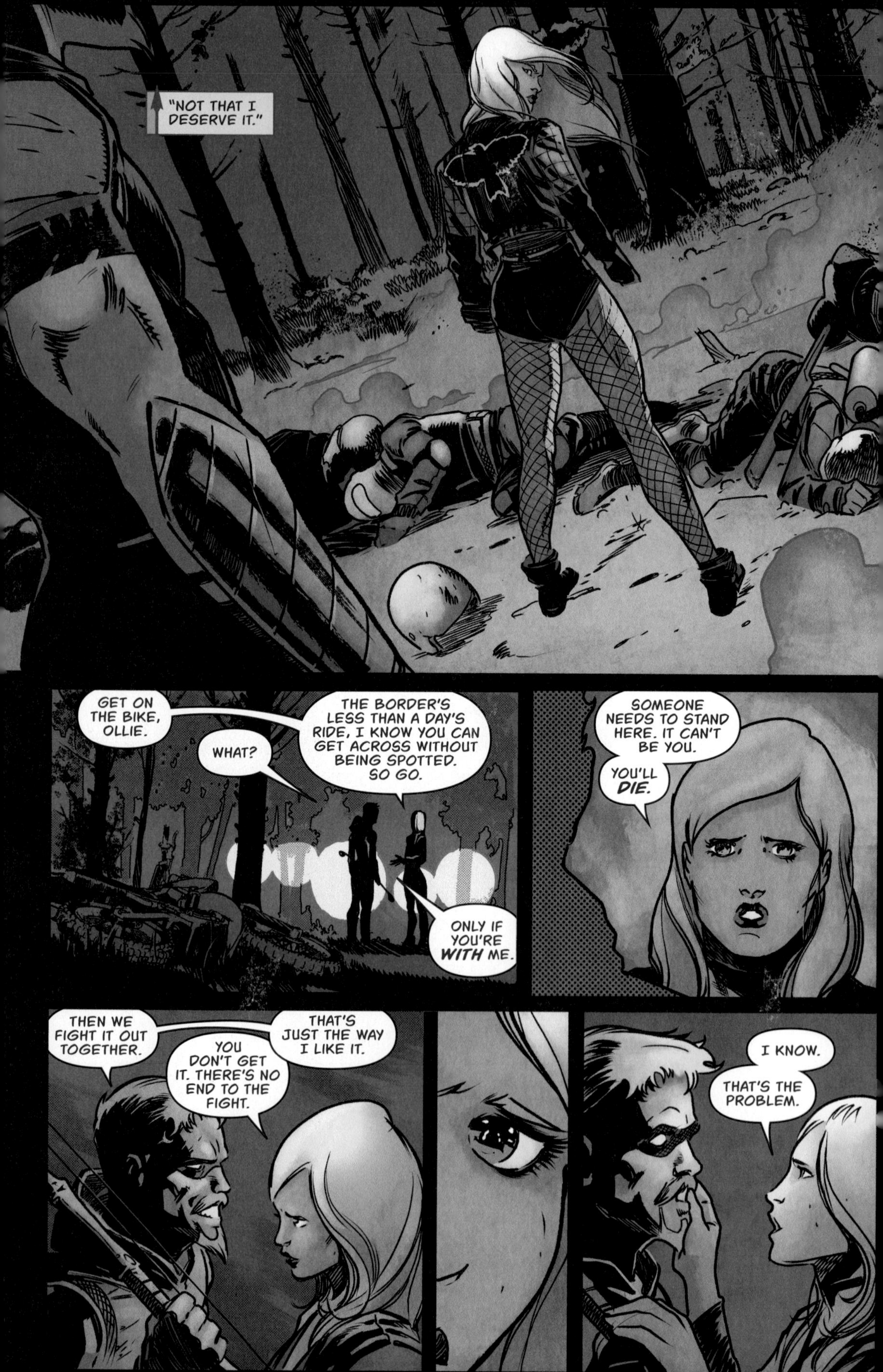
"NOT THAT I DESERVE IT."
GET ON THE BIKE, OLLIE.
THE BORDER'S LESS THAN A DAY'S RIDE, I KNOW YOU CAN GET ACROSS WITHOUT BEING SPOTTED. SO GO.
WHAT?
ONLY IF YOU'RE **WITH** ME.
SOMEONE NEEDS TO STAND HERE. IT CAN'T BE YOU.
YOU'LL **DIE**.
THEN WE FIGHT IT OUT TOGETHER.
THAT'S JUST THE WAY I LIKE IT.
YOU DON'T GET IT. THERE'S NO END TO THE FIGHT.
I KNOW.
THAT'S THE PROBLEM.

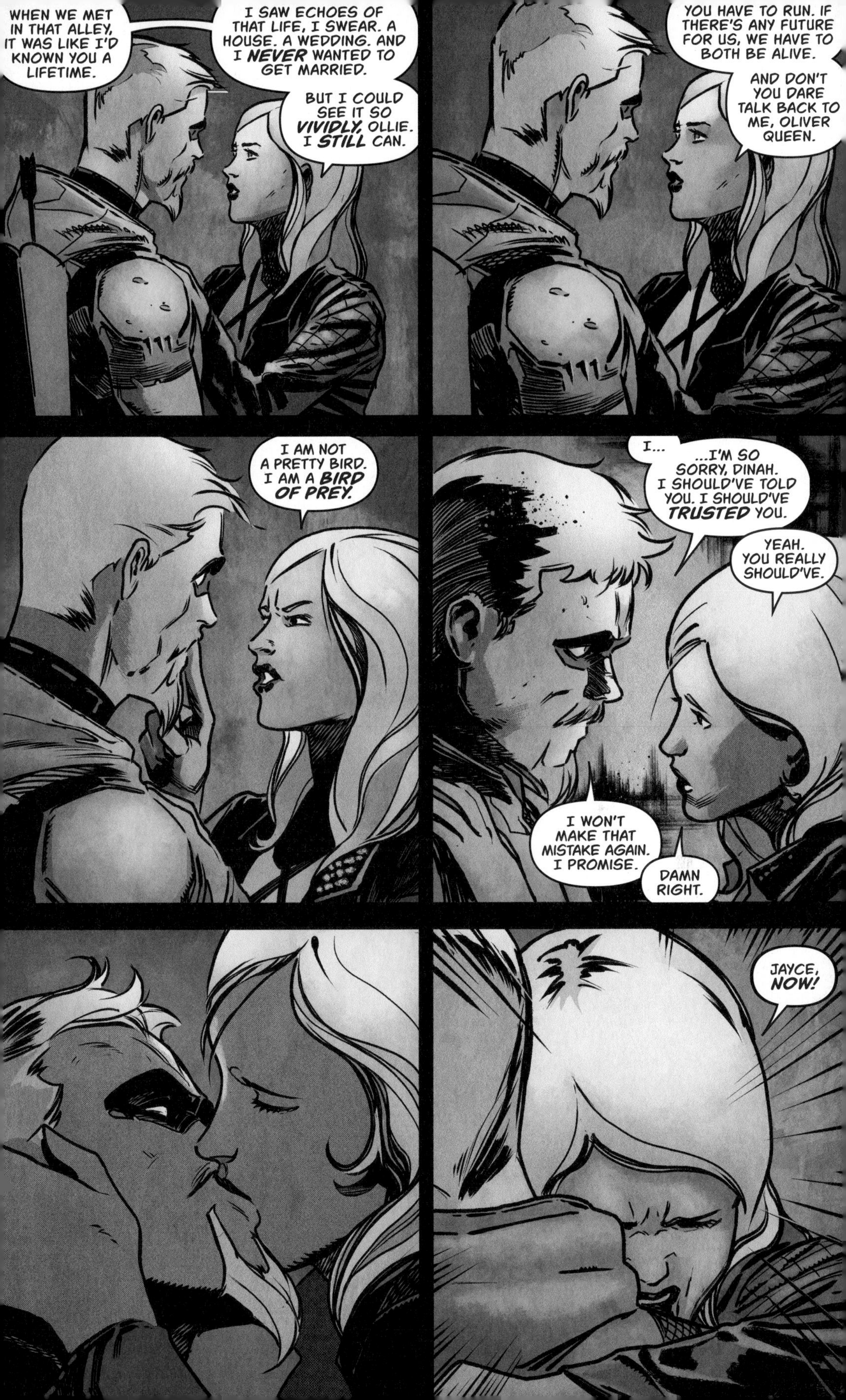
WHEN WE MET IN THAT ALLEY, IT WAS LIKE I'D KNOWN YOU A LIFETIME.
I SAW ECHOES OF THAT LIFE, I SWEAR. A HOUSE. A WEDDING. AND I NEVER WANTED TO GET MARRIED.
BUT I COULD SEE IT SO VIVIDLY, OLLIE. I STILL CAN.
YOU HAVE TO RUN. IF THERE'S ANY FUTURE FOR US, WE HAVE TO BOTH BE ALIVE.
AND DON'T YOU DARE TALK BACK TO ME, OLIVER QUEEN.
I AM NOT A PRETTY BIRD. I AM A BIRD OF PREY.
I...
...I'M SO SORRY, DINAH. I SHOULD'VE TOLD YOU. I SHOULD'VE TRUSTED YOU.
YEAH. YOU REALLY SHOULD'VE.
I WON'T MAKE THAT MISTAKE AGAIN. I PROMISE.
DAMN RIGHT.
JAYCE, NOW!

two.

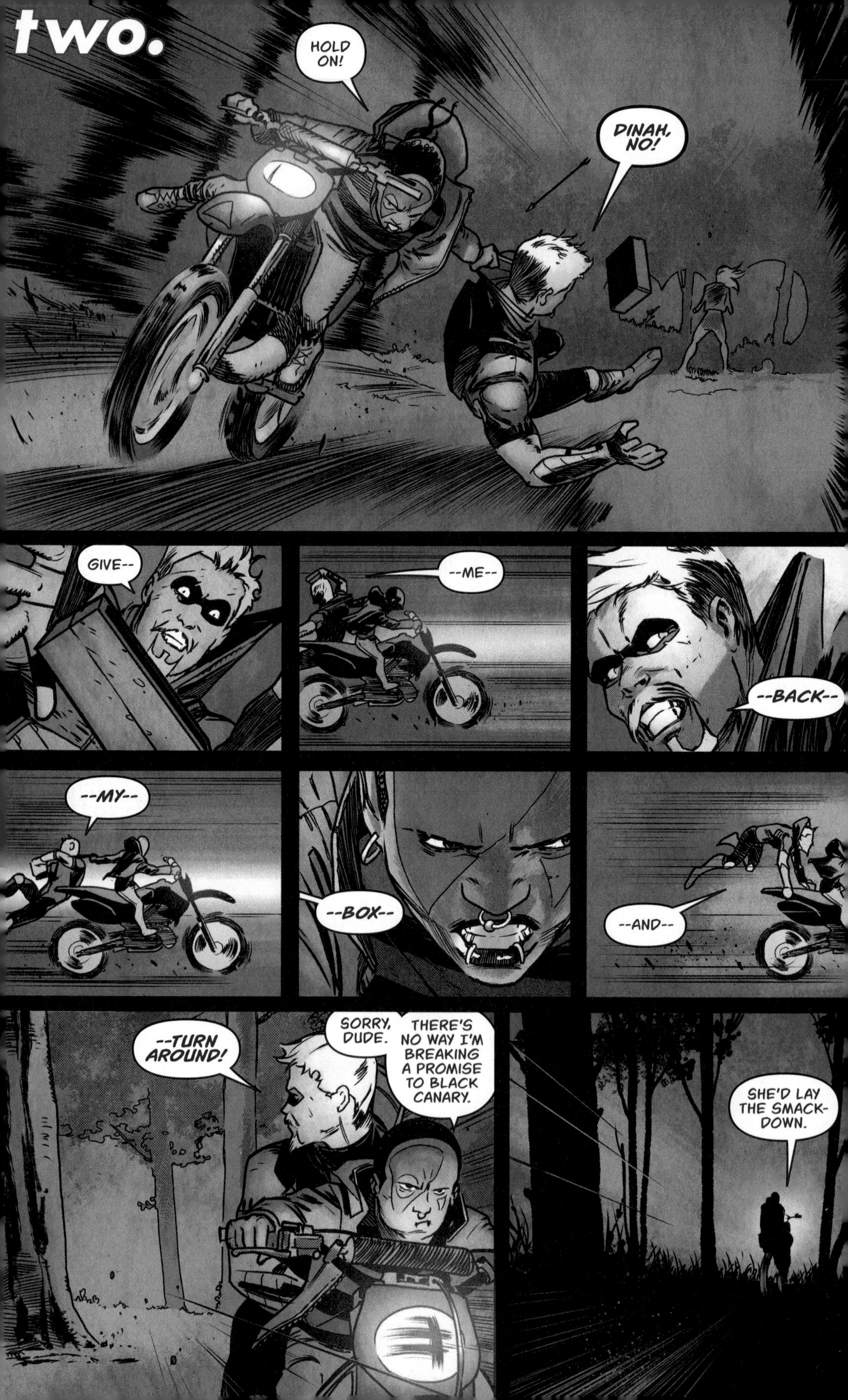

HOLD ON!
DINAH, NO!
GIVE--
--ME--
--BACK--
--MY--
--BOX--
--AND--
--TURN AROUND!
SORRY, DUDE.
THERE'S NO WAY I'M BREAKING A PROMISE TO BLACK CANARY.
SHE'D LAY THE SMACK-DOWN.

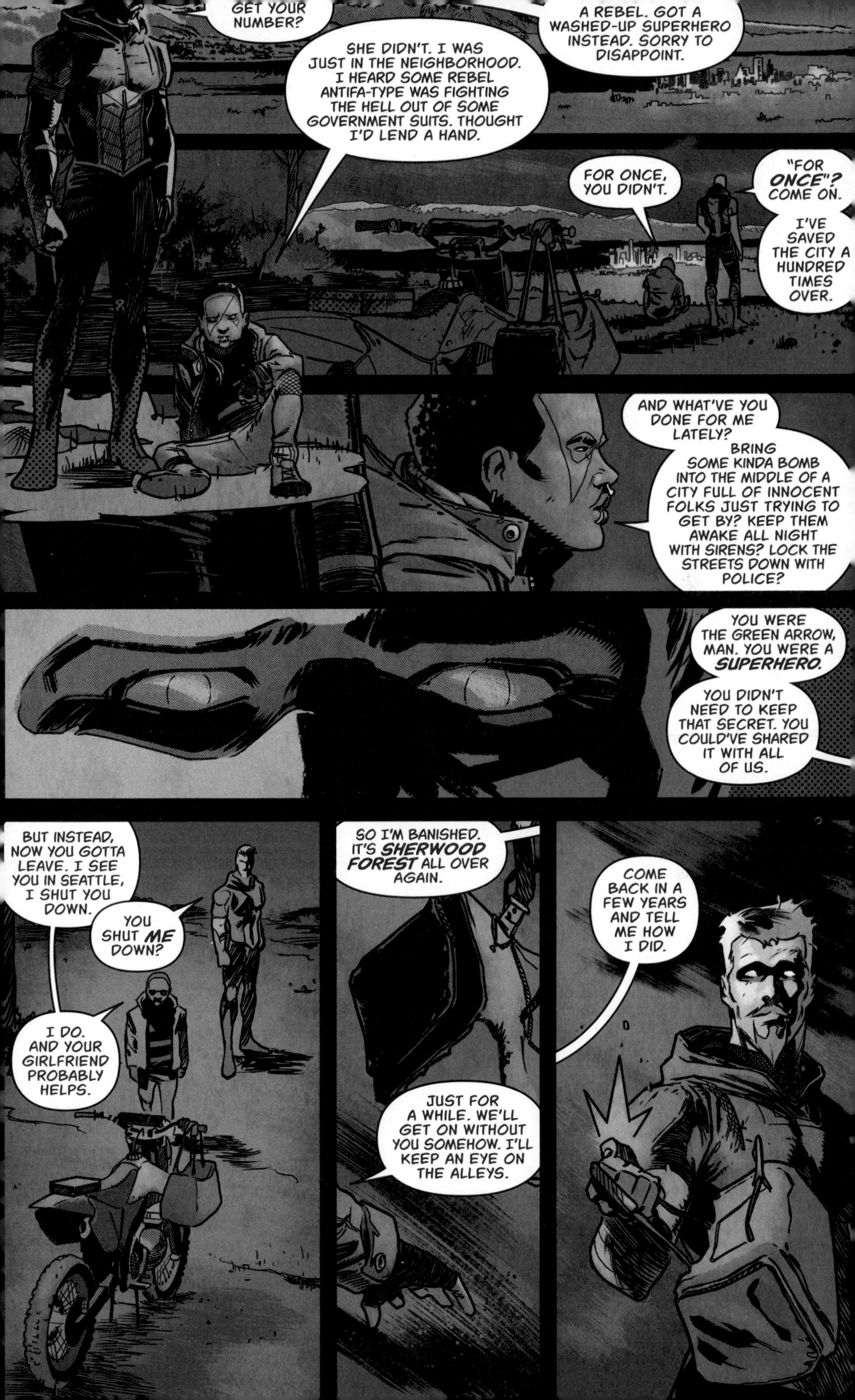

GET YOUR NUMBER?
SHE DIDN'T. I WAS JUST IN THE NEIGHBORHOOD. I HEARD SOME REBEL ANTIFA-TYPE WAS FIGHTING THE HELL OUT OF SOME GOVERNMENT SUITS. THOUGHT I'D LEND A HAND.
A REBEL. GOT A WASHED-UP SUPERHERO INSTEAD. SORRY TO DISAPPOINT.
FOR ONCE, YOU DIDN'T.
"FOR ONCE"? COME ON.
I'VE SAVED THE CITY A HUNDRED TIMES OVER.
AND WHAT'VE YOU DONE FOR ME LATELY?
BRING SOME KINDA BOMB INTO THE MIDDLE OF A CITY FULL OF INNOCENT FOLKS JUST TRYING TO GET BY? KEEP THEM AWAKE ALL NIGHT WITH SIRENS? LOCK THE STREETS DOWN WITH POLICE?
YOU WERE THE GREEN ARROW, MAN. YOU WERE A SUPERHERO.
YOU DIDN'T NEED TO KEEP THAT SECRET. YOU COULD'VE SHARED IT WITH ALL OF US.
BUT INSTEAD, NOW YOU GOTTA LEAVE. I SEE YOU IN SEATTLE, I SHUT YOU DOWN.
YOU SHUT ME DOWN?
I DO. AND YOUR GIRLFRIEND PROBABLY HELPS.
SO I'M BANISHED. IT'S SHERWOOD FOREST ALL OVER AGAIN.
JUST FOR A WHILE. WE'LL GET ON WITHOUT YOU SOMEHOW. I'LL KEEP AN EYE ON THE ALLEYS.
COME BACK IN A FEW YEARS AND TELL ME HOW I DID.

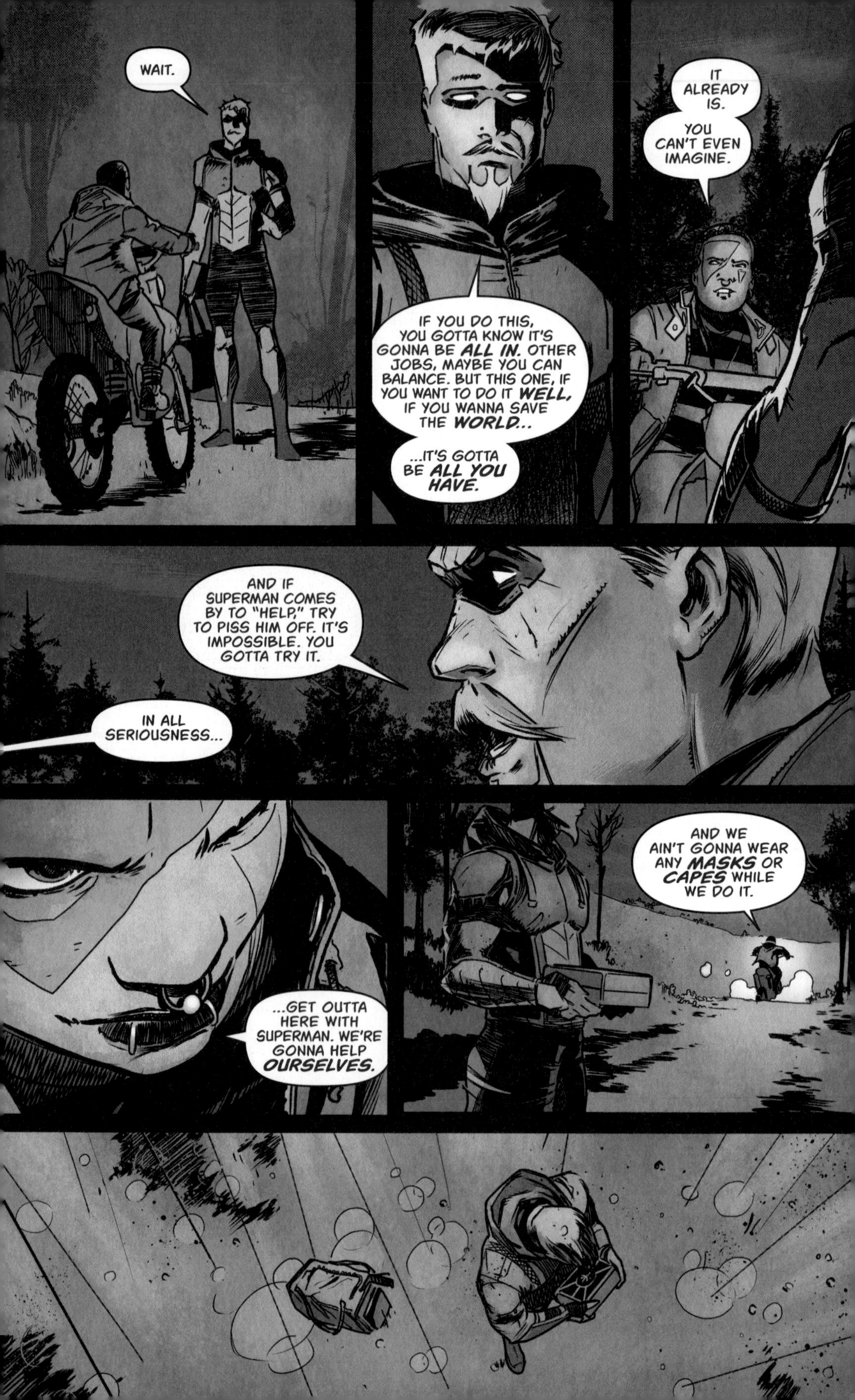
WAIT.
IF YOU DO THIS, YOU GOTTA KNOW IT'S GONNA BE ALL IN. OTHER JOBS, MAYBE YOU CAN BALANCE. BUT THIS ONE, IF YOU WANT TO DO IT WELL, IF YOU WANNA SAVE THE WORLD...
...IT'S GOTTA BE ALL YOU HAVE.
IT ALREADY IS.
YOU CAN'T EVEN IMAGINE.
AND IF SUPERMAN COMES BY TO "HELP," TRY TO PISS HIM OFF. IT'S IMPOSSIBLE. YOU GOTTA TRY IT.
IN ALL SERIOUSNESS...
...GET OUTTA HERE WITH SUPERMAN. WE'RE GONNA HELP OURSELVES.
AND WE AIN'T GONNA WEAR ANY MASKS OR CAPES WHILE WE DO IT.

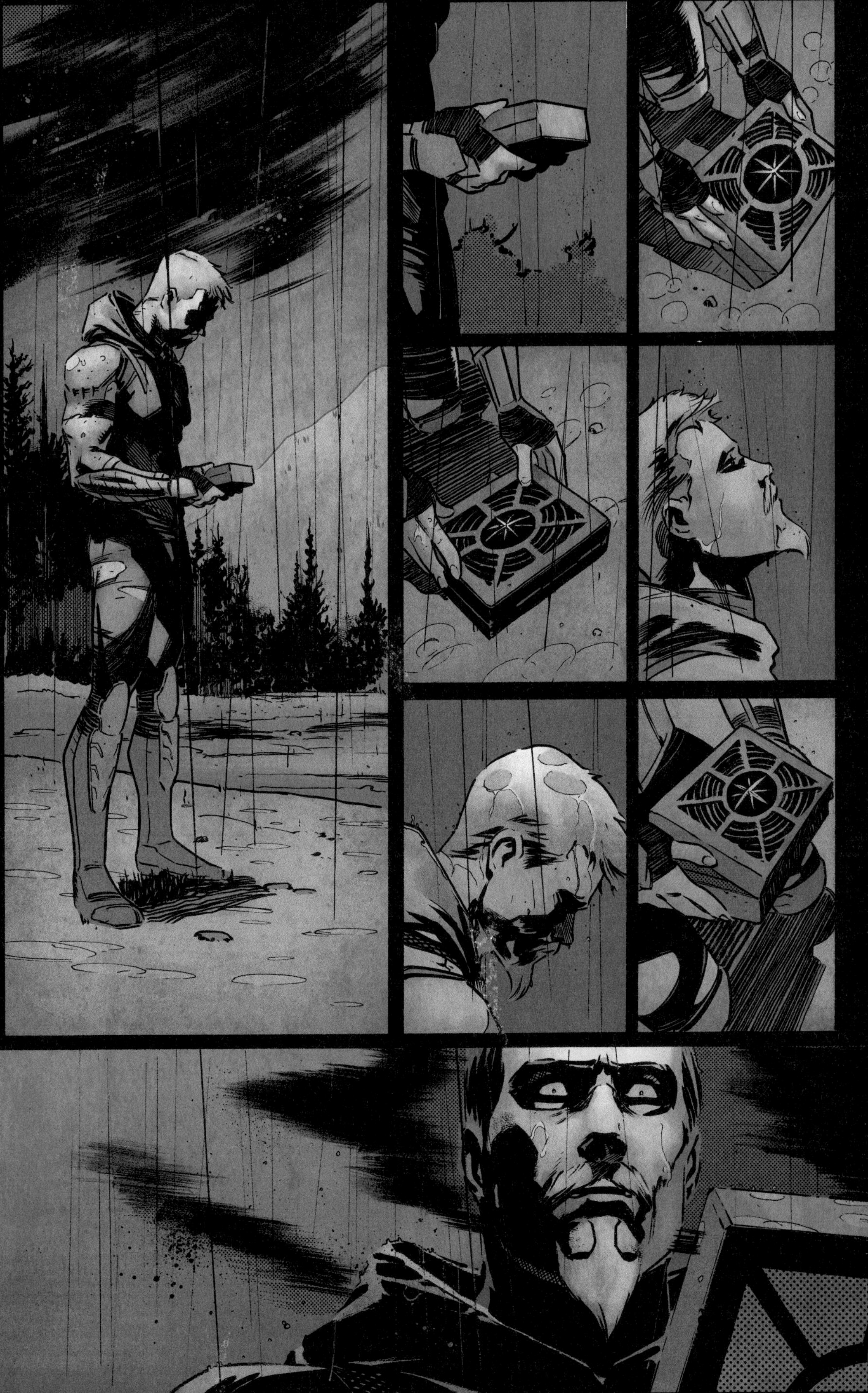

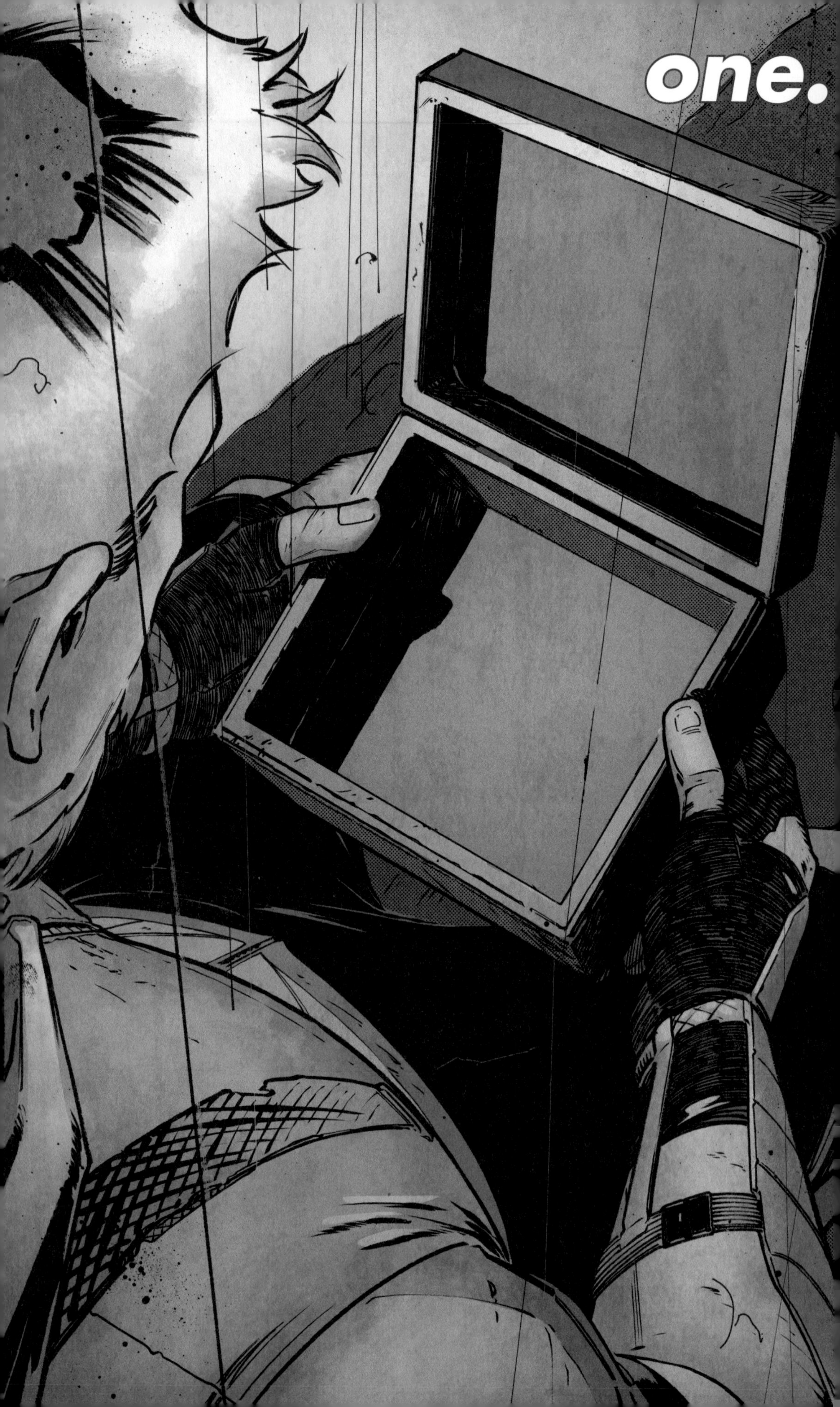
one.

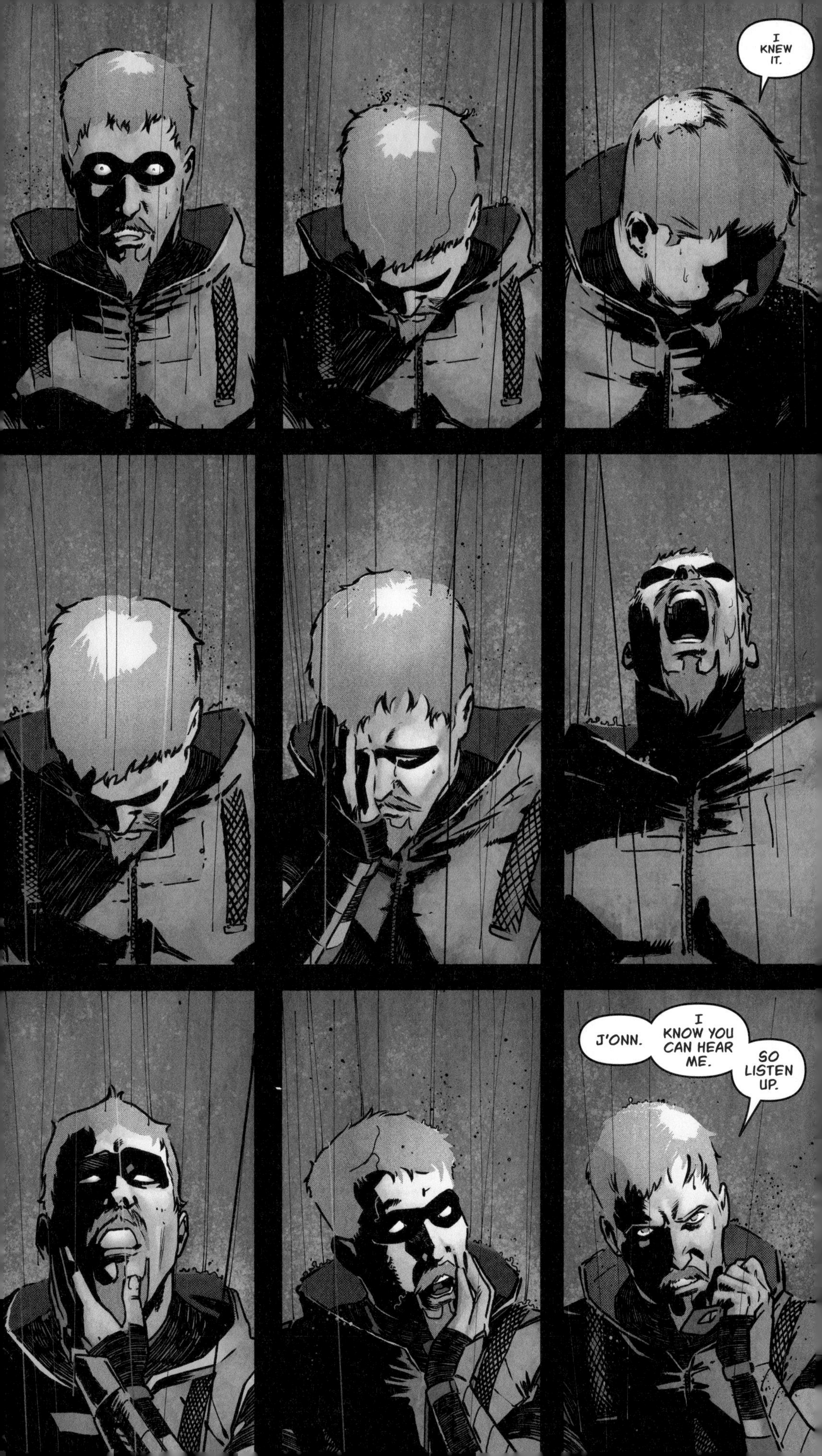
I KNEW IT.
J'ONN.
I KNOW YOU CAN HEAR ME.
SO LISTEN UP.

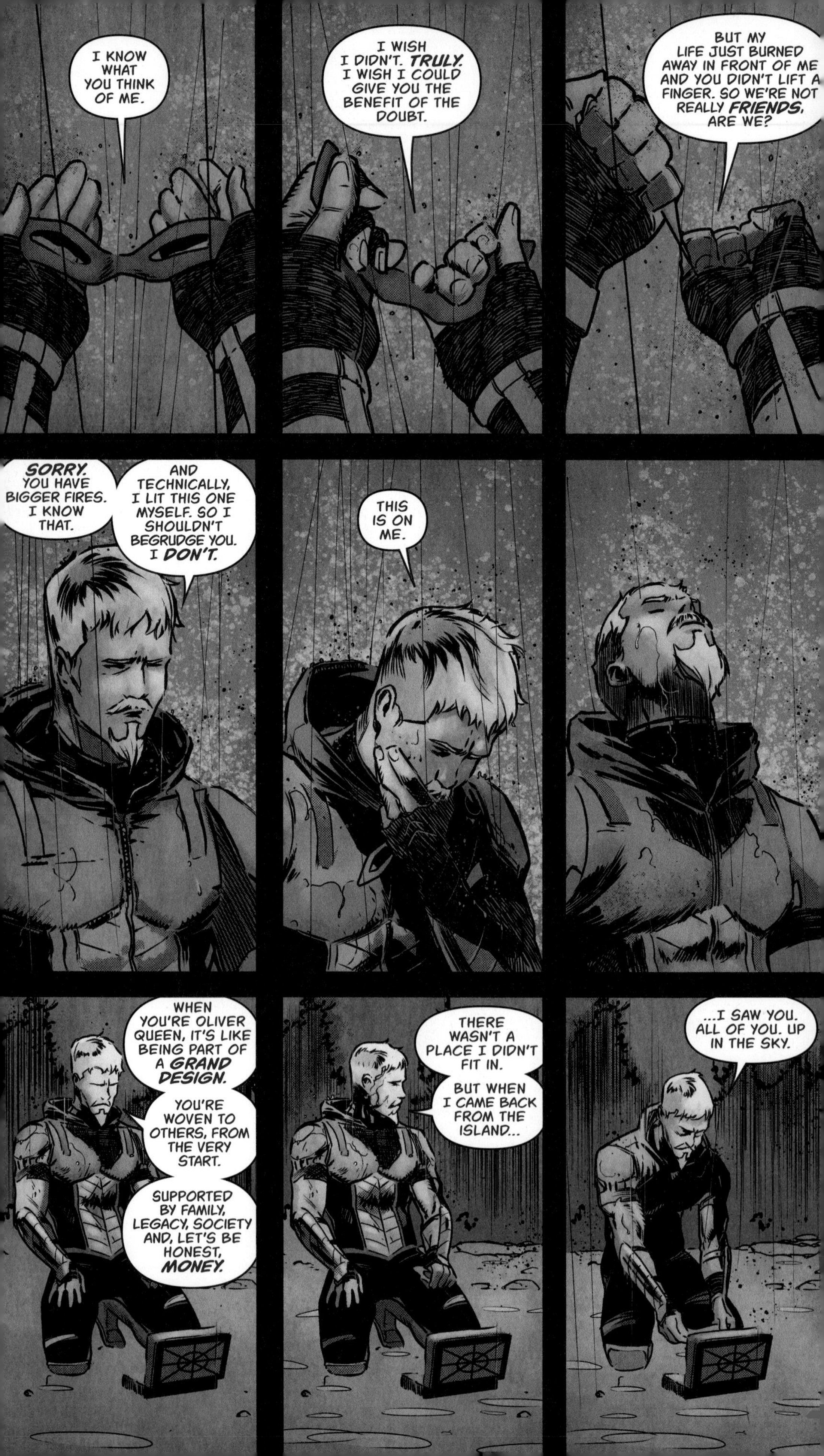
I KNOW WHAT YOU THINK OF ME.
I WISH I DIDN'T. TRULY. I WISH I COULD GIVE YOU THE BENEFIT OF THE DOUBT.
BUT MY LIFE JUST BURNED AWAY IN FRONT OF ME AND YOU DIDN'T LIFT A FINGER. SO WE'RE NOT REALLY FRIENDS, ARE WE?
SORRY. YOU HAVE BIGGER FIRES. I KNOW THAT.
AND TECHNICALLY, I LIT THIS ONE MYSELF. SO I SHOULDN'T BEGRUDGE YOU. I DON'T.
THIS IS ON ME.
WHEN YOU'RE OLIVER QUEEN, IT'S LIKE BEING PART OF A GRAND DESIGN.
YOU'RE WOVEN TO OTHERS, FROM THE VERY START.
SUPPORTED BY FAMILY, LEGACY, SOCIETY AND, LET'S BE HONEST, MONEY.
THERE WASN'T A PLACE I DIDN'T FIT IN.
BUT WHEN I CAME BACK FROM THE ISLAND...
...I SAW YOU. ALL OF YOU. UP IN THE SKY.

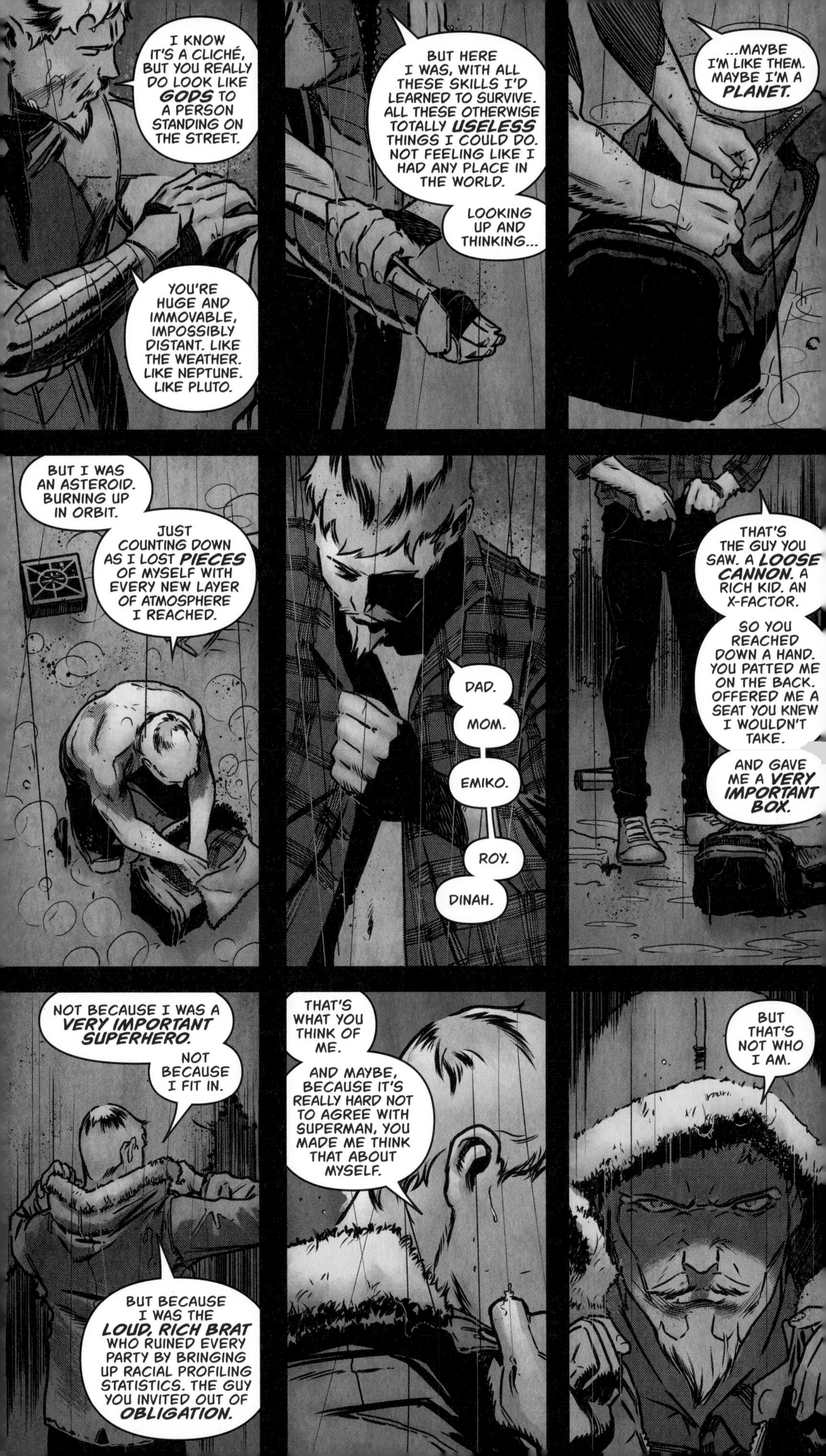
I KNOW IT'S A CLICHÉ, BUT YOU REALLY DO LOOK LIKE GODS TO A PERSON STANDING ON THE STREET.
YOU'RE HUGE AND IMMOVABLE, IMPOSSIBLY DISTANT. LIKE THE WEATHER. LIKE NEPTUNE. LIKE PLUTO.
BUT HERE I WAS, WITH ALL THESE SKILLS I'D LEARNED TO SURVIVE. ALL THESE OTHERWISE TOTALLY USELESS THINGS I COULD DO. NOT FEELING LIKE I HAD ANY PLACE IN THE WORLD.
LOOKING UP AND THINKING...
...MAYBE I'M LIKE THEM. MAYBE I'M A PLANET.
BUT I WAS AN ASTEROID. BURNING UP IN ORBIT.
JUST COUNTING DOWN AS I LOST PIECES OF MYSELF WITH EVERY NEW LAYER OF ATMOSPHERE I REACHED.
DAD.
MOM.
EMIKO.
ROY.
DINAH.
THAT'S THE GUY YOU SAW. A LOOSE CANNON. A RICH KID. AN X-FACTOR.
SO YOU REACHED DOWN A HAND. YOU PATTED ME ON THE BACK. OFFERED ME A SEAT YOU KNEW I WOULDN'T TAKE.
AND GAVE ME A VERY IMPORTANT BOX.
NOT BECAUSE I WAS A VERY IMPORTANT SUPERHERO.
NOT BECAUSE I FIT IN.
BUT BECAUSE I WAS THE LOUD, RICH BRAT WHO RUINED EVERY PARTY BY BRINGING UP RACIAL PROFILING STATISTICS. THE GUY YOU INVITED OUT OF OBLIGATION.
THAT'S WHAT YOU THINK OF ME.
AND MAYBE, BECAUSE IT'S REALLY HARD NOT TO AGREE WITH SUPERMAN, YOU MADE ME THINK THAT ABOUT MYSELF.
BUT THAT'S NOT WHO I AM.

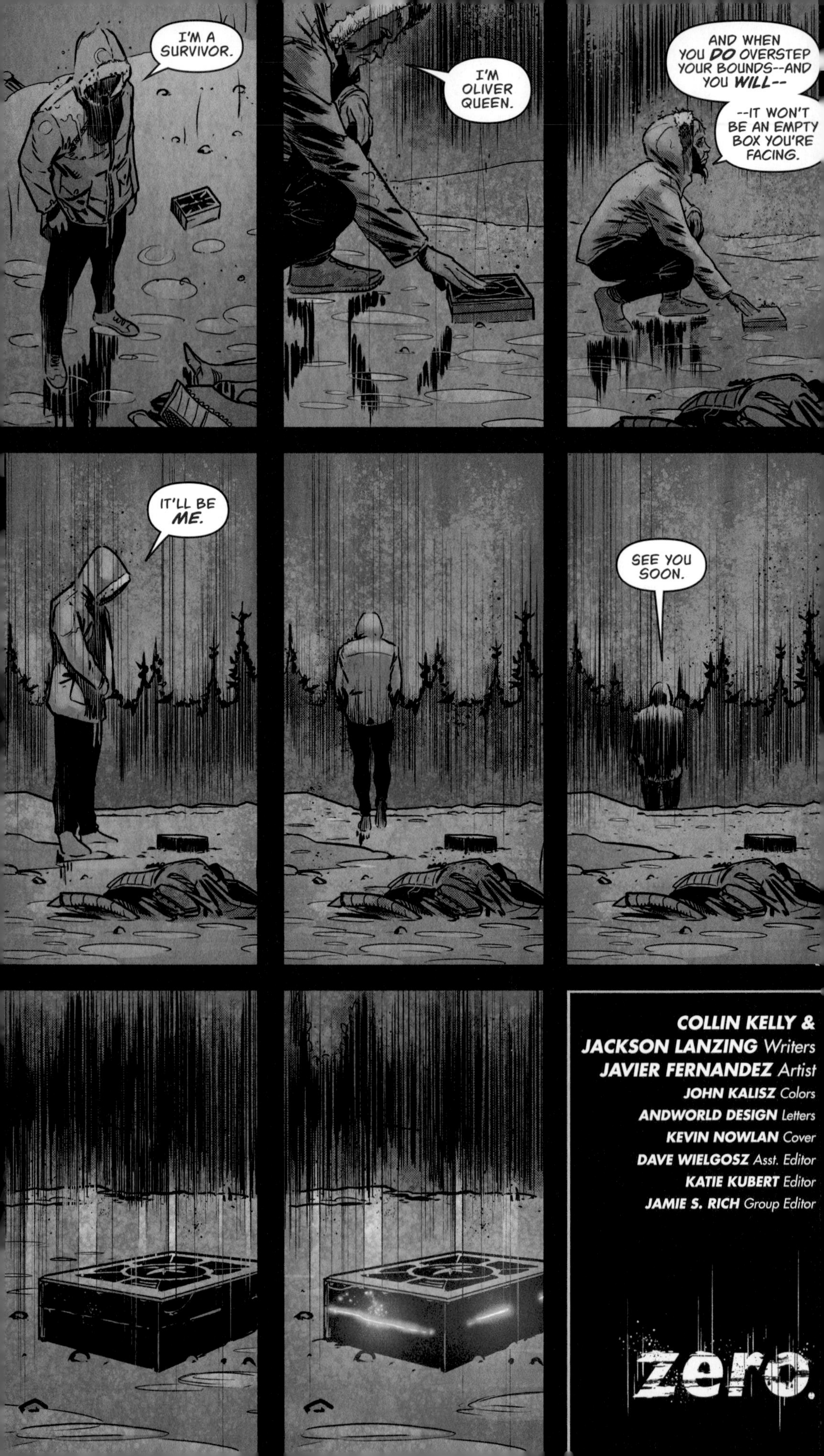
I'M A SURVIVOR.
I'M OLIVER QUEEN.
AND WHEN YOU DO OVERSTEP YOUR BOUNDS--AND YOU WILL--
--IT WON'T BE AN EMPTY BOX YOU'RE FACING.
IT'LL BE ME.
SEE YOU SOON.
COLLIN KELLY & JACKSON LANZING Writers
JAVIER FERNANDEZ Artist
JOHN KALISZ Colors
ANDWORLD DESIGN Letters
KEVIN NOWLAN Cover
DAVE WIELGOSZ Asst. Editor
KATIE KUBERT Editor
JAMIE S. RICH Group Editor
zero.

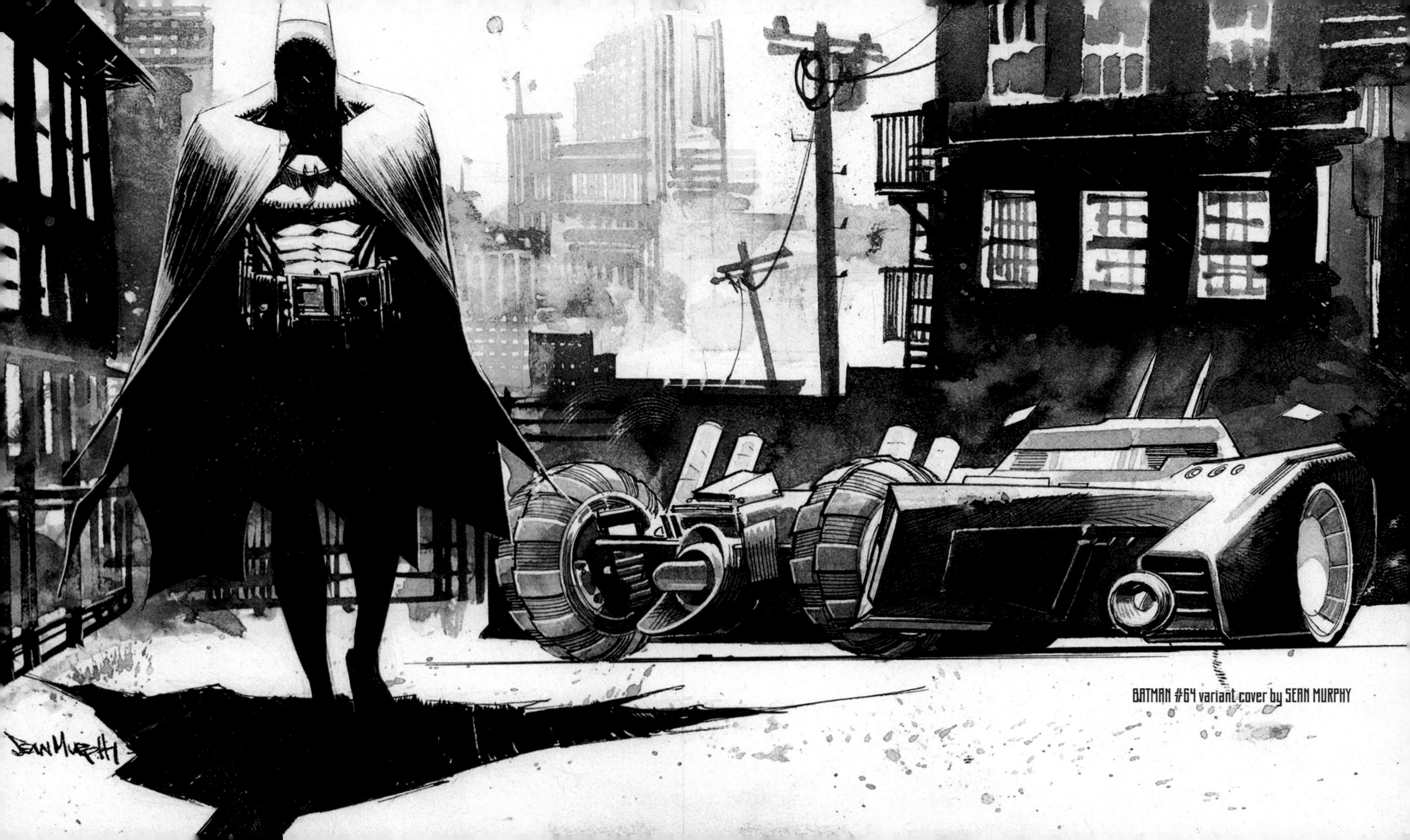

BATMAN #64 variant cover by SEAN MURPHY

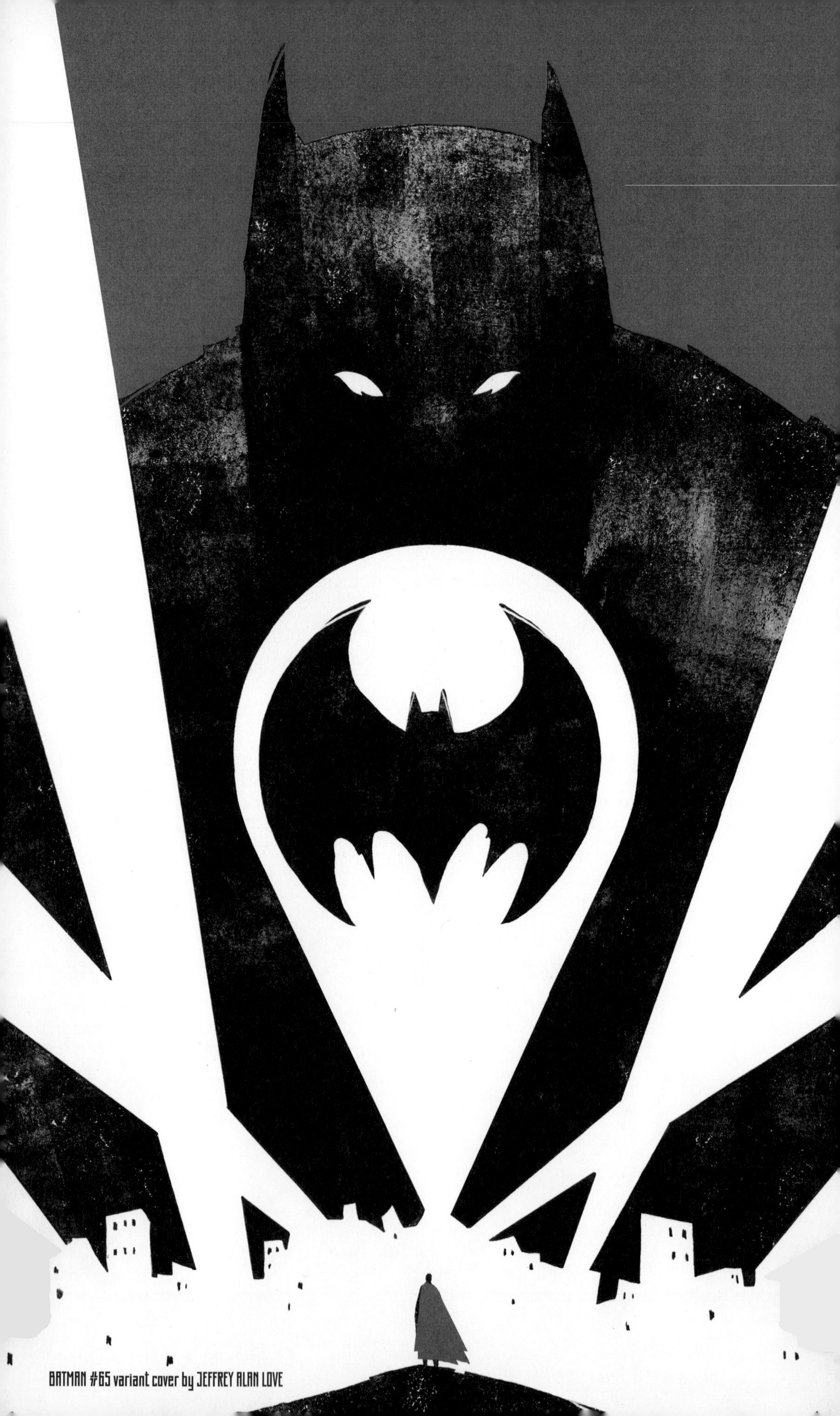

BATMAN #65 variant cover by JEFFREY ALAN LOVE

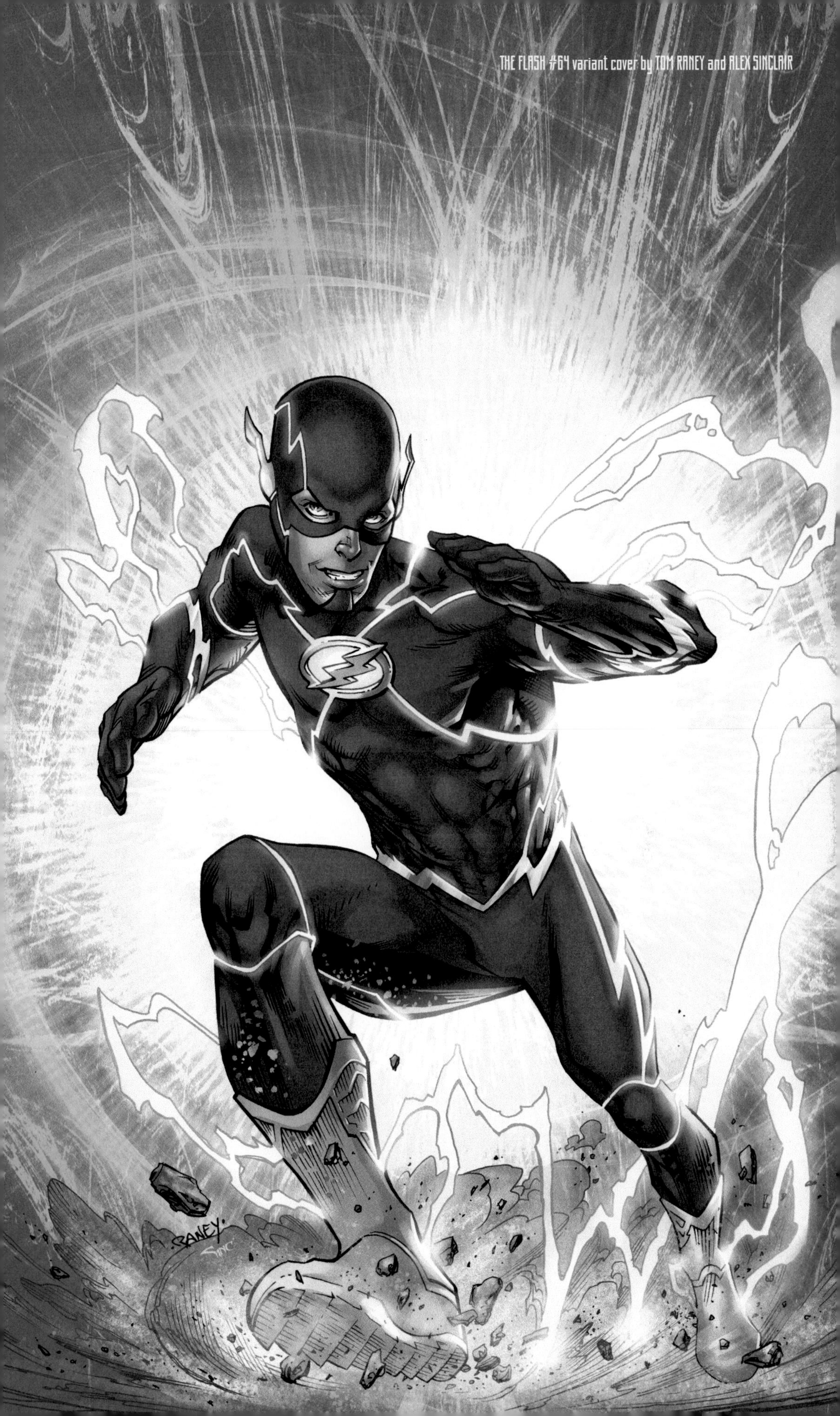
RANEY
THE FLASH #64 variant cover by TOM RANEY and ALEX SINCLAIR

THE FLASH #65 variant cover by MICHAEL GOLDEN

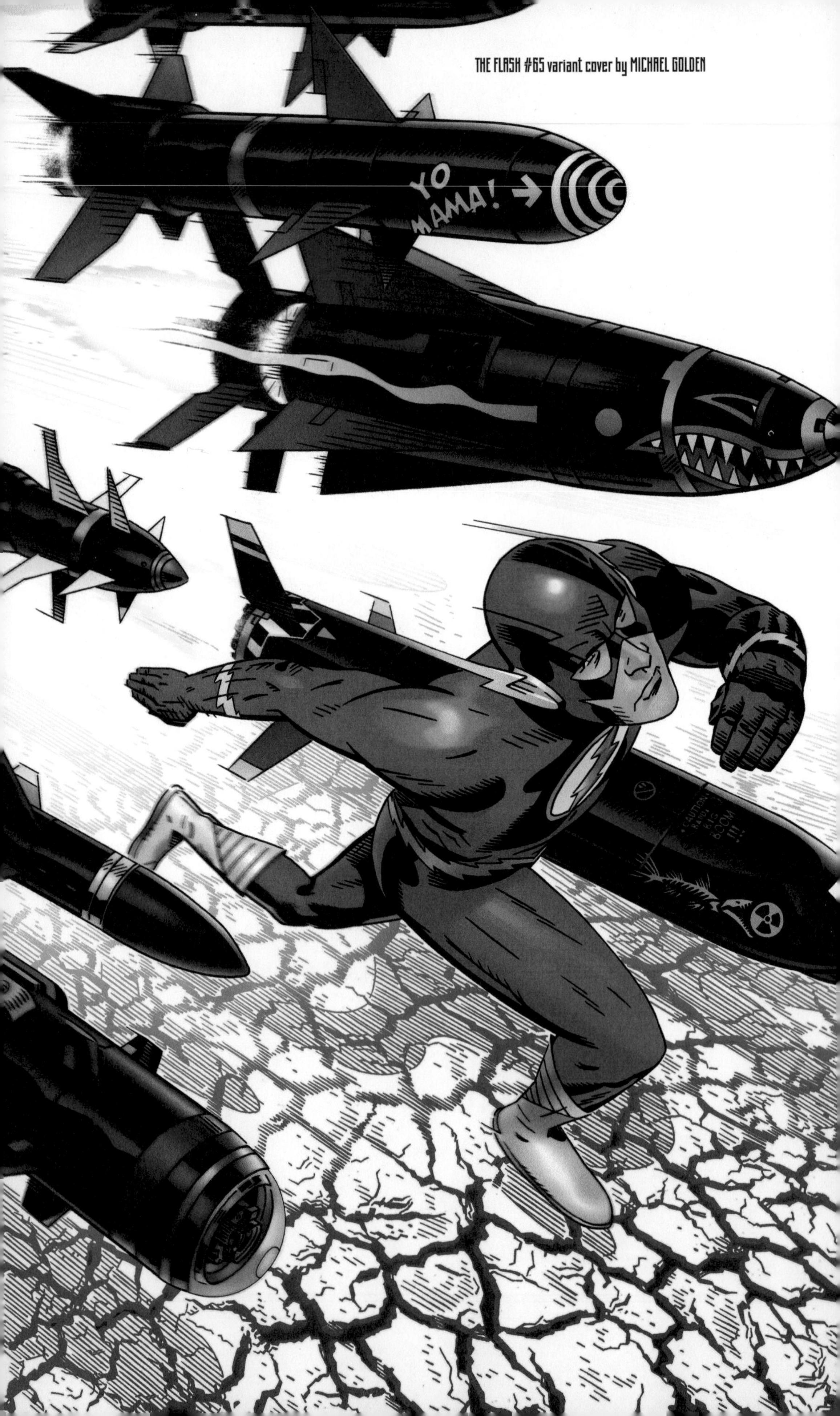
YO MAMA! →
CAUTION!
BIG
BOOM
!!!

GREEN ARROW #45 variant cover by KAARE ANDREWS

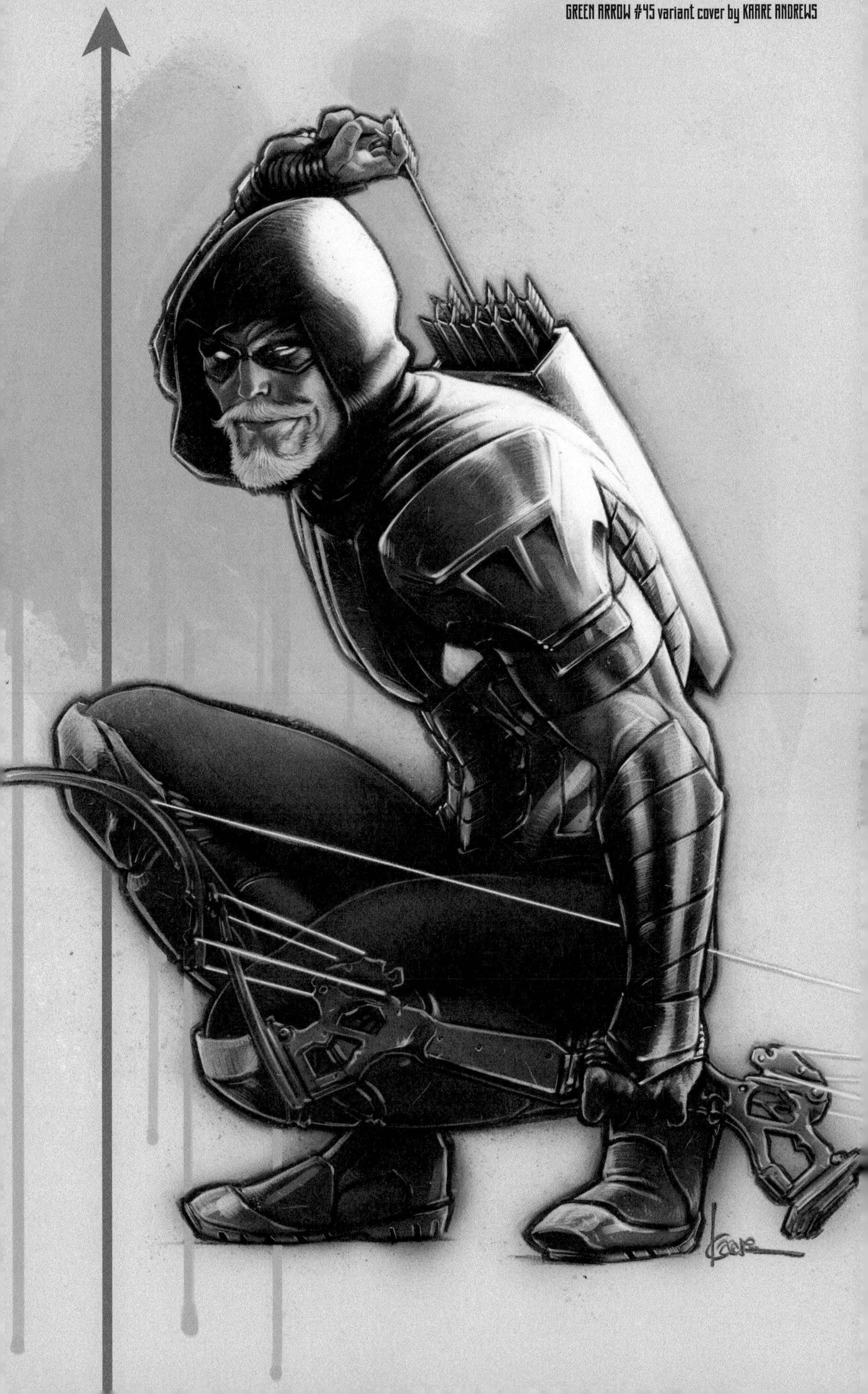

GREEN ARROW #48 variant cover by NEAL ADAMS

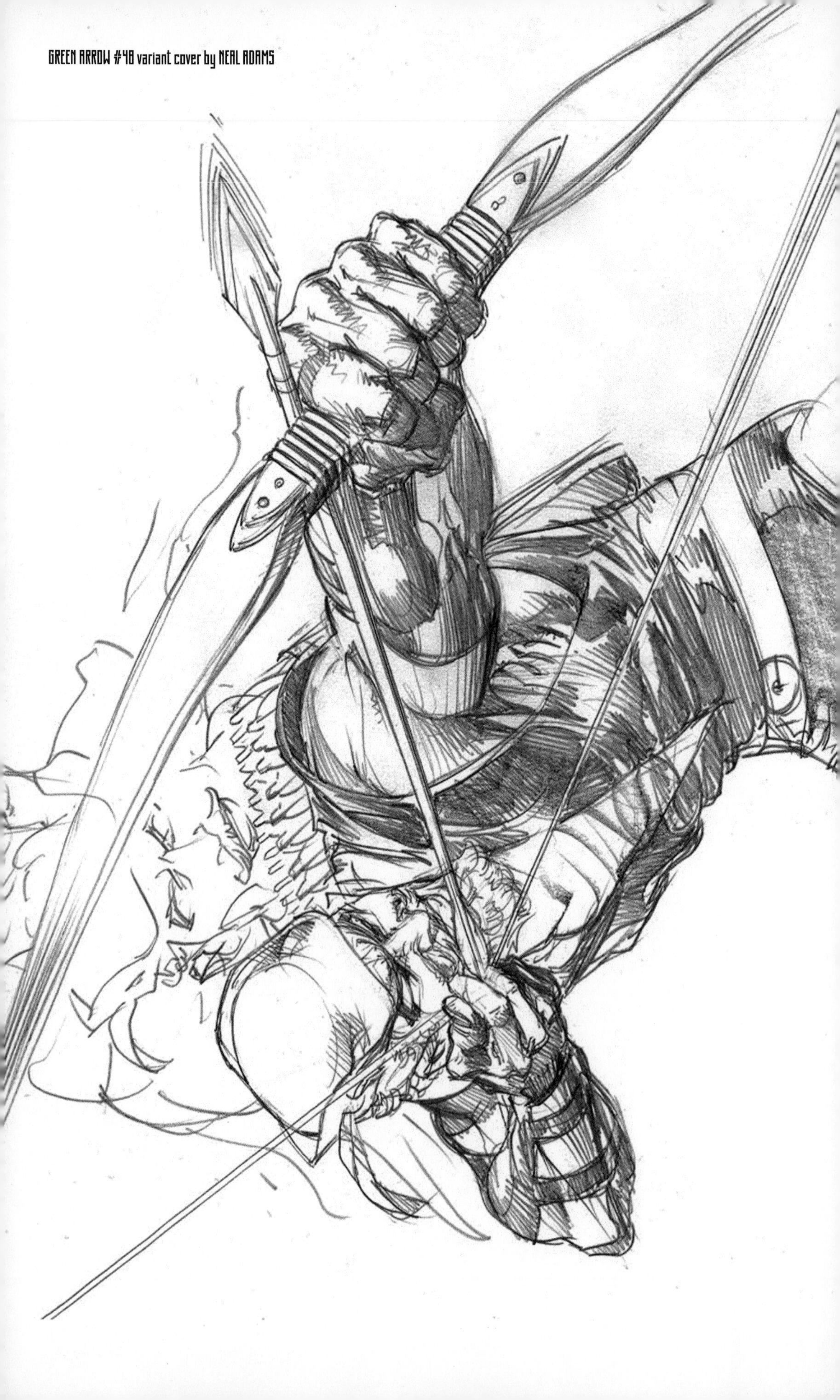

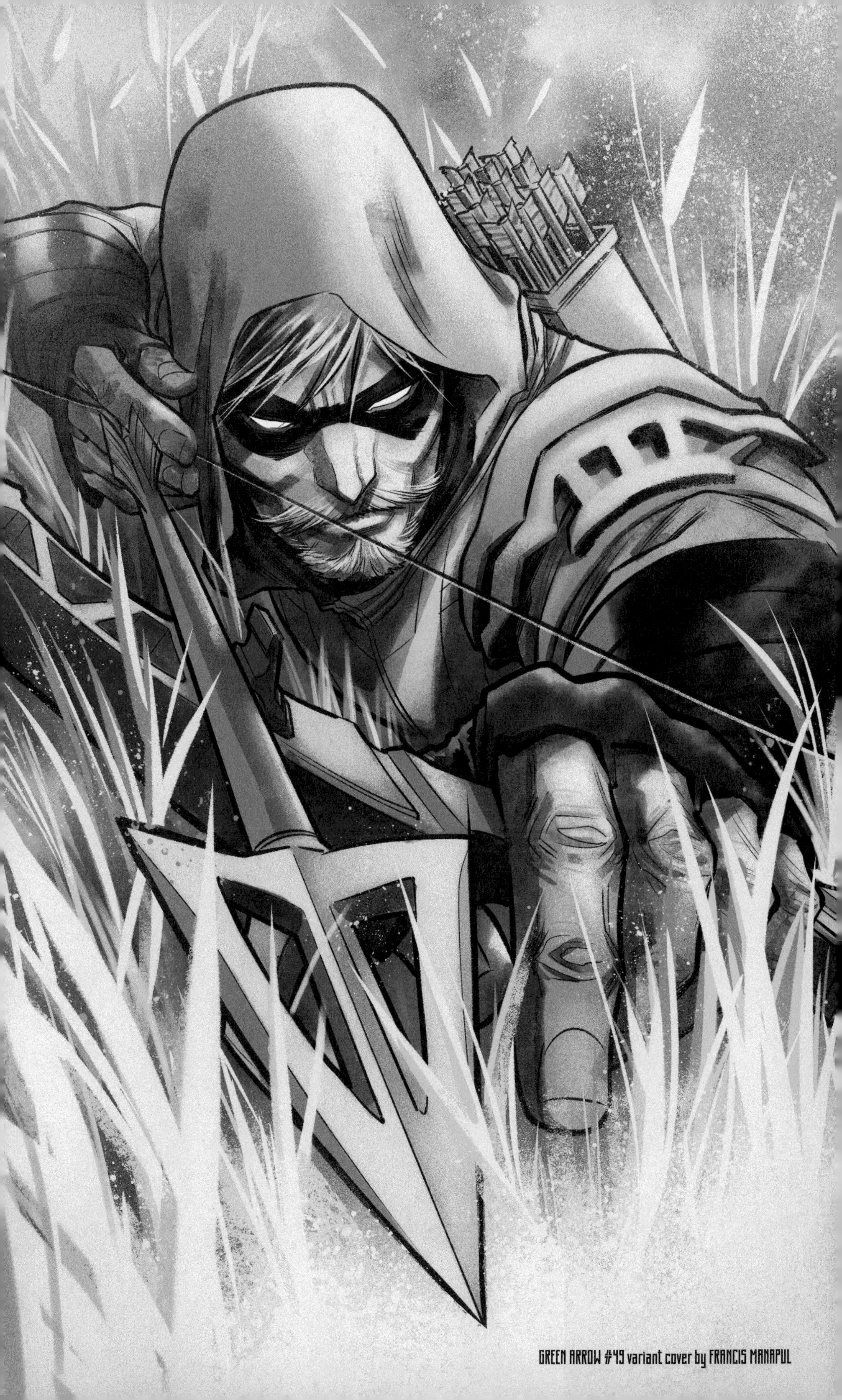

GREEN ARROW #49 variant cover by FRANCIS MANAPUL

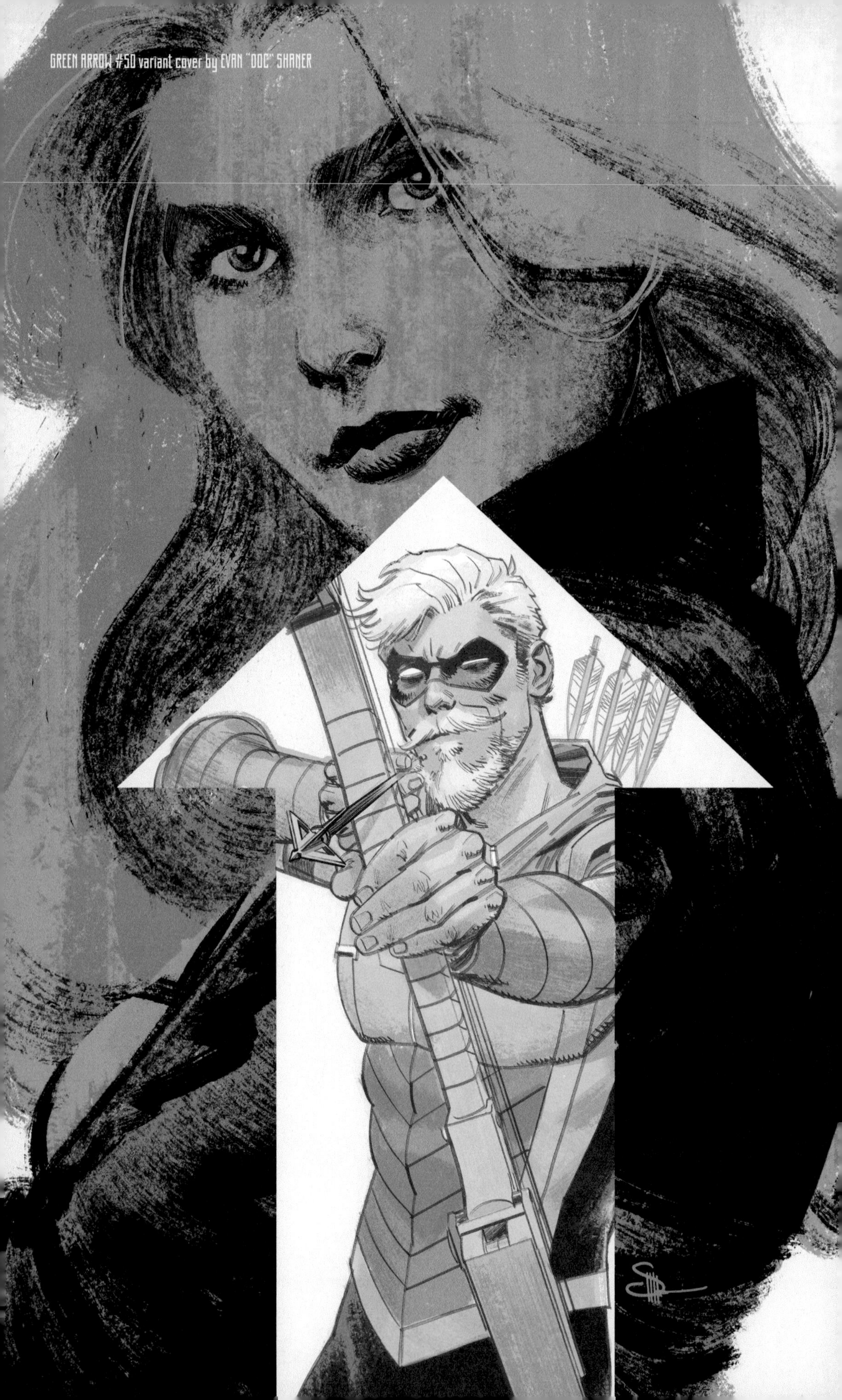
GREEN ARROW #50 variant cover by EVAN "DOC" SHANER